Comparative
World Data

Comparative World Data

·

A Statistical Handbook for Social Science

Georg P. Müller
With the Collaboration of Volker Bornschier

The Johns Hopkins University Press
Baltimore and London

The Johns Hopkins University Press, 701 West 40th Street, Baltimore, Maryland 21211
The Johns Hopkins Press Ltd., London

The paper used in this publication meets the minimum requirements of American National Standard for Information Sciences—Permanence of Paper for Printed Library Materials, ANSI Z39.48-1984.

Library of Congress Cataloging-in-Publication Data

Müller, Georg P., 1949–
   Comparative world data.

   Bibliography: p.
   1. Statistics.   I. Bornschier, Volker, 1944–
II. Title.
HA155.M85   1988   519.5   88-45391
ISBN 0-8018-3734-0
ISBN 0-8018-3770-7 (with three 5.25″ diskettes)
ISBN 0-8018-3805-3 (with two 3.5″ diskettes)

CONTENTS

PREFACE   vii

CHAPTER 1:   AN OVERVIEW   1

    On the Objectives of the Compendium   3

    The Contents of the Country Profiles   5

    The Contents of the Variable Descriptions   9

CHAPTER 2:   ON THE USE OF THE COMPENDIUM   13

    The Tasks for Which the Compendium Is Made   15

    • The Analysis of International Rank Orders   15

    • The Analysis of Reactions Induced by the World System   16

    • The Analysis of International Exchange Relations   17

    On the Use of the Variables   19

    On the Use of the Exploratory Methods   23

    • An Overview   23

    • The Identification of Groups of Countries with Similar Properties   23

    • The Identification of Differences between the Median
      Values of the Members and the Nonmembers of a Group of Nations   24

    • The Identification of Diachronic Changes   26

    • The Identification of Correlations between Variables   27

    • The Identification of Isomorphies between Exchange Relations   29

CHAPTER 3: THE VARIABLE DESCRIPTIONS   33

Measures Describing Socioeconomic Development   35

Measures Describing National Power   50

Measures Describing National Autonomy   59

Measures Describing National Prestige   67

Measures Describing Reactions of Political Movements   76

Measures Describing Reactions of Governments   79

Measures Describing Reactions of Entrepreneurs   86

Measures Describing Reactions of Individuals   92

Measures Describing International Exchange Relations   95

CHAPTER 4: THE COUNTRY PROFILES   101

APPENDIX   483

Footnotes to the Country Profiles   485

List of Countries   491

Organization and Use of the Computer Diskettes   493

Table A: Critical Values $t_{N,p}$ for One-Sided Binomial Tests   496

PREFACE

About ten years ago, *V. Bornschier* and *P. Heintz* from the Sociological Institute of the University of Zurich (Switzerland) edited *Compendium of Data for World-System Analysis.*[1] Although the publication was sold only as a mimeographed brochure and was distributed informally, the demand for this data collection passed far beyond the original expectations of its editors. As a result of this success the decision was made to prepare a second edition of this handbook. Originally this new edition was conceived as a slightly enlarged update of the first one. However, as time went on the new edition became more and more a handbook in its own right, with a new title, many new variables, and a completely different presentation of the data:

- Unlike the first handbook, the present edition can be used as an *encyclopedia of the international system:* Alphabetically organized by country names, it offers statistical profiles for 128 countries with country-specific information about society, politics, and economics.
- Unlike the first compendium, this handbook contains information about the complex network of the *international exchange relations* that are based, among others, on the flows of capital, ideas, people, and commodities.
- As a new feature of this edition, the aforementioned country profiles are organized in such a way that simple hypotheses about correlations between variables, group-specific growth rates, etc. can be *tested without computers.* Cross references to countries with similar properties and percentile rankings allow the reader to do exploratory data analyses with paper and pencil.
- Since the first compendium appeared on the market the personal computer has become a commonly used instrument on the desk of many social scientists. Hence we no longer distribute our data on the big and voluminous tape reels for mainframe computers. Instead, the user of this book has the option to purchase the data of this book on *PC diskettes.* In this way, more sophisticated statistical investigations that go beyond the level of the aforementioned exploratory data analyses can easily be done on a PC system.

The realization of our editorial plans would not have been possible without a generous grant from *SNF*, the national science foundation of Switzerland. The grant allowed us to employ three people who contributed substantially to the production of this book. *Urs Germann* and *Maria Stettler* helped to compile the figures for this book, and *Sandro Cortali* wrote the computer programs for the production of the graphics and the country profiles. Their attentive and reliable work is acknowledged with great appreciation. In addition, we would like to thank those institutions that granted us permission to use their data in this book for modest fees or at no cost. We especially recognize the generosity of the following seventeen institutions:
- Freedom House (New York)
- International Labour Office (ILO) (Geneva)
- International Monetary Fund (IMF) (Washington, D.C.)
- International Progress Organization (IPO) (Vienna)
- Organisation for Economic Co-operation and Development (OECD) (Paris)
- Pinter Publishers (London)
- Stockholm International Peace Research Institute (SIPRI) (Solna, Sweden)
- UNESCO (Paris)
- United Nations Centre on Transnational Corporations (UNCTC) (New York)

---

[1] V. Bornschier and P. Heintz, eds., *Compendium of Data for World-System Analysis. A Sourcebook of Data Based on the Study of MNCs, Economic Policy and National Development.* Reworked and enlarged by Thanh-Huyen Ballmer-Cao and Jürg Scheidegger. Sociological Institute of the University of Zürich. Zürich, 1979.

- United Nations Conference on Trade and Development (UNCTAD) (Geneva)
- United Nations Publications Board (New York)
- United States Arms Control and Disarmament Agency (Washington, D.C.)
- University Center at Binghamton (State University of New York) (Binghamton, N.Y.)
- Wissenschaftszentrum Berlin (Berlin)
- World Bank (Washington, D.C.)
- World Health Organization (WHO) (Geneva)
- World Intellectual Property Organization (WIPO) (Geneva)

And last, but not least, we would like to express our gratitude to the *staffs* of the *Johns Hopkins University Press* in Baltimore and the *Campus Verlag* in Frankfort. They have helped us to review the text and to organize this first edition of the handbook.

CHAPTER 1

AN OVERVIEW

ON THE OBJECTIVES OF THE COMPENDIUM

During the last fifteen years there has been a growing awareness of the interdependence of the world. Many processes that first affected only a few countries have turned out to be relevant for many others. The spread of Islamic militancy and the growing indebtedness of the third world are only two of the more prominent examples of this kind. This interdependence suggests the existence of a *world system* that we conceive of as a very extended and complex *field of various types of interactions.*[1] This field is shaped not only by the policies of national governments. On the contrary, there are many *other* actors who heavily influence the dynamics of this system: Multinational corporations that affect the internal income distribution of their host countries are just one example of the importance of nongovernmental actors. Other examples are the International Monetary Fund, labor unions, and guerrilla movements.

One of the *key objectives* of this data compendium is the *description* of this global field of interactions. However, this field is so complex that a complete realization of this goal is unrealistic. Hence we have tried to *reduce* this *complexity* in several ways:

First, all information in this compendium refers to *national societies.* In spite of this simplification we do *not* deny the importance of nongovernmental actors in the dynamics of the world system. Rather we assume that most of these actors are so closely tied to national societies that their behavior and their properties can be described in terms of the behavior and properties of nations. For example, we describe political strikes of students or workers by strike rates that are attributes of the nations of origin of these groups.

Second, our compendium refers to the *decade of the seventies* only. This simplification can be justified in two ways. On the one hand, the sixties are relatively well documented in an earlier version of this handbook which was edited in 1979 by V. Bornschier and P. Heintz.[2] On the other hand, during the time period covered by this compendium the world system underwent some remarkable changes, such as the exponential increase of the oil prices and the end of the monetary system with fixed exchange rates. Hence we have decided to confine our description to this interesting but insufficiently described decade of the seventies.

Third, our compendium contains only variables that are relevant for the following types of analyses:
a) The analysis of *international rank orders* that are based on the uneven participation of national societies in scarce goods such as wealth or military strength.
b) The analysis of *reactions* induced by the world system. Such reactions can be the response of a national government or of any other social actor that adapts its behavior to new risks or chances of the world system.
c) The analysis of *international exchange relations.* Such exchange relations can be initiated either by national governments or by other nationally tied actors such as entrepreneurs investing abroad or emigrating individuals.

Fourth, we have confined our description of the *international exchange relations* to the interactions with those *three partners* of a nation that are *most important* with regard to a given exchange relation. This way interaction matrices with thousands of elements can be compressed to a manageable size.

---

[1] For an overview of the different concepts of *world system* see V. Bornschier, "Weltsystem," in D. Nohlen, ed., *Pipers Wörterbuch zur Politik,* vol. 5 (München, 1984), pp. 535 ff.
[2] For the corresponding bibliographical reference see *footnote 1* on p. vii.

A data compendium like the present one potentially performs a least three different functions. One of these functions is the *testing of hypotheses* by means of the usual statistical methods. A second one is the *provision of encyclopedic information* about countries. Finally a data collection should also be a *heuristic device for theory construction*. The performance with regard to these three functions differs from one data collection to another. Most of them are well suited for hypothesis testing. Moreover, data compendia that present their information in country profiles can easily be used as encyclopedias. However, with regard to their heuristic functions for theory construction most of the existing data collections are less satisfactory. Hence the second *key objective* of this compendium is the *promotion of exploratory data analysis* [3] as an instrument for theory construction. With regard to this objective the data are presented in such a way that empirical regularities can be discovered *without resort to computer resources*. More precisely, this compendium is designed in such a way that paper, pencil, and a simple pocket calculator are sufficient to get preliminary answers to the following kinds of questions:

a) Which nations have similar properties as the one under consideration?

b) Is there a difference between the median values of the members and the nonmembers of a group of nations?

c) Did the members of a group experience an upward or a downward mobility?

d) Is there a significant correlation between two variables?

e) Are the structures of two exchange relations isomorphic or not?

The methodology to answer these questions is described in *chapter 2*. It is based on *percentile information* and *cross references* to nations with similar structural properties.

To realize the aforementioned objectives we have collected data for 128 nations, 51 variables, and 1 to 3 timepoints/timeintervals. These data are presented in two principal chapters. One of them is a collection of alphabetically ordered *country profiles* (chapter 4). The other one consists of *variable descriptions* with detailed summary statistics (chapter 3). In the following two sections the content of these two chapters is described in full detail.

---

[3] By *exploratory data analysis* we mean a preliminary probing of data. Hence we follow the spirit of J. Tukey, *Exploratory Data Analysis* (Reading, Mass., 1977). However, we do *not* follow the techniques outlined in this book.

THE CONTENTS OF THE COUNTRY PROFILES

Above all, the key objectives of this compendium are realized by means of the country profiles in *chapter 4*. For every nation that was politically independent sometime between 1960 and 1980 and that simultaneously had at least 1 million inhabitants there is a country profile with all the relevant information about the country considered. The country profiles are *ordered alphabetically by country*. A complete list of the countries profiled is provided in the *appendix*.

All country profiles have the same layout, which is illustrated by the following facsimile:

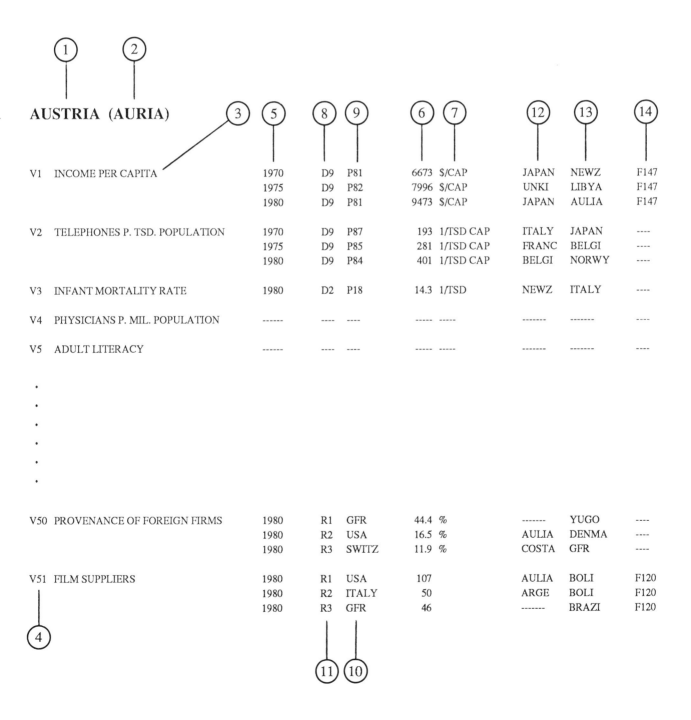

AUSTRIA (AURIA) ③	⑤	⑧	⑨	⑥	⑦	⑫	⑬	⑭
V1 INCOME PER CAPITA	1970	D9	P81	6673	$/CAP	JAPAN	NEWZ	F147
	1975	D9	P82	7996	$/CAP	UNKI	LIBYA	F147
	1980	D9	P81	9473	$/CAP	JAPAN	AULIA	F147
V2 TELEPHONES P. TSD. POPULATION	1970	D9	P87	193	1/TSD CAP	ITALY	JAPAN	----
	1975	D9	P85	281	1/TSD CAP	FRANC	BELGI	----
	1980	D9	P84	401	1/TSD CAP	BELGI	NORWY	----
V3 INFANT MORTALITY RATE	1980	D2	P18	14.3	1/TSD	NEWZ	ITALY	----
V4 PHYSICIANS P. MIL. POPULATION	-------	----	----	----- -----		-------	-------	----
V5 ADULT LITERACY	-------	----	----	----- -----		-------	-------	----

.
.
.
.
.
.

V50 PROVENANCE OF FOREIGN FIRMS	1980	R1	GFR	44.4	%	-------	YUGO	----
	1980	R2	USA	16.5	%	AULIA	DENMA	----
	1980	R3	SWITZ	11.9	%	COSTA	GFR	----
V51 FILM SUPPLIERS	1980	R1	USA	107		AULIA	BOLI	F120
	1980	R2	ITALY	50		ARGE	BOLI	F120
	1980	R3	GFR	46		-------	BRAZI	F120

The information contained in this layout is defined as follows:

1: *Full name of the country* to which the profile refers.

2: *Short name of country (1).*

3: *Full name of the variable* to which the following data lines refer.

4: *Short name of variable (3).*

5: *Timepoint or timeinterval.*

6: *Value.*

7: *Units* of value (6).

8: *Decile* to which value (6) belongs. The deciles are denoted as D1, D2, D3, ... , D10, where D1 contains the lowest values (6) and D10 the highest ones. If several countries have identical values (6) a *common mean* decile is assigned to all these countries. Generally, for different timepoints/timeintervals (5) there are different systems of decile boundaries. However, two values (6) have been classified by the *same* system of deciles if they refer to timepoints/timeintervals that differ by not more than *2 years* from the *same* timepoint/timeinterval 1970, 1975, 1980, 1970-1974, 1975-1979, or 1970-1979.

9: *Percentile* to which value (6) belongs. The percentiles are denoted by P1, P2, P3, ... , P100, where P1 contains the lowest values (6) and P100 the highest ones. If several countries have identical values (6) a *common mean* percentile is assigned to all these countries. Generally, for different timepoints/timeintervals (5) there are different systems of percentiles. However, two values (6) have been classified by the *same* system of percentiles if they refer to timepoints/timeintervals (5) that differ by not more than *1 year* from the *same* timepoint/timeinterval 1970, 1975, 1980, 1970-1974, 1975-1979, or 1970-1979.

10: *Partners* of country (1) with regard to a variable (3) that describes an exchange relation.

11: *Rank* of a partner nation (10) with regard to a variable (3) that describes an exchange relation. The ranks are denoted by R1, R2, and R3, where R1 represents the highest and R3 the lowest rank.

12: *Predecessor nation* in an ordered chain of countries. The components and the structure of such a chain depend on the type of the variable (3). A chain of nations contains only countries with values (6) that refer to timepoints/ timeintervals (5) that differ at most by 2 years from the *same* timepoint/timeinterval 1970, 1975, 1980, 1970-1974, 1975-1979, or 1970-1979. The ordering of the chains depends on the type of the variable (3):

a) For the variables V1 to V34 and V41 to V46, which have been measured on *ordinal, interval, or ratio scales,* the chains are normally ordered by *increasing values (6)* of the members of the chain. However, if the values of 2 or more countries are identical the ordering of the chain is based on the *short names (2)* of these countries. Hence, the first 3 nations of example (A) are ordered by their short names whereas the ordering of the last 3 countries is based on their values (6).

Example A: Predecessors with regard to V26.

Country ordered by position in the chain	Predecessor	Value of V26	Timepoint
ALGER	--------	0.00	1970
IRAN	ALGER	0.00	1970
NIGRA	IRAN	0.00	1970
.	.	.	.
.	.	.	.
FRANC	NETH	0.69	1970
LIBYA	FRANC	2.01	1970
SAUDI	LIBYA	5.59	1970

b) For the variables V35 to V40, which have been measured on *nominal scales,* the predecessor of nation (1) is that country that has the *same value (6)* as nation (1) and that precedes nation (1) with regard to the alphabetic order of the short names of the countries. Hence example (B) consists of 2 *independent* chains of nations with 2 different values on a nominal scale. Each chain is ordered by the short names of its member countries.

Example B: Predecessors with regard to V36.

Country ordered by position in the chain	Predecessor	Value of V36	Timepoint
AFGHA	--------	0	1980
ALBA	AFGHA	0	1980
ANGO	ALBA	0	1980
.	.	.	.
.	.	.	.
ZIMBA	ZAMBI	0	1980
ALGER	-------	1	1980
ECUA	ALGER	1	1980
GABON	ECUA	1	1980
.	.	.	.
.	.	.	.
VENE	UNARE	1	1980

c) For the variables V47 to V51, which describe *exchange relations,* the corresponding chains are organized in the following way: Nations that belong to the same chain *always* have the *same partner (10)* with regard to the exchange relation considered. Besides, these chains are ordered in such a way that nations for which the stated partner (10) has a higher rank (11) always precede those other nations for which the same partner (10) has a lower rank (11). If the stated partner (10) has for several nations the same rank (11) the nations are ordered by their alphabetic short names. From this definition it follows that for a variable like *film suppliers (V51)* there are several chains of nations. One of them consists of all the nations for which INDIA is an important film supplier (see example C). The first 4 nations of this chain are those for which INDIA occupies rank R1. Hence these nations are ordered by their alphabetic short name. For the following nations, ISRA, JORDA, KUWAI, ... , the film supplier INDIA occupies rank R2. This second group of nations is also ordered alphabetically. It is followed by a third group of alphabetically ordered nations for which INDIA always occupies rank R3.

Example C: Predecessors with regard to V51.

Country ordered by position in the chain	Predecessor	Rank of partner	Partner with regard to V51	Timepoint
MOROC	--------	R1	INDIA	1982
RWAN	MOROC	R1	INDIA	1980
SOMA	RWAN	R1	INDIA	1982
TANZA	SOMA	R1	INDIA	1980
ISRA	TANZA	R2	INDIA	1980
JORDA	ISRA	R2	INDIA	1980
KUWAI	JORDA	R2	INDIA	1980
.	.	.	.	.
.	.	.	.	.
.	.	.	.	.
YENO	TRITO	R2	INDIA	1980
ALGER	YENO	R3	INDIA	1980
.	.	.	.	.
.	.	.	.	.
.	.	.	.	.
SUDAN	SRILA	R3	INDIA	1979

13: Successor nation in the chain defined before. Hence the composition and the ordering of the chain are the same as for the *predecessor nation.*

14: Reference to a *footnote* in the first part of the *appendix.*

THE CONTENTS OF THE VARIABLE DESCRIPTIONS

In order to give the reader additional information about the variables in the country profiles, we supply in *chapter 3* detailed descriptions for all 51 variables used in this compendium. Each of these variable descriptions contains the following information:

a) Two *short names* of the variable considered.

b) The *definition* of the variable.

c) The *computational procedure* used for the variable considered. This information is omitted whenever the computational procedure is identical to the theoretical definition (b).

d) The *scaling* of the variable, which informs the user about the type and the units of the scale used for the measurement of the variable considered.

e) The *quality of data,* which informs the user among other things about their crossnational and diachronic comparability.

f) The *availability of data* measured by the approximate number of observations referring to a certain timepoint/timeinterval.

g) The *sources* used for the data collection.

h) A *statistical overview* containing summary statistics. These summary statistics are generally based on information that differs by not more than 2 years from the timepoints/timeintervals 1970, 1975, 1980, 1970-1974, 1975-1979, or 1970-1979. The scope and the presentation of these summary statistics depend on the variable to which they refer.

For the variables V1 to V34 and V41 to V46, which have been measured on *ordinal, interval,* or *ratio scales,* the statistical overviews are presented in the following way:

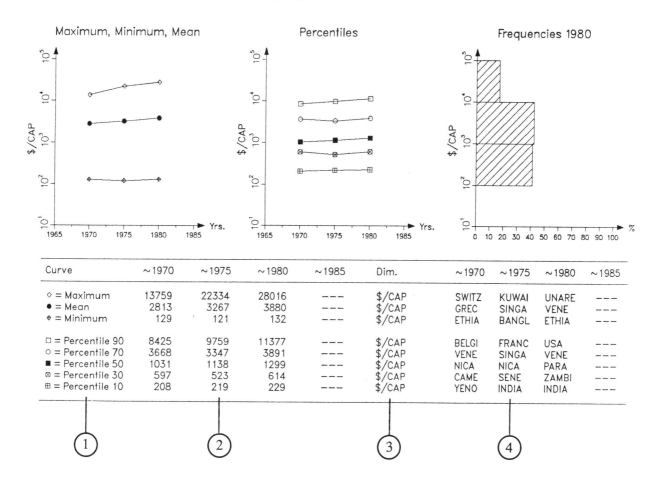

Curve	~1970	~1975	~1980	~1985	Dim.	~1970	~1975	~1980	~1985
◇ = Maximum	13759	22334	28016	---	$/CAP	SWITZ	KUWAI	UNARE	---
● = Mean	2813	3267	3880	---	$/CAP	GREC	SINGA	VENE	---
⟠ = Minimum	129	121	132	---	$/CAP	ETHIA	BANGL	ETHIA	---
□ = Percentile 90	8425	9759	11377	---	$/CAP	BELGI	FRANC	USA	---
○ = Percentile 70	3668	3347	3891	---	$/CAP	VENE	SINGA	VENE	---
■ = Percentile 50	1031	1138	1299	---	$/CAP	NICA	NICA	PARA	---
⊗ = Percentile 30	597	523	614	---	$/CAP	CAME	SENE	ZAMBI	---
⊞ = Percentile 10	208	219	229	---	$/CAP	YENO	INDIA	INDIA	---

Legend to the preceding sample graphic:

1: Statistical measure.

2: Value of the statistical measure (1).

3: Units attached to the value (2).

4: Key Nation = Nation that occupies the position *closest* to value (2) on the variable under consideration. If several countries have the same position on this variable the *key nation* is the first nation in the alphabetic order of the short names of these countries.[4]

In some cases the preceding graphic contains no *diagram*. However, the definitions of the elements of the corresponding *table* remain the same.

For the variables V35 to V40, which have been measured on *nominal scales*, the following standard layout is used for the statistical overviews:

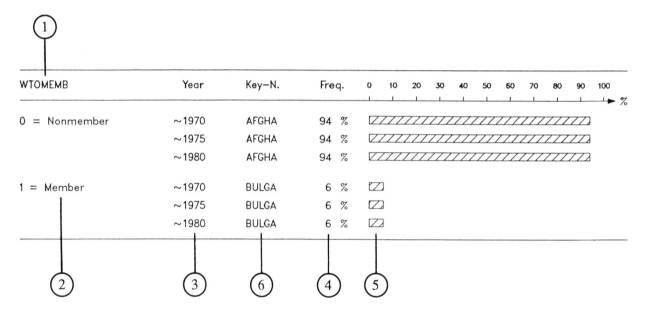

Legend to the preceding sample graphic:

1: Variable to which the graphic refers.

2: Value of variable (1) to which the following lines refer.

3: Approximate year to which the line refers.

4: Percentage of all countries with value (2).

5: Visualization of percentage (4).

6: Key Nation = First nation in the alphabetic order of the countries with value (2) on variable (1). Hence the *key nation* is the first nation in the corresponding chain of countries shown in the *country profiles.*

---

[4] The percentiles in the *statistical overviews* are based on a *different sample* than the percentiles shown in the *country profiles* (see pp. 6 and 9). In certain cases this results in minor differences between the percentile information of the statistical overviews and the corresponding information shown in the country profiles of the *key nations.*

For the variables V47 to V51, which describe *exchange relations,* the statistical overviews are presented in tables of the following kind:

Rank—R1 Patent Suppliers

	Year	Holder	Key—N.	Freq.	0 10 20 30 40 50 60 70 80 90 100 %
Position 1:	~1970	USA	ARGE	64 %	/////////////////
	~1980	USA	ARGE	64 %	/////////////////
Position 2:	~1970	GFR	AURIA	14 %	////
	~1980	GFR	AURIA	19 %	//////
Position 3:	~1970	UNKI	BURU	10 %	///
	~1980	FRANC	CUBA	8 %	//

Legend to the preceding sample graphic:

1: Variable to which the graphic refers.

2: Position of a partner nation on a scale that measures the percentage of all countries for which this nation is the *most important* interaction partner with regard to variable (1). The positions are denoted by cardinal numbers, where position 1 represents the top of the scale.

3: Approximate *year* to which the line refers.

4: Holder of position (2).

5: Percentage of all countries for which the holder (4) of the position (2) is the *most important* interaction partner.

6: Visualization of percentage (5).

7: Key Nation = First nation in the alphabetic order of the countries for which nation (4) is the *most important* interaction partner with regard to variable (1). Hence the *key nation* is the first nation in the corresponding chain of countries shown in the *country profiles.*

CHAPTER 2

ON THE USE OF THE COMPENDIUM

THE TASKS FOR WHICH THE COMPENDIUM IS MADE

The Analysis of International Rank Orders

One of the three principal purposes for which this compendium has been prepared is the analysis of *international rank orders*. International rank orders are the result of *differences* with regard to national participation in *highly valued scarce goods* such as military strength, national wealth, or human capital. This means that *international rank orders* are much more than theoretical constructions: They constitute *social stratifications* of national societies which are relevant for these societies in terms of their collective fears and aspirations. This stratified nature of the world system has led us to focus the contents of the compendium on research questions of the following kind: [1]
- What is the shape of the stratification pyramid of a given rank order?
- Which are the nations belonging to a given stratum of the international system?
- Are certain strata or groups of nations more mobile than others and what are the reasons for this mobility?

To make the answers to these questions easier the user of this compendium is offered 34 variables that refer to the following types of international stratification:
- *Socioeconomic development,* which has been the key dimension in the political discussion about national progress since World War II.
- *National power,* the dimension underlying most of the current discussion on military and economic hegemony.
- *National autonomy,* which, among others, is the ultimate value guiding the complaints of nationalist movements about colonial and neocolonial dependency.
- *National prestige,* a dimension of the world system which describes widely respected national achievements in the fields of human rights, sports, scientific research, etc.

Each of these four dimensions is described by a different set of variables. More detailed information on these variables is given on pp. 19 ff.

To study the structure and the dynamics of rank orders *in depth* it is recommended that one use the resources of a computer. However, for *preliminary* analyses the compendium provides several tools for the exploration of rank orders by paper and pencil methods. Among these tools the following ones are of special importance for the purposes discussed in this chapter:
- *Statistical overviews in the variable descriptions.* These provide the user with information on the shape and the dynamics of the different international stratification systems. Such information is especially useful for the assessment of *international inequality* and for the analysis of upward or downward *mobility of the different strata.*
- *Cross references of the country profiles* which point to predecessor/successor nations with similar structural properties. By following a chain of cross references it is relatively easy to identify a group of nations belonging to a given stratum of the international system. This way the reader gets an overview of the *composition of the different strata.*
- *Percentile ranks of the country profiles.* Since percentile ranks are relatively subtle measures for all kinds of changes they are well suited for the analysis of the *mobility of nations.* The greater the difference between the percentile ranks on a given variable at two different timepoints the higher the relative mobility with regard to the corresponding rank

---

[1] For a detailed overview of the research questions relevant to the stratification paradigm see P. Heintz, ed., *A Macrosociological Theory of Societal Systems,* vols. 1 and 2 (Bern, 1972); P. Heintz, *The Future of Development* (Bern, 1973).

order. It is obvious that the mobility of an *individual* country can easily be identified by looking at its percentile ranks. However, the identification of the collective mobility of *groups of nations* is not possible without the use of statistical methods. Hence we have developed a paper and pencil test that allows the user to decide whether a group has experienced an upward or downward mobility. This test is described on pp. 26 ff.

The Analysis of Reactions Induced by the World System

By definition the world system is the most comprehensive social system that can be imagined. Consequently the dynamics of this system are caused by the system itself. This means on the one hand that the social behavior of the actors of this system is induced by the system itself. Among others the world system offers and withdraws chances to realize aspirations of its actors that use these chances in a more or less rational way. In addition, the system diffuses new values, technologies, and other innovations that are adapted by its actors either voluntarily or due to external pressures. On the other hand the behavior of the actors of the system tends to change the system itself. For instance, by using their chances on the world market of textiles some of the *third world* countries are influencing not only their own industrial structure but also the one of the *first world*. On the grounds of this interplay between reactive behavior and the dynamics of the world system the contents of this compendium focus among others on the following research questions:[2]

- Which nations are similar with regard to their reactions to the world system?
- What are the effects of the world system on the behavior of the different groups of actors?
- What are the effects of the behavior of the different groups of actors on international rank orders and on the world system in general?

To answer the aforementioned questions the variables in this compendium describe four types of reactions that are considered to be especially relevant for the dynamics of the world system:

- *Reactions of governments.* Among others, they are induced by pressures for compliance with international norms, such as the respect for civil rights, by the perception of military threat, by changes of the world economy, etc. In turn, the governmental reactions influence the further diffusion of these norms, the military power distribution, and the dynamics of the world economy.
- *Reactions of entrepreneurs.* Directly or indirectly they are guided by the ups and downs of the world economy, which determine among others their chances for successful investments and exports. Conversely the entrepreneurs influence the pace of the world economy by their investment and export policies.
- *Reactions of political movements,* such as labor unions, student groups, guerrillas, etc. These reactions generally oppose the presence of *foreign* power groups such as foreign companies, foreign air bases, or foreign economic advisors to their own government. If successful, they change the structure of the world system by reducing national dependencies on these foreign power groups.

---

[2] For a detailed overview of the research questions on the reactions induced by the world system see among others: C. Kegley and P. McGowan, eds., *The Political Economy of Foreign Policy Behavior* (Beverly Hills, 1981); V. Bornschier, C. Chase-Dunn, and R. Rubinson, "Cross-national Evidence of the Effects of Foreign Investment and Aid on Economic Growth and Inequality: A Survey of Findings and a Reanalysis," *AJS* 84 (1978): 651 ff.

- *Reactions of individuals.* Among others they are induced by the cycles of the world economy that affect national economies and the structural chances of individuals. The reactions on externally induced structural chances can be *rational,* as in the case of parental investments in the schooling of children, or *anomic,* as in the case of increasing rates of suicides and homicides.

All in all there are 29 variables describing the aforementioned categories of reactive behavior. A complete overview of these variables is given on pp. 19 ff.

For an analysis of the causes and effects of reactive behavior there are exploratory methods that are supported by the following tools:
- By the *cross references of the country profiles* which point to other countries with similar reactive behavior. These cross references simplify the *identification of groups of actors with similar reactions* to the world system.
- By the *percentile ranks of the country profiles.* For the purposes discussed in this chapter they can be used in two ways. *First* they are useful for studying the *effects of the world system on the behavioral changes* of certain groups of actors. *Second* they help to assess the *effects of reactive behavior on the mobility of nations.* In both cases groups of nations with given properties have to be analyzed with regard to the changes of the percentile ranks of their members. To assess the randomness of such changes there is a paper and pencil test, which is described on pp. 26 ff.
- By the *decile ranks of the country profiles.* In this context they are useful for the analysis of the *causes of reactive behavior. First,* decile ranks allow the user to determine whether the members of a group with given properties are above or below the global median of the reaction variable under consideration. *Second,* decile ranks help to identify correlations between behavioral and causal variables. If two variables are correlated positively nations should occupy more or less the same decile ranks on the two variables. Both methods are conceptualized as exploratory paper and pencil tests. Their details are described on pp. 24 ff. and pp. 27 ff.

The Analysis of International Exchange Relations

At the beginning of *chapter 1* the world system was conceptualized as a very complex field of various types of interactions. While some of these interactions are taking place *within national boundaries* many others are *crossing these boundaries.* Interactions of this second type generally involve actors with different national identities. Hence they can be described by the *international exchange* of capital, ideas, people, or commodities. Some of these international exchange relations constitute international dependencies and international spheres of influence. For this reason the compendium has been conceptualized in such a way that it is suitable for finding answers to the following research questions: [3]
- Which nations belong to a *sphere of influence* that is constituted by a common interaction partner?
- What are the effects of the spheres of influence on the *mobility chances* of the nations belonging to these spheres?
- Are there *isomorphies* between various kinds of exchange structures so that these exchange relations are reinforcing on the grounds of their similar topologies?

---

[3] For additional details concerning these research questions see: D. Snyder and E. Kick, "Structural Position in the World System and Economic Growth, 1955-1970: A Multiple-Network Analysis of Transnational Interactions," *AJS* 84 (1979) : 1096 ff. ; J. Galtung, "A Structural Theory of Imperialism," *Journal of Peace Research* 8 (1971): 81 ff.

Due to the great number of international flows, descriptions of international exchange relations tend to be very expensive. This has compelled us to reduce the complexity of our data description in two ways:

- We have confined our description of international flows to those three partners of a nation that are most important with regard to a given exchange relation. In other words, instead of describing each of the 128 nations by their exchange relations with all the other 127 countries we describe these nations by their *3 most important* exchange relations.
- We have confined our description of the international flows to a relatively small set of variables. An overview of the use of these variables is given on pp. 19 ff.

In this compendium the analysis of international exchange relations is not only supported by data on international flows. To study these data the compendium also supplies the following tools for exploratory data analysis:

- *Cross references of the country profiles* which point to predecessor/successor nations all having the *same interaction* partner with regard to a given exchange relation. Hence chains of cross references inform about *spheres of influence* that are characterized by a common exchange partner.
- Information on the *identity of the most important partners* with regard to the different exchange relations. This information is contained in the *country profiles* and can be used to search for hidden *isomorphies between exchange structures*. The existence of such an isomorphy means that the *observed* probability of interacting with the *same* partner nation in *two different* fields of exchange is higher than the *theoretical* probability derived from the assumption of *random* interactions. Obviously isomorphisms cannot be uncovered without using statistical methods. Hence we have developed a relatively easy method for *exploring* hidden isomorphies that is based on the use of paper, pencil, and a simple pocket calculator. The method is described on pp. 29 ff. It is suited not only for *comparing different types of exchange relations* but also as a method for analyzing the *stability of exchange structures* by comparing these structures at two successive timepoints.

ON THE USE OF THE VARIABLES

Most of the variables contained in this compendium can easily be used for very different purposes. In spite of this fact we would like to give a short overview of the use of these variables for those three types of analyses that have been discussed in the preceding chapter. Hence the following pages contain a table that describes the use of these variables

a) for analyses of international *rank orders,*

b) for analyses of *international exchange relations,*

c) for analyses of *reactions* induced by the world system.

Table A: On the use of the variables for different types of analyses.[4]

Variable	Analyses of rank orders	Analyses of exchange relations	Analyses of reactions
V1 Income per Capita	DEV_1	------	------
V2 Telephones p. Tsd. Population	DEV_1	------	------
V3 Infant Mortality Rate	DEV_2	------	------
V4 Physicians p. Mil. Population	DEV_2	------	------
V5 Adult Literacy	DEV_3	------	IND_2
V6 Duration of Schooling	DEV_3	------	IND_2
V7 Student Enrollment Ratio	DEV_3 , PR_1	------	IND_2
V8 Share of Agricultural Labor	DEV_4	------	------
V9 Share of Industrial Labor	DEV_4	------	------
V10 Share of Service Labor	DEV_4	------	------
V11 Share of Academic Labor	DEV_4 , PR_1	------	------
V12 Share of Self-Employed Labor	DEV_4	------	------
V13 Military Expenditures	POW_1	------	GOV_3
V14 Military Manpower	POW_1	------	GOV_3
V15 Men at Age 20 - 30	POW_1	------	------

[4] The table entries are explained at the end of the table.

Table A: Continued from the preceding page.

Variable	Analyses of rank orders	Analyses of exchange relations	Analyses of reactions
V16 Population	POW_2	------	------
V17 Gross Domestic Product	POW_3	------	------
V18 Share in World Imports	POW_3	------	------
V19 Share in World Exports	POW_3	------	------
V20 GDP Share of Imports	AUT_1	------	GOV_4
V21 GDP Share of Exports	AUT_1	------	GOV_4 , ENT_2
V22 Export Partner Concentration	AUT_1	------	------
V23 Total Debt as % of GDP	AUT_2	------	GOV_4
V24 Share of New Foreign Patents	AUT_3	------	------
V25 Foreign Property as % of GDP	AUT_2	------	GOV_4
V26 GNP Share of Development Aid	PR_2	------	GOV_2
V27 Share in Nobel Prize Winners	PR_1	------	------
V28 GDP Share of Manufacturing	DEV_4 , PR_3	------	ENT_1
V29 Export Share of Manufactures	DEV_4 , PR_3	------	ENT_2
V30 Lack of Civil Liberties	DEV_5 , PR_2	------	GOV_2
V31 Lack of Political Rights	DEV_5 , PR_2	------	GOV_2
V32 Riots	------	------	PM_1
V33 Protest Demonstrations	------	------	PM_2
V34 Political Strikes	------	------	PM_2
V35 Member of the Nonaligned Movement	------	------	GOV_1
V36 Member of the OPEC	------	------	GOV_1

Table A: Continued from the preceding page.

Variable	Analyses of rank orders	Analyses of exchange relations	Analyses of reactions
V37 Member of the OECD	------	------	GOV_1
V38 Member of the CMEA	------	------	GOV_1
V39 Member of the WTO	------	------	GOV_1
V40 Member of the NATO	------	------	GOV_1
V41 GDP Share of Investments	------	------	ENT_1
V42 GDP Share of Agriculture	DEV_4	------	ENT_1
V43 GDP Share of Industry	DEV_4	------	ENT_1
V44 GDP Share of Services	DEV_4	------	ENT_1
V45 Homicides p. Mil. Population	------	------	IND_1
V46 Suicides p. Mil. Population	------	------	IND_1
V47 Import Partners	------	EX_1	------
V48 Export Partners	------	EX_1	------
V49 Patent Suppliers	------	EX_2	------
V50 Provenance of Foreign Firms	------	EX_3	------
V51 Film Suppliers	------	EX_2	------

Legend to table A:

AUT_1 - AUT_3 : Indicators for national *autonomy*.
AUT_1 : Indicators for national autonomy with regard to *foreign trade*.
AUT_2 : Indicators for national autonomy with regard to *foreign capital*.
AUT_3 : Indicators for national autonomy with regard to *foreign technology*.

DEV_1 - DEV_5 : Indicators for *socioeconomic development*.
DEV_1 : Indicators for the *wealth* of a nation.
DEV_2 : Indicators for the *health situation* of a nation.
DEV_3 : Indicators for the *educational situation* of a nation.
DEV_4 : Indicators for the *differentiation of a national economy*.

DEV_5 :　　　　　Indicators for the opportunities for *political self-realization.*

$ENT_1 - ENT_2$:　Indicators for the *reactions of entrepreneurs.*
ENT_1 :　　　　Indicators for *investment policies.*
ENT_2 :　　　　Indicators for *export policies.*

$EX_1 - EX_3$:　　Indicators describing international *exchange relations.*
EX_1 :　　　　　Indicators describing the exchange of *commodities.*
EX_2 :　　　　　Indicators describing the exchange of *information.*
EX_3 :　　　　　Indicators describing the exchange of *capital.*

$GOV_1 - GOV_4$:　Indicators for the *reactions of governments.*
GOV_1 :　　　　　Indicators for *international coalition formation.*
GOV_2 :　　　　　Indicators for *compliance with the norms of the world system.*
GOV_3 :　　　　　Indicators for the *military policy* of a government.
GOV_4 :　　　　　Indicators for the *foreign economic policy* of a government.

$IND_1 - IND_2$:　Indicators for the *reactions of individuals.*
IND_1 :　　　　　Indicators for *anomic* reactions.
IND_2 :　　　　　Indicators for *status striving* by acquiring additional education.

$PM_1 - PM_2$:　　Indicators for the *reactions of political movements.*
PM_1 :　　　　　Indicators for *unstructured articulation of dissent.*
PM_2 :　　　　　Indicators for *structured articulation of dissent.*

$POW_1 - POW_3$:　Indicators for the *power* of a nation in the international system.
POW_1 :　　　　　Indicators for the *military* power of a nation. In this book military power is measured by *Military Expenditures, Military Manpower*, and *Men at Age 20 - 30*. The first two indicators measure real *military strength* the third one describes the *base of recruitment* for front-line fighters.
POW_2 :　　　　　Indicators for the *military* and *economic* power of a nation. *Population* as the only indicator belonging to this category is a resource for military and economic goals.
POW_3 :　　　　　Indicators for the *economic* power of a nation. In this book economic power is measured by the productive capacities (see *Gross Domestic Product*) and by the degree of control over the world trade (see *Share in World Imports* and *Share in World Exports*).

$PR_1 - PR_3$:　　Indicators for the *prestige* of a nation in the world system.
PR_1 :　　　　　Indicators for national prestige which is based on the *scientific capacity* of a nation.
PR_2 :　　　　　Indicators for national prestige which is based on the *compliance with the norms of the world system.*
PR_3 :　　　　　Indicators for national prestige which is based on the *modernity of the national economy.* The indicators belonging to this category reflect the fact that the production of *manufactures* is prestigious on the grounds of its know-how intensity.

ON THE USE OF THE EXPLORATORY METHODS

An Overview

One of the key objectives of this compendium is the promotion of exploratory data analysis. For this reason this data collection contains among others cross references to countries with similar properties and information on the national percentile and decile ranks. By means of these tools the reader is able to do the following types of exploratory data analyses:

a) *The identification of groups of countries with similar properties:* For the analysis of international rank orders it can be used to get an overview of the *composition of strata*. For the analysis of international exchange relations it is of use for the uncovering of *spheres of influence* of dominant exchange partners. For the analysis of reactions induced by the world system it is useful for finding groups of actors with *similar patterns of reactions.*

b) *The identification of differences between the median values of the members and the nonmembers of a group of nations:* Among others the method can be used for the analysis of the *causes of group-specific reactions* to the world system.

c) *The identification of diachronic changes:* It is suited for the analysis of rank orders, exchange relations, and reactive behavior. A major field of its application are investigations in the *causes of mobility of nations*. Another field of application is the study of the *effects of the world system on the behavioral changes* of certain groups of actors.

d) *The identification of correlations between variables:* Among others it can be used for the analysis of reactions induced by the world system. By correlating behavioral and causal variables the method imparts insights into the *causes of reactive behavior.*

e) *The identification of isomorphies between exchange relations:* Its primary application is the analysis of international exchange relations. It helps the user to *identify reinforcing structures of dependency.*

The details concerning these types of exploratory data analyses are described in the following paragraphs. Each of these paragraphs describes among others the *objective*, the *rationale*, the *method*, and an *exemplary application* of the given type of analysis.

The Identification of Groups of Countries with Similar Properties

Objective:

The identification of those countries which have *similar* properties with regard to a given variable. Depending on the type of this variable the *similarity of properties* has different meanings. With regard to the *interaction variables* V47 to V51, two countries are similar if a *common* partner nation occupies for both countries the same rank R1, R2, or R3. With regard to the variables V1 to V34 and V41 to V46, which have been measured on *ordinal, ratio,* or *interval scales,* nations are similar if their positions on one of these scales are between the boundaries of a relatively narrow interval. With regard to the *nominal scales* of the variables V35 to V40 two nations are similar if they occupy *identical* values on one of these variables.

Rationale:

On the grounds of the preceding definition of similarity the cross references in the *country profiles* point to successors and predecessors with *similar* properties. Hence it is possible to get an overview of the countries with similar properties just by following the chains of successors/predecessors in the *country profiles.*

Method:

- *Step 1:* Find a nation that has the property you are interested in. To make this task easier the *statistical overview* in the corresponding *variable description* contains information on so-called *key nations* with the appropriate properties.

- *Step 2:* Look for the *country profile* of the aforementioned *key nation* and follow the chain of the predecessors/ successors with regard to the variable you are interested in.

- *Step 3:* Stop the search process of *step 2* if you reach the end of the chain or if a successor/predecessor has properties that are too different from the ones you are interested in.

Example:

- *Task:* Find all nations that were members of the OPEC in 1980.

- *Step 1:* Consult the *statistical overview* of the *variable description* for V36. According to this table ALGER (= Algeria) is the *Key-N(ation)* of the alphabetically ordered chain of countries for which OPECMEMB=1 in 1980.

- *Step 2:* Consult the *country profile* for ALGER (= Algeria). Since Algeria is the first country in the chain, the other members of the OPEC can easily be found. According to the country profiles the successor to Algeria with regard to V36 in 1980 is ECUA (= Ecuador) and the successors to Ecuador are GABON, INDO (= Indonesia), IRAN, etc.

- *Step 3:* Stop the search process of *step 2* when you encounter VENE (= Venezuela) as the *last country* of the chain for which there is no successor nation.

The Identification of Differences between the Median Values of the Members and the Nonmembers of a Group of Nations

Objective:

Test of the hypothesis that the median value M_+ of the *members* of a group of nations with regard to a given variable is greater/lower than the corresponding median value M_- of the *nonmembers* of the same group.

Rationale:

The following test is based on the *null hypothesis* that the members and the nonmembers have the *same* median value. Since the *full sample* is the union of the members and the nonmembers of a group the null hypothesis implies that
$$M_- = M_+ = M$$
where M is the median of the full sample. If the null hypothesis were true about 50% of the observations of the given group should have values that are greater than the common median M. This means that under the null hypothesis 50% of the observations of the given group should belong to the deciles D6, D7, D8, D9, or D10. Deviations from this hypothesis can be tested by means of a *binomial test*. If a deviation is statistically significant the null hypothesis is rejected. This means that the members and the nonmembers of the given group have different median values M_+ and M_-. Unfortunately the results of the test procedure described below are slightly biased. Due to the sampling procedure used in this test the theoretical distribution of the test statistic is *hypergeometric* and *not* binomial. However, for the practical purposes of exploratory data analysis the binomial distribution with the parameter p = 0.50 is a good approximation of the theoretical one.

Method:

- *Step 1:* Identify the members of the group as described in the preceding chapter. While following the chain of successor/ predecessor nations two statistics should be established:
  n = Number of observations of group members that belong to the deciles D6, D7, ... , D10.
  N = Total number of valid observations of group members.

- *Step 2:* Consult *table A* of the appendix and determine for the given N and for p = 0.50 the critical value $t_{N,p}$ of the binomial distribution.

- *Step 3:* Check whether
  $$n \geq t_{N,p} \quad \text{or} \quad N-n \geq t_{N,p}.$$
  If $n \geq t_{N,p}$ it is assured at the 10% level of significance that the median M_+ of the members of the group is *greater* than the median M_- of the nonmembers. If $N-n \geq t_{N,p}$ it is assured at the 10% level of significance that the median M_+ of the members of the group is *lower* than the median M_- of the nonmembers.

Example:

- *Task:* Test the hypothesis that in 1975 the countries with the highest *Income per Capita (V1)* had a *lower* median value on the variable *Lack of Civil Liberties (V30)* than the other countries of the world system.

- *Step 1:* To identify the group of nations with the highest *Income per Capita (V1)* we first consult the *variable description* of V1 and look for the key nation which represented in 1975 the percentile P90. In our example this key nation is FRANC (= France). Following the chain of successors of the key nation France we encounter 8 other nations until we reach the top of the chain. As the *country profiles* show, neither France nor these other 8 nations belong to the deciles D6 to D10 of the variable *Lack of Civil Liberties (V30)*. Hence
  $N = 9$ = Number of observations.
  $n = 0$ = Number of observations belonging to the categories D6 to D10.
  $N-n = 9$ = Number of observations belonging to the categories D1 to D5.

- *Step 2:* To find the critical value $t_{N,p}$ we consult *table A* of the appendix. For N = 9 and p = 0.50 the table shows that $t_{N,p} = 7$.

- *Step 3:* For the test of the hypothesis that nations with a high *Income per Capita (V1)* have *lower* median values with regard to their *Lack of Civil Liberties (V30)* than the rest of the other countries we need to compare (N-n) with $t_{N,p}$. Since $9 = N-n > t_{N,p} = 7$ our original hypothesis is confirmed.

The Identification of Diachronic Changes

Objective:

Test of the hypothesis that the upward/downward movements that the members of a group of nations experience during a given timeinterval with regard to a given variable are not "at random." By definition diachronic changes are *at random* if upward and downward movements have the *same probabilities.* In this case the group experiences neither an upward nor a downward mobility.

Rationale:

The test is based on the *null hypothesis* that upward and downward movements are at random. Hence, if the null hypothesis is true 50% of the nations that have changed their position within a timeinterval should have experienced an upward movement. Deviations from this norm can be tested by a *binomial test.* If the deviations are significant the null hypothesis is rejected and the members of the group are said to have experienced either an upward or a downward movement.

Method:

- *Step 1:* Identify the members of the group as described above. While following the chain of the predecessor/successor nations the following two statistics should be established:
  n = Number of countries in the group that have experienced an *upward* movement with regard to the given variable. Depending on the intentions of the researcher n can be calculated either on the grounds of *absolute* or *relative* changes. A *relative* change is a change of the *percentile rank.* An *absolute* change is a change of the *value* of a nation with regard to the given variable.
  N = Number of countries that have experienced either an upward or a downward movement where the measure for this movement must be the same as for the calculation of n. Hence N *excludes* all countries that have experienced neither an upward nor a downward movement.

- *Step 2:* Consult *table A* of the appendix and determine for the given N and for p = 0.50 the critical value $t_{N,p}$ of the binomial distribution.

- *Step 3:* Check whether
  $n \geq t_{N,p}$ or $N-n \geq t_{N,p}$.

If $n \geq t_{N,p}$ it is assured at the 10% level of significance that the group has experienced an *upward* movement. If $N-n \geq t_{N,p}$ it is assured at the 10% level of significance that the group has experienced a *downward* movement.

Example:

- *Task:* Test the hypothesis that between 1975 and 1980 the OPEC countries experienced a *downward* mobility with regard to the *percentile rank* of their *Military Expenditures (V13)*.

- *Step 1:* To identify the countries that were members of the OPEC in 1975 we first consult the *variable description* of V36 (= *Member of the OPEC*). According to this variable description the alphabetically ordered chain of the members of the OPEC begins with ALGER (= Algeria). Following this chain we encounter 8 nations that have changed their position with regard to their percentile rank on the variable V13 (= *Military Expenditures*). *Three* of these nations have experienced an upward mobility. Hence
$N = 8$ = Number of countries that have been mobile.
$n = 3$ = Number of countries that have moved upward.
$N-n = 5$ = Number of countries that have moved downward.

- *Step 2:* To find the critical value $t_{N,p}$ we consult *table A* of the appendix. For $N = 8$ and $p = 0.50$ the table shows that $t_{N,p} = 7$.

- *Step 3:* For the test of the hypothesis that the OPEC countries have moved *downward* with regard to their *Military Expenditures (V13)* we need to compare (N-n) with $t_{N,p}$. Since $5 = N-n < t_{N,p} = 7$ the disproportion between the upward and the downward movers is probably the result of a *random process* and does *not* point to a systematic change of the military power of the OPEC.

The Identification of Correlations between Variables

Objective:

Test the hypothesis that the higher the rank of a country with regard to a variable v_i the higher/lower the rank of this country with regard to another variable v_j .

Rationale:

If the aforesaid hypothesis is true all the observations should be concentrated in one of the *main diagonals* of the following two diagrams:

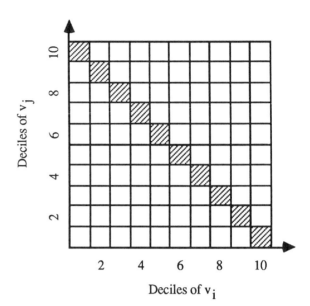

Positive Correlation   Negative Correlation

Deciles of v_j Deciles of v_j

Deciles of v_i Deciles of v_i

Hence our *null hypothesis* is based on the assumption that the observations are more or less dispersed along the rows and the columns of the aforementioned diagrams. More precisely we assume that for any two observations x_i and x_j and for any two deciles $D_i r$ and $D_j s$ which refer to the variables v_i and v_j

$$\mathbf{prob}(\mathbf{x_j} \in \mathbf{D_j r} \mid \mathbf{x_i} \in \mathbf{D_i s}) = 0.10 .$$

Hence

$$\sum_{r=1}^{10} \mathbf{prob}(\mathbf{x_j} \in \mathbf{D_j r} \text{ and } \mathbf{x_i} \in \mathbf{D_i r}) = \sum_{r=1}^{10} \mathbf{prob}(\mathbf{x_j} \in \mathbf{D_j r} \mid \mathbf{x_i} \in \mathbf{D_i r}) \cdot \mathbf{prob}(\mathbf{x_i} \in \mathbf{D_i r}) = \sum_{r=1}^{10} 0.10 \cdot 0.10 = 0.10 .$$

This means that the null hypothesis implies a 10% chance that a pair (x_i , x_j) belongs to the main diagonal $(D_i 1 , D_j 1)$, $(D_i 2 , D_j 2)$, ... , $(D_i 10 , D_j 10)$. Similarly it can be shown that the same rule also holds for the other diagonal $(D_i 1 , D_j 10)$, $(D_i 2 , D_j 9)$, ... , $(D_i 10 , D_j 1)$. Deviations from these rules can easily be identified by means of *binomial tests*. If there are too many observations belonging to one of the main diagonals then there is a significant positive/ negative correlation between the variables v_i and v_j .

Method:

- *Step 1:* Fix the value of
  N = Number of observations in the test sample.
  The value of N depends on the acceptable beta-error and on the acceptable costs of the test. Samples with 10 to 20 observations are relatively good compromises between the risk of a beta-error and the costs of the test.

- *Step 2:* Browse through the *country profiles* and choose at random N nations with valid observations for the variables v_i and v_j . It is acceptable if a country appears several times in the same random sample. If you suppose that the cor-relation between v_i and v_j is *positive* you should determine at the same time
  n_+ = Number of observations (x_i , x_j) in the sample for which the *decile rank* of x_i with regard to v_i is the *same* as the decile rank of x_j with regard to v_j .
  If you suppose that the correlation between v_i and v_j is *negative* you should determine at the same time

n_- = Number of observations (x_i, x_j) in the sample for which the *sum* of the *decile ranks* of x_i and x_j with regard to the corresponding variables v_i and v_j *equals 11.*

- *Step 3:* Consult *table A* of the appendix and determine for the sample size N and for the probability p = 0.10 the critical value of $t_{N,p}$.

- *Step 4:* Check whether

$n_+ \geq t_{N,p}$ or $n_- \geq t_{N,p}$.

If $n_+ \geq t_{N,p}$ the correlation between v_i and v_j is *positive* at the 10% level of significance. If $n_- \geq t_{N,p}$ the correlation between v_i and v_j is *negative* at the 10% level of significance.

Example

- *Task:* Test the hypothesis that in 1980 there was a *positive* correlation between the variables *Income per Capita (V1)* and *Telephones p. Tsd. Population (V2).*

- *Step 1:* To fix the sample size we set N = 10.

- *Step 2:* To compile a test sample we browse *at random* through the *country profiles.* The sample we get this way consists of AULIA (= Australia), IRE (= Ireland), KUWAI (= Kuwait), PANA (= Panama), SINGA (= Singapore), SYRIA, CHILE, KENYA, MEXI (= Mexico), and PANA (= Panama). For 5 out of these 10 nations the decile rank on V1 is *identical* with the decile rank on V2. Hence N = 10 and $n_+ = 5$.

- *Step 3:* To find the critical value $t_{N,p}$ we consult *table A* in the appendix. For N = 10 and p = 0.10 the table shows that $t_{N,p} = 3$.

- *Step 4:* For the test of the hypothesis that there is a positive correlation between V1 and V2 we compare $t_{N,p}$ and n_+. Since $5 = n_+ > t_{N,p} = 3$ the aforementioned correlation is positive at the 10% level of significance.

The Identification of Isomorphies between Exchange Relations

Objective:

Test the hypothesis that the *most important* partner C_i with regard to a given exchange relation r_i tends to be *identical* to the *most important* partner C_j with regard to another relation r_j.

Rationale:

A perfect isomorphy between two relations r_i and r_j implies for the most important partners C_i and C_j a deterministic coupling between the events $C_i = c$ and $C_j = c$. Hence the following methodology is based on the *null hypothesis* that the events $C_i = c$ and $C_j = c$ are *statistically independent.* More precisely it is assumed that

$$\text{prob}(C_i = c \text{ and } C_j = c) = \text{prob}(C_i = c) \cdot \text{prob}(C_j = c).$$

Consequently

$$\text{prob}(C_i = C_j) = \sum_c \text{prob}(C_i = c \text{ and } C_j = c) = \sum_c \text{prob}(C_i = c) \cdot \text{prob}(C_j = c).$$

Theoretically this implication of the null hypothesis is testable by means of a *binomial test* with parameter

$$p = \sum_c \text{prob}(C_i = c) \cdot \text{prob}(C_j = c).$$

However, in practice the compendium contains the frequency counts that are needed to estimate $\text{prob}(C_i = c)$ and $\text{prob}(C_j = c)$ only for a limited set M of nations. Hence the parameter p of this binomial test is *approximated* by

$$[\sum_{c \in M} \text{prob}(C_i = c) \cdot \text{prob}(C_j = c)] + (1 - \sum_{c \in M} \text{prob}(C_i = c)) \cdot (1 - \sum_{c \in M} \text{prob}(C_j = c)).$$

It can be shown that the value of this surrogate measure is *always greater* than the true value of p. This fact tends to bias the results of the aforementioned binomial test. In certain cases the test is not able to uncover isomorphies existing between the exchange relations r_i and r_j.

Method

- *Step 1:* Fix the value of
  N = Number of observations in the test sample.
  The value of N depends on the acceptable beta-error and on the acceptable costs of the test. Samples with 10 to 20 observations are relatively good compromises between the risk of a beta-error and the costs of the test.

- *Step 2:* Browse through the *country profiles* and choose *at random* N nations with valid observations of the exchange relations r_i and r_j. It is acceptable if a country appears several times in the same random sample. Count at the same time
  n = Number of observations in the random sample for which the most important partner C_i with regard to the exchange relation r_i is *identical* to the most important partner C_j with regard to the exchange relation r_j.

- *Step 3:* Consult the *variable descriptions* relating to r_i and r_j, use the available frequency counts in the *statistical overviews* as estimates for the probabilities $\text{prob}(C_i = c)$ and $\text{prob}(C_j = c)$, and determine the parameter

$$p = [\sum_{c \in M} \text{prob}(C_i = c) \cdot \text{prob}(C_j = c)] + (1 - \sum_{c \in M} \text{prob}(C_i = c)) \cdot (1 - \sum_{c \in M} \text{prob}(C_j = c)).$$

- *Step 4:* Consult *table A* of the appendix and determine for the sample size N (see *step 1*) and for the probability p (see *step 3*) the critical value $t_{N,p}$. To find an appropriate table entry the parameter p has to be rounded to the nearest multiple of 0.05.

- *Step 5:* Check whether
  $n \geq t_{N,p}$.
  If this inequality holds there is an isomorphism between the exchange relations r_i and r_j at the 10% level of significance. If $n < t_{N,p}$ there is either no isomorphism or a beta-error that may be caused by an inadequate estimate of the parameter p.

Example

- *Task:* Test the hypothesis that in 1980 the exchange relations described by the variables *Provenance of Foreign Firms (V50)* and *Patent Suppliers (V49)* were isomorphic.

- *Step 1:* To fix the sample size we set N = 10.

- *Step 2:* To compile a test sample we browse *at random* through the *country profiles*. The sample we get this way consists of CANA (= Canada), FRANC (= France), IRE (= Ireland), SRILA (= Sri Lanka), URU (= Uruguay), GREC (= Greece), TUNIS (= Tunisia), SPAIN, PAKI (= Pakistan), and INDIA. For 7 of these 10 countries the rank R1 patent supplier is identical to the rank R1 provenance of foreign firms. Hence n = 7.

- *Step 3:* For the estimation of the parameter p we consult the *variable descriptions* of V49 (= *Patent Suppliers*) and V50 (= *Provenance of Foreign Firms*). According to these variable descriptions the USA and FRANC (= France) are the only countries for which the statistical overviews allow the computation of the terms $prob(C_i = c) \cdot prob(C_j = c)$. Hence

$$p = 0.64 \cdot 0.52 + 0.08 \cdot 0.14 + (1 - 0.64 - 0.08) \cdot (1 - 0.52 - 0.14) = 0.44$$
$$\quad \text{(USA)} \qquad \text{(FRANC)} \qquad\qquad\qquad \text{(others)}$$

- *Step 4:* To find the critical value $t_{N,p}$ we consult *table A* in the appendix. For N = 10 and p = 0.45 the table shows that $t_{N,p} = 8$.

- *Step 5:* For the test of our original hypothesis we compare n with $t_{N,p}$. Since $7 = n < t_{N,p} = 8$ there is no statistical confirmation for the existence of an isomorphy between the exchange relations described by the variables V49 and V50. As stated before this may have to do with the *biased* estimation of p.

CHAPTER 3

THE VARIABLE DESCRIPTIONS

MEASURES DESCRIBING SOCIOECONOMIC DEVELOPMENT

INCOME PER CAPITA (V1)

Short Names:
V1 or GDP/POP.

Definition:
Income per Capita = The given country's gross domestic product (GDP) per inhabitant accumulated during the year stated and valued at constant market prices and exchange rates of the year 1980.

Computational Procedure:
For the computation of the *Income per Capita* the formula
$(1000 \cdot G) / P$
was used, where
G = The country's gross domestic product for the given year, valued at constant prices and exchange rates of the year 1980 and expressed in *thousand* million U.S. dollars. For the computation of G the same procedure was used as for the variable V17.
P = The population of the aforementioned country, expressed in million capita.

Statistical Overview:

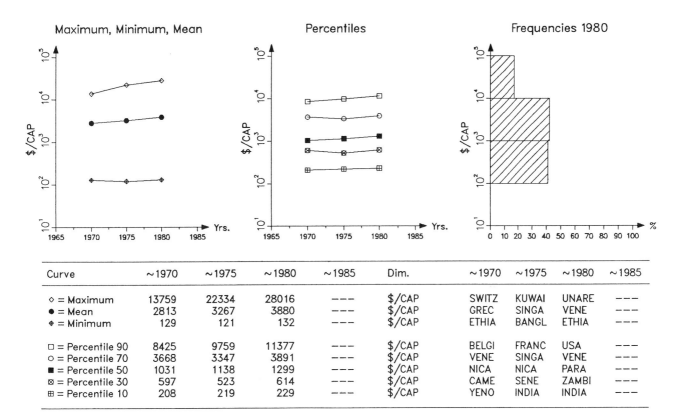

Curve	~1970	~1975	~1980	~1985	Dim.	~1970	~1975	~1980	~1985
◇ = Maximum	13759	22334	28016	---	$/CAP	SWITZ	KUWAI	UNARE	---
● = Mean	2813	3267	3880	---	$/CAP	GREC	SINGA	VENE	---
✦ = Minimum	129	121	132	---	$/CAP	ETHIA	BANGL	ETHIA	---
□ = Percentile 90	8425	9759	11377	---	$/CAP	BELGI	FRANC	USA	---
○ = Percentile 70	3668	3347	3891	---	$/CAP	VENE	SINGA	VENE	---
■ = Percentile 50	1031	1138	1299	---	$/CAP	NICA	NICA	PARA	---
⊗ = Percentile 30	597	523	614	---	$/CAP	CAME	SENE	ZAMBI	---
⊞ = Percentile 10	208	219	229	---	$/CAP	YENO	INDIA	INDIA	---

Scaling:
Ratio scale. Units: U.S. dollars per capita ($/CAP).

Quality of Data:
Unless stated otherwise by footnotes in the country profiles the quality of the data allows *diachronic* and *crossnational* comparisons of the *Income per Capita.*

Availability:
- About 80 observations relating to 1-year intervals between 1968 and 1972.
- About 80 observations relating to 1-year intervals between 1973 and 1977.
- About 90 observations relating to 1-year intervals between 1978 and 1982.

Sources:
- United Nations. *Demographic Yearbook, Historical Supplement.* New York, 1979, tab. 1.
- United Nations. *Demographic Yearbook 1983.* New York, 1985, tab. 5.
- International Monetary Fund (IMF). *International Financial Statistics, Yearbook 1985.* Washington, D.C., 1985.
- World Bank. *World Tables,* 3rd ed. Baltimore, 1984, vol. 1, Economic Data Sheets 1.
- World Bank. *1983 World Bank Atlas.* Washington, D.C., 1983.

TELEPHONES P. TSD. POPULATION (V2)

Short Names:
V2 or PHONES/POP.

Definition:
Telephones p. Tsd. Population = Number of telephones in operation per thousand inhabitants of the given country.

Scaling:
Ratio scale. Units: 1 / thousand capita (1/TSD CAP).

Quality of Data:
Unless stated otherwise by footnotes in the country profiles the quality of the data allows *diachronic* and *crossnational* comparisons of the *Telephones p. Tsd. Population.*

Availability:
- About 100 observations relating to timepoints between 1968 and 1972.
- About 110 observations relating to timepoints between 1973 and 1977.
- About 90 observations relating to timepoints between 1978 and 1982.

Sources:
- Main source: United Nations. *Statistical Yearbook 1982.* New York, 1985, tab. 181.
- Supplementary source 1: United Nations. *Statistical Yearbook 1978.* New York, 1979, tab. 167.
- Supplementary source 2: United Nations. *Statistical Yearbook 1977.* New York, 1978, tab. 168.
- Supplementary source 3: United Nations. *Statistical Yearbook 1974.* New York, 1975, tab. 163.

Statistical Overview:

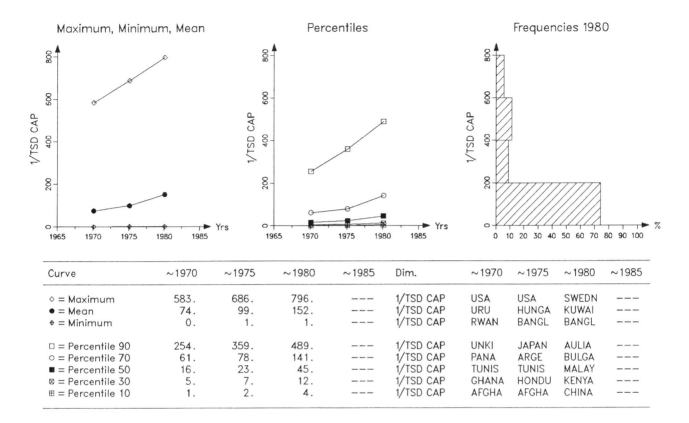

Curve	~1970	~1975	~1980	~1985	Dim.	~1970	~1975	~1980	~1985
◇ = Maximum	583.	686.	796.	---	1/TSD CAP	USA	USA	SWEDN	---
● = Mean	74.	99.	152.	---	1/TSD CAP	URU	HUNGA	KUWAI	---
⊕ = Minimum	0.	1.	1.	---	1/TSD CAP	RWAN	BANGL	BANGL	---
□ = Percentile 90	254.	359.	489.	---	1/TSD CAP	UNKI	JAPAN	AULIA	---
○ = Percentile 70	61.	78.	141.	---	1/TSD CAP	PANA	ARGE	BULGA	---
■ = Percentile 50	16.	23.	45.	---	1/TSD CAP	TUNIS	TUNIS	MALAY	---
⊗ = Percentile 30	5.	7.	12.	---	1/TSD CAP	GHANA	HONDU	KENYA	---
⊞ = Percentile 10	1.	2.	4.	---	1/TSD CAP	AFGHA	AFGHA	CHINA	---

INFANT MORTALITY RATE (V3)

Short Names:
V3 or IMORT.

Definition:
Infant Mortality Rate = Number of children who died during the given year at the age of 0.0 to 12.0 months per 1000 children born alive during the same year.

Scaling:
Ratio scale. Units: 1 / thousand (1/TSD).

Quality of Data:
Unless stated otherwise by footnotes in the country profiles the quality of the data allows *crossnational* comparisons of the *Infant Mortality Rate*. However, a major share of the data are estimates that refer to the *period 1975-1980* (see footnote F5).

Availability:
About 120 observations relating to 1-year intervals between 1978 and 1982.

Statistical Overview:

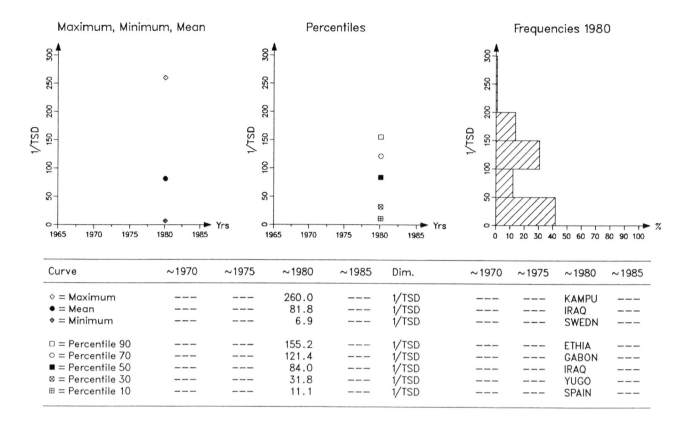

Curve	~1970	~1975	~1980	~1985	Dim.	~1970	~1975	~1980	~1985
◇ = Maximum	---	---	260.0	---	1/TSD	---	---	KAMPU	---
● = Mean	---	---	81.8	---	1/TSD	---	---	IRAQ	---
⊕ = Minimum	---	---	6.9	---	1/TSD	---	---	SWEDN	---
□ = Percentile 90	---	---	155.2	---	1/TSD	---	---	ETHIA	---
○ = Percentile 70	---	---	121.4	---	1/TSD	---	---	GABON	---
■ = Percentile 50	---	---	84.0	---	1/TSD	---	---	IRAQ	---
⊠ = Percentile 30	---	---	31.8	---	1/TSD	---	---	YUGO	---
⊞ = Percentile 10	---	---	11.1	---	1/TSD	---	---	SPAIN	---

Sources:

- Main source: United Nations. *Demographic Yearbook 1983.* New York, 1985, tab. 15.
- Supplementary sources: Ibid. Several other editions.

PHYSICIANS P. MIL. POPULATION (V4)

Short Names:
V4 or PHYSI/POP.

Definition:

Physicians p. Mil. Population = Number of physicians practicing in a given country per million inhabitants of the given country. The professional group of the *physicians* is defined in accordance with the definition given in World Health Organization, *World Health Statistics Annual 1972,* vol. 3 (Geneva, 1976), pp. iv, 236.

Scaling:
Ratio scale. Units: 1 / million (1/MIL).

Statistical Overview:

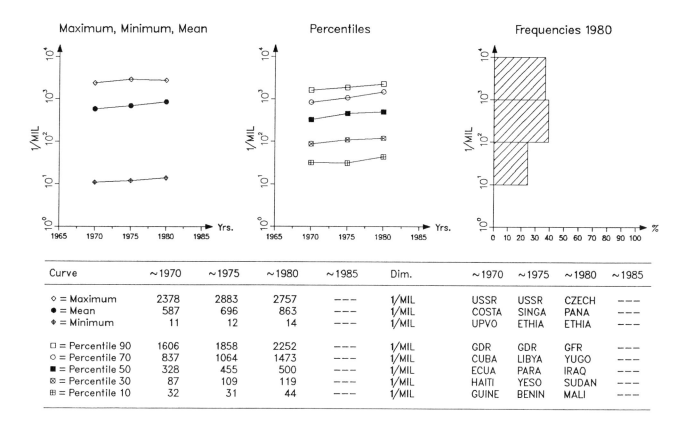

Curve	~1970	~1975	~1980	~1985	Dim.	~1970	~1975	~1980	~1985
◇ = Maximum	2378	2883	2757	– – –	1/MIL	USSR	USSR	CZECH	– – –
● = Mean	587	696	863	– – –	1/MIL	COSTA	SINGA	PANA	– – –
⬧ = Minimum	11	12	14	– – –	1/MIL	UPVO	ETHIA	ETHIA	– – –
□ = Percentile 90	1606	1858	2252	– – –	1/MIL	GDR	GDR	GFR	– – –
○ = Percentile 70	837	1064	1473	– – –	1/MIL	CUBA	LIBYA	YUGO	– – –
■ = Percentile 50	328	455	500	– – –	1/MIL	ECUA	PARA	IRAQ	– – –
⊗ = Percentile 30	87	109	119	– – –	1/MIL	HAITI	YESO	SUDAN	– – –
⊞ = Percentile 10	32	31	44	– – –	1/MIL	GUINE	BENIN	MALI	– – –

Quality of Data:

Unless stated otherwise by footnotes in the country profiles the quality of the data allows *crossnational* comparisons of the *Physicians p. Mil. Population.* However, the validity of *diachronic* comparisons is generally not assured.

Availability:

- About 90 observations relating to timepoints between 1968 and 1972.
- About 100 observations relating to timepoints between 1973 and 1977.
- About 80 observations relating to timepoints between 1978 and 1982.

Sources:

- Number of physicians: World Health Organization (WHO). *World Health Statistics Annual,* several editions. Geneva, several years, tab., "Medical and Allied Health Personnel."
- Population figures for the years around 1970: United Nations. *Demographic Yearbook, Historical Supplement.* New York, 1979, tab. 1.
- Population figures for the years around 1975 and 1980: United Nations. *Demographic Yearbook 1983.* New York, 1985, tab. 5.

ADULT LITERACY (V5)

Short Names:
V5 or LITERACY.

Definition:
Adult Literacy = Percentage share of the population at age 15 and over that is able to read *and* write.

Scaling:
Ratio scale. Units: %.

Quality of Data:
Unless stated otherwise by footnotes in the country profiles the quality of the data allows *crossnational* comparisons of *Adult Literacy*. However, the validity of *diachronic* comparisons is not assured.

Availability:
- About 40 observations relating to timepoints between 1968 and 1972.
- About 40 observations relating to timepoints between 1978 and 1982.

Sources:
UNESCO. *Statistical Yearbook,* several editions. Paris, several years.

Statistical Overview:

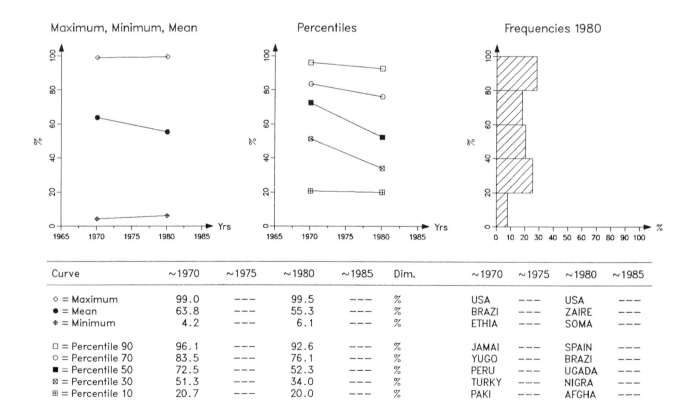

Curve	~1970	~1975	~1980	~1985	Dim.	~1970	~1975	~1980	~1985
◇ = Maximum	99.0	---	99.5	---	%	USA	---	USA	---
● = Mean	63.8	---	55.3	---	%	BRAZI	---	ZAIRE	---
✦ = Minimum	4.2	---	6.1	---	%	ETHIA	---	SOMA	---
□ = Percentile 90	96.1	---	92.6	---	%	JAMAI	---	SPAIN	---
○ = Percentile 70	83.5	---	76.1	---	%	YUGO	---	BRAZI	---
■ = Percentile 50	72.5	---	52.3	---	%	PERU	---	UGADA	---
⊗ = Percentile 30	51.3	---	34.0	---	%	TURKY	---	NIGRA	---
⊞ = Percentile 10	20.7	---	20.0	---	%	PAKI	---	AFGHA	---

DURATION OF SCHOOLING (V6)

Short Names:
V6 or DURSCHOOL.

Definition:
Duration of Schooling = Average time spent on the acquisition of primary and secondary education.

Computational Procedure:
For the computation of the Duration of Schooling the formula
$(0.01 \cdot E) \cdot D$
was used, where
E = Percentage share of the population acquiring primary or secondary education in the age group corresponding to this level of schooling.
D = Duration of a *complete normal* curriculum for acquiring primary and secondary education.
Since E includes students who do not belong to the population at the appropriate age the *Duration of Schooling* published in this book does not exactly correspond to the theoretical definition given above.

Scaling:
Ratio scale. Units: Years (YR).

Statistical Overview:

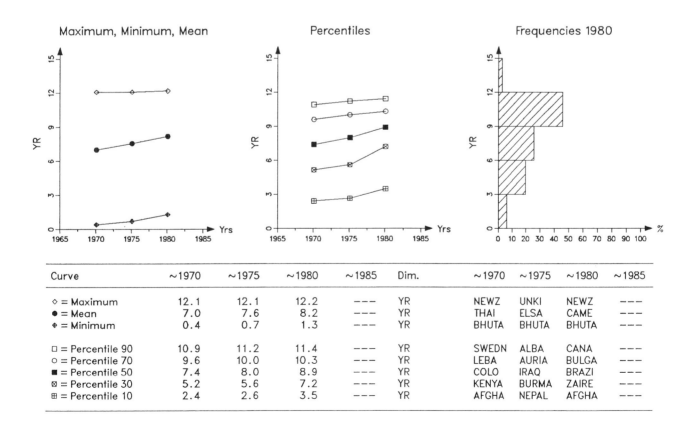

Curve	~1970	~1975	~1980	~1985	Dim.	~1970	~1975	~1980	~1985
◇ = Maximum	12.1	12.1	12.2	---	YR	NEWZ	UNKI	NEWZ	---
● = Mean	7.0	7.6	8.2	---	YR	THAI	ELSA	CAME	---
⬧ = Minimum	0.4	0.7	1.3	---	YR	BHUTA	BHUTA	BHUTA	---
□ = Percentile 90	10.9	11.2	11.4	---	YR	SWEDN	ALBA	CANA	---
○ = Percentile 70	9.6	10.0	10.3	---	YR	LEBA	AURIA	BULGA	---
■ = Percentile 50	7.4	8.0	8.9	---	YR	COLO	IRAQ	BRAZI	---
⊗ = Percentile 30	5.2	5.6	7.2	---	YR	KENYA	BURMA	ZAIRE	---
⊞ = Percentile 10	2.4	2.6	3.5	---	YR	AFGHA	NEPAL	AFGHA	---

Quality of Data:
Unless stated otherwise by footnotes in the country profiles the quality of the data allows *diachronic* and *crossnational* comparisons of the *Duration of Schooling*. However, as stated before, there are slight discrepancies between the theoretical definition of the *Duration of Schooling* and the corresponding computational procedure.

Availability:
- About 100 observations relating to timepoints between 1968 and 1972.
- About 110 observations relating to timepoints between 1973 and 1977.
- About 120 observations relating to timepoints between 1978 and 1982.

Sources:
UNESCO. *Statistical Yearbook 1985*. Paris, 1985, tab. 3.2

STUDENT ENROLLMENT RATIO (V7)

Short Names:
V7 or STUDENROL.

Definition:
Student Enrollment Ratio = Percentage share of the population at the age of 20 to 24 years which is enrolled at an academic educational institution.

Computational Procedure:
For the computation of the *Student Enrollment Ratio* the formula
$100 \cdot (S / P)$
was used, where
S = Number of people who are enrolled at an academic educational institution.
P = Number of people aged 20 to 24 years.
Since S includes students who do not belong to the population at the age of 20 to 24 years, the *Student Enrollment Ratio* published in this book does not exactly correspond to the theoretical definition given above.

Scaling:
Ratio scale. Units: %.

Quality of Data:
Due to the aforementioned difference between the theoretical definition and the computational procedure the student enrollment ratios published in this book are somewhat biased. However, unless stated otherwise by footnotes in the country profiles the quality of the data allows *diachronic* and *crossnational* comparisons.

Availability:
- About 110 observations relating to timepoints between 1968 and 1972.
- About 120 observations relating to timepoints between 1973 and 1977.
- About 120 observations relating to timepoints between 1978 and 1982.

Statistical Overview:

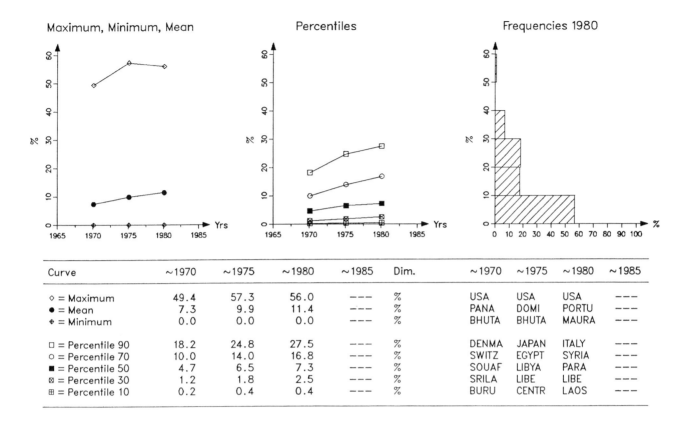

Curve	~1970	~1975	~1980	~1985	Dim.	~1970	~1975	~1980	~1985
◇ = Maximum	49.4	57.3	56.0	– – –	%	USA	USA	USA	– – –
● = Mean	7.3	9.9	11.4	– – –	%	PANA	DOMI	PORTU	– – –
✦ = Minimum	0.0	0.0	0.0	– – –	%	BHUTA	BHUTA	MAURA	– – –
□ = Percentile 90	18.2	24.8	27.5	– – –	%	DENMA	JAPAN	ITALY	– – –
○ = Percentile 70	10.0	14.0	16.8	– – –	%	SWITZ	EGYPT	SYRIA	– – –
■ = Percentile 50	4.7	6.5	7.3	– – –	%	SOUAF	LIBYA	PARA	– – –
⊗ = Percentile 30	1.2	1.8	2.5	– – –	%	SRILA	LIBE	LIBE	– – –
⊞ = Percentile 10	0.2	0.4	0.4	– – –	%	BURU	CENTR	LAOS	– – –

Sources:
UNESCO. *Statistical Yearbook,* several editions. Paris, several years.

SHARE OF AGRICULTURAL LABOR (V8)

Short Names:
V8 or AGRILAB.

Definition:
Share of Agricultural Labor = Percentage share of the *agriculture, animal husbandry* and *forestry workers, fishermen,* and *hunters* in that part of the economically active population that is classifiable by occupation. Armed forces, persons who are unemployed, or persons who are seeking their first job do *not* belong to the *economically active population.* *Agriculture, animal husbandry* and *forestry workers, fishermen,* and *hunters* are defined as category *6* of the *International Standard Classification of Occupations (ISCO-1968).*

Scaling:
Ratio scale. Units: %.

Statistical Overview:

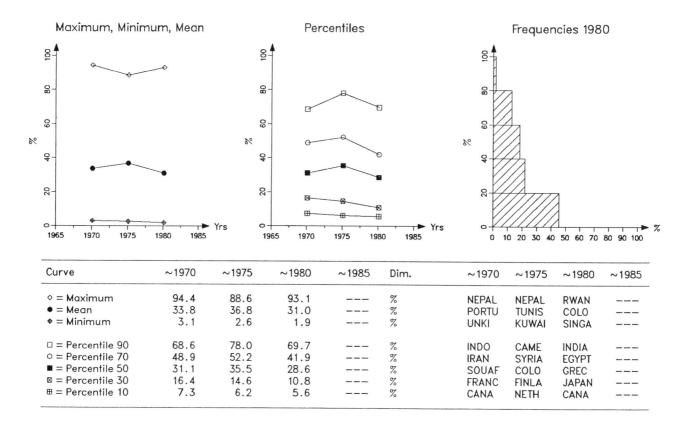

Curve	~1970	~1975	~1980	~1985	Dim.	~1970	~1975	~1980	~1985
◇ = Maximum	94.4	88.6	93.1	---	%	NEPAL	NEPAL	RWAN	---
● = Mean	33.8	36.8	31.0	---	%	PORTU	TUNIS	COLO	---
✦ = Minimum	3.1	2.6	1.9	---	%	UNKI	KUWAI	SINGA	---
□ = Percentile 90	68.6	78.0	69.7	---	%	INDO	CAME	INDIA	---
○ = Percentile 70	48.9	52.2	41.9	---	%	IRAN	SYRIA	EGYPT	---
■ = Percentile 50	31.1	35.5	28.6	---	%	SOUAF	COLO	GREC	---
⊗ = Percentile 30	16.4	14.6	10.8	---	%	FRANC	FINLA	JAPAN	---
⊞ = Percentile 10	7.3	6.2	5.6	---	%	CANA	NETH	CANA	---

Quality of Data:

Unless stated otherwise by footnotes in the country profiles the quality of the data allows *crossnational* comparisons of the *Share of Agricultural Labor.* However, the validity of *diachronic* comparisons is generally not assured.

Availability:

- About 60 observations relating to timepoints between 1968 and 1972.
- About 50 observations relating to timepoints between 1973 and 1977.
- About 60 observations relating to timepoints between 1978 and 1982.

Sources:

International Labour Office (ILO). *Year Book of Labour Statistics,* several editions. Geneva, several years, tab. 2B.

SHARE OF INDUSTRIAL LABOR (V9)

Short Names:
V9 or INDULAB.

Definition:
Share of Industrial Labor = Percentage share of the *production and related workers, transport equipment operators,* and

laborers in that part of the economically active population that is classifiable by occupation. Armed forces, persons who are unemployed, or persons who are seeking their first job do *not* belong to the *economically active population. Production and related workers, transport equipment operators,* and *laborers* are defined as the categories *7 - 9* of the *International Standard Classification of Occupations (ISCO-1968).*

Scaling:
Ratio scale. Units: %.

Quality of Data:
Unless stated otherwise by footnotes in the country profiles the quality of the data allows *crossnational* comparisons of the *Share of Industrial Labor.* However, the validity of *diachronic* comparisons is generally not assured.

Availability:
- About 40 observations relating to timepoints between 1968 and 1972.
- About 50 observations relating to timepoints between 1973 and 1977.
- About 60 observations relating to timepoints between 1978 and 1982.

Sources:
International Labour Office (ILO). *Year Book of Labour Statistics,* several editions. Geneva, several years, tab. 2B.

Statistical Overview:

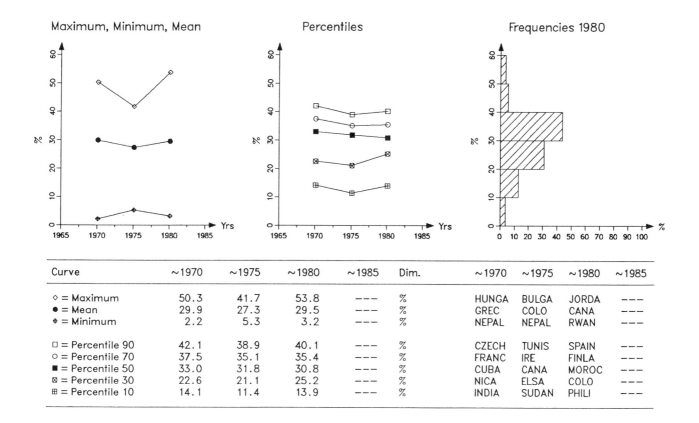

Curve	~1970	~1975	~1980	~1985	Dim.	~1970	~1975	~1980	~1985
◇ = Maximum	50.3	41.7	53.8	---	%	HUNGA	BULGA	JORDA	---
● = Mean	29.9	27.3	29.5	---	%	GREC	COLO	CANA	---
✦ = Minimum	2.2	5.3	3.2	---	%	NEPAL	NEPAL	RWAN	---
□ = Percentile 90	42.1	38.9	40.1	---	%	CZECH	TUNIS	SPAIN	---
○ = Percentile 70	37.5	35.1	35.4	---	%	FRANC	IRE	FINLA	---
■ = Percentile 50	33.0	31.8	30.8	---	%	CUBA	CANA	MOROC	---
⊗ = Percentile 30	22.6	21.1	25.2	---	%	NICA	ELSA	COLO	---
⊞ = Percentile 10	14.1	11.4	13.9	---	%	INDIA	SUDAN	PHILI	---

SHARE OF SERVICE LABOR (V10)

Short Names:
V10 or SERVILAB.

Definition:
Share of Service Labor = Percentage share of the *service, administrative, managerial, sales,* and the *clerical and related workers* in that part of the economically active population that is classifiable by occupation. Armed forces, persons who are unemployed, or persons who are seeking their first job do *not* belong to the *economically active population.* The *service, administrative, managerial, sales,* and the *clerical and related workers* are defined as the categories *2 - 5* of the *International Standard Classification of Occupations (ISCO-1968).*

Scaling:
Ratio scale. Units: %.

Quality of Data:
Unless stated otherwise by footnotes in the country profiles the quality of the data allows *crossnational* comparisons of the *Share of Service Labor.* However, the validity of *diachronic* comparisons is generally not assured.

Statistical Overview:

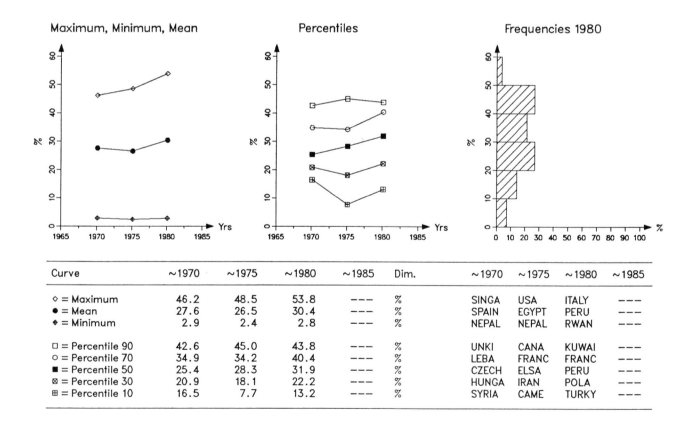

Curve	~1970	~1975	~1980	~1985	Dim.	~1970	~1975	~1980	~1985
◇ = Maximum	46.2	48.5	53.8	---	%	SINGA	USA	ITALY	---
● = Mean	27.6	26.5	30.4	---	%	SPAIN	EGYPT	PERU	---
◆ = Minimum	2.9	2.4	2.8	---	%	NEPAL	NEPAL	RWAN	---
□ = Percentile 90	42.6	45.0	43.8	---	%	UNKI	CANA	KUWAI	---
○ = Percentile 70	34.9	34.2	40.4	---	%	LEBA	FRANC	FRANC	---
■ = Percentile 50	25.4	28.3	31.9	---	%	CZECH	ELSA	PERU	---
⊠ = Percentile 30	20.9	18.1	22.2	---	%	HUNGA	IRAN	POLA	---
⊞ = Percentile 10	16.5	7.7	13.2	---	%	SYRIA	CAME	TURKY	---

Availability:
- About 40 observations relating to timepoints between 1968 and 1972.
- About 40 observations relating to timepoints between 1973 and 1977.
- About 60 observations relating to timepoints between 1978 and 1982.

Sources:
International Labour Office (ILO). *Year Book of Labour Statistics,* several editions. Geneva, several years, tab. 2B.

SHARE OF ACADEMIC LABOR (V11)

Short Names:
V11 or ACALAB.

Definition:
Share of Academic Labor = Percentage share of the *professional, technical, and related workers* in that part of the economically active population that is classifiable by occupation. Armed forces, persons who are unemployed or persons who are seeking their first job do *not* belong to the *economically active population.* The *professional, technical, and related workers* are defined as the categories *0 - 1* of the *International Standard Classification of Occupations (ISCO-1968).*

Statistical Overview:

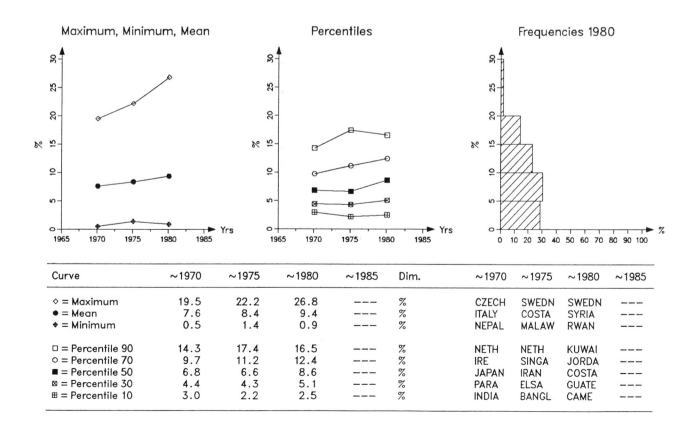

Curve	~1970	~1975	~1980	~1985	Dim.	~1970	~1975	~1980	~1985
◇ = Maximum	19.5	22.2	26.8	---	%	CZECH	SWEDN	SWEDN	---
● = Mean	7.6	8.4	9.4	---	%	ITALY	COSTA	SYRIA	---
◆ = Minimum	0.5	1.4	0.9	---	%	NEPAL	MALAW	RWAN	---
□ = Percentile 90	14.3	17.4	16.5	---	%	NETH	NETH	KUWAI	---
○ = Percentile 70	9.7	11.2	12.4	---	%	IRE	SINGA	JORDA	---
■ = Percentile 50	6.8	6.6	8.6	---	%	JAPAN	IRAN	COSTA	---
⊠ = Percentile 30	4.4	4.3	5.1	---	%	PARA	ELSA	GUATE	---
⊞ = Percentile 10	3.0	2.2	2.5	---	%	INDIA	BANGL	CAME	---

Scaling:
Ratio scale. Units: %.

Quality of Data:
Unless stated otherwise by footnotes in the country profiles the quality of the data allows *crossnational* comparisons of the *Share of Academic Labor.* However, the validity of *diachronic* comparisons is generally not assured.

Availability:
- About 40 observations relating to timepoints between 1968 and 1972.
- About 40 observations relating to timepoints between 1973 and 1977.
- About 60 observations relating to timepoints between 1978 and 1982.

Sources:
International Labour Office (ILO). *Year Book of Labour Statistics,* several editions. Geneva, several years, tab. 2B.

SHARE OF SELF-EMPLOYED LABOR (V12)

Short Names:
V12 or SELFLAB.

Definition:
Share of Self-Employed Labor = Percentage share of the employers and own-account workers in the economically active population that is classifiable by status. Armed forces, persons who are unemployed or not classifiable by status, or persons who are seeking their first job do *not* belong to the *economically active population.*

Scaling:
Ratio scale. Units: %.

Quality of Data:
Unless stated otherwise by footnotes in the country profiles the quality of the data allows *crossnational* comparisons of the *Share of Self-Employed Labor.* However, the validity of *diachronic* comparisons is generally not assured.

Availability:
- About 40 observations relating to timepoints between 1968 and 1972.
- About 40 observations relating to timepoints between 1973 and 1977.
- About 40 observations relating to timepoints between 1978 and 1982.

Sources:
International Labour Office (ILO). *Year Book of Labour Statistics,* several editions. Geneva, several years, tab. 2B.

Statistical Overview:

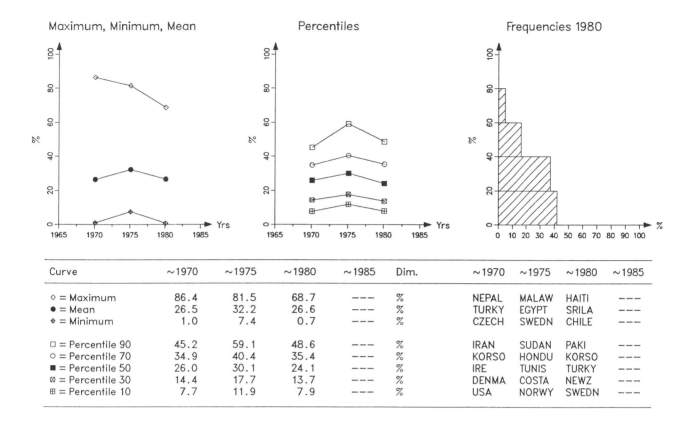

Curve	~1970	~1975	~1980	~1985	Dim.	~1970	~1975	~1980	~1985
◇ = Maximum	86.4	81.5	68.7	---	%	NEPAL	MALAW	HAITI	---
● = Mean	26.5	32.2	26.6	---	%	TURKY	EGYPT	SRILA	---
✦ = Minimum	1.0	7.4	0.7	---	%	CZECH	SWEDN	CHILE	---
□ = Percentile 90	45.2	59.1	48.6	---	%	IRAN	SUDAN	PAKI	---
○ = Percentile 70	34.9	40.4	35.4	---	%	KORSO	HONDU	KORSO	---
■ = Percentile 50	26.0	30.1	24.1	---	%	IRE	TUNIS	TURKY	---
⊗ = Percentile 30	14.4	17.7	13.7	---	%	DENMA	COSTA	NEWZ	---
⊞ = Percentile 10	7.7	11.9	7.9	---	%	USA	NORWY	SWEDN	---

OTHER IMPORTANT VARIABLES

- Lack of Civil Liberties (V30).
- Lack of Political Rights (V31).
- GDP Share of Agriculture (V42).
- GDP Share of Industry (V43).
- GDP Share of Services (V44).
- GDP Share of Manufacturing (V28).
- Export Share of Manufactures (V29).

MEASURES DESCRIBING NATIONAL POWER

MILITARY EXPENDITURES (V13)

Short Names:
V13 or MILEXP.

Definition:
Military Expenditures = The given country's military expenditure for the year stated, valued at constant prices and exchange rates of the year 1980.

Computational Procedure:
For the computation of the *Military Expenditures* the formula
$(0.01 \cdot M) \cdot G$
was used, where
M = The given country's percentage share of the military expenditures in the gross domestic product of the year stated.
G = The country's gross domestic product for the given year, valued at constant prices and exchange rates of the year 1980 and expressed in thousand million U.S. dollars. For the computation of G the same procedure was used as for the variable V17.

Statistical Overview:

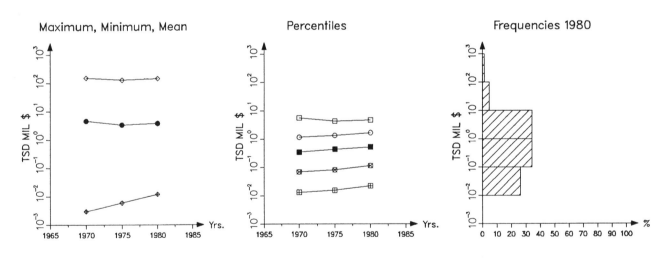

Curve	~1970	~1975	~1980	~1985	Dim.	~1970	~1975	~1980	~1985
◇ = Maximum	152.009	129.169	144.175	–––	TSD MIL $	USA	USA	USA	–––
● = Mean	4.623	3.383	3.815	–––	TSD MIL $	JAPAN	AULIA	AULIA	–––
✦ = Minimum	0.003	0.006	0.012	–––	TSD MIL $	MALAW	LIBE	SIERA	–––
□ = Percentile 90	5.549	4.282	4.676	–––	TSD MIL $	JAPAN	INDIA	CANA	–––
○ = Percentile 70	1.160	1.344	1.669	–––	TSD MIL $	DENMA	ARCE	NORWY	–––
■ = Percentile 50	0.344	0.432	0.520	–––	TSD MIL $	NEWZ	HUNGA	HUNGA	–––
⊗ = Percentile 30	0.069	0.081	0.114	–––	TSD MIL $	GUATE	BOLI	NICA	–––
⊞ = Percentile 10	0.013	0.015	0.022	–––	TSD MIL $	NIGER	BURU	BURU	–––

Scaling:
Ratio scale. Units: Thousand million U.S. dollars (TSD MIL $).

Quality of Data:
Unless stated otherwise by footnotes in the country profiles the quality of the data allows *diachronic* and *crossnational* comparisons of the *Military Expenditures.*

Availability:
- About 60 observations relating to 1-year intervals between 1968 and 1972.
- About 80 observations relating to 1-year intervals between 1973 and 1977.
- About 90 observations relating to 1-year intervals between 1978 and 1982.

Sources:
- SIPRI. *SIPRI Yearbook 1980.* London, 1980, tab. 1A.3, 1A.4.
- SIPRI. *SIPRI Yearbook 1985.* London, 1985, tab. 7A.4, 7A.5.
- International Monetary Fund (IMF). *International Financial Statistics, Yearbook 1985.* Washington, D.C., 1985.
- World Bank. *World Tables,* 3rd ed. Baltimore, 1984, vol. 1, Economic Data Sheets 1.
- World Bank. *1983 World Bank Atlas.* Washington, D.C., 1983.

MILITARY MANPOWER (V14)

Short Names:
V14 or MILPOP.

Definition:
Military Manpower = Number of people belonging to the *active-duty* military forces of the given country. Hence, *reserve forces* are *not* included in the *Military Manpower.*

Scaling:
Ratio scale. Units: Thousand capita (TSD CAP).

Quality of Data:
Unless stated otherwise by footnotes in the country profiles the quality of the data allows *diachronic* and *crossnational* comparisons of the *Military Manpower.*

Availability:
- About 110 observations relating to timepoints between 1968 and 1972.
- About 120 observations relating to timepoints between 1973 and 1977.
- About 120 observations relating to timepoints between 1978 and 1982.

Sources:
U. S. Arms Control and Disarmament Agency. *World Military Expenditures and Arms Transfers,* several editions. Washington, D.C., several years.

Statistical Overview:

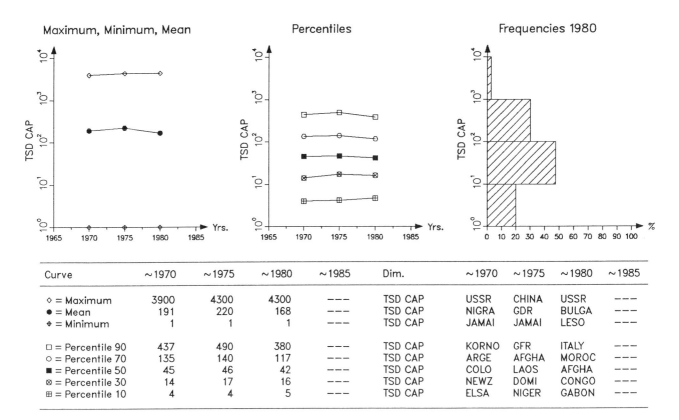

Curve	~1970	~1975	~1980	~1985	Dim.	~1970	~1975	~1980	~1985
◇ = Maximum	3900	4300	4300	---	TSD CAP	USSR	CHINA	USSR	---
● = Mean	191	220	168	---	TSD CAP	NIGRA	GDR	BULGA	---
⬦ = Minimum	1	1	1	---	TSD CAP	JAMAI	JAMAI	LESO	---
□ = Percentile 90	437	490	380	---	TSD CAP	KORNO	GFR	ITALY	---
○ = Percentile 70	135	140	117	---	TSD CAP	ARGE	AFGHA	MOROC	---
■ = Percentile 50	45	46	42	---	TSD CAP	COLO	LAOS	AFGHA	---
⊗ = Percentile 30	14	17	16	---	TSD CAP	NEWZ	DOMI	CONGO	---
⊞ = Percentile 10	4	4	5	---	TSD CAP	ELSA	NIGER	GABON	---

MEN AT AGE 20 - 30 (V15)

Short Names:
V15 or MEN20-30.

Definition:
Men at Age 20 - 30 = Number of *male* inhabitants who are at the age between 20.0 and 30.0 years.

Scaling:
Ratio scale. Units: Thousand capita (TSD CAP).

Quality of Data:
Unless stated otherwise by footnotes in the country profiles the quality of the data allows *diachronic* and *crossnational* comparisons.

Statistical Overview:

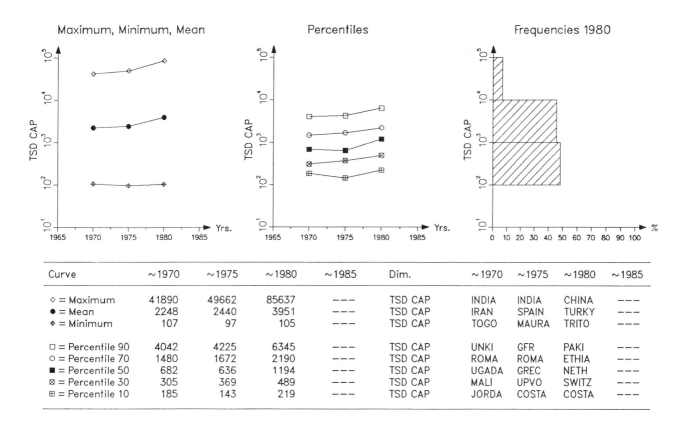

Curve	~1970	~1975	~1980	~1985	Dim.	~1970	~1975	~1980	~1985
◇ = Maximum	41890	49662	85637	– – –	TSD CAP	INDIA	INDIA	CHINA	– – –
● = Mean	2248	2440	3951	– – –	TSD CAP	IRAN	SPAIN	TURKY	– – –
⊕ = Minimum	107	97	105	– – –	TSD CAP	TOGO	MAURA	TRITO	– – –
□ = Percentile 90	4042	4225	6345	– – –	TSD CAP	UNKI	GFR	PAKI	– – –
○ = Percentile 70	1480	1672	2190	– – –	TSD CAP	ROMA	ROMA	ETHIA	– – –
■ = Percentile 50	682	636	1194	– – –	TSD CAP	UGADA	GREC	NETH	– – –
⊗ = Percentile 30	305	369	489	– – –	TSD CAP	MALI	UPVO	SWITZ	– – –
⊞ = Percentile 10	185	143	219	– – –	TSD CAP	JORDA	COSTA	COSTA	– – –

Availability:

- About 70 observations relating to timepoints between 1968 and 1972.
- About 80 observations relating to timepoints between 1973 and 1977.
- About 80 observations relating to timepoints between 1978 and 1982.

Sources:

United Nations. *Demographic Yearbook,* several editions. New York, several years.

POPULATION (V16)

Short Names:

V16 or POP.

Definition:

Population = Number of people de facto living in the given country.

Scaling:

Ratio scale. Units: Million capita (MIL CAP).

Statistical Overview:

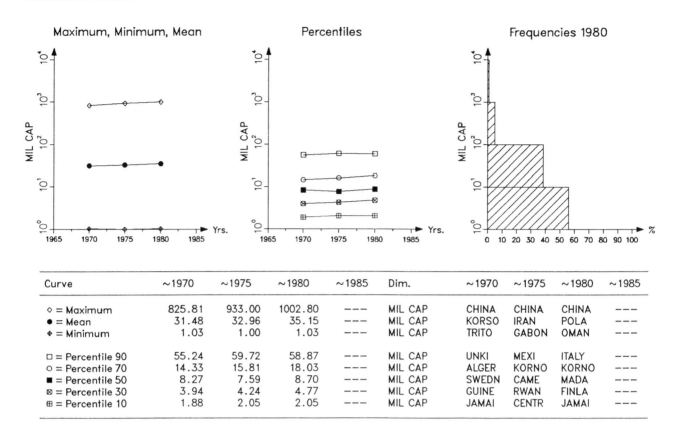

| Maximum, Minimum, Mean | Percentiles | Frequencies 1980 |

Curve	~1970	~1975	~1980	~1985	Dim.	~1970	~1975	~1980	~1985
◇ = Maximum	825.81	933.00	1002.80	---	MIL CAP	CHINA	CHINA	CHINA	---
● = Mean	31.48	32.96	35.15	---	MIL CAP	KORSO	IRAN	POLA	---
✦ = Minimum	1.03	1.00	1.03	---	MIL CAP	TRITO	GABON	OMAN	---
□ = Percentile 90	55.24	59.72	58.87	---	MIL CAP	UNKI	MEXI	ITALY	---
○ = Percentile 70	14.33	15.81	18.03	---	MIL CAP	ALGER	KORNO	KORNO	---
■ = Percentile 50	8.27	7.59	8.70	---	MIL CAP	SWEDN	CAME	MADA	---
⊗ = Percentile 30	3.94	4.24	4.77	---	MIL CAP	GUINE	RWAN	FINLA	---
⊞ = Percentile 10	1.88	2.05	2.05	---	MIL CAP	JAMAI	CENTR	JAMAI	---

Quality of Data:

Unless stated otherwise by footnotes in the country profiles the quality of the data allows *diachronic* comparisons. However, due to different national concepts of the *de jure population* (see appendix, footnote F147) the validity of *crossnational* comparisons is slightly limited if population figures refer to this concept.

Availability:

- About 110 observations relating to timepoints between 1968 and 1972.
- About 120 observations relating to timepoints between 1973 and 1977.
- About 130 observations relating to timepoints between 1978 and 1982.

Sources:

- United Nations. *Demographic Yearbook, Historical Supplement.* New York, 1979, tab. 1.
- United Nations. *Demographic Yearbook 1983.* New York, 1985, tab. 5.

GROSS DOMESTIC PRODUCT (V17)

Short Names:
V17 or GDP.

Definition:
Gross Domestic Product = The given country's gross domestic product of the year stated, valued at constant prices and exchange rates of the year 1980.

Computational Procedure:
For the computation of the *Gross Domestic Product* the formula
$(A / B) \cdot G$
was used, where
A = The given country's gross national product of the year 1980 at constant average 1979-81 exchange rates and market prices and expressed in *U.S. dollars.* (Source: World Bank. *1983 World Bank Atlas.*)
B = The given country's gross national product of the year 1980 at current market prices and expressed in the country's *national currency.* (Source: World Bank. *World Tables.*) Hence, the term (A / B) approximates the average exchange rate of the year 1980.
G = The given country's gross *domestic* product of the year stated, valued at constant prices of the year 1980 and expressed in the country's *national currency.*

Scaling:
Ratio scale. Units: Thousand million U.S. dollars (TSD MIL $).

Statistical Overview:

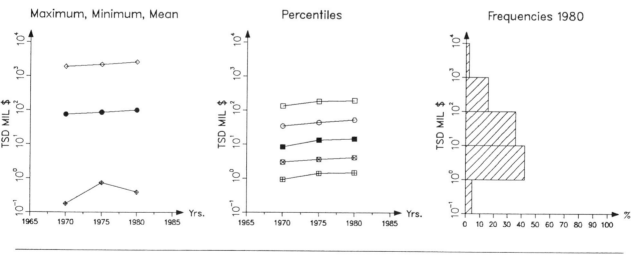

Curve	~1970	~1975	~1980	~1985	Dim.	~1970	~1975	~1980	~1985
◇ = Maximum	1924.160	2174.560	2588.420	---	TSD MIL $	USA	USA	USA	---
● = Mean	75.147	85.894	99.459	---	TSD MIL $	MEXI	SWITZ	SWITZ	---
✦ = Minimum	0.178	0.732	0.389	---	TSD MIL $	LESO	BURU	LESO	---
□ = Percentile 90	133.470	183.225	194.376	---	TSD MIL $	SPAIN	SPAIN	SPAIN	---
○ = Percentile 70	34.216	43.725	52.823	---	TSD MIL $	FINLA	KORSO	NORWY	---
■ = Percentile 50	8.432	13.413	14.613	---	TSD MIL $	LIBYA	MOROC	SYRIA	---
⊗ = Percentile 30	3.026	3.654	4.145	---	TSD MIL $	ETHIA	ZAMBI	ETHIA	---
⊞ = Percentile 10	0.931	1.415	1.488	---	TSD MIL $	HAITI	HONDU	HAITI	---

Quality of Data:
Unless stated otherwise by footnotes in the country profiles the quality of the data allows *diachronic* and *crossnational* comparisons of the *Gross Domestic Product.*

Availability:
- About 80 observations relating to 1-year intervals between 1968 and 1972.
- About 90 observations relating to 1-year intervals between 1973 and 1977.
- About 90 observations relating to 1-year intervals between 1978 and 1982.

Sources:
- International Monetary Fund (IMF). *International Financial Statistics, Yearbook 1985.* Washington, D.C., 1985.
- World Bank. *World Tables,* 3rd ed. Baltimore, 1984, vol. 1, Economic Data Sheets 1.
- World Bank. *1983 World Bank Atlas.* Washington, D.C., 1983.

SHARE IN WORLD IMPORTS (V18)

Short Names:
V18 or WIMPSHARE.

Definition:
Share in World Imports = Per thousand share of the commodity imports of the given country in the sum of the cif-values of the commodities that have been imported for domestic use by all the nations of the world during the given year.

Scaling:
Ratio scale. Units: 1 / thousand (1/TSD).

Quality of Data:
Unless stated otherwise by footnotes in the country profiles the quality of the data allows *diachronic* comparisons of the data. However, the validity of some *crossnational* comparisons is limited since the trade statistics of many countries are based on the *general trade* concept, which includes commodities that are imported for *re-export.*

Availability:
- About 110 observations relating to 1-year intervals between 1968 and 1972.
- About 120 observations relating to 1-year intervals between 1973 and 1977.
- About 120 observations relating to 1-year intervals between 1978 and 1982.

Sources:
United Nations. *Yearbook of International Trade Statistics 1983.* New York, 1985, vol. 1, Special Table A.

Statistical Overview:

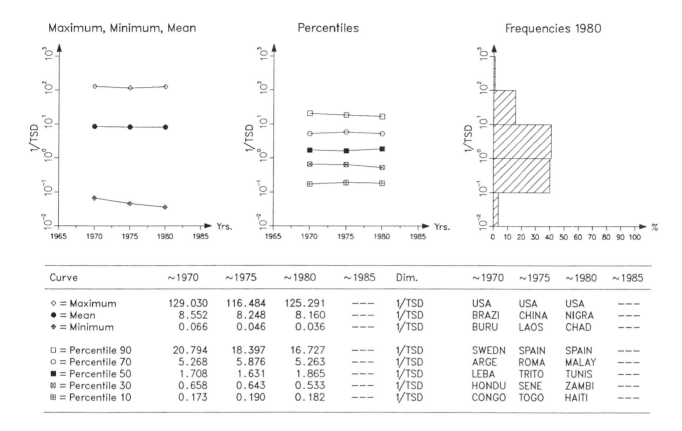

Curve	~1970	~1975	~1980	~1985	Dim.	~1970	~1975	~1980	~1985
◇ = Maximum	129.030	116.484	125.291	---	1/TSD	USA	USA	USA	---
● = Mean	8.552	8.248	8.160	---	1/TSD	BRAZI	CHINA	NIGRA	---
✦ = Minimum	0.066	0.046	0.036	---	1/TSD	BURU	LAOS	CHAD	---
□ = Percentile 90	20.794	18.397	16.727	---	1/TSD	SWEDN	SPAIN	SPAIN	---
○ = Percentile 70	5.268	5.876	5.263	---	1/TSD	ARGE	ROMA	MALAY	---
■ = Percentile 50	1.708	1.631	1.865	---	1/TSD	LEBA	TRITO	TUNIS	---
⊠ = Percentile 30	0.658	0.643	0.533	---	1/TSD	HONDU	SENE	ZAMBI	---
⊞ = Percentile 10	0.173	0.190	0.182	---	1/TSD	CONGO	TOGO	HAITI	---

SHARE IN WORLD EXPORTS (V19)

Short Names:
V19 or WEXPSHARE.

Definition:
Share in World Exports = Per thousand share of the commodity exports of the given country in the sum of the fob-values of the indigenously produced commodities that have been exported by all the nations of the world during the given year.

Scaling:
Ratio scale. Units: 1 / thousand (1/TSD).

Quality of Data:
Unless stated otherwise by footnotes in the country profiles the quality of the data allows *diachronic* comparisons of the data. However, the validity of some *crossnational* comparisons is limited since the trade statistics of many countries are based on the *general trade* concept, which includes *re-exports* of commodities of *foreign* origin.

Availability:

- About 110 observations relating to 1-year intervals between 1968 and 1972.
- About 120 observations relating to 1-year intervals between 1973 and 1977.
- About 120 observations relating to 1-year intervals between 1978 and 1982.

Sources:

United Nations. *Yearbook of International Trade Statistics 1983.* New York, 1985, vol. 1, Special Table A.

Statistical Overview:

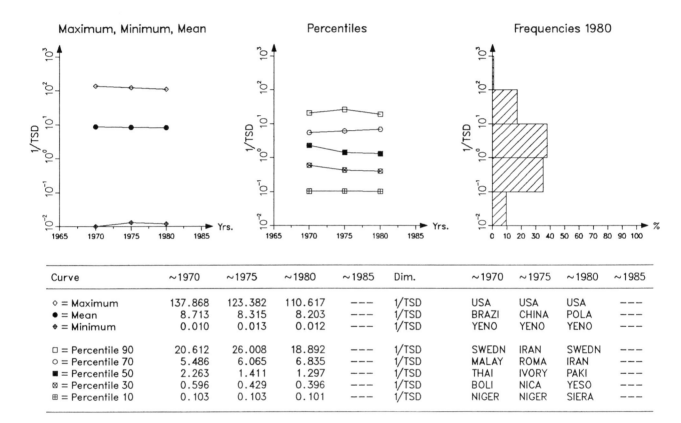

Curve	~1970	~1975	~1980	~1985	Dim.	~1970	~1975	~1980	~1985
◇ = Maximum	137.868	123.382	110.617	---	1/TSD	USA	USA	USA	---
● = Mean	8.713	8.315	8.203	---	1/TSD	BRAZI	CHINA	POLA	---
◈ = Minimum	0.010	0.013	0.012	---	1/TSD	YENO	YENO	YENO	---
□ = Percentile 90	20.612	26.008	18.892	---	1/TSD	SWEDN	IRAN	SWEDN	---
○ = Percentile 70	5.486	6.065	6.835	---	1/TSD	MALAY	ROMA	IRAN	---
■ = Percentile 50	2.263	1.411	1.297	---	1/TSD	THAI	IVORY	PAKI	---
⊠ = Percentile 30	0.596	0.429	0.396	---	1/TSD	BOLI	NICA	YESO	---
⊞ = Percentile 10	0.103	0.103	0.101	---	1/TSD	NIGER	NIGER	SIERA	---

MEASURES DESCRIBING NATIONAL AUTONOMY

GDP SHARE OF IMPORTS (V20)

Short Names:
V20 or IMP/GDP.

Definition:
GDP Share of Imports = Percentage share of the cif-valued commodity imports for domestic use in the gross domestic product that the given country has accumulated during the year stated.

Scaling:
Ratio scale. Units: %.

Quality of Data:
Unless stated otherwise by footnotes in the country profiles the quality of the data allows *diachronic* comparisons of the *GDP Share of Imports*. However, the validity of some *crossnational* comparisons is limited since the trade statistics of many countries are based on the *general trade* concept, which includes commodities that are imported for *re-export*.

Statistical Overview:

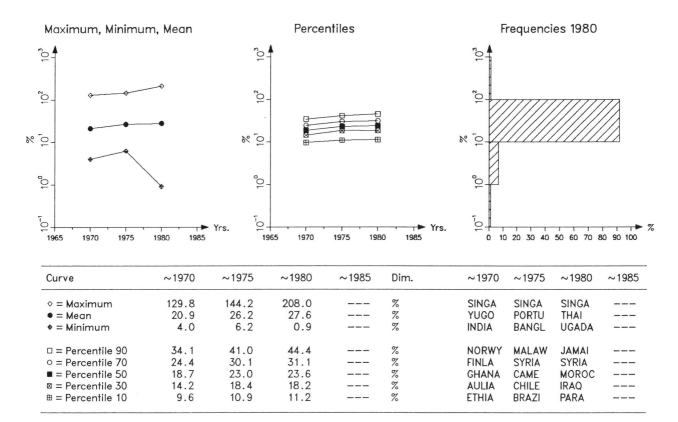

Curve	~1970	~1975	~1980	~1985	Dim.	~1970	~1975	~1980	~1985
◇ = Maximum	129.8	144.2	208.0	---	%	SINGA	SINGA	SINGA	---
● = Mean	20.9	26.2	27.6	---	%	YUGO	PORTU	THAI	---
✦ = Minimum	4.0	6.2	0.9	---	%	INDIA	BANGL	UGADA	---
□ = Percentile 90	34.1	41.0	44.4	---	%	NORWY	MALAW	JAMAI	---
○ = Percentile 70	24.4	30.1	31.1	---	%	FINLA	SYRIA	SYRIA	---
■ = Percentile 50	18.7	23.0	23.6	---	%	GHANA	CAME	MOROC	---
⊗ = Percentile 30	14.2	18.4	18.2	---	%	AULIA	CHILE	IRAQ	---
⊞ = Percentile 10	9.6	10.9	11.2	---	%	ETHIA	BRAZI	PARA	---

Availability:
- About 90 observations relating to 1-year intervals between 1968 and 1972.
- About 100 observations relating to 1-year intervals between 1973 and 1977.
- About 110 observations relating to 1-year intervals between 1978 and 1982.

Sources:
- Trade figures: United Nations. *Yearbook of International Trade Statistics 1983.* New York, 1985, vol. 1, Special Table A.
- Exchange rates: World Bank. *World Tables,* 3rd ed. Baltimore, 1984, vol. 1, Economic Data Sheets 1, row "Foreign exchange rates."
- Main source for GDP statistics: International Monetary Fund (IMF). *International Financial Statistics, Yearbook 1985.* Washington, D.C., 1985, row 99b.
- Supplementary source for GDP statistics: World Bank. *World Tables,* 3rd ed. Baltimore, 1984, vol. 1, Economic Data Sheets 1, row "GDP at market prices, current price figures."

GDP SHARE OF EXPORTS (V21)

Short Names:
V21 or EXP/GDP.

Definition:
GDP Share of Exports = Percentage share of the fob-value of the indigenously produced commodity exports in the gross domestic product that the given country has accumulated during the year stated.

Scaling:
Ratio scale. Units: %.

Quality of Data:
Unless stated otherwise by footnotes in the country profiles the quality of the data allows *diachronic* comparisons of the *GDP Share of Exports.* However, the validity of some *crossnational* comparisons is limited since the trade statistics of many countries are based on the *general trade* concept, which includes *re-exports* of commodities of *foreign* origin.

Availability:
- About 90 observations relating to 1-year intervals between 1968 and 1972.
- About 100 observations relating to 1-year intervals between 1973 and 1977.
- About 110 observations relating to 1-year intervals between 1978 and 1982.

Statistical Overview:

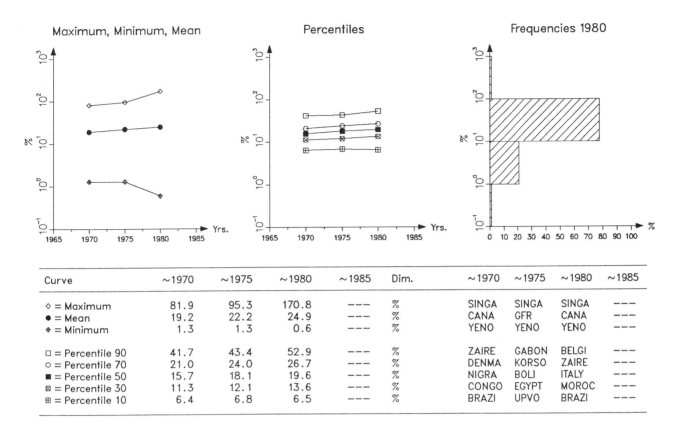

Curve	~1970	~1975	~1980	~1985	Dim.	~1970	~1975	~1980	~1985
◇ = Maximum	81.9	95.3	170.8	---	%	SINGA	SINGA	SINGA	---
● = Mean	19.2	22.2	24.9	---	%	CANA	GFR	CANA	---
✦ = Minimum	1.3	1.3	0.6	---	%	YENO	YENO	YENO	---
□ = Percentile 90	41.7	43.4	52.9	---	%	ZAIRE	GABON	BELGI	---
○ = Percentile 70	21.0	24.0	26.7	---	%	DENMA	KORSO	ZAIRE	---
■ = Percentile 50	15.7	18.1	19.6	---	%	NIGRA	BOLI	ITALY	---
⊗ = Percentile 30	11.3	12.1	13.6	---	%	CONGO	EGYPT	MOROC	---
⊞ = Percentile 10	6.4	6.8	6.5	---	%	BRAZI	UPVO	BRAZI	---

Sources:
- Trade figures: United Nations. *Yearbook of International Trade Statistics 1983.* New York, 1985, vol. 1, Special Table A.
- Exchange rates: World Bank. *World Tables,* 3rd ed. Baltimore, 1984, vol. 1, Economic Data Sheets 1, row "Foreign exchange rates."
- Main source for GDP statistics: International Monetary Fund (IMF). *International Financial Statistics, Yearbook 1985.* Washington, D.C., 1985, row 99b.
- Supplementary source for GDP statistics: World Bank. *World Tables,* 3rd ed. Baltimore, 1984, vol. 1, Economic Data Sheets 1, row "GDP at market prices, current price figures."

EXPORT PARTNER CONCENTRATION (V22)

Short Names:
V22 or EXPACONC.

Definition:
Export Partner Concentration = Percentage share of the 1-year cumulation of the commodity exports of the given country that have been supplied to that nation that consumes the greatest share of the aforementioned exports.

Statistical Overview:

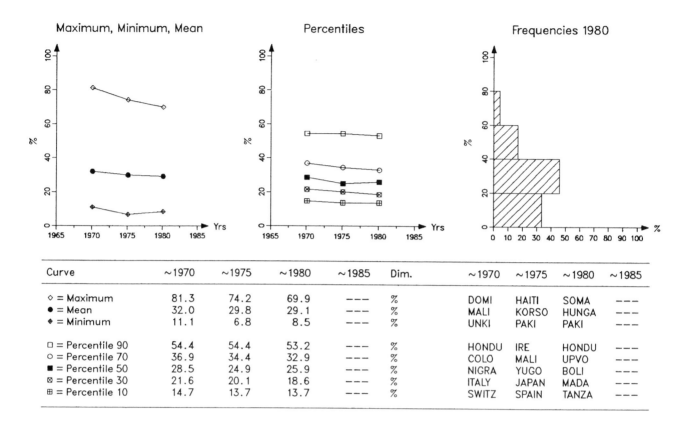

Curve	~1970	~1975	~1980	~1985	Dim.	~1970	~1975	~1980	~1985
◇ = Maximum	81.3	74.2	69.9	---	%	DOMI	HAITI	SOMA	---
● = Mean	32.0	29.8	29.1	---	%	MALI	KORSO	HUNGA	---
✦ = Minimum	11.1	6.8	8.5	---	%	UNKI	PAKI	PAKI	---
□ = Percentile 90	54.4	54.4	53.2	---	%	HONDU	IRE	HONDU	---
○ = Percentile 70	36.9	34.4	32.9	---	%	COLO	MALI	UPVO	---
■ = Percentile 50	28.5	24.9	25.9	---	%	NIGRA	YUGO	BOLI	---
⊗ = Percentile 30	21.6	20.1	18.6	---	%	ITALY	JAPAN	MADA	---
⊞ = Percentile 10	14.7	13.7	13.7	---	%	SWITZ	SPAIN	TANZA	---

Scaling:
Ratio scale. Units: %.

Quality of Data:
Unless stated otherwise by footnotes in the country profiles the quality of the data allows *diachronic* and *crossnational* comparisons of the *Export Partner Concentration.*

Availability:
- About 100 observations relating to 1-year intervals between 1968 and 1972.
- About 110 observations relating to 1-year intervals between 1973 and 1977.
- About 100 observations relating to 1-year intervals between 1978 and 1982.

Sources:
United Nations. *Yearbook of International Trade Statistics,* several editions. New York, several years.

TOTAL DEBT AS % OF GDP (V23)

Short Names:
V23 or DEBT/GDP.

Definition:
Total Debt as % of GDP = Gross external liabilities of the given country as % of the gross domestic product that the country has accumulated during the year stated. *Gross external liabilities* are defined as the sum of *public long-term debts, private debts not guaranteed by a public entity, short-term debts,* and the *use of IMF credits.* The *Gross external liabilities* are *not* offset against external assets.

Scaling:
Ratio scale. Units: %.

Quality of Data:
Unless stated otherwise by footnotes in the country profiles the quality of the data allows *crossnational* comparisons of the *Total Debt as % of GDP*.

Availability:
About 70 observations relating to timepoints between 1978 and 1982.

Statistical Overview:

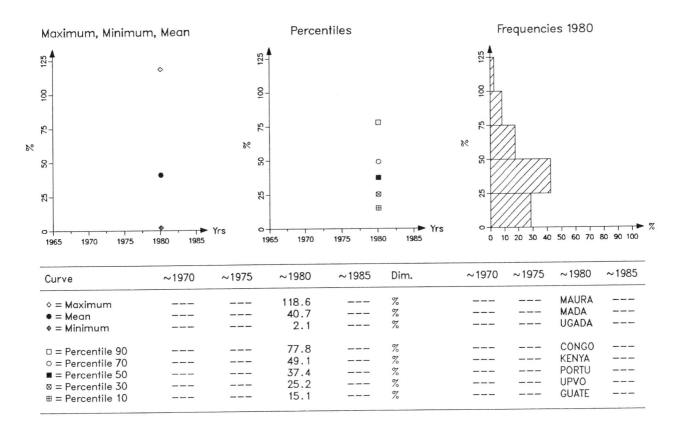

Curve	~1970	~1975	~1980	~1985	Dim.	~1970	~1975	~1980	~1985
◇ = Maximum	---	---	118.6	---	%	---	---	MAURA	---
● = Mean	---	---	40.7	---	%	---	---	MADA	---
⊕ = Minimum	---	---	2.1	---	%	---	---	UGADA	---
□ = Percentile 90	---	---	77.8	---	%	---	---	CONGO	---
○ = Percentile 70	---	---	49.1	---	%	---	---	KENYA	---
■ = Percentile 50	---	---	37.4	---	%	---	---	PORTU	---
⊠ = Percentile 30	---	---	25.2	---	%	---	---	UPVO	---
⊞ = Percentile 10	---	---	15.1	---	%	---	---	GUATE	---

Sources:

- Source for exchange rates: World Bank. *World Tables,* 3rd ed. Baltimore, 1984, vol. 1, Economic Data Sheets 1, row "Foreign exchange rate."
- Main source for gross domestic product: International Monetary Fund (IMF). *International Financial Statistics, Yearbook 1985.* Washington, D.C., 1985, row 99b.
- Supplementary source for gross domestic product: World Bank. *World Tables,* 3rd ed. Baltimore, 1984, vol. 1, Economic Data Sheets 1, row "GDP at current market prices."
- Source for gross external liabilities: World Bank. *World Debt Tables, 1985-86 Edition.* Washington, D.C., 1986.

SHARE OF NEW FOREIGN PATENTS (V24)

Short Names:
V24 or FORPAT.

Definition:
Share of New Foreign Patents = Percentage share of the patents of *nonresidents* in the total of all patents that were *granted* during the year stated. *Inventor's certificates* used in some East European countries are considered to be equivalent to *patents.*

Statistical Overview:

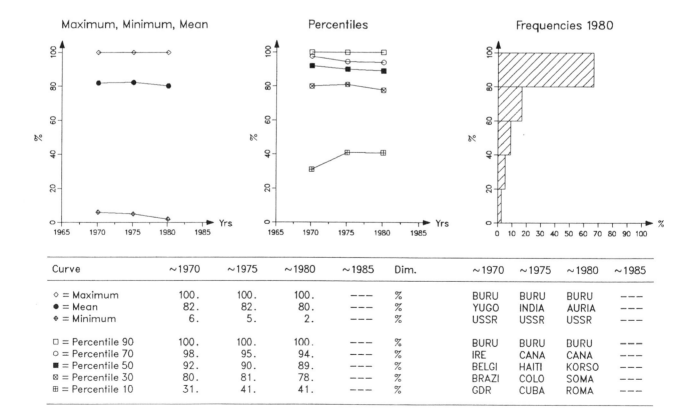

Curve	~1970	~1975	~1980	~1985	Dim.	~1970	~1975	~1980	~1985
◇ = Maximum	100.	100.	100.	---	%	BURU	BURU	BURU	---
● = Mean	82.	82.	80.	---	%	YUGO	INDIA	AURIA	---
✆ = Minimum	6.	5.	2.	---	%	USSR	USSR	USSR	---
□ = Percentile 90	100.	100.	100.	---	%	BURU	BURU	BURU	---
○ = Percentile 70	98.	95.	94.	---	%	IRE	CANA	CANA	---
■ = Percentile 50	92.	90.	89.	---	%	BELGI	HAITI	KORSO	---
⊗ = Percentile 30	80.	81.	78.	---	%	BRAZI	COLO	SOMA	---
⊞ = Percentile 10	31.	41.	41.	---	%	GDR	CUBA	ROMA	---

Scaling:
Ratio scale. Units: %.

Quality of Data:
Unless stated otherwise by footnotes in the country profiles the quality of the data allows *diachronic* and *crossnational* comparisons of the *Share of New Foreign Patents.*

Availability:
- About 80 observations relating to 1-year intervals between 1968 and 1972.
- About 80 observations relating to 1-year intervals between 1973 and 1977.
- About 80 observations relating to 1-year intervals between 1978 and 1982.

Sources:
World Intellectual Property Organization (WIPO). *100 Years Protection of Industrial Property.* Geneva, 1983, series B, tab. II.

FOREIGN PROPERTY AS % OF GDP (V25)

Short Names:
V25 or FORPRO/GDP.

Definition:
Foreign Property as % of GDP = End-of-year-stocks of the *DAC* countries' foreign direct investments in a given host country as % of the gross domestic product that the host country has accumulated during the year stated. In 1971 the *DAC (= Development Assistance Committee)* comprised Australia, Austria, Belgium, Canada, Denmark, France, West Germany, Italy, Japan, the Netherlands, Norway, Portugal, Sweden, Switzerland, the United Kingdom, and the USA. In 1975 and 1980 the DAC had two additional members, namely Finland and New Zealand, whereas Portugal was no longer a member of this organization.

Scaling:
Ratio scale. Units: %.

Quality of Data:
Unless stated otherwise by footnotes in the country profiles the quality of the data allows *crossnational* comparisons of the *Foreign Property as % of GDP.* However, changes in the composition of the DAC between 1971 and 1975 affects the validity of *diachronic* comparisons.

Availability:
- About 70 observations relating to timepoints between 1968 and 1972.
- About 80 observations relating to timepoints between 1973 and 1977.
- About 80 observations relating to timepoints between 1978 and 1982.

Statistical Overview:

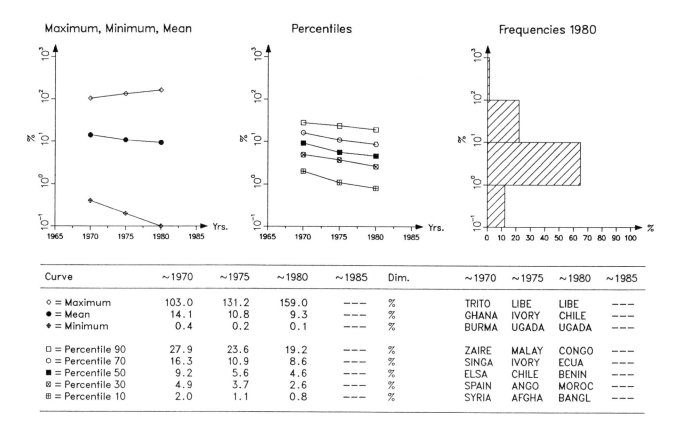

Curve	~1970	~1975	~1980	~1985	Dim.	~1970	~1975	~1980	~1985
◇ = Maximum	103.0	131.2	159.0	---	%	TRITO	LIBE	LIBE	---
● = Mean	14.1	10.8	9.3	---	%	GHANA	IVORY	CHILE	---
◈ = Minimum	0.4	0.2	0.1	---	%	BURMA	UGADA	UGADA	---
□ = Percentile 90	27.9	23.6	19.2	---	%	ZAIRE	MALAY	CONGO	---
○ = Percentile 70	16.3	10.9	8.6	---	%	SINGA	IVORY	ECUA	---
■ = Percentile 50	9.2	5.6	4.6	---	%	ELSA	CHILE	BENIN	---
⊗ = Percentile 30	4.9	3.7	2.6	---	%	SPAIN	ANGO	MOROC	---
⊞ = Percentile 10	2.0	1.1	0.8	---	%	SYRIA	AFGHA	BANGL	---

Sources:

- Source for exchange rates: World Bank. *World Tables,* 3rd ed. Baltimore, 1984, vol. 1, Economic Data Sheets 1, row "Foreign exchange rate."
- Main source for gross domestic product: International Monetary Fund (IMF). *International Financial Statistics, Yearbook 1985.* Washington, D.C., 1985, row 99b.
- Supplementary source for gross domestic product: World Bank. *World Tables,* 3rd ed. Baltimore, 1984, vol. 1, Economic Data Sheets 1, row "GDP at current market prices."
- Source 1 for foreign direct investments: OECD. *Coopération pour le développement, Examen 1973.* Paris, 1973, tab. IV-4.
- Source 2 for foreign direct investments: OECD. *Development Co-Operation, 1977 Review.* Paris, 1977, p. 208, col. 2.
- Source 3 for foreign direct investments: OECD. *Development Co-Operation, 1980 Review.* Paris, 1980, p. 165.

MEASURES DESCRIBING NATIONAL PRESTIGE

GNP SHARE OF DEVELOPMENT AID (V26)

Short Names:
V26 or AID/GNP.

Definition:
GNP Share of Development Aid = Percentage share of the *net* outflow of governmental development aid in the gross domestic product that the donor country has accumulated during the given year. The *net* outflow of development aid is defined as the difference between disbursements and repayments of development aid. Hence the *GNP Share of Development Aid* can be *negative* if the repayments exceed the actual disbursements of the donor country.

Scaling:
Ratio scale. Units: %.

Quality of Data:
Generally, the quality of the data allows *diachronic* and *crossnational* comparisons of the *GNP Share of Development Aid*. However, since 1979 the figures of the OECD countries have included administrative costs. Therefore, they are not strictly comparable with the figures for earlier years.

Statistical Overview:

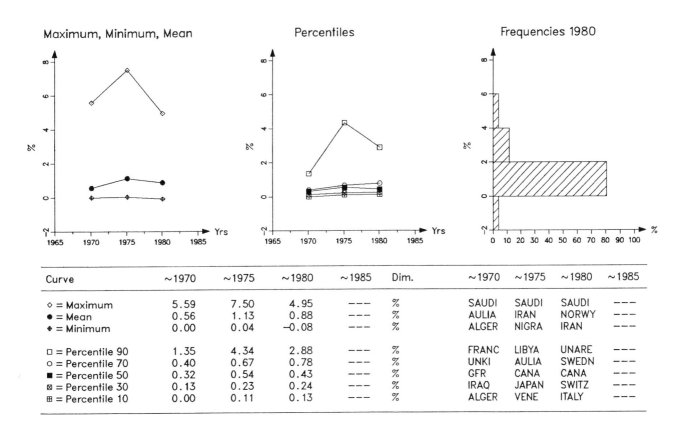

Curve	~1970	~1975	~1980	~1985	Dim.	~1970	~1975	~1980	~1985
◇ = Maximum	5.59	7.50	4.95	— — —	%	SAUDI	SAUDI	SAUDI	— — —
● = Mean	0.56	1.13	0.88	— — —	%	AULIA	IRAN	NORWY	— — —
✦ = Minimum	0.00	0.04	−0.08	— — —	%	ALGER	NIGRA	IRAN	— — —
□ = Percentile 90	1.35	4.34	2.88	— — —	%	FRANC	LIBYA	UNARE	— — —
○ = Percentile 70	0.40	0.67	0.78	— — —	%	UNKI	AULIA	SWEDN	— — —
■ = Percentile 50	0.32	0.54	0.43	— — —	%	GFR	CANA	CANA	— — —
⊗ = Percentile 30	0.13	0.23	0.24	— — —	%	IRAQ	JAPAN	SWITZ	— — —
⊞ = Percentile 10	0.00	0.11	0.13	— — —	%	ALGER	VENE	ITALY	— — —

Availability:
- About 20 observations relating to 1-year intervals between 1968 and 1972.
- About 30 observations relating to 1-year intervals between 1973 and 1977.
- About 30 observations relating to 1-year intervals between 1978 and 1982.

Sources:
OECD. *Twenty-Five Years of Development Co-Operation.* Paris 1985, tab. 14, 26.

SHARE IN NOBEL PRIZE WINNERS (V27)

Short Names:
V27 or NOPRIWI.

Definition:
Share in Nobel Prize Winners = Percentage share of the global community of winners of the *scientific* Nobel Prizes for a 10-year period who are citizens of the given country.

Computational procedure:
For the computation of the *Share in Nobel Prize Winners* the formula
$$100 \cdot (N / T)$$
was used, where
N = Number of scientists who received during a 10-year interval a Nobel Prize in physics, chemistry, medicine/physiology, or economics and who were citizens of the given country. For the computation of N the scientists who were citizens of two nations have been counted twice.
T = Total number of scientists of any nationality who received during the same 10-year interval a Nobel Price in physics, chemistry, medicine/physiology, or economics. For the computation of T the scientists who were citizens of two nations have been counted twice.

Scaling:
Ratio scale. Units: %.

Quality of Data:
Unless stated otherwise by footnotes in the country profiles the quality of the data allows *crossnational* comparisons of the *Share in Nobel Prize Winners.*

Availability:
About 120 observations relating to the 10-year interval 1970-1979.

Sources:
- Main source: *Grand Dictionnaire Encyclopédique Larousse.* Paris, 1984, vol.7, pp. 7406 ff.
- Supplementary Source: *Archiv der Gegenwart,* several editions. Bonn and Sankt Augustin, several years.

Statistical Overview:

	1970-79	Dim.	1970-79
Maximum	53.8	%	USA
Mean	0.9	%	ARGE
Minimum	0.0	%	AFGHA
Percentile 90	1.3	%	ARGE
Percentile 70	0.0	%	AFGHA
Percentile 50	0.0	%	AFGHA
Percentile 30	0.0	%	AFGHA
Percentile 10	0.0	%	AFGHA

GDP SHARE OF MANUFACTURING (V28)

Short Names:
V28 or MANU/GDP.

Definition:
GDP Share of Manufacturing = Percentage share of the contribution of *manufacturing* to the gross domestic product at current market prices that the given country has accumulated during the year stated.

Scaling:
Ratio scale. Units: %.

Quality of Data:
Unless stated otherwise by footnotes in the country profiles the quality of the data allows *diachronic* and *crossnational* comparisons of the *GDP Share of Manufacturing.*

Availability:
- About 80 observations relating to 1-year intervals between 1968 and 1972.
- About 80 observations relating to 1-year intervals between 1973 and 1977.
- About 80 observations relating to 1-year intervals between 1978 and 1982.

Sources:
World Bank. *World Tables,* 3rd ed. Baltimore, 1984, vol. 1, Economic Data Sheets 1.

Statistical Overview:

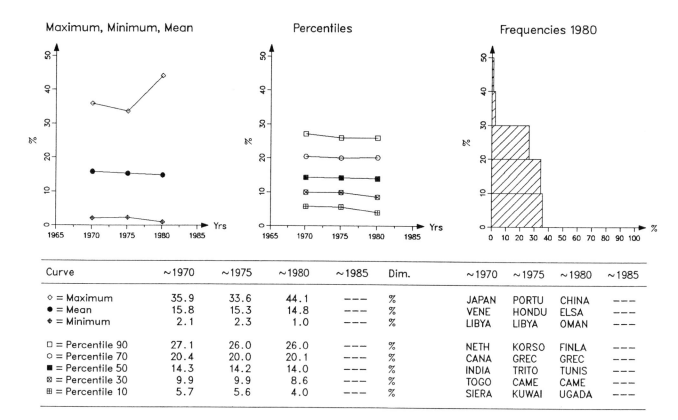

| Maximum, Minimum, Mean | Percentiles | Frequencies 1980 |

Curve	~1970	~1975	~1980	~1985	Dim.	~1970	~1975	~1980	~1985
◇ = Maximum	35.9	33.6	44.1	---	%	JAPAN	PORTU	CHINA	---
● = Mean	15.8	15.3	14.8	---	%	VENE	HONDU	ELSA	---
✦ = Minimum	2.1	2.3	1.0	---	%	LIBYA	LIBYA	OMAN	---
□ = Percentile 90	27.1	26.0	26.0	---	%	NETH	KORSO	FINLA	---
○ = Percentile 70	20.4	20.0	20.1	---	%	CANA	GREC	GREC	---
■ = Percentile 50	14.3	14.2	14.0	---	%	INDIA	TRITO	TUNIS	---
⊗ = Percentile 30	9.9	9.9	8.6	---	%	TOGO	CAME	CAME	---
⊞ = Percentile 10	5.7	5.6	4.0	---	%	SIERA	KUWAI	UGADA	---

EXPORT SHARE OF MANUFACTURES (V29)

Short Names:

V29 or MANEXSHARE.

Definition:

Export Share of Manufactures = Percentage share of the exports of *manufactures* in the fob-value of all commodities from indigenous production that the given country has exported during the year stated.

Computational Procedure:

For the computation of the *Export Share of Manufactures* the formula

$$100 \cdot (E5 + E6 + E7 + E8 - E67 - E68) / E$$

was used, where

$E5$ = Fob-value of the indigenously produced *chemicals* that the given country has exported during the year stated and that belong to category 5 of the Standard International Trade Classification (SITC).

$E6$ = Fob-value of the indigenously produced *basic manufactures* that the given country has exported during the year stated and that belong to category 6 of the SITC.

$E7$ = Fob-value of the indigenously produced *machines and transport equipment* that the given country has exported during the year stated and that belong to category 7 of the SITC.

$E8$ = Fob-value of the exports of indigenously produced *other manufactures* that the given country has exported during the year stated and that belong to category *8* of the SITC.

$E67$ = Fob-value of the exports of the indigenously produced *iron and steel* that the given country has exported during the year stated and that belong to category *67* of the SITC.

$E68$ = Fob-value of the exports of the indigenously produced *non-ferrous metals* that the given country has exported during the year stated and that belong to category *68* of the SITC.

E = Fob-value of *all* indigenously produced commodities that the given country has exported during the year stated.

Scaling:
Ratio scale. Units: %.

Quality of Data:
Unless stated otherwise by footnotes in the country profiles the quality of the data allows *diachronic* and *crossnational* comparisons of the *Export Share of Manufactures.*

Availability:
- About 60 observations relating to 1-year intervals between 1968 and 1972.
- About 70 observations relating to 1-year intervals between 1973 and 1977.
- About 50 observations relating to 1-year intervals between 1978 and 1982.

Statistical Overview:

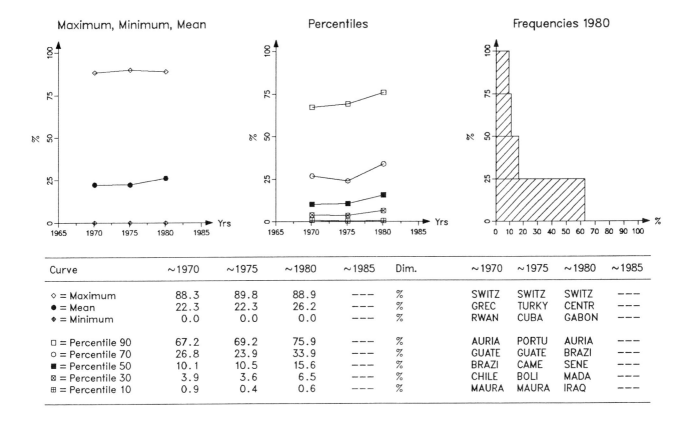

Curve	~1970	~1975	~1980	~1985	Dim.	~1970	~1975	~1980	~1985
◇ = Maximum	88.3	89.8	88.9	---	%	SWITZ	SWITZ	SWITZ	---
● = Mean	22.3	22.3	26.2	---	%	GREC	TURKY	CENTR	---
✦ = Minimum	0.0	0.0	0.0	---	%	RWAN	CUBA	GABON	---
□ = Percentile 90	67.2	69.2	75.9	---	%	AURIA	PORTU	AURIA	---
○ = Percentile 70	26.8	23.9	33.9	---	%	GUATE	GUATE	BRAZI	---
■ = Percentile 50	10.1	10.5	15.6	---	%	BRAZI	CAME	SENE	---
⊠ = Percentile 30	3.9	3.6	6.5	---	%	CHILE	BOLI	MADA	---
⊞ = Percentile 10	0.9	0.4	0.6	---	%	MAURA	MAURA	IRAQ	---

Sources:
- Main source: United Nations. *Handbook of International Trade and Development Statistics, Supplement 1985.* New York, 1985, tab. 4.1 .
- Supplementary source: United Nations. *Yearbook of International Trade Statistics,* several editions. New York, several years.

LACK OF CIVIL LIBERTIES (V30)

Short Names:
V30 or CIVLIB.

Definition:
- *Lack of Civil Liberties = 1* if the given country has a political system "in which the rule of law is unshaken. Freedom of expression is both possible and evident in a variety of news media" (C. L. Taylor and D. A. Jodice, *World Handbook of Political and Social Indicators,* 3rd ed. (New Haven and London, 1983), vol. 1, pp. 64, 65).
- *Lack of Civil Liberties = 2* if the given country has a political system "that aspires to the above level of civil rights but is unable to achieve it because of violence, ignorance, or unavailability of the media, or because it has restrictive laws that seem to be greater than are needed for maintaining order" (ibid.).
- *Lack of Civil Liberties = 3* if the given country has a political system "that has the trappings of civil liberty and whose government may be successfully opposed in the courts, although it may be threatened or have unresolvable political deadlocks and may have to rely often upon martial law, jailing for sedition, and suppression of publications" (ibid.).
- *Lack of Civil Liberties = 4* if the given country has a political system "in which there are broad areas of freedom but also broad areas of illegality" (ibid.).
- *Lack of Civil Liberties = 5* if the given country has a political system "in which civil rights are often denied but in which there is no doctrine on which the denial is based. The media are often weak, controlled by the government, and censored" (ibid.).
- *Lack of Civil Liberties = 6* if the given country has a political system "in which no civil rights are thought to take priority over the rights of the state, although criticism is allowed to be stated in limited ways" (ibid.).
- *Lack of Civil Liberties = 7* if the given country has a political system "of which the outside world never hears criticism, except when it is condemned by the state. Citizens have no rights in relation to the state" (ibid.).

Scaling:
Dimensionless ordinal scale.

Quality of Data:
Unless stated otherwise by footnotes in the country profiles the quality of the data allows *diachronic* and *crossnational* comparisons of the *Lack of Civil Liberties.*

Statistical Overview:

CIVLIB	Year	Key—N.	Freq.	0 10 20 30 40 50 60 70 80 90 100 %
1 = Most civil liberties	~1975	AULIA	12 %	
	~1980	AULIA	12 %	
2	~1975	COLO	10 %	
	~1980	ECUA	10 %	
3	~1975	ELSA	10 %	
	~1980	BANGL	12 %	
4	~1975	ANGO	13 %	
	~1980	GHANA	6 %	
5	~1975	BOLI	18 %	
	~1980	ARGE	22 %	
6	~1975	AFGHA	23 %	
	~1980	ALGER	22 %	
7 = Least civil liberties	~1975	ALBA	14 %	
	~1980	AFGHA	16 %	

Availability:
- About 130 observations relating to timepoints between 1973 and 1977.
- About 130 observations relating to timepoints between 1978 and 1982.

Sources:
R. Gastil. *Freedom in the World, edition 1983-84.* Westport, 1984, pp. 457 ff.

LACK OF POLITICAL RIGHTS (V31)

Short Names:
V31 or POLRIGHTS.

Definition:
- *Lack of Political Rights = 1* if the given country has a political system "in which the great majority of persons or families has both the right and the opportunity to participate in the electoral process. Political parties may be freely formed for the purpose of making the right to compete for public office fairly general" (C. L. Taylor and D. A. Jodice, *World Handbook of Political and Social Indicators,* 3rd ed. (New Haven and London, 1983), vol. 1, pp. 60, 61).

- *Lack of Political Rights = 2* if the given country has a political system "with an open process, which does not always work well, however, due to extreme poverty, a feudal social structure, violence, or other limitations on potential participants or results. As is the case with countries coded 1, a leader or party can be voted out of office" (ibid.).
- *Lack of Political Rights = 3* if the given country has a political system "in which people may elect their leaders or representatives, but in which coups d'état, large-scale interference with election results, and often nondemocratic procedures occur" (ibid.).
- *Lack of Political Rights = 4* if the given country has a political system "in which full democratic elections are blocked constitutionally or have little significance in determining power distributions" (ibid.).
- *Lack of Political Rights = 5* if the given country has a political system "in which elections are either closely controlled or limited, or in which the results have little significance" (ibid.).
- *Lack of Political Rights = 6* if the given country has a political system "without elections or with elections involving only a single list of candidates in which voting is largely a matter of demonstrating support for the system. Nevertheless, there is some distribution of political power" (ibid.).
- *Lack of Political Rights = 7* if the given country has a political system "that is a tyranny without legitimacy either in tradition or in international party doctrine" (ibid.).

Scaling:
Dimensionless ordinal scale.

Quality of Data:
Unless stated otherwise by footnotes in the country profiles the quality of the data allows *diachronic* and *crossnational* comparisons of the *Lack of Political Rights*.

Statistical Overview:

POLRIGHTS	Year	Key–N.	Freq.	
1 = Most pol. rights	~1975	AULIA	14 %	
	~1980	AULIA	13 %	
2	~1975	ARGE	10 %	
	~1980	COLO	14 %	
3	~1975	MALAY	2 %	
	~1980	BANGL	5 %	
4	~1975	BANGL	7 %	
	~1980	BRAZI	6 %	
5	~1975	CONGO	16 %	
	~1980	BHUTA	17 %	
6	~1975	ALGER	25 %	
	~1980	ALGER	25 %	
7 = Least pol. rights	~1975	AFGHA	25 %	
	~1980	AFGHA	20 %	

Availability:
- About 130 observations relating to timepoints between 1973 and 1977.
- About 130 observations relating to timepoints between 1978 and 1982.

Sources:
R. Gastil. *Freedom in the World, edition 1983-84.* Westport, 1984, pp. 457 ff.

OTHER IMPORTANT VARIABLES

- Share of Academic Labor (V11).
- Student Enrollment Ratio (V7).

MEASURES DESCRIBING REACTIONS OF

POLITICAL MOVEMENTS

RIOTS (V32)

Short Names:
V32 or RIOTS.

Definition:
Riots = Number of riots that have taken place during the given *5-year* period. A *riot* is defined as a spontaneous outbreak of violence carried on by an excited or confused mass.

Scaling:
Dimensionless ratio scale.

Quality of Data:
Unless stated otherwise by footnotes in the country profiles the quality of the data allows *diachronic* and *crossnational* comparisons.

Availability:
- About 120 observations relating to the 5-year interval 1970-1974.
- About 120 observations relating to the 5-year interval 1975-1979.

Sources:
C. L. Taylor. *Dataset ZA-1132 of the Zentralarchiv für empirische Sozialforschung.* Köln, 1985, variable V802.

Statistical Overview:

	1970-74	1975-79	Dim.	1970-74	1975-79
Maximum	210.	177.		UNKI	SPAIN
Mean	10.	10.		BOLI	CENTR
Minimum	0.	0.		AFGHA	AFGHA
Percentile 90	37.	28.		SOUAF	PERU
Percentile 70	6.	5.		MADA	BOLI
Percentile 50	2.	2.		BENIN	BENIN
Percentile 30	0.	0.		AFGHA	AFGHA
Percentile 10	0.	0.		AFGHA	AFGHA

PROTEST DEMONSTRATIONS (V33)

Short Names:
V33 or PROTESTS.

Definition:
Protest Demonstrations = Number of protest demonstrations that have taken place during the given *5-year* period. A *protest demonstration* is defined as an organized nonviolent gathering of people protesting against a government.

Scaling:
Dimensionless ratio scale.

Quality of Data:
Unless stated otherwise by footnotes in the country profiles the quality of the data allows *diachronic* and *crossnational* comparisons.

Availability:
- About 120 observations relating to the 5-year interval 1970-1974.
- About 120 observations relating to the 5-year interval 1975-1979.

Sources:
C. L. Taylor. *Dataset ZA-1132 of the Zentralarchiv für empirische Sozialforschung.* Köln, 1985, variable V800.

Statistical Overview:

	1970-74	1975-79	Dim.	1970-74	1975-79
Maximum	624.	581.		USA	USA
Mean	21.	20.		AULIA	PHILI
Minimum	0.	0.		ALBA	ALBA
Percentile 90	45.	41.		VISO	GREC
Percentile 70	8.	10.		GUATE	BOLI
Percentile 50	2.	3.		GDR	AFGHA
Percentile 30	1.	1.		AFGHA	CENTR
Percentile 10	0.	0.		ALBA	ALBA

POLITICAL STRIKES (V34)

Short Names:
V34 or POLSTRIKES.

Definition:
Political Strikes = Number of political strikes that have taken place during the given *5-year* period. A *political strike* is defined as a strike of workers or students that is organized to protest against a government. This definition excludes all forms of strikes that primarily aim at the realization of *economic* goals.

Scaling:
Dimensionless ratio scale.

Quality of Data:
Unless stated otherwise by footnotes in the country profiles the quality of the data allows *diachronic* and *crossnational* comparisons.

Availability:
- About 120 observations relating to the 5-year interval 1970-1974.
- About 120 observations relating to the 5-year interval 1975-1979.

Sources:
C. L. Taylor. *Dataset ZA-1132 of the Zentralarchiv für empirische Sozialforschung.* Köln, 1985, variable V805.

Statistical Overview:

	1970-74	1975-79	Dim.	1970-74	1975-79
Maximum	113.	114.		UNKI	SPAIN
Mean	5.	4.		PERU	GREC
Minimum	0.	0.		AFGHA	AFGHA
Percentile 90	14.	12.		ARGE	IRAN
Percentile 70	1.	2.		AULIA	AULIA
Percentile 50	0.	0.		AFGHA	AFGHA
Percentile 30	0.	0.		AFGHA	AFGHA
Percentile 10	0.	0.		AFGHA	AFGHA

MEASURES DESCRIBING REACTIONS OF

GOVERNMENTS

MEMBER OF THE NONALIGNED MOVEMENT (V35)

Short Names:
V35 or NONALMEMB.

Definition:
- *Member of the Nonaligned Movement = 1* if the country has been a *full* member of the *Nonaligned Movement* at any time of the year stated. Hence, *guests* and *observers* are *not* considered to be members of the *Nonaligned Movement*.
- *Member of the Nonaligned Movement = 0* if the country has *never* been a *full* member of the *Nonaligned Movement* during the year stated.

Scaling:
Dimensionless nominal scale.

Quality of Data:
The quality of the data allows *diachronic* and *crossnational* comparisons of the membership in the *Nonaligned Movement*.

Availability:
- About 110 observations relating to 1-year intervals between 1968 and 1972.
- About 120 observations relating to 1-year intervals between 1973 and 1977.
- About 130 observations relating to 1-year intervals between 1978 and 1982.

Sources:
- A. S. Banks and W. Overstreet. *Political Handbook of the World 1981.* New York, 1981, pp. 607 ff.
- K. P. Sauvant. "Organizational Infrastructure for Self-Reliance: The Non-Aligned Countries and the Group of 77." In H. Köchler, ed. *The Principles of Non-Alignment.* Vienna, 1982, pp. 186 ff., tab. 1.
- *Keesing's Contemporary Archives.* London and Bristol, several years.
- P. Willetts. *The Non-Aligned in Havana.* London, 1981, pp. 64-67, 284 ff.

Statistical Overview:

NONALMEMB	Year	Key-N.	Freq.	
0 = Nonmember	~1970	ALBA	58 %	▨▨▨▨▨
	~1975	ALBA	46 %	▨▨▨
	~1980	ALBA	42 %	▨▨▨
1 = Member	~1970	AFGHA	42 %	▨▨▨
	~1975	AFGHA	54 %	▨▨▨▨
	~1980	AFGHA	58 %	▨▨▨▨▨

MEMBER OF THE OPEC (V36)

Short Names:
V36 or OPECMEMB.

Definition:
- *Member of the OPEC = 1* if the country has been a *full* member of the *OPEC (= Organization of Petroleum Exporting Countries)* at any time of the year stated.
- *Member of the OPEC = 0* if the country has *never* been a *full* member of the *OPEC* during the year stated.

Scaling:
Dimensionless nominal scale.

Quality of Data:
The quality of the data allows *diachronic* and *crossnational* comparisons of OPEC membership.

Availability:
- About 120 observations relating to 1-year intervals between 1968 and 1972.
- About 130 observations relating to 1-year intervals between 1973 and 1977.
- About 130 observations relating to 1-year intervals between 1978 and 1982.

Sources:
- A. S. Banks and W. Overstreet. *Political Handbook of the World 1982-1983.* New York, 1983, pp. 629 ff.
- H. W. Degenhardt. *Treaties and Alliances of the World,* 3rd ed. Harlow, 1981, pp. 98 ff.

Statistical Overview:

OPECMEMB	Year	Key–N.	Freq.	0 10 20 30 40 50 60 70 80 90 100 %
0 = Nonmember	~1970	AFGHA	94 %	////////////////////////////////
	~1975	AFGHA	91 %	///////////////////////////////
	~1980	AFGHA	90 %	///////////////////////////////
1 = Member	~1970	ALGER	6 %	/
	~1975	ALGER	9 %	//
	~1980	ALGER	10 %	//

MEMBER OF THE OECD (V37)

Short Names:
V37 or OECDMEMB.

Definition:
- *Member of the OECD = 1* if the country has been a *full* member of the OECD (= Organisation for Economic Cooperation and Development) at any time of the year stated.
- *Member of the OECD = 0* if the country has *never* been a *full* member of the OECD during the year stated.

Scaling:
Dimensionless nominal scale.

Quality of Data:
The quality of the data allows *diachronic* and *crossnational* comparisons of OECD membership.

Availability:
- About 120 observations relating to 1-year intervals between 1968 and 1972.
- About 130 observations relating to 1-year intervals between 1973 and 1977.
- About 130 observations relating to 1-year intervals between 1978 and 1982.

Sources:
- H. W. Degenhardt. *Treaties and Alliances of the World,* 3rd ed. Harlow, 1981, pp. 156 ff.
- A. S. Banks and W. Overstreet. *Political Handbook of the World 1982-1983.* New York, 1983, pp. 623 ff.

Statistical Overview:

OECDMEMB	Year	Key–N.	Freq.	
0 = Nonmember	~1970	AFGHA	83 %	
	~1975	AFGHA	82 %	
	~1980	AFGHA	82 %	
1 = Member	~1970	AURIA	17 %	
	~1975	AULIA	18 %	
	~1980	AULIA	18 %	

MEMBER OF THE CMEA (V38)

Short Names:
V38 or CMEAMEMB.

Definition:
- *Member of the CMEA = 1* if the country has been a *full* member of the CMEA (= Council for Mutual Economic Assistance) at any time of the year stated.
- *Member of the CMEA = 0* if the country has *never* been a *full* member of the CMEA during the year stated.

Scaling:
Dimensionless nominal scale.

Quality of Data:
The quality of the data allows *diachronic* and *crossnational* comparisons of CMEA membership.

Availability:
- About 120 observations relating to 1-year intervals between 1968 and 1972.
- About 130 observations relating to 1-year intervals between 1973 and 1977.
- About 130 observations relating to 1-year intervals between 1978 and 1982.

Sources:
- A. S. Banks and W. Overstreet. *Political Handbook of the World 1982-1983.* New York, 1983, pp. 594 ff.
- H. W. Degenhardt. *Treaties and Alliances of the World,* 3rd ed. Harlow, 1981, pp. 202 ff.

Statistical Overview:

CMEAMEMB	Year	Key–N.	Freq.	0 10 20 30 40 50 60 70 80 90 100 %
0 = Nonmember	~1970	AFGHA	93 %	/////////////////////////////////
	~1975	AFGHA	93 %	/////////////////////////////////
	~1980	AFGHA	92 %	////////////////////////////////
1 = Member	~1970	BULGA	7 %	//
	~1975	BULGA	7 %	//
	~1980	BULGA	8 %	//

MEMBER OF THE WTO (V39)

Short Names:
V39 or WTOMEMB.

Definition:
- *Member of the WTO = 1* if the country has been a member of the WTO (= Warsaw Treaty Organization) at any time of the year stated.
- *Member of the WTO = 0* if the country has *never* been a member of the WTO during the year stated.

Scaling:
Dimensionless nominal scale.

Quality of Data:
The quality of the data allows *diachronic* and *crossnational* comparisons of WTO membership.

Availability:
- About 120 observations relating to 1-year intervals between 1968 and 1972.
- About 130 observations relating to 1-year intervals between 1973 and 1977.
- About 130 observations relating to 1-year intervals between 1978 and 1982.

Sources:
- H. W. Degenhardt. *Treaties and Alliances of the World,* 3rd ed. Harlow, 1981, pp. 197 ff.
- A. S. Banks and W. Overstreet. *Political Handbook of the World 1982-1983.* New York, 1983, pp. 698 ff.

Statistical Overview:

WTOMEMB	Year	Key–N.	Freq.	0 10 20 30 40 50 60 70 80 90 100 %
0 = Nonmember	~1970	AFGHA	94 %	////////////////////////////////
	~1975	AFGHA	94 %	////////////////////////////////
	~1980	AFGHA	94 %	////////////////////////////////
1 = Member	~1970	BULGA	6 %	//
	~1975	BULGA	6 %	//
	~1980	BULGA	6 %	//

MEMBER OF THE NATO (V40)

Short Names:
V40 or NATOMEMB.

Definition:
- *Member of the NATO = 1* if the country has been a *full* member of the NATO (= North Atlantic Treaty Organization) at any time of the year stated.
- *Member of the NATO = 0* if the country has *never* been a *full* member of the NATO during the year stated.

Scaling:
Dimensionless nominal scale.

Quality of Data:
The quality of the data allows *diachronic* and *crossnational* comparisons of NATO membership.

Availability:
- About 120 observations relating to 1-year intervals between 1968 and 1972.
- About 130 observations relating to 1-year intervals between 1973 and 1977.
- About 130 observations relating to 1-year intervals between 1978 and 1982.

Sources:
- A. S. Banks and W. Overstreet. *Political Handbook of the World 1982-1983.* New York, 1983, pp. 620 ff.
- H. W. Degenhardt. *Treaties and Alliances of the World,* 3rd ed. Harlow, 1981, pp. 164 ff.
- *Fischer Weltalmanach 1986.* Frankfurt, 1985, pp. 684 ff.

Statistical Overview:

NATOMEMB	Year	Key–N.	Freq.	
0 = Nonmember	~1970	AFGHA	89 %	
	~1975	AFGHA	90 %	
	~1980	AFGHA	90 %	
1 = Member	~1970	BELGI	11 %	
	~1975	BELGI	10 %	
	~1980	BELGI	10 %	

OTHER IMPORTANT VARIABLES

- Military Expenditures (V13).
- Military Manpower (V14).
- Foreign Property as % of GDP (V25).
- Total Debt as % of GDP (V23).
- GDP Share of Imports (V20).
- GDP Share of Exports (V21).
- GNP Share of Development Aid (V26).
- Lack of Civil Liberties (V30).
- Lack of Political Rights (V31).

MEASURES DESCRIBING REACTIONS OF

ENTREPRENEURS

GDP SHARE OF INVESTMENTS (V41)

Short Names:
V41 or INVEST/GDP.

Definition:
GDP Share of Investments = Percentage share of the gross domestic product of the given year that has been used as gross domestic investment.

Computational Procedure:
For the computation of the *GDP Share of Investments* the formula
$100 \cdot (I / P)$
was used, where
I = Gross domestic *investments* of the given year, valued at current market prices.
P = Gross domestic *product* of the given year, valued at current market prices.

Statistical Overview:

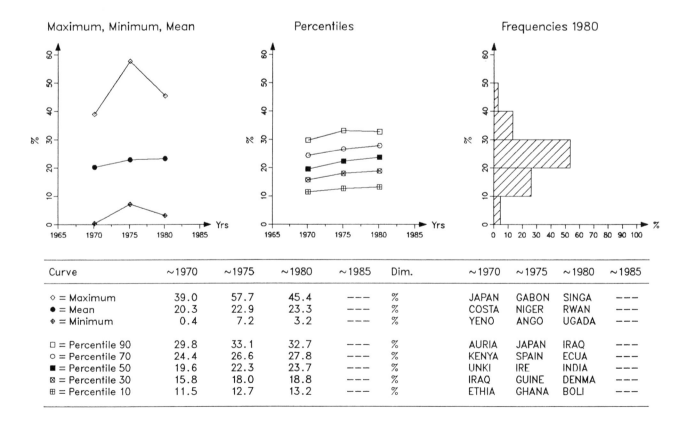

Curve	~1970	~1975	~1980	~1985	Dim.	~1970	~1975	~1980	~1985
◇ = Maximum	39.0	57.7	45.4	---	%	JAPAN	GABON	SINGA	---
● = Mean	20.3	22.9	23.3	---	%	COSTA	NIGER	RWAN	---
⊕ = Minimum	0.4	7.2	3.2	---	%	YENO	ANGO	UGADA	---
□ = Percentile 90	29.8	33.1	32.7	---	%	AURIA	JAPAN	IRAQ	---
○ = Percentile 70	24.4	26.6	27.8	---	%	KENYA	SPAIN	ECUA	---
■ = Percentile 50	19.6	22.3	23.7	---	%	UNKI	IRE	INDIA	---
⊗ = Percentile 30	15.8	18.0	18.8	---	%	IRAQ	GUINE	DENMA	---
⊞ = Percentile 10	11.5	12.7	13.2	---	%	ETHIA	GHANA	BOLI	---

Scaling:
Ratio scale. Units: %.

Quality of Data:
Unless stated otherwise by footnotes in the country profiles the quality of the data allows *diachronic* and *crossnational* comparisons of the *GDP Share of Investments.*

Availability:
- About 100 observations relating to 1-year intervals between 1968 and 1972.
- About 100 observations relating to 1-year intervals between 1973 and 1977.
- About 110 observations relating to 1-year intervals between 1978 and 1982.

Sources:
World Bank. *World Tables,* 3rd ed. Baltimore, 1984, vol. 1, Economic Data Sheets 1.

GDP SHARE OF AGRICULTURE (V42)

Short Names:
V42 or AGRI/GDP.

Definition:
GDP Share of Agriculture = Percentage share of the contribution of *agriculture, forestry, hunting,* and *fishing* to the gross domestic product at current market prices that the given country has accumulated during the year stated.

Scaling:
Ratio scale. Units: %.

Quality of Data:
Unless stated otherwise by footnotes in the country profiles the quality of the data allows *diachronic* and *crossnational* comparisons of the *GDP Share of Agriculture.*

Availability:
- About 90 observations relating to 1-year intervals between 1968 and 1972.
- About 100 observations relating to 1-year intervals between 1973 and 1977.
- About 100 observations relating to 1-year intervals between 1978 and 1982.

Sources:
World Bank. *World Tables,* 3rd ed. Baltimore, 1984, vol. 1, Economic Data Sheets 1.

Statistical Overview:

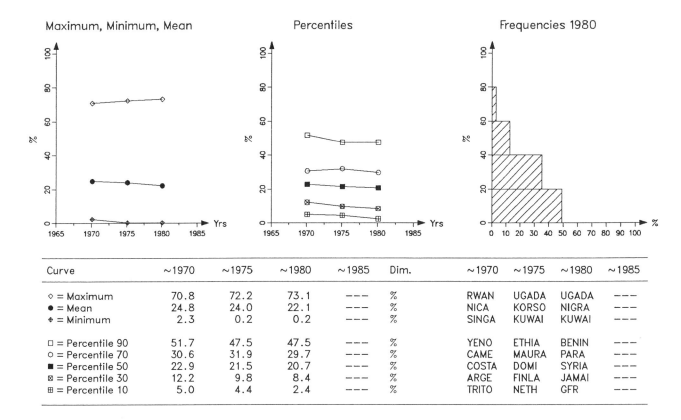

Curve	~1970	~1975	~1980	~1985	Dim.	~1970	~1975	~1980	~1985
◇ = Maximum	70.8	72.2	73.1	---	%	RWAN	UGADA	UGADA	---
● = Mean	24.8	24.0	22.1	---	%	NICA	KORSO	NIGRA	---
⊕ = Minimum	2.3	0.2	0.2	---	%	SINGA	KUWAI	KUWAI	---
□ = Percentile 90	51.7	47.5	47.5	---	%	YENO	ETHIA	BENIN	---
○ = Percentile 70	30.6	31.9	29.7	---	%	CAME	MAURA	PARA	---
■ = Percentile 50	22.9	21.5	20.7	---	%	COSTA	DOMI	SYRIA	---
⊠ = Percentile 30	12.2	9.8	8.4	---	%	ARGE	FINLA	JAMAI	---
⊞ = Percentile 10	5.0	4.4	2.4	---	%	TRITO	NETH	GFR	---

GDP SHARE OF INDUSTRY (V43)

Short Names:
V43 or INDU/GDP.

Definition:
GDP Share of Industry = Percentage share of the contribution of *mining, manufacturing, construction* and the production and distribution of *electricity, gas* and *water* to the gross domestic product at current market prices that the given country has accumulated during the year stated.

Scaling:
Ratio scale. Units: %.

Quality of Data:
Unless stated otherwise by footnotes in the country profiles the quality of the data allows *diachronic* and *crossnational* comparisons of the *GDP Share of Industry*.

Statistical Overview:

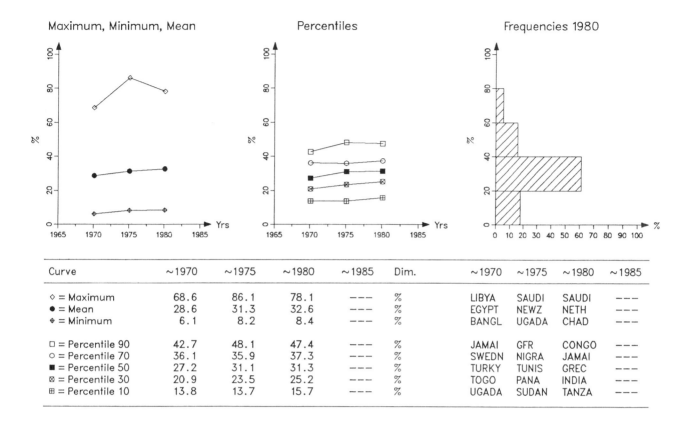

Curve	~1970	~1975	~1980	~1985	Dim.	~1970	~1975	~1980	~1985
◇ = Maximum	68.6	86.1	78.1	———	%	LIBYA	SAUDI	SAUDI	———
● = Mean	28.6	31.3	32.6	———	%	EGYPT	NEWZ	NETH	———
⊕ = Minimum	6.1	8.2	8.4	———	%	BANGL	UGADA	CHAD	———
□ = Percentile 90	42.7	48.1	47.4	———	%	JAMAI	GFR	CONGO	———
○ = Percentile 70	36.1	35.9	37.3	———	%	SWEDN	NIGRA	JAMAI	———
■ = Percentile 50	27.2	31.1	31.3	———	%	TURKY	TUNIS	GREC	———
⊗ = Percentile 30	20.9	23.5	25.2	———	%	TOGO	PANA	INDIA	———
⊞ = Percentile 10	13.8	13.7	15.7	———	%	UGADA	SUDAN	TANZA	———

Availability:
- About 90 observations relating to 1-year intervals between 1968 and 1972.
- About 100 observations relating to 1-year intervals between 1973 and 1977.
- About 100 observations relating to 1-year intervals between 1978 and 1982.

Sources:
World Bank. *World Tables,* 3rd ed. Baltimore, 1984, vol. 1, Economic Data Sheets 1.

GDP SHARE OF SERVICES (V44)

Short Names:
V44 or SERVI/GDP.

Definition:
GDP Share of Services = Percentage share of the contribution of the *service industry* to the gross domestic product at current market prices that the given country has accumulated during the year stated.

Statistical Overview:

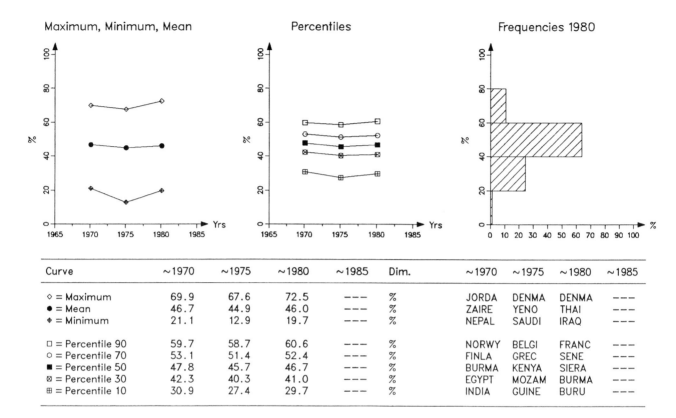

	Maximum, Minimum, Mean	Percentiles	Frequencies 1980

Curve	~1970	~1975	~1980	~1985	Dim.	~1970	~1975	~1980	~1985
◇ = Maximum	69.9	67.6	72.5	---	%	JORDA	DENMA	DENMA	---
● = Mean	46.7	44.9	46.0	---	%	ZAIRE	YENO	THAI	---
✦ = Minimum	21.1	12.9	19.7	---	%	NEPAL	SAUDI	IRAQ	---
□ = Percentile 90	59.7	58.7	60.6	---	%	NORWY	BELGI	FRANC	---
○ = Percentile 70	53.1	51.4	52.4	---	%	FINLA	GREC	SENE	---
■ = Percentile 50	47.8	45.7	46.7	---	%	BURMA	KENYA	SIERA	---
⊗ = Percentile 30	42.3	40.3	41.0	---	%	EGYPT	MOZAM	BURMA	---
⊞ = Percentile 10	30.9	27.4	29.7	---	%	INDIA	GUINE	BURU	---

Computational Procedure:
For the computation of the *GDP Share of Services* the formula
100 - A - I
was used, where
A = GDP-Share of Agriculture (= V42)
I = GDP-Share of Industry (= V43)

Scaling:
Ratio scale. Units: %.

Quality of Data:
Unless stated otherwise by footnotes in the country profiles the quality of the data allows *diachronic* and *crossnational* comparisons of the *GDP Share of Services.*

Availability:
- About 90 observations relating to 1-year intervals between 1968 and 1972.
- About 100 observations relating to 1-year intervals between 1973 and 1977.
- About 90 observations relating to 1-year intervals between 1978 and 1982.

Sources:
World Bank. *World Tables,* 3rd ed. Baltimore, 1984, vol. 1, Economic Data Sheets 1.

OTHER IMPORTANT VARIABLES

- GDP Share of Exports (V21).
- Export Share of Manufactures (V29).
- GDP Share of Manufacturing (V28).

MEASURES DESCRIBING REACTIONS OF

INDIVIDUALS

HOMICIDES P. MIL. POPULATION (V45)

Short Names:
V45 or HOCID/POP.

Definition:
Homicides p. Mil. Population = Cases of death per million inhabitants that have been caused during the year stated by homicides or injuries purposely inflicted by other persons.

Scaling:
Ratio scale. Units: 1 / million capita (1/MIL CAP).

Quality of Data:
The quality of the data is generally bad. For many countries the number of *undetermined* cases of violent death equals up to *50%* of the sum of all cases of homicide or suicide. Hence *diachronic* and *crossnational* comparisons are only of limited value.

Statistical Overview:

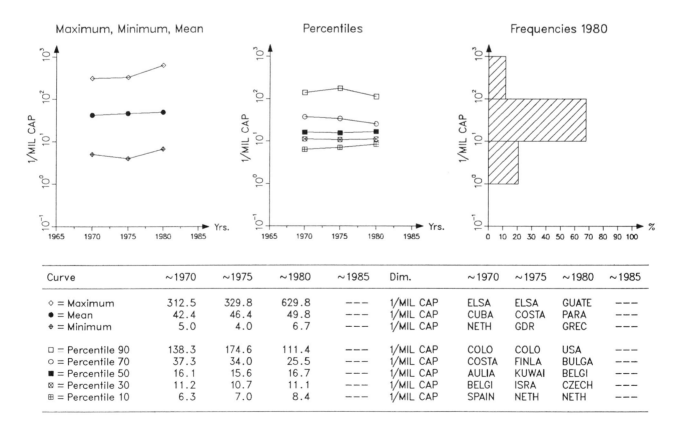

Curve	~1970	~1975	~1980	~1985	Dim.	~1970	~1975	~1980	~1985
◇ = Maximum	312.5	329.8	629.8	---	1/MIL CAP	ELSA	ELSA	GUATE	---
● = Mean	42.4	46.4	49.8	---	1/MIL CAP	CUBA	COSTA	PARA	---
⊕ = Minimum	5.0	4.0	6.7	---	1/MIL CAP	NETH	GDR	GREC	---
□ = Percentile 90	138.3	174.6	111.4	---	1/MIL CAP	COLO	COLO	USA	---
○ = Percentile 70	37.3	34.0	25.5	---	1/MIL CAP	COSTA	FINLA	BULGA	---
■ = Percentile 50	16.1	15.6	16.7	---	1/MIL CAP	AULIA	KUWAI	BELGI	---
⊠ = Percentile 30	11.2	10.7	11.1	---	1/MIL CAP	BELGI	ISRA	CZECH	---
⊞ = Percentile 10	6.3	7.0	8.4	---	1/MIL CAP	SPAIN	NETH	NETH	---

Availability:
- About 40 observations relating to 1-year intervals between 1968 and 1972.
- About 40 observations relating to 1-year intervals between 1973 and 1977.
- About 30 observations relating to 1-year intervals between 1978 and 1982.

Sources:
- Death statistics: World Health Organization. *World Health Statistics Annual,* several editions. Geneva, several years, chapter "Deaths According to Cause," causes "Homicide and injury purposely inflicted by other persons" and "Homicide and injury purposely inflicted by other persons; legal intervention."
- Source 1 for population figures: United Nations. *Demographic Yearbook, Historical Supplement.* New York, 1979, tab. 1.
- Source 2 for population figures: United Nations. *Demographic Yearbook 1983.* New York, 1985, tab. 5.

SUICIDES P. MIL. POPULATION (V46)

Short Names:
V46 or SUCID/POP.

Definition:
Suicides p. Mil. Population = Cases of death per million inhabitants that have been caused by suicides or self-inflicted injuries.

Scaling:
Ratio scale. Units: 1 / million capita (1/MIL CAP).

Quality of Data:
The quality of the data is generally bad. For many countries the number of cases of *undetermined* violent death equals up to *50%* of the sum of all cases of homicide or suicide. Hence *diachronic* and *crossnational* comparisons are only of limited value.

Availability:
- About 40 observations relating to 1-year intervals between 1968 and 1972.
- About 40 observations relating to 1-year intervals between 1973 and 1977.
- About 30 observations relating to 1-year intervals between 1978 and 1982.

Sources:
- Death statistics: World Health Organization. *World Health Statistics Annual,* several editions. Geneva, several years, chapter "Deaths According to Cause," cause "Suicide and self inflicted injury," cause BE49 on the B-List 1965, and cause BE49 on the B-List 1955.
- Source 1 for population figures: United Nations. *Demographic Yearbook, Historical Supplement.* New York, 1979, tab. 1.
- Source 2 for population figures: United Nations. *Demographic Yearbook 1983.* New York, 1985, tab. 5.

Statistical Overview:

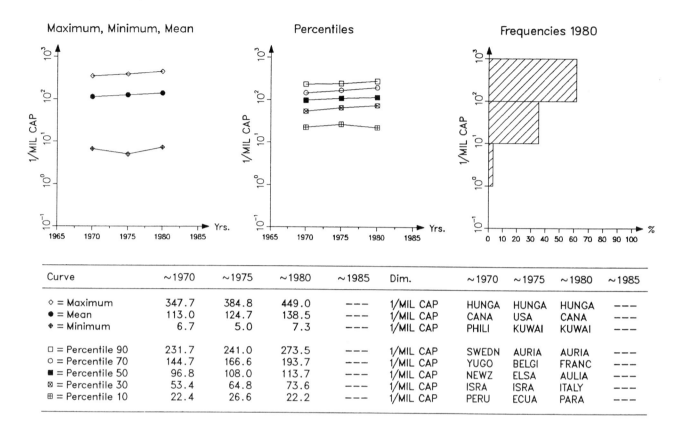

Curve	~1970	~1975	~1980	~1985	Dim.	~1970	~1975	~1980	~1985
◇ = Maximum	347.7	384.8	449.0	---	1/MIL CAP	HUNGA	HUNGA	HUNGA	---
● = Mean	113.0	124.7	138.5	---	1/MIL CAP	CANA	USA	CANA	---
✦ = Minimum	6.7	5.0	7.3	---	1/MIL CAP	PHILI	KUWAI	KUWAI	---
□ = Percentile 90	231.7	241.0	273.5	---	1/MIL CAP	SWEDN	AURIA	AURIA	---
○ = Percentile 70	144.7	166.6	193.7	---	1/MIL CAP	YUGO	BELGI	FRANC	---
■ = Percentile 50	96.8	108.0	113.7	---	1/MIL CAP	NEWZ	ELSA	AULIA	---
⊠ = Percentile 30	53.4	64.8	73.6	---	1/MIL CAP	ISRA	ISRA	ITALY	---
⊞ = Percentile 10	22.4	26.6	22.2	---	1/MIL CAP	PERU	ECUA	PARA	---

OTHER IMPORTANT VARIABLES

- Adult Literacy (V5).
- Duration of Schooling (V6).
- Student Enrollment Ratio (V7).

MEASURES DESCRIBING

INTERNATIONAL EXCHANGE RELATIONS

IMPORT PARTNERS (V47)

Short Names:
V47 or IMPPART.

Definition:
- *Value* = Percentage share of the total commodity imports that the country under consideration has received from a partner nation during the year stated.
- *Partner Nation* = Nation that has one of the three highest ranks on the scale defined before.

Scaling:
Ratio scale. Units: %.

Quality of Data:
Unless stated otherwise by footnotes in the country profiles the quality of the data allows *diachronic* and *crossnational* comparisons.

Statistical Overview:

Rank—R1 Import Partners

	Year	Holder	Key—N.	Freq.	
Position 1:	~1970	USA	ARGE	30 %	
	~1980	USA	ARGE	27 %	
Position 2:	~1970	FRANC	ALGER	15 %	
	~1980	FRANC	ALGER	13 %	
Position 3:	~1970	UNKI	GHANA	14 %	
	~1980	JAPAN	BURMA	12 %	
Position 4:	~1970	GFR	AURIA	13 %	
	~1980	GFR	AURIA	10 %	
Position 5:	~1970	USSR	AFGHA	10 %	
	~1980	USSR	AFGHA	10 %	

Availability:
- For each of the 3 ranks of the partner nations there are about 100 observations relating to 1-year intervals between 1968 and 1972.
- For each of the 3 ranks of the partner nations there are about 100 observations relating to 1-year intervals between 1978 and 1982.

Sources:

United Nations. *Yearbook of International Trade Statistics,* several editions. New York, several years.

EXPORT PARTNERS (V48)

Short Names:

V48 or EXPPART.

Definition:
- *Value* = Percentage share of the total commodity exports that the country under consideration has supplied to a partner nation during the year stated.
- *Partner Nation* = Nation that has one of the three highest ranks on the scale defined before.

Scaling:

Ratio scale. Units: %.

Statistical Overview:

Rank–R1 Export Partners

	Year	Holder	Key–N.	Freq.	0 10 20 30 40 50 60 70 80 90 100 %
Position 1:	~1970	USA	BRAZI	28 %	
	~1980	USA	ALGER	28 %	
Position 2:	~1970	FRANC	ALGER	14 %	
	~1980	GFR	AURIA	14 %	
Position 3:	~1970	GFR	AURIA	12 %	
	~1980	JAPAN	AULIA	11 %	
Position 4:	~1970	UNKI	BOLI	12 %	
	~1980	USSR	AFGHA	11 %	
Position 5:	~1970	USSR	AFGHA	9 %	
	~1980	FRANC	CENTR	9 %	

Quality of Data:
Unless stated otherwise by footnotes in the country profiles the quality of the data allows *diachronic* and *crossnational* comparisons.

Availability:
- For each of the 3 ranks of the partner nations there are about 100 observations relating to 1-year intervals between 1968 and 1972.
- For each of the 3 ranks of the partner nations there are between 90 and 100 observations relating to 1-year intervals between 1978 and 1982.

Sources:
United Nations. *Yearbook of International Trade Statistics,* several editions. New York, several years.

PATENT SUPPLIERS (V49)

Short Names:
V49 or PATSUPPL.

Definition:
- *Value* = Number of patents that the country under consideration has *granted* to inventors from a partner nation during the year stated. *Inventor's certificates* used in some East European countries are considered to be equivalent to *patents* used in the rest of the world. For statistical reasons there are no data for nations that have granted fewer than 10 patents to foreigners.
- *Partner Nation* = Nation that has one of the three highest ranks on the scale defined before.

Scaling:
Dimensionless ratio scale.

Statistical Overview:

Rank—R1 Patent Suppliers

	Year	Holder	Key–N.	Freq.	
Position 1:	~1970	USA	ARGE	64 %	
	~1980	USA	ARGE	64 %	
Position 2:	~1970	GFR	AURIA	14 %	
	~1980	GFR	AURIA	19 %	
Position 3:	~1970	UNKI	BURU	10 %	
	~1980	FRANC	CUBA	8 %	

Quality of Data:

Unless stated otherwise by footnotes in the country profiles the quality of the data allows *crossnational* comparisons. However, the validity of *diachronic* comparisons is not assured.

Availability:

- For each of the 3 ranks of the partner nations there are about 80 observations relating to 1-year intervals between 1968 and 1972.
- For each of the 3 ranks of the partner nations there are about 70 observations relating to 1-year intervals between 1978 and 1982.

Sources:

World Intellectual Property Organization (WIPO). *Industrial Property Statistics* (= Annex of WIPO. *Industrial Property / La Propriété industrielle*) , several editions. Geneva, several years.

PROVENANCE OF FOREIGN FIRMS (V50)

Short Names:

V50 or PROFORFIRM.

Definition:

- *Value* = Percentage share of a partner nation in the total number of foreign enterprises operating in the country under consideration. For statistical reasons the values and nations have been *omitted* if there were fewer than 10 foreign enterprises in the country stated.
- *Partner Nation* = Nation that has one of the three highest ranks on the scale defined before.

Scaling:

Ratio scale. Units: %.

Statistical Overview:

Rank—R1 Provenance of Foreign Firms

	Year	Holder	Key—N.	Freq.	0 10 20 30 40 50 60 70 80 90 100
Position 1:	~1970	---	---	. %	|
	~1980	USA	ARGE	52 %	////////////
Position 2:	~1970	---	---	. %	|
	~1980	UNKI	ANGO	25 %	//////
Position 3:	~1970	---	---	. %	|
	~1980	FRANC	ALGER	14 %	///

Quality of Data:

Since the completeness of the foreign enterprise statistics varies from country to country the validity of *crossnational* comparisons is slightly limited.

Availability:

For each of the 3 ranks of the partner nations there are between 80 and 90 observations relating to timepoints between 1978 and 1982.

Sources:

United Nations Centre on Transnational Corporations. *Transnational Corporations in the World Development, Third Survey.* New York, 1983, Annex Table II.19.

FILM SUPPLIERS (V51)

Short Names:

V51 or FILMSUPPL.

Definition:

- *Value* = Number of foreign films that the country under consideration has received from a partner nation during the year stated. For statistical reasons these values and the corresponding partner nations have been *omitted* if the total number of *all* foreign films that the given country has *imported* during the year stated was lower than 10.
- *Partner Nation* = Nation that has one of the three highest ranks on the scale defined before and that belongs to a group of six important film producers. This group comprises the *USA, France, Italy, India,* the *USSR,* and the *United Kingdom.*

Scaling:

Dimensionless ratio scale.

Statistical Overview:

Rank—R1 Film Suppliers

	Year	Holder	Key—N.	Freq.	0 10 20 30 40 50 60 70 80 90 100 %
Position 1:	~1970	---	---	. %	
	~1980	USA	ALGER	71 %	▨▨▨▨▨▨▨▨▨▨
Position 2:	~1970	---	---	. %	
	~1980	USSR	BULGA	15 %	▨▨
Position 3:	~1970	---	---	. %	
	~1980	INDIA	MOROC	6 %	▨

Quality of Data:
Unless stated otherwise by footnotes in the country profiles the quality of the data allows *crossnational* comparisons.

Availability:
For each of the 3 ranks of the partner nations there are about 70 observations relating to 1-year intervals between 1978 and 1982.

Sources:
- UNESCO. *Statistical Yearbook 1984.* Paris, 1984, tab. 8.2.
- UNESCO. *Statistical Yearbook 1985.* Paris, 1985, tab. 9.2.

CHAPTER 4

THE COUNTRY PROFILES

AFGHANISTAN (AFGHA)

V1	INCOME PER CAPITA	------	----	----	----- -----	-------	-------	----
V2	TELEPHONES P. TSD. POPULATION	1970	D1	P7	1 1/TSD CAP	RWAN	BURMA	----
		1975	D2	P12	2 1/TSD CAP	UPVO	GUINE	----
		1980	D1	P7	2 1/TSD CAP	ZAIRE	NIGER	----
V3	INFANT MORTALITY RATE	------	----	----	----- -----	-------	-------	----
V4	PHYSICIANS P. MIL. POPULATION	1971	D3	P24	62 1/MIL	KAMPU	SENE	----
V5	ADULT LITERACY	1980	D2	P12	20.0 %	NIGER	SAUDI	----
V6	DURATION OF SCHOOLING	1970	D1	P10	2.3 YR	NEPAL	BURU	----
		1975	D1	P9	2.5 YR	YENO	CHAD	F29
		1980	D2	P10	3.5 YR	YENO	SENE	----
V7	STUDENT ENROLLMENT RATIO	1970	D3	P24	0.7 %	GUINE	ZAIRE	----
		1975	D3	P21	1.0 %	SOMA	GHANA	----
		1979	D3	P24	1.7 %	ZAMBI	PAPUA	----
V8	SHARE OF AGRICULTURAL LABOR	1979	D9	P92	60.7 %	TURKY	ZIMBA	F46
V9	SHARE OF INDUSTRIAL LABOR	1979	D5	P40	28.5 %	KORSO	SRILA	F46
V10	SHARE OF SERVICE LABOR	1979	D1	P5	8.2 %	BANGL	INDIA	F46
V11	SHARE OF ACADEMIC LABOR	1979	D2	P11	2.6 %	THAI	HAITI	F46
V12	SHARE OF SELF-EMPLOYED LABOR	------	----	----	----- -----	-------	-------	----
V13	MILITARY EXPENDITURES	------	----	----	----- -----	-------	-------	----
V14	MILITARY MANPOWER	1970	D7	P65	91 TSD CAP	AULIA	CANA	----
		1975	D7	P70	130 TSD CAP	CUBA	IRAQ	----
		1980	D6	P51	43 TSD CAP	AURIA	ANGO	----
V15	MEN AT AGE 20 - 30	------	----	----	----- -----	-------	-------	----
V16	POPULATION	1980	D7	P67	15.95 MIL CAP	CZECH	KENYA	----
V17	GROSS DOMESTIC PRODUCT	------	----	----	----- -----	-------	-------	----
V18	SHARE IN WORLD IMPORTS	1970	D2	P17	0.337 1/TSD	MALAW	LAOS	F30
		1975	D3	P23	0.384 1/TSD	LIBE	MADA	F30
		1980	D2	P17	0.269 1/TSD	TOGO	CONGO	F30
V19	SHARE IN WORLD EXPORTS	1970	D2	P20	0.274 1/TSD	MONGO	MAURA	F30
		1975	D3	P23	0.254 1/TSD	MONGO	ETHIA	F30
		1980	D3	P28	0.353 1/TSD	LIBE	ELSA	F30
V20	GDP SHARE OF IMPORTS	1970	D2	P20	12.1 %	COLO	HAITI	F30
		1975	D3	P27	18.0 %	PERU	GFR	F30
		1980	D3	P24	17.1 %	SPAIN	URU	F30
V21	GDP SHARE OF EXPORTS	1970	D2	P16	9.3 %	NIGER	JAPAN	F30
		1975	D3	P28	11.5 %	JAPAN	PARA	F30
		1980	D6	P58	21.8 %	CAME	NIGER	F30

V22	EXPORT PARTNER CONCENTRATION	1970	D8	P74	38.4 %	BOLI	BENIN	----
		1975	D8	P75	38.7 %	JAMAI	HUNGA	----
		1980	D10	P94	59.3 %	HAITI	TRITO	----
V23	TOTAL DEBT AS % OF GDP	------	----	----	----- -----	-------	-------	----
V24	SHARE OF NEW FOREIGN PATENTS	------	----	----	----- -----	-------	-------	----
V25	FOREIGN PROPERTY AS % OF GDP	1971	D1	P7	1.5 %	EGYPT	SUDAN	----
		1975	D1	P10	1.0 %	IRAQ	SYRIA	----
		1978	D1	----	0.5 %	SAUDI	IRAQ	----
V26	GNP SHARE OF DEVELOPMENT AID	------	----	----	----- -----	-------	-------	----
V27	SHARE IN NOBEL PRIZE WINNERS	1970-79	D5	P45	0.0 %	-------	ALBA	----
V28	GDP SHARE OF MANUFACTURING	------	----	----	----- -----	-------	-------	----
V29	EXPORT SHARE OF MANUFACTURES	------	----	----	----- -----	-------	-------	----
V30	LACK OF CIVIL LIBERTIES	1975	D8	P74	6	VISO	ALGER	----
		1980	D10	P92	7	ZAIRE	ALBA	----
V31	LACK OF POLITICAL RIGHTS	1975	D9	P88	7	YUGO	ALBA	----
		1980	D9	P90	7	ZAIRE	ALBA	----
V32	RIOTS	1970-74	D2	P19	0	-------	ALBA	----
		1975-79	D2	P20	0	-------	ALBA	----
V33	PROTEST DEMONSTRATIONS	1970-74	D4	P37	1	YESO	BURMA	----
		1975-79	D5	P49	3	TANZA	INDO	----
V34	POLITICAL STRIKES	1970-74	D3	P29	0	-------	ALBA	----
		1975-79	D3	P29	0	-------	ALBA	----
V35	MEMBER OF THE NONALIGNED MMT.	1970	----	----	1	-------	ALGER	----
		1976	----	----	1	-------	ALGER	----
		1981	----	----	1	-------	ALGER	----
V36	MEMBER OF THE OPEC	1970	----	----	0	-------	ALBA	----
		1975	----	----	0	-------	ALBA	----
		1980	----	----	0	-------	ALBA	----
V37	MEMBER OF THE OECD	1970	----	----	0	-------	ALBA	----
		1975	----	----	0	-------	ALBA	----
		1980	----	----	0	-------	ALBA	----
V38	MEMBER OF THE CMEA	1970	----	----	0	-------	ALBA	----
		1975	----	----	0	-------	ALBA	----
		1980	----	----	0	-------	ALBA	----
V39	MEMBER OF THE WTO	1970	----	----	0	-------	ALBA	----
		1975	----	----	0	-------	ALBA	----
		1980	----	----	0	-------	ALBA	----
V40	MEMBER OF THE NATO	1970	----	----	0	-------	ALBA	----
		1975	----	----	0	-------	ALBA	----
		1980	----	----	0	-------	ALBA	----

V41	GDP SHARE OF INVESTMENTS	1970	D1	P4	5.5	%	BANGL	NEPAL	----
		1975	D1	P7	9.8	%	NEPAL	BURMA	----
		1978	D2	----	13.9	%	PERU	SENE	----
V42	GDP SHARE OF AGRICULTURE	------	----	----	-----	-----	-------	-------	----
V43	GDP SHARE OF INDUSTRY	------	----	----	-----	-----	-------	-------	----
V44	GDP SHARE OF SERVICES	------	----	----	-----	-----	-------	-------	----
V45	HOMICIDES P. MIL. POPULATION	------	----	----	-----	-----	-------	-------	----
V46	SUICIDES P. MIL. POPULATION	------	----	----	-----	-----	-------	-------	----
V47	IMPORT PARTNERS	1970	R1	USSR	34.2	%	-------	BULGA	----
		1970	R2	JAPAN	17.4	%	THAI	BOLI	----
		1970	R3	INDIA	11.6	%	SUDAN	-------	----
		1980	R1	USSR	52.7	%	-------	BULGA	----
		1980	R2	JAPAN	17.8	%	UNARE	AULIA	----
V48	EXPORT PARTNERS	1970	R1	USSR	38.4	%	-------	BULGA	----
		1970	R2	UNKI	16.1	%	YESO	CANA	----
		1970	R3	INDIA	15.8	%	SUDAN	EGYPT	----
		1980	R1	USSR	59.3	%	-------	ARGE	----
		1980	R2	INDIA	7.8	%	-------	-------	----
		1980	R3	PAKI	7.4	%	BANGL	-------	----
V49	PATENT SUPPLIERS	------	----	----	-----	-----	-------	-------	----
V50	PROVENANCE OF FOREIGN FIRMS	------	----	----	-----	-----	-------	-------	----
V51	FILM SUPPLIERS	------	----	----	-----	-----	-------	-------	----

ALBANIA (ALBA)

V1	INCOME PER CAPITA	------	----	----	-----	-----	-------	-------	----
V2	TELEPHONES P. TSD. POPULATION	------	----	----	-----	-----	-------	-------	----
V3	INFANT MORTALITY RATE	1980	D5	P42	49.5	1/TSD	CHINA	THAI	F5
V4	PHYSICIANS P. MIL. POPULATION	1972	D8	----	847	1/MIL	CUBA	VENE	----
		1977	D7	----	1052	1/MIL	CUBA	LIBYA	----
V5	ADULT LITERACY	------	----	----	-----	-----	-------	-------	----
V6	DURATION OF SCHOOLING	1970	D9	P82	10.3	YR	GREC	BULGA	----
		1977	D10	----	11.2	YR	CUBA	FRANC	----
		1980	D9	P87	11.2	YR	ITALY	ROMA	----

V7	STUDENT ENROLLMENT RATIO	1970	D6	P59	6.4	%	INDIA	MONGO	----
		1977	D5	----	6.2	%	IRAN	LIBYA	----
		1980	D5	P44	5.4	%	TRITO	TUNIS	----
V8	SHARE OF AGRICULTURAL LABOR	------	----	----	-----	-----	-------	-------	----
V9	SHARE OF INDUSTRIAL LABOR	------	----	----	-----	-----	-------	-------	----
V10	SHARE OF SERVICE LABOR	------	----	----	-----	-----	-------	-------	----
V11	SHARE OF ACADEMIC LABOR	------	----	----	-----	-----	-------	-------	----
V12	SHARE OF SELF-EMPLOYED LABOR	------	----	----	-----	-----	-------	-------	----
V13	MILITARY EXPENDITURES	------	----	----	-----	-----	-------	-------	----
V14	MILITARY MANPOWER	1970	D6	P51	52	TSD CAP	ZAIRE	AURIA	----
		1975	D6	P54	52	TSD CAP	SUDAN	VENE	----
		1980	D6	P53	52	TSD CAP	SINGA	LIBYA	----
V15	MEN AT AGE 20 - 30	------	----	----	-----	-----	-------	-------	----
V16	POPULATION	1970	D2	P14	2.14	MIL CAP	SINGA	JORDA	----
		1975	D2	P15	2.40	MIL CAP	SINGA	LIBYA	----
		1980	D2	P14	2.67	MIL CAP	TOGO	LEBA	----
V17	GROSS DOMESTIC PRODUCT	------	----	----	-----	-----	-------	-------	----
V18	SHARE IN WORLD IMPORTS	------	----	----	-----	-----	-------	-------	----
V19	SHARE IN WORLD EXPORTS	------	----	----	-----	-----	-------	-------	----
V20	GDP SHARE OF IMPORTS	------	----	----	-----	-----	-------	-------	----
V21	GDP SHARE OF EXPORTS	------	----	----	-----	-----	-------	-------	----
V22	EXPORT PARTNER CONCENTRATION	------	----	----	-----	-----	-------	-------	----
V23	TOTAL DEBT AS % OF GDP	------	----	----	-----	-----	-------	-------	----
V24	SHARE OF NEW FOREIGN PATENTS	------	----	----	-----	-----	-------	-------	----
V25	FOREIGN PROPERTY AS % OF GDP	------	----	----	-----	-----	-------	-------	----
V26	GNP SHARE OF DEVELOPMENT AID	------	----	----	-----	-----	-------	-------	----
V27	SHARE IN NOBEL PRIZE WINNERS	1970-79	D5	P45	0.0	%	AFGHA	ALGER	----
V28	GDP SHARE OF MANUFACTURING	------	----	----	-----	-----	-------	-------	----
V29	EXPORT SHARE OF MANUFACTURES	------	----	----	-----	-----	-------	-------	----
V30	LACK OF CIVIL LIBERTIES	1975	D10	P93	7		ZAIRE	BULGA	----
		1980	D10	P92	7		AFGHA	ANGO	----
V31	LACK OF POLITICAL RIGHTS	1975	D9	P88	7		AFGHA	BENIN	----
		1980	D9	P90	7		AFGHA	ANGO	----
V32	RIOTS	1970-74	D2	P19	0		AFGHA	AURIA	----
		1975-79	D2	P20	0		AFGHA	ALGER	----

V33	PROTEST DEMONSTRATIONS	1970-74	D2	P15	0	-------	ALGER	----
		1975-79	D2	P13	0	-------	ALGER	----
V34	POLITICAL STRIKES	1970-74	D3	P29	0	AFGHA	ALGER	----
		1975-79	D3	P29	0	AFGHA	ALGER	----
V35	MEMBER OF THE NONALIGNED MMT.	1970	----	----	0	-------	ARGE	----
		1976	----	----	0	-------	AULIA	----
		1981	----	----	0	-------	AULIA	----
V36	MEMBER OF THE OPEC	1970	----	----	0	AFGHA	ARGE	----
		1975	----	----	0	AFGHA	ANGO	----
		1980	----	----	0	AFGHA	ANGO	----
V37	MEMBER OF THE OECD	1970	----	----	0	AFGHA	ALGER	----
		1975	----	----	0	AFGHA	ALGER	----
		1980	----	----	0	AFGHA	ALGER	----
V38	MEMBER OF THE CMEA	1970	----	----	0	AFGHA	ALGER	F8
		1975	----	----	0	AFGHA	ALGER	F8
		1980	----	----	0	AFGHA	ALGER	F8
V39	MEMBER OF THE WTO	1970	----	----	0	AFGHA	ALGER	----
		1975	----	----	0	AFGHA	ALGER	----
		1980	----	----	0	AFGHA	ALGER	----
V40	MEMBER OF THE NATO	1970	----	----	0	AFGHA	ALGER	----
		1975	----	----	0	AFGHA	ALGER	----
		1980	----	----	0	AFGHA	ALGER	----
V41	GDP SHARE OF INVESTMENTS	------	----	----	----- -----	-------	-------	----
V42	GDP SHARE OF AGRICULTURE	------	----	----	----- -----	-------	-------	----
V43	GDP SHARE OF INDUSTRY	------	----	----	----- -----	-------	-------	----
V44	GDP SHARE OF SERVICES	------	----	----	----- -----	-------	-------	----
V45	HOMICIDES P. MIL. POPULATION	------	----	----	----- -----	-------	-------	----
V46	SUICIDES P. MIL. POPULATION	------	----	----	----- -----	-------	-------	----
V47	IMPORT PARTNERS	------	----	----	----- -----	-------	-------	----
V48	EXPORT PARTNERS	------	----	----	----- -----	-------	-------	----
V49	PATENT SUPPLIERS	------	----	----	----- -----	-------	-------	----
V50	PROVENANCE OF FOREIGN FIRMS	------	----	----	----- -----	-------	-------	----
V51	FILM SUPPLIERS	------	----	----	----- -----	-------	-------	----

ALGERIA (ALGER)

V1	INCOME PER CAPITA	1970	D6	P58	1316	$/CAP	BRAZI	PANA	F210
		1975	D6	P60	1529	$/CAP	PANA	HUNGA	F147
		1980	D7	P61	2120	$/CAP	MEXI	BRAZI	F147
V2	TELEPHONES P. TSD. POPULATION	1970	D5	P48	13	1/TSD CAP	IRAQ	NICA	----
		1975	D5	P41	14	1/TSD CAP	PAPUA	PARA	----
		1980	D4	P38	25	1/TSD CAP	NICA	PERU	----
V3	INFANT MORTALITY RATE	1980	D8	P74	125.0	1/TSD	NIGRA	CAME	F5
V4	PHYSICIANS P. MIL. POPULATION	1969	D4	P38	122	1/MIL	ZAMBI	TUNIS	F147
		1976	D4	P38	210	1/MIL	GABON	TUNIS	F147
		1979	D5	P45	380	1/MIL	JAMAI	IRAN	F147
V5	ADULT LITERACY	1971	D2	P17	26.4	%	MOROC	GHANA	----
		1982	D4	----	44.7	%	LAOS	TANZA	----
V6	DURATION OF SCHOOLING	1970	D4	P35	6.0	YR	IRAQ	INDO	----
		1975	D5	P46	7.7	YR	IRAN	GABON	----
		1980	D5	P44	8.5	YR	NICA	LESO	----
V7	STUDENT ENROLLMENT RATIO	1970	D4	P39	1.9	%	THAI	NEPAL	----
		1975	D4	P41	3.2	%	CONGO	MOROC	----
		1980	D5	P42	4.9	%	GUINE	BURMA	----
V8	SHARE OF AGRICULTURAL LABOR	1977	D5	----	24.2	%	LIBYA	JAMAI	F46
V9	SHARE OF INDUSTRIAL LABOR	1977	D9	----	38.8	%	FRANC	TUNIS	F46
V10	SHARE OF SERVICE LABOR	1977	D6	----	29.0	%	COSTA	LIBYA	F46
V11	SHARE OF ACADEMIC LABOR	1977	D6	----	8.0	%	SPAIN	URU	F46
V12	SHARE OF SELF-EMPLOYED LABOR	1977	D4	----	22.8	%	COSTA	IRE	F46
V13	MILITARY EXPENDITURES	1975	D6	P53	0.571	TSD MIL $	MEXI	FINLA	----
		1980	D6	P58	0.831	TSD MIL $	PORTU	VENE	----
V14	MILITARY MANPOWER	1970	D7	P62	80	TSD CAP	SYRIA	MEXI	----
		1975	D7	P62	80	TSD CAP	CANA	BELGI	----
		1980	D7	P68	101	TSD CAP	BELGI	NETH	----
V15	MEN AT AGE 20 - 30	1982	D7	----	1614	TSD CAP	MOROC	ROMA	F184
V16	POPULATION	1970	D7	P70	14.33	MIL CAP	SUDAN	CZECH	F162
		1975	D8	P72	16.02	MIL CAP	KORNO	GDR	F22
		1980	D8	P72	18.67	MIL CAP	TANZA	SUDAN	F22
V17	GROSS DOMESTIC PRODUCT	1970	D6	P60	18.858	TSD MIL $	THAI	NEWZ	----
		1975	D7	P64	24.495	TSD MIL $	NEWZ	COLO	----
		1980	D7	P69	39.586	TSD MIL $	GREC	FINLA	----
V18	SHARE IN WORLD IMPORTS	1970	D7	P61	3.787	1/TSD	NEWZ	PHILI	----
		1975	D8	P72	6.600	1/TSD	BULGA	NIGRA	----
		1980	D7	P68	5.141	1/TSD	ARGE	VENE	----

V19 SHARE IN WORLD EXPORTS	1970	D6	P59	3.217	1/TSD	ZAMBI	IRE	----
	1975	D7	P69	5.363	1/TSD	BULGA	KORSO	----
	1980	D8	P74	7.825	1/TSD	MEXI	POLA	----
V20 GDP SHARE OF IMPORTS	1970	D8	P80	27.1	%	ZAMBI	SIERA	----
	1975	D10	P92	42.1	%	MALAW	NETH	----
	1980	D6	P55	24.8	%	TANZA	ITALY	----
V21 GDP SHARE OF EXPORTS	1970	D8	P74	21.8	%	UGADA	NORWY	----
	1975	D9	P82	33.0	%	ZAMBI	PAPUA	----
	1980	D9	P84	36.8	%	JAMAI	HUNGA	----
V22 EXPORT PARTNER CONCENTRATION	1970	D9	P89	53.6	%	JAMAI	BULGA	----
	1975	D6	P53	26.8	%	KUWAI	CAME	----
	1980	D9	P86	48.1	%	PANA	OMAN	----
V23 TOTAL DEBT AS % OF GDP	1980	D7	P63	43.9	%	CHAD	CHILE	----
V24 SHARE OF NEW FOREIGN PATENTS	------	----	----	-----	-----	-------	-------	----
V25 FOREIGN PROPERTY AS % OF GDP	1971	D3	P24	4.4	%	GREC	IRAQ	----
	1975	D3	P23	2.5	%	THAI	INDIA	----
	1978	D2	----	1.5	%	LESO	EGYPT	----
V26 GNP SHARE OF DEVELOPMENT AID	1970	D1	P11	0.00	%	-------	IRAN	----
	1975	D3	P25	0.21	%	SWITZ	AURIA	----
	1980	D2	P15	0.20	%	ITALY	VENE	----
V27 SHARE IN NOBEL PRIZE WINNERS	1970-79	D5	P45	0.0	%	ALBA	AULIA	----
V28 GDP SHARE OF MANUFACTURING	1970	D5	P49	14.0	%	HONDU	INDIA	----
	1975	D4	P34	10.1	%	ZAIRE	TUNIS	----
	1980	D5	P42	11.1	%	ETHIA	INDO	----
V29 EXPORT SHARE OF MANUFACTURES	1970	D4	P34	4.3	%	IRAN	SOMA	----
	1975	D3	P21	1.4	%	LIBE	PAPUA	----
	1980	D1	P4	0.2	%	GABON	CUBA	----
V30 LACK OF CIVIL LIBERTIES	1975	D8	P74	6		AFGHA	BENIN	----
	1980	D8	P74	6		ZIMBA	BENIN	----
V31 LACK OF POLITICAL RIGHTS	1975	D7	P63	6		ZAMBI	ANGO	----
	1980	D7	P67	6		ZAMBI	ARGE	----
V32 RIOTS	1970-74	D5	P43	1		ZAMBI	CAME	----
	1975-79	D2	P20	0		ALBA	AULIA	----
V33 PROTEST DEMONSTRATIONS	1970-74	D2	P15	0		ALBA	BENIN	----
	1975-79	D2	P13	0		ALBA	BENIN	----
V34 POLITICAL STRIKES	1970-74	D3	P29	0		ALBA	AURIA	----
	1975-79	D3	P29	0		ALBA	AURIA	----
V35 MEMBER OF THE NONALIGNED MMT.	1970	----	----	1		AFGHA	BURU	----
	1976	----	----	1		AFGHA	ANGO	----
	1981	----	----	1		AFGHA	ANGO	----
V36 MEMBER OF THE OPEC	1970	----	----	1		-------	INDO	----
	1975	----	----	1		-------	ECUA	----
	1980	----	----	1		-------	ECUA	----

V37 MEMBER OF THE OECD	1970	----	----	0		ALBA	ARGE	----
	1975	----	----	0		ALBA	ANGO	----
	1980	----	----	0		ALBA	ANGO	----
V38 MEMBER OF THE CMEA	1970	----	----	0		ALBA	ARGE	----
	1975	----	----	0		ALBA	ANGO	----
	1980	----	----	0		ALBA	ANGO	----
V39 MEMBER OF THE WTO	1970	----	----	0		ALBA	ARGE	----
	1975	----	----	0		ALBA	ANGO	----
	1980	----	----	0		ALBA	ANGO	----
V40 MEMBER OF THE NATO	1970	----	----	0		ALBA	ARGE	----
	1975	----	----	0		ALBA	ANGO	----
	1980	----	----	0		ALBA	ANGO	----
V41 GDP SHARE OF INVESTMENTS	1970	D10	P97	36.4 %		HUNGA	SINGA	----
	1975	D10	P99	50.0 %		ZAMBI	GABON	----
	1980	D10	P97	39.9 %		MAURA	JORDA	----
V42 GDP SHARE OF AGRICULTURE	1970	D3	P25	10.1 %		SOUAF	SPAIN	----
	1975	D3	P27	8.8 %		SOUAF	SPAIN	----
	1980	D3	P22	6.4 %		VENE	ITALY	----
V43 GDP SHARE OF INDUSTRY	1970	D8	P77	38.5 %		UNKI	MAURA	----
	1975	D10	P92	51.0 %		YUGO	TRITO	----
	1980	D10	P94	57.1 %		TRITO	GABON	----
V44 GDP SHARE OF SERVICES	1970	D7	P62	51.4 %		IVORY	ECUA	----
	1975	D3	P30	40.2 %		TRITO	MOZAM	----
	1980	D2	P21	36.5 %		LIBE	NIGRA	----
V45 HOMICIDES P. MIL. POPULATION	------	----	----	----- -----		-------	-------	----
V46 SUICIDES P. MIL. POPULATION	------	----	----	----- -----		-------	-------	----
V47 IMPORT PARTNERS	1970	R1	FRANC	42.4 %		-------	BENIN	----
	1970	R2	GFR	10.0 %		YUGO	BRAZI	----
	1970	R3	USA	8.0 %		ZAIRE	CAME	----
	1980	R1	FRANC	23.2 %		-------	BENIN	----
	1980	R2	GFR	13.7 %		SWITZ	CAME	----
	1980	R3	ITALY	11.9 %		TUNIS	GFR	----
V48 EXPORT PARTNERS	1970	R1	FRANC	53.6 %		-------	BENIN	----
	1970	R2	GFR	12.9 %		URU	BRAZI	----
	1970	R3	USSR	4.9 %		YUGO	FINLA	----
	1980	R1	USA	48.1 %		-------	BANGL	----
	1980	R2	FRANC	13.4 %		SPAIN	BELGI	----
	1980	R3	GFR	12.4 %		SPAIN	COSTA	----
V49 PATENT SUPPLIERS	------	----	----	----- -----		-------	-------	----
V50 PROVENANCE OF FOREIGN FIRMS	1980	R1	FRANC	52.5 %		-------	BENIN	----
	1980	R2	USA	17.9 %		VENE	AULIA	----
	1980	R3	GFR	8.9 %		TURKY	ARGE	----
V51 FILM SUPPLIERS	1980	R1	USA	43		-------	ARGE	F119
	1980	R2	FRANC	33		HAITI	AULIA	F119
	1980	R3	INDIA	18		YENO	ETHIA	F119

ANGOLA (ANGO)

V1	INCOME PER CAPITA	------	----	----		----- -----	-------	-------	----
V2	TELEPHONES P. TSD. POPULATION	1980	D3	P22	7	1/TSD CAP	SRILA	GHANA	----
V3	INFANT MORTALITY RATE	1980	D10	P94	160.4	1/TSD	NEPAL	BENIN	F5
V4	PHYSICIANS P. MIL. POPULATION	------	----	----		----- -----	-------	-------	----
V5	ADULT LITERACY	------	----	----		----- -----	-------	-------	----
V6	DURATION OF SCHOOLING	1980	D4	P37	8.0	YR	THAI	EGYPT	----
V7	STUDENT ENROLLMENT RATIO	1980	D1	P6	0.3	%	MOZAM	BHUTA	----
V8	SHARE OF AGRICULTURAL LABOR	------	----	----		----- -----	-------	-------	----
V9	SHARE OF INDUSTRIAL LABOR	------	----	----		----- -----	-------	-------	----
V10	SHARE OF SERVICE LABOR	------	----	----		----- -----	-------	-------	----
V11	SHARE OF ACADEMIC LABOR	------	----	----		----- -----	-------	-------	----
V12	SHARE OF SELF-EMPLOYED LABOR	------	----	----		----- -----	-------	-------	----
V13	MILITARY EXPENDITURES	------	----	----		----- -----	-------	-------	----
V14	MILITARY MANPOWER	1975	D5	P44	30	TSD CAP	SINGA	SOMA	----
		1980	D6	P52	47	TSD CAP	AFGHA	SINGA	----
V15	MEN AT AGE 20 - 30	------	----	----		----- -----	-------	-------	----
V16	POPULATION	1975	D5	P44	6.52	MIL CAP	SWITZ	IVORY	----
		1980	D5	P46	7.72	MIL CAP	AURIA	IVORY	----
V17	GROSS DOMESTIC PRODUCT	------	----	----		----- -----	-------	-------	----
V18	SHARE IN WORLD IMPORTS	1979	D3	P25	0.403	1/TSD	ETHIA	ZAIRE	----
V19	SHARE IN WORLD EXPORTS	1979	D4	P31	0.406	1/TSD	YESO	HONDU	----
V20	GDP SHARE OF IMPORTS	1979	D2	P17	14.4	%	COLO	CHAD	----
V21	GDP SHARE OF EXPORTS	1979	D4	P31	14.1	%	MOROC	CHAD	----
V22	EXPORT PARTNER CONCENTRATION	------	----	----		----- -----	-------	-------	----
V23	TOTAL DEBT AS % OF GDP	------	----	----		----- -----	-------	-------	----
V24	SHARE OF NEW FOREIGN PATENTS	------	----	----		----- -----	-------	-------	----
V25	FOREIGN PROPERTY AS % OF GDP	1975	D3	P30	3.7	%	MOROC	ETHIA	----
		1978	D3	----	2.5	%	GHANA	MOROC	----
V26	GNP SHARE OF DEVELOPMENT AID	------	----	----		----- -----	-------	-------	----
V27	SHARE IN NOBEL PRIZE WINNERS	------	----	----		----- -----	-------	-------	----

V28	GDP SHARE OF MANUFACTURING	1975	D1	P3	4.0	%	LIBYA	GUINE	F16
		1980	D1	P4	2.6	%	LIBYA	KUWAI	F16
V29	EXPORT SHARE OF MANUFACTURES	------	----	----	-----	-----	-------	-------	----
V30	LACK OF CIVIL LIBERTIES	1975	D4	P39	4		TURKY	ARGE	----
		1980	D10	P92	7		ALBA	BULGA	----
V31	LACK OF POLITICAL RIGHTS	1975	D7	P63	6		ALGER	BOLI	----
		1980	D9	P90	7		ALBA	BENIN	----
V32	RIOTS	------	----	----	-----	-----	-------	-------	----
V33	PROTEST DEMONSTRATIONS	------	----	----	-----	-----	-------	-------	----
V34	POLITICAL STRIKES	------	----	----	-----	-----	-------	-------	----
V35	MEMBER OF THE NONALIGNED MMT.	1976	----	----	1		ALGER	ARGE	----
		1981	----	----	1		ALGER	ARGE	----
V36	MEMBER OF THE OPEC	1975	----	----	0		ALBA	ARGE	----
		1980	----	----	0		ALBA	ARGE	----
V37	MEMBER OF THE OECD	1975	----	----	0		ALGER	ARGE	----
		1980	----	----	0		ALGER	ARGE	----
V38	MEMBER OF THE CMEA	1975	----	----	0		ALGER	ARGE	----
		1980	----	----	0		ALGER	ARGE	----
V39	MEMBER OF THE WTO	1975	----	----	0		ALGER	ARGE	----
		1980	----	----	0		ALGER	ARGE	----
V40	MEMBER OF THE NATO	1975	----	----	0		ALGER	ARGE	----
		1980	----	----	0		ALGER	ARGE	----
V41	GDP SHARE OF INVESTMENTS	1975	D1	P1	7.2	%	-------	UGADA	----
		1980	D1	P4	8.6	%	CENTR	MOZAM	----
V42	GDP SHARE OF AGRICULTURE	1975	D8	P80	40.6	%	NIGER	UPVO	F16
		1980	D9	P87	43.1	%	MALAW	MOZAM	F16
V43	GDP SHARE OF INDUSTRY	1975	D6	P60	33.2	%	MEXI	IRE	F16
		1980	D5	P46	30.2	%	PAPUA	TURKY	F16
V44	GDP SHARE OF SERVICES	1975	D1	P9	26.2	%	IRAQ	BANGL	F16
		1980	D1	P6	26.7	%	KUWAI	GHANA	F16
V45	HOMICIDES P. MIL. POPULATION	------	----	----	-----	-----	-------	-------	----
V46	SUICIDES P. MIL. POPULATION	------	----	----	-----	-----	-------	-------	----
V47	IMPORT PARTNERS	------	----	----	-----	-----	-------	-------	----
V48	EXPORT PARTNERS	------	----	----	-----	-----	-------	-------	----
V49	PATENT SUPPLIERS	------	----	----	-----	-----	-------	-------	----
V50	PROVENANCE OF FOREIGN FIRMS	1980	R1	UNKI	46.6	%	-------	AULIA	----
		1980	R2	-------	15.0	%	-------	-------	----
		1980	R3	-------	15.0	%	-------	-------	----

V51	FILM SUPPLIERS	1979	R1	FRANC	34	-------	HAITI	F118
		1979	R2	USA	28	ZAMBI	BULGA	F118
		1979	R3	USSR	26	ROMA	EGYPT	F118

ARGENTINA (ARGE)

V1	INCOME PER CAPITA	1980	D7	P66	2568	$/CAP	CHILE	URU	----
V2	TELEPHONES P. TSD. POPULATION	1970	D8	P73	68	1/TSD CAP	TRITO	LEBA	----
		1975	D8	P69	78	1/TSD CAP	POLA	SOUAF	----
		1980	D6	P60	93	1/TSD CAP	USSR	PANA	----
V3	INFANT MORTALITY RATE	1980	D4	P33	33.2	1/TSD	CHILE	MALAY	----
V4	PHYSICIANS P. MIL. POPULATION	1969	D10	P95	1935	1/MIL	BULGA	HUNGA	F2
		1975	D10	P90	1869	1/MIL	GDR	BELGI	----
V5	ADULT LITERACY	1970	D9	P84	92.6	%	SPAIN	ITALY	----
V6	DURATION OF SCHOOLING	1970	D8	P71	9.7	YR	USSR	SPAIN	----
		1975	D8	P75	10.2	YR	YUGO	HUNGA	----
		1981	D8	P72	10.4	YR	TRITO	MEXI	----
V7	STUDENT ENROLLMENT RATIO	1970	D9	P81	14.0	%	IRE	POLA	----
		1975	D10	P94	27.2	%	NEWZ	FINLA	----
		1980	D8	P79	21.6	%	PANA	YUGO	----
V8	SHARE OF AGRICULTURAL LABOR	1970	D3	P30	15.4	%	AURIA	FRANC	F66
V9	SHARE OF INDUSTRIAL LABOR	1970	D7	P68	36.6	%	USA	FRANC	F66
V10	SHARE OF SERVICE LABOR	1970	D9	P88	40.0	%	NETH	UNKI	F66
V11	SHARE OF ACADEMIC LABOR	1970	D6	P58	8.0	%	PERU	POLA	F66
V12	SHARE OF SELF-EMPLOYED LABOR	1970	D5	P49	22.9	%	ITALY	IRE	F66
V13	MILITARY EXPENDITURES	1976	D7	P70	1.317	TSD MIL $	LIBYA	DENMA	F62
		1980	D8	P71	1.885	TSD MIL $	NORWY	UNARE	F62
V14	MILITARY MANPOWER	1970	D8	P71	140	TSD CAP	NETH	CUBA	----
		1975	D8	P72	160	TSD CAP	IRAQ	BULGA	----
		1980	D8	P75	155	TSD CAP	PERU	BULGA	----
V15	MEN AT AGE 20 - 30	1970	D8	P74	1813	TSD CAP	CANA	IRAN	----
		1975	D8	P76	2055	TSD CAP	CANA	BURMA	F2
		1980	D7	P68	2154	TSD CAP	ZAIRE	ETHIA	----
V16	POPULATION	1970	D8	P78	23.75	MIL CAP	SOUAF	ETHIA	F4
		1975	D8	P79	26.05	MIL CAP	SOUAF	ETHIA	----
		1980	D8	P78	28.24	MIL CAP	COLO	SOUAF	----
V17	GROSS DOMESTIC PRODUCT	1976	D8	P80	65.856	TSD MIL $	NIGRA	SAUDI	----
		1980	D8	P79	72.519	TSD MIL $	AURIA	NIGRA	----

V18	SHARE IN WORLD IMPORTS	1970	D7	P70	5.103	1/TSD	VENE	BULGA	----
		1975	D7	P63	4.342	1/TSD	EGYPT	ISRA	----
		1980	D7	P67	5.139	1/TSD	GREC	ALGER	----
V19	SHARE IN WORLD EXPORTS	1970	D8	P71	5.652	1/TSD	MALAY	ROMA	----
		1975	D7	P62	3.379	1/TSD	THAI	MEXI	----
		1980	D7	P63	4.019	1/TSD	THAI	INDIA	----
V20	GDP SHARE OF IMPORTS	1970	D1	P7	7.3	%	TURKY	BURMA	----
		1975	D1	P7	9.9	%	MEXI	SAUDI	----
		1980	D1	P4	6.9	%	BURMA	CHINA	----
V21	GDP SHARE OF EXPORTS	1970	D2	P14	7.6	%	ETHIA	NIGER	----
		1975	D2	P15	7.5	%	RWAN	BURU	----
		1980	D1	P7	5.2	%	TURKY	INDIA	----
V22	EXPORT PARTNER CONCENTRATION	1970	D2	P14	15.3	%	YUGO	LEBA	----
		1975	D1	P3	10.1	%	UNKI	SWEDN	----
		1980	D4	P35	20.1	%	GHANA	KUWAI	----
V23	TOTAL DEBT AS % OF GDP	1980	D2	P17	17.8	%	BURU	ETHIA	----
V24	SHARE OF NEW FOREIGN PATENTS	1970	D3	P27	78	%	UNKI	FINLA	----
		1975	D2	P20	71	%	SOUAF	SWITZ	----
		1980	D3	P22	65	%	IRAQ	FRANC	----
V25	FOREIGN PROPERTY AS % OF GDP	1971	D5	P47	8.2	%	CHILE	BENIN	----
		1975	D5	P43	5.0	%	LIBYA	CHAD	----
		1978	D6	----	5.1	%	ELSA	MEXI	----
V26	GNP SHARE OF DEVELOPMENT AID	------	----	----	-----	-----	-------	-------	----
V27	SHARE IN NOBEL PRIZE WINNERS	1970-79	D9	P90	1.3	%	ZAMBI	CANA	----
V28	GDP SHARE OF MANUFACTURING	1970	D10	P94	30.0	%	FRANC	BELGI	----
		1975	D10	P98	31.9	%	JAPAN	PORTU	----
		1980	D9	P87	25.3	%	NICA	BELGI	----
V29	EXPORT SHARE OF MANUFACTURES	1970	D6	P54	12.3	%	SYRIA	KENYA	----
		1975	D7	P69	23.6	%	BRAZI	CENTR	----
		1980	D6	P55	21.4	%	COLO	GUATE	----
V30	LACK OF CIVIL LIBERTIES	1975	D4	P39	4		ANGO	BANGL	----
		1980	D6	P52	5		PERU	BHUTA	----
V31	LACK OF POLITICAL RIGHTS	1975	D2	P20	2		USA	COLO	----
		1980	D7	P67	6		ALGER	CAME	----
V32	RIOTS	1970-74	D9	P89	22		PORTU	SOUAF	----
		1975-79	D8	P72	6		PHILI	MEXI	----
V33	PROTEST DEMONSTRATIONS	1970-74	D9	P89	37		INDIA	ISRA	----
		1975-79	D9	P82	18		THAI	CHILE	----
V34	POLITICAL STRIKES	1970-74	D10	P91	14		KORSO	ETHIA	----
		1975-79	D9	P87	9		USA	ITALY	----
V35	MEMBER OF THE NONALIGNED MMT.	1970	----	----	0		ALBA	AULIA	----
		1976	----	----	1		ANGO	BANGL	----
		1981	----	----	1		ANGO	BANGL	----

V36	MEMBER OF THE OPEC	1970	----	----	0		ALBA	AULIA	----
		1975	----	----	0		ANGO	AULIA	----
		1980	----	----	0		ANGO	AULIA	----
V37	MEMBER OF THE OECD	1970	----	----	0		ALGER	AULIA	----
		1975	----	----	0		ANGO	BANGL	----
		1980	----	----	0		ANGO	BANGL	----
V38	MEMBER OF THE CMEA	1970	----	----	0		ALGER	AULIA	----
		1975	----	----	0		ANGO	AULIA	----
		1980	----	----	0		ANGO	AULIA	----
V39	MEMBER OF THE WTO	1970	----	----	0		ALGER	AULIA	----
		1975	----	----	0		ANGO	AULIA	----
		1980	----	----	0		ANGO	AULIA	----
V40	MEMBER OF THE NATO	1970	----	----	0		ALGER	AULIA	----
		1975	----	----	0		ANGO	AULIA	----
		1980	----	----	0		ANGO	AULIA	----
V41	GDP SHARE OF INVESTMENTS	1970	D6	P56	21.1 %		CANA	PHILI	----
		1975	D7	P68	25.9 %		UPVO	AURIA	----
		1980	D6	P59	25.7 %		ITALY	COLO	----
V42	GDP SHARE OF AGRICULTURE	1970	D3	P30	12.2 %		FINLA	MEXI	----
		1975	D4	P32	10.1 %		FINLA	NEWZ	----
		1980	D4	P32	8.8 %		JAMAI	MEXI	----
V43	GDP SHARE OF INDUSTRY	1970	D9	P81	40.1 %		VENE	SOUAF	----
		1975	D9	P85	42.7 %		ITALY	PORTU	----
		1980	D8	P74	37.9 %		ECUA	EGYPT	----
V44	GDP SHARE OF SERVICES	1970	D5	P48	47.7 %		JAPAN	AURIA	----
		1975	D6	P58	47.2 %		CENTR	BENIN	----
		1980	D8	P73	53.3 %		BOLI	JAPAN	----
V45	HOMICIDES P. MIL. POPULATION	1970	D9	P81	70.8 1/MIL CAP		PARA	ECUA	F154
		1981	D8	P79	38.4 1/MIL CAP		FINLA	PARA	F2
V46	SUICIDES P. MIL. POPULATION	1970	D6	P53	97.1 1/MIL CAP		NEWZ	URU	F2
		1981	D4	P34	77.3 1/MIL CAP		THAI	UNKI	F2
V47	IMPORT PARTNERS	1970	R1	USA	24.9 %		-------	AULIA	----
		1970	R2	BRAZI	11.0 %		URU	-------	----
		1970	R3	GFR	11.0 %		VENE	BOLI	----
		1980	R1	USA	22.6 %		-------	AULIA	----
		1980	R2	BRAZI	10.2 %		URU	CHILE	----
		1980	R3	GFR	9.3 %		YUGO	BULGA	----
V48	EXPORT PARTNERS	1970	R1	ITALY	15.3 %		-------	IRAQ	----
		1970	R2	NETH	10.4 %		CHILE	CAME	----
		1970	R3	USA	8.9 %		TURKY	GFR	----
		1980	R1	USSR	20.1 %		AFGHA	BULGA	----
		1980	R2	BRAZI	9.5 %		URU	CHILE	----
		1980	R3	USA	8.9 %		UNKI	CHILE	----

V49 PATENT SUPPLIERS	1970	R1	USA	2244		-------	AULIA	----
	1970	R2	GFR	602		YUGO	BELGI	----
	1970	R3	SWITZ	497		SRILA	AURIA	----
	1980	R1	USA	1166		-------	AULIA	----
	1980	R2	GFR	380		YUGO	BELGI	----
	1980	R3	FRANC	255		SYRIA	BELGI	----
V50 PROVENANCE OF FOREIGN FIRMS	1980	R1	USA	51.2	%	-------	BANGL	----
	1980	R2	UNKI	11.0	%	ZIMBA	BANGL	----
	1980	R3	GFR	9.2	%	ALGER	CANA	----
V51 FILM SUPPLIERS	1980	R1	USA	143		ALGER	AULIA	F118
	1980	R2	ITALY	52		JORDA	AURIA	F118
	1980	R3	FRANC	45		TURKY	CUBA	F118

AUSTRALIA (AULIA)

V1 INCOME PER CAPITA	1970	D9	P88	8224	$/CAP	CANA	FRANC	F4
	1975	D9	P85	8922	$/CAP	FINLA	SAUDI	F147
	1980	D9	P83	9617	$/CAP	AURIA	FINLA	F147
V2 TELEPHONES P. TSD. POPULATION	1971	D10	P94	324	1/TSD CAP	NORWY	DENMA	----
	1975	D10	P92	382	1/TSD CAP	NETH	FINLA	----
	1980	D9	P90	489	1/TSD CAP	UNKI	FINLA	----
V3 INFANT MORTALITY RATE	1980	D1	P9	10.7	1/TSD	CANA	BELGI	----
V4 PHYSICIANS P. MIL. POPULATION	1971	D9	P79	1245	1/MIL	ROMA	NETH	----
	1976	D8	P78	1525	1/MIL	URU	FRANC	F147
	1980	D8	P75	1779	1/MIL	POLA	CANA	F147
V5 ADULT LITERACY	------	----	----	----- -----		-------	-------	----
V6 DURATION OF SCHOOLING	1970	D10	P92	11.0	YR	SWEDN	FRANC	----
	1975	D9	P84	10.8	YR	SPAIN	SWEDN	----
	1980	D8	P79	10.8	YR	ISRA	CUBA	----
V7 STUDENT ENROLLMENT RATIO	1970	D9	P86	16.6	%	YUGO	ITALY	----
	1975	D9	P87	24.0	%	ISRA	FRANC	----
	1980	D9	P84	25.4	%	COSTA	FRANC	----
V8 SHARE OF AGRICULTURAL LABOR	1971	D2	P18	8.2	%	SWITZ	DENMA	F67
	1976	D2	P18	8.0	%	CANA	NORWY	----
	1981	D2	P21	6.9	%	SWITZ	NORWY	----
V9 SHARE OF INDUSTRIAL LABOR	1976	D9	P80	38.0	%	SINGA	NEWZ	----
	1981	D8	P70	36.0	%	FINLA	NEWZ	----
V10 SHARE OF SERVICE LABOR	1976	D9	P83	41.4	%	URU	NETH	----
	1981	D8	P76	42.4	%	COLO	VENE	----
V11 SHARE OF ACADEMIC LABOR	1976	D8	P72	12.6	%	IRE	KUWAI	----
	1981	D8	P78	14.7	%	GFR	HUNGA	----

V12	SHARE OF SELF-EMPLOYED LABOR	1971	D3	P24	12.7	%	SWITZ	NEWZ	F67
		1976	D2	P15	14.0	%	KUWAI	NEWZ	----
		1981	D4	P34	14.6	%	NEWZ	YUGO	----
V13	MILITARY EXPENDITURES	1970	D9	P85	3.519	TSD MIL $	SWEDN	NETH	F4
		1975	D9	P86	3.420	TSD MIL $	NIGRA	SWEDN	----
		1980	D9	P88	3.857	TSD MIL $	SPAIN	INDIA	----
V14	MILITARY MANPOWER	1970	D7	P65	86	TSD CAP	KAMPU	AFGHA	F1
		1975	D6	P58	70	TSD CAP	KAMPU	MOROC	F1
V15	MEN AT AGE 20 - 30	1971	D7	P61	1039	TSD CAP	NEPAL	GDR	----
		1976	D7	P63	1126	TSD CAP	VENE	GDR	----
		1981	D6	P56	1284	TSD CAP	VENE	GDR	F22
V16	POPULATION	1970	D7	P64	12.51	MIL CAP	NEPAL	SRILA	F4
		1975	D7	P67	13.89	MIL CAP	NETH	CZECH	F22
		1980	D7	P64	14.69	MIL CAP	NETH	SRILA	F22
V17	GROSS DOMESTIC PRODUCT	1970	D9	P86	102.883	TSD MIL $	SWEDN	INDIA	----
		1975	D9	P87	123.931	TSD MIL $	SWEDN	INDIA	----
		1980	D9	P86	141.276	TSD MIL $	SWEDN	MEXI	----
V18	SHARE IN WORLD IMPORTS	1970	D9	P89	15.327	1/TSD	GDR	SWITZ	F49
		1975	D9	P86	12.196	1/TSD	DENMA	GDR	F49
		1980	D9	P85	10.963	1/TSD	KORSO	SINGA	F49
V19	SHARE IN WORLD EXPORTS	1970	D9	P89	15.207	1/TSD	GDR	SWITZ	F30
		1975	D9	P88	13.632	1/TSD	POLA	SWITZ	F30
		1980	D9	P87	11.038	1/TSD	LIBYA	IRAQ	F30
V20	GDP SHARE OF IMPORTS	1970	D4	P31	14.2	%	LIBYA	IRAQ	F49
		1975	D2	P16	12.7	%	PARA	MOZAM	F49
		1980	D3	P22	15.9	%	GABON	SPAIN	F49
V21	GDP SHARE OF EXPORTS	1970	D5	P44	13.3	%	ITALY	DOMI	F30
		1975	D4	P37	13.6	%	YUGO	PHILI	F30
		1980	D4	P39	15.6	%	YUGO	HAITI	F30
V22	EXPORT PARTNER CONCENTRATION	1970	D5	P47	27.0	%	LIBYA	PARA	----
		1975	D7	P63	30.4	%	KORSO	NETH	----
		1980	D5	P48	25.2	%	JAPAN	MOROC	----
V23	TOTAL DEBT AS % OF GDP	------	----	----	-----	-----	-------	-------	----
V24	SHARE OF NEW FOREIGN PATENTS	1970	D5	P43	89	%	GUATE	HONDU	----
		1975	D6	P57	92	%	DENMA	BELGI	----
		1980	D7	P65	93	%	TRITO	BANGL	----
V25	FOREIGN PROPERTY AS % OF GDP	------	----	----	-----	-----	-------	-------	----
V26	GNP SHARE OF DEVELOPMENT AID	1970	D9	P83	0.62	%	BELGI	NETH	----
		1975	D7	P68	0.65	%	FRANC	NORWY	----
		1980	D6	P56	0.48	%	GFR	BELGI	----
V27	SHARE IN NOBEL PRIZE WINNERS	1970-79	D5	P45	0.0	%	ALGER	BENIN	----
V28	GDP SHARE OF MANUFACTURING	1970	D9	P89	26.5	%	USA	NETH	----
		1975	D8	P79	22.9	%	NEWZ	MEXI	----
		1979	D8	P72	20.6	%	THAI	TURKY	----

V29	EXPORT SHARE OF MANUFACTURES	------	----	----	----- -----	-------	-------	----
V30	LACK OF CIVIL LIBERTIES	1975	D1	P7	1	-------	AURIA	----
		1980	D1	P7	1	-------	AURIA	----
V31	LACK OF POLITICAL RIGHTS	1975	D1	P8	1	-------	AURIA	----
		1980	D1	P8	1	-------	AURIA	----
V32	RIOTS	1970-74	D7	P64	4	YUGO	BURU	----
		1975-79	D2	P20	0	ALGER	AURIA	----
V33	PROTEST DEMONSTRATIONS	1970-74	D9	P84	21	CANA	JAPAN	----
		1975-79	D8	P74	12	TURKY	JAPAN	----
V34	POLITICAL STRIKES	1970-74	D7	P64	1	ZAMBI	BENIN	----
		1975-79	D8	P73	2	USSR	BURMA	----
V35	MEMBER OF THE NONALIGNED MMT.	1970	----	----	0	ARGE	AURIA	----
		1976	----	----	0	ALBA	AURIA	----
		1981	----	----	0	ALBA	AURIA	----
V36	MEMBER OF THE OPEC	1970	----	----	0	ARGE	AURIA	----
		1975	----	----	0	ARGE	AURIA	----
		1980	----	----	0	ARGE	AURIA	----
V37	MEMBER OF THE OECD	1970	----	----	0	ARGE	BENIN	----
		1975	----	----	1	-------	AURIA	----
		1980	----	----	1	-------	AURIA	----
V38	MEMBER OF THE CMEA	1970	----	----	0	ARGE	AURIA	----
		1975	----	----	0	ARGE	AURIA	----
		1980	----	----	0	ARGE	AURIA	----
V39	MEMBER OF THE WTO	1970	----	----	0	ARGE	AURIA	----
		1975	----	----	0	ARGE	AURIA	----
		1980	----	----	0	ARGE	AURIA	----
V40	MEMBER OF THE NATO	1970	----	----	0	ARGE	AURIA	----
		1975	----	----	0	ARGE	AURIA	----
		1980	----	----	0	ARGE	AURIA	----
V41	GDP SHARE OF INVESTMENTS	1970	D8	P80	27.3 %	KORSO	ISRA	F20
		1975	D6	P56	23.5 %	MALAY	MEXI	F20
		1980	D6	P52	24.3 %	OMAN	VENE	F20
V42	GDP SHARE OF AGRICULTURE	1970	D2	P15	6.1 %	SAUDI	JAPAN	----
		1975	D2	P18	5.5 %	DENMA	JAPAN	----
		1979	D3	P25	6.8 %	SOUAF	SPAIN	----
V43	GDP SHARE OF INDUSTRY	1970	D9	P83	40.5 %	SOUAF	YUGO	----
		1975	D8	P78	37.6 %	SPAIN	FRANC	----
		1979	D7	P67	36.4 %	TUNIS	BELGI	----
V44	GDP SHARE OF SERVICES	1970	D8	P74	53.4 %	COSTA	CAME	----
		1975	D9	P85	56.9 %	URU	SYRIA	----
		1979	D9	P86	56.8 %	FINLA	NEWZ	----
V45	HOMICIDES P. MIL. POPULATION	1970	D5	P49	15.3 1/MIL CAP	AURIA	SINGA	F154
		1975	D6	P52	16.3 1/MIL CAP	KUWAI	AURIA	F153
		1980	D6	P61	19.1 1/MIL CAP	ITALY	URU	F147

V46	SUICIDES P. MIL. POPULATION	1970	D7	P66	124.0	1/MIL CAP	BULGA	CUBA	F2
		1975	D6	P54	110.0	1/MIL CAP	ELSA	SINGA	F150
		1980	D5	P46	109.4	1/MIL CAP	NEWZ	USA	F147
V47	IMPORT PARTNERS	1970	R1	USA	25.5	%	ARGE	BOLI	----
		1970	R2	UNKI	21.4	%	ZAMBI	CANA	----
		1970	R3	JAPAN	12.9	%	USA	BRAZI	----
		1980	R1	USA	21.8	%	ARGE	BANGL	----
		1980	R2	JAPAN	17.0	%	AFGHA	BANGL	----
		1980	R3	UNKI	9.3	%	SWEDN	DENMA	----
V48	EXPORT PARTNERS	1970	R1	JAPAN	27.0	%	-------	INDIA	----
		1970	R2	USA	13.0	%	VENE	BOLI	----
		1970	R3	UNKI	11.5	%	ZAMBI	BURU	----
		1980	R1	JAPAN	25.2	%	-------	CHILE	----
		1980	R2	USA	9.9	%	VENE	EGYPT	----
V49	PATENT SUPPLIERS	1970	R1	USA	2846		ARGE	BELGI	----
		1970	R2	UNKI	899		UGADA	COSTA	----
		1970	R3	GFR	476		URU	EGYPT	----
		1980	R1	USA	3613		ARGE	BANGL	----
		1980	R2	UNKI	874		TANZA	IRE	----
		1980	R3	JAPAN	802		SINGA	FRANC	----
V50	PROVENANCE OF FOREIGN FIRMS	1980	R1	UNKI	53.5	%	ANGO	ETHIA	----
		1980	R2	USA	26.7	%	ALGER	AURIA	----
		1980	R3	NEWZ	4.8	%	-------	-------	----
V51	FILM SUPPLIERS	1980	R1	USA	273		ARGE	AURIA	F118
		1980	R2	FRANC	67		ALGER	DENMA	F118
		1980	R3	UNKI	66		ZAMBI	BOLI	F118

AUSTRIA (AURIA)

V1	INCOME PER CAPITA	1970	D9	P81	6673	$/CAP	JAPAN	NEWZ	F147
		1975	D9	P82	7996	$/CAP	UNKI	LIBYA	F147
		1980	D9	P81	9473	$/CAP	JAPAN	AULIA	F147
V2	TELEPHONES P. TSD. POPULATION	1970	D9	P87	193	1/TSD CAP	ITALY	JAPAN	----
		1975	D9	P85	281	1/TSD CAP	FRANC	BELGI	----
		1980	D9	P84	401	1/TSD CAP	BELGI	NORWY	----
V3	INFANT MORTALITY RATE	1980	D2	P18	14.3	1/TSD	NEWZ	ITALY	----
V4	PHYSICIANS P. MIL. POPULATION	------	----	----	----- -----		-------	-------	----
V5	ADULT LITERACY	------	----	----	----- -----		-------	-------	----
V6	DURATION OF SCHOOLING	1970	D8	P78	10.1	YR	ISRA	GFR	----
		1975	D8	P71	10.0	YR	KORSO	CZECH	----
		1980	D7	P59	9.7	YR	SRILA	DOMI	----

V7	STUDENT ENROLLMENT RATIO	1970	D8	P77	11.7	%	PERU	GFR	----
		1975	D8	P80	18.9	%	IRE	UNKI	----
		1980	D9	P82	23.9	%	SPAIN	COSTA	----
V8	SHARE OF AGRICULTURAL LABOR	1971	D3	P28	14.1	%	CZECH	ARGE	----
		1975	D3	P28	12.4	%	NEWZ	TRITO	----
		1981	D3	P28	8.9	%	FRANC	HUNGA	----
V9	SHARE OF INDUSTRIAL LABOR	1971	D9	P81	40.2	%	SWITZ	SINGA	----
		1975	D10	P95	40.6	%	IRAN	BULGA	----
		1981	D9	P81	38.1	%	GFR	KUWAI	----
V10	SHARE OF SERVICE LABOR	1971	D8	P76	36.8	%	NEWZ	SWEDN	----
		1981	D8	P70	41.3	%	ISRA	CHILE	----
V11	SHARE OF ACADEMIC LABOR	1971	D7	P67	8.9	%	CUBA	SINGA	----
		1981	D7	P66	11.7	%	POLA	JORDA	----
V12	SHARE OF SELF-EMPLOYED LABOR	------	----	----	-----	-----	-------	-------	----
V13	MILITARY EXPENDITURES	1970	D6	P58	0.560	TSD MIL $	PERU	SYRIA	----
		1975	D6	P58	0.728	TSD MIL $	THAI	PERU	----
		1980	D6	P60	0.889	TSD MIL $	VENE	MOROC	----
V14	MILITARY MANPOWER	1970	D6	P52	55	TSD CAP	ALBA	MALAY	----
		1975	D6	P52	50	TSD CAP	LAOS	COLO	----
		1980	D5	P50	40	TSD CAP	NORWY	AFGHA	----
V15	MEN AT AGE 20 - 30	1970	D4	P38	528	TSD CAP	ECUA	SWITZ	F22
		1975	D5	P45	518	TSD CAP	ECUA	GUATE	F22
		1980	D4	P30	551	TSD CAP	TUNIS	ZIMBA	F22
V16	POPULATION	1970	D5	P49	7.43	MIL CAP	MADA	SWEDN	F22
		1975	D5	P49	7.52	MIL CAP	SYRIA	CAME	F22
		1980	D5	P45	7.51	MIL CAP	GUATE	ANGO	F22
V17	GROSS DOMESTIC PRODUCT	1970	D8	P77	49.580	TSD MIL $	NIGRA	DENMA	----
		1975	D8	P76	60.127	TSD MIL $	DENMA	SOUAF	----
		1980	D8	P77	71.141	TSD MIL $	INDO	ARGE	----
V18	SHARE IN WORLD IMPORTS	1970	D9	P82	10.691	1/TSD	YUGO	POLA	----
		1975	D9	P82	10.333	1/TSD	CZECH	NORWY	----
		1980	D9	P88	11.920	1/TSD	BRAZI	SAUDI	----
V19	SHARE IN WORLD EXPORTS	1970	D9	P84	9.105	1/TSD	VENE	DENMA	----
		1975	D8	P78	8.580	1/TSD	CHINA	SPAIN	----
		1980	D8	P78	8.764	1/TSD	GDR	KORSO	----
V20	GDP SHARE OF IMPORTS	1970	D8	P72	24.5	%	FINLA	TOGO	----
		1975	D6	P57	24.9	%	SWEDN	YUGO	----
		1980	D8	P73	31.8	%	OMAN	CONGO	----
V21	GDP SHARE OF EXPORTS	1970	D7	P65	19.8	%	CANA	TANZA	----
		1975	D6	P59	20.0	%	CANA	KENYA	----
		1980	D7	P62	22.8	%	NEWZ	GFR	----
V22	EXPORT PARTNER CONCENTRATION	1970	D4	P38	23.4	%	SRILA	ZAMBI	----
		1975	D4	P40	21.9	%	TURKY	LIBYA	----
		1980	D7	P66	30.8	%	CAME	POLA	----
V23	TOTAL DEBT AS % OF GDP	------	----	----	-----	-----	-------	-------	----

V24 SHARE OF NEW FOREIGN PATENTS	1970	D4	P37	86 %	LEBA	GUATE	----
	1975	D4	P33	83 %	INDIA	VENE	----
	1980	D4	P33	79 %	UNKI	ISRA	----
V25 FOREIGN PROPERTY AS % OF GDP	------	----	----	----- -----	-------	-------	----
V26 GNP SHARE OF DEVELOPMENT AID	1970	D3	P25	0.07 %	FINLA	IRAQ	----
	1975	D3	P25	0.21 %	ALGER	JAPAN	----
	1980	D3	P26	0.23 %	FINLA	SWITZ	----
V27 SHARE IN NOBEL PRIZE WINNERS	1970-79	D10	P97	3.8 %	USSR	BELGI	----
V28 GDP SHARE OF MANUFACTURING	1970	D10	P98	33.7 %	PORTU	JAPAN	----
	1975	D10	P96	28.6 %	FRANC	JAPAN	----
	1980	D10	P94	28.0 %	PERU	KORSO	----
V29 EXPORT SHARE OF MANUFACTURES	1970	D10	P91	68.2 %	FRANC	ISRA	----
	1975	D10	P92	73.5 %	PORTU	ISRA	----
	1980	D9	P89	73.2 %	YUGO	GFR	----
V30 LACK OF CIVIL LIBERTIES	1975	D1	P7	1	AULIA	BELGI	----
	1980	D1	P7	1	AULIA	BELGI	----
V31 LACK OF POLITICAL RIGHTS	1975	D1	P8	1	AULIA	BELGI	----
	1980	D1	P8	1	AULIA	BELGI	----
V32 RIOTS	1970-74	D2	P19	0	ALBA	BELGI	----
	1975-79	D2	P20	0	AULIA	BANGL	----
V33 PROTEST DEMONSTRATIONS	1970-74	D6	P59	4	TUNIS	BELGI	----
	1975-79	D7	P64	6	SWITZ	BELGI	----
V34 POLITICAL STRIKES	1970-74	D3	P29	0	ALGER	BELGI	----
	1975-79	D3	P29	0	ALGER	BANGL	----
V35 MEMBER OF THE NONALIGNED MMT.	1970	----	----	0	AULIA	BELGI	----
	1976	----	----	0	AULIA	BELGI	----
	1981	----	----	0	AULIA	BELGI	----
V36 MEMBER OF THE OPEC	1970	----	----	0	AULIA	BELGI	----
	1975	----	----	0	AULIA	BANGL	----
	1980	----	----	0	AULIA	BANGL	----
V37 MEMBER OF THE OECD	1970	----	----	1	-------	BELGI	----
	1975	----	----	1	AULIA	BELGI	----
	1980	----	----	1	AULIA	BELGI	----
V38 MEMBER OF THE CMEA	1970	----	----	0	AULIA	BELGI	----
	1975	----	----	0	AULIA	BANGL	----
	1980	----	----	0	AULIA	BANGL	----
V39 MEMBER OF THE WTO	1970	----	----	0	AULIA	BELGI	----
	1975	----	----	0	AULIA	BANGL	----
	1980	----	----	0	AULIA	BANGL	----
V40 MEMBER OF THE NATO	1970	----	----	0	AULIA	BENIN	----
	1975	----	----	0	AULIA	BANGL	----
	1980	----	----	0	AULIA	BANGL	----

V41 GDP SHARE OF INVESTMENTS	1970	D9	P90	29.7	%	VENE	NORWY	----
	1975	D7	P69	26.1	%	ARGE	SPAIN	----
	1980	D8	P78	28.8	%	PANA	PARA	----
V42 GDP SHARE OF AGRICULTURE	1970	D3	P21	6.9	%	CHILE	VENE	----
	1975	D2	P14	5.0	%	CANA	FRANC	----
	1980	D2	P17	4.4	%	FRANC	DENMA	----
V43 GDP SHARE OF INDUSTRY	1970	D10	P94	45.4	%	IRAQ	JAPAN	----
	1975	D9	P81	40.9	%	BELGI	ZAMBI	----
	1980	D8	P79	39.9	%	ZAMBI	NORWY	----
V44 GDP SHARE OF SERVICES	1970	D5	P48	47.7	%	ARGE	BURMA	----
	1975	D8	P79	54.1	%	SPAIN	LESO	----
	1980	D9	P82	55.7	%	YENO	MEXI	----
V45 HOMICIDES P. MIL. POPULATION	1970	D5	P47	15.1	1/MIL CAP	CZECH	AULIA	F149
	1975	D6	P54	16.5	1/MIL CAP	AULIA	SINGA	F149
	1980	D4	P43	12.1	1/MIL CAP	SWEDN	NEWZ	F147
V46 SUICIDES P. MIL. POPULATION	1970	D10	P91	240.8	1/MIL CAP	SWEDN	CZECH	F147
	1975	D10	P91	241.1	1/MIL CAP	DENMA	FINLA	F147
	1980	D9	P88	257.3	1/MIL CAP	FINLA	SRILA	F147
V47 IMPORT PARTNERS	1970	R1	GFR	41.2	%	-------	BELGI	----
	1970	R2	SWITZ	7.4	%	-------	-------	----
	1970	R3	UNKI	6.8	%	TOGO	BENIN	----
	1980	R1	GFR	40.8	%	-------	BELGI	----
	1980	R2	ITALY	9.1	%	SOMA	ETHIA	----
	1980	R3	SWITZ	5.0	%	-------	-------	----
V48 EXPORT PARTNERS	1970	R1	GFR	23.4	%	-------	BELGI	----
	1970	R2	SWITZ	10.4	%	-------	TURKY	----
	1970	R3	ITALY	9.7	%	URU	BRAZI	----
	1980	R1	GFR	30.8	%	-------	BELGI	----
	1980	R2	ITALY	11.0	%	SYRIA	ETHIA	----
	1980	R3	SWITZ	7.5	%	-------	ZAIRE	----
V49 PATENT SUPPLIERS	1971	R1	GFR	3288		-------	BULGA	----
	1971	R2	USA	973		ZAMBI	CHINA	----
	1971	R3	SWITZ	876		ARGE	BELGI	----
	1980	R1	GFR	2044		-------	BULGA	----
	1980	R2	USA	602		ZAMBI	BULGA	----
	1980	R3	SWITZ	559		TANZA	CHILE	----
V50 PROVENANCE OF FOREIGN FIRMS	1980	R1	GFR	44.4	%	-------	YUGO	----
	1980	R2	USA	16.5	%	AULIA	DENMA	----
	1980	R3	SWITZ	11.9	%	COSTA	GFR	----
V51 FILM SUPPLIERS	1980	R1	USA	107		AULIA	BOLI	F120
	1980	R2	ITALY	50		ARGE	BOLI	F120
	1980	R3	GFR	46		-------	BRAZI	F120

BANGLADESH (BANGL)

V1	INCOME PER CAPITA	1975	D1	P2	121	$/CAP	-------	ETHIA	----
		1980	D1	P3	138	$/CAP	ETHIA	NEPAL	----
V2	TELEPHONES P. TSD. POPULATION	1975	D1	P5	1	1/TSD CAP	-------	BURMA	----
		1981	D1	P3	1	1/TSD CAP	-------	BURMA	----
V3	INFANT MORTALITY RATE	1980	D9	P83	139.6	1/TSD	BOLI	BURU	F5
V4	PHYSICIANS P. MIL. POPULATION	1972	D4	----	98	1/MIL	CONGO	MADA	F2
		1977	D3	----	79	1/MIL	MOROC	SUDAN	----
		1981	D3	P28	111	1/MIL	MADA	ZAMBI	----
V5	ADULT LITERACY	------	----	----	----- -----		-------	-------	----
V6	DURATION OF SCHOOLING	1975	D3	P29	5.2	YR	SAUDI	CENTR	F4
		1980	D2	P15	4.6	YR	MOZAM	PAPUA	----
V7	STUDENT ENROLLMENT RATIO	1975	D4	P38	2.6	%	PAPUA	MALAY	F4
		1980	D4	P36	3.0	%	UNARE	MADA	----
V8	SHARE OF AGRICULTURAL LABOR	1974	D10	P93	79.1	%	CAME	MALAW	----
		1981	D10	P98	79.1	%	CAME	RWAN	F46
V9	SHARE OF INDUSTRIAL LABOR	1974	D1	P9	11.2	%	MALAW	SUDAN	----
		1981	D1	P3	11.2	%	HAITI	CAME	F46
V10	SHARE OF SERVICE LABOR	1974	D2	P12	7.8	%	CAME	TURKY	----
		1981	D1	P3	7.8	%	CAME	AFGHA	F46
V11	SHARE OF ACADEMIC LABOR	1974	D1	P8	1.9	%	MALI	INDO	----
		1981	D1	P5	1.9	%	COLO	TUNIS	F46
V12	SHARE OF SELF-EMPLOYED LABOR	1974	D8	P80	46.8	%	THAI	YENO	----
		1981	D9	P93	46.8	%	PARA	PAKI	F46
V13	MILITARY EXPENDITURES	1975	D3	P29	0.077	TSD MIL $	GHANA	BOLI	----
		1980	D4	P36	0.179	TSD MIL $	ZAIRE	TUNIS	----
V14	MILITARY MANPOWER	1975	D7	P66	100	TSD CAP	SAUDI	CHILE	----
		1980	D7	P65	71	TSD CAP	SWEDN	CANA	----
V15	MEN AT AGE 20 - 30	1975	D10	P93	6799	TSD CAP	MEXI	BRAZI	F2
		1981	D10	P92	7109	TSD CAP	PAKI	JAPAN	F2
V16	POPULATION	1971	D10	P93	69.77	MIL CAP	GFR	BRAZI	F4
		1975	D10	P94	78.96	MIL CAP	PAKI	BRAZI	----
		1980	D10	P94	88.68	MIL CAP	PAKI	JAPAN	----
V17	GROSS DOMESTIC PRODUCT	1975	D5	P48	9.541	TSD MIL $	SINGA	SYRIA	----
		1980	D5	P49	12.246	TSD MIL $	SINGA	SYRIA	----
V18	SHARE IN WORLD IMPORTS	1975	D4	P39	0.962	1/TSD	GHANA	ZAIRE	F30
		1980	D5	P43	0.962	1/TSD	YENO	SRILA	F30
V19	SHARE IN WORLD EXPORTS	1975	D3	P27	0.346	1/TSD	MADA	HONDU	F30
		1980	D3	P29	0.370	1/TSD	ELSA	YESO	F30

V20	GDP SHARE OF IMPORTS	1975	D1	P1	6.2 %	-------	UGADA	F30
		1980	D2	P20	15.4 %	INDO	GABON	F30
V21	GDP SHARE OF EXPORTS	1975	D1	P2	2.1 %	YENO	MEXI	F30
		1980	D1	P8	5.8 %	INDIA	CHINA	F30
V22	EXPORT PARTNER CONCENTRATION	1975	D2	P19	15.8 %	BRAZI	ISRA	----
		1980	D1	P6	11.7 %	CHILE	SWEDN	----
V23	TOTAL DEBT AS % OF GDP	1980	D5	P42	31.5 %	MEXI	BENIN	----
V24	SHARE OF NEW FOREIGN PATENTS	1976	D7	P62	93 %	BELGI	MEXI	----
		1980	D7	P65	93 %	AULIA	BOLI	----
V25	FOREIGN PROPERTY AS % OF GDP	1975	D1	P5	0.6 %	YUGO	EGYPT	----
		1978	D1	----	0.8 %	NEPAL	SUDAN	----
V26	GNP SHARE OF DEVELOPMENT AID	------	----	----	----- -----	-------	-------	----
V27	SHARE IN NOBEL PRIZE WINNERS	------	----	----	----- -----	-------	-------	----
V28	GDP SHARE OF MANUFACTURING	------	----	----	----- -----	-------	-------	----
V29	EXPORT SHARE OF MANUFACTURES	------	----	----	----- -----	-------	-------	----
V30	LACK OF CIVIL LIBERTIES	1975	D4	P39	4	ARGE	BHUTA	----
		1980	D3	P29	3	VENE	BOLI	----
V31	LACK OF POLITICAL RIGHTS	1975	D4	P31	4	PAPUA	BHUTA	----
		1980	D4	P31	3	UPVO	BOLI	----
V32	RIOTS	1975-79	D2	P20	0	AURIA	BHUTA	----
V33	PROTEST DEMONSTRATIONS	1975-79	D6	P54	4	URU	BRAZI	----
V34	POLITICAL STRIKES	1975-79	D3	P29	0	AURIA	BELGI	----
V35	MEMBER OF THE NONALIGNED MMT.	1976	----	----	1	ARGE	BENIN	----
		1981	----	----	1	ARGE	BENIN	----
V36	MEMBER OF THE OPEC	1975	----	----	0	AURIA	BELGI	----
		1980	----	----	0	AURIA	BELGI	----
V37	MEMBER OF THE OECD	1975	----	----	0	ARGE	BENIN	----
		1980	----	----	0	ARGE	BENIN	----
V38	MEMBER OF THE CMEA	1975	----	----	0	AURIA	BELGI	----
		1980	----	----	0	AURIA	BELGI	----
V39	MEMBER OF THE WTO	1975	----	----	0	AURIA	BELGI	----
		1980	----	----	0	AURIA	BELGI	----
V40	MEMBER OF THE NATO	1975	----	----	0	AURIA	BENIN	----
		1980	----	----	0	AURIA	BENIN	----
V41	GDP SHARE OF INVESTMENTS	1972	D1	----	4.7 %	BURU	AFGHA	----
		1975	D1	P5	8.1 %	MOZAM	NEPAL	----
		1980	D3	P24	16.7 %	SIERA	SUDAN	----

V42	GDP SHARE OF AGRICULTURE	1972	D10	----	59.6	%	SOMA	NEPAL	----
		1975	D10	P97	62.5	%	SOMA	BURU	----
		1980	D10	P94	53.4	%	ETHIA	BURU	----
V43	GDP SHARE OF INDUSTRY	1972	D1	----	6.1	%	-------	RWAN	----
		1975	D1	P6	11.3	%	NEPAL	YENO	----
		1980	D1	P6	12.7	%	SOMA	BURMA	----
V44	GDP SHARE OF SERVICES	1972	D2	----	34.3	%	UGADA	LIBE	----
		1975	D1	P9	26.2	%	ANGO	GUINE	----
		1980	D2	P18	33.9	%	TANZA	CHAD	----
V45	HOMICIDES P. MIL. POPULATION	------	----	----	-----	-----	-------	-------	----
V46	SUICIDES P. MIL. POPULATION	------	----	----	-----	-----	-------	-------	----
V47	IMPORT PARTNERS	1980	R1	USA	15.3	%	AULIA	BOLI	----
		1980	R2	JAPAN	13.7	%	AULIA	CANA	----
		1980	R3	SINGA	9.4	%	-------	MALAY	----
V48	EXPORT PARTNERS	1980	R1	USA	11.7	%	ALGER	BOLI	----
		1980	R2	PAKI	9.5	%	-------	AFGHA	----
		1980	R3	IRAN	5.4	%	-------	PAKI	----
V49	PATENT SUPPLIERS	1979	R1	USA	18		AULIA	BELGI	----
		1979	R2	SWITZ	15		SIERA	COLO	----
		1979	R3	ITALY	14		-------	HONDU	----
V50	PROVENANCE OF FOREIGN FIRMS	1980	R1	USA	42.4	%	ARGE	BELGI	----
		1980	R2	UNKI	36.3	%	ARGE	BENIN	----
V51	FILM SUPPLIERS	------	----	----	-----	-----	-------	-------	----

BELGIUM (BELGI)

V1	INCOME PER CAPITA	1970	D9	P90	8357	$/CAP	FRANC	NETH	F147
		1975	D10	P91	9809	$/CAP	FRANC	USA	F147
		1980	D9	P89	11224	$/CAP	FRANC	USA	F147
V2	TELEPHONES P. TSD. POPULATION	1970	D9	P88	211	1/TSD CAP	JAPAN	GFR	----
		1975	D9	P86	285	1/TSD CAP	AURIA	GFR	----
		1980	D9	P83	369	1/TSD CAP	ITALY	AURIA	----
V3	INFANT MORTALITY RATE	1980	D1	P10	11.0	1/TSD	AULIA	SPAIN	----
V4	PHYSICIANS P. MIL. POPULATION	1970	D9	P87	1541	1/MIL	POLA	USA	F147
		1975	D10	P91	1890	1/MIL	ARGE	GFR	F147
		1980	D10	P96	2491	1/MIL	BULGA	HUNGA	F147
V5	ADULT LITERACY	------	----	----	-----	-----	-------	-------	----
V6	DURATION OF SCHOOLING	1970	D10	P95	11.2	YR	JAPAN	GDR	----
		1975	D9	P87	11.0	YR	ITALY	DENMA	----
		1980	D9	P88	11.3	YR	ROMA	CANA	----

V7	STUDENT ENROLLMENT RATIO	1970	D9	P90	17.5 %		NEWZ	DENMA	----
		1975	D9	P86	22.7 %		USSR	ISRA	----
		1980	D9	P89	26.7 %		JORDA	GFR	----
V8	SHARE OF AGRICULTURAL LABOR	1970	D1	P8	4.8 %		SINGA	NETH	----
V9	SHARE OF INDUSTRIAL LABOR	1970	D10	P96	47.5 %		ITALY	HUNGA	----
V10	SHARE OF SERVICE LABOR	1970	D8	P71	36.1 %		LEBA	NEWZ	----
V11	SHARE OF ACADEMIC LABOR	1970	D8	P79	11.7 %		HUNGA	UNKI	----
V12	SHARE OF SELF-EMPLOYED LABOR	1970	D4	P36	15.3 %		FINLA	FRANC	----
V13	MILITARY EXPENDITURES	1970	D8	P78	2.357 TSD MIL $		SPAIN	NIGRA	----
		1975	D9	P82	2.939 TSD MIL $		BRAZI	TURKY	----
		1980	D9	P84	3.660 TSD MIL $		SOUAF	KORSO	----
V14	MILITARY MANPOWER	1970	D7	P69	110 TSD CAP		ISRA	NETH	----
		1975	D7	P62	87 TSD CAP		ALGER	MEXI	----
		1980	D7	P67	86 TSD CAP		MALAY	ALGER	----
V15	MEN AT AGE 20 - 30	1970	D5	P46	663 TSD CAP		BULGA	SWEDN	F22
		1975	D6	P59	759 TSD CAP		CUBA	CHILE	F22
		1981	D5	P45	786 TSD CAP		CUBA	PORTU	F22
V16	POPULATION	1970	D6	P57	9.66 MIL CAP		IRAQ	UGADA	F22
		1975	D6	P57	9.79 MIL CAP		MOZAM	GHANA	F22
		1980	D6	P55	9.85 MIL CAP		CUBA	PORTU	F22
V17	GROSS DOMESTIC PRODUCT	1970	D9	P82	80.724 TSD MIL $		MEXI	SWITZ	----
		1975	D9	P83	96.035 TSD MIL $		SWITZ	MEXI	----
		1980	D9	P84	110.561 TSD MIL $		SAUDI	SWEDN	----
V18	SHARE IN WORLD IMPORTS	1970	D10	P92	34.380 1/TSD		SWEDN	USSR	F50
		1975	D10	P92	33.873 1/TSD		SWEDN	CANA	F50
		1980	D10	P94	35.042 1/TSD		USSR	NETH	F50
V19	SHARE IN WORLD EXPORTS	1970	D10	P92	36.981 1/TSD		SWEDN	NETH	F31
		1975	D10	P91	32.872 1/TSD		IRAN	SAUDI	F31
		1980	D10	P91	32.398 1/TSD		SWEDN	CANA	F31
V20	GDP SHARE OF IMPORTS	1970	D10	P97	42.7 %		NETH	LIBE	F135
		1975	D10	P95	47.2 %		IRE	PANA	F135
		1980	D10	P96	58.1 %		SRILA	LIBE	F135
V21	GDP SHARE OF EXPORTS	1970	D10	P93	43.4 %		MALAY	MAURA	F135
		1975	D10	P92	44.1 %		GABON	LIBYA	F135
		1980	D9	P90	52.3 %		CONGO	MALAY	F135
V22	EXPORT PARTNER CONCENTRATION	1970	D5	P42	24.6 %		TUNIS	YESO	F135
		1975	D5	P42	22.3 %		LIBE	NEWZ	F135
		1980	D4	P38	21.4 %		TURKY	IVORY	F135
V23	TOTAL DEBT AS % OF GDP	------	----	----	----- -----		-------	-------	----
V24	SHARE OF NEW FOREIGN PATENTS	1970	D5	P53	92 %		TURKY	COSTA	----
		1975	D6	P57	92 %		AULIA	BANGL	----
		1980	D4	P40	86 %		URU	NETH	----
V25	FOREIGN PROPERTY AS % OF GDP	------	----	----	----- -----		-------	-------	----

V26	GNP SHARE OF DEVELOPMENT AID	1970	D8	P77	0.46	%	CANA	AULIA	----
		1975	D6	P58	0.60	%	DENMA	FRANC	----
		1980	D6	P60	0.50	%	AULIA	FRANC	----
V27	SHARE IN NOBEL PRIZE WINNERS	1970-79	D10	P97	3.8	%	AURIA	SWEDN	----
V28	GDP SHARE OF MANUFACTURING	1970	D10	P95	32.1	%	ARGE	PORTU	----
		1975	D10	P94	27.4	%	SWEDN	FRANC	----
		1980	D9	P89	25.4	%	ARGE	ZIMBA	----
V29	EXPORT SHARE OF MANUFACTURES	1970	D9	P86	57.5	%	LEBA	PORTU	F31
		1975	D9	P84	61.7	%	JAMAI	SPAIN	F31
		1980	D8	P80	59.3	%	HAITI	SPAIN	F31
V30	LACK OF CIVIL LIBERTIES	1975	D1	P7	1		AURIA	CANA	----
		1980	D1	P7	1		AURIA	CANA	----
V31	LACK OF POLITICAL RIGHTS	1975	D1	P8	1		AURIA	CANA	----
		1980	D1	P8	1		AURIA	CANA	----
V32	RIOTS	1970-74	D2	P19	0		AURIA	BHUTA	----
		1975-79	D6	P60	3		SWITZ	GUATE	----
V33	PROTEST DEMONSTRATIONS	1970-74	D6	P59	4		AURIA	LAOS	----
		1975-79	D7	P64	6		AURIA	ETHIA	----
V34	POLITICAL STRIKES	1970-74	D3	P29	0		AURIA	BHUTA	----
		1975-79	D3	P29	0		BANGL	BENIN	----
V35	MEMBER OF THE NONALIGNED MMT.	1970	----	----	0		AURIA	BHUTA	----
		1976	----	----	0		AURIA	BOLI	----
		1981	----	----	0		AURIA	BRAZI	----
V36	MEMBER OF THE OPEC	1970	----	----	0		AURIA	BENIN	----
		1975	----	----	0		BANGL	BENIN	----
		1980	----	----	0		BANGL	BENIN	----
V37	MEMBER OF THE OECD	1970	----	----	1		AURIA	CANA	----
		1975	----	----	1		AURIA	CANA	----
		1980	----	----	1		AURIA	CANA	----
V38	MEMBER OF THE CMEA	1970	----	----	0		AURIA	BENIN	----
		1975	----	----	0		BANGL	BENIN	----
		1980	----	----	0		BANGL	BENIN	----
V39	MEMBER OF THE WTO	1970	----	----	0		AURIA	BENIN	----
		1975	----	----	0		BANGL	BENIN	----
		1980	----	----	0		BANGL	BENIN	----
V40	MEMBER OF THE NATO	1970	----	----	1		-------	CANA	----
		1975	----	----	1		-------	CANA	----
		1980	----	----	1		-------	CANA	----
V41	GDP SHARE OF INVESTMENTS	1970	D7	P68	24.0	%	PORTU	NEWZ	----
		1975	D5	P48	21.6	%	CAME	COSTA	----
		1980	D4	P34	21.1	%	INDO	NETH	----
V42	GDP SHARE OF AGRICULTURE	1970	D1	P7	3.6	%	GFR	CANA	----
		1975	D1	P7	2.9	%	UNKI	GFR	----
		1980	D1	P9	2.1	%	OMAN	TRITO	----

V43 GDP SHARE OF INDUSTRY	1970	D9	P88	42.3	%	PORTU	IRAN	----
	1975	D8	P80	38.5	%	CHILE	AURIA	----
	1980	D7	P68	36.7	%	AULIA	MALAY	----
V44 GDP SHARE OF SERVICES	1970	D8	P77	54.1	%	VENE	SYRIA	----
	1975	D9	P90	58.6	%	NEWZ	NORWY	----
	1980	D10	P91	61.2	%	FRANC	CANA	----
V45 HOMICIDES P. MIL. POPULATION	1970	D3	P30	11.0	1/MIL CAP	POLA	PORTU	F149
	1975	D2	P18	9.1	1/MIL CAP	GREC	IRE	F149
	1979	D5	P52	16.1	1/MIL CAP	DENMA	YUGO	F147
V46 SUICIDES P. MIL. POPULATION	1970	D8	P78	164.7	1/MIL CAP	FRANC	SRILA	F147
	1975	D7	P71	162.2	1/MIL CAP	FRANC	CUBA	F147
	1979	D8	P79	214.8	1/MIL CAP	GFR	SWITZ	F147
V47 IMPORT PARTNERS	1970	R1	GFR	23.3	%	AURIA	DENMA	F50
	1970	R2	FRANC	17.1	%	UPVO	CUBA	F50
	1970	R3	NETH	14.6	%	GFR	LIBE	F50
	1980	R1	GFR	19.7	%	AURIA	DENMA	F50
	1980	R2	NETH	16.5	%	GFR	CENTR	F50
	1980	R3	FRANC	14.5	%	ZAIRE	BURU	F50
V48 EXPORT PARTNERS	1970	R1	GFR	24.6	%	AURIA	CONGO	F135
	1970	R2	FRANC	19.8	%	TUNIS	IRAQ	F135
	1970	R3	NETH	19.4	%	TOGO	COLO	F135
	1980	R1	GFR	21.4	%	AURIA	DENMA	F135
	1980	R2	FRANC	19.6	%	ALGER	BENIN	F135
	1980	R3	NETH	15.3	%	TRITO	CAME	F135
V49 PATENT SUPPLIERS	1970	R1	USA	4585		AULIA	BOLI	----
	1970	R2	GFR	3884		ARGE	BOLI	----
	1970	R3	SWITZ	1427		AURIA	BOLI	----
	1980	R1	USA	1602		BANGL	BOLI	----
	1980	R2	GFR	860		ARGE	BOLI	----
	1980	R3	FRANC	626		ARGE	BRAZI	----
V50 PROVENANCE OF FOREIGN FIRMS	1980	R1	USA	23.4	%	BANGL	BOLI	----
	1980	R2	NETH	19.5	%	-------	DOMI	----
	1980	R3	UNKI	17.5	%	VENE	BRAZI	----
V51 FILM SUPPLIERS	-------	----	----	-----	-----	-------	-------	----

BENIN [1] (BENIN)

V1	INCOME PER CAPITA	1970	D2	P15	262	$/CAP	TANZA	INDO	----
		1975	D2	P16	267	$/CAP	TANZA	ZAIRE	----
		1980	D2	P16	301	$/CAP	PAKI	SIERA	F35
V2	TELEPHONES P. TSD. POPULATION	1971	D3	P22	3	1/TSD CAP	ZAIRE	LESO	----
		1974	D2	P17	3	1/TSD CAP	ZAIRE	INDIA	----
V3	INFANT MORTALITY RATE	1980	D10	P94	160.4	1/TSD	ANGO	MALI	F5
V4	PHYSICIANS P. MIL. POPULATION	1970	D2	P13	34	1/MIL	CAME	TOGO	----
		1975	D1	P12	31	1/MIL	NEPAL	UGADA	----
		1980	D2	P15	60	1/MIL	SIERA	PAPUA	----
V5	ADULT LITERACY	1980	D3	P26	27.9	%	BURU	CENTR	F21
V6	DURATION OF SCHOOLING	1970	D2	P13	2.7	YR	CHAD	NIGRA	F4
		1975	D2	P18	4.0	YR	SUDAN	NIGRA	----
		1980	D2	P17	5.3	YR	PAPUA	HAITI	----
V7	STUDENT ENROLLMENT RATIO	1970	D1	P8	0.1	%	YENO	CENTR	----
		1975	D2	P19	0.8	%	YENO	KENYA	----
		1981	D3	P26	1.9	%	SUDAN	PAKI	----
V8	SHARE OF AGRICULTURAL LABOR	------	----	----	-----	-----	-------	-------	----
V9	SHARE OF INDUSTRIAL LABOR	------	----	----	-----	-----	-------	-------	----
V10	SHARE OF SERVICE LABOR	------	----	----	-----	-----	-------	-------	----
V11	SHARE OF ACADEMIC LABOR	------	----	----	-----	-----	-------	-------	----
V12	SHARE OF SELF-EMPLOYED LABOR	------	----	----	-----	-----	-------	-------	----
V13	MILITARY EXPENDITURES	1975	D1	P6	0.013	TSD MIL $	MALAW	NEPAL	----
		1980	D1	P6	0.021	TSD MIL $	NEPAL	COSTA	----
V14	MILITARY MANPOWER	1970	D1	P4	2	TSD CAP	JAMAI	CENTR	----
		1975	D1	P6	3	TSD CAP	COSTA	CENTR	----
		1980	D1	P9	4	TSD CAP	PAPUA	CENTR	----
V15	MEN AT AGE 20 - 30	1975	D2	P12	196	TSD CAP	URU	SIERA	F2
		1979	D1	P8	194	TSD CAP	NICA	URU	----
V16	POPULATION	1970	D2	P19	2.72	MIL CAP	SIERA	SOMA	----
		1975	D3	P23	3.11	MIL CAP	HONDU	SOMA	----
		1980	D3	P23	3.42	MIL CAP	IRE	HONDU	F35
V17	GROSS DOMESTIC PRODUCT	1970	D1	P5	0.714	TSD MIL $	BURU	TOGO	----
		1975	D1	P6	0.831	TSD MIL $	LIBE	SIERA	----
		1980	D1	P7	1.030	TSD MIL $	TOGO	SIERA	----

_____

[1] Formerly known as Dahomey.

V18 SHARE IN WORLD IMPORTS	1970	D2	P13	0.193	1/TSD	CHAD	PARA	----
	1975	D2	P15	0.217	1/TSD	SIERA	UGADA	----
	1979	D2	P12	0.190	1/TSD	HAITI	SIERA	----
V19 SHARE IN WORLD EXPORTS	1970	D2	P12	0.105	1/TSD	NIGER	MALI	----
	1975	D1	P4	0.037	1/TSD	LAOS	BURU	----
	1979	D1	P3	0.028	1/TSD	LAOS	BURU	----
V20 GDP SHARE OF IMPORTS	1970	D8	P74	25.5	%	TANZA	NICA	----
	1975	D9	P85	37.3	%	PAPUA	ZAMBI	----
	1979	D8	P76	35.2	%	MALI	SENE	----
V21 GDP SHARE OF EXPORTS	1970	D5	P42	13.1	%	MOROC	ITALY	----
	1975	D1	P7	6.1	%	INDIA	MOZAM	----
	1979	D1	P5	5.1	%	NEPAL	TURKY	----
V22 EXPORT PARTNER CONCENTRATION	1970	D8	P75	39.4	%	AFGHA	PHILI	----
	1975	D6	P58	27.2	%	IVORY	THAI	----
	1980	D6	P58	28.3	%	YUGO	EGYPT	----
V23 TOTAL DEBT AS % OF GDP	1980	D5	P44	33.8	%	BANGL	TURKY	----
V24 SHARE OF NEW FOREIGN PATENTS	------	----	----	-----	-----	-------	-------	----
V25 FOREIGN PROPERTY AS % OF GDP	1971	D5	P48	8.3	%	ARGE	ELSA	----
	1975	D6	P51	5.7	%	TANZA	NICA	----
	1978	D5	----	4.6	%	PAKI	MAURA	----
V26 GNP SHARE OF DEVELOPMENT AID	------	----	----	-----	-----	-------	-------	----
V27 SHARE IN NOBEL PRIZE WINNERS	1970-79	D5	P45	0.0	%	AULIA	BHUTA	----
V28 GDP SHARE OF MANUFACTURING	------	----	----	-----	-----	-------	-------	----
V29 EXPORT SHARE OF MANUFACTURES	1970	D6	P51	10.5	%	MOROC	SYRIA	----
	1978	D4	----	8.2	%	SYRIA	CHILE	----
V30 LACK OF CIVIL LIBERTIES	1975	D8	P74	6		ALGER	CONGO	----
	1980	D8	P74	6		ALGER	BURMA	----
V31 LACK OF POLITICAL RIGHTS	1975	D9	P88	7		ALBA	BULGA	----
	1980	D9	P90	7		ANGO	BULGA	----
V32 RIOTS	1970-74	D6	P53	2		YENO	BRAZI	----
	1975-79	D6	P53	2		ZAMBI	CANA	----
V33 PROTEST DEMONSTRATIONS	1970-74	D2	P15	0		ALGER	BHUTA	----
	1975-79	D2	P13	0		ALGER	BHUTA	----
V34 POLITICAL STRIKES	1970-74	D7	P64	1		AULIA	BURMA	----
	1975-79	D3	P29	0		BELGI	BHUTA	----
V35 MEMBER OF THE NONALIGNED MMT.	1976	----	----	1		BANGL	BHUTA	----
	1981	----	----	1		BANGL	BHUTA	----
V36 MEMBER OF THE OPEC	1970	----	----	0		BELGI	BHUTA	----
	1975	----	----	0		BELGI	BHUTA	----
	1980	----	----	0		BELGI	BHUTA	----

V37	MEMBER OF THE OECD	1970	----	----	0		AULIA	BHUTA	----
		1975	----	----	0		BANGL	BHUTA	----
		1980	----	----	0		BANGL	BHUTA	----
V38	MEMBER OF THE CMEA	1970	----	----	0		BELGI	BHUTA	----
		1975	----	----	0		BELGI	BHUTA	----
		1980	----	----	0		BELGI	BHUTA	----
V39	MEMBER OF THE WTO	1970	----	----	0		BELGI	BHUTA	----
		1975	----	----	0		BELGI	BHUTA	----
		1980	----	----	0		BELGI	BHUTA	----
V40	MEMBER OF THE NATO	1970	----	----	0		AURIA	BHUTA	----
		1975	----	----	0		BANGL	BHUTA	----
		1980	----	----	0		BANGL	BHUTA	----
V41	GDP SHARE OF INVESTMENTS	1970	D3	P26	15.2	%	TOGO	MALI	----
		1975	D3	P26	17.6	%	SUDAN	COLO	----
		1980	D6	P55	24.8	%	VENE	GFR	----
V42	GDP SHARE OF AGRICULTURE	1970	D9	P85	45.3	%	MALI	GHANA	F16
		1975	D8	P78	37.8	%	PARA	NIGER	F16
		1980	D10	P91	47.9	%	BURMA	TANZA	F16
V43	GDP SHARE OF INDUSTRY	1970	D1	P8	11.7	%	NEPAL	UGADA	F16
		1975	D2	P12	14.5	%	SUDAN	CAME	F16
		1980	D1	P3	10.1	%	CHAD	GHANA	F16
V44	GDP SHARE OF SERVICES	1970	D4	P33	43.0	%	NIGRA	TURKY	F16
		1975	D6	P59	47.7	%	ARGE	ECUA	F16
		1980	D4	P36	42.0	%	COLO	ZAIRE	F16
V45	HOMICIDES P. MIL. POPULATION	------	----	----	----- -----		-------	-------	----
V46	SUICIDES P. MIL. POPULATION	------	----	----	----- -----		-------	-------	----
V47	IMPORT PARTNERS	1970	R1	FRANC	42.2	%	ALGER	CAME	----
		1970	R2	NETH	5.6	%	-------	GFR	----
		1970	R3	UNKI	5.4	%	AURIA	BURMA	----
		1980	R1	FRANC	22.9	%	ALGER	CAME	----
		1980	R2	UNKI	10.5	%	ZAMBI	KENYA	----
		1980	R3	INDIA	7.7	%	-------	-------	----
V48	EXPORT PARTNERS	1970	R1	FRANC	39.4	%	ALGER	CAME	----
		1970	R2	JAPAN	9.7	%	ZAMBI	ECUA	----
		1970	R3	NIGRA	9.3	%	NIGER	-------	----
		1980	R1	NETH	28.3	%	-------	TOGO	----
		1980	R2	FRANC	15.3	%	BELGI	CAME	----
		1980	R3	JAPAN	10.3	%	USA	BRAZI	----
V49	PATENT SUPPLIERS	------	----	----	----- -----		-------	-------	----
V50	PROVENANCE OF FOREIGN FIRMS	1980	R1	FRANC	60.7	%	ALGER	CAME	----
		1980	R2	UNKI	14.2	%	BANGL	BOLI	----
		1980	R3	-------	7.1	%	-------	-------	----
V51	FILM SUPPLIERS	------	----	----	----- -----		-------	-------	----

BHUTAN (BHUTA)

V1	INCOME PER CAPITA	------	----	----	----- -----	-------	-------	----
V2	TELEPHONES P. TSD. POPULATION	------	----	----	----- -----	-------	-------	----
V3	INFANT MORTALITY RATE	1980	D10	P92	156.3 1/TSD	SOMA	NEPAL	F5
V4	PHYSICIANS P. MIL. POPULATION	------	----	----	----- -----	-------	-------	----
V5	ADULT LITERACY	------	----	----	----- -----	-------	-------	----
V6	DURATION OF SCHOOLING	1970	D1	P1	0.4 YR	-------	SOMA	----
		1976	D1	P1	0.7 YR	-------	UPVO	----
		1982	D1	----	1.3 YR	-------	UPVO	F35
V7	STUDENT ENROLLMENT RATIO	1970	D1	P4	0.0 %	-------	CHAD	----
		1975	D1	P2	0.0 %	-------	MAURA	----
		1980	D1	P6	0.3 %	ANGO	MALI	----
V8	SHARE OF AGRICULTURAL LABOR	------	----	----	----- -----	-------	-------	----
V9	SHARE OF INDUSTRIAL LABOR	------	----	----	----- -----	-------	-------	----
V10	SHARE OF SERVICE LABOR	------	----	----	----- -----	-------	-------	----
V11	SHARE OF ACADEMIC LABOR	------	----	----	----- -----	-------	-------	----
V12	SHARE OF SELF-EMPLOYED LABOR	------	----	----	----- -----	-------	-------	----
V13	MILITARY EXPENDITURES	------	----	----	----- -----	-------	-------	----
V14	MILITARY MANPOWER	------	----	----	----- -----	-------	-------	----
V15	MEN AT AGE 20 - 30	------	----	----	----- -----	-------	-------	----
V16	POPULATION	1970	D1	P2	1.05 MIL CAP	TRITO	CONGO	----
		1975	D1	P4	1.16 MIL CAP	TRITO	CONGO	----
		1980	D1	P4	1.28 MIL CAP	TRITO	KUWAI	----
V17	GROSS DOMESTIC PRODUCT	------	----	----	----- -----	-------	-------	----
V18	SHARE IN WORLD IMPORTS	------	----	----	----- -----	-------	-------	----
V19	SHARE IN WORLD EXPORTS	------	----	----	----- -----	-------	-------	----
V20	GDP SHARE OF IMPORTS	------	----	----	----- -----	-------	-------	----
V21	GDP SHARE OF EXPORTS	------	----	----	----- -----	-------	-------	----
V22	EXPORT PARTNER CONCENTRATION	------	----	----	----- -----	-------	-------	----
V23	TOTAL DEBT AS % OF GDP	------	----	----	----- -----	-------	-------	----
V24	SHARE OF NEW FOREIGN PATENTS	------	----	----	----- -----	-------	-------	----
V25	FOREIGN PROPERTY AS % OF GDP	------	----	----	----- -----	-------	-------	----
V26	GNP SHARE OF DEVELOPMENT AID	------	----	----	----- -----	-------	-------	----

V27	SHARE IN NOBEL PRIZE WINNERS	1970-79	D5	P45	0.0 %	BENIN	BOLI	----
V28	GDP SHARE OF MANUFACTURING	------	----	----	----- -----	-------	-------	----
V29	EXPORT SHARE OF MANUFACTURES	------	----	----	----- -----	-------	-------	----
V30	LACK OF CIVIL LIBERTIES	1975	D4	P39	4	BANGL	BRAZI	----
		1980	D6	P52	5	ARGE	CHILE	----
V31	LACK OF POLITICAL RIGHTS	1975	D4	P31	4	BANGL	BRAZI	----
		1980	D5	P47	5	ZIMBA	EGYPT	----
V32	RIOTS	1970-74	D2	P19	0	BELGI	BULGA	----
		1975-79	D2	P20	0	BANGL	BULGA	----
V33	PROTEST DEMONSTRATIONS	1970-74	D2	P15	0	BENIN	BULGA	----
		1975-79	D2	P13	0	BENIN	BULGA	----
V34	POLITICAL STRIKES	1970-74	D3	P29	0	BELGI	BRAZI	----
		1975-79	D3	P29	0	BENIN	BULGA	----
V35	MEMBER OF THE NONALIGNED MMT.	1970	----	----	0	BELGI	BOLI	----
		1976	----	----	1	BENIN	BURMA	----
		1981	----	----	1	BENIN	BOLI	----
V36	MEMBER OF THE OPEC	1970	----	----	0	BENIN	BOLI	----
		1975	----	----	0	BENIN	BOLI	----
		1980	----	----	0	BENIN	BOLI	----
V37	MEMBER OF THE OECD	1970	----	----	0	BENIN	BOLI	----
		1975	----	----	0	BENIN	BOLI	----
		1980	----	----	0	BENIN	BOLI	----
V38	MEMBER OF THE CMEA	1970	----	----	0	BENIN	BOLI	----
		1975	----	----	0	BENIN	BOLI	----
		1980	----	----	0	BENIN	BOLI	----
V39	MEMBER OF THE WTO	1970	----	----	0	BENIN	BOLI	----
		1975	----	----	0	BENIN	BOLI	----
		1980	----	----	0.0	BENIN	BOLI	----
V40	MEMBER OF THE NATO	1970	----	----	0	BENIN	BOLI	----
		1975	----	----	0	BENIN	BOLI	----
		1980	----	----	0	BENIN	BOLI	----
V41	GDP SHARE OF INVESTMENTS	------	----	----	----- -----	-------	-------	----
V42	GDP SHARE OF AGRICULTURE	------	----	----	----- -----	-------	-------	----
V43	GDP SHARE OF INDUSTRY	------	----	----	----- -----	-------	-------	----
V44	GDP SHARE OF SERVICES	------	----	----	----- -----	-------	-------	----
V45	HOMICIDES P. MIL. POPULATION	------	----	----	----- -----	-------	-------	----
V46	SUICIDES P. MIL. POPULATION	------	----	----	----- -----	-------	-------	----
V47	IMPORT PARTNERS	------	----	----	----- -----	-------	-------	----
V48	EXPORT PARTNERS	------	----	----	----- -----	-------	-------	----

V49	PATENT SUPPLIERS	------	----	----	-----	-----	-------	-------	----
V50	PROVENANCE OF FOREIGN FIRMS	------	----	----	-----	-----	-------	-------	----
V51	FILM SUPPLIERS	------	----	----	-----	-----	-------	-------	----

BOLIVIA (BOLI)

V1	INCOME PER CAPITA	1975	D3	P28	502	$/CAP	GHANA	HONDU	----
		1980	D3	P29	513	$/CAP	SENE	HONDU	----
V2	TELEPHONES P. TSD. POPULATION	------	----	----	-----	-----	-------	-------	----
V3	INFANT MORTALITY RATE	1980	D9	P82	138.2	1/TSD	LAOS	BANGL	F5
V4	PHYSICIANS P. MIL. POPULATION	1974	D6	P52	472	1/MIL	PARA	SOUAF	----
V5	ADULT LITERACY	------	----	----	-----	-----	-------	-------	----
V6	DURATION OF SCHOOLING	1970	D5	P48	7.3	YR	THAI	BRAZI	----
		1975	D6	P54	8.3	YR	KENYA	COLO	----
		1980	D5	P42	8.4	YR	ZAMBI	NICA	----
V7	STUDENT ENROLLMENT RATIO	1970	D7	P68	9.3	%	SYRIA	CHILE	----
		1975	D7	P66	11.7	%	CUBA	HUNGA	----
		1980	D7	P68	16.5	%	URU	GREC	----
V8	SHARE OF AGRICULTURAL LABOR	1976	D7	P63	48.4	%	ELSA	KORSO	F67
V9	SHARE OF INDUSTRIAL LABOR	------	----	----	-----	-----	-------	-------	----
V10	SHARE OF SERVICE LABOR	------	----	----	-----	-----	-------	-------	----
V11	SHARE OF ACADEMIC LABOR	------	----	----	-----	-----	-------	-------	----
V12	SHARE OF SELF-EMPLOYED LABOR	1976	D9	P92	50.8	%	PAKI	SUDAN	F67
V13	MILITARY EXPENDITURES	1975	D3	P30	0.080	TSD MIL $	BANGL	IVORY	----
		1980	D3	P23	0.076	TSD MIL $	SENE	CAME	----
V14	MILITARY MANPOWER	1970	D4	P34	17	TSD CAP	UGADA	DOMI	----
		1975	D4	P35	20	TSD CAP	YESO	ECUA	----
		1980	D4	P39	24	TSD CAP	YESO	DOMI	----
V15	MEN AT AGE 20 - 30	1980	D3	P26	447	TSD CAP	CHAD	SWITZ	F2
V16	POPULATION	1975	D4	P35	4.89	MIL CAP	DOMI	SENE	----
		1980	D4	P36	5.60	MIL CAP	DOMI	SENE	----
V17	GROSS DOMESTIC PRODUCT	1970	D2	P18	1.851	TSD MIL $	NIGER	PARA	----
		1975	D2	P18	2.457	TSD MIL $	PAPUA	NICA	----
		1980	D2	P20	2.875	TSD MIL $	SENE	MADA	----

V18	SHARE IN WORLD IMPORTS	1970	D3	P22	0.479	1/TSD	LIBE	BURMA	----
		1975	D3	P30	0.614	1/TSD	URU	SENE	----
		1980	D3	P22	0.324	1/TSD	MADA	GABON	----
V19	SHARE IN WORLD EXPORTS	1970	D4	P31	0.606	1/TSD	TUNIS	ECUA	----
		1975	D4	P34	0.508	1/TSD	PAPUA	CAME	----
		1980	D4	P37	0.520	1/TSD	PAPUA	SRILA	----
V20	GDP SHARE OF IMPORTS	1970	D4	P39	15.2	%	ITALY	CANA	----
		1975	D5	P49	22.7	%	THAI	UNKI	----
		1980	D2	P12	12.7	%	PARA	IRAN	----
V21	GDP SHARE OF EXPORTS	1970	D6	P58	18.2	%	SENE	MALAW	----
		1975	D5	P50	18.1	%	MOROC	ITALY	----
		1980	D6	P52	19.8	%	KENYA	ELSA	----
V22	EXPORT PARTNER CONCENTRATION	1970	D8	P73	38.1	%	GDR	AFGHA	----
		1975	D7	P65	31.2	%	NETH	POLA	----
		1980	D5	P50	25.7	%	MOROC	JORDA	F136
V23	TOTAL DEBT AS % OF GDP	1980	D8	P76	51.4	%	TANZA	MALI	----
V24	SHARE OF NEW FOREIGN PATENTS	1970	D5	P49	90	%	SRILA	DENMA	----
		1975	D4	P40	87	%	NEWZ	ECUA	----
		1980	D7	P65	93	%	BANGL	MEXI	----
V25	FOREIGN PROPERTY AS % OF GDP	1971	D4	P36	6.2	%	THAI	BURU	----
		1975	D4	P32	4.1	%	ETHIA	SPAIN	----
		1978	D4	----	3.7	%	LIBYA	CHAD	----
V26	GNP SHARE OF DEVELOPMENT AID	------	----	----	-----	-----	-------	-------	
V27	SHARE IN NOBEL PRIZE WINNERS	1970-79	D5	P45	0.0	%	BHUTA	BRAZI	----
V28	GDP SHARE OF MANUFACTURING	1970	D6	P51	14.4	%	INDIA	JAMAI	----
		1975	D5	P47	13.1	%	MALAW	IVORY	----
		1980	D5	P49	13.5	%	TRITO	TUNIS	----
V29	EXPORT SHARE OF MANUFACTURES	1970	D3	P27	3.0	%	NIGER	UPVO	----
		1975	D3	P30	3.5	%	MOZAM	SRILA	F29
		1979	D3	P21	2.3	%	INDO	CAME	----
V30	LACK OF CIVIL LIBERTIES	1975	D6	P54	5		ZAMBI	BURMA	----
		1980	D3	P29	3		BANGL	BRAZI	----
V31	LACK OF POLITICAL RIGHTS	1975	D7	P63	6		ANGO	CAME	----
		1980	D4	P31	3		BANGL	GUATE	----
V32	RIOTS	1970-74	D8	P79	10		TURKY	EGYPT	----
		1975-79	D7	P69	5		MADA	BRAZI	----
V33	PROTEST DEMONSTRATIONS	1970-74	D6	P54	3		VINO	ECUA	----
		1975-79	D8	P71	10		NEPAL	EGYPT	----
V34	POLITICAL STRIKES	1970-74	D9	P81	4		TAIWA	COLO	----
		1975-79	D10	P99	21		NIGRA	SPAIN	----
V35	MEMBER OF THE NONALIGNED MMT.	1970	----	----	0		BHUTA	BRAZI	----
		1976	----	----	0		BELGI	BRAZI	----
		1981	----	----	1		BHUTA	BURU	----

V36	MEMBER OF THE OPEC	1970	----	----	0		BHUTA	BRAZI	----
		1975	----	----	0		BHUTA	BRAZI	----
		1980	----	----	0		BHUTA	BRAZI	----
V37	MEMBER OF THE OECD	1970	----	----	0		BHUTA	BRAZI	----
		1975	----	----	0		BHUTA	BRAZI	----
		1980	----	----	0		BHUTA	BRAZI	----
V38	MEMBER OF THE CMEA	1970	----	----	0		BHUTA	BRAZI	----
		1975	----	----	0		BHUTA	BRAZI	----
		1980	----	----	0		BHUTA	BRAZI	----
V39	MEMBER OF THE WTO	1970	----	----	0		BHUTA	BRAZI	----
		1975	----	----	0		BHUTA	BRAZI	----
		1980	----	----	0		BHUTA	BRAZI	----
V40	MEMBER OF THE NATO	1970	----	----	0		BHUTA	BRAZI	----
		1975	----	----	0		BHUTA	BRAZI	----
		1980	----	----	0		BHUTA	BRAZI	----
V41	GDP SHARE OF INVESTMENTS	1970	D4	P37	17.1 %		CAME	INDIA	----
		1975	D6	P59	23.9 %		TURKY	CANA	----
		1980	D1	P10	13.2 %		GUINE	CHAD	----
V42	GDP SHARE OF AGRICULTURE	1970	D5	P44	18.1 %		PORTU	GREC	----
		1975	D5	P46	18.2 %		SYRIA	GREC	----
		1980	D5	P47	17.8 %		GREC	COSTA	----
V43	GDP SHARE OF INDUSTRY	1970	D6	P57	30.2 %		URU	SINGA	----
		1975	D5	P48	29.8 %		MALAY	GREC	----
		1980	D5	P42	29.0 %		ZAIRE	JORDA	----
V44	GDP SHARE OF SERVICES	1970	D7	P65	51.7 %		SOUAF	CHILE	----
		1975	D8	P71	52.0 %		IRE	ELSA	----
		1980	D8	P72	53.2 %		ELSA	ARGE	----
V45	HOMICIDES P. MIL. POPULATION	-------	----	----	----- -----		-------	-------	----
V46	SUICIDES P. MIL. POPULATION	-------	----	----	----- -----		-------	-------	----
V47	IMPORT PARTNERS	1970	R1	USA	34.0 %		AULIA	BRAZI	F137
		1970	R2	JAPAN	12.3 %		AFGHA	BURU	F137
		1970	R3	GFR	10.7 %		ARGE	BURU	F137
		1980	R1	USA	28.5 %		BANGL	BRAZI	----
		1980	R2	ARGE	11.0 %		-------	PARA	----
		1980	R3	JAPAN	9.7 %		YENO	CAME	----
V48	EXPORT PARTNERS	1970	R1	UNKI	38.1 %		-------	DENMA	----
		1970	R2	USA	34.8 %		AULIA	CHILE	----
		1970	R3	JAPAN	9.6 %		YESO	CANA	----
		1980	R1	USA	25.7 %		BANGL	BRAZI	F136
		1980	R2	ARGE	23.7 %		PARA	URU	F136
		1980	R3	UNKI	6.9 %		ZAMBI	CANA	F136

V49	PATENT SUPPLIERS	1970	R1	USA	80		BELGI	BRAZI	----
		1970	R2	GFR	21		BELGI	BRAZI	----
		1970	R3	SWITZ	20		BELGI	BULGA	----
		1980	R1	USA	43		BELGI	BRAZI	----
		1980	R2	GFR	15		BELGI	BRAZI	----
		1980	R3	SPAIN	11		ECUA	-------	----
V50	PROVENANCE OF FOREIGN FIRMS	1980	R1	USA	68.6	%	BELGI	BRAZI	----
		1980	R2	UNKI	5.9	%	BENIN	CANA	----
		1980	R3	-------	4.4	%	-------	-------	----
V51	FILM SUPPLIERS	1979	R1	USA	175		AURIA	BRAZI	F120
		1979	R2	ITALY	64		AURIA	BRAZI	F120
		1979	R3	UNKI	18		AULIA	COLO	F120

BRAZIL (BRAZI)

V1	INCOME PER CAPITA	1970	D6	P56	1258	$/CAP	HUNGA	ALGER	F211
		1975	D7	P65	1813	$/CAP	CHILE	PORTU	F159
		1980	D7	P62	2180	$/CAP	ALGER	PORTU	F220
V2	TELEPHONES P. TSD. POPULATION	1970	D6	P57	21	1/TSD CAP	SYRIA	KORSO	----
		1975	D6	P54	30	1/TSD CAP	LIBYA	CUBA	----
V3	INFANT MORTALITY RATE	1980	D5	P49	79.0	1/TSD	EGYPT	ZIMBA	F5
V4	PHYSICIANS P. MIL. POPULATION	1969	D7	P63	525	1/MIL	SOUAF	PERU	F159
V5	ADULT LITERACY	1970	D5	P41	66.2	%	NICA	DOMI	----
		1978	D8	----	76.1	%	ZIMBA	MEXI	----
V6	DURATION OF SCHOOLING	1971	D5	P48	7.3	YR	BOLI	GHANA	----
		1975	D5	P49	7.9	YR	TUNIS	IRAQ	----
		1980	D6	P49	8.9	YR	GABON	UNARE	----
V7	STUDENT ENROLLMENT RATIO	1970	D6	P52	5.1	%	COLO	IRAQ	----
		1975	D7	P64	10.7	%	MEXI	CUBA	----
		1980	D7	P59	11.9	%	PORTU	KUWAI	----
V8	SHARE OF AGRICULTURAL LABOR	1970	D7	P65	46.5	%	PERU	YUGO	F22
V9	SHARE OF INDUSTRIAL LABOR	1970	D3	P29	22.3	%	KORSO	PANA	F22
V10	SHARE OF SERVICE LABOR	1970	D6	P51	26.1	%	PORTU	SPAIN	F22
V11	SHARE OF ACADEMIC LABOR	1970	D4	P39	5.0	%	MALAY	SRILA	F22
V12	SHARE OF SELF-EMPLOYED LABOR	1970	D8	P77	35.7	%	KORSO	PANA	F22
V13	MILITARY EXPENDITURES	1975	D8	P80	2.493	TSD MIL $	INDO	BELGI	----
		1980	D7	P65	1.375	TSD MIL $	KUWAI	PAKI	----

V14	MILITARY MANPOWER	1970	D9	P88	375	TSD CAP	SPAIN	UNKI	----
		1975	D9	P89	455	TSD CAP	TURKY	KORNO	----
		1980	D10	P93	450	TSD CAP	EGYPT	PAKI	----
V15	MEN AT AGE 20 - 30	1970	D10	P92	7210	TSD CAP	GFR	INDO	F194
		1975	D10	P95	8775	TSD CAP	BANGL	JAPAN	F185
		1980	D10	P95	10462	TSD CAP	JAPAN	INDO	F185
V16	POPULATION	1970	D10	P94	92.52	MIL CAP	BANGL	JAPAN	F163
		1975	D10	P95	104.94	MIL CAP	BANGL	JAPAN	F23
		1980	D10	P96	121.29	MIL CAP	JAPAN	INDO	F164
V17	GROSS DOMESTIC PRODUCT	1970	D9	P89	116.388	TSD MIL $	NETH	SPAIN	----
		1975	D10	P91	190.278	TSD MIL $	SPAIN	CANA	----
		1980	D10	P93	264.389	TSD MIL $	CANA	ITALY	----
V18	SHARE IN WORLD IMPORTS	1970	D8	P80	8.582	1/TSD	FINLA	YUGO	----
		1975	D9	P89	14.953	1/TSD	SWITZ	SPAIN	----
		1980	D9	P87	11.760	1/TSD	SINGA	AURIA	----
V19	SHARE IN WORLD EXPORTS	1970	D9	P83	8.732	1/TSD	IRAN	VENE	F32
		1975	D9	P82	9.895	1/TSD	CZECH	DENMA	F32
		1980	D9	P83	10.110	1/TSD	VENE	KUWAI	F32
V20	GDP SHARE OF IMPORTS	1970	D1	P5	6.7	%	MEXI	TURKY	----
		1975	D1	P10	10.9	%	SAUDI	NEPAL	----
		1979	D1	P6	8.3	%	GHANA	INDIA	----
V21	GDP SHARE OF EXPORTS	1970	D1	P10	6.4	%	NEPAL	GREC	----
		1975	D2	P11	7.0	%	UPVO	USA	----
		1979	D1	P10	6.5	%	CHINA	RWAN	----
V22	EXPORT PARTNER CONCENTRATION	1970	D5	P43	24.7	%	YESO	ELSA	----
		1975	D2	P18	15.4	%	GHANA	BANGL	----
		1980	D3	P20	17.4	%	INDIA	SAUDI	----
V23	TOTAL DEBT AS % OF GDP	1980	D4	P36	28.0	%	YUGO	PAPUA	----
V24	SHARE OF NEW FOREIGN PATENTS	1970	D4	P31	80	%	SWEDN	ITALY	----
		1975	D6	P54	91	%	PHILI	DENMA	----
		1980	D6	P57	91	%	PHILI	CHILE	----
V25	FOREIGN PROPERTY AS % OF GDP	1971	D6	P58	10.3	%	TUNIS	NICA	----
		1975	D6	P59	7.3	%	GUATE	ELSA	----
		1978	D7	----	6.5	%	NIGER	COLO	----
V26	GNP SHARE OF DEVELOPMENT AID	------	----	----	----- -----		-------	-------	----
V27	SHARE IN NOBEL PRIZE WINNERS	1970-79	D5	P45	0.0	%	BOLI	BULGA	----
V28	GDP SHARE OF MANUFACTURING	------	----	----	----- -----		-------	-------	----
V29	EXPORT SHARE OF MANUFACTURES	1970	D5	P49	9.7	%	MALI	MOROC	----
		1975	D7	P68	23.3	%	COSTA	ARGE	----
		1980	D7	P68	32.8	%	COSTA	ELSA	----
V30	LACK OF CIVIL LIBERTIES	1975	D4	P39	4		BHUTA	CAME	----
		1980	D3	P29	3		BOLI	COLO	----
V31	LACK OF POLITICAL RIGHTS	1975	D4	P31	4		BHUTA	DOMI	----
		1980	D4	P36	4		MOROC	GHANA	----

V32	RIOTS	1970-74	D6	P53	2		BENIN	BURMA	----
		1975-79	D7	P69	5		BOLI	GHANA	----
V33	PROTEST DEMONSTRATIONS	1970-74	D7	P64	5		TAIWA	COLO	----
		1975-79	D6	P54	4		BANGL	CHAD	----
V34	POLITICAL STRIKES	1970-74	D3	P29	0		BHUTA	BULGA	----
		1975-79	D9	P83	6		MEXI	COLO	----
V35	MEMBER OF THE NONALIGNED MMT.	1970	----	----	0		BOLI	BULGA	----
		1976	----	----	0		BOLI	BULGA	----
		1981	----	----	0		BELGI	BULGA	----
V36	MEMBER OF THE OPEC	1970	----	----	0		BOLI	BULGA	----
		1975	----	----	0		BOLI	BULGA	----
		1980	----	----	0		BOLI	BULGA	----
V37	MEMBER OF THE OECD	1970	----	----	0		BOLI	BULGA	----
		1975	----	----	0		BOLI	BULGA	----
		1980	----	----	0		BOLI	BULGA	----
V38	MEMBER OF THE CMEA	1970	----	----	0		BOLI	BURMA	----
		1975	----	----	0		BOLI	BURMA	----
		1980	----	----	0		BOLI	BURMA	----
V39	MEMBER OF THE WTO	1970	----	----	0		BOLI	BURMA	----
		1975	----	----	0		BOLI	BURMA	----
		1980	----	----	0		BOLI	BURMA	----
V40	MEMBER OF THE NATO	1970	----	----	0		BOLI	BULGA	----
		1975	----	----	0		BOLI	BULGA	----
		1980	----	----	0		BOLI	BULGA	----
V41	GDP SHARE OF INVESTMENTS	1970	D7	P64	22.7 %		TANZA	MEXI	----
		1975	D8	P73	27.3 %		GREC	TOGO	----
		1979	D4	P30	19.8 %		DENMA	CHILE	----
V42	GDP SHARE OF AGRICULTURE	------	----	----	----- -----		-------	-------	----
V43	GDP SHARE OF INDUSTRY	------	----	----	----- -----		-------	-------	----
V44	GDP SHARE OF SERVICES	------	----	----	----- -----		-------	-------	----
V45	HOMICIDES P. MIL. POPULATION	------	----	----	----- -----		-------	-------	----
V46	SUICIDES P. MIL. POPULATION	------	----	----	----- -----		-------	-------	----
V47	IMPORT PARTNERS	1970	R1	USA	32.3 %		BOLI	CANA	----
		1970	R2	GFR	12.6 %		ALGER	CAME	----
		1970	R3	JAPAN	6.3 %		AULIA	CANA	----
		1980	R1	USA	18.5 %		BOLI	CANA	----
		1980	R2	IRAQ	15.8 %		TURKY	MOROC	----
		1980	R3	SAUDI	8.7 %		ZAMBI	CANA	----

V48 EXPORT PARTNERS	1970	R1	USA	24.7 %	-------	BURU	----
	1970	R2	GFR	8.6 %	ALGER	BURU	----
	1970	R3	ITALY	7.2 %	AURIA	ETHIA	----
	1980	R1	USA	17.4 %	BOLI	CAME	----
	1980	R2	GFR	6.6 %	UNKI	COLO	----
	1980	R3	JAPAN	6.1 %	BENIN	BURMA	----
V49 PATENT SUPPLIERS	1970	R1	USA	1054	BOLI	CANA	----
	1970	R2	GFR	218	BOLI	BURU	----
	1970	R3	FRANC	198	ZAIRE	ISRA	----
	1979	R1	USA	619	BOLI	BURU	----
	1979	R2	GFR	232	BOLI	BURU	----
	1979	R3	FRANC	126	BELGI	EGYPT	----
V50 PROVENANCE OF FOREIGN FIRMS	1980	R1	USA	47.8 %	BOLI	CANA	----
	1980	R2	GFR	11.9 %	YUGO	CAME	----
	1980	R3	UNKI	9.4 %	BELGI	DENMA	----
V51 FILM SUPPLIERS	1980	R1	USA	210	BOLI	COLO	F119
	1980	R2	ITALY	132	BOLI	COLO	F119
	1980	R3	GFR	20	AURIA	FRANC	F119

BULGARIA (BULGA)

V1 INCOME PER CAPITA	------	----	----		----- -----	-------	-------	----
V2 TELEPHONES P. TSD. POPULATION	1970	D7	P68	56	1/TSD CAP	USSR	POLA	----
	1975	D8	P70	89	1/TSD CAP	SOUAF	URU	----
	1980	D7	P70	141	1/TSD CAP	PORTU	KUWAI	----
V3 INFANT MORTALITY RATE	1980	D3	P23	20.2	1/TSD	CUBA	COSTA	----
V4 PHYSICIANS P. MIL. POPULATION	1970	D10	P94	1863	1/MIL	ITALY	ARGE	----
	1975	D10	P97	2153	1/MIL	MONGO	CZECH	----
	1980	D10	P95	2460	1/MIL	SWITZ	BELGI	----
V5 ADULT LITERACY	------	----	----		----- -----	-------	-------	----
V6 DURATION OF SCHOOLING	1970	D9	P82	10.3	YR	ALBA	CHILE	----
	1975	D8	P80	10.6	YR	PANA	IRE	----
	1980	D8	P69	10.3	YR	PANA	ECUA	----
V7 STUDENT ENROLLMENT RATIO	1970	D9	P83	14.4	%	UNKI	NORWY	----
	1975	D9	P81	19.2	%	UNKI	YUGO	----
	1980	D7	P66	15.7	%	EGYPT	URU	----
V8 SHARE OF AGRICULTURAL LABOR	1975	D4	P43	19.7	%	VENE	SPAIN	----
V9 SHARE OF INDUSTRIAL LABOR	1975	D10	P98	41.7	%	AURIA	-------	----
V10 SHARE OF SERVICE LABOR	1975	D5	P46	21.3	%	ECUA	KORSO	----

V11	SHARE OF ACADEMIC LABOR	1975	D9	P89	17.3	%	FRANC	NETH	----
V12	SHARE OF SELF-EMPLOYED LABOR	------	----	----	-----	-----	-------	-------	----
V13	MILITARY EXPENDITURES	------	----	----	-----	-----	-------	-------	----
V14	MILITARY MANPOWER	1970	D8	P75	175	TSD CAP	BURMA	THAI	----
		1975	D8	P72	175	TSD CAP	ARGE	ISRA	----
		1980	D8	P76	162	TSD CAP	ARGE	BURMA	----
V15	MEN AT AGE 20 - 30	1971	D5	P44	651	TSD CAP	GHANA	BELGI	----
		1975	D6	P56	682	TSD CAP	PORTU	CUBA	----
		1980	D4	P36	650	TSD CAP	GUATE	ECUA	----
V16	POPULATION	1970	D6	P51	8.49	MIL CAP	SWEDN	CUBA	----
		1975	D6	P53	8.72	MIL CAP	SWEDN	GREC	----
		1980	D6	P51	8.86	MIL CAP	MADA	SYRIA	----
V17	GROSS DOMESTIC PRODUCT	------	----	----	-----	-----	-------	-------	----
V18	SHARE IN WORLD IMPORTS	1970	D8	P71	5.516	1/TSD	ARGE	GREC	F49
		1975	D8	P71	5.950	1/TSD	ROMA	ALGER	F49
		1980	D7	P65	4.705	1/TSD	PORTU	UNARE	F49
V19	SHARE IN WORLD EXPORTS	1970	D8	P73	6.389	1/TSD	ROMA	INDIA	F30
		1975	D7	P68	5.354	1/TSD	INDIA	ALGER	F30
		1980	D7	P67	5.197	1/TSD	HUNGA	YUGO	F30
V20	GDP SHARE OF IMPORTS	------	----	----	-----	-----	-------	-------	----
V21	GDP SHARE OF EXPORTS	------	----	----	-----	-----	-------	-------	----
V22	EXPORT PARTNER CONCENTRATION	1970	D9	P90	53.8	%	ALGER	HONDU	----
		1975	D10	P91	54.6	%	IRE	CUBA	----
		1980	D9	P89	49.9	%	INDO	HONDU	----
V23	TOTAL DEBT AS % OF GDP	------	----	----	-----	-----	-------	-------	----
V24	SHARE OF NEW FOREIGN PATENTS	1970	D2	P13	42	%	JAPAN	GFR	----
		1975	D2	P13	47	%	GDR	GFR	----
		1980	D1	P8	29	%	POLA	USA	----
V25	FOREIGN PROPERTY AS % OF GDP	------	----	----	-----	-----	-------	-------	----
V26	GNP SHARE OF DEVELOPMENT AID	------	----	----	-----	-----	-------	-------	----
V27	SHARE IN NOBEL PRIZE WINNERS	1970-79	D5	P45	0.0	%	BRAZI	BURMA	----
V28	GDP SHARE OF MANUFACTURING	------	----	----	-----	-----	-------	-------	----
V29	EXPORT SHARE OF MANUFACTURES	------	----	----	-----	-----	-------	-------	----
V30	LACK OF CIVIL LIBERTIES	1975	D10	P93	7		ALBA	BURU	----
		1980	D10	P92	7		ANGO	BURU	----
V31	LACK OF POLITICAL RIGHTS	1975	D9	P88	7		BENIN	BURMA	----
		1980	D9	P90	7		BENIN	BURMA	----
V32	RIOTS	1970-74	D2	P19	0		BHUTA	CENTR	----
		1975-79	D2	P20	0		BHUTA	BURMA	----

V33 PROTEST DEMONSTRATIONS	1970-74	D2	P15	0	BHUTA	BURU	----
	1975-79	D2	P13	0	BHUTA	BURU	----
V34 POLITICAL STRIKES	1970-74	D3	P29	0	BRAZI	BURU	----
	1975-79	D3	P29	0	BHUTA	BURU	----
V35 MEMBER OF THE NONALIGNED MMT.	1970	----	----	0	BRAZI	CANA	----
	1976	----	----	0	BRAZI	CANA	----
	1981	----	----	0	BRAZI	BURMA	----
V36 MEMBER OF THE OPEC	1970	----	----	0	BRAZI	BURMA	----
	1975	----	----	0	BRAZI	BURMA	----
	1980	----	----	0	BRAZI	BURMA	----
V37 MEMBER OF THE OECD	1970	----	----	0	BRAZI	BURMA	----
	1975	----	----	0	BRAZI	BURMA	----
	1980	----	----	0	BRAZI	BURMA	----
V38 MEMBER OF THE CMEA	1970	----	----	1	-------	CZECH	----
	1975	----	----	1	-------	CUBA	----
	1980	----	----	1	-------	CUBA	----
V39 MEMBER OF THE WTO	1970	----	----	1	-------	CZECH	----
	1975	----	----	1	-------	CZECH	----
	1980	----	----	1	-------	CZECH	----
V40 MEMBER OF THE NATO	1970	----	----	0	BRAZI	BURMA	----
	1975	----	----	0	BRAZI	BURMA	----
	1980	----	----	0	BRAZI	BURMA	----
V41 GDP SHARE OF INVESTMENTS	------	----	----	----- -----	-------	-------	----
V42 GDP SHARE OF AGRICULTURE	------	----	----	----- -----	-------	-------	----
V43 GDP SHARE OF INDUSTRY	------	----	----	----- -----	-------	-------	----
V44 GDP SHARE OF SERVICES	------	----	----	----- -----	-------	-------	----
V45 HOMICIDES P. MIL. POPULATION	1970	D7	P64	22.3 1/MIL CAP	CANA	YUGO	F148
	1975	D7	P64	23.3 1/MIL CAP	HUNGA	CANA	F148
	1980	D7	P70	25.1 1/MIL CAP	SRILA	HUNGA	----
V46 SUICIDES P. MIL. POPULATION	1970	D7	P64	119.1 1/MIL CAP	USA	AULIA	----
	1975	D7	P66	129.0 1/MIL CAP	USA	FRANC	----
	1980	D6	P55	136.1 1/MIL CAP	NORWY	CANA	----
V47 IMPORT PARTNERS	1970	R1	USSR	52.2 %	AFGHA	CUBA	----
	1970	R2	GDR	8.6 %	USSR	CZECH	----
	1970	R3	CZECH	5.3 %	-------	GDR	----
	1980	R1	USSR	57.3 %	AFGHA	CUBA	----
	1980	R2	GDR	6.6 %	USSR	CZECH	----
	1980	R3	GFR	4.8 %	ARGE	BURMA	----
V48 EXPORT PARTNERS	1970	R1	USSR	53.8 %	AFGHA	CZECH	----
	1970	R2	GDR	8.7 %	USSR	CZECH	----
	1970	R3	CZECH	4.4 %	-------	GDR	----
	1980	R1	USSR	49.9 %	ARGE	CZECH	----
	1980	R2	GDR	5.5 %	USSR	CZECH	----
	1980	R3	POLA	3.9 %	USSR	CZECH	----

V49	PATENT SUPPLIERS	1970	R1	GFR	128		AURIA	GDR	----
		1970	R2	GDR	86		CZECH	GHANA	----
		1970	R3	SWITZ	53		BOLI	BURU	----
		1980	R1	GFR	125		AURIA	CZECH	----
		1980	R2	USA	113		AURIA	CZECH	----
		1980	R3	USSR	58		-------	-------	----
V50	PROVENANCE OF FOREIGN FIRMS	------	----	----	----- -----		-------	-------	----
V51	FILM SUPPLIERS	1980	R1	USSR	62		-------	CUBA	F117
		1980	R2	USA	15		ANGO	CUBA	F117
		1980	R3	ITALY	9		YUGO	FINLA	F117

BURMA (BURMA)

V1	INCOME PER CAPITA	1970	D1	P4	138	$/CAP	MALAW	NEPAL	----
		1975	D1	P4	138	$/CAP	ETHIA	NEPAL	----
		1980	D1	P6	168	$/CAP	MALAW	UPVO	----
V2	TELEPHONES P. TSD. POPULATION	1970	D1	P7	1	1/TSD CAP	AFGHA	BURU	----
		1975	D1	P5	1	1/TSD CAP	BANGL	BURU	----
		1979	D1	P3	1	1/TSD CAP	BANGL	RWAN	----
V3	INFANT MORTALITY RATE	1980	D6	P60	107.2	1/TSD	TUNIS	GHANA	F5
V4	PHYSICIANS P. MIL. POPULATION	1970	D4	P35	114	1/MIL	MADA	THAI	----
		1975	D4	P37	184	1/MIL	CONGO	GABON	----
		1981	D4	P37	209	1/MIL	CONGO	VINO	----
V5	ADULT LITERACY	1980	D7	P60	65.9	%	CHINA	INDO	F21
V6	DURATION OF SCHOOLING	1970	D4	P33	5.7	YR	INDIA	IRAQ	----
		1975	D3	P31	5.6	YR	CENTR	INDIA	----
		1980	D3	P24	5.9	YR	OMAN	SAUDI	----
V7	STUDENT ENROLLMENT RATIO	1970	D4	P40	2.2	%	NEPAL	HONDU	----
		1975	D4	P34	2.2	%	ZAMBI	NEPAL	----
		1981	D5	P42	5.1	%	ALGER	TRITO	----
V8	SHARE OF AGRICULTURAL LABOR	------	----	----	----- -----		-------	-------	----
V9	SHARE OF INDUSTRIAL LABOR	------	----	----	----- -----		-------	-------	----
V10	SHARE OF SERVICE LABOR	------	----	----	----- -----		-------	-------	----
V11	SHARE OF ACADEMIC LABOR	------	----	----	----- -----		-------	-------	----
V12	SHARE OF SELF-EMPLOYED LABOR	------	----	----	----- -----		-------	-------	----
V13	MILITARY EXPENDITURES	1970	D5	P43	0.209	TSD MIL $	IRE	MOROC	----
		1975	D4	P39	0.157	TSD MIL $	TANZA	URU	----
		1980	D4	P40	0.237	TSD MIL $	URU	TANZA	F62

V14 MILITARY MANPOWER	1970	D8	P73	174 TSD CAP	HUNGA	BULGA	----
	1975	D8	P75	209 TSD CAP	GREC	CZECH	----
	1980	D8	P77	179 TSD CAP	BULGA	ISRA	----
V15 MEN AT AGE 20 - 30	1973	D8	----	2195 TSD CAP	ARGE	IRAN	F2
	1979	D8	P72	2487 TSD CAP	CANA	SPAIN	F2
V16 POPULATION	1970	D8	P80	27.03 MIL CAP	ETHIA	IRAN	----
	1975	D9	P81	30.17 MIL CAP	ETHIA	IRAN	----
	1980	D9	P80	33.64 MIL CAP	ETHIA	POLA	----
V17 GROSS DOMESTIC PRODUCT	1970	D4	P36	3.736 TSD MIL $	KENYA	CAME	----
	1975	D4	P33	4.158 TSD MIL $	TANZA	GHANA	----
	1980	D4	P36	5.653 TSD MIL $	ZIMBA	ZAIRE	----
V18 SHARE IN WORLD IMPORTS	1970	D3	P23	0.509 1/TSD	BOLI	MADA	F30
	1975	D2	P17	0.275 1/TSD	UGADA	MALAW	F30
	1980	D1	P9	0.172 1/TSD	NEPAL	UPVO	F30
V19 SHARE IN WORLD EXPORTS	1970	D3	P24	0.344 1/TSD	PANA	ETHIA	F30
	1975	D2	P17	0.196 1/TSD	JORDA	YESO	F30
	1980	D3	P22	0.236 1/TSD	NICA	SENE	F30
V20 GDP SHARE OF IMPORTS	1970	D1	P8	7.7 %	ARGE	JAPAN	F30
	1975	D1	P4	7.0 %	USA	INDIA	F30
	1980	D1	P2	6.1 %	UGADA	ARGE	F30
V21 GDP SHARE OF EXPORTS	1970	D1	P7	4.9 %	TURKY	UPVO	F30
	1975	D1	P5	4.8 %	TURKY	INDIA	F30
	1980	D2	P17	8.2 %	GHANA	MEXI	F30
V22 EXPORT PARTNER CONCENTRATION	1975	D2	P13	14.1 %	NEPAL	CHILE	----
	1978	D1	----	12.9 %	SWEDN	NEWZ	----
V23 TOTAL DEBT AS % OF GDP	1980	D4	P33	25.9 %	ELSA	YUGO	----
V24 SHARE OF NEW FOREIGN PATENTS	------	----	----	----- -----	-------	-------	----
V25 FOREIGN PROPERTY AS % OF GDP	1971	D1	P2	0.4 %	-------	YUGO	----
	1975	D2	P14	1.5 %	TURKY	MALI	----
	1978	D2	----	1.4 %	IRAN	LESO	----
V26 GNP SHARE OF DEVELOPMENT AID	------	----	----	----- -----	-------	-------	----
V27 SHARE IN NOBEL PRIZE WINNERS	1970-79	D5	P45	0.0 %	BULGA	BURU	----
V28 GDP SHARE OF MANUFACTURING	1970	D4	P35	10.4 %	ZAMBI	CAME	----
	1975	D3	P27	9.0 %	MALI	MOZAM	----
	1980	D4	P36	9.5 %	BURU	TANZA	----
V29 EXPORT SHARE OF MANUFACTURES	1970	D2	P19	1.5 %	SRILA	ETHIA	----
	1975	D3	P28	3.1 %	SOMA	MOZAM	----
V30 LACK OF CIVIL LIBERTIES	1975	D6	P54	5	BOLI	CHILE	----
	1980	D8	P74	6	BENIN	CAME	----
V31 LACK OF POLITICAL RIGHTS	1975	D9	P88	7	BULGA	BURU	----
	1980	D9	P90	7	BULGA	BURU	----
V32 RIOTS	1970-74	D6	P53	2	BRAZI	CZECH	----
	1975-79	D2	P20	0	BULGA	BURU	----

V33	PROTEST DEMONSTRATIONS	1970-74	D4	P37	1	AFGHA	CHAD	----
		1975-79	D6	P59	5	UGADA	ELSA	----
V34	POLITICAL STRIKES	1970-74	D7	P64	1	BENIN	CAME	----
		1975-79	D8	P73	2	AULIA	CENTR	----
V35	MEMBER OF THE NONALIGNED MMT.	1976	----	----	1	BHUTA	BURU	----
		1981	----	----	0	BULGA	CANA	----
V36	MEMBER OF THE OPEC	1970	----	----	0	BULGA	BURU	----
		1975	----	----	0	BULGA	BURU	----
		1980	----	----	0	BULGA	BURU	----
V37	MEMBER OF THE OECD	1970	----	----	0	BULGA	BURU	----
		1975	----	----	0	BULGA	BURU	----
		1980	----	----	0	BULGA	BURU	----
V38	MEMBER OF THE CMEA	1970	----	----	0	BRAZI	BURU	----
		1975	----	----	0	BRAZI	BURU	----
		1980	----	----	0	BRAZI	BURU	----
V39	MEMBER OF THE WTO	1970	----	----	0	BRAZI	BURU	----
		1975	----	----	0	BRAZI	BURU	----
		1980	----	----	0	BRAZI	BURU	----
V40	MEMBER OF THE NATO	1970	----	----	0	BULGA	BURU	----
		1975	----	----	0	BULGA	BURU	----
		1980	----	----	0	BULGA	BURU	----
V41	GDP SHARE OF INVESTMENTS	1970	D3	P22	14.2 %	EGYPT	GHANA	----
		1975	D1	P8	10.0 %	AFGHA	ETHIA	----
		1980	D4	P36	21.5 %	SWEDN	MALAW	----
V42	GDP SHARE OF AGRICULTURE	1970	D8	P79	38.0 %	TOGO	NIGRA	----
		1975	D9	P90	47.1 %	MALAW	ETHIA	----
		1980	D9	P90	46.5 %	RWAN	BENIN	----
V43	GDP SHARE OF INDUSTRY	1970	D2	P10	14.2 %	UGADA	ETHIA	----
		1975	D1	P3	10.8 %	UGADA	BURU	----
		1980	D1	P6	12.7 %	BANGL	SUDAN	----
V44	GDP SHARE OF SERVICES	1970	D5	P50	47.8 %	AURIA	SRILA	----
		1975	D4	P37	42.1 %	PAPUA	PARA	----
		1980	D3	P30	40.8 %	EGYPT	TRITO	----
V45	HOMICIDES P. MIL. POPULATION	------	----	----	----- -----	-------	-------	----
V46	SUICIDES P. MIL. POPULATION	------	----	----	----- -----	-------	-------	----
V47	IMPORT PARTNERS	1970	R1	JAPAN	24.8 %	-------	INDO	----
		1970	R2	INDIA	16.4 %	-------	EGYPT	----
		1970	R3	UNKI	8.8 %	BENIN	CUBA	----
		1979	R1	JAPAN	34.1 %	-------	INDO	----
		1979	R2	USA	12.4 %	VENE	ELSA	----
		1979	R3	GFR	9.2 %	BULGA	COLO	----
V48	EXPORT PARTNERS	1978	R1	SINGA	12.9 %	-------	MALAY	----
		1978	R2	SRILA	12.3 %	-------	-------	----
		1978	R3	JAPAN	11.5 %	BRAZI	INDIA	----

V49	PATENT SUPPLIERS	------	----	----	-----	-----	-------	-------	----
V50	PROVENANCE OF FOREIGN FIRMS	------	----	----	-----	-----	-------	-------	----
V51	FILM SUPPLIERS	------	----	----	-----	-----	-------	-------	----

BURUNDI (BURU)

V1	INCOME PER CAPITA	1970	D1	P7	178	$/CAP	NEPAL	SRILA	F4
		1975	D1	P9	196	$/CAP	UPVO	INDIA	----
		1980	D1	P8	225	$/CAP	UPVO	ZAIRE	----
V2	TELEPHONES P. TSD. POPULATION	1970	D1	P7	1	1/TSD CAP	BURMA	CHAD	----
		1975	D1	P5	1	1/TSD CAP	BURMA	CHAD	----
V3	INFANT MORTALITY RATE	1980	D9	P84	148.5	1/TSD	BANGL	MAURA	F5
V4	PHYSICIANS P. MIL. POPULATION	1970	D1	P7	17	1/MIL	CHAD	NIGER	----
		1974	D1	P7	22	1/MIL	MALI	CHAD	----
V5	ADULT LITERACY	1980	D3	P23	26.8	%	PAKI	BENIN	F21
V6	DURATION OF SCHOOLING	1970	D2	P11	2.5	YR	AFGHA	CHAD	----
		1975	D1	P5	1.7	YR	NIGER	MAURA	----
		1980	D1	P3	2.1	YR	MALI	NIGER	F35
V7	STUDENT ENROLLMENT RATIO	1970	D2	P13	0.2	%	YESO	ETHIA	----
		1975	D1	P9	0.3	%	UPVO	ETHIA	----
		1980	D2	P13	0.6	%	ETHIA	SIERA	----
V8	SHARE OF AGRICULTURAL LABOR	------	----	----	-----	-----	-------	-------	----
V9	SHARE OF INDUSTRIAL LABOR	------	----	----	-----	-----	-------	-------	----
V10	SHARE OF SERVICE LABOR	------	----	----	-----	-----	-------	-------	----
V11	SHARE OF ACADEMIC LABOR	------	----	----	-----	-----	-------	-------	----
V12	SHARE OF SELF-EMPLOYED LABOR	------	----	----	-----	-----	-------	-------	----
V13	MILITARY EXPENDITURES	1975	D1	P10	0.015	TSD MIL $	NIGER	COSTA	----
		1980	D1	P9	0.022	TSD MIL $	HAITI	JAMAI	----
V14	MILITARY MANPOWER	1970	D1	P7	3	TSD CAP	TOGO	MAURA	----
		1975	D2	P17	7	TSD CAP	LIBE	CONGO	----
		1980	D2	P16	7	TSD CAP	UGADA	HAITI	----
V15	MEN AT AGE 20 - 30	1971	D2	P18	222	TSD CAP	NEWZ	NIGER	F22
V16	POPULATION	1970	D3	P27	3.62	MIL CAP	ELSA	CHAD	F4
		1975	D3	P27	3.74	MIL CAP	ISRA	ELSA	----
		1980	D3	P27	4.12	MIL CAP	NORWY	CHAD	----

V17	GROSS DOMESTIC PRODUCT	1970	D1	P4	0.644	TSD MIL $	MALAW	BENIN	----
		1975	D1	P2	0.732	TSD MIL $	-------	MALAW	----
		1980	D1	P4	0.926	TSD MIL $	LIBE	MALAW	----
V18	SHARE IN WORLD IMPORTS	1970	D1	P1	0.066	1/TSD	-------	RWAN	----
		1975	D1	P2	0.068	1/TSD	LAOS	CENTR	----
		1980	D1	P4	0.082	1/TSD	LAOS	RWAN	----
V19	SHARE IN WORLD EXPORTS	1970	D1	P5	0.077	1/TSD	UPVO	RWAN	----
		1975	D1	P4	0.037	1/TSD	BENIN	RWAN	----
		1980	D1	P4	0.033	1/TSD	BENIN	CHAD	----
V20	GDP SHARE OF IMPORTS	1970	D2	P14	10.1	%	PERU	PARA	----
		1975	D2	P19	14.7	%	NIGER	SPAIN	----
		1980	D3	P26	17.5	%	URU	ETHIA	----
V21	GDP SHARE OF EXPORTS	1970	D3	P28	11.0	%	THAI	CHAD	----
		1975	D2	P16	7.6	%	ARGE	MALI	----
		1980	D2	P14	6.8	%	UPVO	PARA	----
V22	EXPORT PARTNER CONCENTRATION	1970	D10	P92	57.0	%	HONDU	SENE	----
		1975	D9	P83	45.9	%	INDO	ECUA	----
V23	TOTAL DEBT AS % OF GDP	1980	D2	P15	17.2	%	LESO	ARGE	----
V24	SHARE OF NEW FOREIGN PATENTS	1970	D9	P90	100	%	ZAMBI	CUBA	F19
		1975	D10	P92	100	%	SINGA	GHANA	F19
		1980	D10	P94	100	%	NIGRA	GHANA	----
V25	FOREIGN PROPERTY AS % OF GDP	1971	D4	P38	6.3	%	BOLI	MEXI	----
		1975	D5	P45	5.2	%	CHAD	KUWAI	----
		1978	D5	----	4.3	%	TANZA	PARA	----
V26	GNP SHARE OF DEVELOPMENT AID	------	----	----	-----	-----	-------	-------	----
V27	SHARE IN NOBEL PRIZE WINNERS	1970-79	D5	P45	0.0	%	BURMA	CAME	----
V28	GDP SHARE OF MANUFACTURING	1970	D2	P12	6.8	%	SIERA	CHAD	F16
		1975	D2	P20	7.3	%	SUDAN	PAPUA	F16
		1980	D4	P35	9.4	%	ECUA	BURMA	F16
V29	EXPORT SHARE OF MANUFACTURES	------	----	----	-----	-----	-------	-------	----
V30	LACK OF CIVIL LIBERTIES	1975	D10	P93	7		BULGA	CENTR	----
		1980	D10	P92	7		BULGA	CONGO	----
V31	LACK OF POLITICAL RIGHTS	1975	D9	P88	7		BURMA	CENTR	----
		1980	D9	P90	7		BURMA	CENTR	----
V32	RIOTS	1970-74	D7	P64	4		AULIA	COLO	----
		1975-79	D2	P20	0		BURMA	CAME	----
V33	PROTEST DEMONSTRATIONS	1970-74	D2	P15	0		BULGA	CAME	----
		1975-79	D2	P13	0		BULGA	CAME	----
V34	POLITICAL STRIKES	1970-74	D3	P29	0		BULGA	CENTR	----
		1975-79	D3	P29	0		BULGA	CAME	----
V35	MEMBER OF THE NONALIGNED MMT.	1970	----	----	1		ALGER	CAME	----
		1976	----	----	1		BURMA	CAME	----
		1981	----	----	1		BOLI	CAME	----

V36 MEMBER OF THE OPEC	1970	----	----	0		BURMA	CAME	----
	1975	----	----	0		BURMA	CAME	----
	1980	----	----	0		BURMA	CAME	----
V37 MEMBER OF THE OECD	1970	----	----	0		BURMA	CAME	----
	1975	----	----	0		BURMA	CAME	----
	1980	----	----	0		BURMA	CAME	----
V38 MEMBER OF THE CMEA	1970	----	----	0		BURMA	CAME	----
	1975	----	----	0		BURMA	CAME	----
	1980	----	----	0		BURMA	CAME	----
V39 MEMBER OF THE WTO	1970	----	----	0		BURMA	CAME	----
	1975	----	----	0		BURMA	CAME	----
	1980	----	----	0		BURMA	CAME	----
V40 MEMBER OF THE NATO	1970	----	----	0		BURMA	CAME	----
	1975	----	----	0		BURMA	CAME	----
	1980	----	----	0		BURMA	CAME	----
V41 GDP SHARE OF INVESTMENTS	1970	D1	P3	4.5 %		YENO	BANGL	----
	1975	D1	P3	7.7 %		UGADA	MOZAM	----
	1980	D2	P13	14.4 %		SENE	HAITI	----
V42 GDP SHARE OF AGRICULTURE	1970	D10	P98	68.2 %		NEPAL	RWAN	F16
	1975	D10	P98	64.8 %		BANGL	NEPAL	F16
	1980	D10	P95	54.5 %		BANGL	CHAD	F16
V43 GDP SHARE OF INDUSTRY	1970	D1	P3	9.3 %		RWAN	CHAD	F16
	1975	D1	P4	11.0 %		BURMA	NEPAL	F16
	1980	D2	P13	16.1 %		YENO	MOZAM	F16
V44 GDP SHARE OF SERVICES	1970	D1	P4	22.5 %		RWAN	SOMA	F16
	1975	D1	P6	24.2 %		KUWAI	SOMA	F16
	1980	D1	P10	29.4 %		GABON	GUINE	F16
V45 HOMICIDES P. MIL. POPULATION	------	----	----	----- -----		-------	-------	----
V46 SUICIDES P. MIL. POPULATION	------	----	----	----- -----		-------	-------	----
V47 IMPORT PARTNERS	1970	R1	BELGI	18.9 %		-------	RWAN	F142
	1970	R2	JAPAN	12.9 %		BOLI	COSTA	----
	1970	R3	GFR	9.7 %		BOLI	COSTA	----
	1980	R1	BELGI	16.7 %		-------	RWAN	F142
	1980	R2	IRAN	13.5 %		-------	TURKY	----
	1980	R3	FRANC	9.1 %		BELGI	UNKI	----
V48 EXPORT PARTNERS	1970	R1	USA	57.0 %		BRAZI	CANA	----
	1970	R2	GFR	16.1 %		BRAZI	COLO	----
	1970	R3	UNKI	7.7 %		AULIA	CHILE	----
V49 PATENT SUPPLIERS	1969	R1	UNKI	7		-------	GHANA	----
	1969	R2	GFR	3		BRAZI	CANA	----
	1969	R3	SWITZ	1		BULGA	COLO	----
	1980	R1	USA	5		BRAZI	CANA	----
	1980	R2	GFR	2		BRAZI	CHILE	----
	1980	R3	-------	1		-------	-------	----
V50 PROVENANCE OF FOREIGN FIRMS	------	----	----	----- -----		-------	-------	----

V51	FILM SUPPLIERS	------	----	----	----- -----	-------	-------	----

CAMEROON (CAME)

V1	INCOME PER CAPITA	1970	D3	P30	595	$/CAP	SENE	MOROC	----
		1975	D4	P35	637	$/CAP	PHILI	ZAMBI	----
		1980	D4	P35	721	$/CAP	PHILI	ZIMBA	F35
V2	TELEPHONES P. TSD. POPULATION	------	----	----	----- -----		-------	-------	----
V3	INFANT MORTALITY RATE	1980	D8	P75	126.6	1/TSD	ALGER	INDIA	F5
V4	PHYSICIANS P. MIL. POPULATION	1970	D2	P12	33	1/MIL	GUINE	BENIN	----
		1974	D2	P17	48	1/MIL	IVORY	TOGO	----
		1979	D2	P19	72	1/MIL	SOMA	SENE	----
V5	ADULT LITERACY	------	----	----	----- -----		-------	-------	----
V6	DURATION OF SCHOOLING	1970	D4	P38	6.2	YR	INDO	IRAN	----
		1975	D4	P40	7.3	YR	MADA	SRILA	----
		1980	D5	P39	8.2	YR	PARA	TUNIS	----
V7	STUDENT ENROLLMENT RATIO	1970	D3	P21	0.5	%	ZAMBI	NIGRA	----
		1975	D3	P27	1.3	%	ZAIRE	GABON	----
		1980	D3	P21	1.5	%	ZIMBA	LESO	----
V8	SHARE OF AGRICULTURAL LABOR	1976	D9	P91	77.9	%	YENO	BANGL	F94
		1982	D10	----	77.9	%	THAI	BANGL	F99
V9	SHARE OF INDUSTRIAL LABOR	1976	D2	P11	11.9	%	SUDAN	INDO	F94
		1982	D1	----	12.0	%	BANGL	THAI	F99
V10	SHARE OF SERVICE LABOR	1976	D1	P9	7.6	%	MALAW	BANGL	F94
		1982	D1	----	7.6	%	RWAN	BANGL	F99
V11	SHARE OF ACADEMIC LABOR	1976	D2	P13	2.6	%	INDO	THAI	F94
		1982	D1	----	2.5	%	TUNIS	THAI	F99
V12	SHARE OF SELF-EMPLOYED LABOR	1976	D10	P95	63.9	%	SUDAN	NEPAL	F94
		1982	D10	----	64.8	%	INDO	HAITI	F99
V13	MILITARY EXPENDITURES	1970	D4	P34	0.075	TSD MIL $	DOMI	GHANA	----
		1975	D4	P33	0.084	TSD MIL $	IVORY	DOMI	----
		1980	D3	P24	0.079	TSD MIL $	BOLI	ELSA	----
V14	MILITARY MANPOWER	1970	D3	P22	8	TSD CAP	SENE	IRE	----
		1975	D3	P23	10	TSD CAP	KENYA	CHAD	----
		1980	D3	P21	11	TSD CAP	SENE	ELSA	----
V15	MEN AT AGE 20 - 30	1976	D4	P40	475	TSD CAP	FINLA	SWITZ	F22
V16	POPULATION	1970	D5	P47	6.78	MIL CAP	SWITZ	MADA	----
		1975	D5	P50	7.58	MIL CAP	AURIA	MADA	----
		1980	D5	P49	8.50	MIL CAP	ECUA	MADA	F35

V17	GROSS DOMESTIC PRODUCT	1970	D4	P38	4.033	TSD MIL $	BURMA	TRITO	----
		1975	D4	P36	4.829	TSD MIL $	TRITO	KENYA	----
		1980	D4	P39	6.130	TSD MIL $	TRITO	KENYA	----
V18	SHARE IN WORLD IMPORTS	1970	D4	P33	0.729	1/TSD	URU	ECUA	F121
		1975	D4	P32	0.659	1/TSD	ELSA	COSTA	F121
		1980	D4	P40	0.781	1/TSD	GUATE	URU	F121
V19	SHARE IN WORLD EXPORTS	1970	D4	P38	0.740	1/TSD	COSTA	URU	F121
		1975	D4	P35	0.511	1/TSD	BOLI	SENE	F121
		1980	D5	P41	0.693	1/TSD	ZAMBI	KENYA	F121
V20	GDP SHARE OF IMPORTS	1970	D7	P66	22.1	%	SOUAF	SENE	F121
		1975	D5	P50	23.0	%	UNKI	UPVO	F121
		1980	D6	P54	24.7	%	ZIMBA	TANZA	F121
V21	GDP SHARE OF EXPORTS	1970	D8	P72	21.2	%	DENMA	FINLA	F121
		1975	D5	P48	17.2	%	GUATE	GHANA	F121
		1980	D6	P58	21.3	%	ECUA	AFGHA	F121
V22	EXPORT PARTNER CONCENTRATION	1970	D6	P54	29.6	%	ROMA	JAPAN	F121
		1975	D6	P53	26.8	%	ALGER	CONGO	F121
		1980	D7	P65	30.2	%	ZAIRE	AURIA	F121
V23	TOTAL DEBT AS % OF GDP	1980	D6	P53	38.7	%	YENO	MADA	----
V24	SHARE OF NEW FOREIGN PATENTS	------	----	----	-----	-----	-------	-------	----
V25	FOREIGN PROPERTY AS % OF GDP	1971	D8	P74	16.9	%	DOMI	NIGRA	----
		1975	D8	P72	11.5	%	IVORY	INDO	----
		1978	D8	----	9.1	%	MADA	VENE	----
V26	GNP SHARE OF DEVELOPMENT AID	------	----	----	-----	-----	-------	-------	----
V27	SHARE IN NOBEL PRIZE WINNERS	1970-79	D5	P45	0.0	%	BURU	CENTR	----
V28	GDP SHARE OF MANUFACTURING	1970	D4	P36	10.5	%	BURMA	NIGER	----
		1975	D4	P31	9.9	%	NEPAL	ZAIRE	----
		1980	D3	P30	8.5	%	NIGER	MOZAM	----
V29	EXPORT SHARE OF MANUFACTURES	1970	D5	P44	8.4	%	HONDU	TURKY	----
		1975	D5	P51	10.5	%	NIGER	HONDU	----
		1980	D3	P23	3.8	%	BOLI	PARA	----
V30	LACK OF CIVIL LIBERTIES	1975	D4	P39	4		BRAZI	ECUA	----
		1980	D8	P74	6		BURMA	CENTR	----
V31	LACK OF POLITICAL RIGHTS	1975	D7	P63	6		BOLI	CHAD	----
		1980	D7	P67	6		ARGE	CHILE	----
V32	RIOTS	1970-74	D5	P43	1		ALGER	CANA	----
		1975-79	D2	P20	0		BURU	CONGO	----
V33	PROTEST DEMONSTRATIONS	1970-74	D2	P15	0		BURU	CENTR	----
		1975-79	D2	P13	0		BURU	CONGO	----
V34	POLITICAL STRIKES	1970-74	D7	P64	1		BURMA	GFR	----
		1975-79	D3	P29	0		BURU	CHAD	----

V35	MEMBER OF THE NONALIGNED MMT.	1970	----	----	1	BURU	CENTR	----
		1976	----	----	1	BURU	CENTR	----
		1981	----	----	1	BURU	CENTR	----
V36	MEMBER OF THE OPEC	1970	----	----	0	BURU	CANA	----
		1975	----	----	0	BURU	CANA	----
		1980	----	----	0	BURU	CANA	----
V37	MEMBER OF THE OECD	1970	----	----	0	BURU	CENTR	----
		1975	----	----	0	BURU	CENTR	----
		1980	----	----	0	BURU	CENTR	----
V38	MEMBER OF THE CMEA	1970	----	----	0	BURU	CANA	----
		1975	----	----	0	BURU	CANA	----
		1980	----	----	0	BURU	CANA	----
V39	MEMBER OF THE WTO	1970	----	----	0	BURU	CANA	----
		1975	----	----	0	BURU	CANA	----
		1980	----	----	0	BURU	CANA	----
V40	MEMBER OF THE NATO	1970	----	----	0	BURU	CENTR	----
		1975	----	----	0	BURU	CENTR	----
		1980	----	----	0	BURU	CENTR	----
V41	GDP SHARE OF INVESTMENTS	1970	D4	P36	17.0 %	SIERA	BOLI	----
		1975	D5	P46	21.5 %	NICA	BELGI	----
		1980	D5	P40	22.3 %	TANZA	LIBYA	----
V42	GDP SHARE OF AGRICULTURE	1970	D7	P71	30.6 %	TURKY	MALAY	----
		1975	D8	P73	34.0 %	PAKI	KENYA	----
		1980	D7	P69	29.0 %	ZAIRE	YENO	----
V43	GDP SHARE OF INDUSTRY	1970	D2	P18	16.0 %	SOMA	TANZA	----
		1975	D2	P13	15.1 %	BENIN	TANZA	----
		1980	D2	P19	20.2 %	ELSA	LESO	----
V44	GDP SHARE OF SERVICES	1970	D8	P74	53.4 %	AULIA	VENE	----
		1975	D7	P68	50.9 %	ITALY	GREC	----
		1980	D7	P64	50.8 %	ECUA	ITALY	----
V45	HOMICIDES P. MIL. POPULATION	------	----	----	----- -----	-------	-------	----
V46	SUICIDES P. MIL. POPULATION	------	----	----	----- -----	-------	-------	----
V47	IMPORT PARTNERS	1970	R1	FRANC	50.5 %	BENIN	CENTR	F121
		1970	R2	GFR	7.9 %	BRAZI	CENTR	F121
		1970	R3	USA	7.7 %	ALGER	CENTR	F121
		1980	R1	FRANC	44.7 %	BENIN	CENTR	F121
		1980	R2	GFR	8.5 %	ALGER	FINLA	F121
		1980	R3	JAPAN	5.5 %	BOLI	CHILE	F121
V48	EXPORT PARTNERS	1970	R1	FRANC	29.6 %	BENIN	CENTR	F121
		1970	R2	NETH	23.6 %	ARGE	CONGO	F121
		1970	R3	GFR	12.3 %	UNKI	DENMA	F121
		1980	R1	USA	30.2 %	BRAZI	CANA	F121
		1980	R2	FRANC	21.8 %	BENIN	HAITI	F121
		1980	R3	NETH	19.2 %	BELGI	DOMI	F121
V49	PATENT SUPPLIERS	------	----	----	----- -----	-------	-------	----

V50	PROVENANCE OF FOREIGN FIRMS	1980	R1	FRANC	65.0	%	BENIN	CONGO	----
		1980	R2	GFR	9.0	%	BRAZI	MEXI	----
		1980	R3	-------	7.0	%	-------	-------	----
V51	FILM SUPPLIERS	------	----	----	-----	-----	-------	-------	----

CANADA (CANA)

V1	INCOME PER CAPITA	1970	D9	P86	8052	$/CAP	FINLA	AULIA	F147
		1975	D9	P89	9664	$/CAP	NETH	FRANC	F147
		1980	D9	P86	10757	$/CAP	LIBYA	NETH	F147
V2	TELEPHONES P. TSD. POPULATION	1970	D10	P97	454	1/TSD CAP	NEWZ	SWITZ	----
		1975	D10	P96	575	1/TSD CAP	NEWZ	SWITZ	----
		1980	D10	P96	686	1/TSD CAP	DENMA	SWITZ	----
V3	INFANT MORTALITY RATE	1980	D1	P8	10.4	1/TSD	FRANC	AULIA	----
V4	PHYSICIANS P. MIL. POPULATION	1975	D9	P86	1723	1/MIL	NORWY	DENMA	F147
		1979	D8	P76	1819	1/MIL	AULIA	USA	F147
V5	ADULT LITERACY	------	----	----	-----	-----	-------	-------	----
V6	DURATION OF SCHOOLING	1970	D10	P98	12.0	YR	UNKI	USA	F4
		1975	D10	P95	11.4	YR	ROMA	FINLA	----
		1980	D10	P90	11.4	YR	BELGI	FRANC	----
V7	STUDENT ENROLLMENT RATIO	1970	D10	P99	34.6	%	GDR	USA	----
		1975	D10	P99	39.3	%	GDR	USA	----
		1980	D10	P97	36.6	%	LEBA	SWEDN	----
V8	SHARE OF AGRICULTURAL LABOR	1971	D2	P12	7.7	%	NETH	ISRA	F68
		1975	D2	P16	6.7	%	ISRA	AULIA	F68
		1980	D2	P13	5.7	%	SWEDN	ISRA	F68
V9	SHARE OF INDUSTRIAL LABOR	1971	D6	P51	33.7	%	CUBA	SOUAF	F68
		1975	D5	P49	31.8	%	SYRIA	VENE	F68
		1980	D5	P44	29.8	%	SRILA	ISRA	F68
V10	SHARE OF SERVICE LABOR	1971	D10	P93	44.8	%	UNKI	USA	F68
		1975	D10	P89	46.1	%	JAPAN	KUWAI	F68
		1980	D10	P94	49.1	%	SINGA	USA	F68
V11	SHARE OF ACADEMIC LABOR	1971	D9	P88	13.9	%	NEWZ	NETH	F68
		1975	D9	P83	15.1	%	USA	FRANC	F68
		1980	D9	P84	15.4	%	NEWZ	SWITZ	F68
V12	SHARE OF SELF-EMPLOYED LABOR	1971	D2	P15	7.8	%	USA	UNKI	F68
V13	MILITARY EXPENDITURES	1970	D9	P88	4.069	TSD MIL $	NETH	JAPAN	----
		1975	D9	P89	4.080	TSD MIL $	SWEDN	INDIA	----
		1980	D9	P90	4.655	TSD MIL $	INDIA	NETH	----

V14	MILITARY MANPOWER	1970	D7	P67	95	TSD CAP	AFGHA	IRAQ	----
		1975	D7	P61	77	TSD CAP	MALAY	ALGER	----
		1980	D7	P65	80	TSD CAP	BANGL	MALAY	----
V15	MEN AT AGE 20 - 30	1971	D8	P73	1742	TSD CAP	SOUAF	ARGE	F22
		1975	D8	P75	2039	TSD CAP	YUGO	ARGE	F22
		1980	D8	P70	2236	TSD CAP	ETHIA	BURMA	F22
V16	POPULATION	1970	D8	P76	21.32	MIL CAP	COLO	SOUAF	F22
		1975	D8	P77	22.70	MIL CAP	ZAIRE	COLO	F22
		1980	D8	P76	24.04	MIL CAP	YUGO	ZAIRE	F22
V17	GROSS DOMESTIC PRODUCT	1970	D10	P92	171.667	TSD MIL $	SPAIN	ITALY	----
		1975	D10	P92	219.377	TSD MIL $	BRAZI	ITALY	----
		1980	D10	P92	258.596	TSD MIL $	SPAIN	BRAZI	----
V18	SHARE IN WORLD IMPORTS	1970	D10	P93	40.246	1/TSD	USSR	NETH	F49
		1975	D10	P93	37.521	1/TSD	BELGI	NETH	F49
		1980	D10	P92	28.876	1/TSD	SWITZ	USSR	F49
V19	SHARE IN WORLD EXPORTS	1970	D10	P95	51.387	1/TSD	ITALY	FRANC	F30
		1975	D10	P93	37.298	1/TSD	SAUDI	USSR	F30
		1980	D10	P92	32.628	1/TSD	BELGI	NETH	F30
V20	GDP SHARE OF IMPORTS	1970	D4	P40	16.1	%	BOLI	IRAN	F49
		1975	D4	P40	20.6	%	SOUAF	HAITI	F49
		1980	D5	P44	22.7	%	DOMI	NEWZ	F49
V21	GDP SHARE OF EXPORTS	1970	D7	P64	19.4	%	KENYA	AURIA	F30
		1975	D6	P57	19.8	%	TUNIS	AURIA	F30
		1980	D7	P65	24.9	%	MALAW	SWEDN	F30
V22	EXPORT PARTNER CONCENTRATION	1970	D10	P96	65.4	%	PANA	IRE	----
		1975	D10	P96	65.7	%	SOMA	TRITO	----
		1980	D10	P96	63.1	%	TRITO	DOMI	----
V23	TOTAL DEBT AS % OF GDP	------	----	----	----- -----		-------	-------	
V24	SHARE OF NEW FOREIGN PATENTS	1970	D7	P61	95	%	CHILE	COLO	----
		1975	D7	P69	94	%	ZAIRE	DOMI	----
		1980	D7	P72	94	%	TURKY	MALAW	----
V25	FOREIGN PROPERTY AS % OF GDP	------	----	----	----- -----		-------	-------	----
V26	GNP SHARE OF DEVELOPMENT AID	1970	D8	P73	0.41	%	UNKI	BELGI	----
		1975	D5	P50	0.54	%	NEWZ	DENMA	----
		1980	D5	P49	0.43	%	UNKI	GFR	----
V27	SHARE IN NOBEL PRIZE WINNERS	1970-79	D9	P90	1.3	%	ARGE	FRANC	----
V28	GDP SHARE OF MANUFACTURING	1970	D8	P71	20.4	%	ECUA	NICA	----
		1975	D7	P68	19.2	%	ELSA	IRE	----
		1980	D7	P68	19.5	%	SRILA	GREC	----
V29	EXPORT SHARE OF MANUFACTURES	------	----	----	----- -----		-------	-------	----
V30	LACK OF CIVIL LIBERTIES	1975	D1	P7	1		BELGI	COSTA	----
		1980	D1	P7	1		BELGI	COSTA	----
V31	LACK OF POLITICAL RIGHTS	1975	D1	P8	1		BELGI	COSTA	----
		1980	D1	P8	1		BELGI	COSTA	----

V32	RIOTS	1970-74	D5	P43	1		CAME	CHAD	----
		1975-79	D6	P53	2		BENIN	CZECH	----
V33	PROTEST DEMONSTRATIONS	1970-74	D9	P83	20		LEBA	AULIA	----
		1975-79	D7	P69	8		ZAMBI	NEPAL	----
V34	POLITICAL STRIKES	1970-74	D10	P95	17		SPAIN	CHILE	----
		1975-79	D8	P78	3		TANZA	KORSO	----
V35	MEMBER OF THE NONALIGNED MMT.	1970	----	----	0		BULGA	CHILE	----
		1976	----	----	0		BULGA	CHILE	----
		1981	----	----	0		BURMA	CHILE	----
V36	MEMBER OF THE OPEC	1970	----	----	0		CAME	CENTR	----
		1975	----	----	0		CAME	CENTR	----
		1980	----	----	0		CAME	CENTR	----
V37	MEMBER OF THE OECD	1970	----	----	1		BELGI	DENMA	----
		1975	----	----	1		BELGI	DENMA	----
		1980	----	----	1		BELGI	DENMA	----
V38	MEMBER OF THE CMEA	1970	----	----	0		CAME	CENTR	----
		1975	----	----	0		CAME	CENTR	----
		1980	----	----	0		CAME	CENTR	----
V39	MEMBER OF THE WTO	1970	----	----	0		CAME	CENTR	----
		1975	----	----	0		CAME	CENTR	----
		1980	----	----	0		CAME	CENTR	----
V40	MEMBER OF THE NATO	1970	----	----	1		BELGI	DENMA	----
		1975	----	----	1		BELGI	DENMA	----
		1980	----	----	1		BELGI	DENMA	----
V41	GDP SHARE OF INVESTMENTS	1970	D6	P55	21.0	%	HONDU	ARGE	----
		1975	D6	P59	23.9	%	BOLI	PARA	----
		1980	D5	P44	22.7	%	NEWZ	SAUDI	----
V42	GDP SHARE OF AGRICULTURE	1970	D1	P8	3.7	%	BELGI	SWEDN	----
		1975	D2	P13	4.5	%	SWEDN	AURIA	----
		1980	D2	P15	3.9	%	JAPAN	FRANC	----
V43	GDP SHARE OF INDUSTRY	1970	D7	P63	31.7	%	NEWZ	MEXI	----
		1975	D6	P56	32.1	%	MAURA	URU	----
		1980	D6	P56	33.7	%	GUINE	USA	----
V44	GDP SHARE OF SERVICES	1970	D10	P96	64.6	%	PANA	DENMA	----
		1975	D10	P94	63.4	%	UNKI	USA	----
		1980	D10	P92	62.4	%	BELGI	JORDA	----
V45	HOMICIDES P. MIL. POPULATION	1970	D7	P61	20.3	1/MIL CAP	FINLA	BULGA	F149
		1975	D7	P66	27.0	1/MIL CAP	BULGA	URU	F153
		1980	D7	P64	20.6	1/MIL CAP	URU	SRILA	F150
V46	SUICIDES P. MIL. POPULATION	1970	D6	P60	113.2	1/MIL CAP	POLA	USA	F147
		1975	D6	P61	123.7	1/MIL CAP	POLA	USA	F150
		1980	D6	P58	139.7	1/MIL CAP	BULGA	YUGO	F150

V47	IMPORT PARTNERS	1970	R1	USA	71.1	%	BRAZI	CHILE	----
		1970	R2	UNKI	5.3	%	AULIA	ISRA	----
		1970	R3	JAPAN	4.2	%	BRAZI	COLO	----
		1980	R1	USA	70.1	%	BRAZI	CHILE	----
		1980	R2	JAPAN	4.1	%	BANGL	CENTR	----
		1980	R3	SAUDI	3.6	%	BRAZI	INDO	----
V48	EXPORT PARTNERS	1970	R1	USA	65.4	%	BURU	COLO	----
		1970	R2	UNKI	8.9	%	AFGHA	GHANA	----
		1970	R3	JAPAN	4.7	%	BOLI	NEWZ	----
		1980	R1	USA	63.1	%	CAME	COLO	----
		1980	R2	JAPAN	5.9	%	ZAMBI	ECUA	----
		1980	R3	UNKI	4.0	%	BOLI	FINLA	----
V49	PATENT SUPPLIERS	1970	R1	USA	18663		BRAZI	CHILE	----
		1970	R2	GFR	2096		BURU	CHILE	----
		1970	R3	UNKI	1985		ZAMBI	CHILE	----
		1980	R1	USA	13386		BURU	CHILE	----
		1980	R2	JAPAN	1864		USA	GFR	----
		1980	R3	GFR	1835		VENE	COLO	----
V50	PROVENANCE OF FOREIGN FIRMS	1980	R1	USA	65.6	%	BRAZI	CHILE	----
		1980	R2	UNKI	23.2	%	BOLI	CHILE	----
		1980	R3	GFR	2.6	%	ARGE	CHILE	----
V51	FILM SUPPLIERS	------	----	----	----- -----		-------	-------	----

CENTRAL AFRICAN REPUBLIC (CENTR)

V1	INCOME PER CAPITA	------	----	----	----- -----		-------	-------	----
V2	TELEPHONES P. TSD. POPULATION	------	----	----	----- -----		-------	-------	----
V3	INFANT MORTALITY RATE	1980	D9	P88	154.3	1/TSD	YESO	CHAD	F5
V4	PHYSICIANS P. MIL. POPULATION	1975	D2	P15	47	1/MIL	UGADA	IVORY	----
		1980	D1	P9	42	1/MIL	NEPAL	MALI	----
V5	ADULT LITERACY	1980	D3	P29	33.0	%	BENIN	MOZAM	F21
V6	DURATION OF SCHOOLING	1970	D3	P27	4.4	YR	YESO	IVORY	----
		1975	D3	P29	5.2	YR	BANGL	BURMA	----
		1980	D3	P20	5.6	YR	MALAW	RWAN	----
V7	STUDENT ENROLLMENT RATIO	1970	D1	P8	0.1	%	BENIN	CHINA	----
		1975	D2	P11	0.4	%	RWAN	MALAW	----
		1980	D2	P15	0.9	%	SIERA	KENYA	----
V8	SHARE OF AGRICULTURAL LABOR	------	----	----	----- -----		-------	-------	----
V9	SHARE OF INDUSTRIAL LABOR	------	----	----	----- -----		-------	-------	----

V10 SHARE OF SERVICE LABOR	------	---- ----	----- -----		-------	-------	----
V11 SHARE OF ACADEMIC LABOR	------	---- ----	----- -----		-------	-------	----
V12 SHARE OF SELF-EMPLOYED LABOR	------	---- ----	----- -----		-------	-------	----
V13 MILITARY EXPENDITURES	------	---- ----	----- -----		-------	-------	----
V14 MILITARY MANPOWER	1970	D1 P4	2	TSD CAP	BENIN	COSTA	----
	1975	D1 P6	3	TSD CAP	BENIN	GABON	----
	1980	D1 P9	4	TSD CAP	BENIN	MALAW	----
V15 MEN AT AGE 20 - 30	1975	D1 P8	112	TSD CAP	LIBE	YESO	----
V16 POPULATION	1975	D2 P11	2.05	MIL CAP	COSTA	JAMAI	----
	1980	D2 P12	2.33	MIL CAP	COSTA	SINGA	----
V17 GROSS DOMESTIC PRODUCT	------	---- ----	----- -----		-------	-------	----
V18 SHARE IN WORLD IMPORTS	1970	D1 P4	0.102	1/TSD	YENO	SOMA	F121
	1975	D1 P3	0.076	1/TSD	BURU	RWAN	F121
	1980	D1 P2	0.039	1/TSD	CHAD	LAOS	F121
V19 SHARE IN WORLD EXPORTS	1970	D1 P9	0.099	1/TSD	CHAD	CONGO	F121
	1975	D1 P7	0.055	1/TSD	UPVO	CHAD	F121
	1980	D1 P8	0.058	1/TSD	UPVO	SOMA	F121
V20 GDP SHARE OF IMPORTS	1970	D6 P53	19.0	%	MADA	NEWZ	F121
	1975	D3 P30	18.3	%	NIGRA	CHILE	F121
	1980	D1 P9	10.2	%	USA	MEXI	F121
V21 GDP SHARE OF EXPORTS	1970	D6 P56	17.3	%	SRILA	SENE	F121
	1975	D4 P34	12.8	%	NIGER	PORTU	F121
	1980	D4 P33	14.4	%	CHAD	DOMI	F121
V22 EXPORT PARTNER CONCENTRATION	1970	D9 P84	49.7	%	KORSO	ETHIA	F121
	1975	D9 P80	42.0	%	COSTA	EGYPT	F121
	1980	D10 P91	53.4	%	HONDU	SYRIA	F121
V23 TOTAL DEBT AS % OF GDP	1980	D3 P26	22.8	%	PARA	GREC	----
V24 SHARE OF NEW FOREIGN PATENTS	------	---- ----	----- -----		-------	-------	----
V25 FOREIGN PROPERTY AS % OF GDP	1971	D9 P87	23.7	%	GUINE	HONDU	----
	1975	D9 P85	16.0	%	SENE	GUINE	----
	1978	D9 ----	11.6	%	INDO	TOGO	----
V26 GNP SHARE OF DEVELOPMENT AID	------	---- ----	----- -----		-------	-------	----
V27 SHARE IN NOBEL PRIZE WINNERS	1970-79	D5 P45	0.0	%	CAME	CHAD	----
V28 GDP SHARE OF MANUFACTURING	1970	D2 P14	7.8	%	CHAD	SUDAN	----
	1975	D3 P24	8.7	%	CHAD	INDO	----
	1980	D3 P23	6.2	%	CONGO	TOGO	----
V29 EXPORT SHARE OF MANUFACTURES	1970	D8 P77	44.3	%	LAOS	JAMAI	----
	1975	D7 P71	23.7	%	ARGE	GUATE	----
	1980	D7 P65	26.2	%	TURKY	COSTA	----
V30 LACK OF CIVIL LIBERTIES	1975	D10 P93	7		BURU	CHAD	----
	1980	D8 P74	6		CAME	CHAD	----

V31	LACK OF POLITICAL RIGHTS	1975	D9	P88	7		BURU	CHILE	----
		1980	D9	P90	7		BURU	CHAD	----
V32	RIOTS	1970-74	D2	P19	0		BULGA	CONGO	----
		1975-79	D9	P84	10		GFR	JAMAI	----
V33	PROTEST DEMONSTRATIONS	1970-74	D2	P15	0		CAME	CONGO	----
		1975-79	D4	P32	1		YESO	CUBA	----
V34	POLITICAL STRIKES	1970-74	D3	P29	0		BURU	CHAD	----
		1975-79	D8	P73	2		BURMA	CHILE	----
V35	MEMBER OF THE NONALIGNED MMT.	1970	----	----	1		CAME	CHAD	----
		1976	----	----	1		CAME	CHAD	----
		1981	----	----	1		CAME	CHAD	----
V36	MEMBER OF THE OPEC	1970	----	----	0		CANA	CHAD	----
		1975	----	----	0		CANA	CHAD	----
		1980	----	----	0		CANA	CHAD	----
V37	MEMBER OF THE OECD	1970	----	----	0		CAME	CHAD	----
		1975	----	----	0		CAME	CHAD	----
		1980	----	----	0		CAME	CHAD	----
V38	MEMBER OF THE CMEA	1970	----	----	0		CANA	CHAD	----
		1975	----	----	0		CANA	CHAD	----
		1980	----	----	0		CANA	CHAD	----
V39	MEMBER OF THE WTO	1970	----	----	0		CANA	CHAD	----
		1975	----	----	0		CANA	CHAD	----
		1980	----	----	0		CANA	CHAD	----
V40	MEMBER OF THE NATO	1970	----	----	0		CAME	CHAD	----
		1975	----	----	0		CAME	CHAD	----
		1980	----	----	0		CAME	CHAD	----
V41	GDP SHARE OF INVESTMENTS	1970	D5	P45	18.9 %		NICA	IRAN	----
		1975	D2	P18	15.1 %		HAITI	MALI	----
		1980	D1	P3	7.0 %		GHANA	ANGO	----
V42	GDP SHARE OF AGRICULTURE	1970	D8	P77	33.4 %		KENYA	TOGO	----
		1975	D8	P75	35.4 %		KENYA	SIERA	----
		1980	D8	P78	35.8 %		PAPUA	LIBE	----
V43	GDP SHARE OF INDUSTRY	1970	D2	P15	15.7 %		SUDAN	JORDA	----
		1975	D2	P17	17.5 %		MOZAM	MADA	----
		1980	D1	P9	15.0 %		SUDAN	ETHIA	----
V44	GDP SHARE OF SERVICES	1970	D6	P60	50.9 %		JAMAI	IVORY	----
		1975	D6	P57	47.1 %		SENE	ARGE	----
		1980	D6	P59	49.2 %		TOGO	MOROC	----
V45	HOMICIDES P. MIL. POPULATION	------	----	----	----- -----		-------	-------	----
V46	SUICIDES P. MIL. POPULATION	------	----	----	----- -----		-------	-------	----

V47 IMPORT PARTNERS	1970	R1	FRANC	58.3 %	CAME	CHAD	F121
	1970	R2	GFR	8.1 %	CAME	CHILE	F121
	1970	R3	USA	5.8 %	CAME	CONGO	F121
	1980	R1	FRANC	60.7 %	CAME	CONGO	F121
	1980	R2	JAPAN	7.2 %	CANA	COLO	F121
	1980	R3	NETH	3.6 %	BELGI	TOGO	F121
V48 EXPORT PARTNERS	1970	R1	FRANC	49.7 %	CAME	CHAD	F121
	1970	R2	ISRA	14.9 %	-------	-------	F121
	1970	R3	BELGI	12.1 %	NETH	FRANC	F140
	1980	R1	FRANC	53.4 %	-------	GABON	F121
	1980	R2	BELGI	14.9 %	ZAIRE	NETH	F140
	1980	R3	ISRA	8.1 %	-------	EGYPT	F121
V49 PATENT SUPPLIERS	------	----	----	----- -----	-------	-------	----
V50 PROVENANCE OF FOREIGN FIRMS	------	----	----	----- -----	-------	-------	----
V51 FILM SUPPLIERS	------	----	----	----- -----	-------	-------	----

CHAD (CHAD)

V1 INCOME PER CAPITA	------	----	----	----- -----	-------	-------	----
V2 TELEPHONES P. TSD. POPULATION	1970	D1	P7	1 1/TSD CAP	BURU	HAITI	----
	1975	D1	P5	1 1/TSD CAP	BURU	NEPAL	----
V3 INFANT MORTALITY RATE	1980	D9	P88	154.3 1/TSD	CENTR	ETHIA	F5
V4 PHYSICIANS P. MIL. POPULATION	1970	D1	P4	16 1/MIL	ETHIA	BURU	----
	1974	D1	P9	23 1/MIL	BURU	RWAN	----
V5 ADULT LITERACY	------	----	----	----- -----	-------	-------	----
V6 DURATION OF SCHOOLING	1970	D2	P11	2.5 YR	BURU	BENIN	----
	1975	D1	P9	2.5 YR	AFGHA	NEPAL	----
V7 STUDENT ENROLLMENT RATIO	1970	D1	P4	0.0 %	BHUTA	MAURA	----
	1975	D1	P6	0.2 %	NIGER	TANZA	----
V8 SHARE OF AGRICULTURAL LABOR	------	----	----	----- -----	-------	-------	----
V9 SHARE OF INDUSTRIAL LABOR	------	----	----	----- -----	-------	-------	----
V10 SHARE OF SERVICE LABOR	------	----	----	----- -----	-------	-------	----
V11 SHARE OF ACADEMIC LABOR	------	----	----	----- -----	-------	-------	----
V12 SHARE OF SELF-EMPLOYED LABOR	------	----	----	----- -----	-------	-------	----
V13 MILITARY EXPENDITURES	------	----	----	----- -----	-------	-------	----

V14	MILITARY MANPOWER	1970	D2	P19	7	TSD CAP	NICA	KENYA	----
		1975	D3	P24	11	TSD CAP	CAME	IRE	----
V15	MEN AT AGE 20 - 30	1972	D4	----	306	TSD CAP	MALI	TUNIS	F2
		1976	D3	P28	342	TSD CAP	MALAW	NIGER	F2
		1978	D3	----	430	TSD CAP	HAITI	BOLI	F2
V16	POPULATION	1970	D3	P28	3.64	MIL CAP	BURU	RWAN	----
		1975	D3	P29	4.03	MIL CAP	NORWY	RWAN	----
		1980	D3	P28	4.48	MIL CAP	BURU	SOMA	F35
V17	GROSS DOMESTIC PRODUCT	------	----	----	----- -----		-------	-------	----
V18	SHARE IN WORLD IMPORTS	1970	D2	P12	0.184	1/TSD	NIGER	BENIN	----
		1975	D1	P6	0.146	1/TSD	NIGER	HAITI	----
		1980	D1	P1	0.036	1/TSD	-------	CENTR	----
V19	SHARE IN WORLD EXPORTS	1970	D1	P7	0.096	1/TSD	RWAN	CENTR	----
		1975	D1	P7	0.055	1/TSD	CENTR	MALI	----
		1980	D1	P5	0.036	1/TSD	BURU	RWAN	----
V20	GDP SHARE OF IMPORTS	1970	D7	P68	22.6	%	SENE	KORSO	----
		1975	D7	P61	26.6	%	PORTU	FINLA	----
		1980	D2	P18	14.8	%	ANGO	INDO	----
V21	GDP SHARE OF EXPORTS	1970	D3	P29	11.1	%	BURU	CONGO	----
		1975	D3	P22	9.6	%	PAKI	PERU	----
		1980	D4	P32	14.2	%	ANGO	CENTR	----
V22	EXPORT PARTNER CONCENTRATION	1970	D10	P98	70.3	%	IRE	MEXI	----
V23	TOTAL DEBT AS % OF GDP	1980	D6	P60	42.6	%	TUNIS	ALGER	----
V24	SHARE OF NEW FOREIGN PATENTS	------	----	----	----- -----		-------	-------	----
V25	FOREIGN PROPERTY AS % OF GDP	1971	D5	P43	6.9	%	SRILA	IRAN	----
		1975	D5	P43	5.0	%	ARGE	BURU	----
		1978	D5	----	3.9	%	BOLI	SPAIN	----
V26	GNP SHARE OF DEVELOPMENT AID	------	----	----	----- -----		-------	-------	----
V27	SHARE IN NOBEL PRIZE WINNERS	1970-79	D5	P45	0.0	%	CENTR	CHILE	----
V28	GDP SHARE OF MANUFACTURING	1970	D2	P13	7.3	%	BURU	CENTR	----
		1975	D3	P22	8.6	%	PAPUA	CENTR	----
		1980	D2	P11	4.0	%	UGADA	LESO	----
V29	EXPORT SHARE OF MANUFACTURES	1970	D3	P23	1.9	%	KAMPU	LIBE	----
		1975	D5	P43	7.7	%	UPVO	KUWAI	----
V30	LACK OF CIVIL LIBERTIES	1975	D10	P93	7		CENTR	CHINA	----
		1980	D8	P74	6		CENTR	CUBA	----
V31	LACK OF POLITICAL RIGHTS	1975	D7	P63	6		CAME	EGYPT	----
		1980	D9	P90	7		CENTR	CONGO	----
V32	RIOTS	1970-74	D5	P43	1		CANA	COSTA	----
		1975-79	D5	P45	1		YUGO	CHILE	----
V33	PROTEST DEMONSTRATIONS	1970-74	D4	P37	1		BURMA	COSTA	----
		1975-79	D6	P54	4		BRAZI	PERU	----

V34	POLITICAL STRIKES	1970-74	D3	P29	0		CENTR	CHINA	----
		1975-79	D3	P29	0		CAME	CHINA	----
V35	MEMBER OF THE NONALIGNED MMT.	1970	----	----	1		CENTR	CONGO	----
		1976	----	----	1		CENTR	CONGO	----
		1981	----	----	1		CENTR	CONGO	----
V36	MEMBER OF THE OPEC	1970	----	----	0		CENTR	CHILE	----
		1975	----	----	0		CENTR	CHILE	----
		1980	----	----	0		CENTR	CHILE	----
V37	MEMBER OF THE OECD	1970	----	----	0		CENTR	CHILE	----
		1975	----	----	0		CENTR	CHILE	----
		1980	----	----	0		CENTR	CHILE	----
V38	MEMBER OF THE CMEA	1970	----	----	0		CENTR	CHILE	----
		1975	----	----	0		CENTR	CHILE	----
		1980	----	----	0		CENTR	CHILE	----
V39	MEMBER OF THE WTO	1970	----	----	0		CENTR	CHILE	----
		1975	----	----	0		CENTR	CHILE	----
		1980	----	----	0		CENTR	CHILE	----
V40	MEMBER OF THE NATO	1970	----	----	0		CENTR	CHILE	----
		1975	----	----	0		CENTR	CHILE	----
		1980	----	----	0		CENTR	CHILE	----
V41	GDP SHARE OF INVESTMENTS	1970	D2	P16	13.4 %		UGADA	INDO	----
		1975	D4	P32	18.1 %		HONDU	KENYA	----
		1980	D1	P10	13.2 %		BOLI	KUWAI	----
V42	GDP SHARE OF AGRICULTURE	1970	D9	P90	48.6 %		INDIA	MALAW	----
		1975	D10	P93	48.4 %		GHANA	RWAN	----
		1980	D10	P96	57.3 %		BURU	NEPAL	----
V43	GDP SHARE OF INDUSTRY	1970	D1	P4	9.6 %		BURU	YENO	----
		1975	D1	P9	12.7 %		SOMA	LESO	----
		1980	D1	P2	8.4 %		-------	BENIN	----
V44	GDP SHARE OF SERVICES	1970	D3	P28	41.8 %		TANZA	SUDAN	----
		1975	D3	P27	38.9 %		UPVO	NIGER	----
		1980	D2	P19	34.3 %		BANGL	LIBE	----
V45	HOMICIDES P. MIL. POPULATION	------	----	----	----- -----		-------	-------	----
V46	SUICIDES P. MIL. POPULATION	------	----	----	----- -----		-------	-------	----
V47	IMPORT PARTNERS	1970	R1	FRANC	39.8 %		CENTR	CONGO	----
		1970	R2	NIGRA	10.4 %		-------	-------	----
		1970	R3	CONGO	9.9 %		-------	-------	----
V48	EXPORT PARTNERS	1970	R1	FRANC	70.3 %		CENTR	GFR	----
		1970	R2	ZAIRE	11.8 %		-------	-------	----
		1970	R3	CONGO	5.2 %		-------	-------	----
V49	PATENT SUPPLIERS	------	----	----	----- -----		-------	-------	----
V50	PROVENANCE OF FOREIGN FIRMS	------	----	----	----- -----		-------	-------	----
V51	FILM SUPPLIERS	------	----	----	----- -----		-------	-------	----

CHILE (CHILE)

V1	INCOME PER CAPITA	1970	D7	P65	2194 $/CAP	URU	SINGA	----
		1975	D7	P64	1801 $/CAP	MEXI	BRAZI	----
		1980	D7	P65	2378 $/CAP	PORTU	ARGE	----
V2	TELEPHONES P. TSD. POPULATION	1970	D7	P66	40 1/TSD CAP	VENE	USSR	----
		1975	D6	P57	41 1/TSD CAP	KORSO	JAMAI	----
		1980	D6	P52	50 1/TSD CAP	MALAY	SAUDI	----
V3	INFANT MORTALITY RATE	1980	D4	P32	33.0 1/TSD	JAMAI	ARGE	----
V4	PHYSICIANS P. MIL. POPULATION	1977	D6	----	618 1/MIL	TRITO	PERU	----
V5	ADULT LITERACY	1970	D9	P79	89.0 %	ISRA	SPAIN	----
V6	DURATION OF SCHOOLING	1970	D9	P85	10.4 YR	BULGA	DENMA	----
		1975	D10	P97	11.5 YR	NORWY	USA	----
		1980	D10	P93	11.5 YR	USA	NETH	----
V7	STUDENT ENROLLMENT RATIO	1970	D7	P69	9.4 %	BOLI	SWITZ	----
		1975	D8	P73	16.5 %	URU	POLA	----
		1980	D6	P57	10.9 %	COLO	ROMA	----
V8	SHARE OF AGRICULTURAL LABOR	1970	D5	P42	22.7 %	FINLA	VENE	F67
		1981	D4	P44	15.4 %	VENE	IRE	----
V9	SHARE OF INDUSTRIAL LABOR	1981	D8	P74	36.5 %	NEWZ	JAPAN	----
V10	SHARE OF SERVICE LABOR	1981	D8	P72	41.5 %	AURIA	COLO	----
V11	SHARE OF ACADEMIC LABOR	1981	D5	P35	6.7 %	SPAIN	MALAY	----
V12	SHARE OF SELF-EMPLOYED LABOR	1981	D1	P3	0.7 %	-------	HUNGA	----
V13	MILITARY EXPENDITURES	1975	D7	P66	1.233 TSD MIL $	PAKI	KUWAI	----
		1980	D8	P74	1.950 TSD MIL $	UNARE	SWITZ	----
V14	MILITARY MANPOWER	1970	D6	P58	70 TSD CAP	SAUDI	JORDA	----
		1975	D7	P67	110 TSD CAP	BANGL	NETH	----
		1980	D7	P70	116 TSD CAP	NETH	MOROC	----
V15	MEN AT AGE 20 - 30	1970	D5	P48	673 TSD CAP	SWEDN	UGADA	----
		1975	D6	P60	862 TSD CAP	BELGI	HUNGA	F46
		1980	D5	P49	1007 TSD CAP	HUNGA	NETH	----
V16	POPULATION	1970	D6	P55	9.37 MIL CAP	PORTU	IRAQ	----
		1975	D6	P58	10.20 MIL CAP	GHANA	HUNGA	----
		1980	D6	P57	11.10 MIL CAP	HUNGA	GHANA	----
V17	GROSS DOMESTIC PRODUCT	1970	D7	P65	20.557 TSD MIL $	COLO	GREC	----
		1975	D6	P58	18.373 TSD MIL $	PORTU	LIBYA	----
		1980	D6	P60	26.391 TSD MIL $	PAKI	KUWAI	----
V18	SHARE IN WORLD IMPORTS	1970	D6	P57	2.856 1/TSD	TURKY	INDO	----
		1975	D5	P47	1.472 1/TSD	LEBA	VISO	----
		1980	D6	P55	2.498 1/TSD	EGYPT	PAKI	----

V19 SHARE IN WORLD EXPORTS	1970	D7	P66	3.934	1/TSD	NEWZ	NIGRA	----
	1975	D6	P54	1.771	1/TSD	COLO	MOROC	----
	1980	D6	P57	2.340	1/TSD	PORTU	GREC	----
V20 GDP SHARE OF IMPORTS	1970	D2	P18	11.6	%	EGYPT	COLO	----
	1975	D4	P31	18.5	%	CENTR	PAKI	----
	1980	D4	P33	18.7	%	MOZAM	MADA	----
V21 GDP SHARE OF EXPORTS	1970	D5	P47	15.0	%	SUDAN	GUATE	----
	1975	D7	P62	21.5	%	TOGO	GFR	----
	1980	D5	P45	17.0	%	PHILI	FRANC	----
V22 EXPORT PARTNER CONCENTRATION	1970	D2	P13	15.2	%	USSR	YUGO	F122
	1975	D2	P14	14.3	%	BURMA	SUDAN	F122
	1980	D1	P5	11.1	%	UNKI	BANGL	F122
V23 TOTAL DEBT AS % OF GDP	1980	D7	P63	43.9	%	ALGER	HUNGA	----
V24 SHARE OF NEW FOREIGN PATENTS	1970	D6	P58	94	%	MEXI	CANA	----
	1975	D5	P43	88	%	ECUA	GUATE	----
	1980	D6	P57	91	%	BRAZI	ELSA	----
V25 FOREIGN PROPERTY AS % OF GDP	1971	D5	P46	7.7	%	IRAN	ARGE	----
	1975	D5	P49	5.5	%	KUWAI	MEXI	----
	1978	D8	----	9.4	%	VENE	KENYA	----
V26 GNP SHARE OF DEVELOPMENT AID	------	----	----	-----	-----	-------	-------	
V27 SHARE IN NOBEL PRIZE WINNERS	1970-79	D5	P45	0.0	%	CHAD	CHINA	----
V28 GDP SHARE OF MANUFACTURING	1970	D9	P87	25.5	%	SPAIN	USA	----
	1975	D8	P72	20.3	%	SRILA	COLO	----
	1980	D8	P75	21.5	%	UNKI	SWEDN	----
V29 EXPORT SHARE OF MANUFACTURES	1970	D4	P31	4.0	%	UPVO	IRAN	----
	1975	D5	P47	8.3	%	SYRIA	NIGER	----
	1980	D4	P34	8.7	%	BENIN	PANA	----
V30 LACK OF CIVIL LIBERTIES	1975	D6	P54	5		BURMA	ETHIA	----
	1980	D6	P52	5		BHUTA	CHINA	----
V31 LACK OF POLITICAL RIGHTS	1975	D9	P88	7		CENTR	CHINA	----
	1980	D7	P67	6		CAME	CHINA	----
V32 RIOTS	1970-74	D10	P95	55		ITALY	GREC	----
	1975-79	D5	P45	1		CHAD	HONDU	----
V33 PROTEST DEMONSTRATIONS	1970-74	D7	P70	7		VENE	GUATE	----
	1975-79	D9	P82	18		ARGE	IRE	----
V34 POLITICAL STRIKES	1970-74	D10	P96	24		CANA	LEBA	----
	1975-79	D8	P73	2		CENTR	COSTA	----
V35 MEMBER OF THE NONALIGNED MMT.	1970	----	----	0		CANA	CHINA	----
	1976	----	----	0		CANA	CHINA	----
	1981	----	----	0		CANA	CHINA	----
V36 MEMBER OF THE OPEC	1970	----	----	0		CHAD	CHINA	----
	1975	----	----	0		CHAD	CHINA	----
	1980	----	----	0		CHAD	CHINA	----

V37	MEMBER OF THE OECD	1970	----	----	0		CHAD	CHINA	----
		1975	----	----	0		CHAD	CHINA	----
		1980	----	----	0		CHAD	CHINA	----
V38	MEMBER OF THE CMEA	1970	----	----	0		CHAD	CHINA	----
		1975	----	----	0		CHAD	CHINA	----
		1980	----	----	0		CHAD	CHINA	----
V39	MEMBER OF THE WTO	1970	----	----	0		CHAD	CHINA	----
		1975	----	----	0		CHAD	CHINA	----
		1980	----	----	0		CHAD	CHINA	----
V40	MEMBER OF THE NATO	1970	----	----	0		CHAD	CHINA	----
		1975	----	----	0		CHAD	CHINA	----
		1980	----	----	0		CHAD	CHINA	----
V41	GDP SHARE OF INVESTMENTS	1970	D4	P33	16.5 %		SAUDI	LIBYA	----
		1975	D2	P13	13.1 %		MADA	SAUDI	----
		1980	D4	P31	20.7 %		BRAZI	SPAIN	----
V42	GDP SHARE OF AGRICULTURE	1970	D2	P20	6.8 %		JAMAI	AURIA	----
		1975	D3	P22	6.6 %		GABON	IRAQ	----
		1980	D3	P27	7.4 %		SPAIN	IRAQ	----
V43	GDP SHARE OF INDUSTRY	1970	D9	P85	41.4 %		YUGO	LIBE	----
		1975	D8	P79	38.1 %		FRANC	BELGI	----
		1980	D8	P72	37.6 %		JAMAI	ECUA	----
V44	GDP SHARE OF SERVICES	1970	D7	P66	51.8 %		BOLI	MADA	----
		1975	D9	P81	55.3 %		LESO	JAMAI	----
		1980	D8	P77	55.0 %		JAMAI	SYRIA	----
V45	HOMICIDES P. MIL. POPULATION	------	----	----	----- -----		-------	-------	----
V46	SUICIDES P. MIL. POPULATION	------	----	----	----- -----		-------	-------	----
V47	IMPORT PARTNERS	1970	R1	USA	37.0 %		CANA	COLO	----
		1970	R2	GFR	12.4 %		CENTR	COLO	----
		1970	R3	ARGE	10.0 %		PARA	URU	----
		1980	R1	USA	25.4 %		CANA	COLO	----
		1980	R2	BRAZI	8.4 %		ARGE	-------	----
		1980	R3	JAPAN	8.1 %		CAME	DOMI	----
V48	EXPORT PARTNERS	1970	R1	NETH	15.2 %		-------	ARGE	F122
		1970	R2	USA	14.4 %		BOLI	ELSA	F122
		1970	R3	UNKI	12.5 %		BURU	LIBYA	F122
		1980	R1	JAPAN	11.1 %		AULIA	INDO	F122
		1980	R2	BRAZI	10.0 %		ARGE	CONGO	F122
		1980	R3	USA	10.0 %		ARGE	CONGO	F122
V49	PATENT SUPPLIERS	1970	R1	USA	389		CANA	COLO	----
		1970	R2	GFR	167		CANA	CZECH	----
		1970	R3	UNKI	47		CANA	CUBA	----
		1978	R1	USA	210		CANA	COLO	----
		1978	R2	GFR	122		BURU	COSTA	----
		1978	R3	SWITZ	31		AURIA	ELSA	----

V50	PROVENANCE OF FOREIGN FIRMS	1980	R1	USA	51.2 %	CANA	COLO	----
		1980	R2	UNKI	16.8 %	CANA	COLO	----
		1980	R3	GFR	9.6 %	CANA	COLO	----
V51	FILM SUPPLIERS	------	----	----	----- -----	-------	-------	----

CHINA, PEOPLE'S REPUBLIC OF (CHINA)

V1	INCOME PER CAPITA	------	----	----	----- -----	-------	-------	----
V2	TELEPHONES P. TSD. POPULATION	1980	D2	P14	4 1/TSD CAP	SUDAN	INDIA	----
V3	INFANT MORTALITY RATE	1980	D5	P41	49.0 1/TSD	LEBA	ALBA	F5
V4	PHYSICIANS P. MIL. POPULATION	1980	D5	P49	446 1/MIL	SYRIA	IRAQ	----
V5	ADULT LITERACY	1982	D6	----	65.5 %	JORDA	BURMA	----
V6	DURATION OF SCHOOLING	1970	D5	P44	6.8 YR	ELSA	MADA	F4
		1975	D7	P63	9.1 YR	MONGO	MEXI	----
		1980	D4	P34	7.8 YR	HONDU	IRAN	----
V7	STUDENT ENROLLMENT RATIO	1970	D1	P8	0.1 %	CENTR	YESO	----
		1975	D2	P14	0.6 %	MALAW	MALI	----
		1980	D2	P18	1.2 %	HAITI	YENO	----
V8	SHARE OF AGRICULTURAL LABOR	------	----	----	----- -----	-------	-------	----
V9	SHARE OF INDUSTRIAL LABOR	------	----	----	----- -----	-------	-------	----
V10	SHARE OF SERVICE LABOR	------	----	----	----- -----	-------	-------	----
V11	SHARE OF ACADEMIC LABOR	------	----	----	----- -----	-------	-------	----
V12	SHARE OF SELF-EMPLOYED LABOR	------	----	----	----- -----	-------	-------	----
V13	MILITARY EXPENDITURES	------	----	----	----- -----	-------	-------	----
V14	MILITARY MANPOWER	1975	D10	P100	4300 TSD CAP	USSR	-------	F1
V15	MEN AT AGE 20 - 30	1982	D10	----	85637 TSD CAP	INDIA	-------	----
V16	POPULATION	1970	D10	P100	825.81 MIL CAP	INDIA	-------	F4
		1975	D10	P100	933.00 MIL CAP	INDIA	-------	----
		1980	D10	P100	1002.80 MIL CAP	INDIA	-------	----
V17	GROSS DOMESTIC PRODUCT	------	----	----	----- -----	-------	-------	----
V18	SHARE IN WORLD IMPORTS	1970	D8	P76	7.019 1/TSD	MEXI	SINGA	F30
		1975	D8	P77	8.240 1/TSD	KORSO	SOUAF	F30
		1980	D9	P83	9.532 1/TSD	MEXI	DENMA	F30

V19 SHARE IN WORLD EXPORTS	1970	D8	P75	7.205	1/TSD	SOUAF	FINLA	F30
	1975	D8	P77	8.285	1/TSD	NORWY	AURIA	F30
	1980	D8	P79	9.154	1/TSD	KORSO	NORWY	F30
V20 GDP SHARE OF IMPORTS	1980	D1	P4	6.9	%	ARGE	GHANA	F30
V21 GDP SHARE OF EXPORTS	1980	D1	P9	6.4	%	BANGL	BRAZI	F30
V22 EXPORT PARTNER CONCENTRATION	------	----	----	-----	-----	-------	-------	----
V23 TOTAL DEBT AS % OF GDP	------	----	----	-----	-----	-------	-------	----
V24 SHARE OF NEW FOREIGN PATENTS	------	----	----	-----	-----	-------	-------	----
V25 FOREIGN PROPERTY AS % OF GDP	------	----	----	-----	-----	-------	-------	----
V26 GNP SHARE OF DEVELOPMENT AID	------	----	----	-----	-----	-------	-------	----
V27 SHARE IN NOBEL PRIZE WINNERS	1970-79	D5	P45	0.0	%	CHILE	COLO	----
V28 GDP SHARE OF MANUFACTURING	1980	D10	P99	44.1	%	PORTU	-------	----
V29 EXPORT SHARE OF MANUFACTURES	------	----	----	-----	-----	-------	-------	----
V30 LACK OF CIVIL LIBERTIES	1975	D10	P93	7		CHAD	CUBA	----
	1980	D6	P52	5		CHILE	EGYPT	----
V31 LACK OF POLITICAL RIGHTS	1975	D9	P88	7		CHILE	CUBA	----
	1980	D7	P67	6		CHILE	CUBA	----
V32 RIOTS	1970-74	D8	P73	7		THAI	GUATE	----
	1975-79	D7	P65	4		TAIWA	EGYPT	----
V33 PROTEST DEMONSTRATIONS	1970-74	D9	P81	18		ETHIA	LEBA	----
	1975-79	D9	P88	34		POLA	PAKI	----
V34 POLITICAL STRIKES	1970-74	D3	P29	0		CHAD	COSTA	----
	1975-79	D3	P29	0		CHAD	CONGO	----
V35 MEMBER OF THE NONALIGNED MMT.	1970	----	----	0		CHILE	COLO	----
	1976	----	----	0		CHILE	COLO	F30
	1981	----	----	0		CHILE	COLO	----
V36 MEMBER OF THE OPEC	1970	----	----	0		CHILE	COLO	----
	1975	----	----	0		CHILE	COLO	----
	1980	----	----	0		CHILE	COLO	----
V37 MEMBER OF THE OECD	1970	----	----	0		CHILE	COLO	----
	1975	----	----	0		CHILE	COLO	----
	1980	----	----	0		CHILE	COLO	----
V38 MEMBER OF THE CMEA	1970	----	----	0		CHILE	COLO	----
	1975	----	----	0		CHILE	COLO	----
	1980	----	----	0		CHILE	COLO	----
V39 MEMBER OF THE WTO	1970	----	----	0		CHILE	COLO	----
	1975	----	----	0		CHILE	COLO	----
	1980	----	----	0		CHILE	COLO	----

V40	MEMBER OF THE NATO	1970	----	----	0		CHILE	COLO	----
		1975	----	----	0		CHILE	COLO	----
		1980	----	----	0		CHILE	COLO	----
V41	GDP SHARE OF INVESTMENTS	1980	D9	P86	30.6	%	PHILI	KORSO	----
V42	GDP SHARE OF AGRICULTURE	1980	D8	P75	32.9	%	KENYA	NIGER	----
V43	GDP SHARE OF INDUSTRY	------	----	----	-----	-----	-------	-------	----
V44	GDP SHARE OF SERVICES	------	----	----	-----	-----	-------	-------	----
V45	HOMICIDES P. MIL. POPULATION	------	----	----	-----	-----	-------	-------	----
V46	SUICIDES P. MIL. POPULATION	------	----	----	-----	-----	-------	-------	----
V47	IMPORT PARTNERS	------	----	----	-----	-----	-------	-------	----
V48	EXPORT PARTNERS	------	----	----	-----	-----	-------	-------	----
V49	PATENT SUPPLIERS	1970	R1	JAPAN	663		-------	IRAQ	----
		1970	R2	USA	388		AURIA	CONGO	----
		1970	R3	GDR	106		YUGO	-------	----
V50	PROVENANCE OF FOREIGN FIRMS	------	----	----	-----	-----	-------	-------	----
V51	FILM SUPPLIERS	------	----	----	-----	-----	-------	-------	----

COLOMBIA (COLO)

V1	INCOME PER CAPITA	1970	D5	P47	933	$/CAP	KORSO	PERU	----
		1975	D5	P46	1067	$/CAP	IVORY	TUNIS	----
		1980	D5	P48	1209	$/CAP	ECUA	DOMI	----
V2	TELEPHONES P. TSD. POPULATION	1970	D7	P64	38	1/TSD CAP	YUGO	JAMAI	----
		1975	D7	P60	52	1/TSD CAP	MEXI	VENE	----
		1980	D6	P56	64	1/TSD CAP	VENE	MEXI	----
V3	INFANT MORTALITY RATE	1980	D5	P45	59.4	1/TSD	MONGO	GUATE	F5
V4	PHYSICIANS P. MIL. POPULATION	1969	D6	P59	474	1/MIL	NICA	DOMI	----
		1977	D6	----	508	1/MIL	KORSO	DOMI	----
V5	ADULT LITERACY	1981	D9	P80	85.2	%	VINO	SRILA	----
V6	DURATION OF SCHOOLING	1970	D6	P51	7.4	YR	SYRIA	TURKY	----
		1975	D6	P55	8.5	YR	BOLI	LESO	----
		1980	D6	P50	9.0	YR	VENE	KENYA	F35
V7	STUDENT ENROLLMENT RATIO	1970	D6	P51	4.8	%	SOUAF	BRAZI	----
		1975	D6	P53	8.0	%	ELSA	NICA	----
		1980	D6	P56	10.6	%	IRAQ	CHILE	----

V8	SHARE OF AGRICULTURAL LABOR	1973	D5	----	35.3	%	JAMAI	IRAN	----
		1980	D6	P59	30.9	%	YUGO	MEXI	F46
V9	SHARE OF INDUSTRIAL LABOR	1973	D5	----	27.1	%	COSTA	SYRIA	----
		1980	D4	P28	25.4	%	PAKI	PARA	F46
V10	SHARE OF SERVICE LABOR	1973	D7	----	31.6	%	IRE	SPAIN	----
		1980	D8	P74	41.8	%	CHILE	AULIA	F46
V11	SHARE OF ACADEMIC LABOR	1973	D5	----	5.9	%	ECUA	MEXI	----
		1980	D1	P3	1.8	%	RWAN	BANGL	F46
V12	SHARE OF SELF-EMPLOYED LABOR	1973	D5	----	26.3	%	URU	TURKY	----
V13	MILITARY EXPENDITURES	1975	D6	P51	0.434	TSD MIL $	HUNGA	MEXI	F62
		1980	D6	P51	0.524	TSD MIL $	HUNGA	MEXI	----
V14	MILITARY MANPOWER	1970	D5	P49	45	TSD CAP	SOUAF	DENMA	----
		1975	D6	P52	50	TSD CAP	AURIA	ETHIA	----
		1980	D6	P59	60	TSD CAP	VENE	JORDA	----
V15	MEN AT AGE 20 - 30	1973	D8	----	1730	TSD CAP	ROMA	YUGO	F46
V16	POPULATION	1970	D8	P75	20.53	MIL CAP	YUGO	CANA	----
		1975	D8	P77	23.64	MIL CAP	CANA	SOUAF	----
		1980	D8	P77	27.09	MIL CAP	ZAIRE	ARGE	----
V17	GROSS DOMESTIC PRODUCT	1970	D7	P63	19.150	TSD MIL $	PHILI	CHILE	----
		1975	D7	P65	25.228	TSD MIL $	ALGER	PHILI	----
		1980	D7	P65	32.742	TSD MIL $	THAI	PHILI	----
V18	SHARE IN WORLD IMPORTS	1970	D6	P55	2.539	1/TSD	EGYPT	TURKY	----
		1975	D6	P50	1.645	1/TSD	TRITO	SYRIA	----
		1980	D6	P53	2.273	1/TSD	MOROC	EGYPT	----
V19	SHARE IN WORLD EXPORTS	1970	D6	P53	2.346	1/TSD	ISRA	EGYPT	----
		1975	D6	P53	1.672	1/TSD	EGYPT	CHILE	----
		1980	D6	P55	1.977	1/TSD	PERU	TRITO	----
V20	GDP SHARE OF IMPORTS	1970	D2	P19	11.7	%	CHILE	AFGHA	----
		1975	D2	P12	11.4	%	ETHIA	JAPAN	----
		1980	D2	P17	14.0	%	ZAIRE	ANGO	----
V21	GDP SHARE OF EXPORTS	1970	D3	P23	10.2	%	HAITI	PANA	----
		1975	D3	P26	11.2	%	GREC	JAPAN	----
		1980	D3	P27	11.8	%	PAKI	JAPAN	----
V22	EXPORT PARTNER CONCENTRATION	1970	D7	P70	36.8	%	MOROC	EGYPT	----
		1975	D7	P67	32.0	%	POLA	GDR	----
		1980	D6	P53	27.1	%	KORSO	VENE	----
V23	TOTAL DEBT AS % OF GDP	1980	D3	P21	20.8	%	SYRIA	HAITI	----
V24	SHARE OF NEW FOREIGN PATENTS	1970	D7	P61	95	%	CANA	MOROC	----
		1975	D3	P30	80	%	SWEDN	ITALY	F19
		1980	D8	P80	97	%	PORTU	EGYPT	----
V25	FOREIGN PROPERTY AS % OF GDP	1971	D7	P64	11.5	%	KENYA	PERU	----
		1975	D7	P66	9.2	%	NIGRA	DOMI	----
		1978	D7	----	6.5	%	BRAZI	URU	----

V26	GNP SHARE OF DEVELOPMENT AID	------	----	----	----- -----		-------	-------	----
V27	SHARE IN NOBEL PRIZE WINNERS	1970-79	D5	P45	0.0 %	CHINA	CONGO	----
V28	GDP SHARE OF MANUFACTURING	1970	D7	P61	17.5 %	TURKY	DENMA	F16
		1975	D8	P74	20.6 %	CHILE	DOMI	F16
		1980	D8	P78	21.8 %	SWEDN	MALAY	F16
V29	EXPORT SHARE OF MANUFACTURES	1970	D4	P40	8.0 %	MADA	HONDU	----
		1975	D7	P63	20.6 %	SENE	TURKY	----
		1980	D6	P53	19.6 %	SRILA	ARGE	----
V30	LACK OF CIVIL LIBERTIES	1975	D2	P18	2	USA	DOMI	----
		1980	D3	P29	3	BRAZI	DOMI	----
V31	LACK OF POLITICAL RIGHTS	1975	D2	P20	2	ARGE	ELSA	----
		1980	D3	P21	2	VENE	DOMI	----
V32	RIOTS	1970-74	D7	P64	4	BURU	SUDAN	----
		1975-79	D9	P89	20	ISRA	FRANC	----
V33	PROTEST DEMONSTRATIONS	1970-74	D7	P64	5	BRAZI	INDO	----
		1975-79	D9	P87	24	LEBA	POLA	----
V34	POLITICAL STRIKES	1970-74	D9	P81	4	BOLI	JAPAN	----
		1975-79	D9	P83	6	BRAZI	ECUA	----
V35	MEMBER OF THE NONALIGNED MMT.	1970	----	----	0	CHINA	COSTA	----
		1976	----	----	0	CHINA	COSTA	----
		1981	----	----	0	CHINA	COSTA	----
V36	MEMBER OF THE OPEC	1970	----	----	0	CHINA	CONGO	----
		1975	----	----	0	CHINA	CONGO	----
		1980	----	----	0	CHINA	CONGO	----
V37	MEMBER OF THE OECD	1970	----	----	0	CHINA	CONGO	----
		1975	----	----	0	CHINA	CONGO	----
		1980	----	----	0	CHINA	CONGO	----
V38	MEMBER OF THE CMEA	1970	----	----	0	CHINA	CONGO	----
		1975	----	----	0	CHINA	CONGO	----
		1980	----	----	0	CHINA	CONGO	----
V39	MEMBER OF THE WTO	1970	----	----	0	CHINA	CONGO	----
		1975	----	----	0	CHINA	CONGO	----
		1980	----	----	0	CHINA	CONGO	----
V40	MEMBER OF THE NATO	1970	----	----	0	CHINA	CONGO	----
		1975	----	----	0	CHINA	CONGO	----
		1980	----	----	0	CHINA	CONGO	----
V41	GDP SHARE OF INVESTMENTS	1970	D6	P59	22.0 %	PHILI	MAURA	----
		1975	D3	P28	17.8 %	BENIN	SENE	----
		1980	D6	P59	25.7 %	ARGE	DOMI	----
V42	GDP SHARE OF AGRICULTURE	1970	D7	P66	28.6 %	ELSA	MAURA	F16
		1975	D7	P63	29.3 %	TURKY	HONDU	F16
		1980	D7	P64	27.6 %	MAURA	SRILA	F16

V43 GDP SHARE OF INDUSTRY	1970	D5	P48	26.6	%	DOMI	MOROC	F16
	1975	D5	P44	28.3	%	COSTA	PAPUA	F16
	1980	D5	P48	30.7	%	TURKY	NICA	F16
V44 GDP SHARE OF SERVICES	1970	D4	P39	44.8	%	MALAY	TOGO	F16
	1975	D4	P39	42.4	%	PARA	MALAY	F16
	1980	D4	P35	41.7	%	CONGO	BENIN	F16
V45 HOMICIDES P. MIL. POPULATION	1969	D10	P91	144.5	1/MIL CAP	USA	THAI	F154
	1975	D10	P91	183.0	1/MIL CAP	USA	NICA	F154
V46 SUICIDES P. MIL. POPULATION	1969	D2	P16	29.2	1/MIL CAP	COSTA	GUATE	F2
	1975	D2	P15	35.6	1/MIL CAP	GREC	SPAIN	F2
V47 IMPORT PARTNERS	1970	R1	USA	46.3	%	CHILE	COSTA	----
	1970	R2	GFR	8.6	%	CHILE	CONGO	----
	1970	R3	JAPAN	7.0	%	CANA	ECUA	----
	1980	R1	USA	39.5	%	CHILE	COSTA	----
	1980	R2	JAPAN	9.3	%	CENTR	COSTA	----
	1980	R3	GFR	7.2	%	BURMA	CONGO	----
V48 EXPORT PARTNERS	1970	R1	USA	36.8	%	CANA	COSTA	----
	1970	R2	GFR	14.3	%	BURU	COSTA	----
	1970	R3	NETH	5.5	%	BELGI	IRAQ	----
	1980	R1	USA	27.1	%	CANA	COSTA	----
	1980	R2	GFR	18.8	%	BRAZI	HONDU	----
	1980	R3	VENE	7.1	%	DOMI	-------	----
V49 PATENT SUPPLIERS	1970	R1	USA	207		CHILE	COSTA	----
	1970	R2	SWEDN	115		FINLA	COSTA	----
	1970	R3	SWITZ	39		BURU	CZECH	----
	1980	R1	USA	224		CHILE	COSTA	----
	1980	R2	SWITZ	39		BANGL	PHILI	----
	1980	R3	GFR	23		CANA	GHANA	----
V50 PROVENANCE OF FOREIGN FIRMS	1980	R1	USA	73.0	%	CHILE	COSTA	----
	1980	R2	UNKI	5.6	%	CHILE	ECUA	----
	1980	R3	GFR	3.7	%	CHILE	ECUA	----
V51 FILM SUPPLIERS	1982	R1	USA	155		BRAZI	DENMA	F119
	1982	R2	ITALY	42		BRAZI	EGYPT	F119
	1982	R3	UNKI	16		BOLI	DENMA	F119

CONGO, PEOPLE'S REP. OF THE (CONGO)

V1 INCOME PER CAPITA	------	----	----	----- -----		-------	-------	----
V2 TELEPHONES P. TSD. POPULATION	1970	D4	P40	10	1/TSD CAP	ZAMBI	PARA	----
	1974	D4	P31	8	1/TSD CAP	THAI	SENE	----
	1979	D3	P27	11	1/TSD CAP	SENE	THAI	----

V3	INFANT MORTALITY RATE	1980	D8	P80	134.5	1/TSD	IVORY	LAOS	F5
V4	PHYSICIANS P. MIL. POPULATION	1971	D4	P32	91	1/MIL	HAITI	BANGL	----
		1975	D4	P36	158	1/MIL	MALAY	BURMA	----
		1978	D4	----	189	1/MIL	ZIMBA	BURMA	----
V5	ADULT LITERACY	------	----	----	----- -----		-------	-------	----
V6	DURATION OF SCHOOLING	------	----	----	----- -----		-------	-------	----
V7	STUDENT ENROLLMENT RATIO	1970	D4	P37	1.7	%	MALAY	SAUDI	----
		1975	D4	P40	2.9	%	MALAY	ALGER	----
		1980	D5	P46	5.6	%	TUNIS	MOROC	----
V8	SHARE OF AGRICULTURAL LABOR	------	----	----	----- -----		-------	-------	----
V9	SHARE OF INDUSTRIAL LABOR	------	----	----	----- -----		-------	-------	----
V10	SHARE OF SERVICE LABOR	------	----	----	----- -----		-------	-------	----
V11	SHARE OF ACADEMIC LABOR	------	----	----	----- -----		-------	-------	----
V12	SHARE OF SELF-EMPLOYED LABOR	------	----	----	----- -----		-------	-------	----
V13	MILITARY EXPENDITURES	------	----	----	----- -----		-------	-------	----
V14	MILITARY MANPOWER	1970	D2	P16	6	TSD CAP	PANA	HONDU	----
		1975	D2	P17	7	TSD CAP	BURU	GUINE	----
		1980	D3	P30	16	TSD CAP	ZAMBI	GUINE	----
V15	MEN AT AGE 20 - 30	------	----	----	----- -----		-------	-------	----
V16	POPULATION	1970	D1	P3	1.20	MIL CAP	BHUTA	MAURA	----
		1975	D1	P5	1.35	MIL CAP	BHUTA	MAURA	----
		1980	D1	P6	1.53	MIL CAP	KUWAI	MAURA	----
V17	GROSS DOMESTIC PRODUCT	------	----	----	----- -----		-------	-------	----
V18	SHARE IN WORLD IMPORTS	1970	D1	P10	0.172	1/TSD	MAURA	NIGER	F121
		1975	D1	P9	0.187	1/TSD	SOMA	NEPAL	F121
		1980	D2	P18	0.274	1/TSD	AFGHA	MONGO	F121
V19	SHARE IN WORLD EXPORTS	1970	D1	P9	0.099	1/TSD	CENTR	SOMA	F121
		1975	D2	P20	0.204	1/TSD	PARA	MOZAM	F121
		1980	D4	P33	0.456	1/TSD	HONDU	DOMI	F121
V20	GDP SHARE OF IMPORTS	1970	D6	P60	20.8	%	THAI	ELSA	F121
		1975	D5	P46	22.2	%	ECUA	NEWZ	F121
		1980	D8	P74	32.1	%	AURIA	MALI	F121
V21	GDP SHARE OF EXPORTS	1970	D4	P31	11.3	%	CHAD	ECUA	F121
		1975	D7	P67	23.3	%	DENMA	INDO	F121
		1980	D9	P89	52.1	%	GABON	BELGI	F121
V22	EXPORT PARTNER CONCENTRATION	1970	D1	P9	14.2	%	SPAIN	SWITZ	F121
		1975	D6	P55	27.0	%	CAME	ELSA	F121
		1980	D8	P78	39.0	%	NICA	NIGER	F121
V23	TOTAL DEBT AS % OF GDP	1980	D10	P91	79.0	%	LIBE	EGYPT	----
V24	SHARE OF NEW FOREIGN PATENTS	------	----	----	----- -----		-------	-------	----

V25	FOREIGN PROPERTY AS % OF GDP	1971	D10	P94	31.2 %	LIBYA	JAMAI	----
		1975	D9	P90	20.9 %	HONDU	MALAY	----
		1978	D10	----	19.3 %	ZAIRE	PERU	----
V26	GNP SHARE OF DEVELOPMENT AID	------	----	----	----- -----	-------	-------	----
V27	SHARE IN NOBEL PRIZE WINNERS	1970-79	D5	P45	0.0 %	COLO	COSTA	----
V28	GDP SHARE OF MANUFACTURING	1980	D3	P22	6.0 %	SUDAN	CENTR	----
V29	EXPORT SHARE OF MANUFACTURES	1970	D8	P74	28.9 %	ELSA	LAOS	----
		1975	D6	P54	11.6 %	PARA	MALI	----
		1980	D4	P31	6.7 %	MADA	SYRIA	----
V30	LACK OF CIVIL LIBERTIES	1975	D8	P74	6	BENIN	GABON	----
		1980	D10	P92	7	BURU	CZECH	----
V31	LACK OF POLITICAL RIGHTS	1975	D5	P43	5	VISO	INDO	----
		1980	D9	P90	7	CHAD	CZECH	----
V32	RIOTS	1970-74	D2	P19	0	CENTR	CUBA	----
		1975-79	D2	P20	0	CAME	CUBA	----
V33	PROTEST DEMONSTRATIONS	1970-74	D2	P15	0	CENTR	ELSA	----
		1975-79	D2	P13	0	CAME	COSTA	----
V34	POLITICAL STRIKES	1970-74	D8	P74	2	YUGO	DENMA	----
		1975-79	D3	P29	0	CHINA	CUBA	----
V35	MEMBER OF THE NONALIGNED MMT.	1970	----	----	1	CHAD	CUBA	----
		1976	----	----	1	CHAD	CUBA	----
		1981	----	----	1	CHAD	CUBA	----
V36	MEMBER OF THE OPEC	1970	----	----	0	COLO	COSTA	----
		1975	----	----	0	COLO	COSTA	----
		1980	----	----	0	COLO	COSTA	----
V37	MEMBER OF THE OECD	1970	----	----	0	COLO	COSTA	----
		1975	----	----	0	COLO	COSTA	----
		1980	----	----	0	COLO	COSTA	----
V38	MEMBER OF THE CMEA	1970	----	----	0	COLO	COSTA	----
		1975	----	----	0	COLO	COSTA	----
		1980	----	----	0	COLO	COSTA	----
V39	MEMBER OF THE WTO	1970	----	----	0	COLO	COSTA	----
		1975	----	----	0	COLO	COSTA	----
		1980	----	----	0	COLO	COSTA	----
V40	MEMBER OF THE NATO	1970	----	----	0	COLO	COSTA	----
		1975	----	----	0	COLO	COSTA	----
		1980	----	----	0	COLO	COSTA	----
V41	GDP SHARE OF INVESTMENTS	------	----	----	----- -----	-------	-------	----
V42	GDP SHARE OF AGRICULTURE	1970	D5	P42	17.9 %	YUGO	PORTU	----
		1975	D4	P39	14.5 %	PERU	YUGO	----
		1980	D4	P37	11.4 %	NEWZ	YUGO	----

V43	GDP SHARE OF INDUSTRY	1970	D4	P39	23.9 %	SRILA	COSTA	----
		1975	D6	P57	32.4 %	URU	MEXI	----
		1980	D9	P89	47.1 %	PORTU	VENE	----
V44	GDP SHARE OF SERVICES	1970	D9	P88	58.2 %	URU	UNKI	----
		1975	D8	P76	53.1 %	JAPAN	FINLA	----
		1980	D4	P33	41.5 %	PORTU	COLO	----
V45	HOMICIDES P. MIL. POPULATION	------	----	----	----- -----	-------	-------	----
V46	SUICIDES P. MIL. POPULATION	------	----	----	----- -----	-------	-------	----
V47	IMPORT PARTNERS	1970	R1	FRANC	55.1 %	CHAD	GFR	F121
		1970	R2	GFR	8.8 %	COLO	ECUA	F121
		1970	R3	USA	6.3 %	CENTR	FRANC	F121
		1980	R1	FRANC	47.8 %	CENTR	GABON	F121
		1980	R2	GABON	7.0 %	-------	-------	F121
		1980	R3	GFR	5.1 %	COLO	ECUA	F121
V48	EXPORT PARTNERS	1970	R1	GFR	14.2 %	BELGI	ELSA	F121
		1970	R2	NETH	14.0 %	CAME	GFR	F121
		1970	R3	FRANC	12.6 %	MALI	HAITI	F121
		1980	R1	ITALY	39.0 %	-------	EGYPT	F121
		1980	R2	BRAZI	17.3 %	CHILE	PARA	F121
		1980	R3	USA	12.7 %	CHILE	MALAY	F121
V49	PATENT SUPPLIERS	1969	R1	SWITZ	40	-------	SYRIA	----
		1969	R2	USA	25	CHINA	FINLA	----
		1969	R3	-------	14	-------	-------	----
V50	PROVENANCE OF FOREIGN FIRMS	1980	R1	FRANC	42.8 %	CAME	GABON	----
		1980	R2	BELGI	19.0 %	ZAIRE	EGYPT	----
		1980	R3	USA	11.9 %	ZIMBA	GUINE	----
V51	FILM SUPPLIERS	------	----	----	----- -----	-------	-------	----

COSTA RICA (COSTA)

V1	INCOME PER CAPITA	1970	D6	P54	1116 $/CAP	TURKY	HUNGA	F147
		1975	D6	P56	1313 $/CAP	TURKY	SYRIA	F147
		1980	D6	P54	1484 $/CAP	SYRIA	KORSO	F147
V2	TELEPHONES P. TSD. POPULATION	1970	D7	P61	35 1/TSD CAP	ROMA	YUGO	----
		1975	D7	P65	63 1/TSD CAP	YUGO	TRITO	----
		1980	D7	P66	107 1/TSD CAP	URU	SOUAF	----
V3	INFANT MORTALITY RATE	1980	D3	P23	20.2 1/TSD	BULGA	POLA	----
V4	PHYSICIANS P. MIL. POPULATION	1970	D7	P65	617 1/MIL	PERU	PANA	F147
		1976	D7	P59	643 1/MIL	PERU	NICA	F156
		1979	D6	P58	694 1/MIL	PERU	KORSO	F147

V5	ADULT LITERACY	------	----	----	-----	-----	-------	-------	----
V6	DURATION OF SCHOOLING	1970	D6	P60	8.4	YR	TUNIS	PHILI	----
		1975	D6	P59	8.7	YR	MALAY	PHILI	----
		1980	D5	P46	8.7	YR	INDO	GABON	----
V7	STUDENT ENROLLMENT RATIO	1970	D8	P74	10.6	%	CZECH	VENE	----
		1975	D8	P76	17.5	%	VENE	GREC	----
		1980	D9	P83	25.2	%	AURIA	AULIA	----
V8	SHARE OF AGRICULTURAL LABOR	1973	D6	----	37.6	%	TUNIS	MEXI	----
V9	SHARE OF INDUSTRIAL LABOR	1973	D5	----	25.5	%	PAKI	COLO	----
V10	SHARE OF SERVICE LABOR	1973	D6	----	28.4	%	ELSA	ALGER	----
		1980	D9	P83	42.9	%	NETH	SWITZ	F46
V11	SHARE OF ACADEMIC LABOR	1973	D7	----	8.4	%	URU	JAPAN	----
		1980	D5	P46	8.6	%	PERU	JAPAN	F46
V12	SHARE OF SELF-EMPLOYED LABOR	1973	D4	----	17.7	%	JAPAN	ALGER	----
		1980	D5	P44	19.8	%	IRE	ITALY	F46
V13	MILITARY EXPENDITURES	1970	D1	P8	0.009	TSD MIL $	SIERA	LIBE	F4
		1975	D2	P12	0.016	TSD MIL $	BURU	HAITI	----
		1980	D1	P6	0.021	TSD MIL $	BENIN	HAITI	----
V14	MILITARY MANPOWER	1970	D1	P4	2	TSD CAP	CENTR	TOGO	----
		1975	D1	P4	2	TSD CAP	TRITO	BENIN	----
		1980	D1	P6	3	TSD CAP	SIERA	NIGER	----
V15	MEN AT AGE 20 - 30	1973	D2	----	143	TSD CAP	PANA	LIBYA	F22
		1982	D2	----	221	TSD CAP	URU	NEWZ	F186
V16	POPULATION	1970	D1	P9	1.73	MIL CAP	YESO	NICA	F22
		1975	D1	P10	1.97	MIL CAP	YESO	CENTR	F22
		1980	D2	P11	2.25	MIL CAP	JAMAI	CENTR	F22
V17	GROSS DOMESTIC PRODUCT	1970	D3	P21	1.930	TSD MIL $	NICA	PANA	----
		1975	D3	P22	2.587	TSD MIL $	SENE	PARA	----
		1980	D3	P26	3.340	TSD MIL $	JORDA	PANA	----
V18	SHARE IN WORLD IMPORTS	1970	D4	P38	0.955	1/TSD	TUNIS	TANZA	----
		1975	D4	P33	0.764	1/TSD	CAME	JORDA	----
		1980	D4	P37	0.743	1/TSD	DOMI	YESO	----
V19	SHARE IN WORLD EXPORTS	1970	D4	P37	0.736	1/TSD	ELSA	CAME	----
		1975	D4	P37	0.563	1/TSD	SENE	ELSA	----
		1980	D4	P35	0.502	1/TSD	JAMAI	PAPUA	----
V20	GDP SHARE OF IMPORTS	1970	D9	P89	32.2	%	SWITZ	NORWY	----
		1975	D9	P81	35.4	%	KORSO	YENO	----
		1980	D8	P72	31.5	%	SYRIA	OMAN	----
V21	GDP SHARE OF EXPORTS	1970	D8	P78	23.5	%	NICA	VENE	----
		1975	D8	P75	25.1	%	DOMI	NORWY	----
		1980	D6	P55	20.7	%	UNKI	NICA	----
V22	EXPORT PARTNER CONCENTRATION	1970	D8	P79	42.5	%	ZAIRE	ECUA	----
		1975	D8	P80	41.9	%	MALAW	CENTR	----
		1980	D8	P71	34.9	%	UPVO	CZECH	----

V23	TOTAL DEBT AS % OF GDP	1980	D8	P80	56.8	%	IVORY	SUDAN	----
V24	SHARE OF NEW FOREIGN PATENTS	1970	D6	P55	93	%	BELGI	IRAN	----
		1975	D5	P46	89	%	PANA	NETH	----
		1980	D2	P18	59	%	HUNGA	NEPAL	----
V25	FOREIGN PROPERTY AS % OF GDP	1971	D7	P68	15.8	%	GHANA	SINGA	----
		1975	D8	P79	12.7	%	PERU	MALAW	----
		1978	D7	----	8.2	%	HAITI	DOMI	----
V26	GNP SHARE OF DEVELOPMENT AID	------	----	----	----- -----		-------	-------	----
V27	SHARE IN NOBEL PRIZE WINNERS	1970-79	D5	P45	0.0	%	CONGO	CUBA	----
V28	GDP SHARE OF MANUFACTURING	------	----	----	----- -----		-------	-------	----
V29	EXPORT SHARE OF MANUFACTURES	1970	D7	P61	18.0	%	TUNIS	SENE	----
		1975	D7	P66	23.2	%	TURKY	BRAZI	----
		1980	D7	P67	26.7	%	CENTR	BRAZI	----
V30	LACK OF CIVIL LIBERTIES	1975	D1	P7	1		CANA	DENMA	----
		1980	D1	P7	1		CANA	DENMA	----
V31	LACK OF POLITICAL RIGHTS	1975	D1	P8	1		CANA	DENMA	----
		1980	D1	P8	1		CANA	DENMA	----
V32	RIOTS	1970-74	D5	P43	1		CHAD	ECUA	----
		1975-79	D8	P75	7		MEXI	ETHIA	----
V33	PROTEST DEMONSTRATIONS	1970-74	D4	P37	1		CHAD	CUBA	----
		1975-79	D2	P13	0		CONGO	DENMA	----
V34	POLITICAL STRIKES	1970-74	D3	P29	0		CHINA	CUBA	----
		1975-79	D8	P73	2		CHILE	JAPAN	----
V35	MEMBER OF THE NONALIGNED MMT.	1970	----	----	0		COLO	CZECH	----
		1976	----	----	0		COLO	CZECH	----
		1981	----	----	0		COLO	CZECH	----
V36	MEMBER OF THE OPEC	1970	----	----	0		CONGO	CUBA	----
		1975	----	----	0		CONGO	CUBA	----
		1980	----	----	0		CONGO	CUBA	----
V37	MEMBER OF THE OECD	1970	----	----	0		CONGO	CUBA	----
		1975	----	----	0		CONGO	CUBA	----
		1980	----	----	0		CONGO	CUBA	----
V38	MEMBER OF THE CMEA	1970	----	----	0		CONGO	CUBA	----
		1975	----	----	0		CONGO	DENMA	----
		1980	----	----	0		CONGO	DENMA	----
V39	MEMBER OF THE WTO	1970	----	----	0		CONGO	CUBA	----
		1975	----	----	0		CONGO	CUBA	----
		1980	----	----	0		CONGO	CUBA	----
V40	MEMBER OF THE NATO	1970	----	----	0		CONGO	CUBA	----
		1975	----	----	0		CONGO	CUBA	----
		1980	----	----	0		CONGO	CUBA	----

V41	GDP SHARE OF INVESTMENTS	1970	D6	P52	20.5	%	TURKY	MALAY	----
		1975	D5	P48	21.6	%	BELGI	ELSA	----
		1980	D7	P65	26.6	%	TURKY	SWITZ	----
V42	GDP SHARE OF AGRICULTURE	1970	D5	P50	22.5	%	SYRIA	DOMI	----
		1975	D5	P49	20.3	%	ZAIRE	TUNIS	----
		1980	D5	P47	17.8	%	BOLI	MOROC	----
V43	GDP SHARE OF INDUSTRY	1970	D5	P40	24.2	%	CONGO	ECUA	----
		1975	D5	P43	27.4	%	DENMA	COLO	----
		1980	D4	P36	27.0	%	TOGO	DOMI	----
V44	GDP SHARE OF SERVICES	1970	D8	P72	53.3	%	MOROC	AULIA	----
		1975	D8	P74	52.3	%	PERU	JAPAN	----
		1980	D8	P79	55.2	%	NORWY	URU	----
V45	HOMICIDES P. MIL. POPULATION	1970	D8	P71	37.6	1/MIL CAP	URU	TRITO	F149
		1975	D8	P76	47.7	1/MIL CAP	CUBA	TRITO	F149
		1980	D9	P85	57.8	1/MIL CAP	PARA	ECUA	F150
V46	SUICIDES P. MIL. POPULATION	1970	D2	P14	23.7	1/MIL CAP	ECUA	COLO	F147
		1975	D2	P20	40.6	1/MIL CAP	SPAIN	THAI	F147
		1980	D3	P22	54.2	1/MIL CAP	VENE	IRE	F150
V47	IMPORT PARTNERS	1970	R1	USA	34.8	%	COLO	ECUA	----
		1970	R2	JAPAN	9.0	%	BURU	ETHIA	----
		1970	R3	GFR	8.3	%	BURU	EGYPT	----
		1980	R1	USA	34.5	%	COLO	DOMI	----
		1980	R2	JAPAN	10.8	%	COLO	CUBA	----
		1980	R3	VENE	6.8	%	NICA	ELSA	----
V48	EXPORT PARTNERS	1970	R1	USA	42.5	%	COLO	DOMI	----
		1970	R2	GFR	8.2	%	COLO	ETHIA	----
		1970	R3	NICA	5.6	%	-------	-------	----
		1980	R1	USA	34.9	%	COLO	DOMI	----
		1980	R2	NICA	12.4	%	-------	-------	----
		1980	R3	GFR	11.4	%	ALGER	GUATE	----
V49	PATENT SUPPLIERS	1970	R1	USA	24		COLO	DENMA	----
		1970	R2	UNKI	4		AULIA	INDIA	----
		1970	R3	SWEDN	3		COLO	NORWY	----
		1980	R1	USA	12		COLO	ECUA	----
		1980	R2	GFR	4		CHILE	EGYPT	----
		1980	R3	UNKI	2		ZIMBA	DENMA	----
V50	PROVENANCE OF FOREIGN FIRMS	1980	R1	USA	77.5	%	COLO	DOMI	----
		1980	R2	SWITZ	6.6	%	-------	AURIA	----
		1980	R3	JAPAN	5.6	%	PHILI	ELSA	----
V51	FILM SUPPLIERS	-------	----	----	-----	-----	-------	-------	----

CUBA (CUBA)

V1	INCOME PER CAPITA	------	----	----	----- -----	-------	-------	----
V2	TELEPHONES P. TSD. POPULATION	1970	D6	P60	32 1/TSD CAP	MEXI	ROMA	----
		1974	D6	P55	32 1/TSD CAP	BRAZI	KORSO	----
		1979	D5	P48	37 1/TSD CAP	ECUA	TURKY	----
V3	INFANT MORTALITY RATE	1980	D3	P22	19.6 1/TSD	CZECH	BULGA	----
V4	PHYSICIANS P. MIL. POPULATION	1968	D8	----	845 1/MIL	LEBA	ALBA	----
		1974	D7	P65	896 1/MIL	LEBA	ALBA	----
V5	ADULT LITERACY	------	----	----	----- -----	-------	-------	----
V6	DURATION OF SCHOOLING	1970	D8	P75	9.9 YR	JAMAI	ISRA	----
		1975	D9	P89	11.1 YR	GREC	ALBA	----
		1980	D9	P81	10.9 YR	AULIA	GREC	F35
V7	STUDENT ENROLLMENT RATIO	1970	D5	P48	3.7 %	GUATE	PARA	----
		1975	D7	P65	11.0 %	BRAZI	BOLI	----
		1980	D8	P73	19.5 %	PERU	UNKI	----
V8	SHARE OF AGRICULTURAL LABOR	1970	D5	P50	27.2 %	IRE	SOUAF	F70
V9	SHARE OF INDUSTRIAL LABOR	1970	D5	P48	33.0 %	IRE	CANA	F70
V10	SHARE OF SERVICE LABOR	1970	D7	P61	31.3 %	SOUAF	IRE	F70
V11	SHARE OF ACADEMIC LABOR	1970	D7	P63	8.5 %	POLA	AURIA	F70
V12	SHARE OF SELF-EMPLOYED LABOR	1970	D1	P6	1.3 %	CZECH	HUNGA	F72
V13	MILITARY EXPENDITURES	------	----	----	----- -----	-------	-------	----
V14	MILITARY MANPOWER	1970	D8	P71	140 TSD CAP	ARGE	HUNGA	----
		1975	D7	P69	120 TSD CAP	HUNGA	AFGHA	----
		1980	D9	P81	220 TSD CAP	ROMA	GDR	----
V15	MEN AT AGE 20 - 30	1970	D6	P51	698 TSD CAP	UGADA	MALAY	F22
		1975	D6	P58	746 TSD CAP	BULGA	BELGI	F22
		1981	D5	P43	766 TSD CAP	SYRIA	BELGI	----
V16	POPULATION	1970	D6	P52	8.55 MIL CAP	BULGA	GHANA	----
		1975	D6	P54	9.29 MIL CAP	GREC	PORTU	----
		1980	D6	P54	9.72 MIL CAP	GREC	BELGI	----
V17	GROSS DOMESTIC PRODUCT	------	----	----	----- -----	-------	-------	----
V18	SHARE IN WORLD IMPORTS	1970	D7	P64	3.949 1/TSD	THAI	MALAY	----
		1975	D7	P62	4.272 1/TSD	PORTU	EGYPT	----
		1980	D6	P57	3.068 1/TSD	NEWZ	IRAQ	----
V19	SHARE IN WORLD EXPORTS	1970	D6	P60	3.344 1/TSD	IRE	PERU	----
		1975	D7	P64	4.204 1/TSD	IRE	MALAY	----
		1980	D7	P61	2.774 1/TSD	NEWZ	PHILI	----
V20	GDP SHARE OF IMPORTS	------	----	----	----- -----	-------	-------	----

V21	GDP SHARE OF EXPORTS	------	----	----	----- -----	-------	-------	----
V22	EXPORT PARTNER CONCENTRATION	1975	D10	P92	56.3 %	BULGA	MEXI	----
V23	TOTAL DEBT AS % OF GDP	------	----	----	----- -----	-------	-------	----
V24	SHARE OF NEW FOREIGN PATENTS	1970	D9	P90	100 %	BURU	GHANA	----
		1976	D1	P10	37 %	USA	ROMA	----
		1980	D2	P13	46 %	ROMA	GREC	----
V25	FOREIGN PROPERTY AS % OF GDP	------	----	----	----- -----	-------	-------	----
V26	GNP SHARE OF DEVELOPMENT AID	------	----	----	----- -----	-------	-------	----
V27	SHARE IN NOBEL PRIZE WINNERS	1970-79	D5	P45	0.0 %	COSTA	CZECH	----
V28	GDP SHARE OF MANUFACTURING	------	----	----	----- -----	-------	-------	----
V29	EXPORT SHARE OF MANUFACTURES	1970	D1	P7	0.3 %	ZAMBI	NIGRA	----
		1976	D1	P3	0.0 %	-------	UGADA	----
		1980	D1	P6	0.3 %	ALGER	IRAQ	----
V30	LACK OF CIVIL LIBERTIES	1975	D10	P93	7	CHINA	CZECH	----
		1980	D8	P74	6	CHAD	GABON	----
V31	LACK OF POLITICAL RIGHTS	1975	D9	P88	7	CHINA	CZECH	----
		1980	D7	P67	6	CHINA	GABON	----
V32	RIOTS	1970-74	D2	P19	0	CONGO	DENMA	----
		1975-79	D2	P20	0	CONGO	DENMA	----
V33	PROTEST DEMONSTRATIONS	1970-74	D4	P37	1	COSTA	DOMI	----
		1975-79	D4	P32	1	CENTR	IRAQ	----
V34	POLITICAL STRIKES	1970-74	D3	P29	0	COSTA	CZECH	----
		1975-79	D3	P29	0	CONGO	DOMI	----
V35	MEMBER OF THE NONALIGNED MMT.	1970	----	----	1	CONGO	EGYPT	----
		1976	----	----	1	CONGO	EGYPT	----
		1981	----	----	1	CONGO	ECUA	----
V36	MEMBER OF THE OPEC	1970	----	----	0	COSTA	CZECH	----
		1975	----	----	0	COSTA	CZECH	----
		1980	----	----	0	COSTA	CZECH	----
V37	MEMBER OF THE OECD	1970	----	----	0	COSTA	CZECH	----
		1975	----	----	0	COSTA	CZECH	----
		1980	----	----	0	COSTA	CZECH	----
V38	MEMBER OF THE CMEA	1970	----	----	0	COSTA	DENMA	----
		1975	----	----	1	BULGA	CZECH	----
		1980	----	----	1	BULGA	CZECH	----
V39	MEMBER OF THE WTO	1970	----	----	0	COSTA	DENMA	----
		1975	----	----	0	COSTA	DENMA	----
		1980	----	----	0	COSTA	DENMA	----
V40	MEMBER OF THE NATO	1970	----	----	0	COSTA	CZECH	----
		1975	----	----	0	COSTA	CZECH	----
		1980	----	----	0	COSTA	CZECH	CUBA

V41	GDP SHARE OF INVESTMENTS	------	----	----	----- -----	-------	-------	----
V42	GDP SHARE OF AGRICULTURE	------	----	----	----- -----	-------	-------	----
V43	GDP SHARE OF INDUSTRY	------	----	----	----- -----	-------	-------	----
V44	GDP SHARE OF SERVICES	------	----	----	----- -----	-------	-------	----
V45	HOMICIDES P. MIL. POPULATION	1971	D8	P76	44.4 1/MIL CAP	TRITO	PARA	F154
		1975	D8	P74	40.2 1/MIL CAP	FINLA	COSTA	F148
V46	SUICIDES P. MIL. POPULATION	1971	D7	P69	132.5 1/MIL CAP	AULIA	YUGO	F2
		1975	D8	P74	173.1 1/MIL CAP	BELGI	JAPAN	----
V47	IMPORT PARTNERS	1970	R1	USSR	52.7 %	BULGA	CZECH	----
		1970	R2	FRANC	4.6 %	BELGI	ITALY	----
		1970	R3	UNKI	4.5 %	BURMA	DENMA	----
		1980	R1	USSR	60.8 %	BULGA	CZECH	----
		1980	R2	JAPAN	3.8 %	COSTA	ECUA	----
		1980	R3	GDR	3.5 %	CZECH	HUNGA	----
V48	EXPORT PARTNERS	------	----	----	----- -----	-------	-------	----
V49	PATENT SUPPLIERS	1969	R1	GDR	8	-------	CZECH	----
		1969	R2	FRANC	6	TUNIS	GFR	----
		1969	R3	UNKI	4	CHILE	DENMA	----
		1980	R1	FRANC	11	-------	GHANA	----
		1980	R2	CANA	10	-------	TRITO	----
		1980	R3	-------	8	-------	-------	----
V50	PROVENANCE OF FOREIGN FIRMS	------	----	----	----- -----	-------	-------	----
V51	FILM SUPPLIERS	1982	R1	USSR	20	BULGA	CZECH	F120
		1982	R2	USA	11	BULGA	CZECH	F120
		1982	R3	FRANC	10	ARGE	CZECH	F120

CZECHOSLOVAKIA (CZECH)

V1	INCOME PER CAPITA	------	----	----	----- -----	-------	-------	----
V2	TELEPHONES P. TSD. POPULATION	1970	D9	P82	138 1/TSD CAP	SPAIN	ISRA	----
		1975	D9	P79	176 1/TSD CAP	GDR	ISRA	----
		1980	D8	P75	206 1/TSD CAP	GDR	UNARE	----
V3	INFANT MORTALITY RATE	1980	D3	P21	18.4 1/TSD	GREC	CUBA	----
V4	PHYSICIANS P. MIL. POPULATION	1970	D10	P98	2122 1/MIL	HUNGA	USSR	----
		1975	D10	P98	2391 1/MIL	BULGA	USSR	----
		1980	D10	P99	2757 1/MIL	HUNGA	-------	----
V5	ADULT LITERACY	------	----	----	----- -----	-------	-------	----

V6	DURATION OF SCHOOLING	1970	D8	P73	9.8	YR	SPAIN	JAMAI	----
		1975	D8	P71	10.0	YR	AURIA	JAMAI	----
		1980	D7	P65	10.1	YR	USSR	GFR	----
V7	STUDENT ENROLLMENT RATIO	1970	D8	P73	10.4	%	ROMA	COSTA	----
		1975	D7	P68	12.1	%	HUNGA	SYRIA	----
		1980	D8	P71	17.1	%	SYRIA	POLA	----
V8	SHARE OF AGRICULTURAL LABOR	1970	D3	P26	12.1	%	NORWY	AURIA	F73
V9	SHARE OF INDUSTRIAL LABOR	1970	D10	P91	42.9	%	SPAIN	ITALY	F73
V10	SHARE OF SERVICE LABOR	1970	D5	P47	25.4	%	PERU	PORTU	F73
V11	SHARE OF ACADEMIC LABOR	1970	D10	P98	19.5	%	SWEDN	-------	F73
V12	SHARE OF SELF-EMPLOYED LABOR	1970	D1	P3	1.0	%	-------	CUBA	F73
V13	MILITARY EXPENDITURES	------	----	----	-----	-----	-------	-------	----
V14	MILITARY MANPOWER	1970	D8	P79	222	TSD CAP	ROMA	PORTU	----
		1975	D8	P76	210	TSD CAP	BURMA	PORTU	----
		1980	D8	P79	212	TSD CAP	GREC	ROMA	----
V15	MEN AT AGE 20 - 30	1970	D7	P68	1144	TSD CAP	SRILA	ROMA	F22
		1975	D7	P69	1279	TSD CAP	MOROC	PERU	----
		1981	D6	P53	1207	TSD CAP	TANZA	NEPAL	----
V16	POPULATION	1970	D7	P70	14.33	MIL CAP	ALGER	MOROC	----
		1975	D7	P67	14.80	MIL CAP	AULIA	PERU	----
		1980	D7	P66	15.31	MIL CAP	VENE	AFGHA	----
V17	GROSS DOMESTIC PRODUCT	------	----	----	-----	-----	-------	-------	----
V18	SHARE IN WORLD IMPORTS	1970	D9	P84	11.131	1/TSD	POLA	NORWY	F49
		1975	D9	P82	9.986	1/TSD	SINGA	AURIA	F49
		1980	D8	P75	7.385	1/TSD	INDIA	FINLA	F49
V19	SHARE IN WORLD EXPORTS	1970	D9	P87	12.089	1/TSD	POLA	GDR	F30
		1975	D9	P82	9.536	1/TSD	IRAQ	BRAZI	F30
		1980	D8	P73	7.461	1/TSD	FINLA	MEXI	F30
V20	GDP SHARE OF IMPORTS	------	----	----	-----	-----	-------	-------	----
V21	GDP SHARE OF EXPORTS	------	----	----	-----	-----	-------	-------	----
V22	EXPORT PARTNER CONCENTRATION	1972	D7	----	33.9	%	UPVO	NEWZ	----
		1975	D7	P69	33.0	%	GDR	LEBA	----
		1980	D8	P72	35.5	%	COSTA	UNARE	----
V23	TOTAL DEBT AS % OF GDP	------	----	----	-----	-----	-------	-------	----
V24	SHARE OF NEW FOREIGN PATENTS	1970	D1	P7	28	%	USA	KORSO	----
		1975	D1	P7	35	%	POLA	USA	----
		1980	D1	P4	21	%	JAPAN	GDR	----
V25	FOREIGN PROPERTY AS % OF GDP	------	----	----	-----	-----	-------	-------	----
V26	GNP SHARE OF DEVELOPMENT AID	------	----	----	-----	-----	-------	-------	----
V27	SHARE IN NOBEL PRIZE WINNERS	1970-79	D5	P45	0.0	%	CUBA	DOMI	----

V28 GDP SHARE OF MANUFACTURING	------	----	----	----- -----		-------	-------	----
V29 EXPORT SHARE OF MANUFACTURES	------	----	----	----- -----		-------	-------	----
V30 LACK OF CIVIL LIBERTIES	1975	D10	P93	7		CUBA	GDR	----
	1980	D10	P92	7		CONGO	ETHIA	----
V31 LACK OF POLITICAL RIGHTS	1975	D9	P88	7		CUBA	ECUA	----
	1980	D9	P90	7		CONGO	ETHIA	----
V32 RIOTS	1970-74	D6	P53	2		BURMA	IRAQ	----
	1975-79	D6	P53	2		CANA	DOMI	----
V33 PROTEST DEMONSTRATIONS	1970-74	D8	P77	11		THAI	URU	----
	1975-79	D8	P77	13		MEXI	GDR	----
V34 POLITICAL STRIKES	1970-74	D3	P29	0		CUBA	DOMI	----
	1975-79	D7	P63	1		ZAMBI	DENMA	----
V35 MEMBER OF THE NONALIGNED MMT.	1970	----	----	0		COSTA	DENMA	----
	1976	----	----	0		COSTA	DENMA	----
	1981	----	----	0		COSTA	DENMA	----
V36 MEMBER OF THE OPEC	1970	----	----	0		CUBA	DENMA	----
	1975	----	----	0		CUBA	DENMA	----
	1980	----	----	0		CUBA	DENMA	----
V37 MEMBER OF THE OECD	1970	----	----	0		CUBA	DOMI	----
	1975	----	----	0		CUBA	DOMI	----
	1980	----	----	0		CUBA	DOMI	----
V38 MEMBER OF THE CMEA	1970	----	----	1		BULGA	GDR	----
	1975	----	----	1		CUBA	GDR	----
	1980	----	----	1		CUBA	GDR	----
V39 MEMBER OF THE WTO	1970	----	----	1		BULGA	GDR	----
	1975	----	----	1		BULGA	GDR	----
	1980	----	----	1		BULGA	GDR	----
V40 MEMBER OF THE NATO	1970	----	----	0		CUBA	DOMI	----
	1975	----	----	0		CUBA	DOMI	----
	1980	----	----	0		CUBA	DOMI	----
V41 GDP SHARE OF INVESTMENTS	------	----	----	----- -----		-------	-------	----
V42 GDP SHARE OF AGRICULTURE	------	----	----	----- -----		-------	-------	----
V43 GDP SHARE OF INDUSTRY	------	----	----	----- -----		-------	-------	----
V44 GDP SHARE OF SERVICES	------	----	----	----- -----		-------	-------	----
V45 HOMICIDES P. MIL. POPULATION	1970	D5	P44	14.9 1/MIL CAP		GFR	AURIA	F148
	1975	D5	P44	13.2 1/MIL CAP		JAPAN	UNKI	F148
	1981	D3	P31	11.0 1/MIL CAP		SPAIN	NORWY	F2
V46 SUICIDES P. MIL. POPULATION	1970	D10	P94	253.1 1/MIL CAP		AURIA	GDR	----
	1975	D9	P83	219.0 1/MIL CAP		GFR	SWITZ	----
	1981	D8	P73	198.2 1/MIL CAP		SWEDN	GFR	F2

V47	IMPORT PARTNERS	1972	R1	USSR	33.2	%	CUBA	EGYPT	----
		1972	R2	GDR	12.6	%	BULGA	HUNGA	----
		1972	R3	POLA	7.6	%	USSR	-------	----
		1980	R1	USSR	36.0	%	CUBA	ETHIA	----
		1980	R2	GDR	10.5	%	BULGA	CUBA	----
		1980	R3	POLA	7.6	%	USSR	-------	----
V48	EXPORT PARTNERS	1972	R1	USSR	33.9	%	BULGA	EGYPT	----
		1972	R2	GDR	10.9	%	BULGA	EGYPT	----
		1972	R3	POLA	9.3	%	USSR	-------	----
		1980	R1	USSR	35.5	%	BULGA	FINLA	----
		1980	R2	GDR	9.3	%	BULGA	HUNGA	----
		1980	R3	POLA	7.5	%	BULGA	-------	----
V49	PATENT SUPPLIERS	1970	R1	GDR	359		CUBA	BULGA	----
		1970	R2	GFR	285		CHILE	DENMA	----
		1970	R3	SWITZ	118		COLO	GHANA	----
		1980	R1	GFR	421		BULGA	DENMA	----
		1980	R2	USA	275		BULGA	DENMA	----
		1980	R3	GDR	190		-------	HUNGA	----
V50	PROVENANCE OF FOREIGN FIRMS	------	----	----	----- -----		-------	-------	----
V51	FILM SUPPLIERS	1980	R1	USSR	36		CUBA	GDR	F120
		1980	R2	USA	22		CUBA	GDR	F120
		1980	R3	FRANC	14		CUBA	GDR	F120

DENMARK (DENMA)

V1	INCOME PER CAPITA	1970	D10	P97	10104	$/CAP	GFR	SWEDN	F213
		1975	D10	P96	11023	$/CAP	NORWY	SWEDN	F213
		1980	D10	P94	12330	$/CAP	GFR	NORWY	F213
V2	TELEPHONES P. TSD. POPULATION	1970	D10	P95	342	1/TSD CAP	AULIA	NEWZ	F6
		1975	D10	P94	454	1/TSD CAP	FINLA	NEWZ	F6
		1980	D10	P95	641	1/TSD CAP	NEWZ	CANA	F6
V3	INFANT MORTALITY RATE	1980	D1	P5	8.4	1/TSD	NORWY	NETH	F6
V4	PHYSICIANS P. MIL. POPULATION	1970	D9	P84	1434	1/MIL	SWEDN	POLA	F161
		1974	D9	P87	1789	1/MIL	CANA	SWITZ	F160
		1978	D9	----	2073	1/MIL	GDR	SWEDN	F160
V5	ADULT LITERACY	------	----	----	----- -----		-------	-------	----
V6	DURATION OF SCHOOLING	1970	D9	P85	10.4	YR	CHILE	POLA	----
		1975	D9	P87	11.0	YR	BELGI	GREC	----
		1980	D10	P99	12.1	YR	UNKI	NEWZ	----

V7	STUDENT ENROLLMENT RATIO	1970	D10	P91	18.3	%	BELGI	FRANC	----
		1975	D10	P97	29.4	%	SWEDN	GDR	----
		1980	D10	P91	28.6	%	ITALY	ISRA	----
V8	SHARE OF AGRICULTURAL LABOR	1970	D2	P20	10.9	%	AULIA	NEWZ	F67
V9	SHARE OF INDUSTRIAL LABOR	------	----	----	-----	-----	-------	-------	----
V10	SHARE OF SERVICE LABOR	------	----	----	-----	-----	-------	-------	----
V11	SHARE OF ACADEMIC LABOR	------	----	----	-----	-----	-------	-------	----
V12	SHARE OF SELF-EMPLOYED LABOR	1970	D3	P33	14.4	%	NORWY	FINLA	F67
V13	MILITARY EXPENDITURES	1970	D8	P71	1.160	TSD MIL $	GREC	NORWY	----
		1975	D8	P71	1.372	TSD MIL $	ARGE	NORWY	----
		1980	D7	P69	1.540	TSD MIL $	MALAY	NORWY	----
V14	MILITARY MANPOWER	1970	D5	P49	45	TSD CAP	COLO	ETHIA	----
		1975	D5	P46	35	TSD CAP	NEPAL	NORWY	----
		1980	D5	P43	33	TSD CAP	MOZAM	ECUA	----
V15	MEN AT AGE 20 - 30	1970	D4	P35	409	TSD CAP	SYRIA	ECUA	F165
		1976	D4	P35	397	TSD CAP	SENE	MALI	F165
		1980	D3	P22	382	TSD CAP	DOMI	RWAN	F6
V16	POPULATION	1970	D4	P38	4.95	MIL CAP	YENO	MALI	F165
		1975	D4	P38	5.06	MIL CAP	ZAMBI	MALAW	F165
		1980	D4	P33	5.12	MIL CAP	RWAN	NIGER	F165
V17	GROSS DOMESTIC PRODUCT	1970	D8	P78	50.015	TSD MIL $	AURIA	SOUAF	----
		1975	D8	P75	55.774	TSD MIL $	TURKY	AURIA	----
		1980	D8	P75	63.129	TSD MIL $	KORSO	INDO	----
V18	SHARE IN WORLD IMPORTS	1970	D9	P86	13.218	1/TSD	SOUAF	SPAIN	F30
		1975	D9	P85	11.409	1/TSD	IRAN	AULIA	F30
		1980	D9	P84	9.625	1/TSD	CHINA	KORSO	F30
V19	SHARE IN WORLD EXPORTS	1970	D9	P85	10.489	1/TSD	AURIA	POLA	F30
		1975	D9	P83	9.944	1/TSD	BRAZI	KUWAI	F30
		1980	D8	P76	8.626	1/TSD	POLA	GDR	F30
V20	GDP SHARE OF IMPORTS	1970	D9	P84	27.7	%	KENYA	MAURA	F30
		1975	D7	P63	27.6	%	FINLA	LIBYA	F30
		1980	D7	P67	29.8	%	NORWY	FINLA	F30
V21	GDP SHARE OF EXPORTS	1970	D7	P70	20.8	%	TOGO	CAME	F30
		1975	D7	P65	23.2	%	MALAW	CONGO	F30
		1980	D7	P69	26.0	%	SRILA	ZAIRE	F30
V22	EXPORT PARTNER CONCENTRATION	1970	D2	P20	18.9	%	JORDA	GHANA	F123
		1975	D3	P27	18.8	%	ITALY	TUNIS	F123
		1980	D4	P31	18.7	%	MADA	SWITZ	F123
V23	TOTAL DEBT AS % OF GDP	------	----	----	-----	-----	-------	-------	----
V24	SHARE OF NEW FOREIGN PATENTS	1970	D5	P49	90	%	BOLI	NORWY	----
		1975	D6	P54	91	%	BRAZI	AULIA	----
		1980	D5	P46	88	%	NORWY	DOMI	----
V25	FOREIGN PROPERTY AS % OF GDP	------	----	----	-----	-----	-------	-------	----

V26	GNP SHARE OF DEVELOPMENT AID	1970	D7	P65	0.37 %	SWEDN	UNKI	----
		1975	D6	P54	0.55 %	CANA	BELGI	----
		1980	D7	P67	0.74 %	FRANC	SWEDN	----
V27	SHARE IN NOBEL PRIZE WINNERS	1970-79	D10	P94	2.5 %	PAKI	GFR	----
V28	GDP SHARE OF MANUFACTURING	1970	D7	P64	18.5 %	COLO	DOMI	----
		1975	D7	P65	18.1 %	THAI	ELSA	----
		1980	D6	P60	16.3 %	VENE	PAKI	----
V29	EXPORT SHARE OF MANUFACTURES	------	----	----	----- -----	-------	-------	----
V30	LACK OF CIVIL LIBERTIES	1975	D1	P7	1	COSTA	GFR	----
		1980	D1	P7	1	COSTA	IRE	----
V31	LACK OF POLITICAL RIGHTS	1975	D1	P8	1	COSTA	FRANC	----
		1980	D1	P8	1	COSTA	FRANC	----
V32	RIOTS	1970-74	D2	P19	0	CUBA	ELSA	----
		1975-79	D2	P20	0	CUBA	FINLA	----
V33	PROTEST DEMONSTRATIONS	1970-74	D7	P68	6	NIGRA	NICA	----
		1975-79	D2	P13	0	COSTA	DOMI	----
V34	POLITICAL STRIKES	1970-74	D8	P74	2	CONGO	GHANA	----
		1975-79	D7	P63	1	CZECH	GUATE	----
V35	MEMBER OF THE NONALIGNED MMT.	1970	----	----	0	CZECH	DOMI	----
		1976	----	----	0	CZECH	DOMI	----
		1981	----	----	0	CZECH	DOMI	----
V36	MEMBER OF THE OPEC	1970	----	----	0	CZECH	DOMI	----
		1975	----	----	0	CZECH	DOMI	----
		1980	----	----	0	CZECH	DOMI	----
V37	MEMBER OF THE OECD	1970	----	----	1	CANA	FINLA	----
		1975	----	----	1	CANA	FINLA	----
		1980	----	----	1	CANA	FINLA	----
V38	MEMBER OF THE CMEA	1970	----	----	0	CUBA	DOMI	----
		1975	----	----	0	COSTA	DOMI	----
		1980	----	----	0	COSTA	DOMI	----
V39	MEMBER OF THE WTO	1970	----	----	0	CUBA	DOMI	----
		1975	----	----	0	CUBA	DOMI	----
		1980	----	----	0	CUBA	DOMI	----
V40	MEMBER OF THE NATO	1970	----	----	1	CANA	FRANC	----
		1975	----	----	1	CANA	FRANC	----
		1980	----	----	1	CANA	FRANC	----
V41	GDP SHARE OF INVESTMENTS	1970	D8	P74	25.7 %	SWEDN	FRANC	----
		1975	D5	P42	20.9 %	INDIA	TANZA	----
		1980	D3	P29	18.2 %	USA	BRAZI	----
V42	GDP SHARE OF AGRICULTURE	1970	D2	P12	5.6 %	NETH	SAUDI	----
		1975	D2	P16	5.1 %	FRANC	AULIA	----
		1980	D2	P19	4.5 %	AURIA	NORWY	----

V43 GDP SHARE OF INDUSTRY	1970	D6	P54	29.6	%	KORSO	PHILI	----
	1975	D5	P42	27.3	%	EGYPT	COSTA	----
	1980	D3	P27	23.0	%	IVORY	MAURA	----
V44 GDP SHARE OF SERVICES	1970	D10	P97	64.8	%	CANA	SINGA	----
	1975	D10	P99	67.6	%	JORDA	-------	----
	1980	D10	P99	72.5	%	PANA	-------	----
V45 HOMICIDES P. MIL. POPULATION	1970	D2	P13	6.7	1/MIL CAP	SPAIN	SWITZ	F149
	1975	D1	P5	5.7	1/MIL CAP	GDR	SPAIN	F153
	1980	D5	P49	13.1	1/MIL CAP	NEWZ	BELGI	F153
V46 SUICIDES P. MIL. POPULATION	1970	D9	P85	214.1	1/MIL CAP	FINLA	GFR	F147
	1975	D9	P88	240.7	1/MIL CAP	SWITZ	AURIA	F150
	1980	D10	P94	316.0	1/MIL CAP	SRILA	HUNGA	F150
V47 IMPORT PARTNERS	1970	R1	GFR	18.9	%	BELGI	FINLA	F123
	1970	R2	SWEDN	16.0	%	NORWY	FINLA	F123
	1970	R3	UNKI	13.9	%	CUBA	FINLA	F123
	1980	R1	GFR	18.4	%	BELGI	FRANC	F123
	1980	R2	SWEDN	12.8	%	NORWY	FINLA	F123
	1980	R3	UNKI	11.9	%	AULIA	JAMAI	F123
V48 EXPORT PARTNERS	1970	R1	UNKI	18.9	%	BOLI	FINLA	F123
	1970	R2	SWEDN	16.8	%	-------	FINLA	F123
	1970	R3	GFR	12.8	%	CAME	ECUA	F123
	1980	R1	GFR	18.7	%	BELGI	FRANC	F123
	1980	R2	UNKI	14.2	%	PORTU	JAMAI	F123
	1980	R3	SWEDN	12.6	%	FINLA	NORWY	F123
V49 PATENT SUPPLIERS	1970	R1	USA	700		COSTA	ECUA	----
	1970	R2	GFR	683		CZECH	ECUA	----
	1970	R3	UNKI	292		CUBA	FRANC	----
	1980	R1	GFR	324		CZECH	FINLA	----
	1980	R2	USA	322		CZECH	GDR	----
	1980	R3	UNKI	123		COSTA	INDIA	----
V50 PROVENANCE OF FOREIGN FIRMS	1980	R1	SWEDN	26.3	%	-------	FINLA	----
	1980	R2	USA	20.2	%	AURIA	FINLA	----
	1980	R3	UNKI	19.9	%	BRAZI	DOMI	----
V51 FILM SUPPLIERS	1980	R1	USA	137		COLO	EGYPT	F120
	1980	R2	FRANC	20		AULIA	ITALY	F120
	1980	R3	UNKI	19		COLO	INDIA	F120

DOMINICAN REPUBLIC (DOMI)

V1 INCOME PER CAPITA	1970	D5	P43	841	$/CAP	NIGRA	GUATE	F4
	1975	D5	P49	1107	$/CAP	TUNIS	PERU	----
	1980	D5	P49	1227	$/CAP	COLO	TUNIS	----

V2	TELEPHONES P. TSD. POPULATION	1970	D5	P45	12	1/TSD CAP	MOROC	EGYPT	----
		1975	D6	P49	24	1/TSD CAP	TUNIS	ETHIA	----
		1980	D5	P42	29	1/TSD CAP	ETHIA	ZIMBA	----
V3	INFANT MORTALITY RATE	1980	D5	P46	73.0	1/TSD	GUATE	MADA	F5
V4	PHYSICIANS P. MIL. POPULATION	1970	D7	P60	477	1/MIL	COLO	SOUAF	----
		1973	D6	----	536	1/MIL	COLO	TURKY	----
V5	ADULT LITERACY	1970	D5	P44	67.0	%	BRAZI	SINGA	----
V6	DURATION OF SCHOOLING	1970	D6	P55	7.9	YR	VENE	MALAY	----
		1975	D6	P60	8.9	YR	PHILI	ECUA	----
		1980	D7	P59	9.7	YR	AURIA	SINGA	----
V7	STUDENT ENROLLMENT RATIO	1970	D6	P60	6.7	%	MONGO	SINGA	----
		1975	D7	P61	10.1	%	KORSO	PORTU	----
V8	SHARE OF AGRICULTURAL LABOR	1970	D8	P77	53.2	%	PARA	MALAY	----
		1981	D6	P65	32.7	%	SYRIA	TUNIS	F46
V9	SHARE OF INDUSTRIAL LABOR	1970	D4	P36	23.3	%	PARA	PERU	----
		1981	D4	P32	26.4	%	MALAY	ELSA	F46
V10	SHARE OF SERVICE LABOR	1970	D3	P28	20.2	%	GHANA	HUNGA	----
		1981	D6	P54	35.0	%	FINLA	TRITO	F46
V11	SHARE OF ACADEMIC LABOR	1970	D2	P17	3.3	%	KORSO	TURKY	----
		1981	D4	P29	5.9	%	SRILA	MOROC	F46
V12	SHARE OF SELF-EMPLOYED LABOR	1970	D9	P88	40.1	%	GREC	INDO	F74
		1981	D8	P85	40.0	%	RWAN	GUATE	F46
V13	MILITARY EXPENDITURES	1970	D4	P32	0.072	TSD MIL $	GUATE	CAME	----
		1975	D4	P33	0.084	TSD MIL $	CAME	KENYA	----
		1980	D3	P28	0.100	TSD MIL $	MADA	HONDU	----
V14	MILITARY MANPOWER	1970	D4	P34	17	TSD CAP	BOLI	LIBYA	----
		1975	D4	P31	18	TSD CAP	ZAMBI	SRILA	----
		1980	D4	P39	24	TSD CAP	BOLI	ZAIRE	----
V15	MEN AT AGE 20 - 30	1970	D3	P25	273	TSD CAP	ZAMBI	HAITI	----
		1980	D3	P20	371	TSD CAP	ISRA	DENMA	F2
V16	POPULATION	1970	D4	P32	4.06	MIL CAP	NIGER	HAITI	F4
		1975	D4	P34	4.75	MIL CAP	FINLA	BOLI	----
		1980	D4	P35	5.44	MIL CAP	NIGER	BOLI	----
V17	GROSS DOMESTIC PRODUCT	1970	D4	P34	3.414	TSD MIL $	TANZA	KENYA	----
		1975	D4	P38	5.260	TSD MIL $	KENYA	GUATE	----
		1980	D5	P41	6.673	TSD MIL $	KENYA	URU	----
V18	SHARE IN WORLD IMPORTS	1970	D4	P34	0.837	1/TSD	ECUA	GUATE	F49
		1975	D4	P37	0.850	1/TSD	SRILA	TANZA	F49
		1980	D4	P36	0.730	1/TSD	PANA	COSTA	F49
V19	SHARE IN WORLD EXPORTS	1970	D4	P35	0.682	1/TSD	LIBE	ELSA	F30
		1975	D5	P45	1.020	1/TSD	ZAIRE	ECUA	F30
		1980	D4	P34	0.482	1/TSD	CONGO	JAMAI	F30

V20	GDP SHARE OF IMPORTS	1970	D6	P51	18.7	%	GHANA	MADA	F49
		1975	D5	P43	21.5	%	SOMA	GABON	F49
		1980	D5	P43	22.6	%	PAKI	CANA	F49
V21	GDP SHARE OF EXPORTS	1970	D5	P45	14.4	%	AULIA	SUDAN	F30
		1975	D8	P74	24.8	%	SENE	COSTA	F30
		1980	D4	P34	14.5	%	CENTR	EGYPT	F30
V22	EXPORT PARTNER CONCENTRATION	1970	D10	P100	81.3	%	MEXI	-------	F137
		1975	D10	P98	68.8	%	TRITO	LAOS	----
		1980	D10	P97	63.4	%	CANA	MEXI	----
V23	TOTAL DEBT AS % OF GDP	1980	D4	P40	30.2	%	INDO	MEXI	----
V24	SHARE OF NEW FOREIGN PATENTS	1970	D7	P70	97	%	SYRIA	IRE	----
		1976	D7	P69	94	%	CANA	ELSA	----
		1980	D5	P46	88	%	DENMA	VENE	----
V25	FOREIGN PROPERTY AS % OF GDP	1971	D8	P72	16.8	%	SIERA	CAME	----
		1975	D7	P67	9.7	%	COLO	MADA	----
		1978	D7	----	8.2	%	COSTA	SOMA	----
V26	GNP SHARE OF DEVELOPMENT AID	------	----	----	-----	-----	-------	-------	----
V27	SHARE IN NOBEL PRIZE WINNERS	1970-79	D5	P45	0.0	%	CZECH	ECUA	----
V28	GDP SHARE OF MANUFACTURING	1970	D7	P64	18.5	%	DENMA	IRE	----
		1975	D8	P75	20.9	%	COLO	NICA	----
		1980	D6	P54	15.1	%	ELSA	JAMAI	----
V29	EXPORT SHARE OF MANUFACTURES	------	----	----	-----	-----	-------	-------	----
V30	LACK OF CIVIL LIBERTIES	1975	D2	P18	2		COLO	FINLA	----
		1980	D3	P29	3		COLO	ELSA	----
V31	LACK OF POLITICAL RIGHTS	1975	D4	P31	4		BRAZI	GUATE	----
		1980	D3	P21	2		COLO	ECUA	----
V32	RIOTS	1970-74	D7	P68	5		UGADA	INDO	----
		1975-79	D6	P53	2		CZECH	IRAQ	----
V33	PROTEST DEMONSTRATIONS	1970-74	D4	P37	1		CUBA	FINLA	----
		1975-79	D2	P13	0		DENMA	ECUA	----
V34	POLITICAL STRIKES	1970-74	D3	P29	0		CZECH	ECUA	----
		1975-79	D3	P29	0		CUBA	EGYPT	----
V35	MEMBER OF THE NONALIGNED MMT.	1970	----	----	0		DENMA	ECUA	----
		1976	----	----	0		DENMA	ECUA	----
		1981	----	----	0		DENMA	ELSA	----
V36	MEMBER OF THE OPEC	1970	----	----	0		DENMA	ECUA	----
		1975	----	----	0		DENMA	EGYPT	----
		1980	----	----	0		DENMA	EGYPT	----
V37	MEMBER OF THE OECD	1970	----	----	0		CZECH	ECUA	----
		1975	----	----	0		CZECH	ECUA	----
		1980	----	----	0		CZECH	ECUA	----

V38	MEMBER OF THE CMEA	1970	----	----	0		DENMA	ECUA	----
		1975	----	----	0		DENMA	ECUA	----
		1980	----	----	0		DENMA	ECUA	----
V39	MEMBER OF THE WTO	1970	----	----	0		DENMA	ECUA	----
		1975	----	----	0		DENMA	ECUA	----
		1980	----	----	0		DENMA	ECUA	----
V40	MEMBER OF THE NATO	1970	----	----	0		CZECH	ECUA	----
		1975	----	----	0		CZECH	ECUA	----
		1980	----	----	0		CZECH	ECUA	----
V41	GDP SHARE OF INVESTMENTS	1970	D5	P48	19.1	%	SRILA	UNKI	----
		1975	D7	P62	24.5	%	SWEDN	LESO	----
		1980	D6	P59	25.7	%	COLO	PORTU	----
V42	GDP SHARE OF AGRICULTURE	1970	D6	P52	23.2	%	COSTA	ECUA	----
		1975	D5	P51	21.5	%	TUNIS	NICA	----
		1980	D6	P50	20.9	%	SYRIA	EGYPT	----
V43	GDP SHARE OF INDUSTRY	1970	D5	P47	26.1	%	NICA	COLO	----
		1975	D6	P53	31.6	%	NEWZ	ZAIRE	----
		1980	D4	P37	27.6	%	COSTA	LIBE	----
V44	GDP SHARE OF SERVICES	1970	D6	P58	50.7	%	GREC	JAMAI	----
		1975	D6	P54	46.9	%	VENE	MOROC	----
		1980	D7	P69	51.5	%	GREC	SENE	----
V45	HOMICIDES P. MIL. POPULATION	------	----	----	----- -----		-------	-------	----
V46	SUICIDES P. MIL. POPULATION	------	----	----	----- -----		-------	-------	----
V47	IMPORT PARTNERS	1980	R1	USA	44.9	%	COSTA	ECUA	----
		1980	R2	VENE	21.1	%	-------	GUATE	----
		1980	R3	JAPAN	8.0	%	CHILE	GUATE	----
V48	EXPORT PARTNERS	1970	R1	USA	81.3	%	COSTA	ECUA	F137
		1970	R2	BELGI	4.4	%	ZAIRE	HAITI	F139
		1970	R3	SPAIN	3.9	%	-------	-------	F137
		1980	R1	USA	63.4	%	COSTA	ECUA	----
		1980	R2	VENE	12.0	%	-------	COLO	----
		1980	R3	NETH	6.9	%	CAME	MALAW	----
V49	PATENT SUPPLIERS	------	----	----	----- -----		-------	-------	----
V50	PROVENANCE OF FOREIGN FIRMS	1980	R1	USA	75.2	%	COSTA	ECUA	----
		1980	R2	NETH	6.6	%	BELGI	ELSA	----
		1980	R3	UNKI	4.7	%	DENMA	EGYPT	----
V51	FILM SUPPLIERS	------	----	----	----- -----		-------	-------	----

ECUADOR (ECUA)

V1	INCOME PER CAPITA	1970	D4	P36	712	$/CAP	LIBE	ZAMBI	F157
		1975	D5	P44	1030	$/CAP	PARA	IVORY	F157
		1980	D5	P47	1193	$/CAP	IVORY	COLO	F157
V2	TELEPHONES P. TSD. POPULATION	1970	D6	P53	17	1/TSD CAP	TURKY	PERU	----
		1975	D6	P53	27	1/TSD CAP	TURKY	LIBYA	----
		1980	D5	P47	33	1/TSD CAP	SYRIA	CUBA	----
V3	INFANT MORTALITY RATE	------	----	----	-----	-----	-------	-------	----
V4	PHYSICIANS P. MIL. POPULATION	1970	D6	P50	349	1/MIL	IRAQ	LIBYA	F157
		1975	D6	P55	499	1/MIL	SAUDI	KORSO	F157
V5	ADULT LITERACY	------	----	----	-----	-----	-------	-------	----
V6	DURATION OF SCHOOLING	1970	D6	P53	7.6	YR	ZAMBI	VENE	----
		1975	D7	P61	9.0	YR	DOMI	MONGO	----
		1980	D8	P69	10.3	YR	BULGA	TRITO	----
V7	STUDENT ENROLLMENT RATIO	1970	D7	P63	7.9	%	PANA	KORSO	----
		1975	D10	P95	27.9	%	FINLA	SWEDN	----
		1980	D10	P99	37.3	%	SWEDN	USA	----
V8	SHARE OF AGRICULTURAL LABOR	1974	D7	P68	49.3	%	KORSO	SYRIA	----
V9	SHARE OF INDUSTRIAL LABOR	1974	D4	P41	24.1	%	KORSO	PAKI	----
V10	SHARE OF SERVICE LABOR	1974	D5	P43	21.0	%	PHILI	BULGA	----
V11	SHARE OF ACADEMIC LABOR	1974	D5	P46	5.6	%	PHILI	COLO	----
V12	SHARE OF SELF-EMPLOYED LABOR	1974	D7	P65	39.6	%	SYRIA	GUATE	----
V13	MILITARY EXPENDITURES	1970	D4	P37	0.093	TSD MIL $	GHANA	URU	----
		1975	D5	P43	0.172	TSD MIL $	ETHIA	ZAIRE	----
		1980	D4	P38	0.188	TSD MIL $	TUNIS	URU	----
V14	MILITARY MANPOWER	1970	D4	P33	16	TSD CAP	SINGA	UGADA	----
		1975	D4	P35	20	TSD CAP	BOLI	GHANA	----
		1980	D5	P45	35	TSD CAP	DENMA	KAMPU	----
V15	MEN AT AGE 20 - 30	1969	D4	P36	437	TSD CAP	DENMA	AURIA	F187
		1974	D5	P43	503	TSD CAP	SWITZ	AURIA	F166
		1980	D4	P38	665	TSD CAP	BULGA	GREC	F187
V16	POPULATION	1970	D5	P44	5.96	MIL CAP	UPVO	SAUDI	F166
		1975	D5	P46	7.06	MIL CAP	IVORY	KAMPU	F166
		1980	D5	P48	8.35	MIL CAP	SWEDN	CAME	F166
V17	GROSS DOMESTIC PRODUCT	1970	D5	P42	4.246	TSD MIL $	GHANA	GUATE	----
		1975	D5	P45	7.272	TSD MIL $	IVORY	SINGA	----
		1980	D5	P47	9.965	TSD MIL $	IVORY	SINGA	----
V18	SHARE IN WORLD IMPORTS	1970	D4	P34	0.825	1/TSD	CAME	DOMI	F30
		1975	D5	P42	1.037	1/TSD	ZAMBI	PANA	F47
		1980	D5	P45	1.098	1/TSD	SRILA	OMAN	F47

V19	SHARE IN WORLD EXPORTS	1970	D4	P31	0.606	1/TSD	BOLI	LEBA	F30
		1975	D5	P46	1.024	1/TSD	DOMI	SYRIA	F47
		1980	D5	P49	1.243	1/TSD	MOROC	OMAN	F47
V20	GDP SHARE OF IMPORTS	1970	D5	P43	16.4	%	IRAN	GFR	F30
		1975	D5	P45	21.9	%	GABON	CONGO	F47
		1980	D4	P35	19.2	%	LIBYA	SUDAN	F47
V21	GDP SHARE OF EXPORTS	1970	D4	P31	11.3	%	CONGO	SYRIA	F30
		1975	D6	P60	20.8	%	KENYA	TOGO	F47
		1980	D6	P57	21.1	%	NICA	CAME	F47
V22	EXPORT PARTNER CONCENTRATION	1970	D8	P80	42.6	%	COSTA	MALAW	----
		1975	D9	P84	46.4	%	BURU	UPVO	----
		1980	D7	P69	32.5	%	PERU	UPVO	----
V23	TOTAL DEBT AS % OF GDP	1980	D7	P68	48.0	%	SRILA	KENYA	----
V24	SHARE OF NEW FOREIGN PATENTS	1970	D7	P67	96	%	PORTU	EGYPT	----
		1975	D4	P40	87	%	BOLI	CHILE	----
		1980	D9	P87	99	%	SRILA	MALAY	----
V25	FOREIGN PROPERTY AS % OF GDP	1971	D8	P79	18.7	%	ZAMBI	IVORY	----
		1975	D8	P74	11.6	%	INDO	SIERA	----
		1978	D7	----	8.6	%	SOMA	MADA	----
V26	GNP SHARE OF DEVELOPMENT AID	------	----	----	-----	-----	-------	-------	----
V27	SHARE IN NOBEL PRIZE WINNERS	1970-79	D5	P45	0.0	%	DOMI	EGYPT	----
V28	GDP SHARE OF MANUFACTURING	1970	D7	P69	19.5	%	GREC	CANA	----
		1975	D5	P45	12.9	%	PANA	MALAW	----
		1980	D4	P34	8.8	%	PAPUA	BURU	----
V29	EXPORT SHARE OF MANUFACTURES	------	----	----	-----	-----	-------	-------	----
V30	LACK OF CIVIL LIBERTIES	1975	D4	P39	4		CAME	EGYPT	----
		1980	D2	P18	2		USA	FINLA	----
V31	LACK OF POLITICAL RIGHTS	1975	D9	P88	7		CZECH	GDR	----
		1980	D3	P21	2		DOMI	FINLA	----
V32	RIOTS	1970-74	D5	P43	1		COSTA	GHANA	----
		1975-79	D8	P79	8		USSR	LAOS	----
V33	PROTEST DEMONSTRATIONS	1970-74	D6	P54	3		BOLI	SINGA	----
		1975-79	D2	P13	0		DOMI	GUINE	----
V34	POLITICAL STRIKES	1970-74	D3	P29	0		DOMI	ELSA	----
		1975-79	D9	P83	6		COLO	INDIA	----
V35	MEMBER OF THE NONALIGNED MMT.	1970	----	----	0		DOMI	ELSA	----
		1976	----	----	0		DOMI	ELSA	----
		1981	----	----	1		CUBA	EGYPT	----
V36	MEMBER OF THE OPEC	1970	----	----	0		DOMI	EGYPT	----
		1975	----	----	1		ALGER	GABON	----
		1980	----	----	1		ALGER	GABON	----

V37	MEMBER OF THE OECD	1970	----	----	0		DOMI	EGYPT	----
		1975	----	----	0		DOMI	EGYPT	----
		1980	----	----	0		DOMI	EGYPT	----
V38	MEMBER OF THE CMEA	1970	----	----	0		DOMI	EGYPT	----
		1975	----	----	0		DOMI	EGYPT	----
		1980	----	----	0		DOMI	EGYPT	----
V39	MEMBER OF THE WTO	1970	----	----	0		DOMI	EGYPT	----
		1975	----	----	0		DOMI	EGYPT	----
		1980	----	----	0		DOMI	EGYPT	----
V40	MEMBER OF THE NATO	1970	----	----	0		DOMI	EGYPT	----
		1975	----	----	0		DOMI	EGYPT	----
		1980	----	----	0		DOMI	EGYPT	----
V41	GDP SHARE OF INVESTMENTS	1970	D5	P41	18.2 %		NIGER	MOROC	----
		1975	D8	P71	26.7 %		SPAIN	GREC	----
		1980	D8	P70	27.9 %		FINLA	IRE	----
V42	GDP SHARE OF AGRICULTURE	1970	D6	P53	23.9 %		DOMI	LIBE	----
		1975	D5	P44	17.9 %		IRE	MOROC	----
		1980	D4	P39	12.3 %		YUGO	PORTU	----
V43	GDP SHARE OF INDUSTRY	1970	D5	P41	24.6 %		COSTA	THAI	----
		1975	D7	P65	33.9 %		KORSO	PERU	----
		1980	D8	P73	37.7 %		CHILE	ARGE	----
V44	GDP SHARE OF SERVICES	1970	D7	P63	51.5 %		ALGER	SOUAF	----
		1975	D7	P61	48.2 %		BENIN	NICA	----
		1980	D7	P63	50.0 %		GFR	CAME	----
V45	HOMICIDES P. MIL. POPULATION	1971	D9	P83	73.6 1/MIL CAP		ARGE	VENE	F179
		1974	D9	P81	71.6 1/MIL CAP		TRITO	VENE	F158
		1978	D9	----	60.6 1/MIL CAP		COSTA	USA	F158
V46	SUICIDES P. MIL. POPULATION	1971	D2	P12	23.0 1/MIL CAP		PERU	COSTA	F180
		1974	D1	P10	26.4 1/MIL CAP		PARA	GREC	F157
		1978	D2	----	27.3 1/MIL CAP		PARA	GREC	F157
V47	IMPORT PARTNERS	1970	R1	USA	43.6 %		COSTA	ELSA	----
		1970	R2	GFR	11.1 %		CONGO	GDR	----
		1970	R3	JAPAN	9.3 %		COLO	ELSA	----
		1980	R1	USA	38.9 %		DOMI	EGYPT	----
		1980	R2	JAPAN	13.9 %		CUBA	GREC	----
		1980	R3	GFR	7.4 %		CONGO	EGYPT	----
V48	EXPORT PARTNERS	1970	R1	USA	42.6 %		DOMI	ETHIA	----
		1970	R2	JAPAN	17.9 %		BENIN	KORSO	----
		1970	R3	GFR	9.3 %		DENMA	GHANA	----
		1980	R1	USA	32.5 %		DOMI	ELSA	----
		1980	R2	JAPAN	12.3 %		CANA	KORSO	----
		1980	R3	CHILE	8.9 %		-------	-------	----

V49	PATENT SUPPLIERS	1972	R1	USA	47		DENMA	EGYPT	----
		1972	R2	GFR	46		DENMA	FRANC	----
		1972	R3	CANA	13		-------	-------	----
		1980	R1	USA	40		COSTA	EGYPT	----
		1980	R2	SPAIN	10		-------	BOLI	----
V50	PROVENANCE OF FOREIGN FIRMS	1980	R1	USA	72.2	%	DOMI	EGYPT	----
		1980	R2	UNKI	8.3	%	COLO	FRANC	----
		1980	R3	GFR	5.7	%	COLO	FRANC	----
V51	FILM SUPPLIERS	------	----	----	----- -----		-------	-------	----

EGYPT (EGYPT)

V1	INCOME PER CAPITA	------	----	----	----- -----		-------	-------	----
V2	TELEPHONES P. TSD. POPULATION	1970	D5	P45	12	1/TSD CAP	DOMI	IRAQ	----
		1975	D5	P39	13	1/TSD CAP	ZAMBI	PAPUA	----
V3	INFANT MORTALITY RATE	1979	D5	P48	76.4	1/TSD	MADA	BRAZI	----
V4	PHYSICIANS P. MIL. POPULATION	1973	D5	----	427	1/MIL	IRAQ	PARA	----
		1981	D7	P63	1227	1/MIL	VENE	IRE	----
V5	ADULT LITERACY	------	----	----	----- -----		-------	-------	----
V6	DURATION OF SCHOOLING	1970	D5	P42	6.6	YR	HONDU	ELSA	----
		1975	D4	P37	7.0	YR	ZAIRE	GHANA	----
		1980	D4	P37	8.0	YR	ANGO	PARA	----
V7	STUDENT ENROLLMENT RATIO	1970	D7	P65	8.6	%	PORTU	SPAIN	----
		1975	D8	P70	14.0	%	SWITZ	PERU	----
		1980	D7	P65	15.1	%	KORSO	BULGA	----
V8	SHARE OF AGRICULTURAL LABOR	1976	D6	P58	44.5	%	MEXI	ELSA	F97
		1980	D7	P78	41.7	%	ELSA	MOROC	F104
V9	SHARE OF INDUSTRIAL LABOR	1976	D4	P36	22.7	%	MEXI	KORSO	F97
		1980	D3	P21	23.3	%	ITALY	PANA	F104
V10	SHARE OF SERVICE LABOR	1976	D5	P52	24.9	%	KORSO	ELSA	F97
		1980	D4	P31	25.0	%	HUNGA	MALAY	F104
V11	SHARE OF ACADEMIC LABOR	1976	D6	P56	7.9	%	IRAN	SPAIN	F97
		1980	D6	P58	10.1	%	VENE	TRITO	F104
V12	SHARE OF SELF-EMPLOYED LABOR	1976	D6	P53	31.2	%	MEXI	ELSA	F97
		1980	D6	P65	29.8	%	ELSA	MALAY	F104
V13	MILITARY EXPENDITURES	------	----	----	----- -----		-------	-------	----

V14	MILITARY MANPOWER	1970	D9	P83	255	TSD CAP	IRAN	YUGO	----
		1975	D9	P86	400	TSD CAP	IRAN	POLA	----
		1980	D10	P92	447	TSD CAP	POLA	BRAZI	----
V15	MEN AT AGE 20 - 30	1976	D9	P80	2844	TSD CAP	SPAIN	KORSO	----
V16	POPULATION	1970	D9	P83	33.33	MIL CAP	POLA	SPAIN	----
		1975	D9	P85	37.01	MIL CAP	SPAIN	TURKY	----
		1980	D9	P84	42.29	MIL CAP	IRAN	TURKY	----
V17	GROSS DOMESTIC PRODUCT	------	----	----	-----	-----	-------	-------	----
V18	SHARE IN WORLD IMPORTS	1970	D6	P54	2.371	1/TSD	SAUDI	COLO	----
		1975	D7	P63	4.328	1/TSD	CUBA	ARGE	F54
		1980	D6	P54	2.369	1/TSD	COLO	CHILE	F54
V19	SHARE IN WORLD EXPORTS	1970	D6	P54	2.429	1/TSD	COLO	ZAIRE	----
		1975	D6	P52	1.600	1/TSD	TURKY	COLO	----
		1980	D6	P52	1.526	1/TSD	TURKY	IVORY	----
V20	GDP SHARE OF IMPORTS	1970	D2	P17	11.2	%	INDO	CHILE	----
		1975	D8	P79	34.2	%	NORWY	KORSO	F54
		1980	D5	P46	23.2	%	NEWZ	GFR	F53
V21	GDP SHARE OF EXPORTS	1970	D3	P25	10.8	%	PANA	PARA	----
		1975	D4	P31	12.2	%	HAITI	SOMA	----
		1980	D4	P36	14.6	%	DOMI	IRAN	----
V22	EXPORT PARTNER CONCENTRATION	1970	D8	P71	37.0	%	COLO	GDR	----
		1975	D9	P81	43.2	%	CENTR	INDO	----
		1980	D6	P59	28.6	%	BENIN	GUATE	----
V23	TOTAL DEBT AS % OF GDP	1980	D10	P92	82.7	%	CONGO	PANA	----
V24	SHARE OF NEW FOREIGN PATENTS	1970	D7	P67	96	%	ECUA	PHILI	----
		1975	D8	P72	95	%	TURKY	IRAQ	----
		1980	D8	P80	97	%	COLO	HONDU	----
V25	FOREIGN PROPERTY AS % OF GDP	1971	D1	P6	1.1	%	NEPAL	AFGHA	----
		1975	D1	P5	0.6	%	BANGL	NEPAL	----
		1978	D3	----	1.7	%	ALGER	THAI	----
V26	GNP SHARE OF DEVELOPMENT AID	------	----	----	-----	-----	-------	-------	----
V27	SHARE IN NOBEL PRIZE WINNERS	1970-79	D5	P45	0.0	%	ECUA	ELSA	----
V28	GDP SHARE OF MANUFACTURING	------	----	----	-----	-----	-------	-------	----
V29	EXPORT SHARE OF MANUFACTURES	1970	D7	P69	26.1	%	HAITI	GUATE	----
		1975	D8	P77	32.2	%	URU	GREC	----
		1980	D5	P44	10.4	%	KUWAI	HONDU	----
V30	LACK OF CIVIL LIBERTIES	1975	D4	P39	4		ECUA	KENYA	----
		1980	D6	P52	5		CHINA	GUATE	----
V31	LACK OF POLITICAL RIGHTS	1975	D7	P63	6		CHAD	ETHIA	----
		1980	D5	P47	5		BHUTA	ELSA	----
V32	RIOTS	1970-74	D8	P80	11		BOLI	GFR	----
		1975-79	D7	P65	4		CHINA	ELSA	----

V33	PROTEST DEMONSTRATIONS	1970-74	D8	P74	9	YUGO	MEXI	----
		1975-79	D8	P71	10	BOLI	JAMAI	----
V34	POLITICAL STRIKES	1970-74	D8	P78	3	VISO	KAMPU	----
		1975-79	D3	P29	0	DOMI	ELSA	----
V35	MEMBER OF THE NONALIGNED MMT.	1970	----	----	1	CUBA	ETHIA	----
		1976	----	----	1	CUBA	ETHIA	----
		1981	----	----	1	ECUA	ETHIA	----
V36	MEMBER OF THE OPEC	1970	----	----	0	ECUA	ELSA	----
		1975	----	----	0	DOMI	ELSA	----
		1980	----	----	0	DOMI	ELSA	----
V37	MEMBER OF THE OECD	1970	----	----	0	ECUA	ELSA	----
		1975	----	----	0	ECUA	ELSA	----
		1980	----	----	0	ECUA	ELSA	----
V38	MEMBER OF THE CMEA	1970	----	----	0	ECUA	ELSA	----
		1975	----	----	0	ECUA	ELSA	----
		1980	----	----	0	ECUA	ELSA	----
V39	MEMBER OF THE WTO	1970	----	----	0	ECUA	ELSA	----
		1975	----	----	0	ECUA	ELSA	----
		1980	----	----	0	ECUA	ELSA	----
V40	MEMBER OF THE NATO	1970	----	----	0	ECUA	ELSA	----
		1975	----	----	0	ECUA	ELSA	----
		1980	----	----	0	ECUA	ELSA	----
V41	GDP SHARE OF INVESTMENTS	1970	D3	P20	13.9 %	SYRIA	BURMA	----
		1975	D10	P91	33.4 %	JAPAN	YUGO	----
		1979	D10	P92	32.8 %	JAPAN	ZAIRE	----
V42	GDP SHARE OF AGRICULTURE	1970	D7	P68	29.4 %	MAURA	MADA	F16
		1975	D6	P61	29.0 %	PHILI	TURKY	F16
		1980	D6	P51	21.2 %	DOMI	NIGRA	F16
V43	GDP SHARE OF INDUSTRY	1970	D6	P51	28.2 %	TURKY	KORSO	F16
		1975	D5	P41	26.9 %	TOGO	DENMA	F16
		1980	D8	P75	38.1 %	ARGE	ZIMBA	F16
V44	GDP SHARE OF SERVICES	1970	D4	P30	42.4 %	SUDAN	PHILI	F16
		1975	D5	P45	44.1 %	THAI	PAKI	F16
		1980	D3	P29	40.7 %	SOUAF	BURMA	F16
V45	HOMICIDES P. MIL. POPULATION	------	----	----	----- -----	-------	-------	----
V46	SUICIDES P. MIL. POPULATION	------	----	----	----- -----	-------	-------	----
V47	IMPORT PARTNERS	1970	R1	USSR	12.1 %	CZECH	GDR	----
		1970	R2	INDIA	7.9 %	BURMA	SUDAN	----
		1970	R3	GFR	7.8 %	COSTA	ETHIA	----
		1980	R1	USA	19.3 %	ECUA	GUATE	----
		1980	R2	FRANC	10.2 %	UPVO	GFR	----
		1980	R3	GFR	9.6 %	ECUA	ETHIA	----

V48	EXPORT PARTNERS	1970	R1	USSR	37.0 %	CZECH	GDR	----
		1970	R2	GDR	6.0 %	CZECH	HUNGA	----
		1970	R3	INDIA	5.4 %	AFGHA	TANZA	----
		1980	R1	ITALY	28.6 %	CONGO	SYRIA	----
		1980	R2	USA	7.7 %	AULIA	GABON	----
		1980	R3	ISRA	6.0 %	CENTR	-------	----
V49	PATENT SUPPLIERS	1970	R1	USA	72	ECUA	FRANC	----
		1970	R2	USSR	38	-------	-------	----
		1970	R3	GFR	33	AULIA	FINLA	----
		1980	R1	USA	97	ECUA	ELSA	----
		1980	R2	GFR	61	COSTA	ELSA	----
		1980	R3	FRANC	32	BRAZI	GREC	----
V50	PROVENANCE OF FOREIGN FIRMS	1980	R1	USA	29.6 %	ECUA	ELSA	----
		1980	R2	BELGI	14.8 %	CONGO	-------	----
		1980	R3	UNKI	11.1 %	DOMI	FINLA	----
V51	FILM SUPPLIERS	1978	R1	USA	199	DENMA	ETHIA	F118
		1978	R2	ITALY	74	COLO	FRANC	F118
		1978	R3	USSR	26	ANGO	-------	F118

EL SALVADOR (ELSA)

V1	INCOME PER CAPITA	1970	D4	P33	634 $/CAP	MOROC	LIBE	F4
		1975	D4	P37	728 $/CAP	ZAMBI	MOROC	----
		1980	D4	P32	647 $/CAP	ZAMBI	THAI	----
V2	TELEPHONES P. TSD. POPULATION	1970	D5	P42	11 1/TSD CAP	PARA	IRAN	----
		1975	D5	P43	15 1/TSD CAP	PARA	JORDA	----
		1980	D4	P36	19 1/TSD CAP	PARA	NICA	----
V3	INFANT MORTALITY RATE	1980	D4	P39	42.0 1/TSD	SRILA	VENE	----
V4	PHYSICIANS P. MIL. POPULATION	1970	D5	P44	248 1/MIL	GUATE	SRILA	----
		1976	D5	P42	271 1/MIL	INDIA	JAMAI	----
		1980	D5	P41	314 1/MIL	INDIA	HONDU	----
V5	ADULT LITERACY	1971	D4	P36	57.1 %	INDO	NICA	----
V6	DURATION OF SCHOOLING	1970	D5	P42	6.6 YR	EGYPT	CHINA	F4
		1975	D5	P43	7.6 YR	THAI	IRAN	----
		1980	D4	P32	7.6 YR	TANZA	HONDU	----
V7	STUDENT ENROLLMENT RATIO	1970	D5	P46	3.2 %	TRITO	GUATE	----
		1975	D6	P52	7.9 %	PARA	COLO	----
		1980	D4	P39	3.9 %	IRAN	INDO	----
V8	SHARE OF AGRICULTURAL LABOR	1971	D9	P85	57.3 %	MOROC	GHANA	----
		1975	D7	P61	46.4 %	EGYPT	BOLI	----
		1980	D7	P75	40.2 %	PERU	EGYPT	----

V9	SHARE OF INDUSTRIAL LABOR	1971	D2	P16	17.2	%	TURKY	MALAY	----
		1975	D3	P29	21.1	%	GUATE	TURKY	----
		1980	D4	P34	26.9	%	DOMI	MEXI	----
V10	SHARE OF SERVICE LABOR	1971	D4	P33	21.8	%	PARA	MALAY	----
		1975	D5	P55	28.3	%	EGYPT	COSTA	----
		1980	D5	P35	28.6	%	MALAY	GREC	----
V11	SHARE OF ACADEMIC LABOR	1971	D3	P21	3.7	%	IRAN	GHANA	----
		1975	D4	P30	4.3	%	HONDU	YENO	----
		1980	D3	P19	4.3	%	INDIA	TURKY	----
V12	SHARE OF SELF-EMPLOYED LABOR	1971	D6	P59	28.3	%	SRILA	THAI	----
		1975	D6	P56	33.5	%	EGYPT	IRAN	----
		1980	D6	P62	28.7	%	VENE	EGYPT	----
V13	MILITARY EXPENDITURES	1970	D2	P18	0.022	TSD MIL $	HONDU	NICA	----
		1975	D3	P23	0.046	TSD MIL $	PARA	SRILA	----
		1980	D3	P25	0.082	TSD MIL $	CAME	MADA	----
V14	MILITARY MANPOWER	1970	D1	P10	4	TSD CAP	SIERA	MALAW	----
		1975	D3	P20	8	TSD CAP	SENE	MALI	----
		1980	D3	P22	12	TSD CAP	CAME	KUWAI	----
V15	MEN AT AGE 20 - 30	1971	D3	P23	258	TSD CAP	ISRA	ZAMBI	----
V16	POPULATION	1970	D3	P26	3.53	MIL CAP	ISRA	BURU	F4
		1975	D3	P28	4.01	MIL CAP	BURU	NORWY	----
		1980	D3	P29	4.75	MIL CAP	SOMA	FINLA	----
V17	GROSS DOMESTIC PRODUCT	1970	D3	P24	2.238	TSD MIL $	PANA	SENE	----
		1975	D3	P26	2.919	TSD MIL $	MADA	JAMAI	----
		1980	D3	P24	3.075	TSD MIL $	GABON	JORDA	----
V18	SHARE IN WORLD IMPORTS	1970	D3	P30	0.645	1/TSD	YESO	HONDU	----
		1975	D4	P32	0.658	1/TSD	SENE	CAME	----
		1980	D3	P28	0.476	1/TSD	NICA	HONDU	----
V19	SHARE IN WORLD EXPORTS	1970	D4	P36	0.727	1/TSD	DOMI	COSTA	----
		1975	D4	P38	0.585	1/TSD	COSTA	SRILA	----
		1980	D3	P28	0.361	1/TSD	AFGHA	BANGL	----
V20	GDP SHARE OF IMPORTS	1970	D6	P60	20.8	%	CONGO	YUGO	----
		1975	D8	P77	33.4	%	NICA	NORWY	----
		1980	D7	P63	27.4	%	SWEDN	THAI	----
V21	GDP SHARE OF EXPORTS	1970	D8	P76	22.2	%	NORWY	NICA	----
		1975	D8	P79	28.6	%	HONDU	IVORY	----
		1980	D6	P53	20.2	%	BOLI	UNKI	----
V22	EXPORT PARTNER CONCENTRATION	1970	D5	P44	24.8	%	BRAZI	THAI	----
		1975	D6	P56	27.1	%	CONGO	IVORY	----
		1980	D7	P63	29.7	%	HUNGA	NETH	----
V23	TOTAL DEBT AS % OF GDP	1980	D4	P32	25.6	%	UPVO	BURMA	----
V24	SHARE OF NEW FOREIGN PATENTS	1976	D7	P69	94	%	DOMI	TURKY	----
		1980	D6	P57	91	%	CHILE	IRAN	----

V25	FOREIGN PROPERTY AS % OF GDP	1971	D5	P50	9.0 %	BENIN	GUATE	----
		1975	D6	P59	7.3 %	BRAZI	PHILI	----
		1978	D6	----	4.9 %	GUATE	ARGE	----
V26	GNP SHARE OF DEVELOPMENT AID	------	----	----	----- -----	-------	-------	----
V27	SHARE IN NOBEL PRIZE WINNERS	1970-79	D5	P45	0.0 %	EGYPT	ETHIA	----
V28	GDP SHARE OF MANUFACTURING	1970	D7	P66	18.8 %	IRE	GREC	----
		1975	D7	P66	18.6 %	DENMA	CANA	----
		1980	D6	P53	14.6 %	JORDA	DOMI	----
V29	EXPORT SHARE OF MANUFACTURES	1970	D8	P72	27.4 %	GUATE	CONGO	----
		1975	D8	P74	26.2 %	GUATE	URU	----
		1980	D8	P70	34.9 %	BRAZI	URU	----
V30	LACK OF CIVIL LIBERTIES	1975	D3	P27	3	VENE	GUATE	----
		1980	D3	P29	3	DOMI	HONDU	----
V31	LACK OF POLITICAL RIGHTS	1975	D2	P20	2	COLO	FINLA	----
		1980	D5	P47	5	EGYPT	INDO	----
V32	RIOTS	1970-74	D2	P19	0	DENMA	FINLA	----
		1975-79	D7	P65	4	EGYPT	MADA	----
V33	PROTEST DEMONSTRATIONS	1970-74	D2	P15	0	CONGO	GUINE	----
		1975-79	D6	P59	5	BURMA	HONDU	----
V34	POLITICAL STRIKES	1970-74	D3	P29	0	ECUA	FINLA	----
		1975-79	D3	P29	0	EGYPT	ETHIA	----
V35	MEMBER OF THE NONALIGNED MMT.	1970	----	----	0	ECUA	FINLA	----
		1976	----	----	0	ECUA	FINLA	----
		1981	----	----	0	DOMI	FINLA	----
V36	MEMBER OF THE OPEC	1970	----	----	0	EGYPT	ETHIA	----
		1975	----	----	0	EGYPT	ETHIA	----
		1980	----	----	0	EGYPT	ETHIA	----
V37	MEMBER OF THE OECD	1970	----	----	0	EGYPT	ETHIA	----
		1975	----	----	0	EGYPT	ETHIA	----
		1980	----	----	0	EGYPT	ETHIA	----
V38	MEMBER OF THE CMEA	1970	----	----	0	EGYPT	ETHIA	----
		1975	----	----	0	EGYPT	ETHIA	----
		1980	----	----	0	EGYPT	ETHIA	----
V39	MEMBER OF THE WTO	1970	----	----	0	EGYPT	ETHIA	----
		1975	----	----	0	EGYPT	ETHIA	----
		1980	----	----	0	EGYPT	ETHIA	----
V40	MEMBER OF THE NATO	1970	----	----	0	EGYPT	ETHIA	----
		1975	----	----	0	EGYPT	ETHIA	----
		1980	----	----	0	EGYPT	ETHIA	----
V41	GDP SHARE OF INVESTMENTS	1970	D2	P13	12.9 %	GUATE	PERU	----
		1975	D5	P49	22.1 %	COSTA	IRE	----
		1980	D1	P6	10.0 %	MOZAM	ETHIA	----

V42 GDP SHARE OF AGRICULTURE	1970	D7	P65	28.4	%	THAI	COLO	----
	1975	D6	P53	23.0	%	NICA	KORSO	----
	1980	D7	P65	27.7	%	SRILA	HONDU	----
V43 GDP SHARE OF INDUSTRY	1970	D4	P36	23.3	%	HONDU	TUNIS	----
	1975	D4	P36	24.9	%	THAI	TURKY	----
	1980	D2	P18	19.8	%	MALAW	CAME	----
V44 GDP SHARE OF SERVICES	1970	D6	P52	48.3	%	SRILA	ITALY	----
	1975	D8	P73	52.1	%	BOLI	PERU	----
	1980	D8	P71	52.5	%	SENE	BOLI	----
V45 HOMICIDES P. MIL. POPULATION	1970	D10	P98	312.5	1/MIL CAP	GUATE	-------	F148
	1974	D10	P98	329.8	1/MIL CAP	THAI	-------	F154
V46 SUICIDES P. MIL. POPULATION	1970	D4	P37	70.5	1/MIL CAP	VENE	UNKI	----
	1974	D5	P52	108.0	1/MIL CAP	URU	AULIA	F2
V47 IMPORT PARTNERS	1970	R1	USA	29.6	%	ECUA	GUATE	----
	1970	R2	GUATE	19.0	%	-------	HONDU	----
	1970	R3	JAPAN	10.4	%	ECUA	GUATE	----
	1980	R1	GUATE	26.0	%	-------	-------	----
	1980	R2	USA	25.2	%	BURMA	GABON	----
	1980	R3	VENE	17.0	%	COSTA	-------	----
V48 EXPORT PARTNERS	1970	R1	GFR	24.8	%	CONGO	FRANC	----
	1970	R2	USA	21.4	%	CHILE	INDIA	----
	1970	R3	GUATE	17.4	%	-------	-------	----
	1980	R1	USA	29.7	%	ECUA	ETHIA	----
	1980	R2	GUATE	24.1	%	-------	HONDU	----
	1980	R3	COSTA	9.4	%	-------	NICA	----
V49 PATENT SUPPLIERS	1980	R1	USA	17		EGYPT	FRANC	----
	1980	R2	GFR	13		EGYPT	FRANC	----
	1980	R3	SWITZ	6		CHILE	GDR	----
V50 PROVENANCE OF FOREIGN FIRMS	1980	R1	USA	66.3	%	EGYPT	FRANC	----
	1980	R2	NETH	8.6	%	DOMI	HAITI	----
	1980	R3	JAPAN	7.7	%	COSTA	MALAY	----
V51 FILM SUPPLIERS	-------	----	----	-----	-----	-------	-------	----

ETHIOPIA (ETHIA)

V1 INCOME PER CAPITA	1970	D1	P2	129	$/CAP	-------	MALAW	----
	1975	D1	P3	132	$/CAP	BANGL	BURMA	----
	1980	D1	P2	132	$/CAP	-------	BANGL	----
V2 TELEPHONES P. TSD. POPULATION	1970	D2	P16	2	1/TSD CAP	YENO	GUINE	----
	1975	D6	P49	24	1/TSD CAP	DOMI	PERU	----
	1980	D4	P40	28	1/TSD CAP	PERU	DOMI	----

V3	INFANT MORTALITY RATE	1980	D9	P90	154.9	1/TSD	CHAD	SOMA	F5
V4	PHYSICIANS P. MIL. POPULATION	1970	D1	P3	14	1/MIL	UPVO	CHAD	----
		1976	D1	P2	12	1/MIL	-------	NIGER	----
		1980	D1	P2	14	1/MIL	-------	UPVO	----
V5	ADULT LITERACY	1970	D1	P3	4.2	%	-------	NEPAL	----
V6	DURATION OF SCHOOLING	1970	D1	P7	1.3	YR	UPVO	MAURA	----
		1975	D1	P6	1.9	YR	MAURA	MALI	----
		1980	D1	P9	3.4	YR	PAKI	YENO	----
V7	STUDENT ENROLLMENT RATIO	1970	D2	P13	0.2	%	BURU	LAOS	----
		1975	D1	P9	0.3	%	BURU	LAOS	----
		1980	D2	P12	0.5	%	TANZA	BURU	----
V8	SHARE OF AGRICULTURAL LABOR	------	----	----	-----	-----	-------	-------	----
V9	SHARE OF INDUSTRIAL LABOR	------	----	----	-----	-----	-------	-------	----
V10	SHARE OF SERVICE LABOR	------	----	----	-----	-----	-------	-------	----
V11	SHARE OF ACADEMIC LABOR	------	----	----	-----	-----	-------	-------	----
V12	SHARE OF SELF-EMPLOYED LABOR	------	----	----	-----	-----	-------	-------	----
V13	MILITARY EXPENDITURES	1970	D3	P29	0.062	TSD MIL $	SENE	GUATE	----
		1975	D5	P42	0.170	TSD MIL $	URU	ECUA	----
		1980	D5	P45	0.358	TSD MIL $	IRE	NEWZ	----
V14	MILITARY MANPOWER	1970	D5	P49	45	TSD CAP	DENMA	VENE	----
		1975	D6	P52	50	TSD CAP	COLO	SUDAN	----
		1980	D9	P84	250	TSD CAP	THAI	INDO	----
V15	MEN AT AGE 20 - 30	1980	D8	P69	2214	TSD CAP	ARGE	CANA	F2
V16	POPULATION	1970	D8	P79	24.63	MIL CAP	ARGE	BURMA	----
		1975	D8	P80	27.47	MIL CAP	ARGE	BURMA	----
		1980	D8	P80	31.07	MIL CAP	SOUAF	BURMA	----
V17	GROSS DOMESTIC PRODUCT	1970	D4	P30	3.166	TSD MIL $	MADA	ZAMBI	----
		1975	D3	P29	3.615	TSD MIL $	SRILA	ZAMBI	----
		1980	D3	P30	4.088	TSD MIL $	SRILA	PARA	----
V18	SHARE IN WORLD IMPORTS	1970	D3	P25	0.518	1/TSD	MADA	UGADA	F30
		1975	D2	P20	0.326	1/TSD	YENO	YESO	F30
		1980	D3	P24	0.352	1/TSD	MOZAM	ANGO	F30
V19	SHARE IN WORLD EXPORTS	1970	D3	P25	0.389	1/TSD	BURMA	YESO	F30
		1975	D3	P24	0.274	1/TSD	AFGHA	UGADA	F30
		1980	D2	P20	0.213	1/TSD	MONGO	NICA	F30
V20	GDP SHARE OF IMPORTS	1970	D1	P10	9.6	%	JAPAN	URU	F30
		1975	D2	P11	11.1	%	NEPAL	COLO	F30
		1980	D3	P27	17.6	%	BURU	NEPAL	F30
V21	GDP SHARE OF EXPORTS	1970	D2	P13	6.8	%	SPAIN	ARGE	F30
		1975	D2	P19	9.0	%	UGADA	PAKI	F30
		1980	D3	P24	10.4	%	TANZA	URU	F30

V22	EXPORT PARTNER CONCENTRATION	1970	D9	P85	50.4 %	CENTR	YENO	F137
		1975	D3	P29	19.5 %	TUNIS	SAUDI	----
		1980	D3	P25	18.1 %	URU	TUNIS	----
V23	TOTAL DEBT AS % OF GDP	1980	D2	P18	19.6 %	ARGE	SYRIA	----
V24	SHARE OF NEW FOREIGN PATENTS	------	----	----	----- -----	-------	-------	----
V25	FOREIGN PROPERTY AS % OF GDP	1971	D2	P20	3.5 %	SOMA	UGADA	----
		1975	D3	P30	3.7 %	ANGO	BOLI	----
		1978	D4	----	2.8 %	SRILA	RWAN	----
V26	GNP SHARE OF DEVELOPMENT AID	------	----	----	----- -----	-------	-------	----
V27	SHARE IN NOBEL PRIZE WINNERS	1970-79	D5	P45	0.0 %	ELSA	FINLA	----
V28	GDP SHARE OF MANUFACTURING	1970	D2	P19	8.9 %	JORDA	NEPAL	F16
		1975	D4	P39	11.2 %	NIGER	JORDA	F16
		1980	D4	P41	10.9 %	PANA	ALGER	F16
V29	EXPORT SHARE OF MANUFACTURES	1970	D2	P19	1.5 %	BURMA	KAMPU	----
V30	LACK OF CIVIL LIBERTIES	1975	D6	P54	5	CHILE	GHANA	----
		1980	D10	P92	7	CZECH	GDR	----
V31	LACK OF POLITICAL RIGHTS	1975	D7	P63	6	EGYPT	GABON	----
		1980	D9	P90	7	CZECH	GDR	----
V32	RIOTS	1970-74	D9	P85	16	PERU	USSR	----
		1975-79	D8	P75	7	COSTA	JAPAN	----
V33	PROTEST DEMONSTRATIONS	1970-74	D8	P80	16	SWEDN	CHINA	----
		1975-79	D7	P64	6	BELGI	NIGRA	----
V34	POLITICAL STRIKES	1970-74	D10	P91	14	ARGE	PORTU	----
		1975-79	D3	P29	0	ELSA	FINLA	----
V35	MEMBER OF THE NONALIGNED MMT.	1970	----	----	1	EGYPT	GHANA	----
		1976	----	----	1	EGYPT	GABON	----
		1981	----	----	1	EGYPT	GABON	----
V36	MEMBER OF THE OPEC	1970	----	----	0	ELSA	FINLA	----
		1975	----	----	0	ELSA	FINLA	----
		1980	----	----	0	ELSA	FINLA	----
V37	MEMBER OF THE OECD	1970	----	----	0	ELSA	GDR	----
		1975	----	----	0	ELSA	GABON	----
		1980	----	----	0	ELSA	GABON	----
V38	MEMBER OF THE CMEA	1970	----	----	0	ELSA	FINLA	----
		1975	----	----	0	ELSA	FINLA	----
		1980	----	----	0	ELSA	FINLA	----
V39	MEMBER OF THE WTO	1970	----	----	0	ELSA	FINLA	----
		1975	----	----	0	ELSA	FINLA	----
		1980	----	----	0	ELSA	FINLA	----
V40	MEMBER OF THE NATO	1970	----	----	0	ELSA	FINLA	----
		1975	----	----	0	ELSA	FINLA	----
		1980	----	----	0	ELSA	FINLA	----

V41 GDP SHARE OF INVESTMENTS	1970	D2	P10	11.5 %	UPVO	SOMA	----
	1975	D1	P9	10.5 %	BURMA	GHANA	----
	1980	D1	P7	10.1 %	ELSA	GUINE	----
V42 GDP SHARE OF AGRICULTURE	1970	D10	P94	55.8 %	UGADA	NIGER	F16
	1975	D9	P91	47.5 %	BURMA	GHANA	F16
	1980	D10	P93	50.8 %	TANZA	BANGL	F16
V43 GDP SHARE OF INDUSTRY	1970	D2	P11	14.4 %	BURMA	NIGER	F16
	1975	D2	P15	16.8 %	TANZA	MOZAM	F16
	1980	D1	P10	15.6 %	CENTR	TANZA	F16
V44 GDP SHARE OF SERVICES	1970	D1	P8	29.8 %	LIBYA	MALAW	F16
	1975	D2	P20	35.7 %	INDIA	MALAW	F16
	1980	D2	P15	33.6 %	RWAN	TANZA	F16
V45 HOMICIDES P. MIL. POPULATION	------	----	----	----- -----	-------	-------	----
V46 SUICIDES P. MIL. POPULATION	------	----	----	----- -----	-------	-------	----
V47 IMPORT PARTNERS	1970	R1	ITALY	17.6 %	-------	LIBYA	----
	1970	R2	JAPAN	14.7 %	COSTA	GREC	----
	1970	R3	GFR	13.6 %	EGYPT	GHANA	----
	1980	R1	USSR	19.3 %	CZECH	FINLA	----
	1980	R2	ITALY	10.8 %	AURIA	FRANC	----
	1980	R3	GFR	9.5 %	EGYPT	GABON	----
V48 EXPORT PARTNERS	1970	R1	USA	50.4 %	ECUA	GHANA	F137
	1970	R2	GFR	6.7 %	COSTA	GDR	F137
	1970	R3	ITALY	6.2 %	BRAZI	HONDU	F137
	1980	R1	USA	18.1 %	ELSA	GUATE	----
	1980	R2	ITALY	10.1 %	AURIA	FRANC	----
	1980	R3	USSR	9.2 %	YUGO	GHANA	----
V49 PATENT SUPPLIERS	------	----	----	----- -----	-------	-------	----
V50 PROVENANCE OF FOREIGN FIRMS	1980	R1	UNKI	30.7 %	AULIA	GHANA	----
	1980	R2	ITALY	17.9 %	-------	-------	----
	1980	R3	-------	12.8 %	-------	-------	----
V51 FILM SUPPLIERS	1980	R1	USA	140	EGYPT	FINLA	F117
	1980	R2	USSR	89	VINO	INDIA	F117
	1980	R3	INDIA	33	ALGER	INDO	F117

FINLAND (FINLA)

V1 INCOME PER CAPITA	1970	D9	P85	7413 $/CAP	UNKI	CANA	F147
	1975	D9	P84	8865 $/CAP	LIBYA	AULIA	F147
	1980	D9	P84	10212 $/CAP	AULIA	LIBYA	F147

V2	TELEPHONES P. TSD. POPULATION	1970	D10	P91	257	1/TSD CAP	UNKI	NETH	----
		1975	D10	P93	389	1/TSD CAP	AULIA	DENMA	----
		1980	D10	P92	496	1/TSD CAP	AULIA	NETH	----
V3	INFANT MORTALITY RATE	1980	D1	P3	7.6	1/TSD	JAPAN	NORWY	----
V4	PHYSICIANS P. MIL. POPULATION	1981	D9	P84	1987	1/MIL	NORWY	GDR	F147
V5	ADULT LITERACY	------	----	----	----- -----		-------	-------	----
V6	DURATION OF SCHOOLING	1975	D10	P95	11.4	YR	CANA	JAPAN	F146
		1980	D10	P97	11.8	YR	NORWY	UNKI	F146
V7	STUDENT ENROLLMENT RATIO	1975	D10	P94	27.2	%	ARGE	ECUA	----
		1980	D10	P95	32.0	%	JAPAN	LEBA	----
V8	SHARE OF AGRICULTURAL LABOR	1970	D4	P40	20.2	%	LEBA	CHILE	F67
		1975	D4	P36	15.0	%	JAPAN	URU	F98
		1980	D4	P40	12.8	%	NEWZ	VENE	----
V9	SHARE OF INDUSTRIAL LABOR	1975	D7	P68	34.8	%	JAPAN	IRE	F98
		1980	D7	P67	35.3	%	SWITZ	AULIA	----
V10	SHARE OF SERVICE LABOR	1975	D7	P63	32.2	%	MEXI	FRANC	F98
		1980	D6	P52	34.6	%	SPAIN	DOMI	----
V11	SHARE OF ACADEMIC LABOR	1975	D10	P92	18.0	%	NETH	ISRA	F98
		1980	D10	P90	17.3	%	KUWAI	NETH	----
V12	SHARE OF SELF-EMPLOYED LABOR	1970	D3	P33	14.4	%	DENMA	BELGI	F67
		1975	D3	P30	17.2	%	TRITO	JAPAN	F98
		1980	D2	P18	9.8	%	SWITZ	NETH	----
V13	MILITARY EXPENDITURES	1970	D6	P55	0.444	TSD MIL $	HUNGA	PERU	----
		1975	D6	P55	0.580	TSD MIL $	ALGER	MOROC	----
		1980	D6	P54	0.727	TSD MIL $	SINGA	PHILI	----
V14	MILITARY MANPOWER	1970	D5	P46	40	TSD CAP	NORWY	SOUAF	----
		1975	D5	P48	40	TSD CAP	MONGO	YENO	----
		1980	D5	P48	36	TSD CAP	ZIMBA	MONGO	----
V15	MEN AT AGE 20 - 30	1970	D4	P32	397	TSD CAP	TUNIS	SYRIA	F22
		1976	D4	P39	443	TSD CAP	TUNIS	CAME	F22
		1980	D3	P23	406	TSD CAP	RWAN	HAITI	F22
V16	POPULATION	1970	D4	P37	4.61	MIL CAP	MALAW	YENO	F22
		1975	D4	P34	4.71	MIL CAP	NIGER	DOMI	F22
		1980	D4	P30	4.78	MIL CAP	ELSA	GUINE	F22
V17	GROSS DOMESTIC PRODUCT	1970	D7	P70	34.172	TSD MIL $	INDO	NORWY	----
		1975	D7	P68	41.756	TSD MIL $	GREC	NORWY	----
		1980	D7	P70	48.811	TSD MIL $	ALGER	NORWY	----
V18	SHARE IN WORLD IMPORTS	1970	D8	P79	7.941	1/TSD	HUNGA	BRAZI	F30
		1975	D8	P79	8.390	1/TSD	SOUAF	YUGO	F30
		1980	D8	P76	7.626	1/TSD	CZECH	NIGRA	F30
V19	SHARE IN WORLD EXPORTS	1970	D8	P76	7.352	1/TSD	CHINA	HUNGA	F30
		1975	D8	P73	6.280	1/TSD	SOUAF	HUNGA	F30
		1980	D8	P72	7.091	1/TSD	IRAN	CZECH	F30

V20	GDP SHARE OF IMPORTS	1970	D7	P70	24.2	%	KORSO	AURIA	F30
		1975	D7	P62	26.9	%	CHAD	DENMA	F30
		1980	D7	P69	30.3	%	DENMA	UNARE	F30
V21	GDP SHARE OF EXPORTS	1970	D8	P72	21.2	%	CAME	UGADA	F30
		1975	D6	P55	19.4	%	SIERA	TUNIS	F30
		1980	D8	P72	27.4	%	ZIMBA	KORSO	F30
V22	EXPORT PARTNER CONCENTRATION	1970	D2	P17	17.4	%	SUDAN	NORWY	----
		1975	D4	P34	20.6	%	MALAY	GREC	----
		1980	D3	P22	17.6	%	SAUDI	GREC	----
V23	TOTAL DEBT AS % OF GDP	------	----	----	-----	-----	-------	-------	----
V24	SHARE OF NEW FOREIGN PATENTS	1970	D3	P29	79	%	ARGE	SWEDN	----
		1975	D3	P24	78	%	SWITZ	UNKI	----
		1980	D3	P29	77	%	SWITZ	INDIA	----
V25	FOREIGN PROPERTY AS % OF GDP	------	----	----	-----	-----	-------	-------	----
V26	GNP SHARE OF DEVELOPMENT AID	1970	D2	P21	0.06	%	VENE	AURIA	----
		1975	D2	P16	0.17	%	VENE	SWITZ	----
		1980	D3	P23	0.22	%	VENE	AURIA	----
V27	SHARE IN NOBEL PRIZE WINNERS	1970-79	D5	P45	0.0	%	ETHIA	GDR	----
V28	GDP SHARE OF MANUFACTURING	1970	D9	P83	24.3	%	PERU	SWEDN	----
		1975	D9	P85	24.8	%	SINGA	PERU	----
		1980	D9	P91	25.7	%	ZIMBA	FRANC	----
V29	EXPORT SHARE OF MANUFACTURES	------	----	----	-----	-----	-------	-------	----
V30	LACK OF CIVIL LIBERTIES	1975	D2	P18	2		DOMI	FRANC	----
		1980	D2	P18	2		ECUA	FRANC	----
V31	LACK OF POLITICAL RIGHTS	1975	D2	P20	2		ELSA	GREC	----
		1980	D3	P21	2		ECUA	GREC	----
V32	RIOTS	1970-74	D2	P19	0		ELSA	GDR	----
		1975-79	D2	P20	0		DENMA	GDR	----
V33	PROTEST DEMONSTRATIONS	1970-74	D4	P37	1		DOMI	GHANA	----
		1975-79	D5	P42	2		ZAIRE	GHANA	----
V34	POLITICAL STRIKES	1970-74	D3	P29	0		ELSA	GDR	----
		1975-79	D3	P29	0		ETHIA	GDR	----
V35	MEMBER OF THE NONALIGNED MMT.	1970	----	----	0		ELSA	FRANC	----
		1976	----	----	0		ELSA	FRANC	----
		1981	----	----	0		ELSA	FRANC	----
V36	MEMBER OF THE OPEC	1970	----	----	0		ETHIA	FRANC	----
		1975	----	----	0		ETHIA	FRANC	----
		1980	----	----	0		ETHIA	FRANC	----
V37	MEMBER OF THE OECD	1970	----	----	1		DENMA	FRANC	----
		1975	----	----	1		DENMA	FRANC	----
		1980	----	----	1		DENMA	FRANC	----

V38	MEMBER OF THE CMEA	1970	----	----	0		ETHIA	FRANC	----
		1975	----	----	0		ETHIA	FRANC	----
		1980	----	----	0		ETHIA	FRANC	----
V39	MEMBER OF THE WTO	1970	----	----	0		ETHIA	FRANC	----
		1975	----	----	0		ETHIA	FRANC	----
		1980	----	----	0		ETHIA	FRANC	----
V40	MEMBER OF THE NATO	1970	----	----	0		ETHIA	GDR	----
		1975	----	----	0		ETHIA	GABON	----
		1980	----	----	0		ETHIA	GABON	----
V41	GDP SHARE OF INVESTMENTS	1970	D9	P89	29.5	%	SOUAF	VENE	----
		1975	D9	P89	32.7	%	SOUAF	JAPAN	----
		1980	D7	P69	27.7	%	NORWY	ECUA	----
V42	GDP SHARE OF AGRICULTURE	1970	D3	P29	11.4	%	ZAMBI	ARGE	----
		1975	D3	P31	9.8	%	IRAN	ARGE	----
		1980	D3	P30	8.2	%	JORDA	JAMAI	----
V43	GDP SHARE OF INDUSTRY	1970	D7	P69	35.5	%	USA	SWEDN	----
		1975	D8	P75	37.0	%	JAMAI	SPAIN	----
		1980	D7	P64	35.7	%	URU	FRANC	----
V44	GDP SHARE OF SERVICES	1970	D8	P70	53.1	%	SPAIN	MOROC	----
		1975	D8	P77	53.2	%	CONGO	SPAIN	----
		1980	D9	P85	56.1	%	MEXI	AULIA	----
V45	HOMICIDES P. MIL. POPULATION	1970	D6	P59	20.2	1/MIL CAP	HUNGA	CANA	F153
		1975	D8	P71	36.3	1/MIL CAP	URU	CUBA	F149
		1980	D8	P76	33.1	1/MIL CAP	HUNGA	ARGE	F153
V46	SUICIDES P. MIL. POPULATION	1970	D9	P82	213.2	1/MIL CAP	SWITZ	DENMA	F150
		1975	D10	P93	250.1	1/MIL CAP	AURIA	GDR	F147
		1980	D9	P85	256.5	1/MIL CAP	SWITZ	AURIA	F150
V47	IMPORT PARTNERS	1970	R1	GFR	16.5	%	DENMA	FRANC	----
		1970	R2	SWEDN	16.1	%	DENMA	-------	----
		1970	R3	UNKI	13.1	%	DENMA	GREC	----
		1980	R1	USSR	21.0	%	ETHIA	HUNGA	----
		1980	R2	GFR	12.6	%	CAME	HUNGA	----
		1980	R3	SWEDN	12.0	%	DENMA	-------	----
V48	EXPORT PARTNERS	1970	R1	UNKI	17.4	%	DENMA	IRE	----
		1970	R2	SWEDN	15.1	%	DENMA	TRITO	----
		1970	R3	USSR	12.2	%	ALGER	INDIA	----
		1980	R1	USSR	17.6	%	CZECH	HUNGA	----
		1980	R2	SWEDN	16.5	%	-------	DENMA	----
		1980	R3	UNKI	11.3	%	CANA	ITALY	----
V49	PATENT SUPPLIERS	1970	R1	SWEDN	254		-------	COLO	----
		1970	R2	USA	219		CONGO	KENYA	----
		1970	R3	GFR	214		EGYPT	GUATE	----
		1980	R1	GFR	293		DENMA	GDR	----
		1980	R2	SWEDN	280		-------	NORWY	----
		1980	R3	USA	268		ZAIRE	ZIMBA	----

V50	PROVENANCE OF FOREIGN FIRMS	1980	R1	SWEDN	42.4	%	DENMA	NORWY	F116
		1980	R2	USA	21.7	%	DENMA	GHANA	F116
		1980	R3	UNKI	10.6	%	EGYPT	GREC	F116
V51	FILM SUPPLIERS	1980	R1	USA	111		ETHIA	FRANC	F120
		1980	R2	UNKI	21		SYRIA	IRAQ	F120
		1980	R3	ITALY	18		BULGA	HAITI	F120

FRANCE (FRANC)

V1	INCOME PER CAPITA	1970	D9	P89	8286	$/CAP	AULIA	BELGI	F147
		1975	D9	P90	9710	$/CAP	CANA	BELGI	F147
		1980	D9	P88	11188	$/CAP	NETH	BELGI	F147
V2	TELEPHONES P. TSD. POPULATION	1970	D9	P84	172	1/TSD CAP	ISRA	ITALY	----
		1975	D9	P84	262	1/TSD CAP	ITALY	AURIA	----
		1980	D9	P86	459	1/TSD CAP	NORWY	JAPAN	----
V3	INFANT MORTALITY RATE	1980	D1	P7	10.0	1/TSD	SWITZ	CANA	----
V4	PHYSICIANS P. MIL. POPULATION	1970	D9	P82	1339	1/MIL	NETH	SWEDN	F147
		1975	D9	P79	1536	1/MIL	AULIA	NETH	F147
V5	ADULT LITERACY	------	----	----	----- -----		-------	-------	----
V6	DURATION OF SCHOOLING	1970	D10	P92	11.0	YR	AULIA	JAPAN	----
		1975	D10	P91	11.2	YR	ALBA	GDR	----
		1980	D10	P90	11.4	YR	CANA	GDR	----
V7	STUDENT ENROLLMENT RATIO	1970	D10	P92	19.5	%	DENMA	NETH	----
		1975	D9	P89	24.5	%	AULIA	GFR	----
		1980	D9	P84	25.4	%	AULIA	NORWY	----
V8	SHARE OF AGRICULTURAL LABOR	1968	D4	----	16.7	%	ARGE	ITALY	----
		1975	D3	P23	10.3	%	NORWY	NEWZ	----
		1982	D3	----	8.6	%	TRITO	AURIA	----
V9	SHARE OF INDUSTRIAL LABOR	1968	D8	----	37.7	%	ARGE	PORTU	----
		1975	D9	P84	38.5	%	NEWZ	ALGER	----
		1982	D7	----	34.9	%	NORWY	YUGO	----
V10	SHARE OF SERVICE LABOR	1968	D7	----	33.1	%	PANA	LEBA	----
		1975	D8	P66	34.7	%	FINLA	SWEDN	----
		1982	D8	----	40.5	%	NEWZ	ISRA	----
V11	SHARE OF ACADEMIC LABOR	1968	D9	----	12.4	%	SWITZ	NEWZ	----
		1975	D9	P86	16.5	%	CANA	BULGA	----
		1982	D9	----	16.0	%	USA	KUWAI	----
V12	SHARE OF SELF-EMPLOYED LABOR	1968	D4	----	16.3	%	BELGI	SPAIN	----
		1975	D2	P21	14.7	%	NEWZ	SINGA	----

V13	MILITARY EXPENDITURES	1970	D10	P93	17.583	TSD MIL $	ITALY	UNKI	----
		1975	D10	P96	19.701	TSD MIL $	JAPAN	UNKI	----
		1980	D10	P96	24.217	TSD MIL $	SAUDI	UNKI	----
V14	MILITARY MANPOWER	1970	D10	P95	570	TSD CAP	TURKY	KORSO	----
		1975	D10	P94	575	TSD CAP	TAIWA	KORSO	----
		1980	D10	P95	486	TSD CAP	GFR	TURKY	----
V15	MEN AT AGE 20 - 30	1970	D9	P87	3797	TSD CAP	MEXI	ITALY	F22
		1980	D9	P86	4306	TSD CAP	THAI	GFR	F22
V16	POPULATION	1970	D9	P89	50.77	MIL CAP	MEXI	ITALY	F22
		1975	D9	P88	52.70	MIL CAP	PHILI	ITALY	F22
		1980	D9	P88	53.71	MIL CAP	PHILI	VINO	F22
V17	GROSS DOMESTIC PRODUCT	1970	D10	P96	420.656	TSD MIL $	UNKI	GFR	----
		1975	D10	P96	511.726	TSD MIL $	UNKI	GFR	----
		1980	D10	P96	600.909	TSD MIL $	UNKI	GFR	----
V18	SHARE IN WORLD IMPORTS	1970	D10	P97	57.579	1/TSD	JAPAN	UNKI	F33
		1975	D10	P97	59.399	1/TSD	UNKI	JAPAN	F33
		1980	D10	P97	65.859	1/TSD	UNKI	JAPAN	F33
V19	SHARE IN WORLD EXPORTS	1970	D10	P96	57.177	1/TSD	CANA	JAPAN	F33
		1975	D10	P97	59.603	1/TSD	UNKI	JAPAN	F33
		1980	D10	P97	55.670	1/TSD	UNKI	JAPAN	F33
V20	GDP SHARE OF IMPORTS	1970	D3	P27	13.6	%	NIGRA	UPVO	F33
		1975	D3	P23	15.9	%	URU	RWAN	F33
		1980	D4	P38	20.6	%	GUATE	RWAN	F33
V21	GDP SHARE OF EXPORTS	1970	D4	P40	12.7	%	TUNIS	MOROC	F33
		1975	D5	P41	15.4	%	SOUAF	NEWZ	F33
		1980	D5	P45	17.0	%	CHILE	SIERA	F33
V22	EXPORT PARTNER CONCENTRATION	1970	D3	P28	20.8	%	PORTU	UGADA	----
		1975	D2	P20	16.7	%	ISRA	URU	----
		1980	D2	P16	16.1	%	USA	SPAIN	----
V23	TOTAL DEBT AS % OF GDP	------	----	----	-----	-----	-------	-------	----
V24	SHARE OF NEW FOREIGN PATENTS	1970	D2	P20	68	%	HUNGA	PAKI	----
		1975	D2	P16	65	%	KORSO	HUNGA	----
		1980	D3	P23	70	%	ARGE	HAITI	----
V25	FOREIGN PROPERTY AS % OF GDP	------	----	----	-----	-----	-------	-------	----
V26	GNP SHARE OF DEVELOPMENT AID	1970	D9	P89	0.69	%	NETH	LIBYA	----
		1975	D7	P62	0.62	%	BELGI	AULIA	----
		1980	D7	P63	0.63	%	BELGI	DENMA	----
V27	SHARE IN NOBEL PRIZE WINNERS	1970-79	D9	P90	1.3	%	CANA	NETH	----
V28	GDP SHARE OF MANUFACTURING	1970	D10	P93	28.8	%	UNKI	ARGE	----
		1975	D10	P94	27.4	%	BELGI	AURIA	----
		1980	D10	P92	26.2	%	FINLA	PERU	----
V29	EXPORT SHARE OF MANUFACTURES	1970	D9	P89	64.9	%	PORTU	AURIA	----
		1975	D9	P89	67.7	%	LEBA	PORTU	----
		1980	D9	P84	66.7	%	SPAIN	PORTU	----

V30 LACK OF CIVIL LIBERTIES	1975	D2	P18	2	FINLA	GREC	----
	1980	D2	P18	2	FINLA	GFR	----
V31 LACK OF POLITICAL RIGHTS	1975	D1	P8	1	DENMA	GFR	----
	1980	D1	P8	1	DENMA	GFR	----
V32 RIOTS	1970-74	D10	P94	46	SPAIN	ITALY	----
	1975-79	D9	P90	21	COLO	PERU	----
V33 PROTEST DEMONSTRATIONS	1970-74	D10	P97	75	GREC	USSR	----
	1975-79	D10	P92	57	GFR	IRAN	----
V34 POLITICAL STRIKES	1970-74	D10	P97	30	LEBA	ITALY	----
	1975-79	D10	P97	19	PERU	NIGRA	----
V35 MEMBER OF THE NONALIGNED MMT.	1970	----	----	0	FINLA	GDR	----
	1976	----	----	0	FINLA	GDR	----
	1981	----	----	0	FINLA	GDR	----
V36 MEMBER OF THE OPEC	1970	----	----	0	FINLA	GDR	----
	1975	----	----	0	FINLA	GDR	----
	1980	----	----	0	FINLA	GDR	----
V37 MEMBER OF THE OECD	1970	----	----	1	FINLA	GFR	----
	1975	----	----	1	FINLA	GFR	----
	1980	----	----	1	FINLA	GFR	----
V38 MEMBER OF THE CMEA	1970	----	----	0	FINLA	GFR	----
	1975	----	----	0	FINLA	GABON	----
	1980	----	----	0	FINLA	GABON	----
V39 MEMBER OF THE WTO	1970	----	----	0	FINLA	GFR	----
	1975	----	----	0	FINLA	GABON	----
	1980	----	----	0	FINLA	GABON	----
V40 MEMBER OF THE NATO	1970	----	----	1	DENMA	GFR	F13
	1975	----	----	1	DENMA	GFR	F13
	1980	----	----	1	DENMA	GFR	F13
V41 GDP SHARE OF INVESTMENTS	1970	D8	P76	26.1 %	DENMA	MALAW	----
	1975	D6	P53	23.0 %	NIGER	SWITZ	----
	1980	D5	P46	23.1 %	SAUDI	RWAN	----
V42 GDP SHARE OF AGRICULTURE	1970	D2	P18	6.5 %	NORWY	JAMAI	----
	1975	D2	P14	5.0 %	AURIA	DENMA	----
	1980	D2	P16	4.2 %	CANA	AURIA	----
V43 GDP SHARE OF INDUSTRY	1970	D8	P79	38.8 %	MAURA	VENE	----
	1975	D8	P78	37.6 %	AULIA	CHILE	----
	1980	D7	P65	35.8 %	FINLA	TUNIS	----
V44 GDP SHARE OF SERVICES	1970	D8	P80	54.7 %	IRE	MEXI	----
	1975	D9	P87	57.4 %	SYRIA	NEWZ	----
	1980	D9	P90	60.0 %	SINGA	BELGI	----
V45 HOMICIDES P. MIL. POPULATION	1970	D2	P18	7.4 1/MIL CAP	SWITZ	UNKI	F153
	1975	D3	P25	10.1 1/MIL CAP	SWITZ	POLA	F153
	1980	D3	P25	10.1 1/MIL CAP	UNKI	SPAIN	F150

V46	SUICIDES P. MIL. POPULATION	1970	D8	P75	154.3	1/MIL CAP	JAPAN	BELGI	F150
		1975	D7	P69	157.9	1/MIL CAP	BULGA	BELGI	F150
		1980	D7	P69	193.7	1/MIL CAP	JAPAN	SWEDN	F150
V47	IMPORT PARTNERS	1970	R1	GFR	22.3	%	FINLA	GREC	----
		1970	R2	BELGI	11.3	%	ZAIRE	NETH	F142
		1970	R3	USA	10.0	%	CONGO	GFR	----
		1980	R1	GFR	16.2	%	DENMA	GREC	----
		1980	R2	ITALY	9.4	%	ETHIA	TUNIS	----
		1980	R3	BELGI	8.4	%	NETH	-------	F142
V48	EXPORT PARTNERS	1970	R1	GFR	20.8	%	ELSA	GREC	----
		1970	R2	ITALY	11.3	%	YUGO	GREC	----
		1970	R3	BELGI	11.1	%	CENTR	-------	F138
		1980	R1	GFR	16.1	%	DENMA	GREC	----
		1980	R2	ITALY	12.5	%	ETHIA	GREC	----
		1980	R3	BELGI	9.4	%	NETH	-------	F138
V49	PATENT SUPPLIERS	1970	R1	USA	5664		EGYPT	GFR	----
		1970	R2	GFR	4512		ECUA	GREC	----
		1970	R3	UNKI	1708		DENMA	GFR	----
		1980	R1	USA	5581		ELSA	GFR	----
		1980	R2	GFR	5100		ELSA	HONDU	----
		1980	R3	JAPAN	1904		AULIA	NETH	----
V50	PROVENANCE OF FOREIGN FIRMS	1980	R1	USA	28.4	%	ELSA	GFR	F116
		1980	R2	UNKI	24.2	%	ECUA	GFR	F116
		1980	R3	GFR	15.1	%	ECUA	GHANA	F116
V51	FILM SUPPLIERS	1980	R1	USA	148		FINLA	GFR	F119
		1980	R2	ITALY	65		EGYPT	GFR	F119
		1980	R3	GFR	37		BRAZI	ITALY	F119

GABON (GABON)

V1	INCOME PER CAPITA	1980	D7	P69	2812	$/CAP	SOUAF	VENE	F171
V2	TELEPHONES P. TSD. POPULATION	------	----	----	-----	-----	-------	-------	----
V3	INFANT MORTALITY RATE	1980	D8	P71	121.6	1/TSD	SAUDI	LIBE	F5
V4	PHYSICIANS P. MIL. POPULATION	1977	D4	----	201	1/MIL	BURMA	ALGER	F171
V5	ADULT LITERACY	------	----	----	-----	-----	-------	-------	----
V6	DURATION OF SCHOOLING	1975	D5	P46	7.7	YR	ALGER	PARA	----
		1980	D5	P46	8.7	YR	COSTA	BRAZI	----
V7	STUDENT ENROLLMENT RATIO	1975	D3	P27	1.3	%	CAME	IVORY	----
		1982	D4	----	3.3	%	NEPAL	IRAN	----

V8	SHARE OF AGRICULTURAL LABOR	------	----	----	-----	-----	-------	-------	----
V9	SHARE OF INDUSTRIAL LABOR	------	----	----	-----	-----	-------	-------	----
V10	SHARE OF SERVICE LABOR	------	----	----	-----	-----	-------	-------	----
V11	SHARE OF ACADEMIC LABOR	------	----	----	-----	-----	-------	-------	----
V12	SHARE OF SELF-EMPLOYED LABOR	------	----	----	-----	-----	-------	-------	----
V13	MILITARY EXPENDITURES	1980	D2	P18	0.053	TSD MIL $	UPVO	SRILA	F62
V14	MILITARY MANPOWER	1975	D1	P6	3	TSD CAP	CENTR	MAURA	----
		1980	D2	P12	5	TSD CAP	TOGO	RWAN	----
V15	MEN AT AGE 20 - 30	------	----	----	-----	-----	-------	-------	----
V16	POPULATION	1975	D1	P1	1.00	MIL CAP	-------	KUWAI	F170
		1980	D1	P3	1.07	MIL CAP	UNARE	TRITO	F170
V17	GROSS DOMESTIC PRODUCT	1980	D3	P22	3.009	TSD MIL $	MADA	ELSA	----
V18	SHARE IN WORLD IMPORTS	1975	D3	P26	0.518	1/TSD	MOZAM	PAPUA	F121
		1980	D3	P23	0.329	1/TSD	BOLI	MOZAM	F121
V19	SHARE IN WORLD EXPORTS	1975	D5	P48	1.075	1/TSD	SYRIA	PAKI	F121
		1980	D5	P46	1.089	1/TSD	SYRIA	TUNIS	F121
V20	GDP SHARE OF IMPORTS	1975	D5	P44	21.8	%	DOMI	ECUA	F121
		1980	D3	P21	15.7	%	BANGL	AULIA	F121
V21	GDP SHARE OF EXPORTS	1975	D10	P91	43.7	%	NETH	BELGI	F121
		1980	D9	P88	50.8	%	IRE	CONGO	F121
V22	EXPORT PARTNER CONCENTRATION	1975	D8	P72	36.7	%	PAPUA	PHILI	F121
		1980	D5	P42	22.5	%	SUDAN	MALAY	F121
V23	TOTAL DEBT AS % OF GDP	1980	D5	P48	37.3	%	NIGER	SIERA	----
V24	SHARE OF NEW FOREIGN PATENTS	------	----	----	-----	-----	-------	-------	----
V25	FOREIGN PROPERTY AS % OF GDP	1975	D10	P92	28.7	%	MALAY	SINGA	----
		1978	D10	----	32.6	%	SINGA	JAMAI	----
V26	GNP SHARE OF DEVELOPMENT AID	------	----	----	-----	-----	-------	-------	----
V27	SHARE IN NOBEL PRIZE WINNERS	------	----	----	-----	-----	-------	-------	----
V28	GDP SHARE OF MANUFACTURING	------	----	----	-----	-----	-------	-------	----
V29	EXPORT SHARE OF MANUFACTURES	1975	D2	P15	1.0	%	ZAMBI	INDO	----
		1980	D1	P2	0.0	%	-------	ALGER	----
V30	LACK OF CIVIL LIBERTIES	1975	D8	P74	6		CONGO	HAITI	----
		1980	D8	P74	6		CUBA	IRAN	----
V31	LACK OF POLITICAL RIGHTS	1975	D7	P63	6		ETHIA	HAITI	----
		1980	D7	P67	6		CUBA	HAITI	----
V32	RIOTS	------	----	----	-----	-----	-------	-------	----

V33	PROTEST DEMONSTRATIONS	------	----	----	----- -----		-------	-------	----
V34	POLITICAL STRIKES	------	----	----	----- -----		-------	-------	----
V35	MEMBER OF THE NONALIGNED MMT.	1976	----	----	1		ETHIA	GHANA	----
		1981	----	----	1		ETHIA	GHANA	----
V36	MEMBER OF THE OPEC	1975	----	----	1		ECUA	INDO	----
		1980	----	----	1		ECUA	INDO	----
V37	MEMBER OF THE OECD	1975	----	----	0		ETHIA	GDR	----
		1980	----	----	0		ETHIA	GDR	----
V38	MEMBER OF THE CMEA	1975	----	----	0		FRANC	GFR	----
		1980	----	----	0		FRANC	GFR	----
V39	MEMBER OF THE WTO	1975	----	----	0		FRANC	GFR	----
		1980	----	----	0		FRANC	GFR	----
V40	MEMBER OF THE NATO	1975	----	----	0		FINLA	GDR	----
		1980	----	----	0		FINLA	GDR	----
V41	GDP SHARE OF INVESTMENTS	1975	D10	P100	57.7	%	ALGER	-------	----
		1980	D9	P84	29.5	%	NIGER	PHILI	----
V42	GDP SHARE OF AGRICULTURE	1975	D2	P21	6.4	%	VENE	CHILE	----
		1980	D3	P24	6.6	%	ITALY	SOUAF	----
V43	GDP SHARE OF INDUSTRY	1975	D10	P95	61.3	%	IRAN	IRAQ	----
		1980	D10	P95	64.5	%	ALGER	IRAQ	----
V44	GDP SHARE OF SERVICES	1975	D2	P16	32.3	%	RWAN	IRAN	----
		1980	D1	P9	28.9	%	SOMA	BURU	----
V45	HOMICIDES P. MIL. POPULATION	------	----	----	----- -----		-------	-------	----
V46	SUICIDES P. MIL. POPULATION	------	----	----	----- -----		-------	-------	----
V47	IMPORT PARTNERS	1980	R1	FRANC	58.4	%	CONGO	MADA	F121
		1980	R2	USA	9.3	%	ELSA	INDO	F121
		1980	R3	GFR	6.0	%	ETHIA	IRE	F121
V48	EXPORT PARTNERS	1980	R1	FRANC	22.5	%	CENTR	GFR	F121
		1980	R2	USA	13.0	%	EGYPT	INDIA	F121
		1980	R3	BRAZI	12.4	%	PARA	-------	F121
V49	PATENT SUPPLIERS	------	----	----	----- -----		-------	-------	----
V50	PROVENANCE OF FOREIGN FIRMS	1980	R1	FRANC	58.6	%	CONGO	IVORY	----
		1980	R2	-------	8.6	%	-------	-------	----
		1980	R3	-------	8.6	%	-------	-------	----
V51	FILM SUPPLIERS	------	----	----	----- -----		-------	-------	----

GERMAN DEMOCRATIC REPUBLIC [2] (GDR)

V1	INCOME PER CAPITA	------	----	----	----- -----		-------	-------	----
V2	TELEPHONES P. TSD. POPULATION	1970	D8	P80	123 1/TSD CAP	GREC	SPAIN	----
		1975	D8	P78	152 1/TSD CAP	SINGA	CZECH	----
		1980	D8	P74	189 1/TSD CAP	IRE	CZECH	----
V3	INFANT MORTALITY RATE	1980	D2	P14	12.1 1/TSD	SINGA	UNKI	----
V4	PHYSICIANS P. MIL. POPULATION	1970	D9	P89	1598 1/MIL	USA	GREC	F147
		1975	D9	P89	1858 1/MIL	SWITZ	ARGE	F147
		1980	D9	P86	2025 1/MIL	FINLA	DENMA	F147
V5	ADULT LITERACY	------	----	----	----- -----	-------	-------	----
V6	DURATION OF SCHOOLING	1970	D10	P95	11.2 YR	BELGI	NORWY	----
		1975	D10	P91	11.2 YR	FRANC	NETH	----
		1980	D10	P90	11.4 YR	FRANC	USA	F35
V7	STUDENT ENROLLMENT RATIO	1970	D10	P98	32.8 %	USSR	CANA	----
		1975	D10	P98	29.5 %	DENMA	CANA	----
		1980	D10	P94	30.7 %	NETH	JAPAN	----
V8	SHARE OF AGRICULTURAL LABOR	------	----	----	----- -----	-------	-------	----
V9	SHARE OF INDUSTRIAL LABOR	------	----	----	----- -----	-------	-------	----
V10	SHARE OF SERVICE LABOR	------	----	----	----- -----	-------	-------	----
V11	SHARE OF ACADEMIC LABOR	------	----	----	----- -----	-------	-------	----
V12	SHARE OF SELF-EMPLOYED LABOR	------	----	----	----- -----	-------	-------	----
V13	MILITARY EXPENDITURES	------	----	----	----- -----	-------	-------	----
V14	MILITARY MANPOWER	1970	D8	P78	202 TSD CAP	NIGRA	ROMA	----
		1975	D8	P78	220 TSD CAP	PORTU	ROMA	----
		1980	D9	P82	231 TSD CAP	CUBA	THAI	----
V15	MEN AT AGE 20 - 30	1971	D7	P62	1051 TSD CAP	AULIA	PERU	F22
		1975	D7	P65	1138 TSD CAP	AULIA	SRILA	F22
		1980	D6	P58	1349 TSD CAP	AULIA	SRILA	F22
V16	POPULATION	1970	D8	P73	17.06 MIL CAP	MOROC	ROMA	F22
		1975	D8	P72	16.85 MIL CAP	ALGER	MOROC	F22
		1980	D7	P68	16.74 MIL CAP	KENYA	PERU	F22
V17	GROSS DOMESTIC PRODUCT	------	----	----	----- -----	-------	-------	----
V18	SHARE IN WORLD IMPORTS	1970	D9	P88	14.601 1/TSD	SPAIN	AULIA	F49
		1975	D9	P87	12.421 1/TSD	AULIA	POLA	F49
		1980	D8	P80	9.303 1/TSD	SOUAF	POLA	F49

---

[2] Also known as East Germany.

V19	SHARE IN WORLD EXPORTS	1970	D9	P88	14.604	1/TSD	CZECH	AULIA	F30
		1975	D9	P86	11.513	1/TSD	VENE	POLA	F30
		1980	D8	P77	8.674	1/TSD	DENMA	AURIA	F30
V20	GDP SHARE OF IMPORTS	------	----	----	----- -----		-------	-------	----
V21	GDP SHARE OF EXPORTS	------	----	----	----- -----		-------	-------	----
V22	EXPORT PARTNER CONCENTRATION	1970	D8	P72	38.0	%	EGYPT	BOLI	----
		1974	D7	P68	32.7	%	COLO	CZECH	
V23	TOTAL DEBT AS % OF GDP	------	----	----	----- -----		-------	-------	----
V24	SHARE OF NEW FOREIGN PATENTS	1970	D1	P11	31	%	KORSO	JAPAN	----
		1975	D2	P11	45	%	ROMA	BULGA	----
		1980	D1	P6	24	%	CZECH	POLA	----
V25	FOREIGN PROPERTY AS % OF GDP	------	----	----	----- -----		-------	-------	----
V26	GNP SHARE OF DEVELOPMENT AID	------	----	----	----- -----		-------	-------	----
V27	SHARE IN NOBEL PRIZE WINNERS	1970-79	D5	P45	0.0	%	FINLA	GHANA	----
V28	GDP SHARE OF MANUFACTURING	------	----	----	----- -----		-------	-------	----
V29	EXPORT SHARE OF MANUFACTURES	------	----	----	----- -----		-------	-------	----
V30	LACK OF CIVIL LIBERTIES	1975	D10	P93	7		CZECH	GUINE	----
		1980	D10	P92	7		ETHIA	GUINE	----
V31	LACK OF POLITICAL RIGHTS	1975	D9	P88	7		ECUA	GHANA	----
		1980	D9	P90	7		ETHIA	GUINE	----
V32	RIOTS	1970-74	D2	P19	0		FINLA	GUINE	----
		1975-79	D2	P20	0		FINLA	GUINE	----
V33	PROTEST DEMONSTRATIONS	1970-74	D5	P49	2		ZAMBI	IRAQ	----
		1975-79	D8	P77	13		CZECH	NETH	----
V34	POLITICAL STRIKES	1970-74	D3	P29	0		FINLA	GUINE	----
		1975-79	D3	P29	0		FINLA	GFR	----
V35	MEMBER OF THE NONALIGNED MMT.	1970	----	----	0		FRANC	GFR	----
		1976	----	----	0		FRANC	GFR	----
		1981	----	----	0		FRANC	GFR	----
V36	MEMBER OF THE OPEC	1970	----	----	0		FRANC	GFR	----
		1975	----	----	0		FRANC	GFR	----
		1980	----	----	0		FRANC	GFR	----
V37	MEMBER OF THE OECD	1970	----	----	0		ETHIA	GHANA	----
		1975	----	----	0		GABON	GHANA	----
		1980	----	----	0		GABON	GHANA	----
V38	MEMBER OF THE CMEA	1970	----	----	1		CZECH	HUNGA	----
		1975	----	----	1		CZECH	HUNGA	----
		1980	----	----	1		CZECH	HUNGA	----
V39	MEMBER OF THE WTO	1970	----	----	1		CZECH	HUNGA	----
		1975	----	----	1		CZECH	HUNGA	----
		1980	----	----	1		CZECH	HUNGA	----

V40	MEMBER OF THE NATO	1970	----	----	0		FINLA	GHANA	----
		1975	----	----	0		GABON	GHANA	----
		1980	----	----	0		GABON	GHANA	----
V41	GDP SHARE OF INVESTMENTS	------	----	----	----- -----		-------	-------	----
V42	GDP SHARE OF AGRICULTURE	------	----	----	----- -----		-------	-------	----
V43	GDP SHARE OF INDUSTRY	------	----	----	----- -----		-------	-------	----
V44	GDP SHARE OF SERVICES	------	----	----	----- -----		-------	-------	----
V45	HOMICIDES P. MIL. POPULATION	1974	D1	P3	4.0	1/MIL CAP	-------	DENMA	F149
V46	SUICIDES P. MIL. POPULATION	1970	D10	P96	304.6	1/MIL CAP	CZECH	HUNGA	F147
		1974	D10	P96	361.8	1/MIL CAP	FINLA	HUNGA	F147
V47	IMPORT PARTNERS	1970	R1	USSR	40.1	%	EGYPT	HUNGA	----
		1970	R2	GFR	10.6	%	ECUA	IRE	----
		1970	R3	CZECH	9.4	%	BULGA	HUNGA	----
V48	EXPORT PARTNERS	1970	R1	USSR	38.0	%	EGYPT	HUNGA	----
		1970	R2	GFR	9.8	%	ETHIA	HONDU	----
		1970	R3	CZECH	9.6	%	BULGA	HUNGA	----
V49	PATENT SUPPLIERS	1970	R1	GFR	820		BULGA	HUNGA	----
		1970	R2	SWITZ	281		ZAIRE	GUATE	----
		1970	R3	CZECH	176		-------	-------	----
		1980	R1	GFR	372		FINLA	GREC	----
		1980	R2	USA	271		DENMA	GHANA	----
		1980	R3	SWITZ	98		ELSA	GFR	----
V50	PROVENANCE OF FOREIGN FIRMS	------	----	----	----- -----		-------	-------	----
V51	FILM SUPPLIERS	1980	R1	USSR	38		CZECH	HUNGA	F118
		1980	R2	USA	10		CZECH	HAITI	F118
		1980	R3	FRANC	5		CZECH	GFR	F118

GERMANY, FEDERAL REPUBLIC OF [3]) (GFR)

V1	INCOME PER CAPITA	1970	D10	P95	9408	$/CAP	USA	DENMA	F147
		1975	D10	P93	10246	$/CAP	USA	NORWY	F147
		1980	D10	P93	12234	$/CAP	SAUDI	DENMA	F147
V2	TELEPHONES P. TSD. POPULATION	1970	D9	P89	225	1/TSD CAP	BELGI	UNKI	----
		1975	D9	P87	317	1/TSD CAP	BELGI	NORWY	----
		1980	D9	P88	464	1/TSD CAP	JAPAN	UNKI	----
V3	INFANT MORTALITY RATE	1980	D2	P15	12.6	1/TSD	UNKI	USA	----

---

[3]) Also known as West Germany.

V4	PHYSICIANS P. MIL. POPULATION	1975	D10	P92	1986	1/MIL	BELGI	HUNGA	F147
		1980	D10	P90	2265	1/MIL	MONGO	SPAIN	F147
V5	ADULT LITERACY	------	----	----	-----	-----	-------	-------	----
V6	DURATION OF SCHOOLING	1970	D8	P78	10.1	YR	AURIA	HUNGA	----
		1975	D8	P78	10.4	YR	HUNGA	ISRA	----
		1980	D7	P65	10.1	YR	CZECH	JAMAI	----
V7	STUDENT ENROLLMENT RATIO	1970	D8	P78	13.4	%	AURIA	GREC	----
		1975	D9	P89	24.5	%	FRANC	JAPAN	----
		1980	D9	P89	27.3	%	BELGI	ITALY	----
V8	SHARE OF AGRICULTURAL LABOR	1980	D1	P10	5.5	%	USA	SWEDN	----
V9	SHARE OF INDUSTRIAL LABOR	1980	D8	P78	37.3	%	JAPAN	AURIA	----
V10	SHARE OF SERVICE LABOR	1980	D9	P86	43.2	%	SWITZ	KUWAI	----
V11	SHARE OF ACADEMIC LABOR	1980	D8	P74	14.0	%	IRE	AULIA	----
V12	SHARE OF SELF-EMPLOYED LABOR	1980	D2	P13	8.6	%	SWEDN	SWITZ	----
V13	MILITARY EXPENDITURES	1970	D10	P97	19.077	TSD MIL $	UNKI	USA	----
		1975	D10	P98	23.186	TSD MIL $	UNKI	USA	----
		1980	D10	P98	24.703	TSD MIL $	UNKI	USA	----
V14	MILITARY MANPOWER	1970	D10	P93	510	TSD CAP	VINO	TAIWA	----
		1975	D10	P91	495	TSD CAP	KORNO	ITALY	----
		1980	D10	P95	480	TSD CAP	PAKI	FRANC	----
V15	MEN AT AGE 20 - 30	1970	D10	P91	4132	TSD CAP	UNKI	BRAZI	F22
		1975	D10	P90	4225	TSD CAP	ITALY	MEXI	F22
		1980	D9	P88	4606	TSD CAP	FRANC	MEXI	F22
V16	POPULATION	1970	D10	P92	60.71	MIL CAP	NIGRA	BANGL	F22
		1975	D10	P91	61.83	MIL CAP	MEXI	NIGRA	F22
		1980	D10	P91	61.56	MIL CAP	ITALY	MEXI	F22
V17	GROSS DOMESTIC PRODUCT	1970	D10	P97	571.153	TSD MIL $	FRANC	JAPAN	----
		1975	D10	P97	633.509	TSD MIL $	FRANC	JAPAN	----
		1980	D10	P97	753.142	TSD MIL $	FRANC	JAPAN	----
V18	SHARE IN WORLD IMPORTS	1970	D10	P99	91.857	1/TSD	UNKI	USA	----
		1975	D10	P99	83.934	1/TSD	JAPAN	USA	----
		1980	D10	P99	93.157	1/TSD	JAPAN	USA	----
V19	SHARE IN WORLD EXPORTS	1970	D10	P99	111.223	1/TSD	UNKI	USA	----
		1975	D10	P99	104.731	1/TSD	JAPAN	USA	----
		1980	D10	P99	98.119	1/TSD	JAPAN	USA	----
V20	GDP SHARE OF IMPORTS	1970	D5	P43	16.4	%	ECUA	MALI	----
		1975	D3	P28	18.2	%	AFGHA	NIGRA	----
		1980	D5	P47	23.3	%	EGYPT	SOUAF	----
V21	GDP SHARE OF EXPORTS	1970	D7	P61	18.8	%	MALAW	NEWZ	----
		1975	D7	P63	21.8	%	CHILE	MALAW	----
		1980	D7	P64	23.9	%	AURIA	MALAW	----

V22	EXPORT PARTNER CONCENTRATION	1970	D1	P3	12.4 %	PAKI	SWEDN	----
		1975	D1	P6	11.7 %	SWEDN	INDIA	----
		1980	D1	P9	13.4 %	NEWZ	TANZA	----
V23	TOTAL DEBT AS % OF GDP	------	----	----	----- -----	-------	-------	----
V24	SHARE OF NEW FOREIGN PATENTS	1970	D2	P14	50 %	BULGA	GREC	----
		1975	D2	P14	50 %	BULGA	KORSO	----
		1980	D2	P15	51 %	GREC	HUNGA	----
V25	FOREIGN PROPERTY AS % OF GDP	------	----	----	----- -----	-------	-------	----
V26	GNP SHARE OF DEVELOPMENT AID	1970	D5	P51	0.32 %	JAPAN	USA	----
		1975	D5	P43	0.40 %	UNKI	NEWZ	----
		1980	D6	P52	0.44 %	CANA	AULIA	----
V27	SHARE IN NOBEL PRIZE WINNERS	1970-79	D10	P94	2.5 %	DENMA	SWITZ	----
V28	GDP SHARE OF MANUFACTURING	------	----	----	----- -----	-------	-------	----
V29	EXPORT SHARE OF MANUFACTURES	1970	D10	P97	80.1 %	ITALY	SWITZ	----
		1975	D10	P98	77.9 %	KORSO	SWITZ	----
		1980	D10	P91	78.5 %	AURIA	ITALY	----
V30	LACK OF CIVIL LIBERTIES	1975	D1	P7	1	DENMA	JAPAN	----
		1980	D2	P18	2	FRANC	GREC	----
V31	LACK OF POLITICAL RIGHTS	1975	D1	P8	1	FRANC	IRE	----
		1980	D1	P8	1	FRANC	IRE	----
V32	RIOTS	1970-74	D9	P82	12	EGYPT	KAMPU	----
		1975-79	D9	P82	9	UGADA	CENTR	----
V33	PROTEST DEMONSTRATIONS	1970-74	D9	P87	36	SOUAF	INDIA	----
		1975-79	D10	P91	42	GREC	FRANC	----
V34	POLITICAL STRIKES	1970-74	D7	P64	1	CAME	GUATE	----
		1975-79	D3	P29	0	GDR	GUINE	----
V35	MEMBER OF THE NONALIGNED MMT.	1970	----	----	0	GDR	GREC	----
		1976	----	----	0	GDR	GREC	----
		1981	----	----	0	GDR	GREC	----
V36	MEMBER OF THE OPEC	1970	----	----	0	GDR	GHANA	----
		1975	----	----	0	GDR	GHANA	----
		1980	----	----	0	GDR	GHANA	----
V37	MEMBER OF THE OECD	1970	----	----	1	FRANC	GREC	----
		1975	----	----	1	FRANC	GREC	----
		1980	----	----	1	FRANC	GREC	----
V38	MEMBER OF THE CMEA	1970	----	----	0	FRANC	GHANA	----
		1975	----	----	0	GABON	GHANA	----
		1980	----	----	0	GABON	GHANA	----
V39	MEMBER OF THE WTO	1970	----	----	0	FRANC	GHANA	----
		1975	----	----	0	GABON	GHANA	----
		1980	----	----	0	GABON	GHANA	----

V40	MEMBER OF THE NATO	1970	----	----	1		FRANC	GREC	----
		1975	----	----	1		FRANC	GREC	----
		1980	----	----	1		FRANC	GREC	----
V41	GDP SHARE OF INVESTMENTS	1970	D9	P83	27.9 %		PANA	NETH	----
		1975	D4	P40	20.6 %		ITALY	NETH	----
		1980	D6	P55	24.8 %		BENIN	ITALY	----
V42	GDP SHARE OF AGRICULTURE	1970	D1	P6	3.4 %		USA	BELGI	----
		1975	D1	P8	3.0 %		BELGI	TRITO	----
		1980	D1	P10	2.2 %		TRITO	USA	----
V43	GDP SHARE OF INDUSTRY	1970	D10	P96	53.1 %		JAPAN	ZAMBI	----
		1975	D9	P90	48.1 %		LIBE	VENE	----
		1980	D10	P91	47.9 %		VENE	SOUAF	----
V44	GDP SHARE OF SERVICES	1970	D4	P36	43.5 %		TURKY	KORSO	----
		1975	D7	P65	48.9 %		SOUAF	ZAIRE	----
		1980	D7	P62	49.9 %		SUDAN	ECUA	----
V45	HOMICIDES P. MIL. POPULATION	1970	D5	P42	13.9	1/MIL CAP	JAPAN	CZECH	F149
		1975	D4	P37	12.2	1/MIL CAP	SWEDN	ITALY	F149
		1980	D4	P37	11.5	1/MIL CAP	NORWY	SWEDN	F147
V46	SUICIDES P. MIL. POPULATION	1970	D9	P87	214.9	1/MIL CAP	DENMA	SWEDN	F147
		1975	D9	P81	208.6	1/MIL CAP	SRILA	CZECH	F147
		1980	D8	P76	209.0	1/MIL CAP	CZECH	BELGI	F147
V47	IMPORT PARTNERS	1970	R1	FRANC	12.7 %		CONGO	IVORY	----
		1970	R2	NETH	12.2 %		BENIN	BELGI	----
		1970	R3	USA	11.0 %		FRANC	IRE	----
		1980	R1	NETH	11.6 %		-------	BELGI	----
		1980	R2	FRANC	10.8 %		EGYPT	ITALY	----
		1980	R3	ITALY	8.0 %		ALGER	GREC	----
V48	EXPORT PARTNERS	1970	R1	FRANC	12.4 %		CHAD	IVORY	----
		1970	R2	NETH	10.6 %		CONGO	NIGRA	----
		1970	R3	USA	9.1 %		ARGE	GREC	----
		1980	R1	FRANC	13.4 %		GABON	IVORY	----
		1980	R2	NETH	9.5 %		TOGO	GHANA	----
		1980	R3	ITALY	8.6 %		YUGO	HAITI	----
V49	PATENT SUPPLIERS	1970	R1	USA	2882		FRANC	GREC	----
		1970	R2	FRANC	734		CUBA	USSR	----
		1970	R3	UNKI	687		FRANC	JAPAN	----
		1980	R1	USA	3211		FRANC	HAITI	----
		1980	R2	JAPAN	2340		CANA	SIERA	----
		1980	R3	SWITZ	948		GDR	JAMAI	----
V50	PROVENANCE OF FOREIGN FIRMS	1980	R1	USA	29.0 %		FRANC	GREC	F116
		1980	R2	UNKI	20.0 %		FRANC	INDIA	F116
		1980	R3	SWITZ	13.2 %		AURIA	-------	F116
V51	FILM SUPPLIERS	1980	R1	USA	109		FRANC	GREC	F120
		1980	R2	ITALY	53		FRANC	GREC	F120
		1980	R3	FRANC	28		GDR	GREC	F120

GHANA (GHANA)

V1	INCOME PER CAPITA	1970	D3	P25	473	$/CAP	THAI	PHILI	F4
		1975	D3	P26	441	$/CAP	KENYA	BOLI	----
		1980	D2	P20	391	$/CAP	MADA	KENYA	F35
V2	TELEPHONES P. TSD. POPULATION	1970	D3	P30	5	1/TSD CAP	THAI	HONDU	----
		1975	D3	P28	6	1/TSD CAP	SRILA	YESO	----
		1979	D3	P22	7	1/TSD CAP	ANGO	HONDU	----
V3	INFANT MORTALITY RATE	1980	D7	P61	107.3	1/TSD	BURMA	TANZA	F5
V4	PHYSICIANS P. MIL. POPULATION	1975	D3	P29	95	1/MIL	SUDAN	MADA	----
		1981	D4	P33	141	1/MIL	YESO	THAI	----
V5	ADULT LITERACY	1970	D3	P19	30.2	%	ALGER	INDIA	----
V6	DURATION OF SCHOOLING	1970	D5	P48	7.3	YR	BRAZI	SYRIA	F4
		1975	D4	P38	7.2	YR	EGYPT	MADA	----
		1980	D4	P29	7.3	YR	ZAIRE	TURKY	----
V7	STUDENT ENROLLMENT RATIO	1970	D3	P26	0.8	%	ZAIRE	KENYA	----
		1975	D3	P23	1.1	%	AFGHA	YESO	----
		1981	D3	P22	1.6	%	LESO	ZAMBI	----
V8	SHARE OF AGRICULTURAL LABOR	1970	D9	P87	57.4	%	ELSA	INDO	F46
V9	SHARE OF INDUSTRIAL LABOR	1970	D2	P21	19.6	%	MALAY	MOROC	F46
V10	SHARE OF SERVICE LABOR	1970	D3	P26	19.2	%	IRAN	DOMI	F46
V11	SHARE OF ACADEMIC LABOR	1970	D3	P23	3.8	%	ELSA	PORTU	F46
V12	SHARE OF SELF-EMPLOYED LABOR	1970	D10	P95	62.9	%	PARA	NEPAL	F46
V13	MILITARY EXPENDITURES	1970	D4	P36	0.078	TSD MIL $	CAME	ECUA	----
		1975	D3	P28	0.074	TSD MIL $	GUATE	BANGL	----
		1980	D2	P16	0.031	TSD MIL $	LIBE	TRITO	F59
V14	MILITARY MANPOWER	1970	D5	P44	35	TSD CAP	NEPAL	NORWY	----
		1975	D4	P35	20	TSD CAP	ECUA	LEBA	----
		1980	D3	P26	14	TSD CAP	NEWZ	HONDU	----
V15	MEN AT AGE 20 - 30	1970	D5	P43	596	TSD CAP	GREC	BULGA	----
V16	POPULATION	1970	D6	P53	8.61	MIL CAP	CUBA	GREC	F4
		1975	D6	P58	9.87	MIL CAP	BELGI	CHILE	----
		1980	D6	P58	11.54	MIL CAP	CHILE	MOZAM	F35
V17	GROSS DOMESTIC PRODUCT	1970	D5	P41	4.073	TSD MIL $	TUNIS	ECUA	----
		1975	D4	P34	4.353	TSD MIL $	BURMA	TRITO	----
		1980	D4	P32	4.511	TSD MIL $	PARA	TANZA	----
V18	SHARE IN WORLD IMPORTS	1970	D5	P44	1.238	1/TSD	SRILA	KENYA	F30
		1975	D4	P38	0.870	1/TSD	TANZA	BANGL	F30
		1980	D4	P32	0.550	1/TSD	ZAMBI	JAMAI	F30

V19 SHARE IN WORLD EXPORTS	1970	D5	P46	1.460 1/TSD	SRILA	IVORY	F30
	1975	D5	P42	0.921 1/TSD	JAMAI	ZAMBI	F30
	1980	D4	P39	0.575 1/TSD	URU	ZAMBI	F30
V20 GDP SHARE OF IMPORTS	1970	D5	P50	18.6 %	SAUDI	DOMI	F30
	1975	D3	P25	17.2 %	RWAN	PERU	F30
	1980	D1	P5	7.6 %	CHINA	BRAZI	F30
V21 GDP SHARE OF EXPORTS	1970	D7	P68	20.7 %	SWEDN	TOGO	F30
	1975	D5	P49	17.6 %	CAME	MOROC	F30
	1980	D2	P15	7.7 %	PARA	BURMA	F30
V22 EXPORT PARTNER CONCENTRATION	1970	D3	P21	19.0 %	DENMA	ISRA	----
	1975	D2	P17	15.3 %	SWITZ	BRAZI	----
	1980	D4	P33	19.8 %	SWITZ	ARGE	----
V23 TOTAL DEBT AS % OF GDP	------	----	----	----- -----	-------	-------	----
V24 SHARE OF NEW FOREIGN PATENTS	1970	D9	P90	100 %	CUBA	HAITI	----
	1975	D10	P92	100 %	BURU	JAMAI	----
	1980	D10	P94	100 %	BURU	KENYA	----
V25 FOREIGN PROPERTY AS % OF GDP	1971	D7	P67	14.2 %	PERU	COSTA	----
	1975	D6	P54	6.5 %	NICA	PAKI	----
	1978	D3	----	2.4 %	NIGRA	ANGO	----
V26 GNP SHARE OF DEVELOPMENT AID	------	----	----	----- -----	-------	-------	----
V27 SHARE IN NOBEL PRIZE WINNERS	1970-79	D5	P45	0.0 %	GDR	GREC	----
V28 GDP SHARE OF MANUFACTURING	1970	D4	P38	11.4 %	NIGER	KENYA	----
	1975	D5	P49	13.9 %	IVORY	TRITO	----
	1980	D3	P27	7.2 %	SOMA	LIBE	----
V29 EXPORT SHARE OF MANUFACTURES	------	----	----	----- -----	-------	-------	----
V30 LACK OF CIVIL LIBERTIES	1975	D6	P54	5	ETHIA	INDO	----
	1980	D4	P38	4	UPVO	KENYA	----
V31 LACK OF POLITICAL RIGHTS	1975	D9	P88	7	GDR	GUINE	----
	1980	D4	P36	4	BRAZI	KORSO	----
V32 RIOTS	1970-74	D5	P43	1	ECUA	HUNGA	----
	1975-79	D7	P69	5	BRAZI	LEBA	----
V33 PROTEST DEMONSTRATIONS	1970-74	D4	P37	1	FINLA	HAITI	----
	1975-79	D5	P42	2	FINLA	HAITI	----
V34 POLITICAL STRIKES	1970-74	D8	P74	2	DENMA	PHILI	----
	1975-79	D10	P94	15	UNKI	SOUAF	----
V35 MEMBER OF THE NONALIGNED MMT.	1970	----	----	1	ETHIA	GUINE	----
	1976	----	----	1	GABON	GUINE	----
	1981	----	----	1	GABON	GUINE	----
V36 MEMBER OF THE OPEC	1970	----	----	0	GFR	GREC	----
	1975	----	----	0	GFR	GREC	----
	1980	----	----	0	GFR	GREC	----

V37 MEMBER OF THE OECD	1970	----	----	0		GDR	GUATE	----
	1975	----	----	0		GDR	GUATE	----
	1980	----	----	0		GDR	GUATE	----
V38 MEMBER OF THE CMEA	1970	----	----	0		GFR	GREC	----
	1975	----	----	0		GFR	GREC	----
	1980	----	----	0		GFR	GREC	----
V39 MEMBER OF THE WTO	1970	----	----	0		GFR	GREC	----
	1975	----	----	0		GFR	GREC	----
	1980	----	----	0		GFR	GREC	----
V40 MEMBER OF THE NATO	1970	----	----	0		GDR	GUATE	----
	1975	----	----	0		GDR	GUATE	----
	1980	----	----	0		GDR	GUATE	----
V41 GDP SHARE OF INVESTMENTS	1970	D3	P22	14.2 %		BURMA	PAKI	----
	1975	D1	P10	12.7 %		ETHIA	KUWAI	----
	1980	D1	P2	5.8 %		UGADA	CENTR	----
V42 GDP SHARE OF AGRICULTURE	1970	D9	P86	46.5 %		BENIN	INDO	----
	1975	D10	P92	47.7 %		ETHIA	CHAD	----
	1980	D10	P99	61.0 %		SOMA	UGADA	----
V43 GDP SHARE OF INDUSTRY	1970	D3	P21	18.2 %		INDO	MADA	----
	1975	D3	P24	21.0 %		UPVO	PARA	----
	1980	D1	P4	11.4 %		BENIN	SOMA	----
V44 GDP SHARE OF SERVICES	1970	D2	P18	35.3 %		INDO	YENO	----
	1975	D2	P14	31.3 %		LIBYA	RWAN	----
	1980	D1	P7	27.6 %		ANGO	SOMA	----
V45 HOMICIDES P. MIL. POPULATION	------	----	----	----- -----		-------	-------	----
V46 SUICIDES P. MIL. POPULATION	------	----	----	----- -----		-------	-------	----
V47 IMPORT PARTNERS	1970	R1	UNKI	23.6 %		-------	IRAQ	----
	1970	R2	USA	18.1 %		VENE	INDO	----
	1970	R3	GFR	10.6 %		ETHIA	INDO	----
	1980	R1	UNKI	21.8 %		-------	IRE	----
	1980	R2	NIGRA	20.3 %		-------	NIGER	----
	1980	R3	USA	12.1 %		UNARE	IRAQ	----
V48 EXPORT PARTNERS	1970	R1	USA	19.0 %		ETHIA	GUATE	----
	1970	R2	UNKI	19.0 %		CANA	ISRA	----
	1970	R3	GFR	10.3 %		ECUA	GUATE	----
	1980	R1	UNKI	19.8 %		-------	IRE	----
	1980	R2	NETH	18.4 %		GFR	IVORY	----
	1980	R3	USSR	17.6 %		ETHIA	SYRIA	----
V49 PATENT SUPPLIERS	1970	R1	UNKI	22		BURU	IRAQ	----
	1970	R2	GDR	17		BULGA	HUNGA	----
	1970	R3	SWITZ	15		CZECH	GREC	----
	1979	R1	FRANC	8		CUBA	IRAQ	----
	1979	R2	USA	7		GDR	GREC	----
	1979	R3	GFR	6		COLO	IRE	----

V50 PROVENANCE OF FOREIGN FIRMS	1980	R1	UNKI	53.2 %	ETHIA	GUINE	----
	1980	R2	USA	15.5 %	FINLA	IRE	----
	1980	R3	GFR	10.6 %	FRANC	INDIA	----
V51 FILM SUPPLIERS	------	----	----	----- -----	-------	-------	----

GREECE (GREC)

V1 INCOME PER CAPITA	1970	D7	P69	2774 $/CAP	SOUAF	VENE	F224
	1975	D8	P71	3447 $/CAP	SINGA	VENE	F224
	1980	D8	P71	4007 $/CAP	VENE	SINGA	F224
V2 TELEPHONES P. TSD. POPULATION	1970	D8	P80	120 1/TSD CAP	IRE	GDR	----
	1975	D9	P82	221 1/TSD CAP	SPAIN	ITALY	----
	1980	D8	P77	289 1/TSD CAP	UNARE	SINGA	----
V3 INFANT MORTALITY RATE	1980	D2	P20	17.9 1/TSD	ISRA	CZECH	----
V4 PHYSICIANS P. MIL. POPULATION	1970	D10	P90	1623 1/MIL	GDR	MONGO	----
	1975	D10	P95	2035 1/MIL	HUNGA	MONGO	----
	1980	D10	P92	2435 1/MIL	SPAIN	SWITZ	----
V5 ADULT LITERACY	1971	D8	P71	84.4 %	YUGO	KORSO	----
V6 DURATION OF SCHOOLING	1970	D8	P80	10.2 YR	IRE	ALBA	----
	1975	D9	P87	11.0 YR	DENMA	CUBA	----
	1980	D9	P81	10.9 YR	CUBA	JORDA	----
V7 STUDENT ENROLLMENT RATIO	1970	D8	P79	13.5 %	GFR	IRE	----
	1975	D8	P77	18.3 %	COSTA	PHILI	----
	1979	D7	P69	16.7 %	BOLI	SYRIA	----
V8 SHARE OF AGRICULTURAL LABOR	1971	D7	P63	41.1 %	MEXI	PERU	F66
	1981	D5	P55	28.6 %	PANA	YUGO	F105
V9 SHARE OF INDUSTRIAL LABOR	1971	D5	P43	30.2 %	IRAN	IRE	F66
	1981	D6	P57	32.9 %	VENE	IRE	F105
V10 SHARE OF SERVICE LABOR	1971	D4	P38	23.0 %	MALAY	KORSO	F66
	1981	D5	P37	28.7 %	ELSA	PHILI	F105
V11 SHARE OF ACADEMIC LABOR	1971	D5	P47	5.7 %	NICA	SPAIN	F66
	1981	D6	P54	9.8 %	SYRIA	VENE	F105
V12 SHARE OF SELF-EMPLOYED LABOR	1971	D8	P85	38.9 %	PHILI	DOMI	F66
	1981	D8	P83	37.3 %	PHILI	RWAN	F105
V13 MILITARY EXPENDITURES	1970	D7	P69	1.158 TSD MIL $	KORSO	DENMA	F4
	1975	D8	P77	2.131 TSD MIL $	KORSO	SOUAF	----
	1980	D8	P79	2.190 TSD MIL $	NIGRA	TURKY	----
V14 MILITARY MANPOWER	1970	D8	P76	180 TSD CAP	THAI	NIGRA	----
	1975	D8	P74	191 TSD CAP	ISRA	BURMA	----
	1980	D8	P78	185 TSD CAP	ISRA	CZECH	----

V15 MEN AT AGE 20 - 30	1971	D5	P42	574	TSD CAP	PORTU	GHANA	----
	1975	D6	P53	636	TSD CAP	SWEDN	PORTU	----
	1981	D4	P39	697	TSD CAP	ECUA	MOZAM	----
V16 POPULATION	1970	D6	P54	8.79	MIL CAP	GHANA	PORTU	F167
	1975	D6	P53	9.05	MIL CAP	BULGA	CUBA	F167
	1980	D6	P53	9.64	MIL CAP	SAUDI	CUBA	F167
V17 GROSS DOMESTIC PRODUCT	1970	D7	P66	24.384	TSD MIL $	CHILE	KORSO	----
	1975	D7	P67	31.195	TSD MIL $	PHILI	FINLA	----
	1980	D7	P68	38.628	TSD MIL $	PHILI	ALGER	----
V18 SHARE IN WORLD IMPORTS	1970	D8	P72	5.898	1/TSD	BULGA	ROMA	----
	1975	D7	P69	5.855	1/TSD	INDO	VENE	----
	1980	D7	P67	5.134	1/TSD	UNARE	ARGE	----
V19 SHARE IN WORLD EXPORTS	1970	D5	P50	2.047	1/TSD	TURKY	THAI	----
	1975	D6	P59	2.609	1/TSD	NEWZ	PHILI	----
	1980	D6	P58	2.576	1/TSD	CHILE	ISRA	----
V20 GDP SHARE OF IMPORTS	1970	D6	P56	19.7	%	SRILA	SYRIA	----
	1975	D6	P59	25.6	%	SRILA	PORTU	----
	1980	D6	P59	26.2	%	HAITI	SAUDI	----
V21 GDP SHARE OF EXPORTS	1970	D1	P10	6.4	%	BRAZI	SPAIN	----
	1975	D3	P25	11.0	%	URU	COLO	----
	1980	D3	P29	12.8	%	MADA	MOROC	----
V22 EXPORT PARTNER CONCENTRATION	1970	D3	P25	20.2	%	TURKY	PORTU	----
	1975	D4	P35	21.1	%	FINLA	MADA	----
	1980	D3	P23	17.9	%	FINLA	URU	----
V23 TOTAL DEBT AS % OF GDP	1980	D3	P28	23.5	%	CENTR	THAI	----
V24 SHARE OF NEW FOREIGN PATENTS	1970	D2	P16	51	%	GFR	IRAQ	----
	1975	D1	P4	29	%	JAPAN	POLA	----
	1980	D2	P13	46	%	CUBA	GFR	----
V25 FOREIGN PROPERTY AS % OF GDP	1971	D3	P23	4.2	%	UGADA	ALGER	----
	1975	D4	P34	4.3	%	SPAIN	RWAN	----
	1978	D4	----	3.3	%	MOZAM	LIBYA	----
V26 GNP SHARE OF DEVELOPMENT AID	------	----	----	----- -----		-------	-------	----
V27 SHARE IN NOBEL PRIZE WINNERS	1970-79	D5	P45	0.0	%	GHANA	GUATE	----
V28 GDP SHARE OF MANUFACTURING	1970	D7	P68	19.1	%	ELSA	ECUA	F16
	1975	D7	P70	19.9	%	IRE	SRILA	F16
	1980	D7	P70	19.6	%	CANA	THAI	F16
V29 EXPORT SHARE OF MANUFACTURES	1970	D7	P66	23.3	%	URU	HAITI	----
	1975	D8	P78	37.3	%	EGYPT	HAITI	----
	1980	D8	P74	41.5	%	URU	NETH	----
V30 LACK OF CIVIL LIBERTIES	1975	D2	P18	2		FRANC	IRE	----
	1980	D2	P18	2		GFR	INDIA	----
V31 LACK OF POLITICAL RIGHTS	1975	D2	P20	2		FINLA	INDIA	----
	1980	D3	P21	2		FINLA	INDIA	----

V32	RIOTS	1970-74	D10	P96	63		CHILE	PAKI	----
		1975-79	D9	P87	17		KORSO	ISRA	----
V33	PROTEST DEMONSTRATIONS	1970-74	D10	P96	73		SPAIN	FRANC	----
		1975-79	D9	P90	41		KORSO	GFR	----
V34	POLITICAL STRIKES	1970-74	D9	P89	10		URU	INDIA	----
		1975-79	D8	P79	4		KORSO	MEXI	----
V35	MEMBER OF THE NONALIGNED MMT.	1970	----	----	0		GFR	GUATE	----
		1976	----	----	0		GFR	GUATE	----
		1981	----	----	0		GFR	GUATE	----
V36	MEMBER OF THE OPEC	1970	----	----	0		GHANA	GUATE	----
		1975	----	----	0		GHANA	GUATE	----
		1980	----	----	0		GHANA	GUATE	----
V37	MEMBER OF THE OECD	1970	----	----	1		GFR	IRE	----
		1975	----	----	1		GFR	IRE	----
		1980	----	----	1		GFR	IRE	----
V38	MEMBER OF THE CMEA	1970	----	----	0		GHANA	GUATE	----
		1975	----	----	0		GHANA	GUATE	----
		1980	----	----	0		GHANA	GUATE	----
V39	MEMBER OF THE WTO	1970	----	----	0		GHANA	GUATE	----
		1975	----	----	0		GHANA	GUATE	----
		1980	----	----	0		GHANA	GUATE	----
V40	MEMBER OF THE NATO	1970	----	----	1		GFR	ITALY	----
		1975	----	----	1		GFR	ITALY	F14
		1980	----	----	1		GFR	ITALY	----
V41	GDP SHARE OF INVESTMENTS	1970	D9	P85	28.1 %		NETH	ZAMBI	----
		1975	D8	P72	27.0 %		ECUA	BRAZI	----
		1980	D8	P73	28.2 %		IRE	IVORY	----
V42	GDP SHARE OF AGRICULTURE	1970	D5	P45	18.3 %		BOLI	TUNIS	F16
		1975	D5	P47	18.7 %		BOLI	ZAIRE	F16
		1980	D5	P46	17.4 %		TUNIS	BOLI	F16
V43	GDP SHARE OF INDUSTRY	1970	D7	P60	31.4 %		SIERA	IRE	F16
		1975	D5	P49	30.2 %		BOLI	TUNIS	F16
		1980	D5	P50	31.3 %		NICA	NEWZ	F16
V44	GDP SHARE OF SERVICES	1970	D6	P57	50.3 %		PERU	DOMI	F16
		1975	D7	P70	51.1 %		CAME	IRE	F16
		1980	D7	P68	51.3 %		IVORY	DOMI	F16
V45	HOMICIDES P. MIL. POPULATION	1970	D1	P5	5.8 1/MIL CAP		NETH	NORWY	F154
		1975	D2	P15	7.8 1/MIL CAP		NORWY	BELGI	F154
		1980	D1	P4	6.7 1/MIL CAP		-------	IRE	F2
V46	SUICIDES P. MIL. POPULATION	1970	D2	P21	31.6 1/MIL CAP		GUATE	THAI	F2
		1975	D2	P13	27.5 1/MIL CAP		ECUA	COLO	F2
		1980	D2	P13	32.7 1/MIL CAP		ECUA	SPAIN	F2

V47	IMPORT PARTNERS	1970	R1	GFR	18.6 %	FRANC	IRAN	----
		1970	R2	JAPAN	12.7 %	ETHIA	HAITI	----
		1970	R3	UNKI	8.6 %	FINLA	LIBYA	----
		1980	R1	GFR	13.9 %	FRANC	ITALY	----
		1980	R2	JAPAN	11.1 %	ECUA	HAITI	----
		1980	R3	ITALY	8.2 %	GFR	NIGER	----
V48	EXPORT PARTNERS	1970	R1	GFR	20.2 %	FRANC	ITALY	----
		1970	R2	ITALY	10.0 %	FRANC	SAUDI	----
		1970	R3	USA	7.5 %	GFR	INDO	----
		1980	R1	GFR	17.9 %	FRANC	ITALY	----
		1980	R2	ITALY	9.7 %	FRANC	LIBYA	----
		1980	R3	FRANC	7.4 %	YENO	IRE	----
V49	PATENT SUPPLIERS	1970	R1	USA	373	GFR	GUATE	----
		1970	R2	GFR	312	FRANC	IRAN	----
		1970	R3	SWITZ	219	GHANA	HUNGA	----
		1980	R1	GFR	204	GDR	HUNGA	----
		1980	R2	USA	196	GHANA	HUNGA	----
		1980	R3	FRANC	124	EGYPT	IRAN	----
V50	PROVENANCE OF FOREIGN FIRMS	1980	R1	USA	29.7 %	GFR	GUATE	----
		1980	R2	FINLA	18.5 %	-------	ITALY	----
		1980	R3	UNKI	16.3 %	FINLA	INDO	----
V51	FILM SUPPLIERS	1980	R1	USA	154	GFR	INDIA	F119
		1980	R2	ITALY	86	GFR	INDO	F119
		1980	R3	FRANC	70	GFR	KORSO	F119

GUATEMALA (GUATE)

V1	INCOME PER CAPITA	1970	D5	P45	863 $/CAP	DOMI	KORSO	F4
		1975	D5	P42	956 $/CAP	NIGRA	PARA	----
		1980	D5	P43	1085 $/CAP	PERU	JAMAI	----
V2	TELEPHONES P. TSD. POPULATION	1969	D4	P37	8 1/TSD CAP	YESO	SENE	----
		1973	D4	----	10 1/TSD CAP	KENYA	MOROC	----
V3	INFANT MORTALITY RATE	1980	D5	P45	65.9 1/TSD	COLO	DOMI	----
V4	PHYSICIANS P. MIL. POPULATION	1971	D5	P42	222 1/MIL	MALAY	ELSA	----
		1975	D5	P49	390 1/MIL	IRAN	IRAQ	----
V5	ADULT LITERACY	------	----	----	----- -----	-------	-------	----
V6	DURATION OF SCHOOLING	1970	D3	P25	4.2 YR	HAITI	LIBE	----
		1975	D3	P24	4.7 YR	MOROC	IVORY	----
		1980	D2	P19	5.4 YR	HAITI	MALAW	----

V7	STUDENT ENROLLMENT RATIO	1970	D5	P47	3.4	%	ELSA	CUBA	----
		1975	D5	P44	4.0	%	THAI	SAUDI	----
		1980	D6	P50	7.7	%	SAUDI	SINGA	----
V8	SHARE OF AGRICULTURAL LABOR	1973	D8	----	56.7	%	PAKI	HONDU	----
		1981	D9	P88	56.0	%	INDO	TURKY	F106
V9	SHARE OF INDUSTRIAL LABOR	1973	D3	----	20.6	%	PHILI	ELSA	----
		1981	D2	P15	21.5	%	PERU	TURKY	F106
V10	SHARE OF SERVICE LABOR	1973	D4	----	19.1	%	TUNIS	INDO	----
		1981	D2	P13	17.6	%	HAITI	PAKI	F106
V11	SHARE OF ACADEMIC LABOR	1973	D3	----	3.6	%	KORSO	NEPAL	----
		1981	D3	P25	5.0	%	PARA	SRILA	F106
V12	SHARE OF SELF-EMPLOYED LABOR	1973	D7	----	40.2	%	ECUA	HONDU	----
		1981	D9	P88	44.0	%	DOMI	PERU	F106
V13	MILITARY EXPENDITURES	1970	D3	P30	0.069	TSD MIL $	ETHIA	DOMI	----
		1975	D3	P26	0.070	TSD MIL $	SENE	GHANA	----
		1980	D4	P33	0.128	TSD MIL $	ZAMBI	ZAIRE	----
V14	MILITARY MANPOWER	1970	D3	P29	13	TSD CAP	ZAMBI	YENO	----
		1975	D3	P27	13	TSD CAP	HONDU	MADA	----
		1980	D3	P28	15	TSD CAP	HONDU	NICA	----
V15	MEN AT AGE 20 - 30	1975	D5	P45	518	TSD CAP	AURIA	MADA	F22
		1980	D4	P35	620	TSD CAP	SWEDN	BULGA	----
V16	POPULATION	1970	D5	P41	5.27	MIL CAP	TUNIS	IVORY	F4
		1975	D5	P42	6.24	MIL CAP	UPVO	MALI	----
		1980	D5	P44	7.26	MIL CAP	ZIMBA	AURIA	----
V17	GROSS DOMESTIC PRODUCT	1970	D5	P44	4.547	TSD MIL $	ECUA	SINGA	----
		1975	D4	P40	5.968	TSD MIL $	DOMI	TUNIS	----
		1980	D5	P43	7.880	TSD MIL $	URU	TUNIS	----
V18	SHARE IN WORLD IMPORTS	1970	D4	P35	0.856	1/TSD	DOMI	SUDAN	----
		1975	D4	P35	0.806	1/TSD	JORDA	SRILA	----
		1980	D4	P39	0.779	1/TSD	SUDAN	CAME	----
V19	SHARE IN WORLD EXPORTS	1970	D5	P42	0.925	1/TSD	UGADA	SUDAN	----
		1975	D4	P39	0.712	1/TSD	SRILA	KENYA	----
		1980	D5	P44	0.762	1/TSD	ZIMBA	ZAIRE	----
V20	GDP SHARE OF IMPORTS	1970	D4	P38	14.9	%	NIGER	ITALY	----
		1975	D4	P37	20.1	%	KUWAI	IRAN	----
		1980	D4	P37	20.3	%	SUDAN	FRANC	----
V21	GDP SHARE OF EXPORTS	1970	D5	P48	15.2	%	CHILE	PORTU	----
		1975	D5	P47	17.1	%	SYRIA	CAME	----
		1980	D5	P48	19.3	%	PORTU	THAI	----
V22	EXPORT PARTNER CONCENTRATION	1970	D5	P50	28.3	%	TOGO	NIGRA	----
		1975	D5	P45	23.1	%	ZAMBI	SOUAF	----
		1980	D6	P60	28.7	%	EGYPT	HUNGA	----
V23	TOTAL DEBT AS % OF GDP	1980	D1	P10	14.8	%	INDIA	RWAN	----

V24	SHARE OF NEW FOREIGN PATENTS	1970	D4	P39	88	%	AURIA	AULIA	----
		1975	D5	P43	88	%	CHILE	NORWY	----
V25	FOREIGN PROPERTY AS % OF GDP	1971	D6	P52	9.3	%	ELSA	MADA	----
		1975	D6	P57	7.1	%	URU	BRAZI	----
		1978	D6	----	4.8	%	TUNIS	ELSA	----
V26	GNP SHARE OF DEVELOPMENT AID	------	----	----	-----	-----	-------	-------	----
V27	SHARE IN NOBEL PRIZE WINNERS	1970-79	D5	P45	0.0	%	GREC	GUINE	----
V28	GDP SHARE OF MANUFACTURING	------	----	----	-----	-----	-------	-------	----
V29	EXPORT SHARE OF MANUFACTURES	1970	D7	P70	26.7	%	EGYPT	ELSA	----
		1975	D8	P72	24.0	%	CENTR	ELSA	----
		1980	D6	P58	23.4	%	ARGE	MALI	----
V30	LACK OF CIVIL LIBERTIES	1975	D3	P27	3		ELSA	HONDU	----
		1980	D6	P52	5		EGYPT	HAITI	----
V31	LACK OF POLITICAL RIGHTS	1975	D4	P31	4		DOMI	KUWAI	----
		1980	D4	P31	3		BOLI	MALAY	----
V32	RIOTS	1970-74	D8	P73	7		CHINA	SENE	----
		1975-79	D6	P60	3		BELGI	IRE	----
V33	PROTEST DEMONSTRATIONS	1970-74	D8	P72	8		CHILE	TURKY	----
		1975-79	D7	P67	7		PANA	YUGO	----
V34	POLITICAL STRIKES	1970-74	D7	P64	1		GFR	IRAQ	----
		1975-79	D7	P63	1		DENMA	IRE	----
V35	MEMBER OF THE NONALIGNED MMT.	1970	----	----	0		GREC	HAITI	----
		1976	----	----	0		GREC	HAITI	----
		1981	----	----	0		GREC	HAITI	----
V36	MEMBER OF THE OPEC	1970	----	----	0		GREC	GUINE	----
		1975	----	----	0		GREC	GUINE	----
		1980	----	----	0		GREC	GUINE	----
V37	MEMBER OF THE OECD	1970	----	----	0		GHANA	GUINE	----
		1975	----	----	0		GHANA	GUINE	----
		1980	----	----	0		GHANA	GUINE	----
V38	MEMBER OF THE CMEA	1970	----	----	0		GREC	GUINE	----
		1975	----	----	0		GREC	GUINE	----
		1980	----	----	0		GREC	GUINE	----
V39	MEMBER OF THE WTO	1970	----	----	0		GREC	GUINE	----
		1975	----	----	0		GREC	GUINE	----
		1980	----	----	0		GREC	GUINE	----
V40	MEMBER OF THE NATO	1970	----	----	0		GHANA	GUINE	----
		1975	----	----	0		GHANA	GUINE	----
		1980	----	----	0		GHANA	GUINE	----
V41	GDP SHARE OF INVESTMENTS	1970	D2	P12	12.8	%	SOMA	ELSA	----
		1975	D3	P21	16.1	%	SIERA	PAKI	----
		1980	D2	P19	15.9	%	NEPAL	MALI	----
V42	GDP SHARE OF AGRICULTURE	------	----	----	-----	-----	-------	-------	----

V43	GDP SHARE OF INDUSTRY	------	----	----	----- -----		-------	-------	----
V44	GDP SHARE OF SERVICES	------	----	----	----- -----		-------	-------	----
V45	HOMICIDES P. MIL. POPULATION	1970	D10	P96	198.1 1/MIL CAP	THAI	ELSA	F148
		1980	D10	P97	629.8 1/MIL CAP	THAI	-------	F2
V46	SUICIDES P. MIL. POPULATION	1970	D2	P19	31.1 1/MIL CAP	COLO	GREC	----
		1980	D1	P7	12.0 1/MIL CAP	KUWAI	PARA	F2
V47	IMPORT PARTNERS	1970	R1	USA	35.3 %	ELSA	HAITI	----
		1970	R2	ELSA	13.9 %	-------	NICA	----
		1970	R3	JAPAN	10.3 %	ELSA	HONDU	----
		1980	R1	USA	33.7 %	EGYPT	HAITI	----
		1980	R2	VENE	9.4 %	DOMI	HONDU	----
		1980	R3	JAPAN	8.3 %	DOMI	HONDU	----
V48	EXPORT PARTNERS	1970	R1	USA	28.3 %	GHANA	HAITI	----
		1970	R2	ELSA	13.4 %	-------	-------	----
		1970	R3	GFR	11.3 %	GHANA	ISRA	----
		1980	R1	USA	28.7 %	ETHIA	HAITI	----
		1980	R2	ELSA	12.3 %	-------	-------	----
		1980	R3	GFR	8.0 %	COSTA	LIBYA	----
V49	PATENT SUPPLIERS	1970	R1	USA	56	GREC	HONDU	----
		1970	R2	SWITZ	6	GDR	HONDU	----
		1970	R3	GFR	5	FINLA	INDIA	----
V50	PROVENANCE OF FOREIGN FIRMS	1980	R1	USA	78.2 %	GREC	HAITI	----
		1980	R2	CANA	5.3 %	-------	UNKI	----
		1980	R3	NETH	3.8 %	TOGO	SAUDI	----
V51	FILM SUPPLIERS	------	----	----	----- -----		-------	-------	----

GUINEA (GUINE)

V1	INCOME PER CAPITA	------	----	----	----- -----		-------	-------	----
V2	TELEPHONES P. TSD. POPULATION	1970	D2	P16	2 1/TSD CAP	ETHIA	INDIA	----
		1974	D2	P12	2 1/TSD CAP	AFGHA	INDO	----
V3	INFANT MORTALITY RATE	1980	D10	P97	171.5 1/TSD	YENO	MALAW	F5
V4	PHYSICIANS P. MIL. POPULATION	1971	D2	P11	32 1/MIL	YESO	CAME	----
		1976	D3	P23	63 1/MIL	SENE	NIGRA	----
V5	ADULT LITERACY	------	----	----	----- -----		-------	-------	----
V6	DURATION OF SCHOOLING	1970	D2	P16	2.9 YR	NIGRA	SUDAN	----
		1975	D2	P11	2.8 YR	NEPAL	SOMA	----
		1980	D1	P7	3.1 YR	SOMA	PAKI	----

V7	STUDENT ENROLLMENT RATIO	1970	D3	P23	0.6 %	TOGO	AFGHA	----
		1975	D5	P42	3.3 %	MOROC	THAI	----
		1980	D5	P41	4.4 %	MALAY	ALGER	----
V8	SHARE OF AGRICULTURAL LABOR	------	----	----	----- -----	-------	-------	----
V9	SHARE OF INDUSTRIAL LABOR	------	----	----	----- -----	-------	-------	----
V10	SHARE OF SERVICE LABOR	------	----	----	----- -----	-------	-------	----
V11	SHARE OF ACADEMIC LABOR	------	----	----	----- -----	-------	-------	----
V12	SHARE OF SELF-EMPLOYED LABOR	------	----	----	----- -----	-------	-------	----
V13	MILITARY EXPENDITURES	------	----	----	----- -----	-------	-------	----
V14	MILITARY MANPOWER	1970	D3	P24	9 TSD CAP	MALI	MADA	----
		1975	D2	P17	7 TSD CAP	CONGO	IVORY	----
		1980	D4	P31	17 TSD CAP	CONGO	SRILA	----
V15	MEN AT AGE 20 - 30	------	----	----	----- -----	-------	-------	----
V16	POPULATION	1970	D3	P30	3.92 MIL CAP	NORWY	NIGER	F4
		1975	D4	P31	4.34 MIL CAP	RWAN	HAITI	----
		1980	D4	P31	4.83 MIL CAP	FINLA	HAITI	----
V17	GROSS DOMESTIC PRODUCT	------	----	----	----- -----	-------	-------	----
V18	SHARE IN WORLD IMPORTS	------	----	----	----- -----	-------	-------	----
V19	SHARE IN WORLD EXPORTS	------	----	----	----- -----	-------	-------	----
V20	GDP SHARE OF IMPORTS	------	----	----	----- -----	-------	-------	----
V21	GDP SHARE OF EXPORTS	------	----	----	----- -----	-------	-------	----
V22	EXPORT PARTNER CONCENTRATION	------	----	----	----- -----	-------	-------	----
V23	TOTAL DEBT AS % OF GDP	1980	D9	P86	64.9 %	HONDU	MALAW	----
V24	SHARE OF NEW FOREIGN PATENTS	------	----	----	----- -----	-------	-------	----
V25	FOREIGN PROPERTY AS % OF GDP	1971	D9	P86	22.5 %	SENE	CENTR	----
		1975	D9	P86	17.8 %	CENTR	KENYA	----
		1978	D9	----	13.7 %	ZAMBI	HONDU	----
V26	GNP SHARE OF DEVELOPMENT AID	------	----	----	----- -----	-------	-------	----
V27	SHARE IN NOBEL PRIZE WINNERS	1970-79	D5	P45	0.0 %	GUATE	HAITI	----
V28	GDP SHARE OF MANUFACTURING	1975	D1	P4	4.4 %	ANGO	SAUDI	----
		1980	D1	P8	3.8 %	ZAIRE	UNARE	----
V29	EXPORT SHARE OF MANUFACTURES	------	----	----	----- -----	-------	-------	----
V30	LACK OF CIVIL LIBERTIES	1975	D10	P93	7	GDR	IRAQ	----
		1980	D10	P92	7	GDR	IRAQ	----
V31	LACK OF POLITICAL RIGHTS	1975	D9	P88	7	GHANA	IRAQ	----
		1980	D9	P90	7	GDR	IRAQ	----

V32	RIOTS	1970-74	D2	P19	0		GDR	HAITI	----
		1975-79	D2	P20	0		GDR	HAITI	----
V33	PROTEST DEMONSTRATIONS	1970-74	D2	P15	0		ELSA	HONDU	----
		1975-79	D2	P13	0		ECUA	HUNGA	----
V34	POLITICAL STRIKES	1970-74	D3	P29	0		GDR	HAITI	----
		1975-79	D3	P29	0		GFR	HAITI	----
V35	MEMBER OF THE NONALIGNED MMT.	1970	----	----	1		GHANA	INDIA	----
		1976	----	----	1		GHANA	INDIA	----
		1981	----	----	1		GHANA	INDIA	----
V36	MEMBER OF THE OPEC	1970	----	----	0		GUATE	HAITI	----
		1975	----	----	0		GUATE	HAITI	----
		1980	----	----	0		GUATE	HAITI	----
V37	MEMBER OF THE OECD	1970	----	----	0		GUATE	HAITI	----
		1975	----	----	0		GUATE	HAITI	----
		1980	----	----	0		GUATE	HAITI	----
V38	MEMBER OF THE CMEA	1970	----	----	0		GUATE	HAITI	----
		1975	----	----	0		GUATE	HAITI	----
		1980	----	----	0		GUATE	HAITI	----
V39	MEMBER OF THE WTO	1970	----	----	0		GUATE	HAITI	----
		1975	----	----	0		GUATE	HAITI	----
		1980	----	----	0		GUATE	HAITI	----
V40	MEMBER OF THE NATO	1970	----	----	0		GUATE	HAITI	----
		1975	----	----	0		GUATE	HAITI	----
		1980	----	----	0		GUATE	HAITI	----
V41	GDP SHARE OF INVESTMENTS	1975	D3	P30	17.9 %		SENE	HONDU	----
		1980	D1	P8	11.0 %		ETHIA	BOLI	----
V42	GDP SHARE OF AGRICULTURE	1975	D10	P95	52.4 %		RWAN	SOMA	----
		1980	D9	P82	36.6 %		SUDAN	INDIA	----
V43	GDP SHARE OF INDUSTRY	1975	D3	P21	20.1 %		MALAW	KENYA	----
		1980	D6	P55	33.4 %		NETH	CANA	----
V44	GDP SHARE OF SERVICES	1975	D2	P11	27.5 %		BANGL	LIBE	----
		1980	D2	P11	30.0 %		BURU	INDO	----
V45	HOMICIDES P. MIL. POPULATION	------	----	----	----- -----		-------	-------	----
V46	SUICIDES P. MIL. POPULATION	------	----	----	----- -----		-------	-------	----
V47	IMPORT PARTNERS	------	----	----	----- -----		-------	-------	----
V48	EXPORT PARTNERS	------	----	----	----- -----		-------	-------	----
V49	PATENT SUPPLIERS	------	----	----	----- -----		-------	-------	----
V50	PROVENANCE OF FOREIGN FIRMS	1980	R1	UNKI	32.5 %		GHANA	IRE	----
		1980	R2	FRANC	30.2 %		UPVO	URU	----
		1980	R3	USA	18.6 %		CONGO	MOZAM	----
V51	FILM SUPPLIERS	------	----	----	----- -----		-------	-------	----

HAITI (HAITI)

V1	INCOME PER CAPITA	1970	D2	P12	215 $/CAP	YENO	TANZA	F147
		1975	D2	P12	240 $/CAP	SRILA	PAKI	F147
		1980	D2	P14	285 $/CAP	TANZA	PAKI	F147
V2	TELEPHONES P. TSD. POPULATION	1971	D1	P7	1 1/TSD CAP	CHAD	LAOS	----
		1976	D3	P23	4 1/TSD CAP	VISO	MADA	----
V3	INFANT MORTALITY RATE	1980	D7	P69	120.9 1/TSD	LESO	SAUDI	F5
V4	PHYSICIANS P. MIL. POPULATION	1969	D3	P31	87 1/MIL	LIBE	CONGO	F147
		1973	D4	----	118 1/MIL	LIBE	THAI	F147
V5	ADULT LITERACY	1971	D2	P11	21.3 %	PAKI	MOROC	F22
V6	DURATION OF SCHOOLING	1971	D3	P23	3.9 YR	MOROC	GUATE	----
		1975	D3	P22	4.4 YR	TANZA	LAOS	----
		1980	D2	P17	5.3 YR	BENIN	GUATE	F35
V7	STUDENT ENROLLMENT RATIO	1970	D2	P18	0.4 %	MALAW	SOMA	----
		1975	D2	P16	0.7 %	SIERA	YENO	----
		1980	D2	P17	1.1 %	SOMA	CHINA	----
V8	SHARE OF AGRICULTURAL LABOR	1971	D10	P95	73.7 %	INDIA	THAI	F75
		1982	D10	----	70.2 %	INDIA	THAI	----
V9	SHARE OF INDUSTRIAL LABOR	1971	D1	P6	8.4 %	NEPAL	INDO	F75
		1982	D1	----	9.5 %	RWAN	BANGL	----
V10	SHARE OF SERVICE LABOR	1971	D2	P13	16.8 %	SYRIA	MOROC	F75
		1982	D2	----	17.5 %	ZIMBA	GUATE	----
V11	SHARE OF ACADEMIC LABOR	1971	D1	P6	1.2 %	NEPAL	INDO	F75
		1982	D2	----	2.9 %	AFGHA	PAKI	----
V12	SHARE OF SELF-EMPLOYED LABOR	1982	D10	----	68.7 %	CAME	-------	----
V13	MILITARY EXPENDITURES	1970	D2	P15	0.016 TSD MIL $	PANA	HONDU	----
		1975	D2	P12	0.016 TSD MIL $	COSTA	PANA	----
		1980	D1	P6	0.021 TSD MIL $	COSTA	BURU	----
V14	MILITARY MANPOWER	1970	D3	P27	12 TSD CAP	SRILA	ZAMBI	----
		1975	D2	P14	6 TSD CAP	UPVO	LIBE	----
		1980	D2	P16	7 TSD CAP	BURU	LIBE	----
V15	MEN AT AGE 20 - 30	1971	D3	P27	293 TSD CAP	DOMI	NORWY	F22
		1974	D3	P22	302 TSD CAP	NEWZ	ISRA	F2
		1980	D3	P25	424 TSD CAP	FINLA	CHAD	F2
V16	POPULATION	1970	D4	P33	4.24 MIL CAP	DOMI	ZAMBI	F22
		1975	D4	P32	4.58 MIL CAP	GUINE	NIGER	F22
		1980	D4	P32	5.01 MIL CAP	GUINE	RWAN	F22
V17	GROSS DOMESTIC PRODUCT	1970	D1	P10	0.911 TSD MIL $	SIERA	YENO	----
		1975	D1	P10	1.097 TSD MIL $	UPVO	HONDU	----
		1980	D1	P10	1.430 TSD MIL $	UPVO	NEPAL	----

V18	SHARE IN WORLD IMPORTS	1970	D1	P8	0.157	1/TSD	UPVO	KAMPU	F30
		1975	D1	P7	0.157	1/TSD	CHAD	UPVO	F30
		1980	D2	P11	0.183	1/TSD	UPVO	BENIN	F30
V19	SHARE IN WORLD EXPORTS	1970	D2	P15	0.131	1/TSD	KAMPU	NEPAL	F32
		1975	D1	P9	0.092	1/TSD	MALI	SOMA	F32
		1980	D2	P12	0.113	1/TSD	MALI	MALAW	F32
V20	GDP SHARE OF IMPORTS	1970	D3	P22	12.7	%	AFGHA	SPAIN	F30
		1975	D5	P41	21.0	%	CANA	SOMA	F30
		1980	D6	P57	25.9	%	ITALY	GREC	F30
V21	GDP SHARE OF EXPORTS	1970	D3	P22	10.0	%	SOMA	COLO	----
		1975	D3	P30	11.9	%	PARA	EGYPT	----
		1980	D4	P39	15.6	%	AULIA	SOUAF	----
V22	EXPORT PARTNER CONCENTRATION	1970	D10	P94	60.0	%	SENE	PANA	----
		1975	D10	P100	74.2	%	LAOS	-------	----
		1980	D10	P93	56.6	%	SYRIA	AFGHA	----
V23	TOTAL DEBT AS % OF GDP	1980	D3	P22	20.9	%	COLO	ZIMBA	----
V24	SHARE OF NEW FOREIGN PATENTS	1972	D9	----	100	%	GHANA	JORDA	F19
		1976	D5	P50	90	%	SRILA	HONDU	----
		1980	D3	P24	71	%	FRANC	SWEDN	----
V25	FOREIGN PROPERTY AS % OF GDP	1971	D7	P62	11.1	%	PHILI	KENYA	----
		1975	D7	P69	10.3	%	MADA	IVORY	----
		1978	D7	----	7.9	%	PHILI	COSTA	----
V26	GNP SHARE OF DEVELOPMENT AID	------	----	----	-----	-----	-------	-------	----
V27	SHARE IN NOBEL PRIZE WINNERS	1970-79	D5	P45	0.0	%	GUINE	HONDU	----
V28	GDP SHARE OF MANUFACTURING	------	----	----	-----	-----	-------	-------	----
V29	EXPORT SHARE OF MANUFACTURES	1970	D7	P67	23.7	%	GREC	EGYPT	----
		1975	D8	P80	37.9	%	GREC	NETH	----
		1979	D8	P78	48.0	%	NETH	BELGI	----
V30	LACK OF CIVIL LIBERTIES	1975	D8	P74	6		GABON	HUNGA	----
		1980	D6	P52	5		GUATE	HUNGA	----
V31	LACK OF POLITICAL RIGHTS	1975	D7	P63	6		GABON	HONDU	----
		1980	D7	P67	6		GABON	HONDU	----
V32	RIOTS	1970-74	D2	P19	0		GUINE	HONDU	----
		1975-79	D2	P20	0		GUINE	HUNGA	----
V33	PROTEST DEMONSTRATIONS	1970-74	D4	P37	1		GHANA	HUNGA	----
		1975-79	D5	P42	2		GHANA	MALAY	----
V34	POLITICAL STRIKES	1970-74	D3	P29	0		GUINE	HONDU	----
		1975-79	D3	P29	0		GUINE	HONDU	----
V35	MEMBER OF THE NONALIGNED MMT.	1970	----	----	0		GUATE	HONDU	----
		1976	----	----	0		GUATE	HONDU	----
		1981	----	----	0		GUATE	HONDU	----

V36 MEMBER OF THE OPEC	1970	----	----	0		GUINE	HONDU	----
	1975	----	----	0		GUINE	HONDU	----
	1980	----	----	0		GUINE	HONDU	----
V37 MEMBER OF THE OECD	1970	----	----	0		GUINE	HONDU	----
	1975	----	----	0		GUINE	HONDU	----
	1980	----	----	0		GUINE	HONDU	----
V38 MEMBER OF THE CMEA	1970	----	----	0		GUINE	HONDU	----
	1975	----	----	0		GUINE	HONDU	----
	1980	----	----	0		GUINE	HONDU	----
V39 MEMBER OF THE WTO	1970	----	----	0		GUINE	HONDU	----
	1975	----	----	0		GUINE	HONDU	----
	1980	----	----	0		GUINE	HONDU	----
V40 MEMBER OF THE NATO	1970	----	----	0		GUINE	HONDU	----
	1975	----	----	0		GUINE	HONDU	----
	1980	----	----	0		GUINE	HONDU	----
V41 GDP SHARE OF INVESTMENTS	1970	D1	P8	11.4 %		URU	UPVO	----
	1975	D2	P17	14.7 %		RWAN	CENTR	----
	1980	D2	P14	15.1 %		BURU	ZIMBA	----
V42 GDP SHARE OF AGRICULTURE	------	----	----	----- -----		-------	-------	----
V43 GDP SHARE OF INDUSTRY	------	----	----	----- -----		-------	-------	----
V44 GDP SHARE OF SERVICES	------	----	----	----- -----		-------	-------	----
V45 HOMICIDES P. MIL. POPULATION	------	----	----	----- -----		-------	-------	----
V46 SUICIDES P. MIL. POPULATION	------	----	----	----- -----		-------	-------	----
V47 IMPORT PARTNERS	1970	R1	USA	46.3 %		GUATE	HONDU	----
	1970	R2	JAPAN	9.1 %		GREC	KENYA	----
	1970	R3	ITALY	5.2 %		YUGO	MADA	----
	1980	R1	USA	53.3 %		GUATE	HONDU	----
	1980	R2	JAPAN	5.5 %		GREC	NEWZ	----
	1980	R3	CANA	5.0 %		USA	-------	----
V48 EXPORT PARTNERS	1970	R1	USA	60.0 %		GUATE	HONDU	----
	1970	R2	BELGI	11.6 %		DOMI	NETH	F138
	1970	R3	FRANC	7.0 %		CONGO	IRE	----
	1980	R1	USA	56.6 %		GUATE	HONDU	----
	1980	R2	FRANC	13.2 %		CAME	ITALY	----
	1980	R3	ITALY	12.7 %		GFR	IVORY	----
V49 PATENT SUPPLIERS	1980	R1	USA	8		GFR	HONDU	----
	1980	R2	-------	1		-------	-------	----
	1980	R3	-------	1		-------	-------	----
V50 PROVENANCE OF FOREIGN FIRMS	1980	R1	USA	89.5 %		GUATE	HONDU	----
	1980	R2	NETH	6.2 %		ELSA	MOZAM	----
	1980	R3	-------	2.0 %		-------	-------	----
V51 FILM SUPPLIERS	1980	R1	FRANC	140		ANGO	ALGER	F117
	1980	R2	USA	137		GDR	HUNGA	F117
	1980	R3	ITALY	9		FINLA	HUNGA	F117

HONDURAS (HONDU)

V1	INCOME PER CAPITA	1970	D3	P28	524	$/CAP	PHILI	SENE	----
		1975	D3	P28	502	$/CAP	BOLI	SENE	----
		1980	D3	P30	597	$/CAP	BOLI	ZAMBI	----
V2	TELEPHONES P. TSD. POPULATION	1970	D3	P30	5	1/TSD CAP	GHANA	LIBE	----
		1975	D4	P29	7	1/TSD CAP	YESO	THAI	----
		1979	D3	P24	8	1/TSD CAP	GHANA	SENE	----
V3	INFANT MORTALITY RATE	1980	D6	P52	95.0	1/TSD	KENYA	NICA	F5
V4	PHYSICIANS P. MIL. POPULATION	1971	D5	P46	287	1/MIL	SYRIA	IRAN	----
		1975	D5	P44	297	1/MIL	JAMAI	PHILI	----
		1979	D5	P42	321	1/MIL	ELSA	JAMAI	----
V5	ADULT LITERACY	------	----	----	-----	-----	-------	-------	----
V6	DURATION OF SCHOOLING	1970	D4	P40	6.4	YR	ZAIRE	EGYPT	----
		1975	D4	P32	6.5	YR	INDIA	INDO	----
		1980	D4	P32	7.6	YR	ELSA	CHINA	----
V7	STUDENT ENROLLMENT RATIO	1970	D5	P41	2.3	%	BURMA	INDO	----
		1975	D5	P47	4.6	%	TUNIS	SOUAF	----
		1980	D6	P52	8.2	%	SINGA	LIBYA	----
V8	SHARE OF AGRICULTURAL LABOR	1974	D8	P78	60.6	%	GUATE	THAI	----
V9	SHARE OF INDUSTRIAL LABOR	1974	D2	P19	17.6	%	YENO	THAI	----
V10	SHARE OF SERVICE LABOR	1974	D3	P26	17.7	%	SYRIA	PAKI	----
V11	SHARE OF ACADEMIC LABOR	1974	D3	P26	4.1	%	NEPAL	ELSA	----
V12	SHARE OF SELF-EMPLOYED LABOR	1974	D7	P68	40.3	%	GUATE	PHILI	----
V13	MILITARY EXPENDITURES	1970	D2	P15	0.016	TSD MIL $	HAITI	ELSA	----
		1975	D2	P18	0.030	TSD MIL $	JAMAI	UPVO	----
		1980	D3	P28	0.100	TSD MIL $	DOMI	IVORY	----
V14	MILITARY MANPOWER	1970	D2	P16	6	TSD CAP	CONGO	IVORY	----
		1975	D3	P25	12	TSD CAP	IRE	GUATE	----
		1980	D3	P26	14	TSD CAP	GHANA	GUATE	----
V15	MEN AT AGE 20 - 30	1970	D2	P13	196	TSD CAP	PARA	IRE	F2
		1981	D2	P16	298	TSD CAP	PARA	NORWY	F2
V16	POPULATION	1970	D2	P18	2.64	MIL CAP	LEBA	SIERA	----
		1975	D3	P22	3.09	MIL CAP	NEWZ	BENIN	----
		1980	D3	P24	3.69	MIL CAP	BENIN	ISRA	----
V17	GROSS DOMESTIC PRODUCT	1970	D2	P13	1.383	TSD MIL $	UPVO	JORDA	----
		1975	D2	P11	1.551	TSD MIL $	HAITI	NIGER	----
		1980	D2	P14	2.202	TSD MIL $	NICA	NIGER	----
V18	SHARE IN WORLD IMPORTS	1970	D4	P31	0.666	1/TSD	ELSA	URU	----
		1975	D3	P25	0.444	1/TSD	MADA	MOZAM	----
		1980	D3	P28	0.497	1/TSD	ELSA	PAPUA	----

V19 SHARE IN WORLD EXPORTS	1970	D3	P29	0.571	1/TSD	SENE	NICA	----
	1975	D3	P27	0.346	1/TSD	BANGL	PANA	----
	1980	D4	P32	0.412	1/TSD	ANGO	CONGO	----
V20 GDP SHARE OF IMPORTS	1970	D9	P87	30.6	%	ZAIRE	SWITZ	----
	1975	D9	P83	36.1	%	YENO	PAPUA	----
	1980	D9	P87	41.0	%	TUNIS	MAURA	----
V21 GDP SHARE OF EXPORTS	1970	D9	P83	24.8	%	JAMAI	SWITZ	----
	1975	D8	P78	27.0	%	JAMAI	ELSA	----
	1980	D8	P79	33.0	%	NORWY	ZAMBI	----
V22 EXPORT PARTNER CONCENTRATION	1970	D10	P91	54.6	%	BULGA	BURU	----
	1975	D9	P88	51.9	%	SIERA	YENO	----
	1980	D9	P90	53.1	%	BULGA	CENTR	----
V23 TOTAL DEBT AS % OF GDP	1980	D9	P84	59.1	%	PERU	GUINE	----
V24 SHARE OF NEW FOREIGN PATENTS	1970	D5	P43	89	%	AULIA	ISRA	----
	1976	D5	P50	90	%	HAITI	ISRA	----
	1980	D8	P80	97	%	EGYPT	ZAIRE	----
V25 FOREIGN PROPERTY AS % OF GDP	1971	D9	P88	25.8	%	CENTR	ZAIRE	----
	1975	D9	P88	20.5	%	KENYA	CONGO	----
	1978	D9	----	14.2	%	GUINE	SENE	----
V26 GNP SHARE OF DEVELOPMENT AID	------	----	----	-----	-----	-------	-------	----
V27 SHARE IN NOBEL PRIZE WINNERS	1970-79	D5	P45	0.0	%	HAITI	HUNGA	----
V28 GDP SHARE OF MANUFACTURING	1970	D5	P47	13.8	%	MALAY	ALGER	F16
	1975	D6	P53	15.6	%	TRITO	INDIA	F16
	1980	D6	P58	15.8	%	RWAN	VENE	F16
V29 EXPORT SHARE OF MANUFACTURES	1970	D5	P42	8.1	%	COLO	CAME	----
	1975	D5	P51	10.5	%	CAME	PARA	----
	1980	D5	P46	12.3	%	EGYPT	SENE	----
V30 LACK OF CIVIL LIBERTIES	1975	D3	P27	3		GUATE	INDIA	----
	1980	D3	P29	3		ELSA	JAMAI	----
V31 LACK OF POLITICAL RIGHTS	1975	D7	P63	6		HAITI	HUNGA	----
	1980	D7	P67	6		HAITI	HUNGA	----
V32 RIOTS	1970-74	D2	P19	0		HAITI	IRAN	----
	1975-79	D5	P45	1		CHILE	KAMPU	----
V33 PROTEST DEMONSTRATIONS	1970-74	D2	P15	0		GUINE	IRAN	----
	1975-79	D6	P59	5		ELSA	LIBYA	----
V34 POLITICAL STRIKES	1970-74	D3	P29	0		HAITI	HUNGA	----
	1975-79	D3	P29	0		HAITI	HUNGA	----
V35 MEMBER OF THE NONALIGNED MMT.	1970	----	----	0		HAITI	HUNGA	----
	1976	----	----	0		HAITI	HUNGA	----
	1981	----	----	0		HAITI	HUNGA	----
V36 MEMBER OF THE OPEC	1970	----	----	0		HAITI	HUNGA	----
	1975	----	----	0		HAITI	HUNGA	----
	1980	----	----	0		HAITI	HUNGA	----

V37	MEMBER OF THE OECD	1970	----	----	0		HAITI	HUNGA	----
		1975	----	----	0		HAITI	HUNGA	----
		1980	----	----	0		HAITI	HUNGA	----
V38	MEMBER OF THE CMEA	1970	----	----	0		HAITI	INDIA	----
		1975	----	----	0		HAITI	INDIA	----
		1980	----	----	0		HAITI	INDIA	----
V39	MEMBER OF THE WTO	1970	----	----	0		HAITI	INDIA	----
		1975	----	----	0		HAITI	INDIA	----
		1980	----	----	0		HAITI	INDIA	----
V40	MEMBER OF THE NATO	1970	----	----	0		HAITI	HUNGA	----
		1975	----	----	0		HAITI	HUNGA	----
		1980	----	----	0		HAITI	HUNGA	----
V41	GDP SHARE OF INVESTMENTS	1970	D6	P54	20.9	%	MALAY	CANA	----
		1975	D3	P30	17.9	%	GUINE	CHAD	----
		1980	D7	P63	26.2	%	MEXI	TURKY	----
V42	GDP SHARE OF AGRICULTURE	1970	D8	P74	32.4	%	PARA	KENYA	F16
		1975	D7	P64	29.5	%	COLO	PAPUA	F16
		1980	D7	P66	28.5	%	ELSA	ZAIRE	F16
V43	GDP SHARE OF INDUSTRY	1970	D4	P35	22.2	%	INDIA	ELSA	F16
		1975	D4	P38	25.3	%	TURKY	SRILA	F16
		1980	D4	P34	26.2	%	PARA	TOGO	F16
V44	GDP SHARE OF SERVICES	1970	D5	P41	45.4	%	TOGO	THAI	F16
		1975	D5	P48	45.2	%	YENO	ZAMBI	F16
		1980	D5	P44	45.3	%	PARA	KENYA	F16
V45	HOMICIDES P. MIL. POPULATION	------	----	----	----- -----		-------	-------	----
V46	SUICIDES P. MIL. POPULATION	------	----	----	----- -----		-------	-------	----
V47	IMPORT PARTNERS	1970	R1	USA	41.5	%	HAITI	INDIA	----
		1970	R2	GUATE	12.9	%	ELSA	NICA	----
		1970	R3	JAPAN	8.1	%	GUATE	IRAN	----
		1980	R1	USA	42.2	%	HAITI	JAMAI	----
		1980	R2	VENE	10.4	%	GUATE	JAMAI	----
		1980	R3	JAPAN	9.9	%	GUATE	KENYA	----
V48	EXPORT PARTNERS	1970	R1	USA	54.6	%	HAITI	ISRA	----
		1970	R2	GFR	10.8	%	GDR	LIBE	----
		1970	R3	ITALY	5.4	%	ETHIA	MAURA	----
		1980	R1	USA	53.1	%	HAITI	JAMAI	----
		1980	R2	GFR	12.6	%	COLO	HUNGA	----
		1980	R3	GUATE	4.7	%	ELSA	-------	----
V49	PATENT SUPPLIERS	1970	R1	USA	35		GUATE	INDIA	----
		1970	R2	SWITZ	4		GUATE	KAMPU	----
		1970	R3	-------	3		-------	-------	----
		1980	R1	USA	37		HAITI	INDIA	----
		1980	R2	GFR	9		FRANC	INDIA	----
		1980	R3	ITALY	6		BANGL	YUGO	----

V50	PROVENANCE OF FOREIGN FIRMS	1980	R1	USA	78.6	%	HAITI	INDIA	----
		1980	R2	-------	6.6	%	-------	-------	----
		1980	R3	-------	6.6	%	-------	-------	----
V51	FILM SUPPLIERS	------	----	----	-----	-----	-------	-------	----

HUNGARY (HUNGA)

V1	INCOME PER CAPITA	1970	D6	P55	1257	$/CAP	COSTA	BRAZI	----
		1975	D7	P62	1672	$/CAP	ALGER	MEXI	----
		1980	D6	P59	1969	$/CAP	PANA	MEXI	----
V2	TELEPHONES P. TSD. POPULATION	1970	D8	P77	80	1/TSD CAP	URU	PORTU	----
		1975	D8	P72	99	1/TSD CAP	URU	KAMPU	----
		1980	D7	P68	118	1/TSD CAP	SOUAF	PORTU	----
V3	INFANT MORTALITY RATE	1980	D3	P25	23.2	1/TSD	POLA	PORTU	----
V4	PHYSICIANS P. MIL. POPULATION	1970	D10	P97	1970	1/MIL	ARGE	CZECH	----
		1975	D10	P94	2006	1/MIL	GFR	GREC	----
		1981	D10	P98	2561	1/MIL	BELGI	CZECH	----
V5	ADULT LITERACY	1970	D10	P95	98.0	%	POLA	USA	----
		1980	D10	P95	98.9	%	POLA	USA	----
V6	DURATION OF SCHOOLING	1970	D8	P78	10.1	YR	GFR	IRE	----
		1975	D8	P76	10.3	YR	ARGE	GFR	----
		1980	D8	P77	10.7	YR	YUGO	IRAQ	----
V7	STUDENT ENROLLMENT RATIO	1970	D8	P72	10.1	%	URU	ROMA	----
		1975	D7	P66	11.7	%	BOLI	CZECH	----
		1980	D7	P61	12.8	%	KUWAI	THAI	----
V8	SHARE OF AGRICULTURAL LABOR	1970	D4	P34	18.1	%	ITALY	JAPAN	F76
		1980	D3	P30	10.0	%	AURIA	ITALY	----
V9	SHARE OF INDUSTRIAL LABOR	1970	D10	P98	50.3	%	BELGI	-------	F76
		1980	D10	P96	50.6	%	TRITO	JORDA	----
V10	SHARE OF SERVICE LABOR	1970	D3	P31	20.7	%	DOMI	PARA	F76
		1980	D4	P29	24.7	%	YUGO	EGYPT	----
V11	SHARE OF ACADEMIC LABOR	1970	D8	P76	10.9	%	LEBA	BELGI	F76
		1980	D8	P78	14.7	%	AULIA	NEWZ	----
V12	SHARE OF SELF-EMPLOYED LABOR	1970	D1	P8	2.8	%	CUBA	USA	F78
		1980	D1	P6	2.2	%	CHILE	USA	----
V13	MILITARY EXPENDITURES	1970	D6	P53	0.369	TSD MIL $	JORDA	FINLA	----
		1975	D5	P50	0.431	TSD MIL $	SINGA	COLO	----
		1980	D5	P50	0.517	TSD MIL $	ZIMBA	COLO	----

V14 MILITARY MANPOWER	1970	D8	P72	146	TSD CAP	CUBA	BURMA	----
	1975	D7	P68	118	TSD CAP	NETH	CUBA	----
	1980	D8	P71	119	TSD CAP	MOROC	MEXI	----
V15 MEN AT AGE 20 - 30	1970	D6	P55	768	TSD CAP	VENE	KENYA	----
	1975	D6	P62	874	TSD CAP	CHILE	IRAQ	----
	1980	D5	P48	859	TSD CAP	PORTU	CHILE	----
V16 POPULATION	1970	D6	P60	10.34	MIL CAP	VENE	MALAY	----
	1975	D6	P59	10.53	MIL CAP	CHILE	IRAQ	----
	1980	D6	P56	10.71	MIL CAP	PORTU	CHILE	----
V17 GROSS DOMESTIC PRODUCT	1970	D6	P55	12.995	TSD MIL $	IRE	PERU	----
	1975	D6	P55	17.605	TSD MIL $	PERU	PAKI	----
	1980	D6	P54	21.092	TSD MIL $	PERU	MALAY	----
V18 SHARE IN WORLD IMPORTS	1970	D8	P78	7.549	1/TSD	SINGA	FINLA	F30
	1975	D8	P75	7.895	1/TSD	MEXI	KORSO	F30
	1980	D7	P63	4.502	1/TSD	THAI	PORTU	F30
V19 SHARE IN WORLD EXPORTS	1970	D8	P77	7.387	1/TSD	FINLA	SAUDI	F30
	1975	D8	P74	6.951	1/TSD	FINLA	LIBYA	F30
	1980	D7	P66	4.347	1/TSD	IRE	BULGA	F30
V20 GDP SHARE OF IMPORTS	1970	D10	P98	45.2	%	LIBE	SINGA	F30
	1975	D10	P99	65.4	%	TRITO	SINGA	F30
	1980	D9	P89	41.7	%	MAURA	JAMAI	F30
V21 GDP SHARE OF EXPORTS	1970	D10	P91	41.8	%	ZAIRE	MALAY	F30
	1975	D10	P94	55.5	%	LIBYA	IRAQ	F30
	1980	D9	P85	39.2	%	ALGER	PAPUA	F30
V22 EXPORT PARTNER CONCENTRATION	1970	D7	P65	34.9	%	MADA	POLA	----
	1975	D8	P76	38.8	%	AFGHA	TOGO	----
	1980	D7	P62	29.3	%	GUATE	ELSA	----
V23 TOTAL DEBT AS % OF GDP	1980	D7	P63	43.9	%	CHILE	KORSO	----
V24 SHARE OF NEW FOREIGN PATENTS	1970	D2	P18	62	%	IRAQ	FRANC	----
	1975	D2	P17	66	%	FRANC	SOUAF	----
	1980	D2	P16	57	%	GFR	COSTA	----
V25 FOREIGN PROPERTY AS % OF GDP	------	----	----	-----	-----	-------	-------	----
V26 GNP SHARE OF DEVELOPMENT AID	------	----	----	-----	-----	-------	-------	----
V27 SHARE IN NOBEL PRIZE WINNERS	1970-79	D5	P45	0.0	%	HONDU	INDIA	----
V28 GDP SHARE OF MANUFACTURING	------	----	----	-----	-----	-------	-------	----
V29 EXPORT SHARE OF MANUFACTURES	------	----	----	-----	-----	-------	-------	----
V30 LACK OF CIVIL LIBERTIES	1975	D8	P74	6		HAITI	IRAN	----
	1980	D6	P52	5		HAITI	INDO	----
V31 LACK OF POLITICAL RIGHTS	1975	D7	P63	6		HONDU	IVORY	----
	1980	D7	P67	6		HONDU	IVORY	----
V32 RIOTS	1970-74	D5	P43	1		GHANA	KENYA	----
	1975-79	D2	P20	0		HAITI	INDO	----

V33	PROTEST DEMONSTRATIONS	1970-74	D4	P37	1		HAITI	JORDA	----
		1975-79	D2	P13	0		GUINE	IVORY	----
V34	POLITICAL STRIKES	1970-74	D3	P29	0		HONDU	INDO	----
		1975-79	D3	P29	0		HONDU	INDO	----
V35	MEMBER OF THE NONALIGNED MMT.	1970	----	----	0		HONDU	IRAN	----
		1976	----	----	0		HONDU	IRAN	----
		1981	----	----	0		HONDU	IRE	----
V36	MEMBER OF THE OPEC	1970	----	----	0		HONDU	INDIA	----
		1975	----	----	0		HONDU	INDIA	----
		1980	----	----	0		HONDU	INDIA	----
V37	MEMBER OF THE OECD	1970	----	----	0		HONDU	INDIA	----
		1975	----	----	0		HONDU	INDIA	----
		1980	----	----	0		HONDU	INDIA	----
V38	MEMBER OF THE CMEA	1970	----	----	1		GDR	MONGO	----
		1975	----	----	1		GDR	MONGO	----
		1980	----	----	1		GDR	MONGO	----
V39	MEMBER OF THE WTO	1970	----	----	1		GDR	POLA	----
		1975	----	----	1		GDR	POLA	----
		1980	----	----	1		GDR	POLA	----
V40	MEMBER OF THE NATO	1970	----	----	0		HONDU	INDIA	----
		1975	----	----	0		HONDU	INDIA	----
		1980	----	----	0		HONDU	INDIA	----
V41	GDP SHARE OF INVESTMENTS	1970	D10	P96	33.6 %		TRITO	ALGER	----
		1975	D10	P97	37.8 %		SINGA	ZAMBI	----
		1980	D9	P87	30.7 %		KORSO	LESO	----
V42	GDP SHARE OF AGRICULTURE	------	----	----	----- -----		-------	-------	----
V43	GDP SHARE OF INDUSTRY	------	----	----	----- -----		-------	-------	----
V44	GDP SHARE OF SERVICES	------	----	----	----- -----		-------	-------	----
V45	HOMICIDES P. MIL. POPULATION	1970	D6	P57	19.5 1/MIL CAP		PERU	FINLA	F148
		1975	D7	P61	20.1 1/MIL CAP		PORTU	BULGA	F148
		1980	D8	P73	25.8 1/MIL CAP		BULGA	FINLA	----
V46	SUICIDES P. MIL. POPULATION	1970	D10	P98	347.7 1/MIL CAP		GDR	-------	----
		1975	D10	P98	384.8 1/MIL CAP		GDR	-------	----
		1980	D10	P97	449.0 1/MIL CAP		DENMA	-------	----
V47	IMPORT PARTNERS	1970	R1	USSR	33.1 %		GDR	POLA	----
		1970	R2	GDR	10.4 %		CZECH	POLA	----
		1970	R3	CZECH	7.9 %		GDR	POLA	----
		1980	R1	USSR	27.8 %		FINLA	POLA	----
		1980	R2	GFR	11.7 %		FINLA	IRAQ	----
		1980	R3	GDR	6.9 %		CUBA	POLA	----

V48 EXPORT PARTNERS	1970	R1	USSR	34.9 %	GDR	POLA	----
	1970	R2	GDR	9.4 %	EGYPT	POLA	----
	1970	R3	CZECH	8.0 %	GDR	KAMPU	----
	1980	R1	USSR	29.3 %	FINLA	INDIA	----
	1980	R2	GFR	9.8 %	HONDU	IRE	----
	1980	R3	GDR	6.8 %	CZECH	POLA	----
V49 PATENT SUPPLIERS	1970	R1	GFR	189	GDR	PAKI	----
	1970	R2	GDR	124	GHANA	ROMA	----
	1970	R3	SWITZ	121	GREC	IRAN	----
	1980	R1	GFR	260	GREC	IRAN	----
	1980	R2	USA	170	GREC	IRAN	----
	1980	R3	GDR	105	CZECH	ROMA	----
V50 PROVENANCE OF FOREIGN FIRMS	------	---- ----	----- -----	-------	-------	----
V51 FILM SUPPLIERS	1980	R1	USSR	37	GDR	IRAN	F118
	1980	R2	USA	29	HAITI	IRAN	F118
	1980	R3	ITALY	17	HAITI	IRAN	F118

INDIA (INDIA)

V1 INCOME PER CAPITA	1970	D1	P10	206 $/CAP	SRILA	YENO	F214
	1975	D1	P10	214 $/CAP	BURU	SRILA	F214
	1980	D2	P11	229 $/CAP	ZAIRE	SRILA	F214
V2 TELEPHONES P. TSD. POPULATION	1970	D2	P16	2 1/TSD CAP	GUINE	INDO	----
	1975	D2	P17	3 1/TSD CAP	BENIN	LESO	----
	1979	D2	P14	4 1/TSD CAP	CHINA	MADA	----
V3 INFANT MORTALITY RATE	1980	D8	P76	129.1 1/TSD	CAME	TURKY	F5
V4 PHYSICIANS P. MIL. POPULATION	1975	D4	P41	243 1/MIL	TUNIS	ELSA	F178
	1978	D5	----	279 1/MIL	TUNIS	ELSA	F168
V5 ADULT LITERACY	1971	D3	P22	34.1 %	GHANA	SYRIA	----
V6 DURATION OF SCHOOLING	1970	D4	P32	5.5 YR	TOGO	BURMA	----
	1975	D3	P31	5.6 YR	BURMA	HONDU	----
	1980	D3	P26	6.1 YR	SAUDI	YESO	----
V7 STUDENT ENROLLMENT RATIO	1970	D6	P57	6.2 %	TURKY	ALBA	----
	1975	D6	P55	8.8 %	MONGO	IRAQ	----
	1979	D6	P54	8.7 %	MONGO	IRAQ	----
V8 SHARE OF AGRICULTURAL LABOR	1971	D10	P93	72.4 %	TURKY	HAITI	----
	1981	D9	P94	69.3 %	ZIMBA	HAITI	F108
V9 SHARE OF INDUSTRIAL LABOR	1971	D1	P11	13.5 %	INDO	TURKY	----
	1981	D2	P9	15.4 %	PHILI	ZIMBA	F108

V10	SHARE OF SERVICE LABOR	1971	D1	P8	11.4	%	TURKY	SYRIA	----
		1981	D1	P7	12.1	%	AFGHA	TURKY	F108
V11	SHARE OF ACADEMIC LABOR	1971	D1	P11	2.8	%	INDO	KORSO	----
		1981	D2	P17	3.2	%	INDO	ELSA	F108
V12	SHARE OF SELF-EMPLOYED LABOR	------	----	----	-----	-----	-------	-------	----
V13	MILITARY EXPENDITURES	1970	D9	P81	3.243	TSD MIL $	NIGRA	SWEDN	----
		1975	D9	P90	4.137	TSD MIL $	CANA	NETH	----
		1980	D9	P89	4.453	TSD MIL $	AULIA	CANA	----
V14	MILITARY MANPOWER	1970	D10	P98	1550	TSD CAP	VISO	USA	----
		1975	D10	P97	1670	TSD CAP	VISO	USA	----
		1980	D10	P98	1104	TSD CAP	VINO	USA	----
V15	MEN AT AGE 20 - 30	1971	D10	P99	41890	TSD CAP	USSR	-------	F198
		1974	D10	P99	49662	TSD CAP	USA	-------	F199
		1980	D10	P99	57404	TSD CAP	USA	CHINA	F188
V16	POPULATION	1970	D10	P99	539.08	MIL CAP	USSR	CHINA	F168
		1975	D10	P99	600.76	MIL CAP	USSR	CHINA	F168
		1980	D10	P99	663.60	MIL CAP	USSR	CHINA	F168
V17	GROSS DOMESTIC PRODUCT	1970	D9	P87	111.058	TSD MIL $	AULIA	NETH	----
		1975	D9	P88	128.475	TSD MIL $	AULIA	NETH	----
		1980	D9	P88	151.983	TSD MIL $	MEXI	NETH	----
V18	SHARE IN WORLD IMPORTS	1970	D8	P75	6.398	1/TSD	KORSO	MEXI	F30
		1975	D8	P74	7.024	1/TSD	NIGRA	MEXI	F30
		1980	D8	P74	6.870	1/TSD	ROMA	CZECH	F30
V19	SHARE IN WORLD EXPORTS	1970	D8	P74	6.459	1/TSD	BULGA	SOUAF	F30
		1975	D7	P67	4.970	1/TSD	YUGO	BULGA	F30
		1980	D7	P64	4.197	1/TSD	ARGE	IRE	F30
V20	GDP SHARE OF IMPORTS	1970	D1	P2	4.0	%	-------	USA	F30
		1975	D1	P6	7.5	%	BURMA	MEXI	F30
		1980	D1	P7	8.7	%	BRAZI	USA	F30
V21	GDP SHARE OF EXPORTS	1970	D1	P4	3.8	%	MEXI	USA	F30
		1975	D1	P6	5.1	%	BURMA	BENIN	F30
		1980	D1	P7	5.2	%	ARGE	BANGL	F30
V22	EXPORT PARTNER CONCENTRATION	1970	D1	P7	14.0	%	KAMPU	SPAIN	----
		1975	D1	P6	11.7	%	GFR	SRILA	----
		1980	D2	P18	16.8	%	SPAIN	BRAZI	----
V23	TOTAL DEBT AS % OF GDP	1980	D1	P9	11.9	%	TRITO	GUATE	----
V24	SHARE OF NEW FOREIGN PATENTS	1970	D4	P35	83	%	YUGO	LEBA	----
		1975	D4	P32	82	%	ITALY	AURIA	----
		1980	D3	P29	77	%	FINLA	ITALY	----
V25	FOREIGN PROPERTY AS % OF GDP	1971	D2	P16	2.8	%	KORSO	URU	----
		1975	D3	P25	2.8	%	ALGER	MOZAM	----
		1978	D3	----	2.1	%	UPVO	NIGRA	----
V26	GNP SHARE OF DEVELOPMENT AID	------	----	----	-----	-----	-------	-------	----
V27	SHARE IN NOBEL PRIZE WINNERS	1970-79	D5	P45	0.0	%	HUNGA	INDO	----

V28	GDP SHARE OF MANUFACTURING	1970	D5	P50	14.2	%	ALGER	BOLI	F16
		1975	D6	P53	15.6	%	HONDU	PARA	F16
		1980	D7	P66	17.2	%	MOROC	SRILA	F16
V29	EXPORT SHARE OF MANUFACTURES	------	----	----	----- -----		-------	-------	----
V30	LACK OF CIVIL LIBERTIES	1975	D3	P27	3		HONDU	ISRA	----
		1980	D2	P18	2		GREC	ISRA	----
V31	LACK OF POLITICAL RIGHTS	1975	D2	P20	2		GREC	ISRA	----
		1980	D3	P21	2		GREC	ISRA	----
V32	RIOTS	1970-74	D10	P98	67		PAKI	USA	----
		1975-79	D10	P95	50		PAKI	USA	----
V33	PROTEST DEMONSTRATIONS	1970-74	D9	P87	36		GFR	ARGE	----
		1975-79	D10	P94	71		IRAN	USSR	----
V34	POLITICAL STRIKES	1970-74	D9	P89	10		GREC	KORSO	----
		1975-79	D9	P83	6		ECUA	TURKY	----
V35	MEMBER OF THE NONALIGNED MMT.	1970	----	----	1		GUINE	INDO	----
		1976	----	----	1		GUINE	INDO	----
		1981	----	----	1		GUINE	INDO	----
V36	MEMBER OF THE OPEC	1970	----	----	0		HUNGA	IRE	----
		1975	----	----	0		HUNGA	IRE	----
		1980	----	----	0		HUNGA	IRE	----
V37	MEMBER OF THE OECD	1970	----	----	0		HUNGA	INDO	----
		1975	----	----	0		HUNGA	INDO	----
		1980	----	----	0		HUNGA	INDO	----
V38	MEMBER OF THE CMEA	1970	----	----	0		HONDU	INDO	----
		1975	----	----	0		HONDU	INDO	----
		1980	----	----	0		HONDU	INDO	----
V39	MEMBER OF THE WTO	1970	----	----	0		HONDU	INDO	----
		1975	----	----	0		HONDU	INDO	----
		1980	----	----	0		HONDU	INDO	----
V40	MEMBER OF THE NATO	1970	----	----	0		HUNGA	INDO	----
		1975	----	----	0		HUNGA	INDO	----
		1980	----	----	0		HUNGA	INDO	----
V41	GDP SHARE OF INVESTMENTS	1970	D4	P38	17.3	%	BOLI	USA	----
		1975	D5	P41	20.8	%	NETH	DENMA	----
		1980	D5	P50	23.7	%	ZAMBI	SYRIA	----
V42	GDP SHARE OF AGRICULTURE	1970	D9	P89	47.4	%	INDO	CHAD	F16
		1975	D9	P84	42.0	%	TANZA	MOZAM	F16
		1980	D9	P83	37.3	%	GUINE	UPVO	F16
V43	GDP SHARE OF INDUSTRY	1970	D4	P33	21.7	%	PANA	HONDU	F16
		1975	D3	P29	23.2	%	SENE	PAKI	F16
		1980	D4	P31	25.2	%	SENE	PAKI	F16
V44	GDP SHARE OF SERVICES	1970	D2	P11	30.9	%	MALAW	SAUDI	F16
		1975	D2	P19	34.8	%	INDO	ETHIA	F16
		1980	D3	P23	37.5	%	NIGRA	MALAW	F16

V45	HOMICIDES P. MIL. POPULATION	------	----	----	----- -----	-------	-------	----
V46	SUICIDES P. MIL. POPULATION	------	----	----	----- -----	-------	-------	----
V47	IMPORT PARTNERS	1970	R1	USA	29.0 %	HONDU	ISRA	----
		1970	R2	USSR	7.9 %	SYRIA	IRAQ	----
		1970	R3	CANA	7.0 %	UNKI	JAMAI	----
V48	EXPORT PARTNERS	1970	R1	JAPAN	14.0 %	AULIA	INDO	----
		1970	R2	USA	13.5 %	ELSA	IRE	----
		1970	R3	USSR	13.4 %	FINLA	SYRIA	----
		1980	R1	USSR	16.8 %	HUNGA	NEPAL	----
		1980	R2	USA	11.3 %	GABON	INDO	----
		1980	R3	JAPAN	9.7 %	BURMA	MADA	----
V49	PATENT SUPPLIERS	1970	R1	USA	874	HONDU	IRAN	----
		1970	R2	UNKI	549	COSTA	IRE	----
		1970	R3	GFR	376	GUATE	JAMAI	----
		1980	R1	USA	391	HONDU	IRE	----
		1980	R2	GFR	171	HONDU	ISRA	----
		1980	R3	UNKI	110	DENMA	ISRA	----
V50	PROVENANCE OF FOREIGN FIRMS	1980	R1	USA	39.5 %	HONDU	INDO	----
		1980	R2	UNKI	39.1 %	GFR	ISRA	----
		1980	R3	GFR	6.7 %	GHANA	ISRA	----
V51	FILM SUPPLIERS	1980	R1	USA	25	GREC	INDO	F118
		1980	R2	USSR	16	ETHIA	ROMA	F118
		1980	R3	UNKI	10	DENMA	ISRA	F118

INDONESIA (INDO)

V1	INCOME PER CAPITA	1970	D2	P16	270 $/CAP	BENIN	KENYA	----
		1975	D2	P20	350 $/CAP	YENO	NIGER	----
		1980	D3	P25	460 $/CAP	YENO	LIBE	----
V2	TELEPHONES P. TSD. POPULATION	1970	D2	P16	2 1/TSD CAP	INDIA	SOMA	----
		1975	D2	P12	2 1/TSD CAP	GUINE	LAOS	----
		1980	D1	P9	3 1/TSD CAP	NIGER	SUDAN	----
V3	INFANT MORTALITY RATE	1980	D6	P54	98.7 1/TSD	NICA	UGADA	F5
V4	PHYSICIANS P. MIL. POPULATION	1970	D2	P16	37 1/MIL	TOGO	NIGRA	----
		1975	D2	P19	61 1/MIL	TOGO	KENYA	----
		1979	D3	P22	84 1/MIL	ZAIRE	YENO	F2
V5	ADULT LITERACY	1971	D4	P33	56.6 %	TURKY	ELSA	----
		1980	D7	P63	67.3 %	BURMA	KUWAI	----
V6	DURATION OF SCHOOLING	1970	D4	P36	6.1 YR	ALGER	CAME	----
		1975	D4	P33	6.6 YR	HONDU	NICA	----
		1980	D5	P45	8.6 YR	LESO	COSTA	----

V7	STUDENT ENROLLMENT RATIO	1970	D5	P42	2.6	%	HONDU	TUNIS	----
		1975	D4	P36	2.4	%	NEPAL	PAPUA	----
		1981	D4	P39	3.9	%	ELSA	MALAY	----
V8	SHARE OF AGRICULTURAL LABOR	1971	D9	P89	66.4	%	GHANA	TURKY	----
		1976	D9	P86	66.9	%	TURKY	SUDAN	----
		1980	D9	P86	55.9	%	PAKI	GUATE	----
V9	SHARE OF INDUSTRIAL LABOR	1971	D1	P8	12.3	%	HAITI	INDIA	----
		1976	D2	P14	12.1	%	CAME	YENO	----
		1980	D2	P11	19.2	%	ZIMBA	PERU	----
V10	SHARE OF SERVICE LABOR	1971	D3	P23	19.1	%	SRILA	IRAN	----
		1976	D4	P38	19.1	%	GUATE	PHILI	----
		1980	D3	P21	21.9	%	MOROC	TUNIS	----
V11	SHARE OF ACADEMIC LABOR	1971	D1	P8	2.3	%	HAITI	INDIA	----
		1976	D1	P8	1.9	%	BANGL	CAME	----
		1980	D2	P15	3.1	%	PAKI	INDIA	----
V12	SHARE OF SELF-EMPLOYED LABOR	1971	D9	P90	40.5	%	DOMI	SYRIA	----
		1976	D8	P74	42.5	%	PHILI	THAI	----
		1980	D10	P98	53.3	%	PAKI	CAME	----
V13	MILITARY EXPENDITURES	1975	D8	P79	2.259	TSD MIL $	SOUAF	BRAZI	----
		1980	D8	P76	2.084	TSD MIL $	SWITZ	SYRIA	----
V14	MILITARY MANPOWER	1970	D9	P86	358	TSD CAP	POLA	SPAIN	----
		1975	D9	P81	260	TSD CAP	JAPAN	NIGRA	----
		1980	D9	P84	250	TSD CAP	ETHIA	SYRIA	----
V15	MEN AT AGE 20 - 30	1971	D10	P94	7580	TSD CAP	BRAZI	JAPAN	F36
		1980	D10	P96	11591	TSD CAP	BRAZI	USA	----
V16	POPULATION	1970	D10	P96	119.47	MIL CAP	JAPAN	USA	----
		1975	D10	P96	135.67	MIL CAP	JAPAN	USA	----
		1980	D10	P96	150.96	MIL CAP	BRAZI	USA	----
V17	GROSS DOMESTIC PRODUCT	1970	D7	P68	32.232	TSD MIL $	KORSO	FINLA	----
		1975	D8	P72	47.463	TSD MIL $	KORSO	VENE	----
		1980	D8	P76	69.472	TSD MIL $	DENMA	AURIA	----
V18	SHARE IN WORLD IMPORTS	1970	D6	P58	3.018	1/TSD	CHILE	NIGRA	F37
		1975	D7	P68	5.248	1/TSD	TURKY	GREC	----
		1980	D8	P71	5.282	1/TSD	MALAY	IRE	----
V19	SHARE IN WORLD EXPORTS	1970	D7	P63	3.532	1/TSD	IRAQ	PHILI	F37
		1975	D8	P75	8.106	1/TSD	LIBYA	NORWY	----
		1980	D9	P85	10.977	1/TSD	SPAIN	LIBYA	----
V20	GDP SHARE OF IMPORTS	1970	D2	P16	11.0	%	PARA	EGYPT	F37
		1975	D3	P22	15.7	%	SPAIN	URU	----
		1980	D2	P19	14.9	%	CHAD	BANGL	----
V21	GDP SHARE OF EXPORTS	1970	D4	P36	12.1	%	MALI	YUGO	F37
		1975	D7	P67	23.3	%	CONGO	SWITZ	----
		1980	D8	P77	30.2	%	IVORY	NORWY	----
V22	EXPORT PARTNER CONCENTRATION	1970	D6	P61	33.3	%	NICA	UPVO	----
		1975	D9	P82	43.9	%	EGYPT	BURU	----
		1980	D9	P88	49.3	%	OMAN	BULGA	----

V23	TOTAL DEBT AS % OF GDP	1980	D4	P38	28.8 %	PAPUA	DOMI	----
V24	SHARE OF NEW FOREIGN PATENTS	------	----	----	----- -----	-------	-------	----
V25	FOREIGN PROPERTY AS % OF GDP	1971	D6	P55	9.6 %	MALAW	TUNIS	----
		1975	D8	P72	11.5 %	CAME	ECUA	----
		1978	D8	----	11.2 %	MALAW	CENTR	----
V26	GNP SHARE OF DEVELOPMENT AID	------	----	----	----- -----	-------	-------	----
V27	SHARE IN NOBEL PRIZE WINNERS	1970-79	D5	P45	0.0 %	INDIA	IRAN	----
V28	GDP SHARE OF MANUFACTURING	1970	D3	P25	9.3 %	UGADA	SOMA	----
		1975	D3	P25	8.9 %	CENTR	MALI	----
		1980	D5	P43	11.6 %	ALGER	IVORY	----
V29	EXPORT SHARE OF MANUFACTURES	1970	D2	P13	1.2 %	IRAQ	PERU	----
		1975	D2	P18	1.2 %	GABON	IRAN	----
		1980	D2	P19	2.2 %	NIGER	BOLI	----
V30	LACK OF CIVIL LIBERTIES	1975	D6	P54	5	GHANA	LAOS	----
		1980	D6	P52	5	HUNGA	IVORY	----
V31	LACK OF POLITICAL RIGHTS	1975	D5	P43	5	CONGO	IRAN	----
		1980	D5	P47	5	ELSA	IRAN	----
V32	RIOTS	1970-74	D7	P68	5	DOMI	POLA	----
		1975-79	D2	P20	0	HUNGA	IVORY	----
V33	PROTEST DEMONSTRATIONS	1970-74	D7	P64	5	COLO	NETH	----
		1975-79	D5	P49	3	AFGHA	KENYA	----
V34	POLITICAL STRIKES	1970-74	D3	P29	0	HUNGA	IRAN	----
		1975-79	D3	P29	0	HUNGA	IRAQ	----
V35	MEMBER OF THE NONALIGNED MMT.	1970	----	----	1	INDIA	IRAQ	----
		1976	----	----	1	INDIA	IRAQ	----
		1981	----	----	1	INDIA	IRAN	----
V36	MEMBER OF THE OPEC	1970	----	----	1	ALGER	IRAN	----
		1975	----	----	1	GABON	IRAN	----
		1980	----	----	1	GABON	IRAN	----
V37	MEMBER OF THE OECD	1970	----	----	0	INDIA	IRAN	----
		1975	----	----	0	INDIA	IRAN	----
		1980	----	----	0	INDIA	IRAN	----
V38	MEMBER OF THE CMEA	1970	----	----	0	INDIA	IRAN	----
		1975	----	----	0	INDIA	IRAN	----
		1980	----	----	0	INDIA	IRAN	----
V39	MEMBER OF THE WTO	1970	----	----	0	INDIA	IRAN	----
		1975	----	----	0	INDIA	IRAN	----
		1980	----	----	0	INDIA	IRAN	----
V40	MEMBER OF THE NATO	1970	----	----	0	INDIA	IRAN	----
		1975	----	----	0	INDIA	IRAN	----
		1980	----	----	0	INDIA	IRAN	----

V41 GDP SHARE OF INVESTMENTS	1970	D2	P18	13.6 %	CHAD	SUDAN	----
	1975	D4	P38	20.3 %	PAPUA	ITALY	----
	1980	D4	P33	20.9 %	SPAIN	BELGI	----
V42 GDP SHARE OF AGRICULTURE	1970	D9	P87	47.2 %	GHANA	INDIA	----
	1975	D7	P69	31.7 %	THAI	LESO	----
	1980	D6	P59	24.8 %	TOGO	THAI	----
V43 GDP SHARE OF INDUSTRY	1970	D3	P20	18.0 %	TANZA	GHANA	----
	1975	D7	P64	33.8 %	PHILI	KORSO	----
	1980	D9	P87	43.4 %	YUGO	PORTU	----
V44 GDP SHARE OF SERVICES	1970	D2	P17	34.8 %	ZAMBI	GHANA	----
	1975	D2	P18	34.5 %	IRAN	INDIA	----
	1980	D2	P12	31.8 %	GUINE	NIGER	----
V45 HOMICIDES P. MIL. POPULATION	------	----	----	----- -----	-------	-------	----
V46 SUICIDES P. MIL. POPULATION	------	----	----	----- -----	-------	-------	----
V47 IMPORT PARTNERS	1970	R1	JAPAN	29.5 %	BURMA	KAMPU	----
	1970	R2	USA	17.7 %	GHANA	IRAN	----
	1970	R3	GFR	9.5 %	GHANA	ISRA	----
	1980	R1	JAPAN	31.5 %	BURMA	IRAQ	----
	1980	R2	USA	13.0 %	GABON	IRE	----
	1980	R3	SAUDI	8.9 %	CANA	KORSO	----
V48 EXPORT PARTNERS	1970	R1	JAPAN	33.3 %	INDIA	SAUDI	----
	1970	R2	SINGA	15.8 %	MALAY	-------	----
	1970	R3	USA	14.0 %	GREC	ITALY	----
	1980	R1	JAPAN	49.3 %	CHILE	KUWAI	----
	1980	R2	USA	19.6 %	INDIA	LIBE	----
	1980	R3	SINGA	11.3 %	MALAY	-------	----
V49 PATENT SUPPLIERS	------	----	----	----- -----	-------	-------	----
V50 PROVENANCE OF FOREIGN FIRMS	1980	R1	USA	38.3 %	INDIA	IRAN	----
	1980	R2	JAPAN	20.9 %	KORSO	PHILI	----
	1980	R3	UNKI	12.6 %	GREC	MEXI	----
V51 FILM SUPPLIERS	1980	R1	USA	114	INDIA	IRAQ	F118
	1980	R2	ITALY	29	GREC	LIBYA	F118
	1980	R3	INDIA	26	ETHIA	IRAQ	F118

IRAN (IRAN)

V1 INCOME PER CAPITA	------	----	----	----- -----	-------	-------	----
V2 TELEPHONES P. TSD. POPULATION	1970	D5	P42	11 1/TSD CAP	ELSA	MOROC	----
	1975	D5	P45	20 1/TSD CAP	IRAQ	MONGO	----
	1980	D5	P45	32 1/TSD CAP	TUNIS	SYRIA	----

V3	INFANT MORTALITY RATE	1980	D7	P65	114.8	1/TSD	MOROC	ZAIRE	F5
V4	PHYSICIANS P. MIL. POPULATION	1970	D5	P47	303	1/MIL	HONDU	SAUDI	----
		1974	D5	P48	382	1/MIL	SYRIA	GUATE	----
		1981	D5	P46	384	1/MIL	ALGER	SYRIA	----
V5	ADULT LITERACY	------	----	----	-----	-----	-------	-------	----
V6	DURATION OF SCHOOLING	1970	D4	P38	6.2	YR	CAME	NICA	F4
		1975	D5	P43	7.6	YR	ELSA	ALGER	----
		1981	D4	P35	7.9	YR	CHINA	THAI	F35
V7	STUDENT ENROLLMENT RATIO	1970	D5	P45	3.1	%	LIBYA	TRITO	----
		1975	D5	P48	4.9	%	TRITO	ALBA	----
		1982	D4	----	3.6	%	GABON	ELSA	----
V8	SHARE OF AGRICULTURAL LABOR	1972	D7	----	48.6	%	NICA	SRILA	----
		1976	D6	P51	35.7	%	COLO	TUNIS	----
V9	SHARE OF INDUSTRIAL LABOR	1972	D5	----	28.8	%	SYRIA	GREC	----
		1976	D10	P92	39.6	%	SPAIN	AURIA	----
V10	SHARE OF SERVICE LABOR	1972	D3	----	19.1	%	INDO	GHANA	----
		1976	D3	P32	18.0	%	PAKI	TUNIS	----
V11	SHARE OF ACADEMIC LABOR	1972	D2	----	3.5	%	TURKY	ELSA	----
		1976	D5	P52	6.6	%	MEXI	EGYPT	----
V12	SHARE OF SELF-EMPLOYED LABOR	1972	D10	----	46.1	%	PERU	PARA	----
		1976	D7	P59	34.2	%	ELSA	SYRIA	----
V13	MILITARY EXPENDITURES	------	----	----	-----	-----	-------	-------	----
V14	MILITARY MANPOWER	1970	D9	P82	245	TSD CAP	JAPAN	EGYPT	----
		1975	D9	P86	385	TSD CAP	SPAIN	EGYPT	----
		1980	D9	P87	305	TSD CAP	YUGO	UNKI	----
V15	MEN AT AGE 20 - 30	1971	D8	P76	2311	TSD CAP	ARGE	KORSO	F2
		1976	D8	P78	2351	TSD CAP	BURMA	SPAIN	----
		1981	D8	P75	3244	TSD CAP	SPAIN	POLA	F2
V16	POPULATION	1970	D9	P81	28.66	MIL CAP	BURMA	KORSO	F4
		1975	D9	P81	33.38	MIL CAP	BURMA	POLA	----
		1980	D9	P84	38.35	MIL CAP	KORSO	EGYPT	----
V17	GROSS DOMESTIC PRODUCT	------	----	----	-----	-----	-------	-------	----
V18	SHARE IN WORLD IMPORTS	1970	D7	P68	5.007	1/TSD	PORTU	VENE	----
		1975	D9	P84	11.379	1/TSD	NORWY	DENMA	----
		1980	D8	P73	5.972	1/TSD	IRE	ROMA	----
V19	SHARE IN WORLD EXPORTS	1970	D9	P82	8.362	1/TSD	NORWY	BRAZI	----
		1975	D9	P90	23.067	1/TSD	SWEDN	BELGI	----
		1980	D8	P71	7.067	1/TSD	MALAY	FINLA	----
V20	GDP SHARE OF IMPORTS	1970	D5	P42	16.3	%	CANA	ECUA	----
		1975	D4	P37	20.1	%	GUATE	ITALY	----
		1980	D2	P12	12.7	%	BOLI	TURKY	----

V21	GDP SHARE OF EXPORTS	1970	D9	P85	25.8	%	SWITZ	IRE	----
		1975	D9	P87	39.2	%	ZAIRE	MAURA	----
		1980	D4	P36	14.6	%	EGYPT	MALI	----
V22	EXPORT PARTNER CONCENTRATION	------	----	----	-----	-----	-------	-------	----
V23	TOTAL DEBT AS % OF GDP	------	----	----	-----	-----	-------	-------	----
V24	SHARE OF NEW FOREIGN PATENTS	1970	D6	P55	93	%	COSTA	JAMAI	----
		1975	D8	P79	97	%	PORTU	IRE	----
		1980	D6	P57	91	%	ELSA	PERU	----
V25	FOREIGN PROPERTY AS % OF GDP	1971	D5	P44	7.3	%	CHAD	CHILE	----
		1975	D3	P21	2.3	%	SRILA	PORTU	----
		1978	D2	----	1.3	%	KUWAI	BURMA	----
V26	GNP SHARE OF DEVELOPMENT AID	1970	D1	P11	0.00	%	ALGER	NIGRA	----
		1975	D9	P81	1.22	%	SWEDN	IRAQ	----
		1980	D1	P4	-0.08	%	-------	NIGRA	----
V27	SHARE IN NOBEL PRIZE WINNERS	1970-79	D5	P45	0.0	%	INDO	IRAQ	----
V28	GDP SHARE OF MANUFACTURING	------	----	----	-----	-----	-------	-------	----
V29	EXPORT SHARE OF MANUFACTURES	1970	D4	P31	4.0	%	CHILE	ALGER	----
		1975	D2	P18	1.2	%	INDO	LIBE	----
V30	LACK OF CIVIL LIBERTIES	1975	D8	P74	6		HUNGA	IVORY	----
		1980	D8	P74	6		GABON	JORDA	----
V31	LACK OF POLITICAL RIGHTS	1975	D5	P43	5		INDO	KENYA	----
		1980	D5	P47	5		INDO	KENYA	----
V32	RIOTS	1970-74	D2	P19	0		HONDU	IVORY	----
		1975-79	D10	P98	123		SOUAF	PORTU	----
V33	PROTEST DEMONSTRATIONS	1970-74	D2	P15	0		HONDU	IVORY	----
		1975-79	D10	P93	63		FRANC	INDIA	----
V34	POLITICAL STRIKES	1970-74	D3	P29	0		INDO	JAMAI	----
		1975-79	D10	P91	12		THAI	PAKI	----
V35	MEMBER OF THE NONALIGNED MMT.	1970	----	----	0		HUNGA	IRE	----
		1976	----	----	0		HUNGA	IRE	----
		1981	----	----	1		INDO	IRAQ	----
V36	MEMBER OF THE OPEC	1970	----	----	1		INDO	IRAQ	----
		1975	----	----	1		INDO	IRAQ	----
		1980	----	----	1		INDO	IRAQ	----
V37	MEMBER OF THE OECD	1970	----	----	0		INDO	IRAQ	----
		1975	----	----	0		INDO	IRAQ	----
		1980	----	----	0		INDO	IRAQ	----
V38	MEMBER OF THE CMEA	1970	----	----	0		INDO	IRAQ	----
		1975	----	----	0		INDO	IRAQ	----
		1980	----	----	0		INDO	IRAQ	----
V39	MEMBER OF THE WTO	1970	----	----	0		INDO	IRAQ	----
		1975	----	----	0		INDO	IRAQ	----
		1980	----	----	0		INDO	IRAQ	----

V40	MEMBER OF THE NATO	1970	----	----	0		INDO	IRAQ	----
		1975	----	----	0		INDO	IRAQ	----
		1980	----	----	0		INDO	IRAQ	----
V41	GDP SHARE OF INVESTMENTS	1970	D5	P45	18.9	%	CENTR	JORDA	----
		1975	D8	P80	29.7	%	ISRA	IRAQ	----
V42	GDP SHARE OF AGRICULTURE	1970	D5	P47	19.4	%	TUNIS	MOROC	F16
		1975	D3	P30	9.6	%	JORDA	FINLA	F16
V43	GDP SHARE OF INDUSTRY	1970	D9	P90	42.5	%	BELGI	JAMAI	F16
		1975	D10	P94	57.4	%	TRITO	GABON	F16
V44	GDP SHARE OF SERVICES	1970	D3	P21	38.1	%	IRAQ	UPVO	F16
		1975	D2	P17	33.0	%	GABON	INDO	F16
V45	HOMICIDES P. MIL. POPULATION	------	----	----	-----	-----	-------	-------	----
V46	SUICIDES P. MIL. POPULATION	------	----	----	-----	-----	-------	-------	----
V47	IMPORT PARTNERS	1970	R1	GFR	20.7	%	GREC	ITALY	----
		1970	R2	USA	13.0	%	INDO	JORDA	----
		1970	R3	JAPAN	12.0	%	HONDU	PERU	----
V48	EXPORT PARTNERS	------	----	----	-----	-----	-------	-------	----
V49	PATENT SUPPLIERS	1970	R1	USA	182		INDIA	IRE	----
		1970	R2	GFR	135		GREC	ISRA	----
		1970	R3	SWITZ	74		HUNGA	IRE	----
		1980	R1	GFR	102		HUNGA	POLA	----
		1980	R2	USA	81		HUNGA	KORSO	----
		1980	R3	FRANC	38		GREC	ITALY	----
V50	PROVENANCE OF FOREIGN FIRMS	1980	R1	USA	26.9	%	INDO	ISRA	----
V51	FILM SUPPLIERS	1982	R1	USSR	18		HUNGA	LAOS	F117
		1982	R2	USA	12		HUNGA	MOROC	F117
		1982	R3	ITALY	6		HUNGA	IRE	F117

IRAQ (IRAQ)

V1	INCOME PER CAPITA	------	----	----	-----	-----	-------	-------	----
V2	TELEPHONES P. TSD. POPULATION	1970	D5	P45	12	1/TSD CAP	EGYPT	ALGER	----
		1975	D5	P44	17	1/TSD CAP	JORDA	IRAN	----
V3	INFANT MORTALITY RATE	1980	D5	P50	84.0	1/TSD	ZIMBA	KENYA	F5
V4	PHYSICIANS P. MIL. POPULATION	1970	D5	P49	306	1/MIL	SAUDI	ECUA	----
		1975	D5	P50	405	1/MIL	GUATE	EGYPT	----
		1980	D6	P51	554	1/MIL	CHINA	PARA	----
V5	ADULT LITERACY	------	----	----	-----	-----	-------	-------	----

V6	DURATION OF SCHOOLING	1970	D4	P34	5.9	YR	BURMA	ALGER	----
		1975	D5	P50	8.0	YR	BRAZI	ZAMBI	----
		1980	D8	P77	10.7	YR	HUNGA	ISRA	----
V7	STUDENT ENROLLMENT RATIO	1970	D6	P53	5.2	%	BRAZI	JAMAI	----
		1975	D6	P57	9.0	%	INDIA	KUWAI	----
		1980	D6	P55	9.4	%	INDIA	COLO	----
V8	SHARE OF AGRICULTURAL LABOR	------	----	----	-----	-----	-------	-------	----
V9	SHARE OF INDUSTRIAL LABOR	------	----	----	-----	-----	-------	-------	----
V10	SHARE OF SERVICE LABOR	------	----	----	-----	-----	-------	-------	----
V11	SHARE OF ACADEMIC LABOR	------	----	----	-----	-----	-------	-------	----
V12	SHARE OF SELF-EMPLOYED LABOR	------	----	----	-----	-----	-------	-------	----
V13	MILITARY EXPENDITURES	------	----	----	-----	-----	-------	-------	----
V14	MILITARY MANPOWER	1970	D7	P67	95	TSD CAP	CANA	ISRA	----
		1975	D8	P71	155	TSD CAP	AFGHA	ARGE	----
		1980	D9	P89	350	TSD CAP	SPAIN	ITALY	----
V15	MEN AT AGE 20 - 30	1977	D6	----	1025	TSD CAP	HUNGA	VENE	----
V16	POPULATION	1970	D6	P56	9.44	MIL CAP	CHILE	BELGI	----
		1975	D6	P60	11.12	MIL CAP	HUNGA	UGADA	----
		1980	D7	P60	13.21	MIL CAP	UGADA	MALAY	F35
V17	GROSS DOMESTIC PRODUCT	------	----	----	-----	-----	-------	-------	----
V18	SHARE IN WORLD IMPORTS	1970	D5	P47	1.533	1/TSD	ZAMBI	JAMAI	----
		1975	D7	P66	4.637	1/TSD	SAUDI	TURKY	----
		1978	D6	----	3.122	1/TSD	CUBA	KUWAI	----
V19	SHARE IN WORLD EXPORTS	1970	D7	P62	3.507	1/TSD	PERU	INDO	----
		1975	D9	P81	9.469	1/TSD	NIGRA	CZECH	----
		1980	D9	P88	13.166	1/TSD	AULIA	NIGRA	----
V20	GDP SHARE OF IMPORTS	1970	D4	P31	14.2	%	AULIA	SOMA	----
		1975	D8	P74	30.9	%	SENE	TUNIS	----
		1978	D4	----	18.2	%	VENE	SOMA	----
V21	GDP SHARE OF EXPORTS	1970	D9	P87	30.6	%	IRE	IVORY	----
		1975	D10	P95	60.8	%	HUNGA	LIBE	----
		1979	D10	P93	62.7	%	LIBYA	UNARE	----
V22	EXPORT PARTNER CONCENTRATION	1970	D6	P52	28.6	%	NIGRA	ROMA	----
		1975	D3	P23	17.5	%	SINGA	ROMA	----
V23	TOTAL DEBT AS % OF GDP	------	----	----	-----	-----	-------	-------	----
V24	SHARE OF NEW FOREIGN PATENTS	1970	D2	P17	56	%	GREC	HUNGA	----
		1975	D8	P72	95	%	EGYPT	LIBYA	----
		1980	D2	P20	63	%	NEPAL	ARGE	----
V25	FOREIGN PROPERTY AS % OF GDP	1971	D3	P26	4.5	%	ALGER	RWAN	----
		1975	D1	P8	0.9	%	NEPAL	AFGHA	----
		1978	D1	----	0.6	%	AFGHA	NEPAL	----

V26	GNP SHARE OF DEVELOPMENT AID	1970	D3	P29	0.13	%	AURIA	SWITZ	----
		1975	D9	P85	1.95	%	IRAN	LIBYA	----
		1980	D9	P86	2.35	%	LIBYA	UNARE	----
V27	SHARE IN NOBEL PRIZE WINNERS	1970-79	D5	P45	0.0	%	IRAN	IRE	----
V28	GDP SHARE OF MANUFACTURING	1970	D3	P30	9.7	%	SAUDI	TOGO	F16
		1975	D2	P15	6.0	%	SIERA	UGADA	F16
		1979	D2	P19	5.6	%	YENO	MALI	F16
V29	EXPORT SHARE OF MANUFACTURES	1970	D2	P12	1.0	%	MAURA	INDO	----
		1975	D1	P7	0.2	%	UGADA	NIGRA	----
		1978	D1	----	0.5	%	CUBA	SOMA	----
V30	LACK OF CIVIL LIBERTIES	1975	D10	P93	7		GUINE	KORNO	----
		1980	D10	P92	7		GUINE	KAMPU	----
V31	LACK OF POLITICAL RIGHTS	1975	D9	P88	7		GUINE	KORNO	----
		1980	D9	P90	7		GUINE	KAMPU	----
V32	RIOTS	1970-74	D6	P53	2		CZECH	NETH	----
		1975-79	D6	P53	2		DOMI	LIBE	----
V33	PROTEST DEMONSTRATIONS	1970-74	D5	P49	2		GDR	MADA	----
		1975-79	D4	P32	1		CUBA	KAMPU	----
V34	POLITICAL STRIKES	1970-74	D7	P64	1		GUATE	IRE	----
		1975-79	D3	P29	0		INDO	IVORY	----
V35	MEMBER OF THE NONALIGNED MMT.	1970	----	----	1		INDO	JAMAI	----
		1976	----	----	1		INDO	IVORY	----
		1981	----	----	1		IRAN	IVORY	----
V36	MEMBER OF THE OPEC	1970	----	----	1		IRAN	LIBYA	----
		1975	----	----	1		IRAN	KUWAI	----
		1980	----	----	1		IRAN	KUWAI	----
V37	MEMBER OF THE OECD	1970	----	----	0		IRAN	ISRA	----
		1975	----	----	0		IRAN	ISRA	----
		1980	----	----	0		IRAN	ISRA	----
V38	MEMBER OF THE CMEA	1970	----	----	0		IRAN	IRE	----
		1975	----	----	0		IRAN	IRE	----
		1980	----	----	0		IRAN	IRE	----
V39	MEMBER OF THE WTO	1970	----	----	0		IRAN	IRE	----
		1975	----	----	0		IRAN	IRE	----
		1980	----	----	0		IRAN	IRE	----
V40	MEMBER OF THE NATO	1970	----	----	0		IRAN	IRE	----
		1975	----	----	0		IRAN	IRE	----
		1980	----	----	0		IRAN	IRE	----
V41	GDP SHARE OF INVESTMENTS	1970	D4	P30	15.8	%	SENE	LESO	----
		1975	D9	P81	30.3	%	IRAN	NEWZ	----
		1979	D9	P90	32.7	%	LESO	JAPAN	----
V42	GDP SHARE OF AGRICULTURE	1970	D4	P40	17.3	%	ZAIRE	YUGO	F16
		1975	D3	P23	7.5	%	CHILE	ITALY	F16
		1979	D3	P28	7.7	%	CHILE	JORDA	F16

V43	GDP SHARE OF INDUSTRY	1970	D10	P93	45.1	%	ITALY	AURIA	F16
		1975	D10	P96	66.4	%	GABON	LIBYA	F16
		1979	D10	P96	72.6	%	GABON	LIBYA	F16
V44	GDP SHARE OF SERVICES	1970	D3	P20	37.6	%	YENO	IRAN	F16
		1975	D1	P8	26.1	%	SOMA	ANGO	F16
		1979	D1	P2	19.7	%	-------	SAUDI	F16
V45	HOMICIDES P. MIL. POPULATION	------	----	----	-----	-----	-------	-------	----
V46	SUICIDES P. MIL. POPULATION	------	----	----	-----	-----	-------	-------	----
V47	IMPORT PARTNERS	1970	R1	UNKI	12.0	%	GHANA	IRE	----
		1970	R2	USSR	10.6	%	INDIA	MALI	----
		1970	R3	FRANC	5.9	%	SWITZ	LEBA	----
		1978	R1	JAPAN	20.9	%	INDO	KORSO	----
		1978	R2	GFR	11.3	%	HUNGA	JORDA	----
		1978	R3	USA	10.1	%	GHANA	ITALY	----
V48	EXPORT PARTNERS	1970	R1	ITALY	28.6	%	ARGE	LIBYA	----
		1970	R2	FRANC	15.4	%	BELGI	ITALY	----
		1970	R3	NETH	6.6	%	COLO	LIBE	----
V49	PATENT SUPPLIERS	1971	R1	UNKI	26		GHANA	KENYA	----
		1971	R2	JAPAN	18		CHINA	MEXI	----
		1971	R3	NETH	8		-------	-------	----
		1979	R1	FRANC	16		GHANA	MOROC	----
		1979	R2	-------	11		-------	-------	----
		1979	R3	-------	11		-------	-------	----
V50	PROVENANCE OF FOREIGN FIRMS	------	----	----	-----	-----	-------	-------	----
V51	FILM SUPPLIERS	1980	R1	USA	41		INDO	IRE	F117
		1980	R2	UNKI	40		FINLA	IRE	F117
		1980	R3	INDIA	20		INDO	LIBYA	F117

IRELAND (IRE)

V1	INCOME PER CAPITA	1970	D8	P72	3832	$/CAP	VENE	TRITO	F4
		1975	D8	P73	4416	$/CAP	VENE	TRITO	----
		1980	D8	P74	5156	$/CAP	SINGA	SPAIN	----
V2	TELEPHONES P. TSD. POPULATION	1970	D8	P79	104	1/TSD CAP	PORTU	GREC	----
		1975	D8	P76	138	1/TSD CAP	KUWAI	SINGA	----
		1980	D8	P73	187	1/TSD CAP	KUWAI	GDR	----
V3	INFANT MORTALITY RATE	1980	D2	P12	11.2	1/TSD	SPAIN	SINGA	----
V4	PHYSICIANS P. MIL. POPULATION	1971	D8	P76	1196	1/MIL	NEWZ	ROMA	----
		1975	D8	P72	1186	1/MIL	PORTU	YUGO	----
		1980	D7	P64	1276	1/MIL	EGYPT	JAPAN	----

V5	ADULT LITERACY	------	----	----	-----	-----	-------	-------	----
V6	DURATION OF SCHOOLING	1970	D8	P78	10.1	YR	HUNGA	GREC	----
		1975	D8	P80	10.6	YR	BULGA	POLA	----
		1980	D8	P74	10.5	YR	TOGO	KUWAI	----
V7	STUDENT ENROLLMENT RATIO	1970	D8	P79	13.5	%	GREC	ARGE	----
		1975	D8	P79	18.8	%	PHILI	AURIA	----
		1980	D8	P77	20.7	%	SWITZ	USSR	----
V8	SHARE OF AGRICULTURAL LABOR	1971	D5	P48	26.5	%	SPAIN	CUBA	----
		1977	D5	----	21.4	%	SPAIN	LIBYA	----
		1981	D5	P46	16.4	%	CHILE	SPAIN	----
V9	SHARE OF INDUSTRIAL LABOR	1971	D5	P46	32.2	%	GREC	CUBA	----
		1977	D7	----	35.0	%	FINLA	KUWAI	----
		1981	D7	P59	34.3	%	GREC	NORWY	----
V10	SHARE OF SERVICE LABOR	1971	D7	P63	31.4	%	CUBA	PANA	----
		1977	D6	----	31.1	%	LIBYA	COLO	----
		1981	D7	P58	35.9	%	TRITO	SWEDN	----
V11	SHARE OF ACADEMIC LABOR	1971	D8	P71	9.9	%	SINGA	LEBA	----
		1977	D8	----	12.5	%	SINGA	AULIA	----
		1981	D8	P72	13.5	%	ITALY	GFR	----
V12	SHARE OF SELF-EMPLOYED LABOR	1971	D5	P52	24.7	%	ARGE	TURKY	----
		1977	D4	----	23.4	%	ALGER	LIBYA	----
		1981	D4	P42	19.1	%	JAPAN	COSTA	----
V13	MILITARY EXPENDITURES	1970	D5	P41	0.148	TSD MIL $	URU	BURMA	----
		1975	D5	P45	0.249	TSD MIL $	ZAIRE	JORDA	----
		1980	D5	P44	0.337	TSD MIL $	YENO	ETHIA	----
V14	MILITARY MANPOWER	1970	D3	P22	8	TSD CAP	CAME	MALI	----
		1975	D3	P24	11	TSD CAP	CHAD	HONDU	----
		1980	D4	P33	19	TSD CAP	SRILA	MADA	----
V15	MEN AT AGE 20 - 30	1971	D2	P14	198	TSD CAP	HONDU	URU	----
		1975	D2	P18	226	TSD CAP	PAPUA	SINGA	----
		1979	D2	P12	257	TSD CAP	NEWZ	SINGA	----
V16	POPULATION	1970	D3	P23	2.94	MIL CAP	URU	LAOS	F4
		1975	D3	P24	3.18	MIL CAP	SOMA	LAOS	----
		1980	D3	P22	3.40	MIL CAP	SIERA	BENIN	----
V17	GROSS DOMESTIC PRODUCT	1970	D6	P54	11.265	TSD MIL $	MALAY	HUNGA	----
		1975	D6	P51	14.043	TSD MIL $	MOROC	MALAY	----
		1980	D6	P52	17.531	TSD MIL $	MOROC	PERU	----
V18	SHARE IN WORLD IMPORTS	1970	D7	P67	4.739	1/TSD	ISRA	PORTU	F30
		1975	D6	P60	4.157	1/TSD	PHILI	PORTU	F30
		1980	D8	P72	5.438	1/TSD	INDO	IRAN	F30
V19	SHARE IN WORLD EXPORTS	1970	D6	P59	3.312	1/TSD	ALGER	CUBA	F30
		1975	D7	P63	3.643	1/TSD	MEXI	CUBA	F30
		1980	D7	P65	4.208	1/TSD	INDIA	HUNGA	F30
V20	GDP SHARE OF IMPORTS	1970	D10	P94	40.5	%	JAMAI	NETH	F30
		1975	D10	P94	45.0	%	NETH	BELGI	F30
		1980	D10	P98	59.1	%	LIBE	YENO	F30

V21	GDP SHARE OF EXPORTS	1970	D9	P86	26.7 %	IRAN	IRAQ	F30
		1975	D9	P85	38.0 %	VENE	ZAIRE	F30
		1980	D9	P87	44.5 %	NETH	GABON	F30
V22	EXPORT PARTNER CONCENTRATION	1970	D10	P97	65.8 %	CANA	CHAD	----
		1975	D9	P90	54.2 %	YENO	BULGA	----
		1980	D9	P83	42.7 %	YENO	NIGRA	----
V23	TOTAL DEBT AS % OF GDP	------	----	----	----- -----	-------	-------	----
V24	SHARE OF NEW FOREIGN PATENTS	1970	D8	P74	98 %	DOMI	MALAY	----
		1975	D8	P79	97 %	IRAN	SYRIA	----
		1980	D9	P84	98 %	ZAIRE	SRILA	----
V25	FOREIGN PROPERTY AS % OF GDP	------	----	----	----- -----	-------	-------	----
V26	GNP SHARE OF DEVELOPMENT AID	------	----	----	----- -----	-------	-------	----
V27	SHARE IN NOBEL PRIZE WINNERS	1970-79	D5	P45	0.0 %	IRAQ	ISRA	----
V28	GDP SHARE OF MANUFACTURING	1970	D7	P64	18.5 %	DOMI	ELSA	----
		1975	D7	P69	19.3 %	CANA	GREC	----
V29	EXPORT SHARE OF MANUFACTURES	------	----	----	----- -----	-------	-------	----
V30	LACK OF CIVIL LIBERTIES	1975	D2	P18	2	GREC	ITALY	----
		1980	D1	P7	1	DENMA	JAPAN	----
V31	LACK OF POLITICAL RIGHTS	1975	D1	P8	1	GFR	ITALY	----
		1980	D1	P8	1	GFR	NETH	----
V32	RIOTS	1970-74	D8	P75	8	VENE	ISRA	----
		1975-79	D6	P60	3	GUATE	KENYA	----
V33	PROTEST DEMONSTRATIONS	1970-74	D10	P92	59	PAKI	ITALY	----
		1975-79	D9	P82	18	CHILE	LAOS	----
V34	POLITICAL STRIKES	1970-74	D7	P64	1	IRAQ	IVORY	----
		1975-79	D7	P63	1	GUATE	JAMAI	----
V35	MEMBER OF THE NONALIGNED MMT.	1970	----	----	0	IRAN	ISRA	----
		1976	----	----	0	IRAN	ISRA	----
		1981	----	----	0	HUNGA	ISRA	----
V36	MEMBER OF THE OPEC	1970	----	----	0	INDIA	ISRA	----
		1975	----	----	0	INDIA	ISRA	----
		1980	----	----	0	INDIA	ISRA	----
V37	MEMBER OF THE OECD	1970	----	----	1	GREC	ITALY	----
		1975	----	----	1	GREC	ITALY	----
		1980	----	----	1	GREC	ITALY	----
V38	MEMBER OF THE CMEA	1970	----	----	0	IRAQ	ISRA	----
		1975	----	----	0	IRAQ	ISRA	----
		1980	----	----	0	IRAQ	ISRA	----
V39	MEMBER OF THE WTO	1970	----	----	0	IRAQ	ISRA	----
		1975	----	----	0	IRAQ	ISRA	----
		1980	----	----	0	IRAQ	ISRA	----

V40	MEMBER OF THE NATO	1970	----	----	0		IRAQ	ISRA	----
		1975	----	----	0		IRAQ	ISRA	----
		1980	----	----	0		IRAQ	ISRA	----
V41	GDP SHARE OF INVESTMENTS	1970	D8	P72	24.5	%	SPAIN	SWEDN	----
		1975	D5	P50	22.2	%	ELSA	IVORY	----
		1980	D8	P71	28.1	%	ECUA	GREC	----
V42	GDP SHARE OF AGRICULTURE	1970	D4	P35	14.4	%	URU	JORDA	----
		1975	D5	P42	15.7	%	PORTU	ECUA	----
		1979	D5	P41	12.8	%	PORTU	ZIMBA	----
V43	GDP SHARE OF INDUSTRY	1970	D7	P60	31.4	%	GREC	NEWZ	----
		1975	D6	P60	33.2	%	ANGO	USA	----
V44	GDP SHARE OF SERVICES	1970	D8	P79	54.2	%	SYRIA	FRANC	----
		1975	D7	P70	51.1	%	GREC	BOLI	----
V45	HOMICIDES P. MIL. POPULATION	1975	D3	P21	9.4	1/MIL CAP	BELGI	SWITZ	F154
		1980	D1	P7	6.8	1/MIL CAP	GREC	NETH	F2
V46	SUICIDES P. MIL. POPULATION	1975	D3	P25	46.5	1/MIL CAP	THAI	VENE	F2
		1980	D3	P25	63.2	1/MIL CAP	COSTA	ITALY	F2
V47	IMPORT PARTNERS	1970	R1	UNKI	53.5	%	IRAQ	JORDA	----
		1970	R2	GFR	7.1	%	GDR	IVORY	----
		1970	R3	USA	7.0	%	GFR	ITALY	----
		1980	R1	UNKI	50.8	%	GHANA	NIGRA	----
		1980	R2	USA	8.7	%	INDO	KORSO	----
		1980	R3	GFR	6.9	%	GABON	LIBE	----
V48	EXPORT PARTNERS	1970	R1	UNKI	65.8	%	FINLA	MALAW	----
		1970	R2	USA	10.1	%	INDIA	IVORY	----
		1970	R3	FRANC	3.1	%	HAITI	NETH	----
		1980	R1	UNKI	42.7	%	GHANA	MALAW	----
		1980	R2	GFR	9.6	%	HUNGA	JAPAN	----
		1980	R3	FRANC	7.7	%	GREC	LIBE	----
V49	PATENT SUPPLIERS	1970	R1	USA	235		IRAN	ISRA	----
		1970	R2	UNKI	228		INDIA	JAMAI	----
		1970	R3	SWITZ	101		IRAN	KORSO	----
		1980	R1	USA	446		INDIA	ISRA	----
		1980	R2	UNKI	235		AULIA	JAMAI	----
		1980	R3	GFR	227		GHANA	KORSO	----
V50	PROVENANCE OF FOREIGN FIRMS	1980	R1	UNKI	72.4	%	GUINE	KENYA	----
		1980	R2	USA	15.3	%	GHANA	IVORY	----
		1980	R3	CANA	2.5	%	USA	JAMAI	----
V51	FILM SUPPLIERS	1980	R1	USA	122		IRAQ	ISRA	F119
		1980	R2	UNKI	71		IRAQ	KORSO	F119
		1980	R3	ITALY	9		IRAN	JAPAN	F119

ISRAEL (ISRA)

V1	INCOME PER CAPITA	------	----	----	----- -----	-------	-------	----
V2	TELEPHONES P. TSD. POPULATION	1970	D9	P83	161 1/TSD CAP	CZECH	FRANC	----
		1975	D9	P80	219 1/TSD CAP	CZECH	SPAIN	----
		1980	D8	P79	293 1/TSD CAP	SINGA	SPAIN	----
V3	INFANT MORTALITY RATE	1980	D2	P19	15.1 1/TSD	ITALY	GREC	F7
V4	PHYSICIANS P. MIL. POPULATION	------	----	----	----- -----	-------	-------	----
V5	ADULT LITERACY	1971	D8	P76	87.9 %	KORSO	CHILE	----
V6	DURATION OF SCHOOLING	1970	D8	P76	10.0 YR	CUBA	AURIA	----
		1975	D8	P78	10.4 YR	GFR	PANA	----
		1980	D8	P77	10.7 YR	IRAQ	AULIA	----
V7	STUDENT ENROLLMENT RATIO	1970	D10	P94	20.0 %	PHILI	SWEDN	----
		1975	D9	P87	23.4 %	BELGI	AULIA	F29
		1980	D10	P92	29.1 %	DENMA	NETH	----
V8	SHARE OF AGRICULTURAL LABOR	1972	D2	----	7.8 %	CANA	SWEDN	F80
		1975	D2	P13	6.3 %	NETH	CANA	F79
		1980	D2	P15	5.9 %	CANA	NETH	F79
V9	SHARE OF INDUSTRIAL LABOR	1975	D7	P63	34.3 %	NETH	JAPAN	F79
		1980	D5	P46	30.6 %	CANA	MOROC	F79
V10	SHARE OF SERVICE LABOR	1975	D8	P78	40.0 %	VENE	URU	F79
		1980	D8	P68	41.0 %	FRANC	AURIA	F79
V11	SHARE OF ACADEMIC LABOR	1975	D10	P95	19.4 %	FINLA	SWEDN	F79
		1980	D10	P96	22.6 %	NORWY	SWEDN	F79
V12	SHARE OF SELF-EMPLOYED LABOR	------	----	----	----- -----	-------	-------	----
V13	MILITARY EXPENDITURES	------	----	----	----- -----	-------	-------	----
V14	MILITARY MANPOWER	1970	D7	P68	105 TSD CAP	IRAQ	BELGI	----
		1975	D8	P73	190 TSD CAP	BULGA	GREC	----
		1980	D8	P77	180 TSD CAP	BURMA	GREC	----
V15	MEN AT AGE 20 - 30	1971	D3	P21	254 TSD CAP	NIGER	ELSA	F205
		1975	D3	P23	311 TSD CAP	HAITI	NORWY	F169
		1980	D2	P19	340 TSD CAP	NORWY	DOMI	F169
V16	POPULATION	1970	D3	P25	2.97 MIL CAP	LAOS	ELSA	F7
		1975	D3	P26	3.46 MIL CAP	LAOS	BURU	F169
		1980	D3	P24	3.88 MIL CAP	HONDU	LAOS	F169
V17	GROSS DOMESTIC PRODUCT	------	----	----	----- -----	-------	-------	----
V18	SHARE IN WORLD IMPORTS	1970	D7	P66	4.320 1/TSD	MALAY	IRE	----
		1975	D7	P64	4.521 1/TSD	ARGE	SAUDI	----
		1980	D7	P61	3.841 1/TSD	TURKY	PHILI	----

V19	SHARE IN WORLD EXPORTS	1970	D6	P52	2.340	1/TSD	PAKI	COLO	----
		1975	D6	P57	2.094	1/TSD	TRITO	PORTU	----
		1980	D6	P59	2.651	1/TSD	GREC	NEWZ	----
V20	GDP SHARE OF IMPORTS	------	----	----	-----	-----	-------	-------	----
V21	GDP SHARE OF EXPORTS	------	----	----	-----	-----	-------	-------	----
V22	EXPORT PARTNER CONCENTRATION	1970	D3	P22	19.2	%	GHANA	MAURA	F125
		1975	D2	P20	15.9	%	BANGL	FRANC	F125
V23	TOTAL DEBT AS % OF GDP	------	----	----	-----	-----	-------	-------	----
V24	SHARE OF NEW FOREIGN PATENTS	1970	D5	P43	89	%	HONDU	NETH	----
		1975	D5	P50	90	%	HONDU	PHILI	----
		1980	D4	P35	82	%	AURIA	SPAIN	----
V25	FOREIGN PROPERTY AS % OF GDP	------	----	----	-----	-----	-------	-------	----
V26	GNP SHARE OF DEVELOPMENT AID	------	----	----	-----	-----	-------	-------	----
V27	SHARE IN NOBEL PRIZE WINNERS	1970-79	D5	P45	0.0	%	IRE	ITALY	----
V28	GDP SHARE OF MANUFACTURING	------	----	----	-----	-----	-------	-------	----
V29	EXPORT SHARE OF MANUFACTURES	1970	D10	P93	69.1	%	AURIA	KORSO	----
		1975	D10	P93	73.7	%	AURIA	ITALY	----
		1980	D10	P97	81.3	%	KORSO	SWITZ	----
V30	LACK OF CIVIL LIBERTIES	1975	D3	P27	3		INDIA	KUWAI	----
		1980	D2	P18	2		INDIA	ITALY	----
V31	LACK OF POLITICAL RIGHTS	1975	D2	P20	2		INDIA	JAPAN	----
		1980	D3	P21	2		INDIA	ITALY	----
V32	RIOTS	1970-74	D8	P75	8		IRE	JAPAN	F221
		1975-79	D9	P88	18		GREC	COLO	F221
V33	PROTEST DEMONSTRATIONS	1970-74	D9	P89	41		ARGE	VISO	F221
		1975-79	D10	P95	88		USSR	ITALY	F221
V34	POLITICAL STRIKES	1970-74	D9	P85	8		SOUAF	POLA	F221
		1975-79	D10	P93	13		PAKI	UNKI	F221
V35	MEMBER OF THE NONALIGNED MMT.	1970	----	----	0		IRE	ITALY	----
		1976	----	----	0		IRE	ITALY	----
		1981	----	----	0		IRE	ITALY	----
V36	MEMBER OF THE OPEC	1970	----	----	0		IRE	ITALY	----
		1975	----	----	0		IRE	ITALY	----
		1980	----	----	0		IRE	ITALY	----
V37	MEMBER OF THE OECD	1970	----	----	0		IRAQ	IVORY	----
		1975	----	----	0		IRAQ	IVORY	----
		1980	----	----	0		IRAQ	IVORY	----
V38	MEMBER OF THE CMEA	1970	----	----	0		IRE	ITALY	----
		1975	----	----	0		IRE	ITALY	----
		1980	----	----	0		IRE	ITALY	----

V39 MEMBER OF THE WTO	1970	----	----	0		IRE	ITALY	----
	1975	----	----	0		IRE	ITALY	----
	1980	----	----	0		IRE	ITALY	----
V40 MEMBER OF THE NATO	1970	----	----	0		IRE	IVORY	----
	1975	----	----	0		IRE	IVORY	----
	1980	----	----	0		IRE	IVORY	----
V41 GDP SHARE OF INVESTMENTS	1970	D9	P81	27.4	%	AULIA	PANA	----
	1975	D8	P79	29.4	%	TUNIS	IRAN	----
	1980	D4	P38	21.8	%	MALAW	TANZA	----
V42 GDP SHARE OF AGRICULTURE	------	----	----	----- -----		-------	-------	----
V43 GDP SHARE OF INDUSTRY	------	----	----	----- -----		-------	-------	----
V44 GDP SHARE OF SERVICES	------	----	----	----- -----		-------	-------	----
V45 HOMICIDES P. MIL. POPULATION	1970	D4	P35	11.8	1/MIL CAP	PORTU	NEWZ	F155
	1975	D4	P31	10.7	1/MIL CAP	POLA	NEWZ	F155
V46 SUICIDES P. MIL. POPULATION	1970	D3	P30	49.2	1/MIL CAP	TRITO	ITALY	F152
	1975	D4	P32	70.8	1/MIL CAP	ITALY	UNKI	F152
V47 IMPORT PARTNERS	1970	R1	USA	22.2	%	INDIA	JAMAI	F125
	1970	R2	UNKI	15.7	%	CANA	JAMAI	F125
	1970	R3	GFR	12.0	%	INDO	JORDA	F125
V48 EXPORT PARTNERS	1970	R1	USA	19.2	%	HONDU	JAMAI	F125
	1970	R2	UNKI	10.6	%	GHANA	JAMAI	F125
	1970	R3	GFR	8.6	%	GUATE	IVORY	F125
V49 PATENT SUPPLIERS	1970	R1	USA	507		IRE	ITALY	----
	1970	R2	GFR	197		IRAN	ITALY	----
	1970	R3	FRANC	163		BRAZI	ITALY	----
	1980	R1	USA	651		IRE	ITALY	----
	1980	R2	GFR	232		INDIA	ITALY	----
	1980	R3	UNKI	129		INDIA	JAPAN	----
V50 PROVENANCE OF FOREIGN FIRMS	1980	R1	USA	67.5	%	IRAN	ITALY	----
	1980	R2	UNKI	14.7	%	INDIA	ITALY	----
	1980	R3	GFR	5.0	%	INDIA	IVORY	----
V51 FILM SUPPLIERS	1980	R1	USA	124		IRE	ITALY	F119
	1980	R2	INDIA	47		TANZA	JORDA	F119
	1980	R3	UNKI	18		INDIA	MEXI	F119

ITALY (ITALY)

V1 INCOME PER CAPITA	1970	D8	P77	4914	$/CAP	LIBYA	SAUDI	F147
	1975	D8	P77	5322	$/CAP	SPAIN	JAPAN	F147
	1980	D8	P77	6287	$/CAP	TRITO	NEWZ	F147

V2	TELEPHONES P. TSD. POPULATION	1970	D9	P85	174	1/TSD CAP	FRANC	AURIA	----
		1975	D9	P83	259	1/TSD CAP	GREC	FRANC	----
		1980	D9	P82	337	1/TSD CAP	SPAIN	BELGI	----
V3	INFANT MORTALITY RATE	1980	D2	P18	14.3	1/TSD	AURIA	ISRA	----
V4	PHYSICIANS P. MIL. POPULATION	1970	D10	P93	1808	1/MIL	MONGO	BULGA	F147
V5	ADULT LITERACY	1971	D9	P87	93.9	%	ARGE	JAMAI	----
V6	DURATION OF SCHOOLING	1970	D9	P88	10.5	YR	URU	NETH	----
		1975	D9	P85	10.9	YR	SWEDN	BELGI	----
		1980	D9	P85	11.1	YR	POLA	ALBA	----
V7	STUDENT ENROLLMENT RATIO	1970	D9	P87	16.7	%	AULIA	JAPAN	----
		1975	D10	P91	25.1	%	JAPAN	NETH	----
		1980	D10	P90	27.5	%	GFR	DENMA	----
V8	SHARE OF AGRICULTURAL LABOR	1971	D4	P32	17.4	%	FRANC	HUNGA	----
		1981	D3	P32	10.4	%	HUNGA	JAPAN	----
V9	SHARE OF INDUSTRIAL LABOR	1971	D10	P93	44.4	%	CZECH	BELGI	----
		1981	D3	P19	23.0	%	TURKY	EGYPT	----
V10	SHARE OF SERVICE LABOR	1971	D6	P56	30.5	%	SPAIN	SOUAF	----
		1981	D10	P98	53.8	%	USA	-------	----
V11	SHARE OF ACADEMIC LABOR	1971	D6	P56	7.7	%	PANA	PERU	----
		1981	D8	P70	12.8	%	JORDA	IRE	----
V12	SHARE OF SELF-EMPLOYED LABOR	1971	D5	P47	21.7	%	PORTU	ARGE	----
		1981	D5	P47	20.0	%	COSTA	PORTU	----
V13	MILITARY EXPENDITURES	1970	D10	P92	6.540	TSD MIL $	JAPAN	FRANC	----
		1975	D10	P93	7.368	TSD MIL $	SAUDI	JAPAN	----
		1980	D10	P93	8.683	TSD MIL $	NETH	JAPAN	----
V14	MILITARY MANPOWER	1970	D9	P90	435	TSD CAP	PAKI	KORNO	----
		1975	D10	P91	500	TSD CAP	GFR	PAKI	----
		1980	D9	P90	363	TSD CAP	IRAQ	POLA	----
V15	MEN AT AGE 20 - 30	1971	D9	P88	3836	TSD CAP	FRANC	UNKI	F22
		1976	D9	P89	4096	TSD CAP	UNKI	GFR	F22
		1980	D9	P83	4066	TSD CAP	UNKI	THAI	F22
V16	POPULATION	1970	D9	P90	53.66	MIL CAP	FRANC	UNKI	F22
		1975	D9	P89	55.83	MIL CAP	FRANC	UNKI	F22
		1980	D9	P90	57.07	MIL CAP	UNKI	GFR	F22
V17	GROSS DOMESTIC PRODUCT	1970	D10	P93	263.695	TSD MIL $	CANA	UNKI	----
		1975	D10	P94	297.113	TSD MIL $	CANA	UNKI	----
		1980	D10	P94	358.781	TSD MIL $	BRAZI	UNKI	----
V18	SHARE IN WORLD IMPORTS	1970	D10	P95	45.096	1/TSD	NETH	JAPAN	----
		1975	D10	P95	42.395	1/TSD	USSR	UNKI	----
		1980	D10	P95	48.579	1/TSD	NETH	UNKI	----
V19	SHARE IN WORLD EXPORTS	1970	D10	P94	42.101	1/TSD	USSR	CANA	----
		1975	D10	P94	39.938	1/TSD	USSR	NETH	----
		1980	D10	P95	38.908	1/TSD	USSR	SAUDI	----

V20	GDP SHARE OF IMPORTS	1970	D4	P38	14.9	%	GUATE	BOLI	----
		1975	D4	P37	20.1	%	IRAN	SOUAF	----
		1980	D6	P56	25.2	%	ALGER	HAITI	----
V21	GDP SHARE OF EXPORTS	1970	D5	P42	13.1	%	BENIN	AULIA	----
		1975	D6	P51	18.2	%	BOLI	UNKI	----
		1980	D5	P50	19.6	%	THAI	KENYA	----
V22	EXPORT PARTNER CONCENTRATION	1970	D4	P32	21.6	%	SYRIA	MALAY	----
		1975	D3	P26	18.6	%	SYRIA	DENMA	----
		1980	D3	P27	18.3	%	TUNIS	ROMA	----
V23	TOTAL DEBT AS % OF GDP	------	----	----	-----	-----	-------	-------	----
V24	SHARE OF NEW FOREIGN PATENTS	1970	D4	P31	80	%	BRAZI	YUGO	----
		1974	D3	P30	80	%	COLO	INDIA	----
		1980	D3	P29	77	%	INDIA	SOMA	----
V25	FOREIGN PROPERTY AS % OF GDP	------	----	----	-----	-----	-------	-------	----
V26	GNP SHARE OF DEVELOPMENT AID	1970	D4	P37	0.15	%	SWITZ	NEWZ	----
		1975	D1	P8	0.10	%	NIGRA	VENE	----
		1980	D2	P12	0.17	%	NIGRA	ALGER	----
V27	SHARE IN NOBEL PRIZE WINNERS	1970-79	D5	P45	0.0	%	ISRA	IVORY	----
V28	GDP SHARE OF MANUFACTURING	------	----	----	-----	-----	-------	-------	----
V29	EXPORT SHARE OF MANUFACTURES	1970	D10	P96	79.4	%	KORSO	GFR	----
		1975	D10	P95	75.4	%	ISRA	KORSO	----
		1980	D10	P93	79.0	%	GFR	KORSO	----
V30	LACK OF CIVIL LIBERTIES	1975	D2	P18	2		IRE	JAMAI	----
		1980	D2	P18	2		ISRA	PAPUA	----
V31	LACK OF POLITICAL RIGHTS	1975	D1	P8	1		IRE	JAMAI	----
		1980	D3	P21	2		ISRA	JAMAI	----
V32	RIOTS	1970-74	D10	P95	53		FRANC	CHILE	----
		1975-79	D10	P96	59		USA	SOUAF	----
V33	PROTEST DEMONSTRATIONS	1970-74	D10	P93	60		IRE	KORSO	----
		1975-79	D10	P96	99		ISRA	UNKI	----
V34	POLITICAL STRIKES	1970-74	D10	P98	36		FRANC	USA	----
		1975-79	D9	P87	9		ARGE	PORTU	----
V35	MEMBER OF THE NONALIGNED MMT.	1970	----	----	0		ISRA	IVORY	----
		1976	----	----	0		ISRA	JAPAN	----
		1981	----	----	0		ISRA	JAPAN	----
V36	MEMBER OF THE OPEC	1970	----	----	0		ISRA	IVORY	----
		1975	----	----	0		ISRA	IVORY	----
		1980	----	----	0		ISRA	IVORY	----
V37	MEMBER OF THE OECD	1970	----	----	1		IRE	JAPAN	----
		1975	----	----	1		IRE	JAPAN	----
		1980	----	----	1		IRE	JAPAN	----

V38 MEMBER OF THE CMEA	1970	----	----	0		ISRA	IVORY	----
	1975	----	----	0		ISRA	IVORY	----
	1980	----	----	0		ISRA	IVORY	----
V39 MEMBER OF THE WTO	1970	----	----	0		ISRA	IVORY	----
	1975	----	----	0		ISRA	IVORY	----
	1980	----	----	0		ISRA	IVORY	----
V40 MEMBER OF THE NATO	1970	----	----	1		GREC	NETH	----
	1975	----	----	1		GREC	NETH	----
	1980	----	----	1		GREC	NETH	----
V41 GDP SHARE OF INVESTMENTS	1970	D7	P65	23.1 %		MEXI	PORTU	----
	1975	D4	P38	20.3 %		INDO	GFR	----
	1980	D6	P56	25.1 %		GFR	ARGE	----
V42 GDP SHARE OF AGRICULTURE	1970	D3	P24	8.1 %		VENE	SOUAF	----
	1975	D3	P24	7.7 %		IRAQ	JAMAI	----
	1980	D3	P22	6.4 %		ALGER	GABON	----
V43 GDP SHARE OF INDUSTRY	1970	D10	P92	42.9 %		JAMAI	IRAQ	----
	1975	D9	P84	42.4 %		JAPAN	ARGE	----
	1980	D9	P84	42.7 %		PERU	JAPAN	----
V44 GDP SHARE OF SERVICES	1970	D6	P53	49.0 %		ELSA	NICA	----
	1975	D7	P67	49.9 %		IVORY	CAME	----
	1980	D7	P66	50.9 %		CAME	IVORY	----
V45 HOMICIDES P. MIL. POPULATION	1970	D3	P24	8.3 1/MIL CAP	UNKI	SWEDN	F149
	1975	D4	P40	12.8 1/MIL CAP	GFR	JAPAN	F149
	1980	D6	P58	18.7 1/MIL CAP	YUGO	AULIA	F147
V46 SUICIDES P. MIL. POPULATION	1970	D4	P32	57.5 1/MIL CAP	ISRA	VENE	F147
	1975	D3	P30	55.7 1/MIL CAP	VENE	ISRA	F147
	1980	D3	P28	72.8 1/MIL CAP	IRE	THAI	F147
V47 IMPORT PARTNERS	1970	R1	GFR	19.8 %		IRAN	NETH	----
	1970	R2	FRANC	13.2 %		CUBA	KAMPU	----
	1970	R3	USA	10.3 %		IRE	IVORY	----
	1980	R1	GFR	16.8 %		GREC	NETH	----
	1980	R2	FRANC	14.1 %		GFR	MALI	----
	1980	R3	USA	7.0 %		IRAQ	JORDA	----
V48 EXPORT PARTNERS	1970	R1	GFR	21.6 %		GREC	NETH	----
	1970	R2	FRANC	12.9 %		IRAQ	MALI	----
	1970	R3	USA	10.2 %		INDO	MALAY	----
	1980	R1	GFR	18.3 %		GREC	LIBE	----
	1980	R2	FRANC	15.1 %		HAITI	SWITZ	----
	1980	R3	UNKI	6.1 %		FINLA	-------	----
V49 PATENT SUPPLIERS	1970	R1	USA	7670		ISRA	JAMAI	----
	1970	R2	GFR	5527		ISRA	JAPAN	----
	1970	R3	FRANC	2409		ISRA	LEBA	----
	1980	R1	USA	1807		ISRA	JAMAI	----
	1980	R2	GFR	1675		ISRA	JAPAN	----
	1980	R3	FRANC	659		IRAN	MEXI	----

V50	PROVENANCE OF FOREIGN FIRMS	1980	R1	USA	36.2	%	ISRA	JAMAI	----
		1980	R2	UNKI	14.4	%	ISRA	JAMAI	----
		1980	R3	FINLA	14.3	%	GREC	JAPAN	----
V51	FILM SUPPLIERS	1980	R1	USA	141		ISRA	JAPAN	F120
		1980	R2	FRANC	101		DENMA	JAPAN	F120
		1980	R3	GFR	40		FRANC	NETH	F120

IVORY COAST (IVORY)

V1	INCOME PER CAPITA	1975	D5	P45	1033	$/CAP	ECUA	COLO	----
		1980	D5	P45	1178	$/CAP	JAMAI	ECUA	----
V2	TELEPHONES P. TSD. POPULATION	1970	D4	P34	7	1/TSD CAP	SRILA	KENYA	----
		1975	D4	P33	9	1/TSD CAP	SENE	KENYA	----
		1980	D4	P32	13	1/TSD CAP	MOROC	PHILI	----
V3	INFANT MORTALITY RATE	1980	D8	P79	132.0	1/TSD	PAKI	CONGO	F5
V4	PHYSICIANS P. MIL. POPULATION	1971	D3	P26	64	1/MIL	SENE	SUDAN	----
		1975	D2	P15	47	1/MIL	CENTR	CAME	----
V5	ADULT LITERACY	1980	D4	P38	35.0	%	NIGRA	LAOS	F21
V6	DURATION OF SCHOOLING	1970	D3	P28	4.6	YR	CENTR	RWAN	----
		1975	D3	P25	4.9	YR	GUATE	LIBE	----
		1982	D3	----	6.5	YR	LIBE	ZAIRE	----
V7	STUDENT ENROLLMENT RATIO	1970	D3	P28	0.9	%	KENYA	LIBE	----
		1975	D3	P27	1.3	%	GABON	MADA	----
		1980	D4	P34	2.9	%	SRILA	UNARE	----
V8	SHARE OF AGRICULTURAL LABOR	------	----	----	-----	-----	-------	-------	----
V9	SHARE OF INDUSTRIAL LABOR	------	----	----	-----	-----	-------	-------	----
V10	SHARE OF SERVICE LABOR	------	----	----	-----	-----	-------	-------	----
V11	SHARE OF ACADEMIC LABOR	------	----	----	-----	-----	-------	-------	----
V12	SHARE OF SELF-EMPLOYED LABOR	------	----	----	-----	-----	-------	-------	----
V13	MILITARY EXPENDITURES	1975	D4	P31	0.083	TSD MIL $	BOLI	CAME	----
		1980	D3	P30	0.109	TSD MIL $	HONDU	NICA	----
V14	MILITARY MANPOWER	1970	D2	P16	6	TSD CAP	HONDU	NICA	----
		1975	D2	P17	7	TSD CAP	GUINE	SENE	----
		1980	D2	P14	6	TSD CAP	UPVO	UGADA	----
V15	MEN AT AGE 20 - 30	1975	D5	P50	597	TSD CAP	SYRIA	SWEDN	----
V16	POPULATION	1970	D5	P42	5.31	MIL CAP	GUATE	UPVO	----
		1975	D5	P45	6.77	MIL CAP	ANGO	ECUA	----
		1980	D5	P47	8.25	MIL CAP	ANGO	SWEDN	----

V17 GROSS DOMESTIC PRODUCT	1975	D5	P44	6.993	TSD MIL $	ZAIRE	ECUA	----
	1980	D5	P46	9.720	TSD MIL $	TUNIS	ECUA	----
V18 SHARE IN WORLD IMPORTS	1970	D5	P42	1.169	1/TSD	VISO	SRILA	F30
	1975	D5	P46	1.240	1/TSD	JAMAI	LEBA	F30
	1980	D5	P48	1.470	1/TSD	KENYA	PERU	F30
V19 SHARE IN WORLD EXPORTS	1970	D5	P47	1.495	1/TSD	GHANA	MOROC	F30
	1975	D5	P50	1.349	1/TSD	PAKI	PERU	F30
	1980	D6	P53	1.574	1/TSD	EGYPT	PERU	F30
V20 GDP SHARE OF IMPORTS	1970	D8	P77	26.0	%	PORTU	MALAW	F30
	1975	D7	P67	28.9	%	MOROC	TOGO	F30
	1980	D7	P65	28.5	%	THAI	ZAMBI	F30
V21 GDP SHARE OF EXPORTS	1970	D9	P88	31.4	%	IRAQ	NETH	F30
	1975	D8	P80	30.4	%	ELSA	ZAMBI	F30
	1980	D8	P76	29.7	%	TOGO	INDO	F30
V22 EXPORT PARTNER CONCENTRATION	1970	D6	P58	32.7	%	NETH	PERU	----
	1975	D6	P56	27.1	%	ELSA	BENIN	----
	1980	D4	P39	21.7	%	BELGI	SUDAN	----
V23 TOTAL DEBT AS % OF GDP	1980	D8	P79	56.1	%	MALI	COSTA	----
V24 SHARE OF NEW FOREIGN PATENTS	------	----	----	----- -----		-------	-------	----
V25 FOREIGN PROPERTY AS % OF GDP	1971	D8	P80	18.9	%	ECUA	MALAY	----
	1975	D7	P70	10.8	%	HAITI	CAME	----
	1978	D7	----	6.7	%	URU	PHILI	----
V26 GNP SHARE OF DEVELOPMENT AID	------	----	----	----- -----		-------	-------	----
V27 SHARE IN NOBEL PRIZE WINNERS	1970-79	D5	P45	0.0	%	ITALY	JAMAI	----
V28 GDP SHARE OF MANUFACTURING	1970	D5	P45	13.4	%	MADA	MALAY	----
	1975	D5	P47	13.1	%	BOLI	GHANA	----
	1980	D5	P45	11.9	%	INDO	MALAW	----
V29 EXPORT SHARE OF MANUFACTURES	------	----	----	----- -----		-------	-------	----
V30 LACK OF CIVIL LIBERTIES	1975	D8	P74	6		IRAN	JORDA	----
	1980	D6	P52	5		INDO	KORSO	----
V31 LACK OF POLITICAL RIGHTS	1975	D7	P63	6		HUNGA	JORDA	----
	1980	D7	P67	6		HUNGA	JORDA	----
V32 RIOTS	1970-74	D2	P19	0		IRAN	JAMAI	----
	1975-79	D2	P20	0		INDO	JORDA	----
V33 PROTEST DEMONSTRATIONS	1970-74	D2	P15	0		IRAN	JAMAI	----
	1975-79	D2	P13	0		HUNGA	JORDA	----
V34 POLITICAL STRIKES	1970-74	D7	P64	1		IRE	JORDA	----
	1975-79	D3	P29	0		IRAQ	JORDA	----
V35 MEMBER OF THE NONALIGNED MMT.	1970	----	----	0		ITALY	JAPAN	----
	1976	----	----	1		IRAQ	JAMAI	----
	1981	----	----	1		IRAQ	JAMAI	----

V36 MEMBER OF THE OPEC	1970	----	----	0		ITALY	JAMAI	----
	1975	----	----	0		ITALY	JAMAI	----
	1980	----	----	0		ITALY	JAMAI	----
V37 MEMBER OF THE OECD	1970	----	----	0		ISRA	JAMAI	----
	1975	----	----	0		ISRA	JAMAI	----
	1980	----	----	0		ISRA	JAMAI	----
V38 MEMBER OF THE CMEA	1970	----	----	0		ITALY	JAMAI	----
	1975	----	----	0		ITALY	JAMAI	----
	1980	----	----	0		ITALY	JAMAI	----
V39 MEMBER OF THE WTO	1970	----	----	0		ITALY	JAMAI	----
	1975	----	----	0		ITALY	JAMAI	----
	1980	----	----	0		ITALY	JAMAI	----
V40 MEMBER OF THE NATO	1970	----	----	0		ISRA	JAMAI	----
	1975	----	----	0		ISRA	JAMAI	----
	1980	----	----	0		ISRA	JAMAI	----
V41 GDP SHARE OF INVESTMENTS	1970	D7	P60	22.1	%	MAURA	LIBE	----
	1975	D6	P51	22.4	%	IRE	NIGER	----
	1980	D8	P73	28.2	%	GREC	MALAY	----
V42 GDP SHARE OF AGRICULTURE	1970	D6	P59	27.2	%	KORSO	PHILI	----
	1975	D6	P59	28.8	%	MALAY	PHILI	----
	1980	D7	P61	26.3	%	THAI	MAURA	----
V43 GDP SHARE OF INDUSTRY	1970	D4	P32	21.5	%	TOGO	PANA	----
	1975	D3	P27	21.5	%	NIGER	SENE	----
	1980	D3	P26	22.8	%	SIERA	DENMA	----
V44 GDP SHARE OF SERVICES	1970	D7	P61	51.3	%	CENTR	ALGER	----
	1975	D7	P66	49.7	%	ZAIRE	ITALY	----
	1980	D7	P66	50.9	%	ITALY	GREC	----
V45 HOMICIDES P. MIL. POPULATION	------	----	----	----- -----		-------	-------	----
V46 SUICIDES P. MIL. POPULATION	------	----	----	----- -----		-------	-------	----
V47 IMPORT PARTNERS	1970	R1	FRANC	46.2	%	GFR	MADA	----
	1970	R2	GFR	8.6	%	IRE	LEBA	----
	1970	R3	USA	7.9	%	ITALY	KENYA	----
V48 EXPORT PARTNERS	1970	R1	FRANC	32.7	%	GFR	MADA	----
	1970	R2	USA	18.7	%	IRE	MADA	----
	1970	R3	GFR	9.6	%	ISRA	KORSO	----
	1980	R1	FRANC	21.7	%	GFR	MADA	----
	1980	R2	NETH	13.6	%	GHANA	KUWAI	----
	1980	R3	ITALY	11.5	%	HAITI	SPAIN	----
V49 PATENT SUPPLIERS	------	----	----	----- -----		-------	-------	----
V50 PROVENANCE OF FOREIGN FIRMS	1980	R1	FRANC	62.8	%	GABON	MADA	----
	1980	R2	USA	8.9	%	IRE	KENYA	----
	1980	R3	GFR	6.5	%	ISRA	KENYA	----
V51 FILM SUPPLIERS	------	----	----	----- -----		-------	-------	----

JAMAICA (JAMAI)

V1	INCOME PER CAPITA	1970	D6	P60	1439 $/CAP	PANA	MEXI	----
		1975	D6	P58	1429 $/CAP	SYRIA	PANA	----
		1980	D5	P44	1159 $/CAP	GUATE	IVORY	----
V2	TELEPHONES P. TSD. POPULATION	1970	D7	P64	38 1/TSD CAP	COLO	VENE	----
		1975	D7	P59	50 1/TSD CAP	CHILE	MEXI	----
		1979	D6	P54	54 1/TSD CAP	SAUDI	VENE	----
V3	INFANT MORTALITY RATE	1980	D4	P31	32.4 1/TSD	YUGO	CHILE	F5
V4	PHYSICIANS P. MIL. POPULATION	1970	D6	P54	380 1/MIL	PHILI	TRITO	----
		1974	D5	P43	284 1/MIL	ELSA	HONDU	----
		1979	D5	P44	353 1/MIL	HONDU	ALGER	----
V5	ADULT LITERACY	1970	D10	P90	96.1 %	ITALY	POLA	F25
V6	DURATION OF SCHOOLING	1970	D8	P73	9.8 YR	CZECH	CUBA	F4
		1975	D8	P73	10.1 YR	CZECH	URU	----
		1980	D7	P65	10.1 YR	GFR	URU	----
V7	STUDENT ENROLLMENT RATIO	1970	D6	P54	5.5 %	IRAQ	NICA	----
		1975	D6	P50	6.7 %	LIBYA	PARA	----
		1980	D5	P48	6.2 %	TURKY	PARA	----
V8	SHARE OF AGRICULTURAL LABOR	1976	D5	P48	32.5 %	ALGER	COLO	----
V9	SHARE OF INDUSTRIAL LABOR	1976	D6	P55	32.0 %	VENE	URU	----
V10	SHARE OF SERVICE LABOR	------	----	----	----- -----	-------	-------	----
V11	SHARE OF ACADEMIC LABOR	------	----	----	----- -----	-------	-------	----
V12	SHARE OF SELF-EMPLOYED LABOR	------	----	----	----- -----	-------	-------	----
V13	MILITARY EXPENDITURES	1975	D2	P16	0.023 TSD MIL $	TRITO	HONDU	----
		1980	D1	P9	0.022 TSD MIL $	BURU	TOGO	F59
V14	MILITARY MANPOWER	1970	D1	P1	1 TSD CAP	-------	BENIN	----
		1975	D1	P2	1 TSD CAP	-------	LESO	----
		1980	D1	P3	2 TSD CAP	TRITO	SIERA	----
V15	MEN AT AGE 20 - 30	1970	D1	P3	108 TSD CAP	TOGO	PANA	F22
		1981	D1	P5	169 TSD CAP	PANA	NICA	F46
V16	POPULATION	1970	D1	P10	1.87 MIL CAP	NICA	TOGO	----
		1975	D2	P11	2.05 MIL CAP	CENTR	NICA	----
		1980	D2	P10	2.17 MIL CAP	PANA	COSTA	----
V17	GROSS DOMESTIC PRODUCT	1970	D3	P28	2.690 TSD MIL $	SRILA	MADA	----
		1975	D3	P27	2.930 TSD MIL $	ELSA	SRILA	----
		1980	D2	P17	2.514 TSD MIL $	PAPUA	YENO	----
V18	SHARE IN WORLD IMPORTS	1970	D5	P48	1.582 1/TSD	IRAQ	ZAIRE	F30
		1975	D5	P45	1.237 1/TSD	SUDAN	IVORY	F30
		1980	D4	P33	0.571 1/TSD	GHANA	TANZA	F30

Var	Description	Year	D	P	Value	Unit	Country1	Country2	F
V19	SHARE IN WORLD EXPORTS	1970	D5	P45	1.090	1/TSD	KENYA	SRILA	F30
		1975	D5	P41	0.866	1/TSD	KENYA	GHANA	F30
		1980	D4	P34	0.482	1/TSD	DOMI	COSTA	F30
V20	GDP SHARE OF IMPORTS	1970	D10	P93	37.4	%	MALAY	IRE	F30
		1975	D9	P88	39.4	%	MALAY	MAURA	F30
		1980	D9	P90	44.1	%	HUNGA	NETH	F30
V21	GDP SHARE OF EXPORTS	1970	D9	P82	24.3	%	SIERA	HONDU	F30
		1975	D8	P77	26.6	%	NORWY	HONDU	F30
		1980	D9	P83	36.3	%	NIGRA	ALGER	F30
V22	EXPORT PARTNER CONCENTRATION	1970	D9	P88	53.4	%	SOMA	ALGER	----
		1975	D8	P74	38.4	%	PHILI	AFGHA	----
		1980	D8	P76	37.4	%	PAPUA	NICA	F136
V23	TOTAL DEBT AS % OF GDP	1980	D9	P88	70.8	%	MALAW	LIBE	----
V24	SHARE OF NEW FOREIGN PATENTS	1972	D6	----	93	%	IRAN	MEXI	----
		1975	D10	P92	100	%	GHANA	JORDA	----
V25	FOREIGN PROPERTY AS % OF GDP	1971	D10	P95	64.1	%	CONGO	MAURA	----
		1975	D10	P94	34.0	%	SINGA	ZAIRE	----
		1978	D10	----	34.6	%	GABON	TRITO	----
V26	GNP SHARE OF DEVELOPMENT AID	------	----	----	-----	-----	-------	-------	
V27	SHARE IN NOBEL PRIZE WINNERS	1970-79	D5	P45	0.0	%	IVORY	JAPAN	----
V28	GDP SHARE OF MANUFACTURING	1970	D6	P52	15.7	%	BOLI	VENE	----
		1975	D6	P60	17.0	%	PAKI	TURKY	----
		1980	D6	P55	15.5	%	DOMI	RWAN	----
V29	EXPORT SHARE OF MANUFACTURES	1970	D8	P78	46.3	%	CENTR	SPAIN	----
		1975	D9	P83	54.3	%	NETH	BELGI	----
V30	LACK OF CIVIL LIBERTIES	1975	D2	P18	2		ITALY	LEBA	----
		1980	D3	P29	3		HONDU	MEXI	----
V31	LACK OF POLITICAL RIGHTS	1975	D1	P8	1		ITALY	NETH	----
		1980	D3	P21	2		ITALY	JAPAN	----
V32	RIOTS	1970-74	D2	P19	0		IVORY	KORNO	----
		1975-79	D9	P84	10		CENTR	NIGRA	----
V33	PROTEST DEMONSTRATIONS	1970-74	D2	P15	0		IVORY	KORNO	----
		1975-79	D8	P71	10		EGYPT	TURKY	----
V34	POLITICAL STRIKES	1970-74	D3	P29	0		IRAN	KENYA	----
		1975-79	D7	P63	1		IRE	MOROC	----
V35	MEMBER OF THE NONALIGNED MMT.	1970	----	----	1		IRAQ	JORDA	----
		1976	----	----	1		IVORY	JORDA	----
		1981	----	----	1		IVORY	JORDA	----
V36	MEMBER OF THE OPEC	1970	----	----	0		IVORY	JAPAN	----
		1975	----	----	0		IVORY	JAPAN	----
		1980	----	----	0		IVORY	JAPAN	----

V37	MEMBER OF THE OECD	1970	----	----	0		IVORY	JORDA	----
		1975	----	----	0		IVORY	JORDA	----
		1980	----	----	0		IVORY	JORDA	----
V38	MEMBER OF THE CMEA	1970	----	----	0		IVORY	JAPAN	----
		1975	----	----	0		IVORY	JAPAN	----
		1980	----	----	0		IVORY	JAPAN	----
V39	MEMBER OF THE WTO	1970	----	----	0		IVORY	JAPAN	----
		1975	----	----	0		IVORY	JAPAN	----
		1980	----	----	0		IVORY	JAPAN	----
V40	MEMBER OF THE NATO	1970	----	----	0		IVORY	JAPAN	----
		1975	----	----	0		IVORY	JAPAN	----
		1980	----	----	0		IVORY	JAPAN	----
V41	GDP SHARE OF INVESTMENTS	1970	D10	P92	31.5 %		NORWY	SWITZ	----
		1975	D7	P66	25.6 %		THAI	UPVO	----
		1980	D2	P16	15.4 %		ZIMBA	NICA	----
V42	GDP SHARE OF AGRICULTURE	1970	D2	P19	6.6 %		FRANC	CHILE	----
		1975	D3	P24	7.7 %		ITALY	SOUAF	----
		1980	D4	P31	8.4 %		FINLA	ARGE	----
V43	GDP SHARE OF INDUSTRY	1970	D10	P91	42.7 %		IRAN	ITALY	----
		1975	D8	P74	36.6 %		UNKI	FINLA	----
		1980	D7	P71	37.2 %		PHILI	CHILE	----
V44	GDP SHARE OF SERVICES	1970	D6	P58	50.7 %		DOMI	CENTR	----
		1975	D9	P83	55.7 %		CHILE	MEXI	----
		1980	D8	P75	54.4 %		JAPAN	CHILE	----
V45	HOMICIDES P. MIL. POPULATION	------	----	----	----- -----		-------	-------	----
V46	SUICIDES P. MIL. POPULATION	------	----	----	----- -----		-------	-------	----
V47	IMPORT PARTNERS	1970	R1	USA	43.8 %		ISRA	JAPAN	----
		1970	R2	UNKI	19.2 %		ISRA	MALAY	----
		1970	R3	CANA	9.0 %		INDIA	-------	----
		1980	R1	USA	31.5 %		HONDU	JAPAN	----
		1980	R2	VENE	22.4 %		HONDU	NICA	----
		1980	R3	UNKI	6.7 %		DENMA	KUWAI	----
V48	EXPORT PARTNERS	1970	R1	USA	53.4 %		ISRA	JAPAN	----
		1970	R2	UNKI	16.5 %		ISRA	MAURA	----
		1970	R3	CANA	7.8 %		VENE	LAOS	----
		1980	R1	USA	37.4 %		HONDU	JAPAN	F136
		1980	R2	UNKI	19.4 %		DENMA	SWEDN	F136
		1980	R3	NORWY	10.9 %		-------	SWEDN	F136
V49	PATENT SUPPLIERS	1972	R1	USA	39		ITALY	JAPAN	----
		1972	R2	UNKI	10		IRE	JORDA	----
		1972	R3	GFR	5		INDIA	JORDA	----
		1979	R1	USA	31		ITALY	JAPAN	----
		1979	R2	UNKI	12		IRE	KENYA	----
		1979	R3	SWITZ	5		GFR	KENYA	----

V50	PROVENANCE OF FOREIGN FIRMS	1980	R1	USA	51.4	%	ITALY	JAPAN	----
		1980	R2	UNKI	35.6	%	ITALY	JAPAN	----
		1980	R3	CANA	8.9	%	IRE	TRITO	----
V51	FILM SUPPLIERS	------	----	----	-----	-----	-------	-------	----

JAPAN (JAPAN)

V1	INCOME PER CAPITA	1970	D8	P80	6297	$/CAP	SAUDI	AURIA	----
		1975	D8	P78	7387	$/CAP	ITALY	NEWZ	----
		1980	D8	P80	9063	$/CAP	UNKI	AURIA	----
V2	TELEPHONES P. TSD. POPULATION	1970	D9	P87	193	1/TSD CAP	AURIA	BELGI	----
		1975	D9	P89	356	1/TSD CAP	NORWY	UNKI	----
		1980	D9	P87	460	1/TSD CAP	FRANC	GFR	----
V3	INFANT MORTALITY RATE	1980	D1	P2	7.5	1/TSD	SWEDN	FINLA	----
V4	PHYSICIANS P. MIL. POPULATION	1970	D8	P74	1123	1/MIL	URU	NEWZ	----
		1975	D8	P69	1174	1/MIL	KUWAI	PORTU	----
		1981	D7	P65	1314	1/MIL	IRE	LIBYA	----
V5	ADULT LITERACY	------	----	----	-----	-----	-------	-------	----
V6	DURATION OF SCHOOLING	1970	D10	P92	11.0	YR	FRANC	BELGI	----
		1975	D10	P95	11.4	YR	FINLA	NORWY	----
		1980	D10	P96	11.6	YR	SPAIN	NORWY	----
V7	STUDENT ENROLLMENT RATIO	1970	D9	P88	17.0	%	ITALY	NEWZ	----
		1975	D9	P90	24.6	%	GFR	ITALY	----
		1980	D10	P95	30.9	%	GDR	FINLA	----
V8	SHARE OF AGRICULTURAL LABOR	1970	D4	P36	19.2	%	HUNGA	LEBA	----
		1975	D3	P33	13.8	%	TRITO	FINLA	----
		1980	D4	P34	10.9	%	ITALY	JORDA	----
V9	SHARE OF INDUSTRIAL LABOR	1970	D7	P63	35.6	%	LEBA	USA	----
		1975	D7	P65	34.5	%	ISRA	FINLA	----
		1980	D8	P74	36.5	%	CHILE	GFR	----
V10	SHARE OF SERVICE LABOR	1970	D9	P81	38.4	%	SWEDN	SWITZ	----
		1975	D9	P86	43.4	%	NETH	CANA	----
		1980	D10	P90	44.1	%	KUWAI	SINGA	----
V11	SHARE OF ACADEMIC LABOR	1970	D5	P51	6.8	%	SPAIN	PANA	----
		1975	D7	P63	8.4	%	COSTA	VENE	----
		1980	D5	P46	8.6	%	COSTA	SINGA	----
V12	SHARE OF SELF-EMPLOYED LABOR	1975	D3	P33	17.6	%	FINLA	COSTA	----
		1980	D4	P39	17.1	%	YUGO	IRE	----
V13	MILITARY EXPENDITURES	1970	D9	P90	5.125	TSD MIL $	CANA	ITALY	----
		1975	D10	P95	7.583	TSD MIL $	ITALY	FRANC	----
		1980	D10	P94	9.951	TSD MIL $	ITALY	SAUDI	----

V14 MILITARY MANPOWER	1970	D9	P81	236	TSD CAP	PORTU	IRAN	F1
	1975	D9	P81	237	TSD CAP	SYRIA	INDO	F1
V15 MEN AT AGE 20 - 30	1970	D10	P95	9891	TSD CAP	INDO	USA	----
	1975	D10	P96	9990	TSD CAP	BRAZI	USSR	----
	1980	D10	P93	8490	TSD CAP	BANGL	BRAZI	----
V16 POPULATION	1970	D10	P95	104.35	MIL CAP	BRAZI	INDO	----
	1975	D10	P96	111.57	MIL CAP	BRAZI	INDO	----
	1980	D10	P95	116.81	MIL CAP	BANGL	BRAZI	----
V17 GROSS DOMESTIC PRODUCT	1970	D10	P98	657.090	TSD MIL $	GFR	USA	----
	1975	D10	P98	824.201	TSD MIL $	GFR	USA	----
	1980	D10	P98	1058.597	TSD MIL $	GFR	USA	----
V18 SHARE IN WORLD IMPORTS	1970	D10	P96	56.883	1/TSD	ITALY	FRANC	F39
	1975	D10	P98	63.677	1/TSD	FRANC	GFR	F30
	1980	D10	P98	68.512	1/TSD	FRANC	GFR	F30
V19 SHARE IN WORLD EXPORTS	1970	D10	P97	61.590	1/TSD	FRANC	UNKI	F39
	1975	D10	P98	63.727	1/TSD	FRANC	GFR	F30
	1980	D10	P98	65.038	1/TSD	FRANC	GFR	F30
V20 GDP SHARE OF IMPORTS	1970	D1	P9	9.3	%	BURMA	ETHIA	F39
	1975	D2	P13	11.6	%	COLO	PARA	F30
	1980	D2	P15	13.5	%	TURKY	ZAIRE	F30
V21 GDP SHARE OF EXPORTS	1970	D2	P18	9.5	%	AFGHA	KORSO	F39
	1975	D3	P26	11.2	%	COLO	AFGHA	F30
	1980	D3	P28	12.5	%	COLO	MADA	F30
V22 EXPORT PARTNER CONCENTRATION	1970	D6	P55	31.1	%	CAME	MALI	----
	1975	D4	P31	20.2	%	SAUDI	USA	----
	1980	D5	P47	24.4	%	MALI	AULIA	----
V23 TOTAL DEBT AS % OF GDP	------	----	----	----- -----		-------	-------	----
V24 SHARE OF NEW FOREIGN PATENTS	1970	D1	P11	31	%	GDR	BULGA	----
	1975	D1	P3	21	%	USSR	GREC	----
	1980	D1	P3	18	%	USSR	CZECH	----
V25 FOREIGN PROPERTY AS % OF GDP	------	----	----	----- -----		-------	-------	----
V26 GNP SHARE OF DEVELOPMENT AID	1970	D5	P45	0.23	%	NEWZ	GFR	----
	1975	D4	P31	0.23	%	AURIA	USA	----
	1980	D4	P38	0.32	%	USA	NEWZ	----
V27 SHARE IN NOBEL PRIZE WINNERS	1970-79	D5	P45	0.0	%	JAMAI	JORDA	----
V28 GDP SHARE OF MANUFACTURING	1970	D10	P99	35.9	%	AURIA	-------	----
	1975	D10	P97	29.9	%	AURIA	ARGE	----
	1980	D10	P97	30.3	%	SINGA	PORTU	----
V29 EXPORT SHARE OF MANUFACTURES	------	----	----	----- -----		-------	-------	----
V30 LACK OF CIVIL LIBERTIES	1975	D1	P7	1		GFR	NETH	----
	1980	D1	P7	1		IRE	NETH	----
V31 LACK OF POLITICAL RIGHTS	1975	D2	P20	2		ISRA	LEBA	----
	1980	D3	P21	2		JAMAI	NIGRA	----

V32	RIOTS	1970-74	D8	P78	9		ISRA	NIGRA	----
		1975-79	D8	P75	7		ETHIA	SRILA	----
V33	PROTEST DEMONSTRATIONS	1970-74	D9	P85	27		AULIA	PHILI	----
		1975-79	D8	P74	12		AULIA	MEXI	----
V34	POLITICAL STRIKES	1970-74	D9	P81	4		COLO	PERU	----
		1975-79	D8	P73	2		COSTA	KENYA	----
V35	MEMBER OF THE NONALIGNED MMT.	1970	----	----	0		IVORY	KORNO	----
		1976	----	----	0		ITALY	KORSO	----
		1981	----	----	0		ITALY	KORSO	----
V36	MEMBER OF THE OPEC	1970	----	----	0		JAMAI	JORDA	----
		1975	----	----	0		JAMAI	JORDA	----
		1980	----	----	0		JAMAI	JORDA	----
V37	MEMBER OF THE OECD	1970	----	----	1		ITALY	NETH	----
		1975	----	----	1		ITALY	NETH	----
		1980	----	----	1		ITALY	NETH	----
V38	MEMBER OF THE CMEA	1970	----	----	0		JAMAI	JORDA	----
		1975	----	----	0		JAMAI	JORDA	----
		1980	----	----	0		JAMAI	JORDA	----
V39	MEMBER OF THE WTO	1970	----	----	0		JAMAI	JORDA	----
		1975	----	----	0		JAMAI	JORDA	----
		1980	----	----	0		JAMAI	JORDA	----
V40	MEMBER OF THE NATO	1970	----	----	0		JAMAI	JORDA	----
		1975	----	----	0		JAMAI	JORDA	----
		1980	----	----	0		JAMAI	JORDA	----
V41	GDP SHARE OF INVESTMENTS	1970	D10	P99	39.0 %		SINGA	-------	----
		1975	D9	P90	32.8 %		FINLA	EGYPT	----
		1980	D9	P90	32.7 %		IRAQ	EGYPT	----
V42	GDP SHARE OF AGRICULTURE	1970	D2	P15	6.1 %		AULIA	NORWY	----
		1975	D2	P18	5.5 %		AULIA	NORWY	----
		1980	D2	P14	3.8 %		NETH	CANA	----
V43	GDP SHARE OF INDUSTRY	1970	D10	P95	46.6 %		AURIA	GFR	----
		1975	D9	P83	42.1 %		ZAMBI	ITALY	----
		1980	D9	P85	42.9 %		ITALY	YUGO	----
V44	GDP SHARE OF SERVICES	1970	D5	P47	47.3 %		PARA	ARGE	----
		1975	D8	P75	52.4 %		COSTA	CONGO	----
		1980	D8	P73	53.3 %		ARGE	JAMAI	----
V45	HOMICIDES P. MIL. POPULATION	1970	D4	P40	13.3	1/MIL CAP	NEWZ	GFR	F148
		1975	D5	P42	13.0	1/MIL CAP	ITALY	CZECH	F148
		1980	D2	P19	9.5	1/MIL CAP	SWITZ	UNKI	----
V46	SUICIDES P. MIL. POPULATION	1970	D8	P73	150.7	1/MIL CAP	YUGO	FRANC	----
		1975	D8	P76	179.0	1/MIL CAP	CUBA	SWEDN	----
		1980	D7	P64	175.9	1/MIL CAP	YUGO	FRANC	----

V47 IMPORT PARTNERS	1970	R1	USA	29.5	%	JAMAI	LAOS	----
	1970	R2	AULIA	8.0	%	-------	NEWZ	----
	1970	R3	IRAN	5.3	%	YESO	-------	----
	1980	R1	USA	17.5	%	JAMAI	MEXI	----
	1980	R2	SAUDI	14.0	%	YENO	PANA	----
	1980	R3	INDO	9.4	%	-------	-------	----
V48 EXPORT PARTNERS	1970	R1	USA	31.1	%	JAMAI	KORSO	----
	1970	R2	KORSO	4.2	%	-------	-------	----
	1970	R3	AULIA	3.0	%	-------	-------	----
	1980	R1	USA	24.4	%	JAMAI	KORSO	----
	1980	R2	GFR	4.4	%	IRE	MOROC	----
	1980	R3	KORSO	4.1	%	-------	KUWAI	----
V49 PATENT SUPPLIERS	1970	R1	USA	4774		JAMAI	JORDA	----
	1970	R2	GFR	1572		ITALY	KORSO	----
	1970	R3	UNKI	772		GFR	KAMPU	----
	1980	R1	USA	3968		JAMAI	KENYA	----
	1980	R2	GFR	1336		ITALY	MEXI	----
	1980	R3	UNKI	495		ISRA	PAKI	----
V50 PROVENANCE OF FOREIGN FIRMS	1980	R1	USA	64.7	%	JAMAI	KUWAI	----
	1980	R2	UNKI	8.1	%	JAMAI	KUWAI	----
	1980	R3	FINLA	6.5	%	ITALY	-------	----
V51 FILM SUPPLIERS	1980	R1	USA	141		ITALY	KORSO	F120
	1980	R2	FRANC	25		ITALY	MOZAM	F120
	1980	R3	ITALY	11		IRE	KUWAI	F120

JORDAN (JORDA)

V1 INCOME PER CAPITA	------	----	----	----- -----		-------	-------	----
V2 TELEPHONES P. TSD. POPULATION	1970	D5	P49	14	1/TSD CAP	NICA	MONGO	----
	1973	D5	----	16	1/TSD CAP	ELSA	IRAQ	----
V3 INFANT MORTALITY RATE	------	----	----	----- -----		-------	-------	----
V4 PHYSICIANS P. MIL. POPULATION	------	----	----	----- -----		-------	-------	----
V5 ADULT LITERACY	1979	D6	P58	65.4	%	ZAIRE	CHINA	----
V6 DURATION OF SCHOOLING	1980	D9	P81	10.9	YR	GREC	SWEDN	F17
V7 STUDENT ENROLLMENT RATIO	1980	D9	P88	26.6	%	NEWZ	BELGI	F17
V8 SHARE OF AGRICULTURAL LABOR	1979	D4	P36	11.5	%	JAPAN	NEWZ	----
V9 SHARE OF INDUSTRIAL LABOR	1979	D10	P98	53.8	%	HUNGA	-------	----
V10 SHARE OF SERVICE LABOR	1979	D4	P25	22.3	%	POLA	PARA	----

V11	SHARE OF ACADEMIC LABOR	1979	D8	P68	12.5 %		AURIA	ITALY	----
V12	SHARE OF SELF-EMPLOYED LABOR	------	----	----	----- -----	-------	-------	----
V13	MILITARY EXPENDITURES	1970	D6	P51	0.352 TSD MIL $	NEWZ	HUNGA	F4
		1975	D5	P46	0.318 TSD MIL $	IRE	NEWZ	----
		1980	D5	P48	0.439 TSD MIL $	NEWZ	ZIMBA	----
V14	MILITARY MANPOWER	1970	D6	P58	70 TSD CAP	CHILE	SWEDN	----
		1975	D6	P56	60 TSD CAP	VENE	KAMPU	----
		1980	D7	P61	65 TSD CAP	COLO	SUDAN	----
V15	MEN AT AGE 20 - 30	1971	D1	P10	179 TSD CAP	SINGA	PARA	F201
V16	POPULATION	1970	D2	P15	2.30 MIL CAP	ALBA	PARA	F172
		1975	D2	P17	2.70 MIL CAP	PARA	PAPUA	F172
		1980	D2	P17	2.92 MIL CAP	URU	LIBYA	F181
V17	GROSS DOMESTIC PRODUCT	1970	D2	P14	1.643 TSD MIL $	HONDU	NEPAL	F17
		1975	D2	P13	1.748 TSD MIL $	NIGER	YENO	F17
		1980	D3	P25	3.165 TSD MIL $	ELSA	COSTA	F17
V18	SHARE IN WORLD IMPORTS	1970	D3	P26	0.554 1/TSD	UGADA	SENE	----
		1975	D4	P34	0.801 1/TSD	COSTA	GUATE	----
		1980	D5	P46	1.167 1/TSD	OMAN	KENYA	----
V19	SHARE IN WORLD EXPORTS	1970	D2	P13	0.108 1/TSD	MALI	KAMPU	----
		1975	D2	P16	0.175 1/TSD	MALAW	BURMA	----
		1980	D3	P26	0.287 1/TSD	NIGER	LIBE	----
V20	GDP SHARE OF IMPORTS	------	----	----	----- -----	-------	-------	----
V21	GDP SHARE OF EXPORTS	------	----	----	----- -----	-------	-------	----
V22	EXPORT PARTNER CONCENTRATION	1970	D2	P19	18.7 %	NORWY	DENMA	----
		1975	D1	P9	13.6 %	USSR	SPAIN	----
		1980	D6	P51	26.0 %	BOLI	KORSO	----
V23	TOTAL DEBT AS % OF GDP	------	----	----	----- -----	-------	-------	----
V24	SHARE OF NEW FOREIGN PATENTS	1971	D9	P90	100 %	HAITI	KENYA	----
		1976	D10	P92	100 %	JAMAI	KENYA	----
V25	FOREIGN PROPERTY AS % OF GDP	------	----	----	----- -----	-------	-------	----
V26	GNP SHARE OF DEVELOPMENT AID	------	----	----	----- -----	-------	-------	----
V27	SHARE IN NOBEL PRIZE WINNERS	1970-79	D5	P45	0.0 %	JAPAN	KAMPU	----
V28	GDP SHARE OF MANUFACTURING	1971	D2	P18	8.5 %	ZAIRE	ETHIA	F18
		1975	D4	P39	11.2 %	ETHIA	KENYA	F18
		1980	D6	P52	14.2 %	TUNIS	ELSA	F18
V29	EXPORT SHARE OF MANUFACTURES	------	----	----	----- -----	-------	-------	----
V30	LACK OF CIVIL LIBERTIES	1975	D8	P74	6	IVORY	KAMPU	----
		1980	D8	P74	6	IRAN	LIBYA	----
V31	LACK OF POLITICAL RIGHTS	1975	D7	P63	6	IVORY	KAMPU	----
		1980	D7	P67	6	IVORY	KUWAI	----

V32	RIOTS	1970-74	D9	P87	19		USSR	PHILI	F222
		1975-79	D2	P20	0		IVORY	KORNO	F222
V33	PROTEST DEMONSTRATIONS	1970-74	D4	P37	1		HUNGA	KENYA	F222
		1975-79	D2	P13	0		IVORY	LESO	F222
V34	POLITICAL STRIKES	1970-74	D7	P64	1		IVORY	LIBE	F222
		1975-79	D3	P29	0		IVORY	KAMPU	F222
V35	MEMBER OF THE NONALIGNED MMT.	1970	----	----	1		JAMAI	KAMPU	----
		1976	----	----	1		JAMAI	KAMPU	----
		1981	----	----	1		JAMAI	KAMPU	----
V36	MEMBER OF THE OPEC	1970	----	----	0		JAPAN	KAMPU	----
		1975	----	----	0		JAPAN	KAMPU	----
		1980	----	----	0		JAPAN	KAMPU	----
V37	MEMBER OF THE OECD	1970	----	----	0		JAMAI	KAMPU	----
		1975	----	----	0		JAMAI	KAMPU	----
		1980	----	----	0		JAMAI	KAMPU	----
V38	MEMBER OF THE CMEA	1970	----	----	0		JAPAN	KAMPU	----
		1975	----	----	0		JAPAN	KAMPU	----
		1980	----	----	0		JAPAN	KAMPU	----
V39	MEMBER OF THE WTO	1970	----	----	0		JAPAN	KAMPU	----
		1975	----	----	0		JAPAN	KAMPU	----
		1980	----	----	0		JAPAN	KAMPU	----
V40	MEMBER OF THE NATO	1970	----	----	0		JAPAN	KAMPU	----
		1975	----	----	0		JAPAN	KAMPU	----
		1980	----	----	0		JAPAN	KAMPU	----
V41	GDP SHARE OF INVESTMENTS	1971	D5	P45	18.9 %		IRAN	SRILA	F17
		1975	D9	P86	31.5 %		PHILI	ZAIRE	F17
		1980	D10	P98	41.0 %		ALGER	YENO	F17
V42	GDP SHARE OF AGRICULTURE	1971	D4	P35	14.4 %		IRE	PANA	F18
		1975	D3	P29	9.5 %		SPAIN	IRAN	F18
		1980	D3	P28	7.7 %		IRAQ	FINLA	F18
V43	GDP SHARE OF INDUSTRY	1971	D2	P15	15.7 %		CENTR	SOMA	F18
		1975	D4	P33	24.2 %		SIERA	SYRIA	F18
		1980	D5	P43	29.6 %		BOLI	SRILA	F18
V44	GDP SHARE OF SERVICES	1971	D10	P99	69.9 %		SINGA	-------	F18
		1975	D10	P98	66.3 %		PANA	DENMA	F18
		1980	D10	P93	62.7 %		CANA	USA	F18
V45	HOMICIDES P. MIL. POPULATION	------	----	----	----- -----		-------	-------	----
V46	SUICIDES P. MIL. POPULATION	------	----	----	----- -----		-------	-------	----
V47	IMPORT PARTNERS	1970	R1	UNKI	13.4 %		IRE	KENYA	----
		1970	R2	USA	11.2 %		IRAN	KORSO	----
		1970	R3	GFR	9.0 %		ISRA	KAMPU	----
		1980	R1	SAUDI	17.0 %		-------	KENYA	----
		1980	R2	GFR	9.9 %		IRAQ	LIBYA	----
		1980	R3	USA	8.6 %		ITALY	NETH	----

V48	EXPORT PARTNERS	1970	R1	LEBA	18.7	%	-------	SYRIA	----
		1970	R2	SAUDI	14.2	%	SOMA	-------	----
		1970	R3	SYRIA	12.9	%	-------	LEBA	----
		1980	R1	SAUDI	26.0	%	-------	SOMA	----
		1980	R2	IRAQ	18.9	%	-------	-------	----
		1980	R3	SYRIA	9.5	%	-------	-------	----
V49	PATENT SUPPLIERS	1971	R1	USA	21		JAPAN	KAMPU	----
		1971	R2	UNKI	5		JAMAI	MALAY	----
		1971	R3	GFR	3		JAMAI	KENYA	----
V50	PROVENANCE OF FOREIGN FIRMS	-------	----	----	-----	-----	-------	-------	----
V51	FILM SUPPLIERS	1980	R1	ITALY	260		-------	ARGE	F117
		1980	R2	INDIA	100		ISRA	KUWAI	F117
		1980	R3	USA	80		TANZA	MOZAM	F117

KAMPUCHEA [4] (KAMPU)

V1	INCOME PER CAPITA	-------	----	----	-----	-----	-------	-------	----
V2	TELEPHONES P. TSD. POPULATION	1975	D8	P73	112	1/TSD CAP	HUNGA	PORTU	----
V3	INFANT MORTALITY RATE	1980	D10	P100	260.0	1/TSD	SIERA	-------	F5
V4	PHYSICIANS P. MIL. POPULATION	1971	D3	P22	60	1/MIL	SIERA	AFGHA	----
V5	ADULT LITERACY	-------	----	----	-----	-----	-------	-------	----
V6	DURATION OF SCHOOLING	-------	----	----	-----	-----	-------	-------	----
V7	STUDENT ENROLLMENT RATIO	1970	D4	P33	1.5	%	SUDAN	MOROC	----
V8	SHARE OF AGRICULTURAL LABOR	-------	----	----	-----	-----	-------	-------	----
V9	SHARE OF INDUSTRIAL LABOR	-------	----	----	-----	-----	-------	-------	----
V10	SHARE OF SERVICE LABOR	-------	----	----	-----	-----	-------	-------	----
V11	SHARE OF ACADEMIC LABOR	-------	----	----	-----	-----	-------	-------	----
V12	SHARE OF SELF-EMPLOYED LABOR	-------	----	----	-----	-----	-------	-------	----
V13	MILITARY EXPENDITURES	-------	----	----	-----	-----	-------	-------	----
V14	MILITARY MANPOWER	1970	D7	P64	85	TSD CAP	PERU	AULIA	----
		1975	D6	P57	62	TSD CAP	JORDA	AULIA	----
		1980	D5	P45	35	TSD CAP	ECUA	ZIMBA	----

---

[4] Also known as Cambodia.

V15	MEN AT AGE 20 - 30	------	----	----	----- -----		-------	-------	----
V16	POPULATION	1975	D5	P47	7.10 MIL CAP	ECUA	SAUDI	----
		1980	D5	P42	6.40 MIL CAP	TUNIS	MALI	----
V17	GROSS DOMESTIC PRODUCT	------	----	----	----- -----	-------	-------	----
V18	SHARE IN WORLD IMPORTS	1970	D1	P8	0.157 1/TSD	HAITI	MAURA	----
V19	SHARE IN WORLD EXPORTS	1970	D2	P14	0.121 1/TSD	JORDA	HAITI	----
V20	GDP SHARE OF IMPORTS	------	----	----	----- -----	-------	-------	----
V21	GDP SHARE OF EXPORTS	------	----	----	----- -----	-------	-------	----
V22	EXPORT PARTNER CONCENTRATION	1970	D1	P6	13.8 %	URU	INDIA	----
V23	TOTAL DEBT AS % OF GDP	------	----	----	----- -----	-------	-------	----
V24	SHARE OF NEW FOREIGN PATENTS	------	----	----	----- -----	-------	-------	----
V25	FOREIGN PROPERTY AS % OF GDP	------	----	----	----- -----	-------	-------	----
V26	GNP SHARE OF DEVELOPMENT AID	------	----	----	----- -----	-------	-------	----
V27	SHARE IN NOBEL PRIZE WINNERS	1970-79	D5	P45	0.0 %	JORDA	KENYA	----
V28	GDP SHARE OF MANUFACTURING	------	----	----	----- -----	-------	-------	----
V29	EXPORT SHARE OF MANUFACTURES	1970	D3	P21	1.6 %	ETHIA	CHAD	----
V30	LACK OF CIVIL LIBERTIES	1975	D8	P74	6	JORDA	KORSO	----
		1980	D10	P92	7	IRAQ	KORNO	----
V31	LACK OF POLITICAL RIGHTS	1975	D7	P63	6	JORDA	LIBE	----
		1980	D9	P90	7	IRAQ	KORNO	----
V32	RIOTS	1970-74	D9	P82	12	GFR	MEXI	----
		1975-79	D5	P45	1	HONDU	LESO	----
V33	PROTEST DEMONSTRATIONS	1970-74	D8	P78	13	URU	SWEDN	----
		1975-79	D4	P32	1	IRAQ	KORNO	----
V34	POLITICAL STRIKES	1970-74	D8	P78	3	EGYPT	NIGRA	----
		1975-79	D3	P29	0	JORDA	KORNO	----
V35	MEMBER OF THE NONALIGNED MMT.	1970	----	----	1	JORDA	KENYA	----
		1976	----	----	1	JORDA	KENYA	----
		1981	----	----	1	JORDA	KENYA	----
V36	MEMBER OF THE OPEC	1970	----	----	0	JORDA	KENYA	----
		1975	----	----	0	JORDA	KENYA	----
		1980	----	----	0	JORDA	KENYA	----
V37	MEMBER OF THE OECD	1970	----	----	0	JORDA	KENYA	----
		1975	----	----	0	JORDA	KENYA	----
		1980	----	----	0	JORDA	KENYA	----
V38	MEMBER OF THE CMEA	1970	----	----	0	JORDA	KENYA	----
		1975	----	----	0	JORDA	KENYA	----
		1980	----	----	0	JORDA	KENYA	----

V39	MEMBER OF THE WTO	1970	----	----	0		JORDA	KENYA	----
		1975	----	----	0		JORDA	KENYA	----
		1980	----	----	0		JORDA	KENYA	----
V40	MEMBER OF THE NATO	1970	----	----	0		JORDA	KENYA	----
		1975	----	----	0		JORDA	KENYA	----
		1980	----	----	0		JORDA	KENYA	----
V41	GDP SHARE OF INVESTMENTS	------	----	----	----- -----		-------	-------	----
V42	GDP SHARE OF AGRICULTURE	------	----	----	----- -----		-------	-------	----
V43	GDP SHARE OF INDUSTRY	------	----	----	----- -----		-------	-------	----
V44	GDP SHARE OF SERVICES	------	----	----	----- -----		-------	-------	----
V45	HOMICIDES P. MIL. POPULATION	------	----	----	----- -----		-------	-------	----
V46	SUICIDES P. MIL. POPULATION	------	----	----	----- -----		-------	-------	----
V47	IMPORT PARTNERS	1970	R1	JAPAN	26.1 %		INDO	KORSO	----
		1970	R2	FRANC	23.8 %		ITALY	SWITZ	----
		1970	R3	GFR	7.4 %		JORDA	KORSO	----
V48	EXPORT PARTNERS	1970	R1	VINO	13.8 %		-------	-------	----
		1970	R2	SENE	10.6 %		-------	MALI	----
		1970	R3	CZECH	9.5 %		HUNGA	POLA	----
V49	PATENT SUPPLIERS	1971	R1	USA	5		JORDA	KORSO	----
		1971	R2	SWITZ	4		HONDU	LEBA	----
		1971	R3	UNKI	3		JAPAN	PORTU	----
V50	PROVENANCE OF FOREIGN FIRMS	------	----	----	----- -----		-------	-------	----
V51	FILM SUPPLIERS	------	----	----	----- -----		-------	-------	----

KENYA (KENYA)

V1	INCOME PER CAPITA	1970	D2	P17	328 $/CAP		INDO	SIERA	----
		1975	D3	P25	372 $/CAP		TOGO	GHANA	----
		1980	D3	P21	397 $/CAP		GHANA	TOGO	----
V2	TELEPHONES P. TSD. POPULATION	1970	D4	P34	7 1/TSD CAP		IVORY	PHILI	----
		1975	D4	P33	9 1/TSD CAP		IVORY	GUATE	----
		1980	D3	P30	12 1/TSD CAP		ZAMBI	MOROC	----
V3	INFANT MORTALITY RATE	1980	D6	P51	92.0 1/TSD		IRAQ	HONDU	F5
V4	PHYSICIANS P. MIL. POPULATION	1973	D2	----	61 1/MIL		INDO	MAURA	----
V5	ADULT LITERACY	1980	D5	P46	47.1 %		TUNIS	RWAN	F21

V6	DURATION OF SCHOOLING	1970	D3	P30	5.1	YR	RWAN	TOGO	----
		1975	D6	P53	8.2	YR	VENE	BOLI	----
		1980	D6	P52	9.2	YR	COLO	MALAY	----
V7	STUDENT ENROLLMENT RATIO	1970	D3	P26	0.8	%	GHANA	IVORY	----
		1975	D2	P19	0.8	%	BENIN	LESO	----
		1980	D2	P15	0.9	%	CENTR	SOMA	----
V8	SHARE OF AGRICULTURAL LABOR	------	----	----	-----	-----	-------	-------	----
V9	SHARE OF INDUSTRIAL LABOR	------	----	----	-----	-----	-------	-------	----
V10	SHARE OF SERVICE LABOR	------	----	----	-----	-----	-------	-------	----
V11	SHARE OF ACADEMIC LABOR	------	----	----	-----	-----	-------	-------	----
V12	SHARE OF SELF-EMPLOYED LABOR	------	----	----	-----	-----	-------	-------	----
V13	MILITARY EXPENDITURES	1970	D3	P25	0.041	TSD MIL $	PARA	SENE	F62
		1975	D4	P35	0.085	TSD MIL $	DOMI	TUNIS	F62
		1980	D5	P42	0.252	TSD MIL $	TANZA	YENO	F62
V14	MILITARY MANPOWER	1970	D2	P19	7	TSD CAP	CHAD	SENE	----
		1975	D3	P22	9	TSD CAP	PANA	CAME	----
		1980	D3	P24	13	TSD CAP	KUWAI	NEWZ	----
V15	MEN AT AGE 20 - 30	1969	D6	P57	778	TSD CAP	HUNGA	MOROC	----
V16	POPULATION	1970	D7	P62	11.23	MIL CAP	MALAY	NEPAL	----
		1975	D7	P64	13.41	MIL CAP	VENE	SRILA	----
		1980	D7	P68	16.67	MIL CAP	AFGHA	GDR	----
V17	GROSS DOMESTIC PRODUCT	1970	D4	P35	3.685	TSD MIL $	DOMI	BURMA	----
		1975	D4	P37	4.987	TSD MIL $	CAME	DOMI	----
		1980	D4	P40	6.619	TSD MIL $	CAME	DOMI	----
V18	SHARE IN WORLD IMPORTS	1970	D5	P45	1.331	1/TSD	GHANA	ZAMBI	F30
		1975	D5	P44	1.078	1/TSD	PANA	SUDAN	F30
		1980	D5	P47	1.262	1/TSD	JORDA	IVORY	F30
V19	SHARE IN WORLD EXPORTS	1970	D5	P43	0.972	1/TSD	SUDAN	JAMAI	F30
		1975	D5	P40	0.735	1/TSD	GUATE	JAMAI	F30
		1980	D5	P42	0.696	1/TSD	CAME	ZIMBA	F30
V20	GDP SHARE OF IMPORTS	1970	D9	P83	27.5	%	SIERA	DENMA	F30
		1975	D8	P72	30.5	%	TANZA	SENE	F30
		1980	D8	P80	36.5	%	SWITZ	MALAW	F30
V21	GDP SHARE OF EXPORTS	1970	D7	P63	18.9	%	NEWZ	CANA	F30
		1975	D6	P59	20.0	%	AURIA	ECUA	F30
		1980	D5	P50	19.6	%	ITALY	BOLI	F30
V22	EXPORT PARTNER CONCENTRATION	------	----	----	-----	-----	-------	-------	----
V23	TOTAL DEBT AS % OF GDP	1980	D7	P70	49.1	%	ECUA	PHILI	----
V24	SHARE OF NEW FOREIGN PATENTS	1970	D9	P90	100	%	JORDA	LAOS	----
		1975	D10	P92	100	%	JORDA	LAOS	----
		1980	D10	P94	100	%	GHANA	RWAN	----

V25	FOREIGN PROPERTY AS % OF GDP	1971	D7	P62	11.1 %	HAITI	COLO	----
		1975	D9	P87	20.2 %	GUINE	HONDU	----
		1978	D8	----	9.8 %	CHILE	SIERA	----
V26	GNP SHARE OF DEVELOPMENT AID	------	----	----	----- -----	-------	-------	----
V27	SHARE IN NOBEL PRIZE WINNERS	1970-79	D5	P45	0.0 %	KAMPU	KORNO	----
V28	GDP SHARE OF MANUFACTURING	1970	D4	P40	12.0 %	GHANA	PANA	F16
		1975	D5	P41	12.0 %	JORDA	RWAN	F16
		1980	D5	P47	13.2 %	MALAW	TRITO	F16
V29	EXPORT SHARE OF MANUFACTURES	1970	D6	P56	12.4 %	ARGE	TANZA	----
		1975	D6	P60	13.1 %	MOROC	SENE	----
V30	LACK OF CIVIL LIBERTIES	1975	D4	P39	4	EGYPT	LESO	----
		1980	D4	P38	4	GHANA	KUWAI	----
V31	LACK OF POLITICAL RIGHTS	1975	D5	P43	5	IRAN	KORSO	----
		1980	D5	P47	5	IRAN	LESO	----
V32	RIOTS	1970-74	D5	P43	1	HUNGA	MALAY	----
		1975-79	D6	P60	3	IRE	NETH	----
V33	PROTEST DEMONSTRATIONS	1970-74	D4	P37	1	JORDA	LIBYA	----
		1975-79	D5	P49	3	INDO	NORWY	----
V34	POLITICAL STRIKES	1970-74	D3	P29	0	JAMAI	KORNO	----
		1975-79	D8	P73	2	JAPAN	MALI	----
V35	MEMBER OF THE NONALIGNED MMT.	1970	----	----	1	KAMPU	LAOS	----
		1976	----	----	1	KAMPU	KORNO	----
		1981	----	----	1	KAMPU	KORNO	----
V36	MEMBER OF THE OPEC	1970	----	----	0	KAMPU	KORNO	----
		1975	----	----	0	KAMPU	KORNO	----
		1980	----	----	0	KAMPU	KORNO	----
V37	MEMBER OF THE OECD	1970	----	----	0	KAMPU	KORNO	----
		1975	----	----	0	KAMPU	KORNO	----
		1980	----	----	0	KAMPU	KORNO	----
V38	MEMBER OF THE CMEA	1970	----	----	0	KAMPU	KORNO	----
		1975	----	----	0	KAMPU	KORNO	----
		1980	----	----	0	KAMPU	KORNO	----
V39	MEMBER OF THE WTO	1970	----	----	0	KAMPU	KORNO	----
		1975	----	----	0	KAMPU	KORNO	----
		1980	----	----	0	KAMPU	KORNO	----
V40	MEMBER OF THE NATO	1970	----	----	0	KAMPU	KORNO	----
		1975	----	----	0	KAMPU	KORNO	----
		1980	----	----	0	KAMPU	KORNO	----
V41	GDP SHARE OF INVESTMENTS	1970	D8	P70	24.4 %	NEWZ	SPAIN	----
		1975	D4	P32	18.1 %	CHAD	UNKI	----
		1980	D9	P82	29.2 %	TRITO	NIGER	----
V42	GDP SHARE OF AGRICULTURE	1970	D8	P75	33.3 %	HONDU	CENTR	F16
		1975	D8	P74	34.2 %	CAME	CENTR	F16
		1980	D8	P74	32.5 %	SIERA	CHINA	F16

V43	GDP SHARE OF INDUSTRY	1970	D3	P27	19.8 %	NIGRA	SENE	F16
		1975	D3	P22	20.2 %	GUINE	UPVO	F16
		1980	D3	P23	21.8 %	PANA	RWAN	F16
V44	GDP SHARE OF SERVICES	1970	D5	P44	46.9 %	ZAIRE	PARA	F16
		1975	D5	P50	45.6 %	ZAMBI	TURKY	F16
		1980	D5	P45	45.7 %	HONDU	MADA	F16
V45	HOMICIDES P. MIL. POPULATION	------	----	----	----- -----	-------	-------	----
V46	SUICIDES P. MIL. POPULATION	------	----	----	----- -----	-------	-------	----
V47	IMPORT PARTNERS	1970	R1	UNKI	29.1 %	JORDA	MALAW	F124
		1970	R2	JAPAN	10.7 %	HAITI	PAKI	F124
		1970	R3	USA	8.4 %	IVORY	MALAY	F124
		1980	R1	SAUDI	17.5 %	JORDA	LIBE	F136
		1980	R2	UNKI	16.9 %	BENIN	MALAW	F136
		1980	R3	JAPAN	9.2 %	HONDU	LIBYA	F136
V48	EXPORT PARTNERS	------	----	----	----- -----	-------	-------	----
V49	PATENT SUPPLIERS	1971	R1	UNKI	36	IRAQ	MALAW	----
		1971	R2	USA	31	FINLA	MALAW	----
		1971	R3	GFR	22	JORDA	MOROC	----
		1979	R1	USA	28	JAPAN	MEXI	----
		1979	R2	UNKI	18	JAMAI	NEWZ	----
		1979	R3	SWITZ	16	JAMAI	MALAW	----
V50	PROVENANCE OF FOREIGN FIRMS	1980	R1	UNKI	75.6 %	IRE	MALAW	----
		1980	R2	USA	7.9 %	IVORY	KORSO	----
		1980	R3	GFR	3.8 %	IVORY	MADA	----
V51	FILM SUPPLIERS	------	----	----	----- -----	-------	-------	----

KOREA, NORTH (KORNO)

V1	INCOME PER CAPITA	------	----	----	----- -----	-------	-------	----
V2	TELEPHONES P. TSD. POPULATION	------	----	----	----- -----	-------	-------	----
V3	INFANT MORTALITY RATE	1980	D4	P36	36.7 1/TSD	PANA	URU	F5
V4	PHYSICIANS P. MIL. POPULATION	------	----	----	----- -----	-------	-------	----
V5	ADULT LITERACY	------	----	----	----- -----	-------	-------	----
V6	DURATION OF SCHOOLING	------	----	----	----- -----	-------	-------	----
V7	STUDENT ENROLLMENT RATIO	------	----	----	----- -----	-------	-------	----
V8	SHARE OF AGRICULTURAL LABOR	------	----	----	----- -----	-------	-------	----

V9	SHARE OF INDUSTRIAL LABOR	------	----	----	----- -----		-------	-------	----
V10	SHARE OF SERVICE LABOR	------	----	----	----- -----		-------	-------	----
V11	SHARE OF ACADEMIC LABOR	------	----	----	----- -----		-------	-------	----
V12	SHARE OF SELF-EMPLOYED LABOR	------	----	----	----- -----		-------	-------	----
V13	MILITARY EXPENDITURES	------	----	----	----- -----		-------	-------	----
V14	MILITARY MANPOWER	1970	D10	P91	438	TSD CAP	ITALY	VINO	F1
		1975	D9	P90	470	TSD CAP	BRAZI	GFR	F3
V15	MEN AT AGE 20 - 30	------	----	----	----- -----		-------	-------	----
V16	POPULATION	1970	D7	P68	13.89	MIL CAP	PERU	SUDAN	----
		1975	D8	P71	15.85	MIL CAP	SUDAN	ALGER	----
		1980	D7	P70	17.89	MIL CAP	PERU	TANZA	----
V17	GROSS DOMESTIC PRODUCT	------	----	----	----- -----		-------	-------	----
V18	SHARE IN WORLD IMPORTS	------	----	----	----- -----		-------	-------	----
V19	SHARE IN WORLD EXPORTS	------	----	----	----- -----		-------	-------	----
V20	GDP SHARE OF IMPORTS	------	----	----	----- -----		-------	-------	----
V21	GDP SHARE OF EXPORTS	------	----	----	----- -----		-------	-------	----
V22	EXPORT PARTNER CONCENTRATION	------	----	----	----- -----		-------	-------	----
V23	TOTAL DEBT AS % OF GDP	------	----	----	----- -----		-------	-------	----
V24	SHARE OF NEW FOREIGN PATENTS	------	----	----	----- -----		-------	-------	----
V25	FOREIGN PROPERTY AS % OF GDP	------	----	----	----- -----		-------	-------	----
V26	GNP SHARE OF DEVELOPMENT AID	------	----	----	----- -----		-------	-------	----
V27	SHARE IN NOBEL PRIZE WINNERS	1970-79	D5	P45	0.0	%	KENYA	KORSO	----
V28	GDP SHARE OF MANUFACTURING	------	----	----	----- -----		-------	-------	----
V29	EXPORT SHARE OF MANUFACTURES	------	----	----	----- -----		-------	-------	----
V30	LACK OF CIVIL LIBERTIES	1975	D10	P93	7		IRAQ	LIBYA	----
		1980	D10	P92	7		KAMPU	LAOS	----
V31	LACK OF POLITICAL RIGHTS	1975	D9	P88	7		IRAQ	LIBYA	----
		1980	D9	P90	7		KAMPU	LAOS	----
V32	RIOTS	1970-74	D2	P19	0		JAMAI	LAOS	----
		1975-79	D2	P20	0		JORDA	MALAW	----
V33	PROTEST DEMONSTRATIONS	1970-74	D2	P15	0		JAMAI	LIBE	----
		1975-79	D4	P32	1		KAMPU	LIBE	----
V34	POLITICAL STRIKES	1970-74	D3	P29	0		KENYA	LAOS	----
		1975-79	D3	P29	0		KAMPU	LAOS	----

V35 MEMBER OF THE NONALIGNED MMT.	1970	----	----	0		JAPAN	KORSO	----
	1976	----	----	1		KENYA	KUWAI	----
	1981	----	----	1		KENYA	KUWAI	----
V36 MEMBER OF THE OPEC	1970	----	----	0		KENYA	KORSO	----
	1975	----	----	0		KENYA	KORSO	----
	1980	----	----	0		KENYA	KORSO	----
V37 MEMBER OF THE OECD	1970	----	----	0		KENYA	KORSO	----
	1975	----	----	0		KENYA	KORSO	----
	1980	----	----	0		KENYA	KORSO	----
V38 MEMBER OF THE CMEA	1970	----	----	0		KENYA	KORSO	----
	1975	----	----	0		KENYA	KORSO	----
	1980	----	----	0		KENYA	KORSO	----
V39 MEMBER OF THE WTO	1970	----	----	0		KENYA	KORSO	----
	1975	----	----	0		KENYA	KORSO	----
	1980	----	----	0		KENYA	KORSO	----
V40 MEMBER OF THE NATO	1970	----	----	0		KENYA	KORSO	----
	1975	----	----	0		KENYA	KORSO	----
	1980	----	----	0		KENYA	KORSO	----
V41 GDP SHARE OF INVESTMENTS	------	----	----	----- -----		-------	-------	----
V42 GDP SHARE OF AGRICULTURE	------	----	----	----- -----		-------	-------	----
V43 GDP SHARE OF INDUSTRY	------	----	----	----- -----		-------	-------	----
V44 GDP SHARE OF SERVICES	------	----	----	----- -----		-------	-------	----
V45 HOMICIDES P. MIL. POPULATION	------	----	----	----- -----		-------	-------	----
V46 SUICIDES P. MIL. POPULATION	------	----	----	----- -----		-------	-------	----
V47 IMPORT PARTNERS	------	----	----	----- -----		-------	-------	----
V48 EXPORT PARTNERS	------	----	----	----- -----		-------	-------	----
V49 PATENT SUPPLIERS	------	----	----	----- -----		-------	-------	----
V50 PROVENANCE OF FOREIGN FIRMS	------	----	----	----- -----		-------	-------	----
V51 FILM SUPPLIERS	------	----	----	----- -----		-------	-------	----

KOREA, SOUTH (KORSO)

V1 INCOME PER CAPITA	1970	D5	P46	884 $/CAP	GUATE	COLO	----
	1975	D6	P52	1242 $/CAP	NICA	MALAY	----
	1980	D6	P56	1646 $/CAP	COSTA	MALAY	----

V2	TELEPHONES P. TSD. POPULATION	1970	D6	P57	21	1/TSD CAP	BRAZI	LIBYA	----
		1975	D6	P56	40	1/TSD CAP	CUBA	CHILE	----
		1979	D6	P58	77	1/TSD CAP	MEXI	USSR	----
V3	INFANT MORTALITY RATE	1980	D4	P34	34.0	1/TSD	MALAY	PANA	F5
V4	PHYSICIANS P. MIL. POPULATION	1977	D6	----	505	1/MIL	ECUA	COLO	----
		1981	D6	P58	694	1/MIL	COSTA	TRITO	----
V5	ADULT LITERACY	1970	D8	P73	87.6	%	GREC	ISRA	----
V6	DURATION OF SCHOOLING	1970	D7	P66	9.0	YR	PORTU	SINGA	----
		1975	D7	P70	9.7	YR	USSR	AURIA	----
		1980	D9	P84	11.0	YR	SWEDN	POLA	----
V7	STUDENT ENROLLMENT RATIO	1970	D7	P63	7.9	%	ECUA	PORTU	----
		1975	D7	P60	9.6	%	TURKY	DOMI	----
		1980	D7	P65	14.8	%	NICA	EGYPT	----
V8	SHARE OF AGRICULTURAL LABOR	1970	D8	P75	51.1	%	SYRIA	PARA	----
		1975	D7	P66	49.2	%	BOLI	ECUA	----
		1980	D7	P69	37.6	%	TUNIS	MALAY	----
V9	SHARE OF INDUSTRIAL LABOR	1970	D3	P26	21.8	%	MOROC	BRAZI	----
		1975	D4	P38	23.0	%	EGYPT	ECUA	----
		1980	D5	P38	28.1	%	MEXI	AFGHA	----
V10	SHARE OF SERVICE LABOR	1970	D5	P41	23.8	%	GREC	NICA	----
		1975	D5	P49	24.5	%	BULGA	EGYPT	----
		1980	D5	P41	29.7	%	PHILI	PERU	----
V11	SHARE OF ACADEMIC LABOR	1970	D2	P13	3.2	%	INDIA	DOMI	----
		1975	D3	P20	3.3	%	PAKI	GUATE	----
		1980	D3	P23	4.6	%	ZIMBA	PARA	----
V12	SHARE OF SELF-EMPLOYED LABOR	1970	D7	P75	34.8	%	VENE	BRAZI	----
		1975	D6	P48	30.8	%	TUNIS	MEXI	----
		1980	D8	P77	35.4	%	SYRIA	PHILI	----
V13	MILITARY EXPENDITURES	1970	D7	P67	1.064	TSD MIL $	PORTU	GREC	F4
		1975	D8	P76	1.989	TSD MIL $	SWITZ	GREC	----
		1980	D9	P85	3.734	TSD MIL $	BELGI	SWEDN	----
V14	MILITARY MANPOWER	1970	D10	P96	645	TSD CAP	FRANC	VISO	F1
		1975	D10	P95	630	TSD CAP	FRANC	VINO	F1
V15	MEN AT AGE 20 - 30	1970	D8	P77	2396	TSD CAP	IRAN	SPAIN	----
		1975	D9	P82	2884	TSD CAP	EGYPT	POLA	F22
		1980	D8	P78	3754	TSD CAP	POLA	TURKY	F184
V16	POPULATION	1970	D9	P82	32.24	MIL CAP	IRAN	POLA	----
		1975	D9	P83	35.28	MIL CAP	POLA	SPAIN	----
		1980	D9	P83	38.12	MIL CAP	SPAIN	IRAN	----
V17	GROSS DOMESTIC PRODUCT	1970	D7	P67	28.514	TSD MIL $	GREC	INDO	----
		1975	D8	P71	43.804	TSD MIL $	NORWY	INDO	----
		1980	D8	P74	62.750	TSD MIL $	TURKY	DENMA	----
V18	SHARE IN WORLD IMPORTS	1970	D8	P74	5.977	1/TSD	ROMA	INDIA	F51
		1975	D8	P76	8.003	1/TSD	HUNGA	CHINA	F51
		1980	D9	P84	10.868	1/TSD	DENMA	AULIA	F51

V19 SHARE IN WORLD EXPORTS	1970	D6	P56	2.662 1/TSD	ZAIRE	PORTU	----
	1975	D7	P69	5.799 1/TSD	ALGER	ROMA	----
	1980	D8	P78	8.770 1/TSD	AURIA	CHINA	----
V20 GDP SHARE OF IMPORTS	1970	D7	P68	22.6 %	CHAD	FINLA	F51
	1975	D8	P80	34.4 %	EGYPT	COSTA	F51
	1980	D8	P78	35.8 %	SENE	SWITZ	F51
V21 GDP SHARE OF EXPORTS	1970	D2	P18	9.5 %	JAPAN	URU	----
	1975	D7	P70	24.0 %	SWITZ	SWEDN	----
	1980	D8	P73	28.1 %	FINLA	MAURA	----
V22 EXPORT PARTNER CONCENTRATION	1970	D9	P83	46.8 %	NIGER	CENTR	F126
	1975	D7	P62	30.3 %	NIGRA	AULIA	F126
	1980	D6	P52	26.4 %	JORDA	COLO	F126
V23 TOTAL DEBT AS % OF GDP	1980	D7	P65	47.1 %	HUNGA	SRILA	----
V24 SHARE OF NEW FOREIGN PATENTS	1970	D1	P9	29 %	CZECH	GDR	----
	1975	D2	P15	52 %	GFR	FRANC	----
	1980	D5	P50	89 %	YUGO	NEWZ	----
V25 FOREIGN PROPERTY AS % OF GDP	1971	D2	P15	2.6 %	LESO	INDIA	----
	1975	D4	P38	4.5 %	SOMA	PARA	----
	1978	D4	----	3.0 %	RWAN	PORTU	----
V26 GNP SHARE OF DEVELOPMENT AID	------	----	----	----- -----	-------	-------	----
V27 SHARE IN NOBEL PRIZE WINNERS	1970-79	D5	P45	0.0 %	KORNO	LAOS	----
V28 GDP SHARE OF MANUFACTURING	1970	D8	P75	20.9 %	TRITO	PHILI	----
	1975	D10	P91	26.0 %	UNKI	SWEDN	----
	1980	D10	P94	28.0 %	AURIA	SINGA	----
V29 EXPORT SHARE OF MANUFACTURES	1970	D10	P94	74.9 %	ISRA	ITALY	----
	1975	D10	P96	76.8 %	ITALY	GFR	----
	1980	D10	P95	80.1 %	ITALY	ISRA	----
V30 LACK OF CIVIL LIBERTIES	1975	D8	P74	6	KAMPU	MALAW	----
	1980	D6	P52	5	IVORY	LESO	----
V31 LACK OF POLITICAL RIGHTS	1975	D5	P43	5	KENYA	LAOS	----
	1980	D4	P36	4	GHANA	LEBA	----
V32 RIOTS	1970-74	D10	P91	38	SOUAF	VISO	----
	1975-79	D9	P86	16	NEPAL	GREC	----
V33 PROTEST DEMONSTRATIONS	1970-74	D10	P94	66	ITALY	PORTU	----
	1975-79	D9	P90	38	PAKI	GREC	----
V34 POLITICAL STRIKES	1970-74	D9	P89	10	INDIA	ARGE	----
	1975-79	D8	P78	3	CANA	GREC	----
V35 MEMBER OF THE NONALIGNED MMT.	1970	----	----	0	KORNO	MADA	----
	1976	----	----	0	JAPAN	MEXI	----
	1981	----	----	0	JAPAN	MEXI	----
V36 MEMBER OF THE OPEC	1970	----	----	0	KORNO	LAOS	----
	1975	----	----	0	KORNO	LAOS	----
	1980	----	----	0	KORNO	LAOS	----

V37	MEMBER OF THE OECD	1970	----	----	0		KORNO	LAOS	----
		1975	----	----	0		KORNO	KUWAI	----
		1980	----	----	0		KORNO	KUWAI	----
V38	MEMBER OF THE CMEA	1970	----	----	0		KORNO	LAOS	----
		1975	----	----	0		KORNO	KUWAI	----
		1980	----	----	0		KORNO	KUWAI	----
V39	MEMBER OF THE WTO	1970	----	----	0		KORNO	LAOS	----
		1975	----	----	0		KORNO	KUWAI	----
		1980	----	----	0		KORNO	KUWAI	----
V40	MEMBER OF THE NATO	1970	----	----	0		KORNO	LAOS	----
		1975	----	----	0		KORNO	KUWAI	----
		1980	----	----	0		KORNO	KUWAI	----
V41	GDP SHARE OF INVESTMENTS	1970	D8	P79	26.9 %		THAI	AULIA	----
		1975	D8	P77	29.0 %		SYRIA	TUNIS	----
		1980	D9	P86	30.6 %		CHINA	HUNGA	----
V42	GDP SHARE OF AGRICULTURE	1970	D6	P58	26.9 %		LESO	IVORY	----
		1975	D6	P54	24.5 %		ELSA	LIBE	----
		1980	D5	P44	15.8 %		ZAMBI	TUNIS	----
V43	GDP SHARE OF INDUSTRY	1970	D6	P52	29.5 %		EGYPT	DENMA	----
		1975	D7	P64	33.8 %		INDO	ECUA	----
		1980	D9	P82	40.6 %		NORWY	NIGRA	----
V44	GDP SHARE OF SERVICES	1970	D4	P37	43.6 %		GFR	MALAY	----
		1975	D4	P35	41.7 %		PORTU	PAPUA	----
		1980	D4	P40	43.6 %		SRILA	PAKI	----
V45	HOMICIDES P. MIL. POPULATION	------	----	----	----- -----		-------	-------	----
V46	SUICIDES P. MIL. POPULATION	------	----	----	----- -----		-------	-------	----
V47	IMPORT PARTNERS	1970	R1	JAPAN	40.8 %		KAMPU	MALAY	F126
		1970	R2	USA	29.5 %		JORDA	LIBYA	F126
		1970	R3	GFR	3.4 %		KAMPU	MOROC	F126
		1980	R1	JAPAN	26.2 %		IRAQ	KUWAI	F126
		1980	R2	USA	21.9 %		IRE	KUWAI	F126
		1980	R3	SAUDI	14.7 %		INDO	PAKI	F126
V48	EXPORT PARTNERS	1970	R1	USA	46.8 %		JAPAN	LIBE	F126
		1970	R2	JAPAN	28.1 %		ECUA	MALAY	F126
		1970	R3	GFR	3.3 %		IVORY	MEXI	F126
		1980	R1	USA	26.4 %		JAPAN	LIBYA	F126
		1980	R2	JAPAN	17.3 %		ECUA	NIGER	F126
		1980	R3	SAUDI	5.4 %		SUDAN	-------	F126
V49	PATENT SUPPLIERS	1970	R1	USA	50		KAMPU	LAOS	----
		1970	R2	GFR	12		JAPAN	LAOS	----
		1970	R3	SWITZ	8		IRE	MALAY	----
		1980	R1	JAPAN	725		-------	USA	----
		1980	R2	USA	371		IRAN	MALAW	----
		1980	R3	GFR	117		IRE	MOROC	----

V50	PROVENANCE OF FOREIGN FIRMS	1980	R1	JAPAN	49.1 %	-------	INDO	----
		1980	R2	USA	43.5 %	KENYA	MADA	----
V51	FILM SUPPLIERS	1980	R1	USA	21	JAPAN	KUWAI	F119
		1980	R2	UNKI	6	IRE	NEWZ	F119
		1980	R3	FRANC	4	GREC	MAURA	F119

KUWAIT (KUWAI)

V1	INCOME PER CAPITA	1975	D10	P99	22334 $/CAP	SWITZ	-------	----
		1980	D10	P98	19882 $/CAP	SWITZ	UNARE	----
V2	TELEPHONES P. TSD. POPULATION	1975	D8	P75	130 1/TSD CAP	PORTU	IRE	----
		1980	D8	P72	159 1/TSD CAP	BULGA	IRE	----
V3	INFANT MORTALITY RATE	1980	D3	P28	27.7 1/TSD	TRITO	USSR	----
V4	PHYSICIANS P. MIL. POPULATION	1975	D8	P68	1078 1/MIL	VENE	JAPAN	----
		1980	D8	P72	1704 1/MIL	NEWZ	POLA	----
V5	ADULT LITERACY	1980	D7	P66	67.5 %	INDO	ZIMBA	----
V6	DURATION OF SCHOOLING	1975	D7	P64	9.2 YR	MEXI	PERU	----
		1980	D8	P75	10.6 YR	IRE	YUGO	----
V7	STUDENT ENROLLMENT RATIO	1975	D6	P57	9.0 %	IRAQ	SINGA	----
		1980	D7	P60	12.0 %	BRAZI	HUNGA	----
V8	SHARE OF AGRICULTURAL LABOR	1975	D1	P3	2.6 %	-------	SINGA	----
		1980	D1	P5	2.0 %	SINGA	USA	----
V9	SHARE OF INDUSTRIAL LABOR	1975	D8	P71	35.4 %	IRE	SWEDN	----
		1980	D9	P81	38.1 %	AURIA	SYRIA	----
V10	SHARE OF SERVICE LABOR	1975	D10	P92	48.0 %	CANA	SINGA	----
		1980	D9	P88	43.7 %	GFR	JAPAN	----
V11	SHARE OF ACADEMIC LABOR	1975	D8	P75	14.0 %	AULIA	NEWZ	----
		1980	D9	P88	16.2 %	FRANC	FINLA	----
V12	SHARE OF SELF-EMPLOYED LABOR	1975	D2	P12	12.1 %	NORWY	AULIA	----
		1980	D3	P24	10.1 %	NETH	SINGA	----
V13	MILITARY EXPENDITURES	1975	D7	P68	1.236 TSD MIL $	CHILE	LIBYA	----
		1980	D7	P63	1.250 TSD MIL $	PERU	BRAZI	----
V14	MILITARY MANPOWER	1975	D4	P40	25 TSD CAP	TUNIS	LIBYA	----
		1980	D3	P22	12 TSD CAP	ELSA	KENYA	----
V15	MEN AT AGE 20 - 30	1975	D1	P5	98 TSD CAP	TRITO	LIBE	----
		1980	D1	P2	158 TSD CAP	TRITO	PANA	----
V16	POPULATION	1975	D1	P3	1.01 MIL CAP	GABON	TRITO	----
		1980	D1	P5	1.37 MIL CAP	BHUTA	CONGO	----

V17	GROSS DOMESTIC PRODUCT	1975	D7	P61	22.557 TSD MIL $	THAI	NEWZ	----
		1980	D7	P61	27.239 TSD MIL $	CHILE	UNARE	----
V18	SHARE IN WORLD IMPORTS	1975	D6	P53	2.627 1/TSD	PAKI	PERU	----
		1980	D6	P58	3.184 1/TSD	IRAQ	LIBYA	----
V19	SHARE IN WORLD EXPORTS	1975	D9	P84	10.481 1/TSD	DENMA	VENE	----
		1980	D9	P84	10.241 1/TSD	BRAZI	SPAIN	----
V20	GDP SHARE OF IMPORTS	1975	D4	P35	19.9 %	MADA	GUATE	----
		1980	D6	P51	23.7 %	MOROC	NIGER	----
V21	GDP SHARE OF EXPORTS	1975	D10	P99	76.4 %	SAUDI	SINGA	----
		1980	D10	P98	74.1 %	OMAN	SAUDI	----
V22	EXPORT PARTNER CONCENTRATION	1975	D6	P52	25.5 %	YUGO	ALGER	----
		1980	D4	P35	20.1 %	ARGE	TOGO	----
V23	TOTAL DEBT AS % OF GDP	------	----	----	----- -----	-------	-------	----
V24	SHARE OF NEW FOREIGN PATENTS	------	----	----	----- -----	-------	-------	----
V25	FOREIGN PROPERTY AS % OF GDP	1975	D5	P46	5.4 %	BURU	CHILE	----
		1978	D2	----	1.2 %	MALI	IRAN	----
V26	GNP SHARE OF DEVELOPMENT AID	1975	D10	P93	7.26 %	LIBYA	SAUDI	----
		1980	D10	P93	3.52 %	UNARE	SAUDI	----
V27	SHARE IN NOBEL PRIZE WINNERS	------	----	----	----- -----	-------	-------	----
V28	GDP SHARE OF MANUFACTURING	1975	D1	P10	5.6 %	NIGRA	SOMA	----
		1980	D1	P5	2.8 %	ANGO	ZAIRE	----
V29	EXPORT SHARE OF MANUFACTURES	1975	D5	P43	7.7 %	CHAD	SYRIA	----
		1980	D5	P42	10.2 %	TOGO	EGYPT	----
V30	LACK OF CIVIL LIBERTIES	1975	D3	P27	3	ISRA	LIBE	----
		1980	D4	P38	4	KENYA	LEBA	----
V31	LACK OF POLITICAL RIGHTS	1975	D4	P31	4	GUATE	MEXI	----
		1980	D7	P67	6	JORDA	LIBE	----
V32	RIOTS	------	----	----	----- -----	-------	-------	----
V33	PROTEST DEMONSTRATIONS	------	----	----	----- -----	-------	-------	----
V34	POLITICAL STRIKES	------	----	----	----- -----	-------	-------	----
V35	MEMBER OF THE NONALIGNED MMT.	1976	----	----	1	KORNO	LAOS	----
		1981	----	----	1	KORNO	LAOS	----
V36	MEMBER OF THE OPEC	1975	----	----	1	IRAQ	LIBYA	----
		1980	----	----	1	IRAQ	LIBYA	----
V37	MEMBER OF THE OECD	1975	----	----	0	KORSO	LAOS	----
		1980	----	----	0	KORSO	LAOS	----
V38	MEMBER OF THE CMEA	1975	----	----	0	KORSO	LAOS	----
		1980	----	----	0	KORSO	LAOS	----

V39	MEMBER OF THE WTO	1975	----	----	0	KORSO	LAOS	----
		1980	----	----	0	KORSO	LAOS	----
V40	MEMBER OF THE NATO	1975	----	----	0	KORSO	LAOS	----
		1980	----	----	0	KORSO	LAOS	----
V41	GDP SHARE OF INVESTMENTS	1975	D1	P10	12.7 %	GHANA	MADA	----
		1980	D1	P10	13.2 %	CHAD	PERU	----
V42	GDP SHARE OF AGRICULTURE	1975	D1	P2	0.2 %	-------	SAUDI	----
		1980	D1	P1	0.2 %	-------	UNARE	----
V43	GDP SHARE OF INDUSTRY	1975	D10	P98	78.6 %	LIBYA	SAUDI	----
		1980	D10	P98	77.1 %	LIBYA	SAUDI	----
V44	GDP SHARE OF SERVICES	1975	D1	P5	21.2 %	UGADA	BURU	----
		1980	D1	P5	22.7 %	LIBYA	ANGO	----
V45	HOMICIDES P. MIL. POPULATION	1975	D5	P49	14.9 1/MIL CAP	UNKI	AULIA	F154
		1980	D2	P13	8.8 1/MIL CAP	NETH	SWITZ	F2
V46	SUICIDES P. MIL. POPULATION	1975	D1	P3	5.0 1/MIL CAP	-------	NICA	F2
		1980	D1	P4	7.3 1/MIL CAP	-------	GUATE	F2
V47	IMPORT PARTNERS	1980	R1	JAPAN	21.0 %	KORSO	MALAY	----
		1980	R2	USA	14.5 %	KORSO	LIBE	----
		1980	R3	UNKI	8.6 %	JAMAI	OMAN	----
V48	EXPORT PARTNERS	1980	R1	JAPAN	20.1 %	INDO	MALAY	----
		1980	R2	NETH	11.4 %	IVORY	NIGRA	----
		1980	R3	KORSO	7.6 %	JAPAN	-------	----
V49	PATENT SUPPLIERS	-------	----	----	----- -----	-------	-------	----
V50	PROVENANCE OF FOREIGN FIRMS	1980	R1	USA	50.0 %	JAPAN	LEBA	----
		1980	R2	UNKI	27.7 %	JAPAN	LEBA	----
		1980	R3	-------	5.5 %	-------	-------	----
V51	FILM SUPPLIERS	1980	R1	USA	109	KORSO	LIBYA	F117
		1980	R2	INDIA	86	JORDA	LAOS	F117
		1980	R3	ITALY	36	JAPAN	NORWY	F117

LAOS (LAOS)

V1	INCOME PER CAPITA	-------	----	----	----- -----	-------	-------	----
V2	TELEPHONES P. TSD. POPULATION	1970	D1	P7	1 1/TSD CAP	HAITI	MALI	----
		1975	D2	P12	2 1/TSD CAP	INDO	LIBE	----
V3	INFANT MORTALITY RATE	1980	D9	P81	135.0 1/TSD	CONGO	BOLI	F5
V4	PHYSICIANS P. MIL. POPULATION	-------	----	----	----- -----	-------	-------	----
V5	ADULT LITERACY	1980	D4	P40	43.6 %	IVORY	ALGER	F21

V6	DURATION OF SCHOOLING	1970	D3	P22	3.8	YR	SAUDI	MOROC	----
		1975	D3	P22	4.4	YR	HAITI	MOROC	----
		1980	D3	P22	5.8	YR	RWAN	MOROC	F35
V7	STUDENT ENROLLMENT RATIO	1970	D2	P13	0.2	%	ETHIA	MALI	----
		1974	D1	P9	0.3	%	ETHIA	RWAN	----
		1980	D1	P10	0.4	%	UPVO	MALAW	----
V8	SHARE OF AGRICULTURAL LABOR	------	----	----	-----	-----	-------	-------	----
V9	SHARE OF INDUSTRIAL LABOR	------	----	----	-----	-----	-------	-------	----
V10	SHARE OF SERVICE LABOR	------	----	----	-----	-----	-------	-------	----
V11	SHARE OF ACADEMIC LABOR	------	----	----	-----	-----	-------	-------	----
V12	SHARE OF SELF-EMPLOYED LABOR	------	----	----	-----	-----	-------	-------	----
V13	MILITARY EXPENDITURES	------	----	----	-----	-----	-------	-------	----
V14	MILITARY MANPOWER	1970	D6	P55	62	TSD CAP	PHILI	MOROC	----
		1975	D5	P50	46	TSD CAP	YENO	AURIA	----
		1980	D6	P58	55	TSD CAP	SOMA	VENE	----
V15	MEN AT AGE 20 - 30	------	----	----	-----	-----	-------	-------	----
V16	POPULATION	1970	D3	P24	2.96	MIL CAP	IRE	ISRA	F4
		1975	D3	P25	3.43	MIL CAP	IRE	ISRA	----
		1980	D3	P25	3.90	MIL CAP	ISRA	NORWY	----
V17	GROSS DOMESTIC PRODUCT	------	----	----	-----	-----	-------	-------	----
V18	SHARE IN WORLD IMPORTS	1970	D2	P18	0.343	1/TSD	AFGHA	SIERA	----
		1975	D1	P1	0.046	1/TSD	-------	BURU	----
		1980	D1	P3	0.064	1/TSD	CENTR	BURU	----
V19	SHARE IN WORLD EXPORTS	1970	D1	P2	0.022	1/TSD	YENO	VISO	----
		1975	D1	P2	0.035	1/TSD	YENO	BENIN	----
		1980	D1	P2	0.016	1/TSD	YENO	BENIN	----
V20	GDP SHARE OF IMPORTS	------	----	----	-----	-----	-------	-------	----
V21	GDP SHARE OF EXPORTS	------	----	----	-----	-----	-------	-------	----
V22	EXPORT PARTNER CONCENTRATION	1970	D7	P68	35.7	%	VENE	MOROC	----
		1974	D10	P99	72.8	%	DOMI	HAITI	----
V23	TOTAL DEBT AS % OF GDP	------	----	----	-----	-----	-------	-------	----
V24	SHARE OF NEW FOREIGN PATENTS	1971	D9	P90	100	%	KENYA	MALAW	F19
		1974	D10	P92	100	%	KENYA	MALAY	----
V25	FOREIGN PROPERTY AS % OF GDP	------	----	----	-----	-----	-------	-------	----
V26	GNP SHARE OF DEVELOPMENT AID	------	----	----	-----	-----	-------	-------	----
V27	SHARE IN NOBEL PRIZE WINNERS	1970-79	D5	P45	0.0	%	KORSO	LEBA	----
V28	GDP SHARE OF MANUFACTURING	------	----	----	-----	-----	-------	-------	----

V29	EXPORT SHARE OF MANUFACTURES	1970	D8	P75	30.8	%	CONGO	CENTR	----
		1974	D4	P34	4.1	%	SRILA	MADA	----
V30	LACK OF CIVIL LIBERTIES	1975	D6	P54	5		INDO	MOROC	----
		1980	D10	P92	7		KORNO	MALAW	----
V31	LACK OF POLITICAL RIGHTS	1975	D5	P43	5		KORSO	LESO	----
		1980	D9	P90	7		KORNO	MALI	----
V32	RIOTS	1970-74	D2	P19	0		KORNO	LIBE	----
		1975-79	D8	P79	8		ECUA	PANA	----
V33	PROTEST DEMONSTRATIONS	1970-74	D6	P59	4		BELGI	NEWZ	----
		1975-79	D9	P82	18		IRE	PHILI	----
V34	POLITICAL STRIKES	1970-74	D3	P29	0		KORNO	LIBYA	----
		1975-79	D3	P29	0		KORNO	LESO	----
V35	MEMBER OF THE NONALIGNED MMT.	1970	----	----	1		KENYA	LEBA	----
		1976	----	----	1		KUWAI	LEBA	----
		1981	----	----	1		KUWAI	LEBA	----
V36	MEMBER OF THE OPEC	1970	----	----	0		KORSO	LEBA	----
		1975	----	----	0		KORSO	LEBA	----
		1980	----	----	0		KORSO	LEBA	----
V37	MEMBER OF THE OECD	1970	----	----	0		KORSO	LEBA	----
		1975	----	----	0		KUWAI	LEBA	----
		1980	----	----	0		KUWAI	LEBA	----
V38	MEMBER OF THE CMEA	1970	----	----	0		KORSO	LEBA	----
		1975	----	----	0		KUWAI	LEBA	----
		1980	----	----	0		KUWAI	LEBA	----
V39	MEMBER OF THE WTO	1970	----	----	0		KORSO	LEBA	----
		1975	----	----	0		KUWAI	LEBA	----
		1980	----	----	0		KUWAI	LEBA	----
V40	MEMBER OF THE NATO	1970	----	----	0		KORSO	LEBA	----
		1975	----	----	0		KUWAI	LEBA	----
		1980	----	----	0		KUWAI	LEBA	----
V41	GDP SHARE OF INVESTMENTS	------	----	----	----- -----		-------	-------	----
V42	GDP SHARE OF AGRICULTURE	------	----	----	----- -----		-------	-------	----
V43	GDP SHARE OF INDUSTRY	------	----	----	----- -----		-------	-------	----
V44	GDP SHARE OF SERVICES	------	----	----	----- -----		-------	-------	----
V45	HOMICIDES P. MIL. POPULATION	------	----	----	----- -----		-------	-------	----
V46	SUICIDES P. MIL. POPULATION	------	----	----	----- -----		-------	-------	----
V47	IMPORT PARTNERS	1970	R1	USA	24.3	%	JAPAN	LEBA	----
		1970	R2	THAI	20.6	%	-------	-------	----
		1970	R3	INDO	15.3	%	-------	-------	----
V48	EXPORT PARTNERS	1970	R1	MALAY	35.7	%	-------	SINGA	----
		1970	R2	THAI	27.4	%	-------	YESO	----
		1970	R3	CANA	21.1	%	JAMAI	-------	----

V49 PATENT SUPPLIERS	1972	R1	USA	7		KORSO	LEBA	----
	1972	R2	GFR	2		KORSO	NETH	----
	1972	R3	-------	1		-------	-------	----
V50 PROVENANCE OF FOREIGN FIRMS	------	----	----	-----	-----	-------	-------	----
V51 FILM SUPPLIERS	1980	R1	USSR	91		IRAN	MOZAM	F117
	1980	R2	INDIA	21		KUWAI	MALAY	F117
	1980	R3	-------	0		-------	-------	F117

LEBANON (LEBA)

V1 INCOME PER CAPITA	------	----	----	-----	-----	-------	-------	----
V2 TELEPHONES P. TSD. POPULATION	1970	D8	P73	68	1/TSD CAP	ARGE	SINGA	----
V3 INFANT MORTALITY RATE	1980	D4	P40	48.0	1/TSD	VENE	CHINA	F5
V4 PHYSICIANS P. MIL. POPULATION	1970	D7	P69	769	1/MIL	MEXI	CUBA	----
	1973	D7	----	865	1/MIL	MEXI	CUBA	----
	1979	D9	P80	1863	1/MIL	NETH	URU	----
V5 ADULT LITERACY	------	----	----	-----	-----	-------	-------	----
V6 DURATION OF SCHOOLING	1970	D7	P70	9.5	YR	YUGO	USSR	----
	1980	D7	P61	9.8	YR	SINGA	PERU	----
V7 STUDENT ENROLLMENT RATIO	1970	D10	P96	23.7	%	SWEDN	USSR	----
	1980	D10	P96	33.7	%	FINLA	CANA	----
V8 SHARE OF AGRICULTURAL LABOR	1970	D4	P38	19.5	%	JAPAN	FINLA	----
V9 SHARE OF INDUSTRIAL LABOR	1970	D7	P61	35.2	%	POLA	JAPAN	----
V10 SHARE OF SERVICE LABOR	1970	D8	P68	35.3	%	FRANC	BELGI	----
V11 SHARE OF ACADEMIC LABOR	1970	D8	P73	10.1	%	IRE	HUNGA	----
V12 SHARE OF SELF-EMPLOYED LABOR	1970	D7	P70	32.2	%	NICA	VENE	F74
V13 MILITARY EXPENDITURES	------	----	----	-----	-----	-------	-------	----
V14 MILITARY MANPOWER	1970	D4	P37	19	TSD CAP	URU	SOMA	----
	1975	D4	P35	20	TSD CAP	GHANA	MOZAM	----
	1980	D4	P36	23	TSD CAP	NEPAL	SWITZ	----
V15 MEN AT AGE 20 - 30	------	----	----	-----	-----	-------	-------	----
V16 POPULATION	1970	D2	P17	2.47	MIL CAP	PARA	HONDU	F174
	1975	D2	P19	2.77	MIL CAP	PAPUA	URU	F173
	1980	D2	P14	2.67	MIL CAP	ALBA	NICA	F173
V17 GROSS DOMESTIC PRODUCT	------	----	----	-----	-----	-------	-------	----

V18	SHARE IN WORLD IMPORTS	1970	D5	P50	1.708	1/TSD	LIBYA	PERU	----
		1977	D5	----	1.463	1/TSD	IVORY	CHILE	----
V19	SHARE IN WORLD EXPORTS	1970	D4	P33	0.631	1/TSD	ECUA	SYRIA	----
		1977	D3	----	0.387	1/TSD	PANA	TANZA	----
V20	GDP SHARE OF IMPORTS	------	----	----	-----	-----	-------	-------	----
V21	GDP SHARE OF EXPORTS	------	----	----	-----	-----	-------	-------	----
V22	EXPORT PARTNER CONCENTRATION	1970	D2	P15	15.4	%	ARGE	SUDAN	----
		1977	D7	----	33.3	%	CZECH	MALI	----
V23	TOTAL DEBT AS % OF GDP	------	----	----	-----	-----	-------	-------	----
V24	SHARE OF NEW FOREIGN PATENTS	1970	D4	P36	84	%	INDIA	AURIA	----
		1974	D4	P36	85	%	VENE	NICA	----
V25	FOREIGN PROPERTY AS % OF GDP	------	----	----	-----	-----	-------	-------	----
V26	GNP SHARE OF DEVELOPMENT AID	------	----	----	-----	-----	-------	-------	----
V27	SHARE IN NOBEL PRIZE WINNERS	1970-79	D5	P45	0.0	%	LAOS	LIBE	
V28	GDP SHARE OF MANUFACTURING	------	----	----	-----	-----	-------	-------	
V29	EXPORT SHARE OF MANUFACTURES	1970	D9	P85	57.0	%	YUGO	BELGI	----
		1973	D9	----	66.3	%	YUGO	FRANC	----
V30	LACK OF CIVIL LIBERTIES	1975	D2	P18	2		JAMAI	PAPUA	----
		1980	D4	P38	4		KUWAI	MALAY	----
V31	LACK OF POLITICAL RIGHTS	1975	D2	P20	2		JAPAN	SRILA	----
		1980	D4	P36	4		KORSO	SENE	----
V32	RIOTS	1970-74	D9	P84	13		MEXI	PERU	----
		1975-79	D7	P69	5		GHANA	PHILI	----
V33	PROTEST DEMONSTRATIONS	1970-74	D9	P82	19		CHINA	CANA	----
		1975-79	D9	P85	23		SOUAF	COLO	----
V34	POLITICAL STRIKES	1970-74	D10	P96	24		CHILE	FRANC	----
		1975-79	D10	P95	17		SOUAF	PERU	----
V35	MEMBER OF THE NONALIGNED MMT.	1970	----	----	1		LAOS	LIBE	----
		1976	----	----	1		LAOS	LESO	----
		1981	----	----	1		LAOS	LESO	----
V36	MEMBER OF THE OPEC	1970	----	----	0		LAOS	LIBE	----
		1975	----	----	0		LAOS	LESO	----
		1980	----	----	0		LAOS	LESO	----
V37	MEMBER OF THE OECD	1970	----	----	0		LAOS	LIBE	----
		1975	----	----	0		LAOS	LESO	----
		1980	----	----	0		LAOS	LESO	----
V38	MEMBER OF THE CMEA	1970	----	----	0		LAOS	LIBE	----
		1975	----	----	0		LAOS	LESO	----
		1980	----	----	0		LAOS	LESO	----

Variable		Year			Value		Col1	Col2	Col3
V39	MEMBER OF THE WTO	1970	----	----	0		LAOS	LIBE	----
		1975	----	----	0		LAOS	LESO	----
		1980	----	----	0		LAOS	LESO	----
V40	MEMBER OF THE NATO	1970	----	----	0		LAOS	LIBE	----
		1975	----	----	0		LAOS	LESO	----
		1980	----	----	0		LAOS	LESO	----
V41	GDP SHARE OF INVESTMENTS	------	----	----	----- -----		-------	-------	----
V42	GDP SHARE OF AGRICULTURE	------	----	----	----- -----		-------	-------	----
V43	GDP SHARE OF INDUSTRY	------	----	----	----- -----		-------	-------	----
V44	GDP SHARE OF SERVICES	------	----	----	----- -----		-------	-------	----
V45	HOMICIDES P. MIL. POPULATION	------	----	----	----- -----		-------	-------	----
V46	SUICIDES P. MIL. POPULATION	------	----	----	----- -----		-------	-------	----
V47	IMPORT PARTNERS	1970	R1	USA	12.1	%	LAOS	LIBE	----
		1970	R2	GFR	10.6	%	IVORY	LIBE	----
		1970	R3	FRANC	8.4	%	IRAQ	MEXI	----
V48	EXPORT PARTNERS	1970	R1	SAUDI	15.4	%	-------	SOMA	----
		1970	R2	KUWAI	12.2	%	-------	-------	----
		1970	R3	SYRIA	7.1	%	JORDA	-------	----
V49	PATENT SUPPLIERS	1970	R1	USA	46		LAOS	MALAY	----
		1970	R2	SWITZ	28		KAMPU	PERU	----
		1970	R3	FRANC	23		ITALY	NETH	----
V50	PROVENANCE OF FOREIGN FIRMS	1980	R1	USA	31.5	%	KUWAI	MEXI	----
		1980	R2	UNKI	24.6	%	KUWAI	PAKI	----
		1980	R3	FRANC	13.0	%	URU	YUGO	----
V51	FILM SUPPLIERS	------	----	----	----- -----		-------	-------	----

LESOTHO (LESO)

Variable		Year			Value		Col1	Col2	Col3
V1	INCOME PER CAPITA	------	----	----	----- -----		-------	-------	----
V2	TELEPHONES P. TSD. POPULATION	1971	D3	P22	3	1/TSD CAP	BENIN	MALAW	----
		1974	D2	P17	3	1/TSD CAP	INDIA	PAKI	----
V3	INFANT MORTALITY RATE	1980	D7	P68	120.0	1/TSD	MOZAM	HAITI	F5
V4	PHYSICIANS P. MIL. POPULATION	------	----	----	----- -----		-------	-------	----
V5	ADULT LITERACY	------	----	----	----- -----		-------	-------	----
V6	DURATION OF SCHOOLING	1975	D6	P55	8.5	YR	COLO	SYRIA	----
		1980	D5	P44	8.5	YR	ALGER	INDO	----

V7	STUDENT ENROLLMENT RATIO	1975	D2	P19	0.8	%	KENYA	NIGRA	----
		1978	D3	----	1.5	%	CAME	GHANA	----
V8	SHARE OF AGRICULTURAL LABOR	------	----	----	-----	-----	-------	-------	----
V9	SHARE OF INDUSTRIAL LABOR	------	----	----	-----	-----	-------	-------	----
V10	SHARE OF SERVICE LABOR	------	----	----	-----	-----	-------	-------	----
V11	SHARE OF ACADEMIC LABOR	------	----	----	-----	-----	-------	-------	----
V12	SHARE OF SELF-EMPLOYED LABOR	------	----	----	-----	-----	-------	-------	----
V13	MILITARY EXPENDITURES	------	----	----	-----	-----	-------	-------	----
V14	MILITARY MANPOWER	1975	D1	P2	1	TSD CAP	JAMAI	TRITO	----
		1980	D1	P2	1	TSD CAP	-------	TRITO	----
V15	MEN AT AGE 20 - 30	------	----	----	-----	-----	-------	-------	----
V16	POPULATION	------	----	----	-----	-----	-------	-------	----
V17	GROSS DOMESTIC PRODUCT	1971	D1	P2	0.178	TSD MIL $	-------	MALAW	----
		1980	D1	P2	0.389	TSD MIL $	-------	LIBE	----
V18	SHARE IN WORLD IMPORTS	------	----	----	-----	-----	-------	-------	----
V19	SHARE IN WORLD EXPORTS	------	----	----	-----	-----	-------	-------	----
V20	GDP SHARE OF IMPORTS	------	----	----	-----	-----	-------	-------	----
V21	GDP SHARE OF EXPORTS	------	----	----	-----	-----	-------	-------	----
V22	EXPORT PARTNER CONCENTRATION	------	----	----	-----	-----	-------	-------	----
V23	TOTAL DEBT AS % OF GDP	1980	D2	P14	16.9	%	URU	BURU	----
V24	SHARE OF NEW FOREIGN PATENTS	------	----	----	-----	-----	-------	-------	----
V25	FOREIGN PROPERTY AS % OF GDP	1971	D2	P14	2.5	%	TURKY	KORSO	----
		1975	D2	P18	2.0	%	SAUDI	SRILA	----
		1978	D2	----	1.4	%	BURMA	ALGER	----
V26	GNP SHARE OF DEVELOPMENT AID	------	----	----	-----	-----	-------	-------	----
V27	SHARE IN NOBEL PRIZE WINNERS	------	----	----	-----	-----	-------	-------	----
V28	GDP SHARE OF MANUFACTURING	1971	D1	P9	5.2	%	MAURA	SIERA	F16
		1975	D2	P13	5.7	%	YENO	SIERA	F16
		1980	D2	P12	4.8	%	CHAD	SAUDI	F16
V29	EXPORT SHARE OF MANUFACTURES	------	----	----	-----	-----	-------	-------	----
V30	LACK OF CIVIL LIBERTIES	1975	D4	P39	4		KENYA	MADA	----
		1980	D6	P52	5		KORSO	LIBE	----
V31	LACK OF POLITICAL RIGHTS	1975	D5	P43	5		LAOS	MADA	----
		1980	D5	P47	5		KENYA	NEPAL	----
V32	RIOTS	1975-79	D5	P45	1		KAMPU	POLA	----

V33	PROTEST DEMONSTRATIONS	1975-79	D2	P13	0		JORDA	MADA	----
V34	POLITICAL STRIKES	1975-79	D3	P29	0		LAOS	LIBE	----
V35	MEMBER OF THE NONALIGNED MMT.	1976	----	----	1		LEBA	LIBE	----
		1981	----	----	1		LEBA	LIBE	----
V36	MEMBER OF THE OPEC	1975	----	----	0		LEBA	LIBE	----
		1980	----	----	0		LEBA	LIBE	----
V37	MEMBER OF THE OECD	1975	----	----	0		LEBA	LIBE	----
		1980	----	----	0		LEBA	LIBE	----
V38	MEMBER OF THE CMEA	1975	----	----	0		LEBA	LIBE	----
		1980	----	----	0		LEBA	LIBE	----
V39	MEMBER OF THE WTO	1975	----	----	0		LEBA	LIBE	----
		1980	----	----	0		LEBA	LIBE	----
V40	MEMBER OF THE NATO	1975	----	----	0		LEBA	LIBE	----
		1980	----	----	0		LEBA	LIBE	----
V41	GDP SHARE OF INVESTMENTS	1971	D4	P30	15.8	%	IRAQ	SAUDI	----
		1975	D7	P63	24.6	%	DOMI	MOROC	----
		1980	D9	P88	31.4	%	HUNGA	IRAQ	----
V42	GDP SHARE OF AGRICULTURE	1971	D6	P57	26.0	%	NICA	KORSO	F16
		1975	D7	P69	31.7	%	INDO	MAURA	F16
		1980	D8	P71	31.0	%	PARA	PAKI	F16
V43	GDP SHARE OF INDUSTRY	1971	D1	P6	10.6	%	YENO	NEPAL	F16
		1975	D1	P10	13.1	%	CHAD	SUDAN	F16
		1980	D2	P20	21.3	%	CAME	PANA	F16
V44	GDP SHARE OF SERVICES	1971	D10	P94	63.4	%	USA	PANA	F16
		1975	D8	P80	55.2	%	AURIA	CHILE	F16
		1980	D6	P54	47.7	%	PERU	TUNIS	F16
V45	HOMICIDES P. MIL. POPULATION	------	----	----	----- -----		-------	-------	----
V46	SUICIDES P. MIL. POPULATION	------	----	----	----- -----		-------	-------	----
V47	IMPORT PARTNERS	------	----	----	----- -----		-------	-------	----
V48	EXPORT PARTNERS	------	----	----	----- -----		-------	-------	----
V49	PATENT SUPPLIERS	------	----	----	----- -----		-------	-------	----
V50	PROVENANCE OF FOREIGN FIRMS	------	----	----	----- -----		-------	-------	----
V51	FILM SUPPLIERS	------	----	----	----- -----		-------	-------	----

LIBERIA (LIBE)

V1	INCOME PER CAPITA	1970	D4	P34	637	$/CAP	ELSA	ECUA	F4
		1975	D4	P32	534	$/CAP	THAI	PHILI	----
		1980	D3	P26	472	$/CAP	INDO	SENE	----
V2	TELEPHONES P. TSD. POPULATION	1969	D3	P30	5	1/TSD CAP	HONDU	SRILA	----
		1973	D2	----	2	1/TSD CAP	LAOS	NIGRA	----
V3	INFANT MORTALITY RATE	1980	D8	P71	121.6	1/TSD	GABON	TOGO	F5
V4	PHYSICIANS P. MIL. POPULATION	1969	D3	P30	85	1/MIL	MOROC	HAITI	F2
		1975	D4	P33	110	1/MIL	YESO	HAITI	----
V5	ADULT LITERACY	1980	D2	P18	25.4	%	SAUDI	PAKI	F21
V6	DURATION OF SCHOOLING	1970	D3	P25	4.2	YR	GUATE	YESO	----
		1975	D3	P27	5.0	YR	IVORY	MALAW	----
		1980	D3	P27	6.2	YR	YESO	IVORY	----
V7	STUDENT ENROLLMENT RATIO	1970	D3	P28	0.9	%	IVORY	MADA	----
		1975	D3	P31	1.8	%	SUDAN	PAKI	----
		1979	D4	P31	2.5	%	YESO	VINO	----
V8	SHARE OF AGRICULTURAL LABOR	------	----	----	-----	-----	-------	-------	----
V9	SHARE OF INDUSTRIAL LABOR	------	----	----	-----	-----	-------	-------	----
V10	SHARE OF SERVICE LABOR	------	----	----	-----	-----	-------	-------	----
V11	SHARE OF ACADEMIC LABOR	------	----	----	-----	-----	-------	-------	----
V12	SHARE OF SELF-EMPLOYED LABOR	------	----	----	-----	-----	-------	-------	----
V13	MILITARY EXPENDITURES	1970	D1	P8	0.009	TSD MIL $	COSTA	TOGO	----
		1975	D1	P2	0.006	TSD MIL $	-------	SIERA	----
		1980	D2	P14	0.025	TSD MIL $	PANA	GHANA	----
V14	MILITARY MANPOWER	1970	D2	P13	5	TSD CAP	UPVO	PANA	----
		1975	D2	P14	6	TSD CAP	HAITI	BURU	----
		1980	D2	P16	7	TSD CAP	HAITI	MALI	----
V15	MEN AT AGE 20 - 30	1974	D1	P6	108	TSD CAP	KUWAI	CENTR	----
V16	POPULATION	1970	D1	P6	1.34	MIL CAP	MONGO	PANA	F4
		1975	D1	P7	1.55	MIL CAP	MONGO	PANA	----
		1980	D1	P8	1.87	MIL CAP	YESO	PANA	----
V17	GROSS DOMESTIC PRODUCT	1970	D1	P8	0.854	TSD MIL $	TOGO	SIERA	----
		1975	D1	P5	0.827	TSD MIL $	TOGO	BENIN	----
		1980	D1	P3	0.882	TSD MIL $	LESO	BURU	----
V18	SHARE IN WORLD IMPORTS	1970	D3	P21	0.452	1/TSD	MONGO	BOLI	----
		1975	D3	P22	0.365	1/TSD	YESO	AFGHA	----
		1980	D2	P16	0.260	1/TSD	PARA	TOGO	----
V19	SHARE IN WORLD EXPORTS	1970	D4	P34	0.679	1/TSD	SYRIA	DOMI	----
		1975	D4	P32	0.450	1/TSD	URU	SUDAN	----
		1980	D3	P27	0.295	1/TSD	JORDA	AFGHA	----

V20	GDP SHARE OF IMPORTS	1970	D10	P97	42.7	%	BELGI	HUNGA	----
		1975	D10	P97	54.5	%	PANA	TRITO	----
		1980	D10	P97	58.3	%	BELGI	IRE	----
V21	GDP SHARE OF EXPORTS	1970	D10	P97	60.6	%	LIBYA	SAUDI	----
		1975	D10	P96	64.6	%	IRAQ	TRITO	----
		1980	D10	P96	64.3	%	TRITO	OMAN	----
V22	EXPORT PARTNER CONCENTRATION	1970	D4	P35	22.7	%	TANZA	SRILA	----
		1975	D5	P41	22.0	%	LIBYA	BELGI	----
		1980	D5	P45	24.1	%	PARA	MALI	F136
V23	TOTAL DEBT AS % OF GDP	1980	D9	P90	76.0	%	JAMAI	CONGO	----
V24	SHARE OF NEW FOREIGN PATENTS	------	----	----	-----	-----	-------	-------	----
V25	FOREIGN PROPERTY AS % OF GDP	1971	D10	P98	84.6	%	MAURA	TRITO	----
		1975	D10	P99	131.2	%	PAPUA	-------	----
		1978	D10	----	159.0	%	PAPUA	-------	----
V26	GNP SHARE OF DEVELOPMENT AID	------	----	----	-----	-----	-------	-------	----
V27	SHARE IN NOBEL PRIZE WINNERS	1970-79	D5	P45	0.0	%	LEBA	LIBYA	----
V28	GDP SHARE OF MANUFACTURING	1970	D1	P4	4.0	%	RWAN	YENO	F16
		1975	D1	P7	5.4	%	SAUDI	NIGRA	F16
		1980	D3	P28	7.7	%	GHANA	NIGER	F16
V29	EXPORT SHARE OF MANUFACTURES	1970	D3	P24	2.0	%	CHAD	NIGER	----
		1975	D2	P18	1.2	%	IRAN	ALGER	----
		1980	D2	P16	1.9	%	PAPUA	NIGER	----
V30	LACK OF CIVIL LIBERTIES	1975	D3	P27	3		KUWAI	MALAY	----
		1980	D6	P52	5		LESO	NICA	----
V31	LACK OF POLITICAL RIGHTS	1975	D7	P63	6		KAMPU	MOZAM	----
		1980	D7	P67	6		KUWAI	LIBYA	----
V32	RIOTS	1970-74	D2	P19	0		LAOS	MALAW	----
		1975-79	D6	P53	2		IRAQ	LIBYA	----
V33	PROTEST DEMONSTRATIONS	1970-74	D2	P15	0		KORNO	MALAW	----
		1975-79	D4	P32	1		KORNO	MAURA	----
V34	POLITICAL STRIKES	1970-74	D7	P64	1		JORDA	MADA	----
		1975-79	D3	P29	0		LESO	LIBYA	----
V35	MEMBER OF THE NONALIGNED MMT.	1970	----	----	1		LEBA	LIBYA	----
		1976	----	----	1		LESO	LIBYA	----
		1981	----	----	1		LESO	LIBYA	----
V36	MEMBER OF THE OPEC	1970	----	----	0		LEBA	MADA	----
		1975	----	----	0		LESO	MADA	----
		1980	----	----	0		LESO	MADA	----
V37	MEMBER OF THE OECD	1970	----	----	0		LEBA	LIBYA	----
		1975	----	----	0		LESO	LIBYA	----
		1980	----	----	0		LESO	LIBYA	----

V38 MEMBER OF THE CMEA	1970	----	----	0		LEBA	LIBYA	----
	1975	----	----	0		LESO	LIBYA	----
	1980	----	----	0		LESO	LIBYA	----
V39 MEMBER OF THE WTO	1970	----	----	0		LEBA	LIBYA	----
	1975	----	----	0		LESO	LIBYA	----
	1980	----	----	0		LESO	LIBYA	----
V40 MEMBER OF THE NATO	1970	----	----	0		LEBA	LIBYA	----
	1975	----	----	0		LESO	LIBYA	----
	1980	----	----	0		LESO	LIBYA	----
V41 GDP SHARE OF INVESTMENTS	1970	D7	P61	22.2 %		IVORY	TANZA	----
	1975	D10	P93	34.0 %		YUGO	MAURA	----
	1980	D7	P67	27.3 %		THAI	NORWY	----
V42 GDP SHARE OF AGRICULTURE	1970	D6	P54	24.1 %		ECUA	SENE	F16
	1975	D6	P55	26.6 %		KORSO	TOGO	F16
	1980	D8	P79	35.9 %		CENTR	MADA	F16
V43 GDP SHARE OF INDUSTRY	1970	D9	P86	41.5 %		CHILE	PORTU	F16
	1975	D9	P88	45.2 %		SOUAF	GFR	F16
	1980	D4	P38	28.1 %		DOMI	THAI	F16
V44 GDP SHARE OF SERVICES	1970	D2	P15	34.4 %		BANGL	ZAMBI	F16
	1975	D2	P12	28.2 %		GUINE	LIBYA	F16
	1980	D2	P20	36.0 %		CHAD	ALGER	F16
V45 HOMICIDES P. MIL. POPULATION	------	----	----	----- -----		-------	-------	----
V46 SUICIDES P. MIL. POPULATION	------	----	----	----- -----		-------	-------	----
V47 IMPORT PARTNERS	1970	R1	USA	31.0 %		LEBA	MEXI	----
	1970	R2	GFR	14.5 %		LEBA	MADA	----
	1970	R3	NETH	10.8 %		BELGI	-------	----
	1980	R1	SAUDI	26.8 %		KENYA	TRITO	----
	1980	R2	USA	22.5 %		KUWAI	MALAY	----
	1980	R3	GFR	9.4 %		IRE	MALI	----
V48 EXPORT PARTNERS	1970	R1	USA	22.7 %		KORSO	MEXI	----
	1970	R2	GFR	17.9 %		HONDU	LIBYA	----
	1970	R3	NETH	15.3 %		IRAQ	PANA	----
	1980	R1	GFR	24.1 %		ITALY	NETH	F136
	1980	R2	USA	20.9 %		INDO	MADA	F136
	1980	R3	FRANC	12.7 %		IRE	NETH	F136
V49 PATENT SUPPLIERS	------	----	----	----- -----		-------	-------	----
V50 PROVENANCE OF FOREIGN FIRMS	------	----	----	----- -----		-------	-------	----
V51 FILM SUPPLIERS	------	----	----	----- -----		-------	-------	----

LIBYA (LIBYA)

V1	INCOME PER CAPITA	1970	D8	P76	4237	$/CAP	SPAIN	ITALY	F147
		1975	D9	P83	8684	$/CAP	AURIA	FINLA	F147
		1980	D9	P85	10599	$/CAP	FINLA	CANA	F147
V2	TELEPHONES P. TSD. POPULATION	1970	D6	P57	21	1/TSD CAP	KORSO	MEXI	----
		1973	D6	----	28	1/TSD CAP	ECUA	BRAZI	----
V3	INFANT MORTALITY RATE	1980	D6	P59	107.0	1/TSD	VINO	TUNIS	F5
V4	PHYSICIANS P. MIL. POPULATION	1970	D6	P51	367	1/MIL	ECUA	PHILI	F147
		1975	D7	P66	1064	1/MIL	ALBA	VENE	F147
		1980	D7	P67	1366	1/MIL	JAPAN	YUGO	F147
V5	ADULT LITERACY	------	----	----	----- -----		-------	-------	----
V6	DURATION OF SCHOOLING	------	----	----	----- -----		-------	-------	----
V7	STUDENT ENROLLMENT RATIO	1970	D5	P44	3.0	%	TUNIS	IRAN	----
		1975	D5	P49	6.3	%	ALBA	JAMAI	----
		1979	D6	P52	8.2	%	HONDU	MONGO	----
V8	SHARE OF AGRICULTURAL LABOR	1973	D5	----	22.0	%	IRE	ALGER	----
V9	SHARE OF INDUSTRIAL LABOR	1973	D8	----	37.4	%	SWEDN	SINGA	----
V10	SHARE OF SERVICE LABOR	1973	D6	----	30.1	%	ALGER	IRE	----
V11	SHARE OF ACADEMIC LABOR	1973	D7	----	10.6	%	VENE	SINGA	----
V12	SHARE OF SELF-EMPLOYED LABOR	1973	D4	----	24.3	%	IRE	URU	----
V13	MILITARY EXPENDITURES	1970	D5	P48	0.325	TSD MIL $	SINGA	NEWZ	F61
		1975	D7	P69	1.313	TSD MIL $	KUWAI	ARGE	F59
		1980	D9	P81	2.899	TSD MIL $	TURKY	SOUAF	F59
V14	MILITARY MANPOWER	1970	D4	P36	18	TSD CAP	DOMI	URU	----
		1975	D4	P40	25	TSD CAP	KUWAI	SWITZ	----
		1980	D6	P55	53	TSD CAP	ALBA	TANZA	----
V15	MEN AT AGE 20 - 30	1973	D2	----	168	TSD CAP	COSTA	URU	F22
V16	POPULATION	1970	D2	P12	1.99	MIL CAP	TOGO	SINGA	F22
		1975	D2	P15	2.43	MIL CAP	ALBA	PARA	F22
		1980	D2	P18	2.97	MIL CAP	JORDA	PAPUA	F22
V17	GROSS DOMESTIC PRODUCT	1970	D5	P50	8.432	TSD MIL $	ZAIRE	MOROC	----
		1975	D6	P59	21.102	TSD MIL $	CHILE	THAI	----
		1980	D7	P63	31.480	TSD MIL $	UNARE	THAI	----
V18	SHARE IN WORLD IMPORTS	1970	D5	P50	1.669	1/TSD	ZAIRE	LEBA	F30
		1975	D6	P57	3.897	1/TSD	THAI	MALAY	F30
		1980	D6	P59	3.304	1/TSD	KUWAI	TURKY	F30
V19	SHARE IN WORLD EXPORTS	1970	D8	P79	7.543	1/TSD	SAUDI	SPAIN	F30
		1975	D8	P75	7.806	1/TSD	HUNGA	INDO	F30
		1980	D9	P86	10.982	1/TSD	INDO	AULIA	F30

V20	GDP SHARE OF IMPORTS	1970	D3	P29	13.9 %	UPVO	AULIA	F30
		1975	D7	P64	27.7 %	DENMA	MALI	F30
		1980	D4	P34	19.0 %	MADA	ECUA	F30
V21	GDP SHARE OF EXPORTS	1970	D10	P96	59.2 %	ZAMBI	LIBE	F30
		1975	D10	P93	53.6 %	BELGI	HUNGA	F30
		1980	D10	P92	61.6 %	MALAY	IRAQ	F30
V22	EXPORT PARTNER CONCENTRATION	1970	D5	P46	25.9 %	THAI	AULIA	----
		1975	D4	P40	21.9 %	AURIA	LIBE	----
		1979	D8	P74	36.1 %	UNARE	PAPUA	----
V23	TOTAL DEBT AS % OF GDP	------	----	----	----- -----	-------	-------	----
V24	SHARE OF NEW FOREIGN PATENTS	1975	D8	P75	96 %	IRAQ	PAKI	----
V25	FOREIGN PROPERTY AS % OF GDP	1971	D10	P92	30.5 %	VENE	CONGO	----
		1975	D5	P41	4.9 %	NIGER	ARGE	----
		1978	D4	----	3.4 %	GREC	BOLI	----
V26	GNP SHARE OF DEVELOPMENT AID	1970	D10	P93	2.01 %	FRANC	SAUDI	----
		1975	D9	P89	2.39 %	IRAQ	KUWAI	----
		1980	D9	P82	1.16 %	NETH	IRAQ	----
V27	SHARE IN NOBEL PRIZE WINNERS	1970-79	D5	P45	0.0 %	LIBE	MADA	----
V28	GDP SHARE OF MANUFACTURING	1970	D1	P2	2.1 %	-------	RWAN	F16
		1975	D1	P2	2.3 %	-------	ANGO	F16
		1980	D1	P3	2.3 %	OMAN	ANGO	F16
V29	EXPORT SHARE OF MANUFACTURES	------	----	----	----- -----	-------	-------	----
V30	LACK OF CIVIL LIBERTIES	1975	D10	P93	7	KORNO	MONGO	----
		1980	D8	P74	6	JORDA	MADA	----
V31	LACK OF POLITICAL RIGHTS	1975	D9	P88	7	KORNO	MALAW	----
		1980	D7	P67	6	LIBE	MADA	----
V32	RIOTS	1970-74	D6	P59	3	URU	MOROC	----
		1975-79	D6	P53	2	LIBE	SAUDI	----
V33	PROTEST DEMONSTRATIONS	1970-74	D4	P37	1	KENYA	NEPAL	----
		1975-79	D6	P59	5	HONDU	ROMA	----
V34	POLITICAL STRIKES	1970-74	D3	P29	0	LAOS	MALAW	----
		1975-79	D3	P29	0	LIBE	MADA	----
V35	MEMBER OF THE NONALIGNED MMT.	1970	----	----	1	LIBE	MALAW	----
		1976	----	----	1	LIBE	MADA	----
		1981	----	----	1	LIBE	MADA	----
V36	MEMBER OF THE OPEC	1970	----	----	1	IRAQ	SAUDI	----
		1975	----	----	1	KUWAI	NIGRA	----
		1980	----	----	1	KUWAI	NIGRA	----
V37	MEMBER OF THE OECD	1970	----	----	0	LIBE	MADA	----
		1975	----	----	0	LIBE	MADA	----
		1980	----	----	0	LIBE	MADA	----

V38 MEMBER OF THE CMEA	1970	----	----	0	LIBE	MADA	----
	1975	----	----	0	LIBE	MADA	----
	1980	----	----	0	LIBE	MADA	----
V39 MEMBER OF THE WTO	1970	----	----	0	LIBE	MADA	----
	1975	----	----	0	LIBE	MADA	----
	1980	----	----	0	LIBE	MADA	----
V40 MEMBER OF THE NATO	1970	----	----	0	LIBE	MADA	----
	1975	----	----	0	LIBE	MADA	----
	1980	----	----	0	LIBE	MADA	----
V41 GDP SHARE OF INVESTMENTS	1970	D4	P33	16.5 %	CHILE	SIERA	----
	1975	D9	P82	30.5 %	NEWZ	PANA	----
	1980	D5	P41	22.4 %	CAME	MOROC	----
V42 GDP SHARE OF AGRICULTURE	1970	D1	P3	2.4 %	SINGA	UNKI	F16
	1975	D1	P5	2.3 %	SINGA	UNKI	F16
	1980	D1	P5	1.6 %	SINGA	UNKI	F16
V43 GDP SHARE OF INDUSTRY	1970	D10	P99	68.6 %	SAUDI	-------	F16
	1975	D10	P97	68.0 %	IRAQ	KUWAI	F16
	1980	D10	P97	76.7 %	IRAQ	KUWAI	F16
V44 GDP SHARE OF SERVICES	1970	D1	P7	29.0 %	NIGER	ETHIA	F16
	1975	D2	P13	29.7 %	LIBE	GHANA	F16
	1980	D1	P4	21.7 %	SAUDI	KUWAI	F16
V45 HOMICIDES P. MIL. POPULATION	------	----	----	----- -----	-------	-------	----
V46 SUICIDES P. MIL. POPULATION	------	----	----	----- -----	-------	-------	----
V47 IMPORT PARTNERS	1970	R1	ITALY	21.6 %	ETHIA	SOMA	----
	1970	R2	USA	13.8 %	KORSO	MOROC	----
	1970	R3	UNKI	9.4 %	GREC	NORWY	----
	1980	R1	ITALY	29.5 %	-------	SOMA	----
	1980	R2	GFR	13.3 %	JORDA	MADA	----
	1980	R3	JAPAN	7.5 %	KENYA	MALAW	----
V48 EXPORT PARTNERS	1970	R1	ITALY	25.9 %	IRAQ	SYRIA	----
	1970	R2	GFR	17.5 %	LIBE	MOROC	----
	1970	R3	UNKI	15.1 %	CHILE	SAUDI	----
	1979	R1	USA	36.1 %	KORSO	MEXI	----
	1979	R2	ITALY	18.0 %	GREC	SOMA	----
	1979	R3	GFR	14.8 %	GUATE	MALI	----
V49 PATENT SUPPLIERS	------	----	----	----- -----	-------	-------	----
V50 PROVENANCE OF FOREIGN FIRMS	------	----	----	----- -----	-------	-------	----
V51 FILM SUPPLIERS	1979	R1	USA	102	KUWAI	MALAY	F120
	1979	R2	ITALY	17	INDO	MEXI	F120
	1979	R3	INDIA	9	IRAQ	SRILA	F120

MADAGASCAR (MADA)

V1	INCOME PER CAPITA	1970	D3	P23	414	$/CAP	NIGER	THAI	F4
		1975	D3	P23	369	$/CAP	NIGER	TOGO	----
		1980	D2	P18	346	$/CAP	SIERA	GHANA	----
V2	TELEPHONES P. TSD. POPULATION	1970	D3	P27	4	1/TSD CAP	UGADA	SIERA	----
		1976	D3	P23	4	1/TSD CAP	HAITI	MALAW	----
		1980	D2	P14	4	1/TSD CAP	INDIA	MOZAM	----
V3	INFANT MORTALITY RATE	1980	D5	P47	75.7	1/TSD	DOMI	EGYPT	F5
V4	PHYSICIANS P. MIL. POPULATION	1971	D4	P33	98	1/MIL	BANGL	BURMA	----
		1975	D3	P30	99	1/MIL	GHANA	YESO	----
		1981	D3	P26	101	1/MIL	NIGRA	BANGL	----
V5	ADULT LITERACY	------	----	----	-----	-----	-------	-------	----
V6	DURATION OF SCHOOLING	1970	D5	P44	6.8	YR	CHINA	THAI	----
		1975	D4	P38	7.2	YR	GHANA	CAME	----
V7	STUDENT ENROLLMENT RATIO	1970	D3	P29	1.0	%	LIBE	SRILA	----
		1975	D3	P27	1.3	%	IVORY	SRILA	----
		1980	D4	P36	3.1	%	BANGL	NEPAL	----
V8	SHARE OF AGRICULTURAL LABOR	------	----	----	-----	-----	-------	-------	----
V9	SHARE OF INDUSTRIAL LABOR	------	----	----	-----	-----	-------	-------	----
V10	SHARE OF SERVICE LABOR	------	----	----	-----	-----	-------	-------	----
V11	SHARE OF ACADEMIC LABOR	------	----	----	-----	-----	-------	-------	----
V12	SHARE OF SELF-EMPLOYED LABOR	------	----	----	-----	-----	-------	-------	----
V13	MILITARY EXPENDITURES	1970	D3	P22	0.038	TSD MIL $	NICA	PARA	----
		1975	D3	P21	0.045	TSD MIL $	NICA	PARA	----
		1980	D3	P26	0.086	TSD MIL $	ELSA	DOMI	F62
V14	MILITARY MANPOWER	1970	D3	P24	9	TSD CAP	GUINE	YESO	----
		1975	D3	P27	13	TSD CAP	GUATE	NEWZ	----
		1980	D4	P34	20	TSD CAP	IRE	NEPAL	----
V15	MEN AT AGE 20 - 30	1975	D5	P48	546	TSD CAP	GUATE	SYRIA	F46
V16	POPULATION	1970	D5	P48	6.80	MIL CAP	CAME	AURIA	F4
		1975	D6	P51	7.60	MIL CAP	CAME	SWEDN	----
		1980	D5	P50	8.70	MIL CAP	CAME	BULGA	----
V17	GROSS DOMESTIC PRODUCT	1970	D3	P29	2.815	TSD MIL $	JAMAI	ETHIA	----
		1975	D3	P25	2.808	TSD MIL $	PARA	ELSA	----
		1980	D3	P21	3.008	TSD MIL $	BOLI	GABON	----
V18	SHARE IN WORLD IMPORTS	1970	D3	P24	0.512	1/TSD	BURMA	ETHIA	----
		1975	D3	P24	0.404	1/TSD	AFGHA	HONDU	----
		1980	D3	P21	0.293	1/TSD	NIGER	BOLI	----

V19	SHARE IN WORLD EXPORTS	1970	D3	P26	0.462	1/TSD	YESO	SENE	----
		1975	D3	P25	0.336	1/TSD	UGADA	BANGL	----
		1980	D2	P18	0.201	1/TSD	MOZAM	MONGO	----
V20	GDP SHARE OF IMPORTS	1970	D6	P52	18.9	%	DOMI	CENTR	----
		1975	D4	P34	19.7	%	VENE	KUWAI	----
		1980	D4	P34	18.8	%	CHILE	LIBYA	----
V21	GDP SHARE OF EXPORTS	1970	D6	P53	16.1	%	PHILI	PERU	----
		1975	D5	P43	15.8	%	NEWZ	THAI	----
		1980	D3	P29	12.6	%	JAPAN	GREC	----
V22	EXPORT PARTNER CONCENTRATION	1970	D7	P64	34.2	%	NEWZ	HUNGA	F137
		1975	D4	P36	21.2	%	GREC	PORTU	----
		1980	D3	P30	18.6	%	ZAMBI	DENMA	----
V23	TOTAL DEBT AS % OF GDP	1980	D6	P55	41.2	%	CAME	PAKI	----
V24	SHARE OF NEW FOREIGN PATENTS	------	----	----	-----	-----	-------	-------	----
V25	FOREIGN PROPERTY AS % OF GDP	1971	D6	P52	9.3	%	GUATE	MALAW	----
		1975	D7	P67	9.7	%	DOMI	HAITI	----
		1978	D8	----	9.0	%	ECUA	CAME	----
V26	GNP SHARE OF DEVELOPMENT AID	------	----	----	-----	-----	-------	-------	----
V27	SHARE IN NOBEL PRIZE WINNERS	1970-79	D5	P45	0.0	%	LIBYA	MALAW	----
V28	GDP SHARE OF MANUFACTURING	1970	D5	P44	13.2	%	MALAW	IVORY	----
V29	EXPORT SHARE OF MANUFACTURES	1970	D4	P39	7.2	%	TOGO	COLO	----
		1975	D4	P34	4.1	%	LAOS	PANA	----
		1980	D3	P29	6.2	%	TRITO	CONGO	----
V30	LACK OF CIVIL LIBERTIES	1975	D4	P39	4		LESO	NICA	----
		1980	D8	P74	6		LIBYA	MALI	----
V31	LACK OF POLITICAL RIGHTS	1975	D5	P43	5		LESO	MAURA	----
		1980	D7	P67	6		LIBYA	MALAW	----
V32	RIOTS	1970-74	D7	P70	6		SYRIA	THAI	----
		1975-79	D7	P65	4		ELSA	BOLI	----
V33	PROTEST DEMONSTRATIONS	1970-74	D5	P49	2		IRAQ	MALAY	----
		1975-79	D2	P13	0		LESO	MALAW	----
V34	POLITICAL STRIKES	1970-74	D7	P64	1		LIBE	MAURA	----
		1975-79	D3	P29	0		LIBYA	MALAW	----
V35	MEMBER OF THE NONALIGNED MMT.	1970	----	----	0		KORSO	MEXI	----
		1976	----	----	1		LIBYA	MALAW	----
		1981	----	----	1		LIBYA	MALAW	----
V36	MEMBER OF THE OPEC	1970	----	----	0		LIBE	MALAW	----
		1975	----	----	0		LIBE	MALAW	----
		1980	----	----	0		LIBE	MALAW	----
V37	MEMBER OF THE OECD	1970	----	----	0		LIBYA	MALAW	----
		1975	----	----	0		LIBYA	MALAW	----
		1980	----	----	0		LIBYA	MALAW	----

V38 MEMBER OF THE CMEA	1970	----	----	0		LIBYA	MALAW	----
	1975	----	----	0		LIBYA	MALAW	----
	1980	----	----	0		LIBYA	MALAW	----
V39 MEMBER OF THE WTO	1970	----	----	0		LIBYA	MALAW	----
	1975	----	----	0		LIBYA	MALAW	----
	1980	----	----	0		LIBYA	MALAW	----
V40 MEMBER OF THE NATO	1970	----	----	0		LIBYA	MALAW	----
	1975	----	----	0		LIBYA	MALAW	----
	1980	----	----	0		LIBYA	MALAW	----
V41 GDP SHARE OF INVESTMENTS	1970	D3	P27	15.6	%	MALI	SENE	----
	1975	D2	P12	12.8	%	KUWAI	CHILE	----
	1980	D5	P48	23.5	%	RWAN	ZAMBI	----
V42 GDP SHARE OF AGRICULTURE	1970	D7	P69	29.6	%	EGYPT	TURKY	----
	1975	D9	P82	41.1	%	UPVO	TANZA	----
	1980	D8	P80	36.1	%	LIBE	SUDAN	----
V43 GDP SHARE OF INDUSTRY	1970	D3	P22	18.4	%	GHANA	UPVO	----
	1975	D2	P18	17.9	%	CENTR	RWAN	----
	1980	D2	P16	18.0	%	UPVO	MALAW	----
V44 GDP SHARE OF SERVICES	1970	D7	P68	52.0	%	CHILE	SPAIN	----
	1975	D4	P33	41.0	%	SIERA	PORTU	----
	1980	D5	P46	45.9	%	KENYA	THAI	----
V45 HOMICIDES P. MIL. POPULATION	------	----	----	----- -----		-------	-------	----
V46 SUICIDES P. MIL. POPULATION	------	----	----	----- -----		-------	-------	----
V47 IMPORT PARTNERS	1970	R1	FRANC	54.7	%	IVORY	MALI	----
	1970	R2	GFR	9.1	%	LIBE	MEXI	----
	1970	R3	ITALY	5.9	%	HAITI	SWITZ	----
	1980	R1	FRANC	37.6	%	GABON	MOROC	----
	1980	R2	GFR	9.4	%	LIBYA	NIGRA	----
	1980	R3	IRAQ	8.3	%	URU	ROMA	----
V48 EXPORT PARTNERS	1970	R1	FRANC	34.2	%	IVORY	MAURA	F137
	1970	R2	USA	22.7	%	IVORY	NEWZ	F137
	1970	R3	MALAY	5.9	%	SINGA	-------	F137
	1980	R1	FRANC	18.6	%	IVORY	MALI	----
	1980	R2	USA	17.4	%	LIBE	MALAW	----
	1980	R3	JAPAN	10.5	%	INDIA	MEXI	----
V49 PATENT SUPPLIERS	------	----	----	----- -----		-------	-------	----
V50 PROVENANCE OF FOREIGN FIRMS	1980	R1	FRANC	67.3	%	IVORY	MOROC	----
	1980	R2	USA	7.6	%	KORSO	MALAW	----
	1980	R3	GFR	6.5	%	KENYA	MALAW	----
V51 FILM SUPPLIERS	------	----	----	----- -----		-------	-------	----

MALAWI (MALAW)

V1	INCOME PER CAPITA	1970	D1	P3	133	$/CAP	ETHIA	BURMA	F4
		1975	D1	P6	144	$/CAP	NEPAL	UPVO	----
		1980	D1	P5	156	$/CAP	NEPAL	BURMA	----
V2	TELEPHONES P. TSD. POPULATION	1970	D3	P22	3	1/TSD CAP	LESO	PAKI	----
		1975	D3	P23	4	1/TSD CAP	MADA	SIERA	----
		1979	D2	P19	5	1/TSD CAP	UGADA	TANZA	----
V3	INFANT MORTALITY RATE	1980	D10	P98	178.9	1/TSD	GUINE	SIERA	F5
V4	PHYSICIANS P. MIL. POPULATION	1975	D1	P5	20	1/MIL	UPVO	MALI	----
V5	ADULT LITERACY	------	----	----	----- -----		-------	-------	----
V6	DURATION OF SCHOOLING	1970	D2	P19	3.4	YR	SIERA	SENE	F4
		1975	D3	P27	5.0	YR	LIBE	SAUDI	----
		1980	D2	P19	5.4	YR	GUATE	CENTR	----
V7	STUDENT ENROLLMENT RATIO	1970	D2	P16	0.3	%	TANZA	HAITI	----
		1975	D2	P11	0.4	%	CENTR	CHINA	----
		1980	D1	P10	0.4	%	LAOS	TANZA	----
V8	SHARE OF AGRICULTURAL LABOR	1977	D10	----	86.4	%	BANGL	MALI	----
V9	SHARE OF INDUSTRIAL LABOR	1977	D1	----	8.0	%	MALI	BANGL	----
V10	SHARE OF SERVICE LABOR	1977	D1	----	6.0	%	MALI	CAME	----
V11	SHARE OF ACADEMIC LABOR	1977	D1	----	1.4	%	-------	MALI	----
V12	SHARE OF SELF-EMPLOYED LABOR	1977	D10	----	81.5	%	NEPAL	-------	----
V13	MILITARY EXPENDITURES	1970	D1	P2	0.003	TSD MIL $	-------	SIERA	----
		1975	D1	P4	0.011	TSD MIL $	SIERA	BENIN	----
		1980	D2	P12	0.023	TSD MIL $	TOGO	PANA	F62
V14	MILITARY MANPOWER	1970	D1	P10	4	TSD CAP	ELSA	NIGER	----
		1975	D2	P12	5	TSD CAP	RWAN	NICA	----
		1980	D1	P9	4	TSD CAP	CENTR	TOGO	----
V15	MEN AT AGE 20 - 30	1976	D3	P26	338	TSD CAP	NORWY	CHAD	----
V16	POPULATION	1970	D4	P36	4.44	MIL CAP	SENE	FINLA	F4
		1975	D4	P39	5.24	MIL CAP	DENMA	YENO	----
		1980	D4	P39	5.95	MIL CAP	ZAMBI	UPVO	----
V17	GROSS DOMESTIC PRODUCT	1970	D1	P3	0.591	TSD MIL $	LESO	BURU	----
		1975	D1	P3	0.756	TSD MIL $	BURU	TOGO	----
		1980	D1	P5	0.931	TSD MIL $	BURU	TOGO	----
V18	SHARE IN WORLD IMPORTS	1970	D2	P17	0.259	1/TSD	NEPAL	AFGHA	F55
		1975	D2	P18	0.276	1/TSD	BURMA	MONGO	F30
		1980	D2	P14	0.215	1/TSD	MALI	PARA	F30
V19	SHARE IN WORLD EXPORTS	1970	D2	P17	0.191	1/TSD	TOGO	PARA	F30
		1975	D2	P15	0.159	1/TSD	TOGO	JORDA	F30
		1980	D2	P13	0.143	1/TSD	HAITI	PARA	F30

V20 GDP SHARE OF IMPORTS	1970	D8	P79	26.8 %	IVORY	ZAMBI	F55
	1975	D10	P91	41.0 %	ZAIRE	ALGER	F30
	1980	D9	P81	36.8 %	KENYA	SIERA	F30
V21 GDP SHARE OF EXPORTS	1970	D6	P59	18.7 %	BOLI	GFR	F30
	1975	D7	P64	22.7 %	GFR	DENMA	F30
	1980	D7	P64	23.9 %	GFR	CANA	F30
V22 EXPORT PARTNER CONCENTRATION	1970	D9	P81	46.3 %	ECUA	NIGER	----
	1975	D8	P79	39.9 %	VENE	COSTA	----
	1980	D6	P56	27.6 %	PHILI	YUGO	----
V23 TOTAL DEBT AS % OF GDP	1980	D9	P87	68.5 %	GUINE	JAMAI	----
V24 SHARE OF NEW FOREIGN PATENTS	1970	D9	P90	100 %	LAOS	NIGRA	----
	1975	D9	P82	98 %	SYRIA	ZAMBI	----
	1980	D7	P72	94 %	CANA	MOROC	----
V25 FOREIGN PROPERTY AS % OF GDP	1971	D6	P54	9.4 %	MADA	INDO	----
	1975	D8	P80	13.9 %	COSTA	VENE	----
	1978	D8	----	10.5 %	SIERA	INDO	----
V26 GNP SHARE OF DEVELOPMENT AID	------	----	----	----- -----	-------	-------	----
V27 SHARE IN NOBEL PRIZE WINNERS	1970-79	D5	P45	0.0 %	MADA	MALAY	----
V28 GDP SHARE OF MANUFACTURING	1970	D5	P42	12.7 %	PANA	MADA	F16
	1975	D5	P45	12.9 %	ECUA	BOLI	F16
	1980	D5	P46	12.9 %	IVORY	KENYA	F16
V29 EXPORT SHARE OF MANUFACTURES	------	----	----	----- -----	-------	-------	----
V30 LACK OF CIVIL LIBERTIES	1975	D8	P74	6	KORSO	MALI	----
	1980	D10	P92	7	LAOS	MONGO	----
V31 LACK OF POLITICAL RIGHTS	1975	D9	P88	7	LIBYA	MALI	----
	1980	D7	P67	6	MADA	MAURA	----
V32 RIOTS	1970-74	D2	P19	0	LIBE	MALI	----
	1975-79	D2	P20	0	KORNO	MALAY	----
V33 PROTEST DEMONSTRATIONS	1970-74	D2	P15	0	LIBE	MALI	----
	1975-79	D2	P13	0	MADA	MALI	----
V34 POLITICAL STRIKES	1970-74	D3	P29	0	LIBYA	MALAY	----
	1975-79	D3	P29	0	MADA	MALAY	----
V35 MEMBER OF THE NONALIGNED MMT.	1970	----	-----	1	LIBYA	MALAY	----
	1976	----	----	1	MADA	MALAY	----
	1981	----	----	1	MADA	MALAY	----
V36 MEMBER OF THE OPEC	1970	----	----	0	MADA	MALAY	----
	1975	----	----	0	MADA	MALAY	----
	1980	----	----	0	MADA	MALAY	----
V37 MEMBER OF THE OECD	1970	----	-----	0	MADA	MALAY	----
	1975	----	----	0	MADA	MALAY	----
	1980	----	----	0	MADA	MALAY	----

V38	MEMBER OF THE CMEA	1970	----	----	0		MADA	MALAY	----
		1975	----	----	0		MADA	MALAY	----
		1980	----	----	0		MADA	MALAY	----
V39	MEMBER OF THE WTO	1970	----	----	0		MADA	MALAY	----
		1975	----	----	0		MADA	MALAY	----
		1980	----	----	0		MADA	MALAY	----
V40	MEMBER OF THE NATO	1970	----	----	0		MADA	MALAY	----
		1975	----	----	0		MADA	MALAY	----
		1980	----	----	0		MADA	MALAY	----
V41	GDP SHARE OF INVESTMENTS	1970	D8	P76	26.1 %		FRANC	ZAIRE	----
		1975	D8	P75	28.5 %		TOGO	SYRIA	----
		1980	D4	P37	21.7 %		BURMA	ISRA	----
V42	GDP SHARE OF AGRICULTURE	1970	D9	P91	50.5 %		CHAD	YENO	F16
		1975	D9	P89	44.7 %		MALI	BURMA	F16
		1980	D9	P86	42.6 %		MALI	ANGO	F16
V43	GDP SHARE OF INDUSTRY	1970	D3	P25	18.7 %		UPVO	NIGRA	F16
		1975	D2	P20	19.3 %		RWAN	GUINE	F16
		1980	D2	P17	19.6 %		MADA	ELSA	F16
V44	GDP SHARE OF SERVICES	1970	D1	P9	30.8 %		ETHIA	INDIA	F16
		1975	D3	P21	36.0 %		ETHIA	YUGO	F16
		1980	D3	P24	37.8 %		INDIA	MALAY	F16
V45	HOMICIDES P. MIL. POPULATION	------	----	----	----- -----		-------	-------	----
V46	SUICIDES P. MIL. POPULATION	------	----	----	----- -----		-------	-------	----
V47	IMPORT PARTNERS	1970	R1	UNKI	26.6 %		KENYA	NEWZ	----
		1970	R2	ZIMBA	21.7 %		-------	-------	----
		1970	R3	SOUAF	12.9 %		ZAMBI	-------	F144
		1980	R1	SOUAF	36.9 %		-------	ZAMBI	F144
		1980	R2	UNKI	18.8 %		KENYA	NEPAL	----
		1980	R3	JAPAN	7.0 %		LIBYA	NIGRA	----
V48	EXPORT PARTNERS	1970	R1	UNKI	46.3 %		IRE	NEWZ	----
		1970	R2	ZIMBA	8.5 %		-------	-------	----
		1970	R3	ZAMBI	6.8 %		-------	-------	----
		1980	R1	UNKI	27.6 %		IRE	NEWZ	----
		1980	R2	USA	16.9 %		MADA	NEPAL	----
		1980	R3	NETH	8.6 %		DOMI	MOROC	----
V49	PATENT SUPPLIERS	1969	R1	UNKI	26		KENYA	NIGRA	----
		1969	R2	USA	16		KENYA	MOROC	----
		1969	R3	SOUAF	8		-------	ZAMBI	----
		1980	R1	UNKI	9		-------	TANZA	----
		1980	R2	USA	7		KORSO	MOROC	----
		1980	R3	SWITZ	4		KENYA	NEWZ	----
V50	PROVENANCE OF FOREIGN FIRMS	1980	R1	UNKI	78.0 %		KENYA	MALAY	----
		1980	R2	USA	5.2 %		MADA	MALAY	----
		1980	R3	GFR	4.3 %		MADA	MOROC	----
V51	FILM SUPPLIERS	------	----	----	----- -----		-------	-------	----

MALAYSIA (MALAY)

V1	INCOME PER CAPITA	1970	D5	P50	1028	$/CAP	PERU	NICA	----
		1975	D6	P53	1283	$/CAP	KORSO	TURKY	----
		1980	D6	P57	1662	$/CAP	KORSO	PANA	F35
V2	TELEPHONES P. TSD. POPULATION	1980	D5	P50	45	1/TSD CAP	TURKY	CHILE	----
V3	INFANT MORTALITY RATE	1980	D4	P34	33.3	1/TSD	ARGE	KORSO	F5
V4	PHYSICIANS P. MIL. POPULATION	1971	D5	P41	192	1/MIL	TUNIS	GUATE	----
		1974	D4	P35	134	1/MIL	THAI	CONGO	----
V5	ADULT LITERACY	------	----	----	----- -----		-------	-------	----
V6	DURATION OF SCHOOLING	1970	D6	P55	7.9	YR	DOMI	MEXI	----
		1975	D6	P57	8.6	YR	SYRIA	COSTA	----
		1980	D6	P52	9.2	YR	KENYA	SYRIA	----
V7	STUDENT ENROLLMENT RATIO	1970	D4	P35	1.6	%	SENE	CONGO	----
		1975	D4	P39	2.8	%	BANGL	CONGO	----
		1980	D5	P40	4.1	%	INDO	GUINE	----
V8	SHARE OF AGRICULTURAL LABOR	1970	D9	P79	53.7	%	DOMI	PHILI	----
		1980	D7	P72	39.2	%	KORSO	PERU	----
V9	SHARE OF INDUSTRIAL LABOR	1970	D2	P18	19.4	%	ELSA	GHANA	----
		1980	D4	P30	26.2	%	PARA	DOMI	----
V10	SHARE OF SERVICE LABOR	1970	D4	P36	22.1	%	ELSA	GREC	----
		1980	D5	P33	27.5	%	EGYPT	ELSA	----
V11	SHARE OF ACADEMIC LABOR	1970	D4	P36	4.8	%	SOUAF	BRAZI	----
		1980	D5	P37	7.1	%	CHILE	PORTU	----
V12	SHARE OF SELF-EMPLOYED LABOR	1980	D7	P67	30.8	%	EGYPT	THAI	----
V13	MILITARY EXPENDITURES	1975	D7	P64	1.053	TSD MIL $	PORTU	PAKI	----
		1980	D7	P68	1.508	TSD MIL $	THAI	DENMA	----
V14	MILITARY MANPOWER	1970	D6	P53	58	TSD CAP	AURIA	PHILI	----
		1975	D6	P60	76	TSD CAP	SWEDN	CANA	----
		1980	D7	P66	83	TSD CAP	CANA	BELGI	----
V15	MEN AT AGE 20 - 30	1970	D6	P53	743	TSD CAP	CUBA	VENE	----
V16	POPULATION	1970	D7	P61	10.39	MIL CAP	HUNGA	KENYA	----
		1975	D7	P62	11.90	MIL CAP	UGADA	NEPAL	----
		1980	D7	P61	13.87	MIL CAP	IRAQ	NEPAL	F35
V17	GROSS DOMESTIC PRODUCT	1970	D6	P52	10.683	TSD MIL $	MOROC	IRE	----
		1975	D6	P52	15.262	TSD MIL $	IRE	PERU	----
		1980	D6	P55	23.051	TSD MIL $	HUNGA	NEWZ	----
V18	SHARE IN WORLD IMPORTS	1970	D7	P65	4.254	1/TSD	CUBA	ISRA	F30
		1975	D6	P58	3.907	1/TSD	LIBYA	PHILI	F30
		1980	D7	P70	5.255	1/TSD	VENE	INDO	F30

V19	SHARE IN WORLD EXPORTS	1970	D7	P70	5.375	1/TSD	YUGO	ARGE	F30
		1975	D7	P65	4.377	1/TSD	CUBA	YUGO	F30
		1980	D7	P70	6.486	1/TSD	SOUAF	IRAN	F30
V20	GDP SHARE OF IMPORTS	1970	D10	P92	35.6	%	PANA	JAMAI	F30
		1975	D9	P87	38.2	%	ZAMBI	JAMAI	F30
		1980	D10	P92	45.3	%	NETH	TOGO	F30
V21	GDP SHARE OF EXPORTS	1970	D10	P92	42.5	%	HUNGA	BELGI	F30
		1975	D9	P89	41.2	%	MAURA	NETH	F30
		1980	D10	P91	54.4	%	BELGI	LIBYA	F30
V22	EXPORT PARTNER CONCENTRATION	1970	D4	P32	21.6	%	ITALY	SINGA	F134
		1975	D4	P33	20.3	%	USA	FINLA	F134
		1980	D5	P43	22.8	%	GABON	PARA	F134
V23	TOTAL DEBT AS % OF GDP	------	----	----	-----	-----	-------	-------	----
V24	SHARE OF NEW FOREIGN PATENTS	1969	D8	P74	98	%	IRE	NICA	----
		1974	D10	P92	100	%	LAOS	NEPAL	----
		1980	D9	P87	99	%	ECUA	NICA	----
V25	FOREIGN PROPERTY AS % OF GDP	1971	D9	P82	20.7	%	IVORY	TOGO	----
		1975	D10	P91	24.7	%	CONGO	GABON	----
		1978	D9	----	17.6	%	SENE	ZAIRE	----
V26	GNP SHARE OF DEVELOPMENT AID	------	----	----	-----	-----	-------	-------	----
V27	SHARE IN NOBEL PRIZE WINNERS	1970-79	D5	P45	0.0	%	MALAW	MALI	----
V28	GDP SHARE OF MANUFACTURING	1970	D5	P45	13.4	%	IVORY	HONDU	----
		1975	D7	P63	17.5	%	MOROC	THAI	----
		1980	D8	P79	21.9	%	COLO	SOUAF	----
V29	EXPORT SHARE OF MANUFACTURES	------	----	----	-----	-----	-------	-------	----
V30	LACK OF CIVIL LIBERTIES	1975	D3	P27	3		LIBE	MEXI	----
		1980	D4	P38	4		LEBA	MOROC	----
V31	LACK OF POLITICAL RIGHTS	1975	D3	P27	3		VENE	PAKI	----
		1980	D4	P31	3		GUATE	MEXI	----
V32	RIOTS	1970-74	D5	P43	1		KENYA	NEWZ	----
		1975-79	D2	P20	0		MALAW	MALI	----
V33	PROTEST DEMONSTRATIONS	1970-74	D5	P49	2		MADA	MOROC	----
		1975-79	D5	P42	2		HAITI	NEWZ	----
V34	POLITICAL STRIKES	1970-74	D3	P29	0		MALAW	MALI	----
		1975-79	D3	P29	0		MALAW	MAURA	----
V35	MEMBER OF THE NONALIGNED MMT.	1970	----	----	1		MALAW	MALI	----
		1976	----	----	1		MALAW	MALI	----
		1981	----	----	1		MALAW	MALI	----
V36	MEMBER OF THE OPEC	1970	----	----	0		MALAW	MALI	----
		1975	----	----	0		MALAW	MALI	----
		1980	----	----	0		MALAW	MALI	----

V37 MEMBER OF THE OECD	1970	----	----	0		MALAW	MALI	----
	1975	----	----	0		MALAW	MALI	----
	1980	----	----	0		MALAW	MALI	----
V38 MEMBER OF THE CMEA	1970	----	----	0		MALAW	MALI	----
	1975	----	----	0		MALAW	MALI	----
	1980	----	----	0		MALAW	MALI	----
V39 MEMBER OF THE WTO	1970	----	----	0		MALAW	MALI	----
	1975	----	----	0		MALAW	MALI	----
	1980	----	----	0		MALAW	MALI	----
V40 MEMBER OF THE NATO	1970	----	----	0		MALAW	MALI	----
	1975	----	----	0		MALAW	MALI	----
	1980	----	----	0		MALAW	MALI	----
V41 GDP SHARE OF INVESTMENTS	1970	D6	P53	20.7 %		COSTA	HONDU	----
	1975	D6	P55	23.4 %		SWITZ	AULIA	----
	1980	D8	P75	28.4 %		IVORY	UNARE	----
V42 GDP SHARE OF AGRICULTURE	1970	D8	P72	30.8 %		CAME	PARA	----
	1975	D6	P58	27.9 %		NIGRA	IVORY	----
	1980	D6	P57	24.1 %		PHILI	TOGO	----
V43 GDP SHARE OF INDUSTRY	1970	D5	P43	25.4 %		THAI	SYRIA	----
	1975	D5	P47	29.5 %		NICA	BOLI	----
	1980	D7	P69	36.9 %		BELGI	PHILI	----
V44 GDP SHARE OF SERVICES	1970	D4	P38	43.8 %		KORSO	COLO	----
	1975	D4	P40	42.6 %		COLO	TANZA	----
	1980	D3	P25	39.0 %		MALAW	PHILI	----
V45 HOMICIDES P. MIL. POPULATION	------	----	----	----- -----		-------	-------	----
V46 SUICIDES P. MIL. POPULATION	------	----	----	----- -----		-------	-------	----
V47 IMPORT PARTNERS	1970	R1	JAPAN	17.5 %		KORSO	PHILI	F134
	1970	R2	UNKI	13.5 %		JAMAI	PORTU	F134
	1970	R3	USA	8.6 %		KENYA	NETH	F134
	1980	R1	JAPAN	23.0 %		KUWAI	NEPAL	F134
	1980	R2	USA	15.0 %		LIBE	PORTU	F134
	1980	R3	SINGA	11.7 %		BANGL	PAPUA	F134
V48 EXPORT PARTNERS	1970	R1	SINGA	21.6 %		-------	INDO	F134
	1970	R2	JAPAN	18.3 %		KORSO	MEXI	F134
	1970	R3	USA	13.0 %		ITALY	NIGRA	F134
	1980	R1	JAPAN	22.8 %		KUWAI	OMAN	F134
	1980	R2	SINGA	19.1 %		BURMA	INDO	F134
	1980	R3	USA	16.3 %		CONGO	NEWZ	F134
V49 PATENT SUPPLIERS	1969	R1	USA	187		LEBA	MEXI	----
	1969	R2	UNKI	75		JORDA	SIERA	----
	1969	R3	SWITZ	47		KORSO	NICA	----
V50 PROVENANCE OF FOREIGN FIRMS	1980	R1	UNKI	40.1 %		MALAW	MOZAM	----
	1980	R2	USA	15.0 %		MALAW	MOROC	----
	1980	R3	JAPAN	7.2 %		ELSA	PERU	----

V51 FILM SUPPLIERS	1980	R1	USA	291		LIBYA	MAURA	F119
	1980	R2	INDIA	143		LAOS	MAURA	F119
	1980	R3	-------	0		-------	-------	F119

MALI (MALI)

V1	INCOME PER CAPITA	------	----	----	----- -----		-------	-------	----
V2	TELEPHONES P. TSD. POPULATION	1970	D1	P7	1 1/TSD CAP		LAOS	NEPAL	----
V3	INFANT MORTALITY RATE	1980	D10	P94	160.4 1/TSD		BENIN	UPVO	F5
V4	PHYSICIANS P. MIL. POPULATION	1970	D1	P9	24 1/MIL		RWAN	YESO	----
		1974	D1	P6	21 1/MIL		MALAW	BURU	----
		1978	D1	----	43 1/MIL		CENTR	UGADA	----
V5	ADULT LITERACY	------	----	----	----- -----		-------	-------	----
V6	DURATION OF SCHOOLING	1970	D1	P8	1.8 YR		MAURA	NEPAL	----
		1975	D1	P7	2.0 YR		ETHIA	YENO	----
		1980	D1	P2	2.0 YR		UPVO	BURU	----
V7	STUDENT ENROLLMENT RATIO	1970	D2	P13	0.2 %		LAOS	RWAN	----
		1975	D2	P14	0.6 %		CHINA	SIERA	----
		1980	D1	P6	0.3 %		BHUTA	NIGER	----
V8	SHARE OF AGRICULTURAL LABOR	1976	D10	P96	87.4 %		MALAW	NEPAL	F22
V9	SHARE OF INDUSTRIAL LABOR	1976	D1	P6	7.3 %		NEPAL	MALAW	F22
V10	SHARE OF SERVICE LABOR	1976	D1	P6	3.8 %		NEPAL	MALAW	F22
V11	SHARE OF ACADEMIC LABOR	1976	D1	P3	1.5 %		MALAW	BANGL	F22
V12	SHARE OF SELF-EMPLOYED LABOR	1976	D9	P86	49.6 %		YENO	PAKI	F22
V13	MILITARY EXPENDITURES	------	----	----	----- -----		-------	-------	----
V14	MILITARY MANPOWER	1970	D3	P22	8 TSD CAP		IRE	GUINE	----
		1975	D3	P20	8 TSD CAP		ELSA	PANA	----
		1980	D2	P16	7 TSD CAP		LIBE	MAURA	----
V15	MEN AT AGE 20 - 30	1970	D3	P29	304 TSD CAP		NORWY	CHAD	F2
		1976	D4	P36	418 TSD CAP		DENMA	TUNIS	F22
V16	POPULATION	1970	D4	P39	5.05 MIL CAP		DENMA	TUNIS	F4
		1975	D5	P43	6.29 MIL CAP		GUATE	SWITZ	----
		1980	D5	P43	6.98 MIL CAP		KAMPU	ZIMBA	F35
V17	GROSS DOMESTIC PRODUCT	------	----	----	----- -----		-------	-------	----
V18	SHARE IN WORLD IMPORTS	1970	D1	P6	0.142 1/TSD		SOMA	UPVO	----
		1975	D2	P12	0.195 1/TSD		TOGO	MAURA	----
		1980	D2	P13	0.214 1/TSD		SIERA	MALAW	----

V19	SHARE IN WORLD EXPORTS	1970	D2	P12	0.105	1/TSD	BENIN	JORDA	----
		1975	D1	P8	0.062	1/TSD	CHAD	HAITI	----
		1980	D2	P12	0.103	1/TSD	SIERA	HAITI	----
V20	GDP SHARE OF IMPORTS	1970	D5	P45	17.1	%	GFR	UNKI	----
		1975	D7	P65	27.8	%	LIBYA	MOROC	----
		1980	D8	P75	33.1	%	CONGO	BENIN	----
V21	GDP SHARE OF EXPORTS	1970	D4	P35	12.0	%	SOUAF	INDO	----
		1975	D2	P17	8.5	%	BURU	UGADA	----
		1980	D4	P37	15.5	%	IRAN	YUGO	----
V22	EXPORT PARTNER CONCENTRATION	1970	D6	P56	32.2	%	JAPAN	NETH	----
		1975	D7	P70	34.0	%	LEBA	PAPUA	----
		1980	D5	P46	24.2	%	LIBE	JAPAN	----
V23	TOTAL DEBT AS % OF GDP	1980	D8	P78	53.0	%	BOLI	IVORY	----
V24	SHARE OF NEW FOREIGN PATENTS	------	----	----	-----	-----	-------	-------	----
V25	FOREIGN PROPERTY AS % OF GDP	1971	D2	P11	2.3	%	SYRIA	TURKY	----
		1975	D2	P16	1.6	%	BURMA	SAUDI	----
		1978	D2	----	1.1	%	TURKY	KUWAI	----
V26	GNP SHARE OF DEVELOPMENT AID	------	----	----	-----	-----	-------	-------	----
V27	SHARE IN NOBEL PRIZE WINNERS	1970-79	D5	P45	0.0	%	MALAY	MAURA	----
V28	GDP SHARE OF MANUFACTURING	1970	D3	P27	9.5	%	SOMA	SAUDI	----
		1975	D3	P25	8.9	%	INDO	BURMA	----
		1980	D2	P19	5.6	%	IRAQ	SUDAN	----
V29	EXPORT SHARE OF MANUFACTURES	1970	D5	P47	9.6	%	TURKY	BRAZI	----
		1975	D6	P56	11.7	%	CONGO	TANZA	----
		1979	D6	P58	23.4	%	GUATE	MOROC	----
V30	LACK OF CIVIL LIBERTIES	1975	D8	P74	6		MALAW	MAURA	----
		1980	D8	P74	6		MADA	MAURA	----
V31	LACK OF POLITICAL RIGHTS	1975	D9	P88	7		MALAW	MONGO	----
		1980	D9	P90	7		LAOS	MONGO	----
V32	RIOTS	1970-74	D2	P19	0		MALAW	MAURA	----
		1975-79	D2	P20	0		MALAY	MAURA	----
V33	PROTEST DEMONSTRATIONS	1970-74	D2	P15	0		MALAW	MAURA	----
		1975-79	D2	P13	0		MALAW	MONGO	----
V34	POLITICAL STRIKES	1970-74	D3	P29	0		MALAY	MEXI	----
		1975-79	D8	P73	2		KENYA	PANA	----
V35	MEMBER OF THE NONALIGNED MMT.	1970	----	----	1		MALAY	MAURA	----
		1976	----	----	1		MALAY	MAURA	----
		1981	----	----	1		MALAY	MAURA	----
V36	MEMBER OF THE OPEC	1970	----	----	0		MALAY	MAURA	----
		1975	----	----	0		MALAY	MAURA	----
		1980	----	----	0		MALAY	MAURA	----

V37	MEMBER OF THE OECD	1970	----	----	0	MALAY	MAURA	----
		1975	----	----	0	MALAY	MAURA	----
		1980	----	----	0	MALAY	MAURA	----
V38	MEMBER OF THE CMEA	1970	----	----	0	MALAY	MAURA	----
		1975	----	----	0	MALAY	MAURA	----
		1980	----	----	0	MALAY	MAURA	----
V39	MEMBER OF THE WTO	1970	----	----	0	MALAY	MAURA	----
		1975	----	----	0	MALAY	MAURA	----
		1980	----	----	0	MALAY	MAURA	----
V40	MEMBER OF THE NATO	1970	----	----	0	MALAY	MAURA	----
		1975	----	----	0	MALAY	MAURA	----
		1980	----	----	0	MALAY	MAURA	----
V41	GDP SHARE OF INVESTMENTS	1970	D3	P26	15.2 %	BENIN	MADA	----
		1975	D2	P19	15.4 %	CENTR	SRILA	----
		1980	D2	P19	15.9 %	GUATE	SOMA	----
V42	GDP SHARE OF AGRICULTURE	1970	D9	P84	44.1 %	SUDAN	BENIN	----
		1975	D9	P88	43.9 %	YENO	MALAW	----
		1980	D9	P85	42.0 %	UPVO	MALAW	----
V43	GDP SHARE OF INDUSTRY	------	----	----	----- -----	-------	-------	----
V44	GDP SHARE OF SERVICES	------	----	----	----- -----	-------	-------	----
V45	HOMICIDES P. MIL. POPULATION	------	----	----	----- -----	-------	-------	----
V46	SUICIDES P. MIL. POPULATION	------	----	----	----- -----	-------	-------	----
V47	IMPORT PARTNERS	1970	R1	FRANC	38.4 %	MADA	MOROC	----
		1970	R2	USSR	11.3 %	IRAQ	SUDAN	----
		1970	R3	IVORY	9.7 %	UPVO	SENE	----
		1980	R1	IVORY	29.3 %	-------	UPVO	----
		1980	R2	FRANC	24.4 %	ITALY	SWITZ	----
		1980	R3	GFR	8.9 %	LIBE	NORWY	----
V48	EXPORT PARTNERS	1970	R1	IVORY	32.2 %	-------	UPVO	----
		1970	R2	FRANC	17.1 %	ITALY	CONGO	----
		1970	R3	SENE	15.2 %	KAMPU	-------	----
		1980	R1	FRANC	24.2 %	MADA	MOROC	----
		1980	R2	IVORY	19.3 %	UPVO	-------	----
		1980	R3	GFR	12.6 %	LIBYA	NEPAL	----
V49	PATENT SUPPLIERS	------	----	----	----- -----	-------	-------	----
V50	PROVENANCE OF FOREIGN FIRMS	------	----	----	----- -----	-------	-------	----
V51	FILM SUPPLIERS	------	----	----	----- -----	-------	-------	----

MAURITANIA (MAURA)

V1	INCOME PER CAPITA	------	----	----	----- -----		-------	-------	----
V2	TELEPHONES P. TSD. POPULATION	------	----	----	----- -----		-------	-------	----
V3	INFANT MORTALITY RATE	1980	D9	P84	148.5	1/TSD	BURU	NIGER	F5
V4	PHYSICIANS P. MIL. POPULATION	1970	D2	P19	54	1/MIL	SOMA	SIERA	----
		1975	D2	P19	61	1/MIL	KENYA	SENE	----
V5	ADULT LITERACY	------	----	----	----- -----		-------	-------	----
V6	DURATION OF SCHOOLING	1970	D1	P7	1.3	YR	ETHIA	MALI	----
		1975	D1	P5	1.7	YR	BURU	ETHIA	----
		1980	D1	P5	2.8	YR	NIGER	SOMA	F35
V7	STUDENT ENROLLMENT RATIO	1970	D1	P4	0.0	%	CHAD	NIGER	----
		1975	D1	P2	0.0	%	BHUTA	MOZAM	----
		1980	D1	P2	0.0	%	-------	OMAN	----
V8	SHARE OF AGRICULTURAL LABOR	------	----	----	----- -----		-------	-------	
V9	SHARE OF INDUSTRIAL LABOR	------	----	----	----- -----		-------	-------	----
V10	SHARE OF SERVICE LABOR	------	----	----	----- -----		-------	-------	----
V11	SHARE OF ACADEMIC LABOR	------	----	----	----- -----		-------	-------	----
V12	SHARE OF SELF-EMPLOYED LABOR	------	----	----	----- -----		-------	-------	----
V13	MILITARY EXPENDITURES	------	----	----	----- -----		-------	-------	----
V14	MILITARY MANPOWER	1970	D1	P7	3	TSD CAP	BURU	SIERA	----
		1975	D1	P6	3	TSD CAP	GABON	PAPUA	----
		1980	D2	P19	8	TSD CAP	MALI	PANA	----
V15	MEN AT AGE 20 - 30	1975	D1	P3	97	TSD CAP	-------	TRITO	F2
V16	POPULATION	1970	D1	P5	1.25	MIL CAP	CONGO	MONGO	----
		1975	D1	P5	1.42	MIL CAP	CONGO	MONGO	----
		1980	D1	P7	1.63	MIL CAP	CONGO	MONGO	----
V17	GROSS DOMESTIC PRODUCT	------	----	----	----- -----		-------	-------	----
V18	SHARE IN WORLD IMPORTS	1970	D1	P9	0.169	1/TSD	KAMPU	CONGO	----
		1975	D2	P12	0.195	1/TSD	MALI	PARA	----
		1980	D1	P6	0.139	1/TSD	SOMA	UGADA	----
V19	SHARE IN WORLD EXPORTS	1970	D3	P21	0.284	1/TSD	AFGHA	SIERA	----
		1975	D2	P19	0.199	1/TSD	YESO	PARA	----
		1980	D1	P10	0.097	1/TSD	SOMA	SIERA	----
V20	GDP SHARE OF IMPORTS	1970	D9	P84	27.7	%	DENMA	ZAIRE	----
		1975	D9	P89	39.9	%	JAMAI	ZAIRE	----
		1980	D9	P88	41.4	%	HONDU	HUNGA	----

V21	GDP SHARE OF EXPORTS	1970	D10	P94	44.1	%	BELGI	ZAMBI	----
		1975	D9	P88	39.3	%	IRAN	MALAY	----
		1980	D8	P73	28.1	%	KORSO	SWITZ	----
V22	EXPORT PARTNER CONCENTRATION	1970	D3	P23	19.8	%	ISRA	TURKY	----
V23	TOTAL DEBT AS % OF GDP	1980	D10	P99	118.6	%	NICA	-------	----
V24	SHARE OF NEW FOREIGN PATENTS	------	----	----	----- -----		-------	-------	----
V25	FOREIGN PROPERTY AS % OF GDP	1971	D10	P96	66.2	%	JAMAI	LIBE	----
		1975	D8	P76	12.4	%	SIERA	PERU	----
		1978	D5	----	4.6	%	BENIN	TUNIS	----
V26	GNP SHARE OF DEVELOPMENT AID	------	----	----	----- -----		-------	-------	----
V27	SHARE IN NOBEL PRIZE WINNERS	1970-79	D5	P45	0.0	%	MALI	MEXI	----
V28	GDP SHARE OF MANUFACTURING	1970	D1	P8	4.9	%	NIGRA	LESO	F16
V29	EXPORT SHARE OF MANUFACTURES	1970	D1	P10	0.8	%	NIGRA	IRAQ	----
		1975	D2	P11	0.4	%	YESO	SAUDI	----
V30	LACK OF CIVIL LIBERTIES	1975	D8	P74	6		MALI	MOZAM	----
		1980	D8	P74	6		MALI	NIGER	----
V31	LACK OF POLITICAL RIGHTS	1975	D5	P43	5		MADA	MOROC	----
		1980	D7	P67	6		MALAW	OMAN	----
V32	RIOTS	1970-74	D2	P19	0		MALI	MONGO	----
		1975-79	D2	P20	0		MALI	MONGO	----
V33	PROTEST DEMONSTRATIONS	1970-74	D2	P15	0		MALI	MONGO	----
		1975-79	D4	P32	1		LIBE	RWAN	----
V34	POLITICAL STRIKES	1970-74	D7	P64	1		MADA	NEPAL	----
		1975-79	D3	P29	0		MALAY	MONGO	----
V35	MEMBER OF THE NONALIGNED MMT.	1970	----	----	1		MALI	MOROC	----
		1976	----	----	1		MALI	MOROC	----
		1981	----	----	1		MALI	MOROC	----
V36	MEMBER OF THE OPEC	1970	----	----	0		MALI	MEXI	----
		1975	----	----	0		MALI	MEXI	----
		1980	----	----	0		MALI	MEXI	----
V37	MEMBER OF THE OECD	1970	----	----	0		MALI	MEXI	----
		1975	----	----	0		MALI	MEXI	----
		1980	----	----	0		MALI	MEXI	----
V38	MEMBER OF THE CMEA	1970	----	----	0		MALI	MEXI	----
		1975	----	----	0		MALI	MEXI	----
		1980	----	----	0		MALI	MEXI	----
V39	MEMBER OF THE WTO	1970	----	----	0		MALI	MEXI	----
		1975	----	----	0		MALI	MEXI	----
		1980	----	----	0		MALI	MEXI	----
V40	MEMBER OF THE NATO	1970	----	----	0		MALI	MEXI	----
		1975	----	----	0		MALI	MEXI	----
		1980	----	----	0		MALI	MEXI	----

V41	GDP SHARE OF INVESTMENTS	1970	D6	P59	22.0 %	COLO	IVORY	----
		1975	D10	P94	34.3 %	LIBE	NORWY	----
		1980	D10	P96	36.0 %	YUGO	ALGER	----
V42	GDP SHARE OF AGRICULTURE	1970	D7	P67	29.3 %	COLO	EGYPT	F16
		1975	D7	P71	31.9 %	LESO	PAKI	F16
		1980	D7	P62	27.0 %	IVORY	COLO	F16
V43	GDP SHARE OF INDUSTRY	1970	D8	P77	38.5 %	ALGER	FRANC	F16
		1975	D6	P54	31.7 %	ZAIRE	CANA	F16
		1980	D3	P28	24.3 %	DENMA	SYRIA	F16
V44	GDP SHARE OF SERVICES	1970	D2	P13	32.2 %	SAUDI	UGADA	F16
		1975	D3	P23	36.4 %	YUGO	NIGRA	F16
		1980	D6	P57	48.7 %	ZIMBA	TOGO	F16
V45	HOMICIDES P. MIL. POPULATION	------	----	----	----- -----	-------	-------	----
V46	SUICIDES P. MIL. POPULATION	------	----	----	----- -----	-------	-------	----
V47	IMPORT PARTNERS	------	----	----	----- -----	-------	-------	----
V48	EXPORT PARTNERS	1970	R1	FRANC	19.8 %	MADA	MOROC	----
		1970	R2	UNKI	16.5 %	JAMAI	NORWY	----
		1970	R3	ITALY	14.7 %	HONDU	MOROC	----
V49	PATENT SUPPLIERS	------	----	----	----- -----	-------	-------	----
V50	PROVENANCE OF FOREIGN FIRMS	------	----	----	----- -----	-------	-------	----
V51	FILM SUPPLIERS	1980	R1	USA	100	MALAY	MEXI	F118
		1980	R2	INDIA	60	MALAY	SINGA	F118
		1980	R3	FRANC	28	KORSO	MOROC	F118

MEXICO (MEXI)

V1	INCOME PER CAPITA	1970	D7	P62	1472 $/CAP	JAMAI	PORTU	F147
		1975	D7	P63	1704 $/CAP	HUNGA	CHILE	F147
		1980	D6	P60	2040 $/CAP	HUNGA	ALGER	F147
V2	TELEPHONES P. TSD. POPULATION	1970	D6	P59	31 1/TSD CAP	LIBYA	CUBA	----
		1975	D7	P59	50 1/TSD CAP	JAMAI	COLO	----
		1980	D6	P57	72 1/TSD CAP	COLO	KORSO	----
V3	INFANT MORTALITY RATE	------	----	----	----- -----	-------	-------	----
V4	PHYSICIANS P. MIL. POPULATION	1970	D7	P68	670 1/MIL	PANA	LEBA	F147
		1974	D7	P64	800 1/MIL	PANA	LEBA	F147
V5	ADULT LITERACY	1970	D6	P52	74.2 %	PERU	VENE	----
		1980	D8	P72	82.7 %	BRAZI	SINGA	----

V6	DURATION OF SCHOOLING	1970	D6	P57	8.0	YR	MALAY	PARA	----
		1975	D7	P63	9.1	YR	CHINA	KUWAI	----
		1980	D8	P72	10.4	YR	ARGE	TOGO	----
V7	STUDENT ENROLLMENT RATIO	1970	D6	P55	5.9	%	NICA	TURKY	----
		1975	D7	P63	10.6	%	PORTU	BRAZI	----
		1980	D7	P63	14.1	%	THAI	NICA	----
V8	SHARE OF AGRICULTURAL LABOR	1969	D6	P61	40.3	%	PANA	GREC	F67
		1975	D6	P56	39.3	%	COSTA	EGYPT	F99
		1980	D6	P61	31.5	%	COLO	SYRIA	----
V9	SHARE OF INDUSTRIAL LABOR	1975	D4	P33	22.5	%	TURKY	EGYPT	F99
		1980	D4	P36	27.4	%	ELSA	KORSO	----
V10	SHARE OF SERVICE LABOR	1975	D7	P60	32.0	%	SPAIN	FINLA	F99
		1980	D6	P45	32.8	%	PERU	PORTU	----
V11	SHARE OF ACADEMIC LABOR	1975	D5	P49	6.2	%	COLO	IRAN	F99
		1980	D5	P41	8.3	%	PORTU	PERU	----
V12	SHARE OF SELF-EMPLOYED LABOR	1969	D7	P65	31.3	%	THAI	NICA	F67
		1975	D6	P50	31.1	%	KORSO	EGYPT	F99
		1980	D7	P72	34.7	%	THAI	SYRIA	----
V13	MILITARY EXPENDITURES	1975	D6	P52	0.543	TSD MIL $	COLO	ALGER	----
		1980	D6	P52	0.580	TSD MIL $	COLO	SINGA	----
V14	MILITARY MANPOWER	1970	D7	P62	80	TSD CAP	ALGER	PERU	----
		1975	D7	P64	95	TSD CAP	BELGI	PERU	----
		1980	D8	P72	145	TSD CAP	HUNGA	NIGRA	----
V15	MEN AT AGE 20 - 30	1970	D9	P85	3506	TSD CAP	PHILI	FRANC	F22
		1976	D10	P92	4994	TSD CAP	GFR	BANGL	F184
		1979	D9	P89	5644	TSD CAP	GFR	PAKI	F184
V16	POPULATION	1970	D9	P88	50.70	MIL CAP	PHILI	FRANC	F22
		1975	D10	P91	60.15	MIL CAP	UNKI	GFR	F22
		1980	D10	P92	69.35	MIL CAP	GFR	NIGRA	F22
V17	GROSS DOMESTIC PRODUCT	1970	D9	P81	74.648	TSD MIL $	SOUAF	BELGI	----
		1975	D9	P84	102.484	TSD MIL $	BELGI	SWEDN	----
		1980	D9	P87	141.446	TSD MIL $	AULIA	INDIA	----
V18	SHARE IN WORLD IMPORTS	1970	D8	P75	6.989	1/TSD	INDIA	CHINA	F30
		1975	D8	P75	7.228	1/TSD	INDIA	HUNGA	F30
		1980	D9	P82	9.466	1/TSD	POLA	CHINA	F30
V19	SHARE IN WORLD EXPORTS	1970	D7	P67	4.179	1/TSD	NIGRA	SINGA	F30
		1975	D7	P63	3.415	1/TSD	ARGE	IRE	F30
		1980	D8	P73	7.666	1/TSD	CZECH	ALGER	F30
V20	GDP SHARE OF IMPORTS	1970	D1	P4	6.5	%	USA	BRAZI	F30
		1975	D1	P6	7.5	%	INDIA	ARGE	F30
		1980	D1	P10	10.4	%	CENTR	PARA	F30
V21	GDP SHARE OF EXPORTS	1970	D1	P3	3.7	%	YENO	INDIA	F30
		1975	D1	P3	3.4	%	BANGL	TURKY	F30
		1980	D2	P17	8.2	%	BURMA	USA	F30

V22 EXPORT PARTNER CONCENTRATION	1970	D10	P98	70.3 %	CHAD	DOMI	----
	1975	D10	P93	61.6 %	CUBA	NIGER	----
	1980	D10	P98	65.8 %	DOMI	SOMA	----
V23 TOTAL DEBT AS % OF GDP	1980	D5	P41	30.7 %	DOMI	BANGL	----
V24 SHARE OF NEW FOREIGN PATENTS	1970	D6	P55	93 %	JAMAI	CHILE	----
	1975	D7	P62	93 %	BANGL	MOROC	----
	1980	D7	P65	93 %	BOLI	TURKY	----
V25 FOREIGN PROPERTY AS % OF GDP	1971	D4	P38	6.3 %	BURU	PARA	----
	1975	D5	P49	5.5 %	CHILE	TANZA	----
	1978	D6	----	5.8 %	ARGE	NIGER	----
V26 GNP SHARE OF DEVELOPMENT AID	------	----	----	----- -----	-------	-------	----
V27 SHARE IN NOBEL PRIZE WINNERS	1970-79	D5	P45	0.0 %	MAURA	MONGO	----
V28 GDP SHARE OF MANUFACTURING	1970	D8	P80	23.7 %	SOUAF	PERU	----
	1975	D8	P80	23.3 %	AULIA	SOUAF	----
	1979	D9	P84	23.3 %	NEWZ	PHILI	----
V29 EXPORT SHARE OF MANUFACTURES	------	----	----	----- -----	-------	-------	----
V30 LACK OF CIVIL LIBERTIES	1975	D3	P27	3	MALAY	PORTU	----
	1980	D3	P29	3	JAMAI	NIGRA	----
V31 LACK OF POLITICAL RIGHTS	1975	D4	P31	4	KUWAI	SOUAF	----
	1980	D4	P31	3	MALAY	MOROC	----
V32 RIOTS	1970-74	D9	P82	12	KAMPU	LEBA	----
	1975-79	D8	P72	6	ARGE	COSTA	----
V33 PROTEST DEMONSTRATIONS	1970-74	D8	P74	9	EGYPT	SWITZ	----
	1975-79	D8	P74	12	JAPAN	CZECH	----
V34 POLITICAL STRIKES	1970-74	D3	P29	0	MALI	MONGO	----
	1975-79	D8	P80	5	GREC	BRAZI	----
V35 MEMBER OF THE NONALIGNED MMT.	1970	----	----	0	MADA	MONGO	----
	1976	----	----	0	KORSO	MONGO	----
	1981	----	----	0	KORSO	MONGO	----
V36 MEMBER OF THE OPEC	1970	----	----	0	MAURA	MONGO	----
	1975	----	----	0	MAURA	MONGO	----
	1980	----	----	0	MAURA	MONGO	----
V37 MEMBER OF THE OECD	1970	----	----	0	MAURA	MONGO	----
	1975	----	----	0	MAURA	MONGO	----
	1980	----	----	0	MAURA	MONGO	----
V38 MEMBER OF THE CMEA	1970	----	----	0	MAURA	MOROC	----
	1975	----	----	0	MAURA	MOROC	----
	1980	----	----	0	MAURA	MOROC	----
V39 MEMBER OF THE WTO	1970	----	----	0	MAURA	MONGO	----
	1975	----	----	0	MAURA	MONGO	----
	1980	----	----	0	MAURA	MONGO	----

V40	MEMBER OF THE NATO	1970	----	----	0		MAURA	MONGO	----
		1975	----	----	0		MAURA	MONGO	----
		1980	----	----	0		MAURA	MONGO	----
V41	GDP SHARE OF INVESTMENTS	1970	D7	P64	22.7	%	BRAZI	ITALY	----
		1975	D6	P57	23.7	%	AULIA	TURKY	----
		1979	D7	P62	26.0	%	PAPUA	HONDU	----
V42	GDP SHARE OF AGRICULTURE	1970	D3	P30	12.2	%	ARGE	NEWZ	----
		1975	D4	P34	11.2	%	NEWZ	PANA	----
		1979	D4	P33	9.2	%	ARGE	URU	----
V43	GDP SHARE OF INDUSTRY	1970	D7	P64	32.7	%	CANA	NORWY	----
		1975	D6	P58	33.1	%	CONGO	ANGO	----
		1979	D7	P62	34.9	%	UNKI	URU	----
V44	GDP SHARE OF SERVICES	1970	D9	P81	55.1	%	FRANC	SENE	----
		1975	D9	P83	55.7	%	JAMAI	URU	----
		1979	D9	P83	55.9	%	AURIA	FINLA	----
V45	HOMICIDES P. MIL. POPULATION	------	----	----	----- -----		-------	-------	----
V46	SUICIDES P. MIL. POPULATION	------	----	----	----- -----		-------	-------	----
V47	IMPORT PARTNERS	1970	R1	USA	63.7	%	LIBE	NICA	----
		1970	R2	GFR	7.5	%	MADA	NORWY	----
		1970	R3	FRANC	4.2	%	LEBA	SPAIN	----
		1980	R1	USA	61.6	%	JAPAN	NICA	----
V48	EXPORT PARTNERS	1970	R1	USA	70.3	%	LIBE	NICA	----
		1970	R2	JAPAN	5.7	%	MALAY	NICA	----
		1970	R3	GFR	2.3	%	KORSO	NICA	----
		1980	R1	USA	65.8	%	LIBYA	NICA	----
		1980	R2	SPAIN	8.1	%	-------	-------	----
		1980	R3	JAPAN	4.4	%	MADA	SINGA	----
V49	PATENT SUPPLIERS	1970	R1	USA	3070		MALAY	NETH	----
		1970	R2	JAPAN	724		IRAQ	PHILI	----
		1970	R3	ITALY	650		-------	TRITO	----
		1980	R1	USA	1442		KENYA	NETH	----
		1980	R2	GFR	208		JAPAN	NETH	----
		1980	R3	FRANC	131		ITALY	NIGRA	----
V50	PROVENANCE OF FOREIGN FIRMS	1980	R1	USA	79.7	%	LEBA	NICA	----
		1980	R2	GFR	4.2	%	CAME	SENE	----
		1980	R3	UNKI	3.7	%	INDO	NORWY	----
V51	FILM SUPPLIERS	1980	R1	USA	318		MAURA	NETH	F118
		1980	R2	ITALY	46		LIBYA	NICA	F118
		1980	R3	UNKI	26		ISRA	NICA	F118

MONGOLIA (MONGO)

V1	INCOME PER CAPITA	------	----	----	-----	-----	-------	-------	----
V2	TELEPHONES P. TSD. POPULATION	1970	D5	P50	15	1/TSD CAP	JORDA	TUNIS	----
		1975	D5	P46	21	1/TSD CAP	IRAN	SYRIA	----
V3	INFANT MORTALITY RATE	1980	D5	P44	59.1	1/TSD	THAI	COLO	F5
V4	PHYSICIANS P. MIL. POPULATION	1970	D10	P92	1738	1/MIL	GREC	ITALY	----
		1976	D10	P96	2051	1/MIL	GREC	BULGA	----
		1980	D9	P88	2220	1/MIL	SWEDN	GFR	----
V5	ADULT LITERACY	------	----	----	-----	-----	-------	-------	----
V6	DURATION OF SCHOOLING	1970	D6	P59	8.1	YR	PARA	TUNIS	F4
		1975	D7	P61	9.0	YR	ECUA	CHINA	----
		1979	D6	P55	9.4	YR	SYRIA	PHILI	----
V7	STUDENT ENROLLMENT RATIO	1970	D6	P59	6.4	%	ALBA	DOMI	----
		1975	D6	P54	8.4	%	NICA	INDIA	----
		1979	D6	P53	8.6	%	LIBYA	INDIA	----
V8	SHARE OF AGRICULTURAL LABOR	------	----	----	-----	-----	-------	-------	----
V9	SHARE OF INDUSTRIAL LABOR	------	----	----	-----	-----	-------	-------	----
V10	SHARE OF SERVICE LABOR	------	----	----	-----	-----	-------	-------	----
V11	SHARE OF ACADEMIC LABOR	------	----	----	-----	-----	-------	-------	----
V12	SHARE OF SELF-EMPLOYED LABOR	------	----	----	-----	-----	-------	-------	----
V13	MILITARY EXPENDITURES	------	----	----	-----	-----	-------	-------	----
V14	MILITARY MANPOWER	1975	D5	P48	36	TSD CAP	NORWY	FINLA	----
		1980	D5	P48	36	TSD CAP	FINLA	YENO	----
V15	MEN AT AGE 20 - 30	------	----	----	-----	-----	-------	-------	----
V16	POPULATION	1970	D1	P5	1.25	MIL CAP	MAURA	LIBE	----
		1975	D1	P6	1.45	MIL CAP	MAURA	LIBE	----
		1980	D1	P8	1.66	MIL CAP	MAURA	YESO	----
V17	GROSS DOMESTIC PRODUCT	------	----	----	-----	-----	-------	-------	----
V18	SHARE IN WORLD IMPORTS	1970	D2	P20	0.365	1/TSD	SIERA	LIBE	F30
		1975	D2	P19	0.293	1/TSD	MALAW	YENO	F30
		1980	D2	P19	0.276	1/TSD	CONGO	NIGER	F30
V19	SHARE IN WORLD EXPORTS	1970	D2	P19	0.268	1/TSD	PARA	AFGHA	F30
		1975	D3	P22	0.249	1/TSD	MOZAM	AFGHA	F30
		1980	D2	P19	0.208	1/TSD	MADA	ETHIA	F30
V20	GDP SHARE OF IMPORTS	------	----	----	-----	-----	-------	-------	----
V21	GDP SHARE OF EXPORTS	------	----	----	-----	-----	-------	-------	----
V22	EXPORT PARTNER CONCENTRATION	------	----	----	-----	-----	-------	-------	----

V23	TOTAL DEBT AS % OF GDP	------	---- ----	----- -----	------- -------	----
V24	SHARE OF NEW FOREIGN PATENTS	------	---- ----	----- -----	------- -------	----
V25	FOREIGN PROPERTY AS % OF GDP	------	---- ----	----- -----	------- -------	----
V26	GNP SHARE OF DEVELOPMENT AID	------	---- ----	----- -----	------- -------	----
V27	SHARE IN NOBEL PRIZE WINNERS	1970-79	D5 P45	0.0 %	MEXI MOROC	----
V28	GDP SHARE OF MANUFACTURING	------	---- ----	----- -----	------- -------	----
V29	EXPORT SHARE OF MANUFACTURES	------	---- ----	----- -----	------- -------	----
V30	LACK OF CIVIL LIBERTIES	1975	D10 P93	7	LIBYA SYRIA	----
		1980	D10 P92	7	MALAW MOZAM	----
V31	LACK OF POLITICAL RIGHTS	1975	D9 P88	7	MALI NIGER	----
		1980	D9 P90	7	MALI MOZAM	----
V32	RIOTS	1970-74	D2 P19	0	MAURA NICA	----
		1975-79	D2 P20	0	MAURA MOROC	----
V33	PROTEST DEMONSTRATIONS	1970-74	D2 P15	0	MAURA NORWY	----
		1975-79	D2 P13	0	MALI MOROC	----
V34	POLITICAL STRIKES	1970-74	D3 P29	0	MEXI NETH	----
		1975-79	D3 P29	0	MAURA NETH	----
V35	MEMBER OF THE NONALIGNED MMT.	1970	---- ----	0	MEXI NETH	----
		1976	---- ----	0	MEXI NETH	----
		1981	---- ----	0	MEXI NETH	----
V36	MEMBER OF THE OPEC	1970	---- ----	0	MEXI MOROC	----
		1975	---- ----	0	MEXI MOROC	----
		1980	---- ----	0	MEXI MOROC	----
V37	MEMBER OF THE OECD	1970	---- ----	0	MEXI MOROC	----
		1975	---- ----	0	MEXI MOROC	----
		1980	---- ----	0	MEXI MOROC	----
V38	MEMBER OF THE CMEA	1970	---- ----	1	HUNGA POLA	----
		1975	---- ----	1	HUNGA POLA	----
		1980	---- ----	1	HUNGA POLA	----
V39	MEMBER OF THE WTO	1970	---- ----	0	MEXI MOROC	----
		1975	---- ----	0	MEXI MOROC	----
		1980	---- ----	0	MEXI MOROC	----
V40	MEMBER OF THE NATO	1970	---- ----	0	MEXI MOROC	----
		1975	---- ----	0	MEXI MOROC	----
		1980	---- ----	0	MEXI MOROC	----
V41	GDP SHARE OF INVESTMENTS	------	---- ----	----- -----	------- -------	----
V42	GDP SHARE OF AGRICULTURE	------	---- ----	----- -----	------- -------	----
V43	GDP SHARE OF INDUSTRY	------	---- ----	----- -----	------- -------	----
V44	GDP SHARE OF SERVICES	------	---- ----	----- -----	------- -------	----

V45	HOMICIDES P. MIL. POPULATION	------	----	----	----- -----	-------	-------	----
V46	SUICIDES P. MIL. POPULATION	------	----	----	----- -----	-------	-------	----
V47	IMPORT PARTNERS	------	----	----	----- -----	-------	-------	----
V48	EXPORT PARTNERS	------	----	----	----- -----	-------	-------	----
V49	PATENT SUPPLIERS	------	----	----	----- -----	-------	-------	----
V50	PROVENANCE OF FOREIGN FIRMS	------	----	----	----- -----	-------	-------	----
V51	FILM SUPPLIERS	------	----	----	----- -----	-------	-------	----

MOROCCO (MOROC)

V1	INCOME PER CAPITA	1970	D4	P32	617 $/CAP	CAME	ELSA	F4
		1975	D4	P38	738 $/CAP	ELSA	PAPUA	----
		1980	D4	P40	817 $/CAP	PAPUA	NIGRA	----
V2	TELEPHONES P. TSD. POPULATION	1970	D5	P42	11 1/TSD CAP	IRAN	DOMI	----
		1975	D4	P35	10 1/TSD CAP	GUATE	NICA	----
		1980	D3	P30	12 1/TSD CAP	KENYA	IVORY	----
V3	INFANT MORTALITY RATE	1980	D7	P64	114.4 1/TSD	PAPUA	IRAN	F5
V4	PHYSICIANS P. MIL. POPULATION	1970	D3	P28	75 1/MIL	SUDAN	LIBE	----
		1975	D3	P27	72 1/MIL	PAPUA	BANGL	----
		1981	D2	P13	56 1/MIL	TOGO	SIERA	----
V5	ADULT LITERACY	1971	D2	P14	21.4 %	HAITI	ALGER	F27
V6	DURATION OF SCHOOLING	1970	D3	P22	3.8 YR	LAOS	HAITI	----
		1975	D3	P22	4.4 YR	LAOS	GUATE	----
		1980	D3	P22	5.8 YR	LAOS	OMAN	----
V7	STUDENT ENROLLMENT RATIO	1970	D4	P33	1.5 %	KAMPU	SENE	----
		1975	D4	P41	3.2 %	ALGER	GUINE	----
		1980	D5	P47	6.0 %	CONGO	TURKY	----
V8	SHARE OF AGRICULTURAL LABOR	1971	D9	P83	56.3 %	PHILI	ELSA	F82
		1982	D8	----	42.9 %	EGYPT	SRILA	F110
V9	SHARE OF INDUSTRIAL LABOR	1971	D3	P23	21.0 %	GHANA	KORSO	F82
		1982	D5	----	30.8 %	ISRA	USA	F110
V10	SHARE OF SERVICE LABOR	1971	D2	P17	18.4 %	HAITI	POLA	F82
		1982	D3	----	20.5 %	SYRIA	INDO	F110
V11	SHARE OF ACADEMIC LABOR	1971	D3	P28	4.3 %	PORTU	PARA	F82
		1982	D4	----	5.9 %	DOMI	PHILI	F110
V12	SHARE OF SELF-EMPLOYED LABOR	------	----	----	----- -----	-------	-------	----

V13	MILITARY EXPENDITURES	1970	D5	P44	0.219	TSD MIL $	BURMA	SINGA	----
		1975	D6	P56	0.588	TSD MIL $	FINLA	THAI	----
		1980	D7	P61	1.027	TSD MIL $	AURIA	PERU	----
V14	MILITARY MANPOWER	1970	D6	P56	65	TSD CAP	LAOS	SAUDI	----
		1975	D6	P59	75	TSD CAP	AULIA	SWEDN	----
		1980	D8	P71	117	TSD CAP	CHILE	HUNGA	----
V15	MEN AT AGE 20 - 30	1971	D6	P58	900	TSD CAP	KENYA	NEPAL	F22
		1973	D7	----	1275	TSD CAP	NETH	CZECH	F190
		1978	D7	----	1514	TSD CAP	SUDAN	ALGER	F190
V16	POPULATION	1970	D8	P72	15.52	MIL CAP	CZECH	GDR	F4
		1975	D8	P73	17.31	MIL CAP	GDR	ROMA	----
		1980	D8	P73	20.05	MIL CAP	SUDAN	ROMA	----
V17	GROSS DOMESTIC PRODUCT	1970	D6	P51	9.576	TSD MIL $	LIBYA	MALAY	----
		1975	D5	P50	12.783	TSD MIL $	SYRIA	IRE	----
		1980	D6	P51	16.378	TSD MIL $	SYRIA	IRE	----
V18	SHARE IN WORLD IMPORTS	1970	D6	P52	2.060	1/TSD	PERU	SAUDI	----
		1975	D6	P55	2.825	1/TSD	PERU	NEWZ	----
		1980	D6	P52	2.040	1/TSD	SYRIA	COLO	----
V19	SHARE IN WORLD EXPORTS	1970	D5	P48	1.556	1/TSD	IVORY	TURKY	----
		1975	D6	P55	1.845	1/TSD	CHILE	TRITO	----
		1980	D5	P48	1.204	1/TSD	TUNIS	ECUA	----
V20	GDP SHARE OF IMPORTS	1970	D5	P47	17.8	%	UNKI	PHILI	----
		1975	D7	P66	28.6	%	MALI	IVORY	----
		1980	D5	P50	23.5	%	PHILI	KUWAI	----
V21	GDP SHARE OF EXPORTS	1970	D4	P40	12.7	%	FRANC	BENIN	----
		1975	D5	P50	18.0	%	GHANA	BOLI	----
		1980	D3	P30	13.5	%	GREC	ANGO	----
V22	EXPORT PARTNER CONCENTRATION	1970	D7	P69	36.6	%	LAOS	COLO	----
		1975	D4	P38	21.7	%	PORTU	TURKY	----
		1980	D5	P48	25.2	%	AULIA	BOLI	----
V23	TOTAL DEBT AS % OF GDP	------	----	----	----- -----		-------	-------	----
V24	SHARE OF NEW FOREIGN PATENTS	1970	D7	P61	95	%	COLO	PERU	----
		1975	D7	P62	93	%	MEXI	PERU	----
		1980	D7	P72	94	%	MALAW	PANA	----
V25	FOREIGN PROPERTY AS % OF GDP	1971	D4	P32	5.7	%	UPVO	NIGER	----
		1975	D3	P28	3.3	%	UPVO	ANGO	----
		1978	D3	----	2.6	%	ANGO	SRILA	----
V26	GNP SHARE OF DEVELOPMENT AID	------	----	----	----- -----		-------	-------	----
V27	SHARE IN NOBEL PRIZE WINNERS	1970-79	D5	P45	0.0	%	MONGO	NEPAL	----
V28	GDP SHARE OF MANUFACTURING	1970	D6	P56	16.2	%	THAI	PARA	----
		1975	D7	P61	17.1	%	TURKY	MALAY	----
		1980	D7	P65	17.1	%	ZAMBI	INDIA	----
V29	EXPORT SHARE OF MANUFACTURES	1970	D5	P49	9.7	%	BRAZI	BENIN	----
		1975	D6	P59	12.5	%	TANZA	KENYA	----
		1980	D7	P61	23.5	%	MALI	TURKY	----

V30	LACK OF CIVIL LIBERTIES	1975	D6	P54	5	LAOS	NEPAL	----
		1980	D4	P38	4	MALAY	NEPAL	----
V31	LACK OF POLITICAL RIGHTS	1975	D5	P43	5	MAURA	NICA	----
		1980	D4	P31	3	MEXI	BRAZI	----
V32	RIOTS	1970-74	D6	P59	3	LIBYA	NEPAL	----
		1975-79	D2	P20	0	MONGO	NEWZ	----
V33	PROTEST DEMONSTRATIONS	1970-74	D5	P49	2	MALAY	NIGER	----
		1975-79	D2	P13	0	MONGO	NIGER	----
V34	POLITICAL STRIKES	1970-74	D9	P87	9	POLA	URU	----
		1975-79	D7	P63	1	JAMAI	NEPAL	----
V35	MEMBER OF THE NONALIGNED MMT.	1970	----	----	1	MAURA	NEPAL	----
		1976	----	----	1	MAURA	MOZAM	----
		1981	----	----	1	MAURA	MOZAM	----
V36	MEMBER OF THE OPEC	1970	----	----	0	MONGO	NEPAL	----
		1975	----	----	0	MONGO	MOZAM	----
		1980	----	----	0	MONGO	MOZAM	----
V37	MEMBER OF THE OECD	1970	----	----	0	MONGO	NEPAL	----
		1975	----	----	0	MONGO	MOZAM	----
		1980	----	----	0	MONGO	MOZAM	----
V38	MEMBER OF THE CMEA	1970	----	----	0	MEXI	NEPAL	----
		1975	----	----	0	MEXI	MOZAM	----
		1980	----	----	0	MEXI	MOZAM	----
V39	MEMBER OF THE WTO	1970	----	----	0	MONGO	NEPAL	----
		1975	----	----	0	MONGO	MOZAM	----
		1980	----	----	0	MONGO	MOZAM	----
V40	MEMBER OF THE NATO	1970	----	----	0	MONGO	NEPAL	----
		1975	----	----	0	MONGO	MOZAM	----
		1980	----	----	0	MONGO	MOZAM	----
V41	GDP SHARE OF INVESTMENTS	1970	D5	P42	18.5 %	ECUA	NICA	----
		1975	D7	P65	25.4 %	LESO	THAI	----
		1980	D5	P42	22.6 %	LIBYA	NEWZ	----
V42	GDP SHARE OF AGRICULTURE	1970	D5	P48	19.9 %	IRAN	SYRIA	----
		1975	D5	P44	17.9 %	ECUA	SYRIA	----
		1980	D5	P49	18.1 %	COSTA	SYRIA	----
V43	GDP SHARE OF INDUSTRY	1970	D5	P49	27.0 %	COLO	TURKY	----
		1975	D7	P69	35.2 %	NETH	NIGRA	----
		1980	D6	P53	32.3 %	SWEDN	NETH	----
V44	GDP SHARE OF SERVICES	1970	D8	P70	53.1 %	FINLA	COSTA	----
		1975	D6	P54	46.9 %	DOMI	TOGO	----
		1980	D6	P60	49.6 %	CENTR	SUDAN	----
V45	HOMICIDES P. MIL. POPULATION	------	----	----	----- -----	-------	-------	----
V46	SUICIDES P. MIL. POPULATION	------	----	----	----- -----	-------	-------	----

V47	IMPORT PARTNERS	1970	R1	FRANC	31.0 %	MALI	SENE	----
		1970	R2	USA	11.3 %	LIBYA	NIGRA	----
		1970	R3	GFR	8.8 %	KORSO	NIGRA	----
		1980	R1	FRANC	24.8 %	MADA	NIGER	----
		1980	R2	IRAQ	9.5 %	BRAZI	URU	----
		1980	R3	SPAIN	8.3 %	-------	-------	----
V48	EXPORT PARTNERS	1970	R1	FRANC	36.6 %	MAURA	NIGER	----
		1970	R2	GFR	9.2 %	LIBYA	PANA	----
		1970	R3	ITALY	6.6 %	MAURA	NIGER	----
		1980	R1	FRANC	25.2 %	MALI	NIGER	----
		1980	R2	GFR	8.2 %	JAPAN	NICA	----
		1980	R3	NETH	5.9 %	MALAW	PHILI	----
V49	PATENT SUPPLIERS	1970	R1	FRANC	125	-------	TUNIS	----
		1970	R2	USA	62	MALAW	NIGRA	----
		1970	R3	GFR	59	KENYA	PERU	----
		1980	R1	FRANC	130	IRAQ	TUNIS	----
		1980	R2	USA	74	MALAW	POLA	----
		1980	R3	GFR	39	KORSO	PERU	----
V50	PROVENANCE OF FOREIGN FIRMS	1980	R1	FRANC	58.2 %	MADA	SENE	----
		1980	R2	USA	11.3 %	MALAY	NETH	----
		1980	R3	GFR	4.7 %	MALAW	NETH	----
V51	FILM SUPPLIERS	1982	R1	INDIA	83	-------	RWAN	F119
		1982	R2	USA	73	IRAN	PAKI	F119
		1982	R3	FRANC	53	MAURA	NEWZ	F119

MOZAMBIQUE (MOZAM)

V1	INCOME PER CAPITA	------	----	----	----- -----	-------	-------	----
V2	TELEPHONES P. TSD. POPULATION	1975	D3	P27	5 1/TSD CAP	UGADA	SRILA	----
		1979	D2	P14	4 1/TSD CAP	MADA	PAKI	----
V3	INFANT MORTALITY RATE	1980	D7	P67	119.6 1/TSD	RWAN	LESO	F5
V4	PHYSICIANS P. MIL. POPULATION	1980	D1	P5	26 1/MIL	UPVO	NIGER	----
V5	ADULT LITERACY	1980	D3	P32	33.2 %	CENTR	NIGRA	F21
V6	DURATION OF SCHOOLING	1982	D2	----	4.4 YR	SIERA	BANGL	----
V7	STUDENT ENROLLMENT RATIO	1976	D1	P4	0.1 %	MAURA	NIGER	----
		1980	D1	P3	0.1 %	OMAN	ANGO	----
V8	SHARE OF AGRICULTURAL LABOR	------	----	----	----- -----	-------	-------	----
V9	SHARE OF INDUSTRIAL LABOR	------	----	----	----- -----	-------	-------	----

V10 SHARE OF SERVICE LABOR	------	----	----	-----	-----	-------	-------	----
V11 SHARE OF ACADEMIC LABOR	------	----	----	-----	-----	-------	-------	----
V12 SHARE OF SELF-EMPLOYED LABOR	------	----	----	-----	-----	-------	-------	----
V13 MILITARY EXPENDITURES	------	----	----	-----	-----	-------	-------	----
V14 MILITARY MANPOWER	1975	D4	P35	20	TSD CAP	LEBA	TUNIS	----
	1980	D5	P42	30	TSD CAP	TUNIS	DENMA	----
V15 MEN AT AGE 20 - 30	1980	D5	P40	735	TSD CAP	GREC	SYRIA	F46
V16 POPULATION	1975	D6	P56	9.72	MIL CAP	PORTU	BELGI	----
	1980	D6	P59	12.09	MIL CAP	GHANA	UGADA	----
V17 GROSS DOMESTIC PRODUCT	------	----	----	-----	-----	-------	-------	----
V18 SHARE IN WORLD IMPORTS	1975	D3	P25	0.459	1/TSD	HONDU	GABON	----
	1980	D3	P23	0.349	1/TSD	GABON	ETHIA	----
V19 SHARE IN WORLD EXPORTS	1975	D3	P21	0.231	1/TSD	CONGO	MONGO	----
	1980	D2	P17	0.183	1/TSD	PANA	MADA	----
V20 GDP SHARE OF IMPORTS	1975	D2	P16	12.7	%	AULIA	TURKY	----
	1980	D4	P32	18.4	%	SOMA	CHILE	----
V21 GDP SHARE OF EXPORTS	1975	D1	P8	6.2	%	BENIN	NEPAL	----
	1980	D2	P20	9.4	%	SOMA	SPAIN	----
V22 EXPORT PARTNER CONCENTRATION	1975	D5	P47	23.8	%	SOUAF	NORWY	----
V23 TOTAL DEBT AS % OF GDP	------	----	----	-----	-----	-------	-------	----
V24 SHARE OF NEW FOREIGN PATENTS	------	----	----	-----	-----	-------	-------	----
V25 FOREIGN PROPERTY AS % OF GDP	1975	D3	P26	3.1	%	INDIA	UPVO	----
	1978	D4	----	3.2	%	PORTU	GREC	----
V26 GNP SHARE OF DEVELOPMENT AID	------	----	----	-----	-----	-------	-------	----
V27 SHARE IN NOBEL PRIZE WINNERS	------	----	----	-----	-----	-------	-------	----
V28 GDP SHARE OF MANUFACTURING	1975	D3	P29	9.4	%	BURMA	NEPAL	F16
	1980	D4	P32	8.6	%	CAME	PAPUA	F16
V29 EXPORT SHARE OF MANUFACTURES	1975	D3	P28	3.1	%	BURMA	BOLI	----
V30 LACK OF CIVIL LIBERTIES	1975	D8	P74	6		MAURA	NIGER	----
	1980	D10	P92	7		MONGO	SOMA	----
V31 LACK OF POLITICAL RIGHTS	1975	D7	P63	6		LIBE	NEPAL	----
	1980	D9	P90	7		MONGO	NIGER	----
V32 RIOTS	-------	----	----	-----	-----	-------	-------	----
V33 PROTEST DEMONSTRATIONS	------	----	----	-----	-----	-------	-------	----
V34 POLITICAL STRIKES	------	----	----	-----	-----	-------	-------	----

V35	MEMBER OF THE NONALIGNED MMT.	1976	----	----	1		MOROC	NEPAL	----
		1981	----	----	1		MOROC	NEPAL	----
V36	MEMBER OF THE OPEC	1975	----	----	0		MOROC	NEPAL	----
		1980	----	----	0		MOROC	NEPAL	----
V37	MEMBER OF THE OECD	1975	----	----	0		MOROC	NEPAL	----
		1980	----	----	0		MOROC	NEPAL	----
V38	MEMBER OF THE CMEA	1975	----	----	0		MOROC	NEPAL	----
		1980	----	----	0		MOROC	NEPAL	----
V39	MEMBER OF THE WTO	1975	----	----	0		MOROC	NEPAL	----
		1980	----	----	0		MOROC	NEPAL	----
V40	MEMBER OF THE NATO	1975	----	----	0		MOROC	NEPAL	----
		1980	----	----	0		MOROC	NEPAL	----
V41	GDP SHARE OF INVESTMENTS	1975	D1	P4	7.8 %		BURU	BANGL	----
		1980	D1	P5	9.8 %		ANGO	ELSA	----
V42	GDP SHARE OF AGRICULTURE	1975	D9	P85	42.8 %		INDIA	SUDAN	F16
		1980	D9	P88	43.4 %		ANGO	RWAN	F16
V43	GDP SHARE OF INDUSTRY	1975	D2	P15	16.8 %		ETHIA	CENTR	F16
		1980	D2	P14	16.6 %		BURU	UPVO	F16
V44	GDP SHARE OF SERVICES	1975	D4	P31	40.4 %		ALGER	SIERA	F16
		1980	D3	P27	40.0 %		PHILI	SOUAF	F16
V45	HOMICIDES P. MIL. POPULATION	------	----	----	----- -----		-------	-------	----
V46	SUICIDES P. MIL. POPULATION	------	----	----	----- -----		-------	-------	----
V47	IMPORT PARTNERS	------	----	----	----- -----		-------	-------	----
V48	EXPORT PARTNERS	------	----	----	----- -----		-------	-------	----
V49	PATENT SUPPLIERS	------	----	----	----- -----		-------	-------	----
V50	PROVENANCE OF FOREIGN FIRMS	1980	R1	UNKI	56.7 %		MALAY	NETH	----
		1980	R2	NETH	18.9 %		HAITI	TOGO	----
		1980	R3	USA	16.2 %		GUINE	NEWZ	----
V51	FILM SUPPLIERS	1982	R1	USSR	32		LAOS	POLA	F117
		1982	R2	FRANC	7		JAPAN	NETH	F117
		1982	R3	USA	4		JORDA	-------	F117

NEPAL (NEPAL)

V1	INCOME PER CAPITA	1970	D1	P6	144 $/CAP		BURMA	BURU	F210
		1975	D1	P5	142 $/CAP		BURMA	MALAW	----
		1980	D1	P4	143 $/CAP		BANGL	MALAW	----

V2	TELEPHONES P. TSD. POPULATION	1970	D1	P7	1	1/TSD CAP	MALI	NIGER	----
		1975	D1	P5	1	1/TSD CAP	CHAD	NIGER	----
V3	INFANT MORTALITY RATE	1980	D10	P92	156.3	1/TSD	BHUTA	ANGO	F5
V4	PHYSICIANS P. MIL. POPULATION	1974	D1	P11	27	1/MIL	RWAN	BENIN	----
		1980	D1	P7	35	1/MIL	RWAN	CENTR	----
V5	ADULT LITERACY	1971	D1	P6	12.5	%	ETHIA	TOGO	----
V6	DURATION OF SCHOOLING	1970	D1	P9	1.9	YR	MALI	AFGHA	----
		1975	D1	P10	2.6	YR	CHAD	GUINE	----
		1980	D2	P13	4.3	YR	SUDAN	SIERA	----
V7	STUDENT ENROLLMENT RATIO	1970	D4	P39	1.9	%	ALGER	BURMA	----
		1975	D4	P35	2.3	%	BURMA	INDO	----
		1980	D4	P37	3.2	%	MADA	GABON	----
V8	SHARE OF AGRICULTURAL LABOR	1971	D10	P99	94.4	%	THAI	-------	----
		1976	D10	P98	88.6	%	MALI	-------	----
V9	SHARE OF INDUSTRIAL LABOR	1971	D1	P3	2.2	%	-------	HAITI	----
		1976	D1	P3	5.3	%	-------	MALI	----
V10	SHARE OF SERVICE LABOR	1971	D1	P3	2.9	%	-------	TURKY	----
		1976	D1	P3	2.4	%	-------	MALI	----
V11	SHARE OF ACADEMIC LABOR	1971	D1	P3	0.5	%	-------	HAITI	----
		1976	D3	P23	3.7	%	GUATE	HONDU	----
V12	SHARE OF SELF-EMPLOYED LABOR	1971	D10	P98	86.4	%	GHANA	-------	----
		1976	D10	P98	70.2	%	CAME	MALAW	----
V13	MILITARY EXPENDITURES	1975	D1	P6	0.013	TSD MIL $	BENIN	TOGO	----
		1980	D1	P4	0.020	TSD MIL $	NIGER	BENIN	----
V14	MILITARY MANPOWER	1970	D5	P43	29	TSD CAP	TUNIS	GHANA	----
		1975	D5	P45	32	TSD CAP	SOMA	DENMA	----
		1980	D4	P35	21	TSD CAP	MADA	LEBA	----
V15	MEN AT AGE 20 - 30	1971	D6	P59	922	TSD CAP	MOROC	AULIA	F22
		1981	D6	P53	1207	TSD CAP	CZECH	VENE	F22
V16	POPULATION	1970	D7	P63	11.42	MIL CAP	KENYA	AULIA	F162
		1975	D7	P62	12.59	MIL CAP	MALAY	VENE	----
		1980	D7	P62	14.01	MIL CAP	MALAY	NETH	----
V17	GROSS DOMESTIC PRODUCT	1970	D2	P15	1.645	TSD MIL $	JORDA	NIGER	----
		1975	D2	P15	1.790	TSD MIL $	YENO	PAPUA	----
		1980	D2	P11	2.010	TSD MIL $	HAITI	NICA	----
V18	SHARE IN WORLD IMPORTS	1970	D2	P16	0.253	1/TSD	TOGO	MALAW	F30
		1975	D1	P10	0.188	1/TSD	CONGO	TOGO	F30
		1980	D1	P8	0.167	1/TSD	UGADA	BURMA	F30
V19	SHARE IN WORLD EXPORTS	1970	D2	P16	0.153	1/TSD	HAITI	TOGO	F30
		1975	D2	P12	0.114	1/TSD	NIGER	VISO	F30
		1980	D1	P6	0.040	1/TSD	RWAN	UPVO	F30

V20	GDP SHARE OF IMPORTS	1970	D2	P12	9.7	%	URU	PERU	F58
		1975	D1	P10	10.9	%	BRAZI	ETHIA	F30
		1980	D3	P27	17.6	%	ETHIA	PERU	F30
V21	GDP SHARE OF EXPORTS	1970	D1	P9	5.5	%	UPVO	BRAZI	F58
		1975	D1	P9	6.4	%	MOZAM	UPVO	F30
		1980	D1	P3	4.1	%	UGADA	BENIN	F30
V22	EXPORT PARTNER CONCENTRATION	1975	D2	P12	14.0	%	TANZA	BURMA	F127
		1980	D2	P11	14.2	%	TANZA	PORTU	F127
V23	TOTAL DEBT AS % OF GDP	1980	D1	P4	10.5	%	UGADA	OMAN	----
V24	SHARE OF NEW FOREIGN PATENTS	1974	D10	P92	100	%	MALAY	RWAN	F19
		1980	D2	P19	60	%	COSTA	IRAQ	F19
V25	FOREIGN PROPERTY AS % OF GDP	1971	D1	P4	0.6	%	YUGO	EGYPT	----
		1975	D1	P5	0.6	%	EGYPT	IRAQ	----
		1978	D1	----	0.6	%	IRAQ	BANGL	----
V26	GNP SHARE OF DEVELOPMENT AID	------	----	----	----- -----		-------	-------	----
V27	SHARE IN NOBEL PRIZE WINNERS	1970-79	D5	P45	0.0	%	MOROC	NEWZ	----
V28	GDP SHARE OF MANUFACTURING	1970	D3	P21	9.0	%	ETHIA	TUNIS	----
		1975	D3	P30	9.8	%	MOZAM	CAME	----
		1980	D4	P39	10.2	%	TANZA	PANA	----
V29	EXPORT SHARE OF MANUFACTURES	------	----	----	----- -----		-------	-------	----
V30	LACK OF CIVIL LIBERTIES	1975	D6	P54	5		MOROC	PAKI	----
		1980	D4	P38	4		MOROC	PERU	----
V31	LACK OF POLITICAL RIGHTS	1975	D7	P63	6		MOZAM	NIGRA	----
		1980	D5	P47	5		LESO	NICA	----
V32	RIOTS	1970-74	D6	P59	3		MOROC	SRILA	----
		1975-79	D9	P85	11		NIGRA	KORSO	----
V33	PROTEST DEMONSTRATIONS	1970-74	D4	P37	1		LIBYA	PARA	----
		1975-79	D7	P69	8		CANA	BOLI	----
V34	POLITICAL STRIKES	1970-74	D7	P64	1		MAURA	NIGER	----
		1975-79	D7	P63	1		MOROC	POLA	----
V35	MEMBER OF THE NONALIGNED MMT.	1970	----	----	1		MOROC	NIGRA	----
		1976	----	----	1		MOZAM	NIGER	----
		1981	----	----	1		MOZAM	NICA	----
V36	MEMBER OF THE OPEC	1970	----	----	0		MOROC	NETH	----
		1975	----	----	0		MOZAM	NETH	----
		1980	----	----	0		MOZAM	NETH	----
V37	MEMBER OF THE OECD	1970	----	----	0		MOROC	NEWZ	----
		1975	----	----	0		MOZAM	NICA	----
		1980	----	----	0		MOZAM	NICA	----
V38	MEMBER OF THE CMEA	1970	----	----	0		MOROC	NETH	----
		1975	----	----	0		MOZAM	NETH	----
		1980	----	----	0		MOZAM	NETH	----

V39	MEMBER OF THE WTO	1970	----	----	0	MOROC	NETH	----
		1975	----	----	0	MOZAM	NETH	----
		1980	----	----	0	MOZAM	NETH	----
V40	MEMBER OF THE NATO	1970	----	----	0	MOROC	NEWZ	----
		1975	----	----	0	MOZAM	NEWZ	----
		1980	----	----	0	MOZAM	NEWZ	----
V41	GDP SHARE OF INVESTMENTS	1970	D1	P5	6.0 %	AFGHA	RWAN	----
		1975	D1	P6	9.3 %	BANGL	AFGHA	----
		1980	D2	P17	15.8 %	NICA	GUATE	----
V42	GDP SHARE OF AGRICULTURE	1970	D10	P97	67.5 %	BANGL	BURU	----
		1975	D10	P99	69.7 %	BURU	UGADA	----
		1980	D10	P97	58.6 %	CHAD	SOMA	----
V43	GDP SHARE OF INDUSTRY	1970	D1	P7	11.4 %	LESO	BENIN	----
		1975	D1	P4	11.0 %	BURU	BANGL	----
V44	GDP SHARE OF SERVICES	1970	D1	P2	21.1 %	-------	RWAN	----
		1975	D1	P3	19.3 %	SAUDI	UGADA	----
V45	HOMICIDES P. MIL. POPULATION	------	----	----	----- -----	-------	-------	----
V46	SUICIDES P. MIL. POPULATION	------	----	----	----- -----	-------	-------	----
V47	IMPORT PARTNERS	1980	R1	JAPAN	21.5 %	MALAY	OMAN	F127
		1980	R2	UNKI	11.4 %	MALAW	NORWY	F127
		1980	R3	KORSO	9.8 %	-------	-------	F127
V48	EXPORT PARTNERS	1980	R1	USSR	14.2 %	INDIA	POLA	F127
		1980	R2	USA	11.9 %	MALAW	SAUDI	F127
		1980	R3	GFR	9.3 %	MALI	NIGRA	F127
V49	PATENT SUPPLIERS	------	----	----	----- -----	-------	-------	----
V50	PROVENANCE OF FOREIGN FIRMS	------	----	----	----- -----	-------	-------	----
V51	FILM SUPPLIERS	------	----	----	----- -----	-------	-------	----

NETHERLANDS (NETH)

V1	INCOME PER CAPITA	1970	D10	P91	8583 $/CAP	BELGI	NORWY	F147
		1975	D9	P88	9541 $/CAP	SAUDI	CANA	F147
		1980	D9	P87	11074 $/CAP	CANA	FRANC	F147
V2	TELEPHONES P. TSD. POPULATION	1970	D10	P92	260 1/TSD CAP	FINLA	NORWY	----
		1975	D10	P91	368 1/TSD CAP	UNKI	AULIA	----
		1980	D10	P93	514 1/TSD CAP	FINLA	NEWZ	----
V3	INFANT MORTALITY RATE	1980	D1	P6	8.6 1/TSD	DENMA	SWITZ	----

V4	PHYSICIANS P. MIL. POPULATION	1970	D9	P80	1250	1/MIL	AULIA	FRANC	F147
		1975	D9	P80	1599	1/MIL	FRANC	USA	F147
		1979	D8	P79	1849	1/MIL	USA	LEBA	F147
V5	ADULT LITERACY	------	----	----	----- -----		-------	-------	----
V6	DURATION OF SCHOOLING	1970	D9	P89	10.7	YR	ITALY	SWEDN	----
		1975	D10	P91	11.2	YR	GDR	ROMA	----
		1980	D10	P93	11.5	YR	CHILE	SPAIN	----
V7	STUDENT ENROLLMENT RATIO	1970	D10	P92	19.5	%	FRANC	PHILI	----
		1975	D10	P92	25.2	%	ITALY	NEWZ	----
		1980	D10	P93	30.2	%	ISRA	GDR	----
V8	SHARE OF AGRICULTURAL LABOR	1971	D1	P10	6.8	%	BELGI	CANA	F83
		1977	D2	----	6.2	%	SWEDN	ISRA	----
		1979	D2	P17	6.1	%	ISRA	SWITZ	----
V9	SHARE OF INDUSTRIAL LABOR	1971	D8	P74	38.7	%	PORTU	NEWZ	F83
		1977	D7	----	33.6	%	USA	ISRA	----
		1979	D6	P53	32.4	%	SWEDN	VENE	----
V10	SHARE OF SERVICE LABOR	1971	D9	P86	39.9	%	SWITZ	ARGE	F83
		1977	D9	----	42.7	%	AULIA	JAPAN	----
		1979	D9	P80	42.8	%	VENE	COSTA	----
V11	SHARE OF ACADEMIC LABOR	1971	D10	P91	14.5	%	CANA	USA	F83
		1977	D10	----	17.5	%	BULGA	FINLA	----
		1979	D10	P92	18.8	%	FINLA	NORWY	----
V12	SHARE OF SELF-EMPLOYED LABOR	1977	D1	----	9.9	%	USA	NORWY	----
		1979	D2	P21	10.0	%	FINLA	KUWAI	----
V13	MILITARY EXPENDITURES	1970	D9	P86	3.870	TSD MIL $	AULIA	CANA	F4
		1975	D10	P91	4.428	TSD MIL $	INDIA	SAUDI	----
		1980	D10	P92	4.870	TSD MIL $	CANA	ITALY	----
V14	MILITARY MANPOWER	1970	D7	P70	115	TSD CAP	BELGI	ARGE	----
		1975	D7	P67	112	TSD CAP	CHILE	HUNGA	----
		1980	D7	P69	108	TSD CAP	ALGER	CHILE	----
V15	MEN AT AGE 20 - 30	1971	D7	P65	1117	TSD CAP	PERU	SRILA	F22
		1975	D7	P68	1197	TSD CAP	SRILA	MOROC	F22
		1980	D5	P50	1194	TSD CAP	CHILE	TANZA	F22
V16	POPULATION	1970	D7	P65	13.03	MIL CAP	SRILA	TANZA	F22
		1975	D7	P66	13.65	MIL CAP	SRILA	AULIA	F22
		1980	D7	P63	14.14	MIL CAP	NEPAL	AULIA	F22
V17	GROSS DOMESTIC PRODUCT	1970	D9	P88	111.843	TSD MIL $	INDIA	BRAZI	----
		1975	D9	P89	130.237	TSD MIL $	INDIA	SPAIN	----
		1980	D9	P90	156.582	TSD MIL $	INDIA	SPAIN	----
V18	SHARE IN WORLD IMPORTS	1970	D10	P94	40.445	1/TSD	CANA	ITALY	----
		1975	D10	P94	38.325	1/TSD	CANA	USSR	----
		1980	D10	P95	37.355	1/TSD	BELGI	ITALY	----
V19	SHARE IN WORLD EXPORTS	1970	D10	P92	37.536	1/TSD	BELGI	USSR	----
		1975	D10	P95	40.056	1/TSD	ITALY	UNKI	----
		1980	D10	P93	37.051	1/TSD	CANA	USSR	----

V20	GDP SHARE OF IMPORTS	1970	D10	P95	42.4 %	IRE	BELGI	----
		1975	D10	P92	42.1 %	ALGER	IRE	----
		1980	D10	P91	45.2 %	JAMAI	MALAY	----
V21	GDP SHARE OF EXPORTS	1970	D9	P89	37.2 %	IVORY	ZAIRE	----
		1975	D9	P90	42.4 %	MALAY	GABON	----
		1980	D9	P86	43.7 %	PAPUA	IRE	----
V22	EXPORT PARTNER CONCENTRATION	1970	D6	P57	32.6 %	MALI	IVORY	----
		1975	D7	P64	30.5 %	AULIA	BOLI	----
		1980	D7	P64	29.9 %	ELSA	ZAIRE	----
V23	TOTAL DEBT AS % OF GDP	------	----	----	----- -----	-------	-------	----
V24	SHARE OF NEW FOREIGN PATENTS	1970	D5	P43	89 %	ISRA	SRILA	----
		1975	D5	P46	89 %	COSTA	SRILA	----
		1980	D5	P42	87 %	BELGI	NORWY	----
V25	FOREIGN PROPERTY AS % OF GDP	------	----	----	----- -----	-------	-------	----
V26	GNP SHARE OF DEVELOPMENT AID	1970	D9	P83	0.62 %	AULIA	FRANC	----
		1975	D8	P74	0.74 %	NORWY	SWEDN	----
		1980	D8	P78	0.97 %	NORWY	LIBYA	----
V27	SHARE IN NOBEL PRIZE WINNERS	1970-79	D9	P90	1.3 %	FRANC	PAKI	----
V28	GDP SHARE OF MANUFACTURING	1970	D9	P90	27.0 %	AULIA	UNKI	----
V29	EXPORT SHARE OF MANUFACTURES	1970	D9	P81	51.9 %	SPAIN	YUGO	----
		1975	D8	P81	50.0 %	HAITI	JAMAI	----
		1980	D8	P76	47.2 %	GREC	HAITI	----
V30	LACK OF CIVIL LIBERTIES	1975	D1	P7	1	JAPAN	NEWZ	----
		1980	D1	P7	1	JAPAN	NEWZ	----
V31	LACK OF POLITICAL RIGHTS	1975	D1	P8	1	JAMAI	NEWZ	----
		1980	D1	P8	1	IRE	NEWZ	----
V32	RIOTS	1970-74	D6	P53	2	IRAQ	SWITZ	----
		1975-79	D6	P60	3	KENYA	SYRIA	----
V33	PROTEST DEMONSTRATIONS	1970-74	D7	P64	5	INDO	NIGRA	----
		1975-79	D8	P77	13	GDR	NICA	----
V34	POLITICAL STRIKES	1970-74	D3	P29	0	MONGO	NEWZ	----
		1975-79	D3	P29	0	MONGO	NEWZ	----
V35	MEMBER OF THE NONALIGNED MMT.	1970	----	----	0	MONGO	NEWZ	----
		1976	----	----	0	MONGO	NEWZ	----
		1981	----	----	0	MONGO	NEWZ	----
V36	MEMBER OF THE OPEC	1970	----	----	0	NEPAL	NEWZ	----
		1975	----	----	0	NEPAL	NEWZ	----
		1980	----	----	0	NEPAL	NEWZ	----
V37	MEMBER OF THE OECD	1970	----	----	1	JAPAN	NORWY	----
		1975	----	----	1	JAPAN	NEWZ	----
		1980	----	----	1	JAPAN	NEWZ	----

V38	MEMBER OF THE CMEA	1970	----	----	0		NEPAL	NEWZ	----
		1975	----	----	0		NEPAL	NEWZ	----
		1980	----	----	0		NEPAL	NEWZ	----
V39	MEMBER OF THE WTO	1970	----	----	0		NEPAL	NEWZ	----
		1975	----	----	0		NEPAL	NEWZ	----
		1980	----	----	0		NEPAL	NEWZ	----
V40	MEMBER OF THE NATO	1970	----	----	1		ITALY	NORWY	----
		1975	----	----	1		ITALY	NORWY	----
		1980	----	----	1		ITALY	NORWY	----
V41	GDP SHARE OF INVESTMENTS	1970	D9	P83	27.9 %		GFR	GREC	----
		1975	D4	P40	20.7 %		GFR	INDIA	----
		1980	D4	P35	21.4 %		BELGI	SWEDN	----
V42	GDP SHARE OF AGRICULTURE	1970	D2	P11	5.5 %		TRITO	DENMA	----
		1975	D2	P11	4.4 %		USA	SWEDN	----
		1980	D2	P13	3.5 %		SWEDN	JAPAN	----
V43	GDP SHARE OF INDUSTRY	1970	D8	P72	36.9 %		ZAIRE	SPAIN	----
		1975	D7	P68	34.6 %		SINGA	MOROC	----
		1980	D6	P54	32.6 %		MOROC	GUINE	----
V44	GDP SHARE OF SERVICES	1970	D9	P86	57.6 %		TUNIS	TRITO	----
		1975	D10	P92	61.0 %		SWEDN	UNKI	----
		1980	D10	P96	63.9 %		UNKI	SWEDN	----
V45	HOMICIDES P. MIL. POPULATION	1970	D1	P3	5.0 1/MIL CAP		-------	GREC	F149
		1975	D2	P11	7.0 1/MIL CAP		SPAIN	NORWY	F149
		1980	D1	P10	7.9 1/MIL CAP		IRE	KUWAI	F147
V46	SUICIDES P. MIL. POPULATION	1970	D4	P41	80.6 1/MIL CAP		UNKI	PORTU	F147
		1975	D4	P40	89.3 1/MIL CAP		PORTU	TRITO	F147
		1980	D4	P40	101.1 1/MIL CAP		UNKI	URU	F147
V47	IMPORT PARTNERS	1970	R1	GFR	27.1 %		ITALY	PORTU	----
		1970	R2	BELGI	16.9 %		FRANC	-------	F142
		1970	R3	USA	9.8 %		MALAY	NEWZ	----
		1980	R1	GFR	22.2 %		ITALY	PORTU	----
		1980	R2	BELGI	11.6 %		ZAIRE	FRANC	F142
		1980	R3	USA	8.8 %		JORDA	NEWZ	----
V48	EXPORT PARTNERS	1970	R1	GFR	32.6 %		ITALY	NORWY	----
		1970	R2	BELGI	13.9 %		HAITI	CENTR	F138
		1970	R3	FRANC	10.0 %		IRE	SPAIN	----
		1980	R1	GFR	29.9 %		LIBE	SWEDN	----
		1980	R2	BELGI	15.1 %		CENTR	FRANC	F138
		1980	R3	FRANC	10.6 %		LIBE	PORTU	----
V49	PATENT SUPPLIERS	1970	R1	USA	789		MEXI	NICA	----
		1970	R2	GFR	452		LAOS	NICA	----
		1970	R3	FRANC	223		LEBA	POLA	----
		1980	R1	USA	886		MEXI	NEWZ	----
		1980	R2	GFR	619		MEXI	NORWY	----
		1980	R3	JAPAN	431		FRANC	PHILI	----

V50 PROVENANCE OF FOREIGN FIRMS	1980	R1	UNKI	38.2	%	MOZAM	NEWZ	----
	1980	R2	USA	26.9	%	MOROC	NIGRA	----
	1980	R3	GFR	11.9	%	MOROC	NIGRA	----
V51 FILM SUPPLIERS	1980	R1	USA	141		MEXI	NEWZ	F120
	1980	R2	FRANC	55		MOZAM	SWEDN	F120
	1980	R3	GFR	27		ITALY	YUGO	F120

NEW ZEALAND (NEWZ)

V1 INCOME PER CAPITA	1970	D9	P82	6719	$/CAP	AURIA	UNKI	----
	1975	D8	P79	7462	$/CAP	JAPAN	UNKI	----
	1980	D8	P78	7471	$/CAP	ITALY	UNKI	----
V2 TELEPHONES P. TSD. POPULATION	1970	D10	P96	427	1/TSD CAP	DENMA	CANA	----
	1975	D10	P95	476	1/TSD CAP	DENMA	CANA	----
	1980	D10	P94	560	1/TSD CAP	NETH	DENMA	----
V3 INFANT MORTALITY RATE	1980	D2	P17	12.9	1/TSD	USA	AURIA	----
V4 PHYSICIANS P. MIL. POPULATION	1970	D8	P75	1150	1/MIL	JAPAN	IRE	----
	1975	D8	P75	1334	1/MIL	ROMA	URU	----
	1980	D8	P71	1569	1/MIL	ROMA	KUWAI	----
V5 ADULT LITERACY	------	----	----	-----	-----	-------	-------	----
V6 DURATION OF SCHOOLING	1970	D10	P100	12.1	YR	USA	-------	----
	1975	D10	P99	12.0	YR	USA	UNKI	----
	1980	D10	P100	12.2	YR	DENMA	-------	----
V7 STUDENT ENROLLMENT RATIO	1970	D9	P89	17.4	%	JAPAN	BELGI	----
	1975	D10	P93	25.7	%	NETH	ARGE	----
	1980	D9	P87	26.3	%	PHILI	JORDA	----
V8 SHARE OF AGRICULTURAL LABOR	1971	D3	P22	11.8	%	DENMA	NORWY	----
	1976	D3	P26	10.6	%	FRANC	AURIA	F100
	1981	D4	P38	11.6	%	JORDA	FINLA	F100
V9 SHARE OF INDUSTRIAL LABOR	1971	D8	P74	38.7	%	NETH	SWITZ	----
	1976	D9	P80	38.0	%	AULIA	FRANC	F100
	1981	D8	P70	36.0	%	AULIA	CHILE	F100
V10 SHARE OF SERVICE LABOR	1971	D8	P73	36.7	%	BELGI	AURIA	----
	1976	D8	P72	37.0	%	SWEDN	VENE	F100
	1981	D7	P66	39.4	%	NORWY	FRANC	F100
V11 SHARE OF ACADEMIC LABOR	1971	D9	P86	12.7	%	FRANC	CANA	----
	1976	D8	P78	14.5	%	KUWAI	USA	F100
	1981	D8	P78	14.7	%	HUNGA	CANA	F100
V12 SHARE OF SELF-EMPLOYED LABOR	1971	D3	P26	12.9	%	AULIA	NORWY	----
	1976	D2	P18	14.2	%	AULIA	FRANC	F100
	1981	D3	P31	13.5	%	TRITO	AULIA	F100

V13	MILITARY EXPENDITURES	1970	D5	P50	0.336	TSD MIL $	LIBYA	JORDA	----
		1975	D5	P48	0.368	TSD MIL $	JORDA	SINGA	----
		1980	D5	P47	0.400	TSD MIL $	ETHIA	JORDA	----
V14	MILITARY MANPOWER	1970	D4	P31	14	TSD CAP	YENO	SINGA	----
		1975	D3	P27	13	TSD CAP	MADA	PARA	----
		1980	D3	P24	13	TSD CAP	KENYA	GHANA	----
V15	MEN AT AGE 20 - 30	1971	D2	P17	214	TSD CAP	RWAN	BURU	----
		1975	D3	P20	259	TSD CAP	SINGA	HAITI	----
		1980	D2	P10	255	TSD CAP	COSTA	IRE	----
V16	POPULATION	1970	D3	P21	2.81	MIL CAP	SOMA	URU	----
		1975	D3	P21	3.08	MIL CAP	SIERA	HONDU	----
		1980	D2	P20	3.11	MIL CAP	PAPUA	PARA	----
V17	GROSS DOMESTIC PRODUCT	1970	D7	P61	18.879	TSD MIL $	ALGER	PHILI	----
		1975	D7	P63	22.984	TSD MIL $	KUWAI	ALGER	----
		1980	D6	P57	23.234	TSD MIL $	MALAY	PORTU	----
V18	SHARE IN WORLD IMPORTS	1970	D6	P60	3.750	1/TSD	PAKI	ALGER	F30
		1975	D6	P56	3.454	1/TSD	MOROC	THAI	F30
		1980	D6	P56	2.667	1/TSD	PAKI	CUBA	F30
V19	SHARE IN WORLD EXPORTS	1970	D7	P65	3.905	1/TSD	PHILI	CHILE	F30
		1975	D6	P58	2.455	1/TSD	PORTU	GREC	F30
		1980	D6	P60	2.714	1/TSD	ISRA	CUBA	F30
V20	GDP SHARE OF IMPORTS	1970	D6	P54	19.1	%	CENTR	SRILA	F30
		1975	D5	P47	22.4	%	CONGO	THAI	F30
		1980	D5	P45	23.0	%	CANA	EGYPT	F30
V21	GDP SHARE OF EXPORTS	1970	D7	P61	18.8	%	GFR	KENYA	F30
		1975	D5	P41	15.4	%	FRANC	MADA	F30
		1980	D7	P61	22.7	%	PERU	AURIA	F30
V22	EXPORT PARTNER CONCENTRATION	1970	D7	P63	33.9	%	CZECH	MADA	----
		1975	D5	P44	22.5	%	BELGI	ZAMBI	----
		1980	D1	P8	13.1	%	BURMA	GFR	----
V23	TOTAL DEBT AS % OF GDP	------	----	----	----- -----		-------	-------	----
V24	SHARE OF NEW FOREIGN PATENTS	1976	D4	P38	86	%	NICA	BOLI	----
		1980	D5	P50	89	%	KORSO	ZIMBA	----
V25	FOREIGN PROPERTY AS % OF GDP	------	----	----	----- -----		-------	-------	----
V26	GNP SHARE OF DEVELOPMENT AID	1970	D4	P41	0.22	%	ITALY	JAPAN	----
		1975	D5	P47	0.52	%	GFR	CANA	----
		1980	D5	P41	0.33	%	JAPAN	UNKI	----
V27	SHARE IN NOBEL PRIZE WINNERS	1970-79	D5	P45	0.0	%	NEPAL	NICA	----
V28	GDP SHARE OF MANUFACTURING	1971	D8	P78	22.8	%	PHILI	SOUAF	----
		1975	D8	P77	22.4	%	NICA	AULIA	----
		1980	D9	P83	23.2	%	USA	MEXI	----
V29	EXPORT SHARE OF MANUFACTURES	------	----	----	----- -----		-------	-------	----
V30	LACK OF CIVIL LIBERTIES	1975	D1	P7	1		NETH	NORWY	----
		1980	D1	P7	1		NETH	NORWY	----

V31	LACK OF POLITICAL RIGHTS	1975	D1	P8	1		NETH	NORWY	----
		1980	D1	P8	1		NETH	NORWY	----
V32	RIOTS	1970-74	D5	P43	1		MALAY	NORWY	----
		1975-79	D2	P20	0		MOROC	NIGER	----
V33	PROTEST DEMONSTRATIONS	1970-74	D6	P59	4		LAOS	SRILA	----
		1975-79	D5	P42	2		MALAY	PARA	----
V34	POLITICAL STRIKES	1970-74	D3	P29	0		NETH	NICA	----
		1975-79	D3	P29	0		NETH	NIGER	----
V35	MEMBER OF THE NONALIGNED MMT.	1970	----	----	0		NETH	NICA	----
		1976	----	----	0		NETH	NICA	----
		1981	----	----	0		NETH	NORWY	----
V36	MEMBER OF THE OPEC	1970	----	----	0		NETH	NICA	----
		1975	----	----	0		NETH	NICA	----
		1980	----	----	0		NETH	NICA	----
V37	MEMBER OF THE OECD	1970	----	----	0		NEPAL	NICA	----
		1975	----	----	1		NETH	NORWY	----
		1980	----	----	1		NETH	NORWY	----
V38	MEMBER OF THE CMEA	1970	----	----	0		NETH	NICA	----
		1975	----	----	0		NETH	NICA	----
		1980	----	----	0		NETH	NICA	----
V39	MEMBER OF THE WTO	1970	----	----	0		NETH	NICA	----
		1975	----	----	0		NETH	NICA	----
		1980	----	----	0		NETH	NICA	----
V40	MEMBER OF THE NATO	1970	----	----	0		NEPAL	NICA	----
		1975	----	----	0		NEPAL	NICA	----
		1980	----	----	0		NEPAL	NICA	----
V41	GDP SHARE OF INVESTMENTS	1970	D7	P69	24.3 %		BELGI	KENYA	----
		1975	D9	P81	30.3 %		IRAQ	LIBYA	----
		1980	D5	P42	22.6 %		MOROC	CANA	----
V42	GDP SHARE OF AGRICULTURE	1971	D4	P33	12.6 %		MEXI	URU	----
		1975	D4	P33	10.5 %		ARGE	MEXI	----
		1980	D4	P36	11.3 %		PERU	CONGO	----
V43	GDP SHARE OF INDUSTRY	1971	D7	P62	31.5 %		IRE	CANA	----
		1975	D6	P51	31.3 %		TUNIS	DOMI	----
		1980	D5	P50	31.3 %		GREC	SWEDN	----
V44	GDP SHARE OF SERVICES	1971	D9	P83	55.9 %		SENE	TUNIS	----
		1975	D9	P88	58.2 %		FRANC	BELGI	----
		1980	D9	P87	57.4 %		AULIA	SPAIN	----
V45	HOMICIDES P. MIL. POPULATION	1970	D4	P37	12.5	1/MIL CAP	ISRA	JAPAN	F148
		1975	D4	P31	10.7	1/MIL CAP	ISRA	SWEDN	F148
		1980	D5	P46	12.9	1/MIL CAP	AURIA	DENMA	----
V46	SUICIDES P. MIL. POPULATION	1970	D5	P50	96.4	1/MIL CAP	SINGA	ARGE	----
		1975	D5	P44	95.1	1/MIL CAP	TRITO	NORWY	----
		1980	D5	P43	108.4	1/MIL CAP	URU	AULIA	----

V47	IMPORT PARTNERS	1970	R1	UNKI	27.4	%	MALAW	NIGRA	----
		1970	R2	AULIA	19.8	%	JAPAN	YENO	----
		1970	R3	USA	13.0	%	NETH	SINGA	----
		1980	R1	AULIA	17.6	%	-------	PAPUA	----
		1980	R2	JAPAN	14.4	%	HAITI	PAKI	----
		1980	R3	USA	13.8	%	NETH	PARA	----
V48	EXPORT PARTNERS	1970	R1	UNKI	33.9	%	MALAW	NIGRA	----
		1970	R2	USA	17.1	%	MADA	PARA	----
		1970	R3	JAPAN	9.8	%	CANA	PAKI	----
		1980	R1	UNKI	13.1	%	MALAW	NORWY	----
		1980	R2	AULIA	13.0	%	-------	PAPUA	----
		1980	R3	USA	12.8	%	MALAY	THAI	----
V49	PATENT SUPPLIERS	1980	R1	USA	391		NETH	NIGRA	----
		1980	R2	UNKI	190		KENYA	NIGRA	----
		1980	R3	SWITZ	94		MALAW	SRILA	----
V50	PROVENANCE OF FOREIGN FIRMS	1980	R1	UNKI	46.5	%	NETH	NIGRA	----
		1980	R2	AULIA	27.1	%	PAPUA	-------	----
		1980	R3	USA	17.5	%	MOZAM	-------	----
V51	FILM SUPPLIERS	1979	R1	USA	277		NETH	NICA	F119
		1979	R2	UNKI	75		KORSO	NORWY	F119
		1979	R3	FRANC	54		MOROC	PAKI	F119

NICARAGUA (NICA)

V1	INCOME PER CAPITA	1970	D6	P51	1034	$/CAP	MALAY	TURKY	F4
		1975	D6	P51	1152	$/CAP	PERU	KORSO	F147
		1980	D4	P38	775	$/CAP	ZIMBA	PAPUA	F147
V2	TELEPHONES P. TSD. POPULATION	1970	D5	P48	13	1/TSD CAP	ALGER	JORDA	----
		1975	D4	P35	10	1/TSD CAP	MOROC	PHILI	----
		1979	D4	P37	22	1/TSD CAP	ELSA	ALGER	----
V3	INFANT MORTALITY RATE	1980	D6	P53	97.0	1/TSD	HONDU	INDO	F5
V4	PHYSICIANS P. MIL. POPULATION	1971	D6	P57	460	1/MIL	TURKY	COLO	----
		1975	D7	P60	648	1/MIL	COSTA	SINGA	F150
V5	ADULT LITERACY	1971	D4	P38	57.5	%	ELSA	BRAZI	F22
V6	DURATION OF SCHOOLING	1970	D4	P38	6.2	YR	IRAN	ZAIRE	----
		1975	D4	P35	6.7	YR	INDO	YESO	----
		1980	D5	P42	8.4	YR	BOLI	ALGER	F35
V7	STUDENT ENROLLMENT RATIO	1970	D6	P54	5.5	%	JAMAI	MEXI	----
		1975	D6	P54	8.3	%	COLO	MONGO	----
		1980	D7	P63	14.1	%	MEXI	KORSO	----
V8	SHARE OF AGRICULTURAL LABOR	1971	D7	P69	48.1	%	YUGO	IRAN	F46

V9	SHARE OF INDUSTRIAL LABOR	1971	D4	P33	22.6 %	PANA	PARA	F46
V10	SHARE OF SERVICE LABOR	1971	D5	P43	23.9 %	KORSO	PERU	F46
V11	SHARE OF ACADEMIC LABOR	1971	D5	P43	5.3 %	SRILA	GREC	F46
V12	SHARE OF SELF-EMPLOYED LABOR	1971	D7	P67	31.7 %	MEXI	LEBA	F46
V13	MILITARY EXPENDITURES	1970	D2	P20	0.030 TSD MIL $	ELSA	MADA	F4
		1975	D2	P19	0.043 TSD MIL $	UPVO	MADA	----
		1980	D4	P31	0.116 TSD MIL $	IVORY	ZAMBI	----
V14	MILITARY MANPOWER	1970	D2	P16	6 TSD CAP	IVORY	CHAD	----
		1975	D2	P12	5 TSD CAP	MALAW	SIERA	----
		1980	D3	P28	15 TSD CAP	GUATE	PARA	----
V15	MEN AT AGE 20 - 30	1971	D1	P7	130 TSD CAP	YESO	SINGA	F22
		1980	D1	P6	189 TSD CAP	JAMAI	BENIN	----
V16	POPULATION	1970	D1	P10	1.83 MIL CAP	COSTA	JAMAI	----
		1975	D2	P12	2.16 MIL CAP	JAMAI	TOGO	F22
		1980	D2	P16	2.73 MIL CAP	LEBA	URU	F22
V17	GROSS DOMESTIC PRODUCT	1970	D3	P20	1.893 TSD MIL $	PARA	COSTA	F4
		1975	D2	P19	2.488 TSD MIL $	BOLI	PANA	----
		1980	D2	P13	2.116 TSD MIL $	NEPAL	HONDU	----
V18	SHARE IN WORLD IMPORTS	1970	D3	P28	0.599 1/TSD	SENE	YESO	F30
		1975	D3	P28	0.569 1/TSD	PAPUA	URU	F30
		1980	D3	P27	0.432 1/TSD	ZAIRE	ELSA	F30
V19	SHARE IN WORLD EXPORTS	1970	D3	P29	0.571 1/TSD	HONDU	TUNIS	F30
		1975	D3	P30	0.428 1/TSD	TANZA	URU	F30
		1980	D3	P21	0.225 1/TSD	ETHIA	BURMA	F30
V20	GDP SHARE OF IMPORTS	1970	D8	P75	25.6 %	BENIN	PORTU	F30
		1975	D8	P76	33.2 %	TUNIS	ELSA	F30
		1980	D9	P85	40.7 %	PAPUA	PANA	F30
V21	GDP SHARE OF EXPORTS	1970	D8	P77	23.1 %	ELSA	COSTA	F30
		1975	D8	P72	24.1 %	SWEDN	NIGRA	F30
		1980	D6	P55	20.7 %	COSTA	ECUA	F30
V22	EXPORT PARTNER CONCENTRATION	1970	D6	P60	33.2 %	PERU	INDO	----
		1975	D6	P60	28.0 %	THAI	PARA	----
		1980	D8	P77	38.7 %	JAMAI	CONGO	----
V23	TOTAL DEBT AS % OF GDP	1980	D10	P98	100.8 %	TOGO	MAURA	----
V24	SHARE OF NEW FOREIGN PATENTS	1970	D8	P74	98 %	MALAY	TRITO	----
		1974	D4	P36	85 %	LEBA	NEWZ	----
		1978	D9	----	99 %	MALAY	NIGRA	----
V25	FOREIGN PROPERTY AS % OF GDP	1971	D6	P58	10.3 %	BRAZI	PHILI	----
		1975	D6	P52	5.8 %	BENIN	GHANA	----
		1978	D5	----	4.4 %	PARA	PAKI	----
V26	GNP SHARE OF DEVELOPMENT AID	------	----	----	----- -----	-------	-------	----
V27	SHARE IN NOBEL PRIZE WINNERS	1970-79	D5	P45	0.0 %	NEWZ	NIGER	----

V28	GDP SHARE OF MANUFACTURING	1970	D8	P71	20.4	%	CANA	SINGA	----
		1975	D8	P76	22.1	%	DOMI	NEWZ	----
		1980	D9	P86	25.1	%	PHILI	ARGE	----
V29	EXPORT SHARE OF MANUFACTURES	------	----	----	----- -----		-------	-------	----
V30	LACK OF CIVIL LIBERTIES	1975	D4	P39	4		MADA	NIGRA	----
		1980	D6	P52	5		LIBE	PANA	----
V31	LACK OF POLITICAL RIGHTS	1975	D5	P43	5		MOROC	PARA	----
		1980	D5	P47	5		NEPAL	PANA	----
V32	RIOTS	1970-74	D2	P19	0		MONGO	NIGER	----
		1975-79	D10	P92	34		TURKY	UNKI	----
V33	PROTEST DEMONSTRATIONS	1970-74	D7	P68	6		DENMA	POLA	----
		1975-79	D8	P79	15		NETH	THAI	----
V34	POLITICAL STRIKES	1970-74	D3	P29	0		NEWZ	PANA	----
		1975-79	D9	P89	10		PORTU	THAI	----
V35	MEMBER OF THE NONALIGNED MMT.	1970	----	----	0		NEWZ	NIGER	----
		1976	----	----	0		NEWZ	NORWY	----
		1981	----	----	1		NEPAL	NIGER	----
V36	MEMBER OF THE OPEC	1970	----	----	0		NEWZ	NIGER	----
		1975	----	----	0		NEWZ	NIGER	----
		1980	----	----	0		NEWZ	NIGER	----
V37	MEMBER OF THE OECD	1970	----	----	0		NEWZ	NIGER	----
		1975	----	----	0		NEPAL	NIGER	----
		1980	----	----	0		NEPAL	NIGER	----
V38	MEMBER OF THE CMEA	1970	----	----	0		NEWZ	NIGER	----
		1975	----	----	0		NEWZ	NIGER	----
		1980	----	----	0		NEWZ	NIGER	----
V39	MEMBER OF THE WTO	1970	----	----	0		NEWZ	NIGER	----
		1975	----	----	0		NEWZ	NIGER	----
		1980	----	----	0		NEWZ	NIGER	----
V40	MEMBER OF THE NATO	1970	----	----	0		NEWZ	NIGER	----
		1975	----	----	0		NEWZ	NIGER	----
		1980	----	----	0		NEWZ	NIGER	----
V41	GDP SHARE OF INVESTMENTS	1970	D5	P43	18.6	%	MOROC	CENTR	----
		1975	D5	P45	21.4	%	TRITO	CAME	----
		1980	D2	P16	15.4	%	JAMAI	NEPAL	----
V42	GDP SHARE OF AGRICULTURE	1970	D6	P56	24.9	%	SENE	LESO	----
		1975	D6	P52	22.4	%	DOMI	ELSA	----
		1980	D6	P53	22.6	%	NIGRA	SENE	----
V43	GDP SHARE OF INDUSTRY	1970	D5	P46	25.8	%	SYRIA	DOMI	----
		1975	D5	P46	29.4	%	PAPUA	MALAY	----
		1980	D5	P49	31.1	%	COLO	GREC	----
V44	GDP SHARE OF SERVICES	1970	D6	P55	49.3	%	ITALY	PERU	----
		1975	D7	P61	48.2	%	ECUA	TUNIS	----
		1980	D5	P49	46.3	%	THAI	ZAMBI	----

V45	HOMICIDES P. MIL. POPULATION	1975	D10	P93	185.6	1/MIL CAP	COLO	THAI	F153
V46	SUICIDES P. MIL. POPULATION	1969	D1	P5	14.0	1/MIL CAP	PHILI	PARA	----
		1975	D1	P5	9.3	1/MIL CAP	KUWAI	PARA	F150
V47	IMPORT PARTNERS	1970	R1	USA	36.5	%	MEXI	PAKI	----
		1970	R2	GUATE	7.9	%	HONDU	-------	----
		1970	R3	ELSA	7.8	%	GUATE	-------	----
		1980	R1	USA	27.5	%	MEXI	PAKI	----
		1980	R2	VENE	16.9	%	JAMAI	COSTA	----
		1980	R3	COSTA	13.2	%	-------	-------	----
V48	EXPORT PARTNERS	1970	R1	USA	33.2	%	MEXI	PAKI	----
		1970	R2	JAPAN	14.1	%	MEXI	PHILI	----
		1970	R3	GFR	11.9	%	MEXI	TOGO	----
		1980	R1	USA	38.7	%	MEXI	NIGRA	----
		1980	R2	GFR	13.5	%	MOROC	NORWY	----
		1980	R3	COSTA	8.9	%	ELSA	PANA	----
V49	PATENT SUPPLIERS	1970	R1	USA	128		NETH	NORWY	----
		1970	R2	GFR	35		NETH	NORWY	----
		1970	R3	SWITZ	17		MALAY	NIGRA	----
V50	PROVENANCE OF FOREIGN FIRMS	1980	R1	USA	81.5	%	MEXI	PAKI	----
		1980	R2	-------	4.8	%	-------	-------	----
		1980	R3	-------	4.8	%	-------	-------	----
V51	FILM SUPPLIERS	1980	R1	USA	109		NEWZ	NIGRA	F120
		1980	R2	ITALY	33		MEXI	PERU	F120
		1980	R3	UNKI	19		MEXI	SWEDN	F120

NIGER (NIGER)

V1	INCOME PER CAPITA	1970	D3	P21	411	$/CAP	TOGO	MADA	----
		1975	D3	P22	365	$/CAP	INDO	MADA	----
		1980	D3	P23	435	$/CAP	TOGO	YENO	F35
V2	TELEPHONES P. TSD. POPULATION	1970	D1	P7	1	1/TSD CAP	NEPAL	UPVO	----
		1975	D1	P5	1	1/TSD CAP	NEPAL	RWAN	----
		1979	D1	P7	2	1/TSD CAP	AFGHA	INDO	----
V3	INFANT MORTALITY RATE	1980	D9	P85	151.4	1/TSD	MAURA	SENE	F5
V4	PHYSICIANS P. MIL. POPULATION	1970	D1	P7	17	1/MIL	BURU	RWAN	----
		1975	D1	P3	18	1/MIL	ETHIA	UPVO	----
		1978	D1	----	27	1/MIL	MOZAM	RWAN	----
V5	ADULT LITERACY	1980	D1	P9	9.8	%	YENO	AFGHA	F21
V6	DURATION OF SCHOOLING	1970	D1	P5	1.0	YR	YENO	UPVO	----
		1975	D1	P3	1.4	YR	UPVO	BURU	----
		1981	D1	P4	2.2	YR	BURU	MAURA	----

V7	STUDENT ENROLLMENT RATIO	1970	D1	P4	0.0	%	MAURA	UPVO	----
		1975	D1	P4	0.1	%	MOZAM	CHAD	----
		1980	D1	P6	0.3	%	MALI	RWAN	----
V8	SHARE OF AGRICULTURAL LABOR	------	----	----	-----	-----	-------	-------	----
V9	SHARE OF INDUSTRIAL LABOR	------	----	----	-----	-----	-------	-------	----
V10	SHARE OF SERVICE LABOR	------	----	----	-----	-----	-------	-------	----
V11	SHARE OF ACADEMIC LABOR	------	----	----	-----	-----	-------	-------	----
V12	SHARE OF SELF-EMPLOYED LABOR	------	----	----	-----	-----	-------	-------	----
V13	MILITARY EXPENDITURES	1970	D2	P12	0.015	TSD MIL $	TOGO	PANA	F4
		1975	D1	P9	0.014	TSD MIL $	TOGO	BURU	----
		1979	D1	P3	0.017	TSD MIL $	SIERA	NEPAL	----
V14	MILITARY MANPOWER	1970	D1	P10	4	TSD CAP	MALAW	RWAN	----
		1975	D1	P9	4	TSD CAP	TOGO	RWAN	----
		1980	D1	P6	3	TSD CAP	COSTA	PAPUA	----
V15	MEN AT AGE 20 - 30	1969	D2	P20	253	TSD CAP	BURU	ISRA	F2
		1974	D3	P29	353	TSD CAP	CHAD	UPVO	F2
V16	POPULATION	1970	D4	P31	4.00	MIL CAP	GUINE	DOMI	----
		1975	D4	P33	4.60	MIL CAP	HAITI	FINLA	----
		1980	D4	P34	5.31	MIL CAP	DENMA	DOMI	F35
V17	GROSS DOMESTIC PRODUCT	1970	D2	P17	1.646	TSD MIL $	NEPAL	BOLI	----
		1975	D2	P12	1.677	TSD MIL $	HONDU	JORDA	----
		1980	D2	P15	2.312	TSD MIL $	HONDU	PAPUA	----
V18	SHARE IN WORLD IMPORTS	1970	D2	P11	0.175	1/TSD	CONGO	CHAD	----
		1975	D1	P5	0.111	1/TSD	RWAN	CHAD	----
		1980	D2	P20	0.290	1/TSD	MONGO	MADA	----
V19	SHARE IN WORLD EXPORTS	1970	D1	P10	0.102	1/TSD	SOMA	BENIN	----
		1975	D2	P11	0.104	1/TSD	SOMA	NEPAL	----
		1980	D3	P25	0.284	1/TSD	SUDAN	JORDA	----
V20	GDP SHARE OF IMPORTS	1970	D4	P36	14.5	%	YENO	GUATE	----
		1975	D2	P18	13.7	%	TURKY	BURU	----
		1980	D6	P51	23.7	%	KUWAI	ZIMBA	----
V21	GDP SHARE OF EXPORTS	1970	D2	P15	8.0	%	ARGE	AFGHA	----
		1975	D4	P33	12.4	%	SOMA	CENTR	----
		1980	D6	P60	22.6	%	AFGHA	PERU	----
V22	EXPORT PARTNER CONCENTRATION	1970	D9	P82	46.7	%	MALAW	KORSO	----
		1975	D10	P94	63.7	%	MEXI	SOMA	----
		1980	D8	P79	40.4	%	CONGO	NORWY	----
V23	TOTAL DEBT AS % OF GDP	1980	D5	P46	34.5	%	TURKY	GABON	----
V24	SHARE OF NEW FOREIGN PATENTS	------	----	----	-----	-----	-------	-------	----
V25	FOREIGN PROPERTY AS % OF GDP	1971	D4	P34	5.8	%	MOROC	THAI	----
		1975	D4	P40	4.8	%	PARA	LIBYA	----
		1978	D6	----	6.2	%	MEXI	BRAZI	----

V26	GNP SHARE OF DEVELOPMENT AID	------	----	----	----- -----	-------	-------	----
V27	SHARE IN NOBEL PRIZE WINNERS	1970-79	D5	P45	0.0 %	NICA	NIGRA	----
V28	GDP SHARE OF MANUFACTURING	1970	D4	P37	10.6 %	CAME	GHANA	----
		1975	D4	P37	11.1 %	TANZA	ETHIA	----
		1980	D3	P29	8.4 %	LIBE	CAME	----
V29	EXPORT SHARE OF MANUFACTURES	1970	D3	P26	2.7 %	LIBE	BOLI	----
		1975	D5	P48	8.4 %	CHILE	CAME	----
		1980	D2	P17	2.0 %	LIBE	INDO	----
V30	LACK OF CIVIL LIBERTIES	1975	D8	P74	6	MOZAM	PANA	----
		1980	D8	P74	6	MAURA	OMAN	----
V31	LACK OF POLITICAL RIGHTS	1975	D9	P88	7	MONGO	PANA	----
		1980	D9	P90	7	MOZAM	ROMA	----
V32	RIOTS	1970-74	D2	P19	0	NICA	PANA	----
		1975-79	D2	P20	0	NEWZ	NORWY	----
V33	PROTEST DEMONSTRATIONS	1970-74	D5	P49	2	MOROC	SYRIA	----
		1975-79	D2	P13	0	MOROC	SENE	----
V34	POLITICAL STRIKES	1970-74	D7	P64	1	NEPAL	NORWY	----
		1975-79	D3	P29	0	NEWZ	NORWY	----
V35	MEMBER OF THE NONALIGNED MMT.	1970	----	----	0	NICA	NORWY	----
		1976	----	----	1	NEPAL	NIGRA	----
		1981	----	----	1	NICA	NIGRA	----
V36	MEMBER OF THE OPEC	1970	----	----	0	NICA	NIGRA	----
		1975	----	----	0	NICA	NORWY	----
		1980	----	----	0	NICA	NORWY	----
V37	MEMBER OF THE OECD	1970	----	----	0	NICA	NIGRA	----
		1975	----	----	0	NICA	NIGRA	----
		1980	----	----	0	NICA	NIGRA	----
V38	MEMBER OF THE CMEA	1970	----	----	0	NICA	NIGRA	----
		1975	----	----	0	NICA	NIGRA	----
		1980	----	----	0	NICA	NIGRA	----
V39	MEMBER OF THE WTO	1970	----	----	0	NICA	NIGRA	----
		1975	----	----	0	NICA	NIGRA	----
		1980	----	----	0	NICA	NIGRA	----
V40	MEMBER OF THE NATO	1970	----	----	0	NICA	NIGRA	----
		1975	----	----	0	NICA	NIGRA	----
		1980	----	----	0	NICA	NIGRA	----
V41	GDP SHARE OF INVESTMENTS	1970	D5	P40	18.0 %	USA	ECUA	----
		1975	D6	P52	22.8 %	IVORY	FRANC	----
		1980	D9	P82	29.2 %	KENYA	GABON	----
V42	GDP SHARE OF AGRICULTURE	1970	D10	P95	58.1 %	ETHIA	SOMA	----
		1975	D8	P79	39.4 %	BENIN	ANGO	----
		1980	D8	P76	33.1 %	CHINA	PAPUA	----

V43 GDP SHARE OF INDUSTRY	1970	D2	P13	14.5	%	ETHIA	SUDAN	----
	1975	D3	P26	21.2	%	PARA	IVORY	----
	1980	D6	P59	34.2	%	USA	SPAIN	----
V44 GDP SHARE OF SERVICES	1970	D1	P6	27.4	%	SOMA	LIBYA	----
	1975	D3	P28	39.4	%	CHAD	TRITO	----
	1980	D2	P13	32.7	%	INDO	RWAN	----
V45 HOMICIDES P. MIL. POPULATION	------	----	----	-----	-----	-------	-------	----
V46 SUICIDES P. MIL. POPULATION	------	----	----	-----	-----	-------	-------	----
V47 IMPORT PARTNERS	1980	R1	FRANC	39.1	%	MOROC	SENE	----
	1980	R2	NIGRA	11.6	%	GHANA	SENE	----
	1980	R3	ITALY	7.7	%	GREC	SWITZ	----
V48 EXPORT PARTNERS	1970	R1	FRANC	46.7	%	MOROC	SENE	----
	1970	R2	NIGRA	19.8	%	-------	BENIN	----
	1970	R3	ITALY	14.9	%	MOROC	SUDAN	----
	1980	R1	FRANC	40.4	%	MOROC	SPAIN	----
	1980	R2	JAPAN	15.9	%	KORSO	PAKI	----
	1980	R3	NIGRA	11.6	%	-------	TOGO	----
V49 PATENT SUPPLIERS	------	----	----	-----	-----	-------	-------	----
V50 PROVENANCE OF FOREIGN FIRMS	------	----	----	-----	-----	-------	-------	----
V51 FILM SUPPLIERS	------	----	----	-----	-----	-------	-------	----

NIGERIA (NIGRA)

V1 INCOME PER CAPITA	1970	D5	P42	823	$/CAP	SYRIA	DOMI	F4
	1975	D4	P40	938	$/CAP	PAPUA	GUATE	----
	1980	D5	P41	906	$/CAP	MOROC	PERU	----
V2 TELEPHONES P. TSD. POPULATION	1976	D2	P12	2	1/TSD CAP	LIBE	ZAIRE	----
V3 INFANT MORTALITY RATE	1980	D8	P73	124.1	1/TSD	TOGO	ALGER	F5
V4 PHYSICIANS P. MIL. POPULATION	1972	D2	----	38	1/MIL	INDO	YENO	----
	1975	D3	P23	63	1/MIL	GUINE	SOMA	----
	1980	D3	P25	100	1/MIL	YENO	MADA	----
V5 ADULT LITERACY	1980	D4	P35	34.0	%	MOZAM	IVORY	F21
V6 DURATION OF SCHOOLING	1970	D2	P13	2.7	YR	BENIN	GUINE	----
	1975	D2	P18	4.0	YR	BENIN	PAPUA	----
V7 STUDENT ENROLLMENT RATIO	1970	D3	P21	0.5	%	CAME	SIERA	----
	1975	D2	P19	0.8	%	LESO	SOMA	----
	1980	D3	P28	2.2	%	PAKI	TOGO	----
V8 SHARE OF AGRICULTURAL LABOR	------	----	----	-----	-----	-------	-------	----

V9	SHARE OF INDUSTRIAL LABOR	------	----	----	----- -----		-------	-------	----
V10	SHARE OF SERVICE LABOR	------	----	----	----- -----		-------	-------	----
V11	SHARE OF ACADEMIC LABOR	------	----	----	----- -----		-------	-------	----
V12	SHARE OF SELF-EMPLOYED LABOR	------	----	----	----- -----		-------	-------	----
V13	MILITARY EXPENDITURES	1970	D8	P79	2.466	TSD MIL $	BELGI	INDIA	----
		1975	D9	P85	3.135	TSD MIL $	SPAIN	AULIA	----
		1980	D8	P78	2.103	TSD MIL $	SYRIA	GREC	----
V14	MILITARY MANPOWER	1970	D8	P77	200	TSD CAP	GREC	GDR	----
		1975	D9	P83	270	TSD CAP	INDO	YUGO	----
		1980	D8	P73	150	TSD CAP	MEXI	PERU	----
V15	MEN AT AGE 20 - 30	------	----	----	----- -----		-------	-------	----
V16	POPULATION	1970	D10	P91	56.35	MIL CAP	UNKI	GFR	F4
		1975	D10	P92	67.67	MIL CAP	GFR	PAKI	----
		1980	D10	P92	80.56	MIL CAP	MEXI	PAKI	----
V17	GROSS DOMESTIC PRODUCT	1970	D8	P76	46.355	TSD MIL $	VENE	AURIA	----
		1975	D8	P79	63.470	TSD MIL $	SOUAF	ARGE	----
		1980	D8	P80	73.023	TSD MIL $	ARGE	SOUAF	----
V18	SHARE IN WORLD IMPORTS	1970	D6	P59	3.190	1/TSD	INDO	PAKI	F30
		1975	D8	P73	6.646	1/TSD	ALGER	INDIA	F30
		1980	D8	P77	8.123	1/TSD	FINLA	NORWY	F30
V19	SHARE IN WORLD EXPORTS	1970	D7	P67	3.950	1/TSD	CHILE	MEXI	F30
		1975	D8	P80	9.123	1/TSD	SPAIN	IRAQ	F30
		1980	D9	P89	13.409	1/TSD	IRAQ	SWITZ	F30
V20	GDP SHARE OF IMPORTS	1970	D3	P26	13.5	%	RWAN	FRANC	F30
		1975	D3	P28	18.2	%	GFR	CENTR	F30
		1980	D5	P40	21.1	%	RWAN	UNKI	F30
V21	GDP SHARE OF EXPORTS	1970	D5	P50	15.7	%	PORTU	UNKI	F30
		1975	D8	P72	24.1	%	NICA	SENE	F30
		1980	D9	P82	33.8	%	VENE	JAMAI	F30
V22	EXPORT PARTNER CONCENTRATION	1970	D5	P51	28.5	%	GUATE	IRAQ	F137
		1975	D7	P61	29.0	%	PARA	KORSO	----
		1979	D9	P84	45.3	%	IRE	PANA	----
V23	TOTAL DEBT AS % OF GDP	1980	D1	P6	11.4	%	OMAN	TRITO	----
V24	SHARE OF NEW FOREIGN PATENTS	1970	D9	P90	100	%	MALAW	RWAN	----
		1975	D9	P84	99	%	ZAMBI	SINGA	----
		1978	D9	----	99	%	NICA	BURU	----
V25	FOREIGN PROPERTY AS % OF GDP	1971	D8	P75	17.1	%	CAME	SAUDI	----
		1975	D7	P64	8.8	%	TUNIS	COLO	----
		1978	D3	----	2.1	%	INDIA	GHANA	----
V26	GNP SHARE OF DEVELOPMENT AID	1970	D1	P11	0.00	%	IRAN	VENE	----
		1975	D1	P4	0.04	%	-------	ITALY	----
		1980	D1	P8	0.04	%	IRAN	ITALY	----
V27	SHARE IN NOBEL PRIZE WINNERS	1970-79	D5	P45	0.0	%	NIGER	NORWY	----

V28	GDP SHARE OF MANUFACTURING	1970	D1	P7	4.3	%	YENO	MAURA	F16
		1975	D1	P8	5.5	%	LIBE	KUWAI	F16
		1980	D2	P15	5.4	%	SAUDI	SIERA	F16
V29	EXPORT SHARE OF MANUFACTURES	1970	D1	P8	0.7	%	CUBA	MAURA	----
		1975	D1	P7	0.2	%	IRAQ	RWAN	----
V30	LACK OF CIVIL LIBERTIES	1975	D4	P39	4		NICA	UPVO	----
		1980	D3	P29	3		MEXI	SENE	----
V31	LACK OF POLITICAL RIGHTS	1975	D7	P63	6		NEPAL	PERU	----
		1980	D3	P21	2		JAPAN	PAPUA	----
V32	RIOTS	1970-74	D8	P78	9		JAPAN	TURKY	----
		1975-79	D9	P84	10		JAMAI	NEPAL	----
V33	PROTEST DEMONSTRATIONS	1970-74	D7	P64	5		NETH	DENMA	----
		1975-79	D7	P64	6		ETHIA	PANA	----
V34	POLITICAL STRIKES	1970-74	D8	P78	3		KAMPU	TAIWA	----
		1975-79	D10	P98	20		FRANC	BOLI	----
V35	MEMBER OF THE NONALIGNED MMT.	1970	----	----	1		NEPAL	RWAN	----
		1976	----	----	1		NIGER	PANA	----
		1981	----	----	1		NIGER	OMAN	----
V36	MEMBER OF THE OPEC	1970	----	----	0		NIGER	NORWY	----
		1975	----	----	1		LIBYA	SAUDI	----
		1980	----	----	1		LIBYA	SAUDI	----
V37	MEMBER OF THE OECD	1970	----	----	0		NIGER	PAKI	----
		1975	----	----	0		NIGER	PAKI	----
		1980	----	----	0		NIGER	PAKI	----
V38	MEMBER OF THE CMEA	1970	----	----	0		NIGER	NORWY	----
		1975	----	----	0		NIGER	NORWY	----
		1980	----	----	0		NIGER	NORWY	----
V39	MEMBER OF THE WTO	1970	----	----	0		NIGER	NORWY	----
		1975	----	----	0		NIGER	NORWY	----
		1980	----	----	0		NIGER	NORWY	----
V40	MEMBER OF THE NATO	1970	----	----	0		NIGER	PAKI	----
		1975	----	----	0		NIGER	PAKI	----
		1980	----	----	0		NIGER	PAKI	----
V41	GDP SHARE OF INVESTMENTS	------	----	----	----- -----		-------	-------	----
V42	GDP SHARE OF AGRICULTURE	1970	D8	P80	38.1	%	BURMA	TANZA	F16
		1975	D6	P57	27.3	%	TOGO	MALAY	F16
		1980	D6	P52	22.2	%	EGYPT	NICA	F16
V43	GDP SHARE OF INDUSTRY	1970	D3	P26	19.2	%	MALAW	KENYA	F16
		1975	D8	P71	35.9	%	MOROC	NORWY	F16
		1980	D9	P83	41.2	%	KORSO	PERU	F16
V44	GDP SHARE OF SERVICES	1970	D4	P32	42.7	%	PHILI	BENIN	F16
		1975	D3	P24	36.8	%	MAURA	PHILI	F16
		1980	D3	P22	36.6	%	ALGER	INDIA	F16
V45	HOMICIDES P. MIL. POPULATION	------	----	----	----- -----		-------	-------	----

V46	SUICIDES P. MIL. POPULATION	------	----	----	----- -----		-------	-------	----
V47	IMPORT PARTNERS	1970	R1	UNKI	30.6	%	NEWZ	SOUAF	----
		1970	R2	USA	14.4	%	MOROC	PHILI	----
		1970	R3	GFR	13.0	%	MOROC	PARA	----
		1979	R1	UNKI	17.4	%	IRE	SUDAN	----
		1979	R2	GFR	16.2	%	MADA	POLA	----
		1979	R3	JAPAN	10.8	%	MALAW	TANZA	----
V48	EXPORT PARTNERS	1970	R1	UNKI	28.5	%	NEWZ	PORTU	F137
		1970	R2	NETH	17.0	%	GFR	TOGO	F137
		1970	R3	USA	11.5	%	MALAY	SRILA	F137
		1979	R1	USA	45.3	%	NICA	PANA	----
		1979	R2	NETH	13.6	%	KUWAI	OMAN	----
		1979	R3	GFR	7.8	%	NEPAL	OMAN	----
V49	PATENT SUPPLIERS	1970	R1	UNKI	45		MALAW	SRILA	----
		1970	R2	USA	43		MOROC	PAKI	----
		1970	R3	SWITZ	18		NICA	PAKI	----
		1978	R1	USA	134		NEWZ	NORWY	----
		1978	R2	UNKI	87		NEWZ	SRILA	----
		1978	R3	FRANC	57		MEXI	POLA	----
V50	PROVENANCE OF FOREIGN FIRMS	1980	R1	UNKI	53.6	%	NEWZ	SIERA	----
		1980	R2	USA	16.6	%	NETH	NORWY	----
		1980	R3	GFR	7.0	%	NETH	PAKI	----
V51	FILM SUPPLIERS	1979	R1	USA	105		NICA	NORWY	F119
		1979	R2	-------	0		-------	-------	F119
		1979	R3	-------	0		-------	-------	F119

NORWAY (NORWY)

V1	INCOME PER CAPITA	1970	D10	P93	8836	$/CAP	NETH	USA	F147
		1975	D10	P95	10727	$/CAP	GFR	DENMA	F147
		1980	D10	P95	13335	$/CAP	DENMA	SWEDN	F147
V2	TELEPHONES P. TSD. POPULATION	1970	D10	P93	294	1/TSD CAP	NETH	AULIA	----
		1975	D9	P88	350	1/TSD CAP	GFR	JAPAN	----
		1980	D9	P85	452	1/TSD CAP	AURIA	FRANC	----
V3	INFANT MORTALITY RATE	1980	D1	P4	8.1	1/TSD	FINLA	DENMA	----
V4	PHYSICIANS P. MIL. POPULATION	1975	D9	P84	1717	1/MIL	SWEDN	CANA	F147
		1980	D9	P83	1910	1/MIL	URU	FINLA	F147
V5	ADULT LITERACY	------	----	----	----- -----		-------	-------	----
V6	DURATION OF SCHOOLING	1970	D10	P95	11.2	YR	GDR	UNKI	F4
		1975	D10	P95	11.4	YR	JAPAN	CHILE	----
		1980	D10	P96	11.6	YR	JAPAN	FINLA	----

V7	STUDENT ENROLLMENT RATIO	1970	D9	P85	15.9	%	BULGA	YUGO	----
		1975	D9	P84	22.1	%	SPAIN	USSR	----
		1980	D9	P85	25.5	%	FRANC	PHILI	----
V8	SHARE OF AGRICULTURAL LABOR	1970	D3	P24	11.9	%	NEWZ	CZECH	F84
		1975	D2	P21	10.0	%	AULIA	FRANC	F67
		1980	D2	P23	7.4	%	AULIA	TRITO	F46
V9	SHARE OF INDUSTRIAL LABOR	1980	D7	P61	34.6	%	IRE	FRANC	F46
V10	SHARE OF SERVICE LABOR	1980	D7	P64	38.2	%	PANA	NEWZ	F46
V11	SHARE OF ACADEMIC LABOR	1980	D10	P94	19.8	%	NETH	ISRA	F46
V12	SHARE OF SELF-EMPLOYED LABOR	1970	D3	P29	13.9	%	NEWZ	DENMA	F84
		1975	D1	P9	11.8	%	NETH	KUWAI	F67
V13	MILITARY EXPENDITURES	1970	D8	P72	1.190	TSD MIL $	DENMA	SWITZ	----
		1975	D8	P72	1.381	TSD MIL $	DENMA	SYRIA	----
		1980	D7	P70	1.576	TSD MIL $	DENMA	ARGE	----
V14	MILITARY MANPOWER	1970	D5	P44	35	TSD CAP	GHANA	FINLA	----
		1975	D5	P46	35	TSD CAP	DENMA	MONGO	----
		1980	D5	P49	37	TSD CAP	YENO	AURIA	----
V15	MEN AT AGE 20 - 30	1970	D3	P28	295	TSD CAP	HAITI	MALI	F22
		1975	D3	P25	318	TSD CAP	ISRA	MALAW	F22
		1980	D2	P18	314	TSD CAP	HONDU	ISRA	F22
V16	POPULATION	1970	D3	P29	3.88	MIL CAP	RWAN	GUINE	F22
		1975	D3	P28	4.01	MIL CAP	ELSA	CHAD	F22
		1980	D3	P26	4.09	MIL CAP	LAOS	BURU	F22
V17	GROSS DOMESTIC PRODUCT	1970	D8	P71	34.283	TSD MIL $	FINLA	TURKY	----
		1975	D7	P69	43.016	TSD MIL $	FINLA	KORSO	----
		1980	D8	P71	54.542	TSD MIL $	FINLA	VENE	----
V18	SHARE IN WORLD IMPORTS	1970	D9	P84	11.152	1/TSD	CZECH	SOUAF	F30
		1975	D9	P83	10.678	1/TSD	AURIA	IRAN	F30
		1980	D8	P78	8.253	1/TSD	NIGRA	YUGO	F30
V19	SHARE IN WORLD EXPORTS	1970	D9	P81	7.833	1/TSD	SPAIN	IRAN	F30
		1975	D8	P76	8.256	1/TSD	INDO	CHINA	F30
		1980	D8	P80	9.291	1/TSD	CHINA	SINGA	F30
V20	GDP SHARE OF IMPORTS	1970	D9	P90	33.1	%	COSTA	PANA	F30
		1975	D8	P78	34.1	%	ELSA	EGYPT	F30
		1980	D7	P67	29.3	%	ZAMBI	DENMA	F30
V21	GDP SHARE OF EXPORTS	1970	D8	P75	22.0	%	ALGER	ELSA	F30
		1975	D8	P76	25.4	%	COSTA	JAMAI	F30
		1980	D8	P78	32.1	%	INDO	HONDU	F30
V22	EXPORT PARTNER CONCENTRATION	1970	D2	P18	17.9	%	FINLA	JORDA	----
		1975	D5	P48	23.9	%	MOZAM	PERU	----
		1980	D9	P80	41.4	%	NIGER	YENO	----
V23	TOTAL DEBT AS % OF GDP	------	----	----	----- -----		-------	-------	----

V24 SHARE OF NEW FOREIGN PATENTS	1970	D5	P49	90 %	DENMA	TURKY	----
	1975	D5	P43	88 %	GUATE	PANA	----
	1980	D5	P42	87 %	NETH	DENMA	----
V25 FOREIGN PROPERTY AS % OF GDP	------	----	----	----- -----	-------	-------	----
V26 GNP SHARE OF DEVELOPMENT AID	1970	D6	P57	0.33 %	USA	SWEDN	----
	1975	D7	P68	0.65 %	AULIA	NETH	----
	1980	D8	P75	0.87 %	SWEDN	NETH	----
V27 SHARE IN NOBEL PRIZE WINNERS	1970-79	D5	P45	0.0 %	NIGRA	PANA	----
V28 GDP SHARE OF MANUFACTURING	------	----	----	----- -----	-------	-------	----
V29 EXPORT SHARE OF MANUFACTURES	------	----	----	----- -----	-------	-------	----
V30 LACK OF CIVIL LIBERTIES	1975	D1	P7	1	NEWZ	SWEDN	----
	1980	D1	P7	1	NEWZ	SWEDN	----
V31 LACK OF POLITICAL RIGHTS	1975	D1	P8	1	NEWZ	SWEDN	----
	1980	D1	P8	1	NEWZ	SWEDN	----
V32 RIOTS	1970-74	D5	P43	1	NEWZ	SIERA	----
	1975-79	D2	P20	0	NIGER	PARA	----
V33 PROTEST DEMONSTRATIONS	1970-74	D2	P15	0	MONGO	PANA	----
	1975-79	D5	P49	3	KENYA	SIERA	----
V34 POLITICAL STRIKES	1970-74	D7	P64	1	NIGER	SWEDN	----
	1975-79	D3	P29	0	NIGER	PARA	----
V35 MEMBER OF THE NONALIGNED MMT.	1970	----	----	0	NIGER	PAKI	----
	1976	----	----	0	NICA	PAKI	----
	1981	----	----	0	NEWZ	PAPUA	----
V36 MEMBER OF THE OPEC	1970	----	----	0	NIGRA	PAKI	----
	1975	----	----	0	NIGER	PAKI	----
	1980	----	----	0	NIGER	PAKI	----
V37 MEMBER OF THE OECD	1970	----	----	1	NETH	PORTU	----
	1975	----	----	1	NEWZ	PORTU	----
	1980	----	----	1	NEWZ	PORTU	----
V38 MEMBER OF THE CMEA	1970	----	----	0	NIGRA	PAKI	----
	1975	----	----	0	NIGRA	PAKI	----
	1980	----	----	0	NIGRA	PAKI	----
V39 MEMBER OF THE WTO	1970	----	----	0	NIGRA	PAKI	----
	1975	----	----	0	NIGRA	PAKI	----
	1980	----	----	0	NIGRA	PAKI	----
V40 MEMBER OF THE NATO	1970	----	----	1	NETH	PORTU	----
	1975	----	----	1	NETH	PORTU	----
	1980	----	----	1	NETH	PORTU	----
V41 GDP SHARE OF INVESTMENTS	1970	D10	P91	30.5 %	AURIA	JAMAI	----
	1975	D10	P95	35.2 %	MAURA	SINGA	----
	1980	D7	P68	27.4 %	LIBE	FINLA	----

V42	GDP SHARE OF AGRICULTURE	1970	D2	P17	6.4	%	JAPAN	FRANC	----
		1975	D2	P18	5.5	%	JAPAN	VENE	----
		1980	D2	P19	4.5	%	DENMA	VENE	----
V43	GDP SHARE OF INDUSTRY	1970	D7	P65	33.8	%	MEXI	PERU	----
		1975	D8	P71	35.9	%	NIGRA	SWEDN	----
		1980	D8	P80	40.4	%	AURIA	KORSO	----
V44	GDP SHARE OF SERVICES	1970	D10	P91	59.8	%	UNKI	SWEDN	----
		1975	D9	P90	58.6	%	BELGI	SWEDN	----
		1980	D8	P78	55.1	%	SYRIA	COSTA	----
V45	HOMICIDES P. MIL. POPULATION	1970	D1	P8	6.2	1/MIL CAP	GREC	SPAIN	F149
		1975	D2	P11	7.0	1/MIL CAP	NETH	GREC	F149
		1980	D4	P34	11.2	1/MIL CAP	CZECH	GFR	F149
V46	SUICIDES P. MIL. POPULATION	1970	D5	P46	83.8	1/MIL CAP	PORTU	SINGA	F147
		1975	D5	P47	98.5	1/MIL CAP	NEWZ	URU	F147
		1980	D6	P52	124.0	1/MIL CAP	USA	BULGA	F147
V47	IMPORT PARTNERS	1970	R1	SWEDN	20.1	%	-------	DENMA	----
		1970	R2	GFR	14.4	%	MEXI	PERU	----
		1970	R3	UNKI	12.3	%	LIBYA	PAKI	----
		1980	R1	SWEDN	16.7	%	-------	DENMA	----
		1980	R2	UNKI	14.9	%	NEPAL	SWEDN	----
		1980	R3	GFR	13.8	%	MALI	PERU	----
V48	EXPORT PARTNERS	1970	R1	GFR	17.9	%	NETH	SWITZ	----
		1970	R2	UNKI	17.9	%	MAURA	PAKI	----
		1970	R3	SWEDN	16.2	%	TRITO	-------	----
		1980	R1	UNKI	41.4	%	NEWZ	PORTU	----
		1980	R2	GFR	16.7	%	NICA	PANA	----
		1980	R3	SWEDN	9.2	%	DENMA	-------	----
V49	PATENT SUPPLIERS	1970	R1	USA	575		NICA	PERU	----
		1970	R2	GFR	466		NICA	PORTU	----
		1970	R3	SWEDN	376		COSTA	-------	----
		1980	R1	USA	428		NIGRA	PAKI	----
		1980	R2	GFR	275		NETH	PAKI	----
		1980	R3	SWEDN	273		FINLA	-------	----
V50	PROVENANCE OF FOREIGN FIRMS	1980	R1	SWEDN	33.6	%	FINLA	-------	----
		1980	R2	USA	24.6	%	NIGRA	SOUAF	----
		1980	R3	UNKI	12.5	%	MEXI	PHILI	----
V51	FILM SUPPLIERS	1980	R1	USA	131		NIGRA	PERU	F119
		1980	R2	UNKI	35		NEWZ	SRILA	F119
		1980	R3	ITALY	14		KUWAI	POLA	F119

OMAN (OMAN)

V1	INCOME PER CAPITA	------	----	----	----- -----	-------	-------	----
V2	TELEPHONES P. TSD. POPULATION	------	----	----	----- -----	-------	-------	----
V3	INFANT MORTALITY RATE	------	----	----	----- -----	-------	-------	----
V4	PHYSICIANS P. MIL. POPULATION	1981	D6	P53	587 1/MIL	PARA	SAUDI	----
V5	ADULT LITERACY	------	----	----	----- -----	-------	-------	----
V6	DURATION OF SCHOOLING	1982	D3	----	5.8 YR	MOROC	BURMA	----
V7	STUDENT ENROLLMENT RATIO	1981	D1	P2	0.0 %	MAURA	MOZAM	----
V8	SHARE OF AGRICULTURAL LABOR	------	----	----	----- -----	-------	-------	----
V9	SHARE OF INDUSTRIAL LABOR	------	----	----	----- -----	-------	-------	----
V10	SHARE OF SERVICE LABOR	------	----	----	----- -----	-------	-------	----
V11	SHARE OF ACADEMIC LABOR	------	----	----	----- -----	-------	-------	----
V12	SHARE OF SELF-EMPLOYED LABOR	------	----	----	----- -----	-------	-------	----
V13	MILITARY EXPENDITURES	------	----	----	----- -----	-------	-------	----
V14	MILITARY MANPOWER	------	----	----	----- -----	-------	-------	----
V15	MEN AT AGE 20 - 30	------	----	----	----- -----	-------	-------	----
V16	POPULATION	1981	D1	P1	1.03 MIL CAP	-------	UNARE	----
V17	GROSS DOMESTIC PRODUCT	------	----	----	----- -----	-------	-------	----
V18	SHARE IN WORLD IMPORTS	1981	D5	P45	1.125 1/TSD	ECUA	JORDA	F30
V19	SHARE IN WORLD EXPORTS	1981	D5	P50	1.281 1/TSD	ECUA	PAKI	F30
V20	GDP SHARE OF IMPORTS	1981	D8	P72	31.5 %	COSTA	AURIA	F30
V21	GDP SHARE OF EXPORTS	1981	D10	P97	64.6 %	LIBE	KUWAI	F30
V22	EXPORT PARTNER CONCENTRATION	1981	D9	P87	48.5 %	ALGER	INDO	----
V23	TOTAL DEBT AS % OF GDP	1981	D1	P4	10.5 %	NEPAL	NIGRA	----
V24	SHARE OF NEW FOREIGN PATENTS	------	----	----	----- -----	-------	-------	----
V25	FOREIGN PROPERTY AS % OF GDP	------	----	----	----- -----	-------	-------	----
V26	GNP SHARE OF DEVELOPMENT AID	------	----	----	----- -----	-------	-------	----
V27	SHARE IN NOBEL PRIZE WINNERS	------	----	----	----- -----	-------	-------	----
V28	GDP SHARE OF MANUFACTURING	1981	D1	P2	1.0 %	-------	LIBYA	----
V29	EXPORT SHARE OF MANUFACTURES	------	----	----	----- -----	-------	-------	----

V30	LACK OF CIVIL LIBERTIES	1981	D8	P74	6		NIGER	PAKI	----
V31	LACK OF POLITICAL RIGHTS	1981	D7	P67	6		MAURA	PAKI	----
V32	RIOTS	------	----	----	-----	-----	-------	-------	----
V33	PROTEST DEMONSTRATIONS	------	----	----	-----	-----	-------	-------	----
V34	POLITICAL STRIKES	------	----	----	-----	-----	-------	-------	----
V35	MEMBER OF THE NONALIGNED MMT.	1981	----	----	1		NIGRA	PAKI	----
V36	MEMBER OF THE OPEC	------	----	----	-----	-----	-------	-------	----
V37	MEMBER OF THE OECD	------	----	----	-----	-----	-------	-------	----
V38	MEMBER OF THE CMEA	------	----	----	-----	-----	-------	-------	----
V39	MEMBER OF THE WTO	------	----	----	-----	-----	-------	-------	----
V40	MEMBER OF THE NATO	------	----	----	-----	-----	-------	-------	----
V41	GDP SHARE OF INVESTMENTS	1981	D6	P51	24.1	%	SYRIA	AULIA	----
V42	GDP SHARE OF AGRICULTURE	1981	D1	P7	2.0	%	UNKI	BELGI	----
V43	GDP SHARE OF INDUSTRY	------	----	----	-----	-----	-------	-------	----
V44	GDP SHARE OF SERVICES	------	----	----	-----	-----	-------	-------	----
V45	HOMICIDES P. MIL. POPULATION	------	----	----	-----	-----	-------	-------	----
V46	SUICIDES P. MIL. POPULATION	------	----	----	-----	-----	-------	-------	----
V47	IMPORT PARTNERS	1981	R1	JAPAN	22.6	%	NEPAL	SINGA	----
		1981	R2	UNARE	15.9	%	-------	-------	----
		1981	R3	UNKI	14.5	%	KUWAI	PORTU	----
V48	EXPORT PARTNERS	1981	R1	JAPAN	48.5	%	MALAY	PAPUA	----
		1981	R2	NETH	10.6	%	NIGRA	THAI	----
		1981	R3	GFR	10.6	%	NIGRA	PARA	----
V49	PATENT SUPPLIERS	------	----	----	-----	-----	-------	-------	----
V50	PROVENANCE OF FOREIGN FIRMS	------	----	----	-----	-----	-------	-------	----
V51	FILM SUPPLIERS	------	----	----	-----	-----	-------	-------	----

PAKISTAN (PAKI)

V1	INCOME PER CAPITA	1975	D2	P13	253	$/CAP	HAITI	TANZA	F219
		1980	D2	P15	293	$/CAP	HAITI	BENIN	F219

V2	TELEPHONES P. TSD. POPULATION	1970	D3	P22	3	1/TSD CAP	MALAW	TANZA	F9
		1975	D2	P17	3	1/TSD CAP	LESO	VISO	----
		1980	D2	P14	4	1/TSD CAP	MOZAM	TOGO	----
V3	INFANT MORTALITY RATE	1980	D8	P78	131.2	1/TSD	SUDAN	IVORY	F5
V4	PHYSICIANS P. MIL. POPULATION	------	----	----	----- -----		-------	-------	----
V5	ADULT LITERACY	1972	D2	----	20.7	%	TOGO	HAITI	----
		1981	D2	P20	26.2	%	LIBE	BURU	----
V6	DURATION OF SCHOOLING	1975	D2	P14	3.5	YR	SENE	SIERA	----
		1980	D1	P8	3.2	YR	GUINE	ETHIA	----
V7	STUDENT ENROLLMENT RATIO	1975	D4	P32	1.9	%	LIBE	SENE	----
		1979	D3	P27	2.0	%	BENIN	NIGRA	----
V8	SHARE OF AGRICULTURAL LABOR	1976	D8	P76	54.8	%	PHILI	GUATE	F101
		1980	D8	P84	54.8	%	PHILI	INDO	F101
V9	SHARE OF INDUSTRIAL LABOR	1976	D5	P44	24.3	%	ECUA	COSTA	F101
		1980	D3	P25	24.3	%	PANA	COLO	F101
V10	SHARE OF SERVICE LABOR	1976	D3	P29	17.9	%	HONDU	IRAN	F101
		1980	D2	P15	17.9	%	GUATE	SRILA	F101
V11	SHARE OF ACADEMIC LABOR	1976	D2	P18	3.0	%	SUDAN	KORSO	F101
		1980	D2	P13	3.0	%	HAITI	INDO	F101
V12	SHARE OF SELF-EMPLOYED LABOR	1976	D9	P89	49.8	%	MALI	BOLI	F101
		1980	D10	P95	49.8	%	BANGL	INDO	F101
V13	MILITARY EXPENDITURES	1975	D7	P65	1.202	TSD MIL $	MALAY	CHILE	----
		1980	D7	P66	1.412	TSD MIL $	BRAZI	THAI	----
V14	MILITARY MANPOWER	1970	D9	P89	390	TSD CAP	UNKI	ITALY	F9
		1975	D10	P92	502	TSD CAP	ITALY	TAIWA	----
		1980	D10	P94	467	TSD CAP	BRAZI	GFR	----
V15	MEN AT AGE 20 - 30	1981	D9	P90	6154	TSD CAP	MEXI	BANGL	F203
V16	POPULATION	1975	D10	P93	70.90	MIL CAP	NIGRA	BANGL	F101
		1980	D10	P93	82.14	MIL CAP	NIGRA	BANGL	F101
V17	GROSS DOMESTIC PRODUCT	1975	D6	P56	17.967	TSD MIL $	HUNGA	PORTU	----
		1980	D6	P59	24.101	TSD MIL $	PORTU	CHILE	----
V18	SHARE IN WORLD IMPORTS	1970	D6	P59	3.528	1/TSD	NIGRA	NEWZ	F56
		1975	D6	P52	2.374	1/TSD	SYRIA	KUWAI	F30
		1980	D6	P56	2.608	1/TSD	CHILE	NEWZ	F30
V19	SHARE IN WORLD EXPORTS	1970	D6	P51	2.305	1/TSD	THAI	ISRA	F56
		1975	D5	P49	1.181	1/TSD	GABON	IVORY	F30
		1980	D5	P50	1.297	1/TSD	OMAN	TURKY	F30
V20	GDP SHARE OF IMPORTS	1975	D4	P32	19.0	%	CHILE	VENE	F30
		1980	D5	P42	22.3	%	UNKI	DOMI	F30
V21	GDP SHARE OF EXPORTS	1975	D2	P20	9.1	%	ETHIA	CHAD	F30
		1980	D3	P26	10.8	%	URU	COLO	F30

V22	EXPORT PARTNER CONCENTRATION	1970	D1	P2	11.8 %	UNKI	GFR	F145
		1975	D1	P1	6.8 %	-------	UNKI	----
		1980	D1	P2	8.5 %	-------	USSR	----
V23	TOTAL DEBT AS % OF GDP	1980	D6	P56	41.4 %	MADA	SENE	----
V24	SHARE OF NEW FOREIGN PATENTS	1972	D2	----	71 %	FRANC	URU	----
		1975	D8	P75	96 %	LIBYA	PORTU	----
		1980	D8	P76	96 %	SYRIA	PORTU	----
V25	FOREIGN PROPERTY AS % OF GDP	1975	D6	P55	6.6 %	GHANA	URU	----
		1978	D5	----	4.5 %	NICA	BENIN	----
V26	GNP SHARE OF DEVELOPMENT AID	------	----	----	----- -----	-------	-------	----
V27	SHARE IN NOBEL PRIZE WINNERS	1970-79	D9	P90	1.3 %	NETH	DENMA	----
V28	GDP SHARE OF MANUFACTURING	1975	D6	P58	16.7 %	VENE	JAMAI	F16
		1980	D7	P62	16.5 %	DENMA	PARA	F16
V29	EXPORT SHARE OF MANUFACTURES	------	----	----	----- -----	-------	-------	----
V30	LACK OF CIVIL LIBERTIES	1975	D6	P54	5	NEPAL	PARA	----
		1980	D8	P74	6	OMAN	ROMA	----
V31	LACK OF POLITICAL RIGHTS	1975	D3	P27	3	MALAY	PAPUA	----
		1980	D7	P67	6	OMAN	POLA	----
V32	RIOTS	1970-74	D10	P97	64	GREC	INDIA	F9
		1975-79	D10	P94	47	UNKI	INDIA	----
V33	PROTEST DEMONSTRATIONS	1970-74	D10	P91	48	VISO	IRE	F9
		1975-79	D9	P89	35	CHINA	KORSO	----
V34	POLITICAL STRIKES	1970-74	D10	P93	16	PORTU	SPAIN	F9
		1975-79	D10	P91	12	IRAN	ISRA	----
V35	MEMBER OF THE NONALIGNED MMT.	1970	----	----	0	NORWY	PANA	----
		1976	----	----	0	NORWY	PAPUA	----
		1981	----	----	1	OMAN	PANA	----
V36	MEMBER OF THE OPEC	1970	----	----	0	NORWY	PANA	----
		1975	----	----	0	NORWY	PANA	----
		1980	----	----	0	NORWY	PANA	----
V37	MEMBER OF THE OECD	1970	----	----	0	NIGRA	PANA	----
		1975	----	----	0	NIGRA	PANA	----
		1980	----	----	0	NIGRA	PANA	----
V38	MEMBER OF THE CMEA	1970	----	----	0	NORWY	PANA	----
		1975	----	----	0	NORWY	PANA	----
		1980	----	----	0	NORWY	PANA	----
V39	MEMBER OF THE WTO	1970	----	----	0	NORWY	PANA	----
		1975	----	----	0	NORWY	PANA	----
		1980	----	----	0	NORWY	PANA	----
V40	MEMBER OF THE NATO	1970	----	----	0	NIGRA	PANA	----
		1975	----	----	0	NIGRA	PANA	----
		1980	----	----	0	NIGRA	PANA	----

V41 GDP SHARE OF INVESTMENTS	1972	D3	----	14.2 %	GHANA	PARA	----
	1975	D3	P22	16.2 %	GUATE	PORTU	----
	1980	D3	P26	17.5 %	UPVO	URU	----
V42 GDP SHARE OF AGRICULTURE	1975	D8	P72	32.0 %	MAURA	CAME	F16
	1980	D8	P72	31.1 %	LESO	SIERA	F16
V43 GDP SHARE OF INDUSTRY	1975	D3	P30	23.4 %	INDIA	PANA	F16
	1980	D4	P33	25.3 %	INDIA	PARA	F16
V44 GDP SHARE OF SERVICES	1975	D5	P46	44.6 %	EGYPT	YENO	F16
	1980	D4	P40	43.6 %	KORSO	YUGO	F16
V45 HOMICIDES P. MIL. POPULATION	------	----	----	----- -----	-------	-------	----
V46 SUICIDES P. MIL. POPULATION	------	----	----	----- -----	-------	-------	----
V47 IMPORT PARTNERS	1970	R1	USA	30.8 %	NICA	PARA	F145
	1970	R2	JAPAN	11.1 %	KENYA	RWAN	F145
	1970	R3	UNKI	10.2 %	NORWY	TURKY	F145
	1980	R1	USA	14.1 %	NICA	PANA	----
	1980	R2	JAPAN	10.3 %	NEWZ	PAPUA	----
	1980	R3	SAUDI	9.6 %	KORSO	PHILI	----
V48 EXPORT PARTNERS	1970	R1	USA	11.8 %	NICA	PANA	F145
	1970	R2	UNKI	10.4 %	NORWY	UGADA	F145
	1970	R3	JAPAN	5.9 %	NEWZ	PERU	F145
	1980	R1	CHINA	8.5 %	-------	YENO	----
	1980	R2	JAPAN	7.8 %	NIGER	PERU	----
	1980	R3	IRAN	7.6 %	BANGL	-------	----
V49 PATENT SUPPLIERS	1972	R1	GFR	4	HUNGA	POLA	----
	1972	R2	USA	3	NIGRA	SWITZ	----
	1972	R3	SWITZ	2	NIGRA	PHILI	----
	1980	R1	USA	105	NORWY	PERU	----
	1980	R2	GFR	47	NORWY	PORTU	----
	1980	R3	UNKI	39	JAPAN	SIERA	----
V50 PROVENANCE OF FOREIGN FIRMS	1980	R1	USA	42.5 %	NICA	PANA	----
	1980	R2	UNKI	38.5 %	LEBA	PANA	----
	1980	R3	GFR	4.5 %	NIGRA	PORTU	----
V51 FILM SUPPLIERS	1979	R1	UNKI	19	-------	SYRIA	F118
	1979	R2	USA	16	MOROC	POLA	F118
	1979	R3	FRANC	4	NEWZ	PERU	F118

PANAMA (PANA)

V1 INCOME PER CAPITA	1970	D6	P59	1385 $/CAP	ALGER	JAMAI	F216
	1975	D6	P59	1484 $/CAP	JAMAI	ALGER	----
	1980	D6	P58	1800 $/CAP	MALAY	HUNGA	----

V2	TELEPHONES P. TSD. POPULATION	1970	D7	P70	60	1/TSD CAP	POLA	TRITO	----
		1980	D7	P63	95	1/TSD CAP	ARGE	POLA	----
V3	INFANT MORTALITY RATE	1980	D4	P35	36.0	1/TSD	KORSO	KORNO	F5
V4	PHYSICIANS P. MIL. POPULATION	1970	D7	P66	646	1/MIL	COSTA	MEXI	F85
		1975	D7	P63	750	1/MIL	SINGA	MEXI	F85
		1978	D7	----	856	1/MIL	TRITO	SINGA	F35
V5	ADULT LITERACY	1970	D7	P60	78.3	%	SRILA	THAI	----
		1980	D9	P86	87.1	%	SRILA	THAI	F23
V6	DURATION OF SCHOOLING	1970	D7	P63	8.6	YR	SRILA	PERU	----
		1975	D8	P78	10.4	YR	ISRA	BULGA	----
		1980	D7	P67	10.2	YR	URU	BULGA	----
V7	STUDENT ENROLLMENT RATIO	1970	D7	P62	6.8	%	SINGA	ECUA	----
		1975	D8	P74	17.3	%	POLA	VENE	----
		1980	D8	P78	21.5	%	USSR	ARGE	----
V8	SHARE OF AGRICULTURAL LABOR	1970	D6	P59	38.9	%	POLA	MEXI	F85
		1980	D5	P53	28.1	%	POLA	GREC	F85
V9	SHARE OF INDUSTRIAL LABOR	1970	D3	P29	22.3	%	BRAZI	NICA	F85
		1980	D3	P23	23.8	%	EGYPT	PAKI	F85
V10	SHARE OF SERVICE LABOR	1970	D7	P66	31.7	%	IRE	FRANC	F85
		1980	D7	P62	37.0	%	SWEDN	NORWY	F85
V11	SHARE OF ACADEMIC LABOR	1970	D6	P53	7.1	%	JAPAN	ITALY	F85
		1980	D7	P64	11.1	%	YUGO	POLA	F85
V12	SHARE OF SELF-EMPLOYED LABOR	1970	D8	P80	37.7	%	BRAZI	PHILI	F85
V13	MILITARY EXPENDITURES	1970	D2	P12	0.015	TSD MIL $	NIGER	HAITI	----
		1975	D2	P13	0.020	TSD MIL $	HAITI	TRITO	----
		1980	D2	P12	0.023	TSD MIL $	MALAW	LIBE	F59
V14	MILITARY MANPOWER	1970	D2	P13	5	TSD CAP	LIBE	CONGO	----
		1975	D3	P20	8	TSD CAP	MALI	KENYA	----
		1980	D2	P19	8	TSD CAP	MAURA	SENE	----
V15	MEN AT AGE 20 - 30	1970	D1	P5	113	TSD CAP	JAMAI	YESO	F85
		1975	D1	P9	132	TSD CAP	YESO	COSTA	F193
		1980	D1	P3	163	TSD CAP	KUWAI	JAMAI	F2
V16	POPULATION	1970	D1	P7	1.43	MIL CAP	LIBE	YESO	F175
		1975	D1	P8	1.68	MIL CAP	LIBE	YESO	----
		1980	D1	P9	1.88	MIL CAP	LIBE	JAMAI	----
V17	GROSS DOMESTIC PRODUCT	1970	D3	P23	1.980	TSD MIL $	COSTA	ELSA	----
		1975	D2	P20	2.493	TSD MIL $	NICA	SENE	----
		1980	D3	P27	3.384	TSD MIL $	COSTA	ZAMBI	----
V18	SHARE IN WORLD IMPORTS	1970	D4	P40	1.075	1/TSD	TANZA	SYRIA	F41
		1975	D5	P43	1.048	1/TSD	ECUA	KENYA	----
		1980	D4	P35	0.706	1/TSD	ZIMBA	DOMI	----
V19	SHARE IN WORLD EXPORTS	1970	D3	P23	0.338	1/TSD	SIERA	BURMA	F41
		1975	D3	P28	0.348	1/TSD	HONDU	LEBA	----
		1980	D2	P17	0.176	1/TSD	UGADA	MOZAM	----

V20 GDP SHARE OF IMPORTS	1970	D10	P91	35.0	%	NORWY	MALAY	F41
	1975	D10	P96	51.8	%	BELGI	LIBE	----
	1980	D9	P85	40.7	%	NICA	TUNIS	----
V21 GDP SHARE OF EXPORTS	1970	D3	P24	10.4	%	COLO	EGYPT	F41
	1975	D5	P45	16.6	%	THAI	SYRIA	----
	1980	D3	P22	9.9	%	SPAIN	TANZA	----
V22 EXPORT PARTNER CONCENTRATION	1970	D10	P95	62.1	%	HAITI	CANA	F131
	1979	D9	P85	46.4	%	NIGRA	ALGER	F132
V23 TOTAL DEBT AS % OF GDP	1980	D10	P94	83.4	%	EGYPT	ZAMBI	----
V24 SHARE OF NEW FOREIGN PATENTS	1977	D5	----	88	%	NORWY	COSTA	F19
	1980	D7	P72	94	%	MOROC	SYRIA	----
V25 FOREIGN PROPERTY AS % OF GDP	------	----	----	-----	-----	-------	-------	----
V26 GNP SHARE OF DEVELOPMENT AID	------	----	----	-----	-----	-------	-------	----
V27 SHARE IN NOBEL PRIZE WINNERS	1970-79	D5	P45	0.0	%	NORWY	PARA	----
V28 GDP SHARE OF MANUFACTURING	1970	D5	P41	12.5	%	KENYA	MALAW	----
	1975	D5	P43	12.8	%	RWAN	ECUA	----
	1980	D4	P40	10.4	%	NEPAL	ETHIA	----
V29 EXPORT SHARE OF MANUFACTURES	1975	D4	P36	4.5	%	MADA	TOGO	F131
	1980	D4	P36	8.8	%	CHILE	UPVO	F132
V30 LACK OF CIVIL LIBERTIES	1975	D8	P74	6		NIGER	PERU	----
	1980	D6	P52	5		NICA	PARA	----
V31 LACK OF POLITICAL RIGHTS	1975	D9	P88	7		NIGER	ROMA	----
	1980	D5	P47	5		NICA	PARA	----
V32 RIOTS	1970-74	D2	P19	0		NIGER	PARA	----
	1975-79	D8	P79	8		LAOS	THAI	----
V33 PROTEST DEMONSTRATIONS	1970-74	D2	P15	0		NORWY	PERU	----
	1975-79	D7	P64	6		NIGRA	GUATE	----
V34 POLITICAL STRIKES	1970-74	D3	P29	0		NICA	PARA	----
	1975-79	D8	P73	2		MALI	TANZA	----
V35 MEMBER OF THE NONALIGNED MMT.	1970	----	----	0		PAKI	PARA	----
	1976	----	----	1		NIGRA	PERU	----
	1981	----	----	1		PAKI	PERU	----
V36 MEMBER OF THE OPEC	1970	----	----	0		PAKI	PARA	----
	1975	----	----	0		PAKI	PAPUA	----
	1980	----	----	0		PAKI	PAPUA	----
V37 MEMBER OF THE OECD	1970	----	----	0		PAKI	PARA	----
	1975	----	----	0		PAKI	PAPUA	----
	1980	----	----	0		PAKI	PAPUA	----
V38 MEMBER OF THE CMEA	1970	----	----	0		PAKI	PARA	----
	1975	----	----	0		PAKI	PAPUA	----
	1980	----	----	0		PAKI	PAPUA	----

V39	MEMBER OF THE WTO	1970	----	----	0	PAKI	PARA	----
		1975	----	----	0	PAKI	PAPUA	----
		1980	----	----	0	PAKI	PAPUA	----
V40	MEMBER OF THE NATO	1970	----	----	0	PAKI	PARA	----
		1975	----	----	0	PAKI	PAPUA	----
		1980	----	----	0	PAKI	PAPUA	----
V41	GDP SHARE OF INVESTMENTS	1970	D9	P82	27.8 %	ISRA	GFR	----
		1975	D9	P84	30.8 %	LIBYA	VENE	----
		1980	D8	P76	28.5 %	UNARE	AURIA	----
V42	GDP SHARE OF AGRICULTURE	1970	D4	P36	14.6 %	JORDA	PERU	----
		1975	D4	P34	11.2 %	MEXI	URU	----
		1980	D4	P35	10.0 %	URU	PERU	----
V43	GDP SHARE OF INDUSTRY	1970	D4	P32	21.5 %	IVORY	INDIA	----
		1975	D4	P31	23.5 %	PAKI	SIERA	----
		1980	D3	P22	21.4 %	LESO	KENYA	----
V44	GDP SHARE OF SERVICES	1970	D10	P95	63.9 %	LESO	CANA	----
		1975	D10	P97	65.3 %	SINGA	JORDA	----
		1980	D10	P98	68.6 %	SWEDN	DENMA	----
V45	HOMICIDES P. MIL. POPULATION	------	----	----	----- -----	-------	-------	----
V46	SUICIDES P. MIL. POPULATION	------	----	----	----- -----	-------	-------	----
V47	IMPORT PARTNERS	1980	R1	USA	33.8 %	PAKI	PERU	F129
		1980	R2	SAUDI	18.6 %	JAPAN	SPAIN	F129
V48	EXPORT PARTNERS	1970	R1	USA	62.1 %	PAKI	PERU	F131
		1970	R2	GFR	15.8 %	MOROC	PERU	F131
		1970	R3	NETH	4.2 %	LIBE	PARA	F131
		1979	R1	USA	46.4 %	NIGRA	PERU	F132
		1979	R2	GFR	7.9 %	NORWY	PAPUA	F132
		1979	R3	COSTA	5.7 %	NICA	-------	F132
V49	PATENT SUPPLIERS	------	----	----	----- -----	-------	-------	----
V50	PROVENANCE OF FOREIGN FIRMS	1980	R1	USA	63.8 %	PAKI	PARA	----
		1980	R2	UNKI	10.4 %	PAKI	PAPUA	----
V51	FILM SUPPLIERS	------	----	----	----- -----	-------	-------	----

PAPUA NEW GUINEA (PAPUA)

V1	INCOME PER CAPITA	1975	D4	P39	863 $/CAP	MOROC	NIGRA	----
		1980	D4	P39	797 $/CAP	NICA	MOROC	----
V2	TELEPHONES P. TSD. POPULATION	1975	D5	P39	13 1/TSD CAP	EGYPT	ALGER	----
		1980	D4	P34	16 1/TSD CAP	PHILI	PARA	----

V3	INFANT MORTALITY RATE	1980	D7	P63	110.9	1/TSD	ZAMBI	MOROC	F5
V4	PHYSICIANS P. MIL. POPULATION	1975	D3	P26	69	1/MIL	YENO	MOROC	----
		1980	D2	P17	64	1/MIL	BENIN	SOMA	----
V5	ADULT LITERACY	------	----	----	-----	-----	-------	-------	----
V6	DURATION OF SCHOOLING	1975	D2	P20	4.3	YR	NIGRA	TANZA	----
		1980	D2	P15	4.6	YR	BANGL	BENIN	----
V7	STUDENT ENROLLMENT RATIO	1975	D4	P37	2.5	%	INDO	BANGL	----
		1980	D3	P25	1.8	%	AFGHA	SUDAN	----
V8	SHARE OF AGRICULTURAL LABOR	------	----	----	-----	-----	-------	-------	----
V9	SHARE OF INDUSTRIAL LABOR	------	----	----	-----	-----	-------	-------	----
V10	SHARE OF SERVICE LABOR	------	----	----	-----	-----	-------	-------	----
V11	SHARE OF ACADEMIC LABOR	------	----	----	-----	-----	-------	-------	----
V12	SHARE OF SELF-EMPLOYED LABOR	------	----	----	-----	-----	-------	-------	----
V13	MILITARY EXPENDITURES	------	----	----	-----	-----	-------	-------	----
V14	MILITARY MANPOWER	1977	D1	----	3	TSD CAP	MAURA	TOGO	----
		1980	D1	P6	3	TSD CAP	NIGER	BENIN	----
V15	MEN AT AGE 20 - 30	1976	D2	P16	225	TSD CAP	PARA	IRE	F46
V16	POPULATION	1975	D2	P17	2.70	MIL CAP	JORDA	LEBA	----
		1980	D2	P19	3.00	MIL CAP	LIBYA	NEWZ	----
V17	GROSS DOMESTIC PRODUCT	1975	D2	P17	2.329	TSD MIL $	NEPAL	BOLI	----
		1980	D2	P16	2.392	TSD MIL $	NIGER	JAMAI	----
V18	SHARE IN WORLD IMPORTS	1975	D3	P27	0.524	1/TSD	GABON	NICA	F49
		1980	D3	P29	0.499	1/TSD	HONDU	SENE	F49
V19	SHARE IN WORLD EXPORTS	1975	D4	P33	0.502	1/TSD	SUDAN	BOLI	F30
		1980	D4	P36	0.518	1/TSD	COSTA	BOLI	F30
V20	GDP SHARE OF IMPORTS	1975	D9	P84	36.2	%	HONDU	BENIN	F49
		1980	D9	P84	40.4	%	PORTU	NICA	F49
V21	GDP SHARE OF EXPORTS	1975	D9	P83	33.4	%	ALGER	VENE	F30
		1980	D9	P86	40.8	%	HUNGA	NETH	F30
V22	EXPORT PARTNER CONCENTRATION	1975	D8	P71	35.8	%	MALI	GABON	----
		1980	D8	P75	37.2	%	LIBYA	JAMAI	----
V23	TOTAL DEBT AS % OF GDP	1980	D4	P37	28.4	%	BRAZI	INDO	----
V24	SHARE OF NEW FOREIGN PATENTS	------	----	----	-----	-----	-------	-------	----
V25	FOREIGN PROPERTY AS % OF GDP	1975	D10	P98	53.2	%	TRITO	LIBE	----
		1978	D10	----	43.1	%	TRITO	LIBE	----
V26	GNP SHARE OF DEVELOPMENT AID	------	----	----	-----	-----	-------	-------	----
V27	SHARE IN NOBEL PRIZE WINNERS	------	----	----	-----	-----	-------	-------	----

V28	GDP SHARE OF MANUFACTURING	1975	D3	P21	8.1	%	BURU	CHAD	----
		1980	D4	P32	8.6	%	MOZAM	ECUA	----
V29	EXPORT SHARE OF MANUFACTURES	1975	D3	P23	1.8	%	ALGER	PERU	----
		1979	D2	P14	1.6	%	ZAMBI	LIBE	----
V30	LACK OF CIVIL LIBERTIES	1975	D2	P18	2		LEBA	TRITO	----
		1980	D2	P18	2		ITALY	PORTU	----
V31	LACK OF POLITICAL RIGHTS	1975	D3	P27	3		PAKI	BANGL	----
		1980	D3	P21	2		NIGRA	PORTU	----
V32	RIOTS	------	----	----	-----	-----	-------	-------	----
V33	PROTEST DEMONSTRATIONS	------	----	----	-----	-----	-------	-------	----
V34	POLITICAL STRIKES	------	----	----	-----	-----	-------	-------	----
V35	MEMBER OF THE NONALIGNED MMT.	1976	----	----	0		PAKI	PARA	----
		1981	----	----	0		NORWY	PARA	----
V36	MEMBER OF THE OPEC	1975	----	----	0		PANA	PARA	----
		1980	----	----	0		PANA	PARA	----
V37	MEMBER OF THE OECD	1975	----	----	0		PANA	PARA	----
		1980	----	----	0		PANA	PARA	----
V38	MEMBER OF THE CMEA	1975	----	----	0		PANA	PARA	----
		1980	----	----	0		PANA	PARA	----
V39	MEMBER OF THE WTO	1975	----	----	0		PANA	PARA	----
		1980	----	----	0		PANA	PARA	----
V40	MEMBER OF THE NATO	1975	----	----	0		PANA	PARA	----
		1980	----	----	0		PANA	PARA	----
V41	GDP SHARE OF INVESTMENTS	1975	D4	P37	20.0	%	PERU	INDO	----
		1980	D7	P61	25.9	%	PORTU	MEXI	----
V42	GDP SHARE OF AGRICULTURE	1975	D7	P65	29.7	%	HONDU	SENE	----
		1980	D8	P77	35.2	%	NIGER	CENTR	----
V43	GDP SHARE OF INDUSTRY	1975	D5	P45	28.5	%	COLO	NICA	----
		1979	D5	P45	29.7	%	SRILA	ANGO	----
V44	GDP SHARE OF SERVICES	1975	D4	P36	41.8	%	KORSO	BURMA	----
V45	HOMICIDES P. MIL. POPULATION	------	----	----	-----	-----	-------	-------	----
V46	SUICIDES P. MIL. POPULATION	------	----	----	-----	-----	-------	-------	----
V47	IMPORT PARTNERS	1980	R1	AULIA	40.8	%	NEWZ	-------	----
		1980	R2	JAPAN	18.1	%	PAKI	PERU	----
		1980	R3	SINGA	15.3	%	MALAY	-------	----
V48	EXPORT PARTNERS	1980	R1	JAPAN	37.2	%	OMAN	SAUDI	----
		1980	R2	GFR	24.9	%	PANA	POLA	----
		1980	R3	AULIA	14.3	%	NEWZ	-------	----
V49	PATENT SUPPLIERS	------	----	----	-----	-----	-------	-------	----

V50 PROVENANCE OF FOREIGN FIRMS	1980	R1	AULIA	66.9 %	-------	NEWZ	----
	1980	R2	UNKI	19.4 %	PANA	PERU	----
V51 FILM SUPPLIERS	------	----	----	----- -----	-------	-------	----

PARAGUAY (PARA)

V1 INCOME PER CAPITA	1970	D4	P39	815 $/CAP	TUNIS	SYRIA	F4
	1975	D5	P43	964 $/CAP	GUATE	ECUA	----
	1980	D6	P51	1350 $/CAP	TUNIS	TURKY	----
V2 TELEPHONES P. TSD. POPULATION	1970	D4	P40	10 1/TSD CAP	CONGO	ELSA	----
	1975	D5	P41	14 1/TSD CAP	ALGER	ELSA	----
	1980	D4	P35	18 1/TSD CAP	PAPUA	ELSA	----
V3 INFANT MORTALITY RATE	------	----	----	----- -----	-------	-------	----
V4 PHYSICIANS P. MIL. POPULATION	1972	D6	----	441 1/MIL	TRITO	TURKY	----
	1976	D5	P51	455 1/MIL	EGYPT	BOLI	----
	1979	D6	P51	554 1/MIL	IRAQ	OMAN	----
V5 ADULT LITERACY	1972	D7	----	80.1 %	THAI	PHILI	----
V6 DURATION OF SCHOOLING	1970	D6	P57	8.0 YR	MEXI	MONGO	----
	1975	D5	P46	7.7 YR	GABON	TOGO	----
	1979	D4	P37	8.0 YR	EGYPT	CAME	----
V7 STUDENT ENROLLMENT RATIO	1970	D5	P49	4.3 %	CUBA	SOUAF	----
	1975	D6	P50	6.7 %	JAMAI	ELSA	----
	1978	D5	----	7.2 %	JAMAI	SAUDI	----
V8 SHARE OF AGRICULTURAL LABOR	1972	D8	----	51.4 %	KORSO	DOMI	----
	1982	D8	----	46.6 %	SRILA	PHILI	----
V9 SHARE OF INDUSTRIAL LABOR	1972	D4	----	22.6 %	NICA	DOMI	----
	1982	D4	----	25.8 %	COLO	MALAY	----
V10 SHARE OF SERVICE LABOR	1972	D4	----	21.6 %	HUNGA	ELSA	----
	1982	D4	----	22.9 %	JORDA	YUGO	----
V11 SHARE OF ACADEMIC LABOR	1972	D4	----	4.4 %	MOROC	SYRIA	----
	1982	D3	----	4.7 %	KORSO	GUATE	----
V12 SHARE OF SELF-EMPLOYED LABOR	1972	D10	----	46.6 %	IRAN	GHANA	----
	1982	D9	----	46.1 %	PERU	BANGL	----
V13 MILITARY EXPENDITURES	1970	D3	P22	0.038 TSD MIL $	MADA	KENYA	F4
	1975	D3	P21	0.045 TSD MIL $	MADA	ELSA	----
	1980	D3	P21	0.058 TSD MIL $	SRILA	SENE	----
V14 MILITARY MANPOWER	1975	D3	P29	15 TSD CAP	NEWZ	ZAMBI	----
	1980	D3	P28	15 TSD CAP	NICA	ZAMBI	----

V15 MEN AT AGE 20 - 30	1970	D2	P11	190	TSD CAP	JORDA	HONDU	F2
	1975	D2	P15	211	TSD CAP	SIERA	PAPUA	F2
	1980	D2	P15	284	TSD CAP	SINGA	HONDU	F2
V16 POPULATION	1970	D2	P15	2.30	MIL CAP	JORDA	LEBA	F4
	1975	D2	P16	2.69	MIL CAP	LIBYA	JORDA	----
	1980	D3	P20	3.17	MIL CAP	NEWZ	SIERA	----
V17 GROSS DOMESTIC PRODUCT	1970	D2	P19	1.874	TSD MIL $	BOLI	NICA	----
	1975	D3	P23	2.593	TSD MIL $	COSTA	MADA	----
	1980	D4	P31	4.279	TSD MIL $	ETHIA	GHANA	----
V18 SHARE IN WORLD IMPORTS	1970	D2	P13	0.193	1/TSD	BENIN	TOGO	F48
	1975	D2	P13	0.197	1/TSD	MAURA	SIERA	F48
	1980	D2	P15	0.252	1/TSD	MALAW	LIBE	F48
V19 SHARE IN WORLD EXPORTS	1970	D2	P18	0.204	1/TSD	MALAW	MONGO	----
	1975	D2	P19	0.202	1/TSD	MAURA	CONGO	----
	1980	D2	P14	0.155	1/TSD	MALAW	TOGO	----
V20 GDP SHARE OF IMPORTS	1970	D2	P15	10.8	%	BURU	INDO	F48
	1975	D2	P14	11.8	%	JAPAN	AULIA	F48
	1980	D2	P11	11.6	%	MEXI	BOLI	F48
V21 GDP SHARE OF EXPORTS	1970	D3	P25	10.8	%	EGYPT	THAI	----
	1975	D3	P29	11.7	%	AFGHA	HAITI	----
	1980	D2	P15	7.0	%	BURU	GHANA	----
V22 EXPORT PARTNER CONCENTRATION	1970	D5	P48	27.4	%	AULIA	TOGO	----
	1975	D6	P60	28.5	%	NICA	NIGRA	----
	1980	D5	P44	23.9	%	MALAY	LIBE	----
V23 TOTAL DEBT AS % OF GDP	1980	D3	P25	21.5	%	ZIMBA	CENTR	----
V24 SHARE OF NEW FOREIGN PATENTS	------	----	----	----- -----		-------	-------	----
V25 FOREIGN PROPERTY AS % OF GDP	1971	D5	P41	6.5	%	MEXI	SRILA	----
	1975	D4	P39	4.6	%	KORSO	NIGER	----
	1978	D5	----	4.3	%	BURU	NICA	----
V26 GNP SHARE OF DEVELOPMENT AID	------	----	----	----- -----		-------	-------	----
V27 SHARE IN NOBEL PRIZE WINNERS	1970-79	D5	P45	0.0	%	PANA	PERU	----
V28 GDP SHARE OF MANUFACTURING	1970	D6	P58	16.7	%	MOROC	SRILA	----
	1975	D6	P53	15.6	%	INDIA	ZAMBI	----
	1980	D7	P62	16.5	%	PAKI	ZAMBI	----
V29 EXPORT SHARE OF MANUFACTURES	1975	D5	P51	10.5	%	HONDU	CONGO	----
	1980	D3	P25	4.4	%	CAME	TRITO	----
V30 LACK OF CIVIL LIBERTIES	1975	D6	P54	5		PAKI	PHILI	----
	1980	D6	P52	5		PANA	PHILI	----
V31 LACK OF POLITICAL RIGHTS	1975	D5	P43	5		NICA	PHILI	----
	1980	D5	P47	5		PANA	PERU	----
V32 RIOTS	1970-74	D2	P19	0		PANA	ROMA	----
	1975-79	D2	P20	0		NORWY	ROMA	----

V33	PROTEST DEMONSTRATIONS	1970-74	D4	P37	1	NEPAL	ROMA	----
		1975-79	D5	P42	2	NEWZ	SRILA	----
V34	POLITICAL STRIKES	1970-74	D3	P29	0	PANA	ROMA	----
		1975-79	D3	P29	0	NORWY	PHILI	----
V35	MEMBER OF THE NONALIGNED MMT.	1970	----	----	0	PANA	PERU	----
		1976	----	----	0	PAPUA	PHILI	----
		1981	----	----	0	PAPUA	PHILI	----
V36	MEMBER OF THE OPEC	1970	----	----	0	PANA	PERU	----
		1975	----	----	0	PAPUA	PERU	----
		1980	----	----	0	PAPUA	PERU	----
V37	MEMBER OF THE OECD	1970	----	----	0	PANA	PERU	----
		1975	----	----	0	PAPUA	PERU	----
		1980	----	----	0	PAPUA	PERU	----
V38	MEMBER OF THE CMEA	1970	----	----	0	PANA	PERU	----
		1975	----	----	0	PAPUA	PERU	----
		1980	----	----	0	PAPUA	PERU	----
V39	MEMBER OF THE WTO	1970	----	----	0	PANA	PERU	----
		1975	----	----	0	PAPUA	PERU	----
		1980	----	----	0	PAPUA	PERU	----
V40	MEMBER OF THE NATO	1970	----	----	0	PANA	PERU	----
		1975	----	----	0	PAPUA	PERU	----
		1980	----	----	0	PAPUA	PERU	----
V41	GDP SHARE OF INVESTMENTS	1970	D3	P23	14.7 %	PAKI	TOGO	----
		1975	D6	P60	24.1 %	CANA	SWEDN	----
		1980	D8	P78	28.8 %	AURIA	SOUAF	----
V42	GDP SHARE OF AGRICULTURE	1970	D8	P73	32.1 %	MALAY	HONDU	----
		1975	D8	P77	36.9 %	SIERA	BENIN	----
		1980	D7	P70	29.5 %	YENO	LESO	----
V43	GDP SHARE OF INDUSTRY	1970	D3	P29	20.7 %	SENE	TOGO	----
		1975	D3	P24	21.0 %	GHANA	NIGER	----
		1980	D4	P33	25.3 %	PAKI	HONDU	----
V44	GDP SHARE OF SERVICES	1970	D5	P46	47.2 %	KENYA	JAPAN	----
		1975	D4	P37	42.1 %	BURMA	COLO	----
		1980	D5	P43	45.2 %	YUGO	HONDU	----
V45	HOMICIDES P. MIL. POPULATION	1971	D8	P79	68.8 1/MIL CAP	CUBA	ARGE	F154
		1975	D9	P86	79.9 1/MIL CAP	VENE	USA	F154
		1980	D8	P82	50.2 1/MIL CAP	ARGE	COSTA	F2
V46	SUICIDES P. MIL. POPULATION	1971	D1	P7	16.0 1/MIL CAP	NICA	PERU	F2
		1975	D1	P8	14.5 1/MIL CAP	NICA	ECUA	F2
		1980	D1	P10	17.0 1/MIL CAP	GUATE	ECUA	F2
V47	IMPORT PARTNERS	1970	R1	USA	22.7 %	PAKI	PERU	----
		1970	R2	ARGE	16.7 %	-------	CHILE	----
		1970	R3	GFR	13.7 %	NIGRA	PHILI	----
		1980	R1	BRAZI	27.2 %	-------	URU	F136
		1980	R2	ARGE	20.6 %	BOLI	URU	F136
		1980	R3	USA	9.9 %	NEWZ	SWEDN	F136

V48	EXPORT PARTNERS	1970	R1	ARGE	27.4	%	-------	-------	----
		1970	R2	USA	14.1	%	NEWZ	SINGA	----
		1970	R3	NETH	8.6	%	PANA	PHILI	----
		1980	R1	ARGE	23.9	%	-------	BOLI	----
		1980	R2	BRAZI	13.0	%	CONGO	GABON	----
		1980	R3	GFR	12.4	%	OMAN	PERU	----
V49	PATENT SUPPLIERS	------	----	----	-----	-----	-------	-------	----
V50	PROVENANCE OF FOREIGN FIRMS	1980	R1	USA	38.2	%	PANA	PERU	----
		1980	R2	-------	11.7	%	-------	-------	----
		1980	R3	-------	11.7	%	-------	-------	----
V51	FILM SUPPLIERS	------	----	----	-----	-----	-------	-------	----

PERU (PERU)

V1	INCOME PER CAPITA	1970	D5	P49	980	$/CAP	COLO	MALAY	F211
		1975	D5	P50	1124	$/CAP	DOMI	NICA	F159
		1980	D5	P42	1069	$/CAP	NIGRA	GUATE	F159
V2	TELEPHONES P. TSD. POPULATION	1970	D6	P53	17	1/TSD CAP	ECUA	SYRIA	----
		1975	D6	P52	25	1/TSD CAP	ETHIA	TURKY	----
		1980	D4	P39	27	1/TSD CAP	ALGER	ETHIA	----
V3	INFANT MORTALITY RATE	1980	D6	P56	104.9	1/TSD	SOUAF	VINO	F5
V4	PHYSICIANS P. MIL. POPULATION	1969	D7	P64	526	1/MIL	BRAZI	COSTA	----
		1975	D7	P58	623	1/MIL	CHILE	COSTA	----
		1979	D6	P56	693	1/MIL	TURKY	COSTA	----
V5	ADULT LITERACY	1972	D6	----	72.5	%	PORTU	MEXI	----
V6	DURATION OF SCHOOLING	1970	D7	P65	8.8	YR	PANA	PORTU	F4
		1975	D7	P66	9.4	YR	KUWAI	SINGA	----
		1980	D7	P63	10.0	YR	LEBA	USSR	----
V7	STUDENT ENROLLMENT RATIO	1970	D8	P76	11.4	%	VENE	AURIA	----
		1975	D8	P71	14.6	%	EGYPT	URU	----
		1980	D8	P72	19.4	%	POLA	CUBA	----
V8	SHARE OF AGRICULTURAL LABOR	1972	D7	----	43.2	%	GREC	BRAZI	F86
		1981	D7	P72	39.2	%	MALAY	ELSA	F112
V9	SHARE OF INDUSTRIAL LABOR	1972	D4	----	24.2	%	DOMI	SRILA	F86
		1981	D2	P13	21.4	%	INDO	GUATE	F112
V10	SHARE OF SERVICE LABOR	1972	D5	----	24.7	%	NICA	CZECH	F86
		1981	D5	P43	31.0	%	KORSO	MEXI	F112
V11	SHARE OF ACADEMIC LABOR	1972	D6	----	7.9	%	ITALY	ARGE	F86
		1981	D5	P43	8.5	%	MEXI	COSTA	F112

V12	SHARE OF SELF-EMPLOYED LABOR	1972	D9	----	43.2	%		SYRIA	IRAN	F86
		1981	D9	P90	44.2	%		GUATE	PARA	F112
V13	MILITARY EXPENDITURES	1970	D6	P57	0.483	TSD MIL $		FINLA	AURIA	F4
		1975	D6	P59	0.789	TSD MIL $		AURIA	PHILI	----
		1980	D7	P62	1.054	TSD MIL $		MOROC	KUWAI	F62
V14	MILITARY MANPOWER	1970	D7	P62	80	TSD CAP		MEXI	KAMPU	----
		1975	D7	P64	95	TSD CAP		MEXI	SAUDI	----
		1980	D8	P74	151	TSD CAP		NIGRA	ARGE	----
V15	MEN AT AGE 20 - 30	1970	D7	P64	1083	TSD CAP		GDR	NETH	F2
		1976	D7	P70	1299	TSD CAP		CZECH	ROMA	F2
		1980	D7	P60	1489	TSD CAP		SRILA	SUDAN	F2
V16	POPULATION	1970	D7	P67	13.45	MIL CAP		TANZA	KORNO	F163
		1975	D7	P68	15.16	MIL CAP		CZECH	TANZA	F23
		1980	D7	P69	17.30	MIL CAP		GDR	KORNO	F23
V17	GROSS DOMESTIC PRODUCT	1970	D6	P56	13.185	TSD MIL $		HUNGA	PORTU	----
		1975	D6	P53	17.041	TSD MIL $		MALAY	HUNGA	----
		1980	D6	P53	18.498	TSD MIL $		IRE	HUNGA	----
V18	SHARE IN WORLD IMPORTS	1970	D6	P51	1.874	1/TSD		LEBA	MOROC	----
		1975	D6	P54	2.629	1/TSD		KUWAI	MOROC	----
		1980	D5	P49	1.493	1/TSD		IVORY	TRITO	----
V19	SHARE IN WORLD EXPORTS	1970	D7	P61	3.395	1/TSD		CUBA	IRAQ	----
		1975	D6	P50	1.473	1/TSD		IVORY	TURKY	----
		1980	D6	P54	1.953	1/TSD		IVORY	COLO	----
V20	GDP SHARE OF IMPORTS	1970	D2	P13	10.0	%		NEPAL	BURU	----
		1975	D3	P26	17.7	%		GHANA	AFGHA	----
		1980	D3	P29	17.8	%		NEPAL	VENE	----
V21	GDP SHARE OF EXPORTS	1970	D6	P55	17.1	%		MADA	SRILA	----
		1975	D3	P22	9.6	%		CHAD	SUDAN	----
		1980	D6	P60	22.6	%		NIGER	NEWZ	----
V22	EXPORT PARTNER CONCENTRATION	1970	D6	P59	33.1	%		IVORY	NICA	----
		1975	D5	P49	24.2	%		NORWY	UGADA	----
		1980	D7	P68	32.4	%		POLA	ECUA	----
V23	TOTAL DEBT AS % OF GDP	1980	D9	P83	58.0	%		SUDAN	HONDU	----
V24	SHARE OF NEW FOREIGN PATENTS	1972	D7	----	95	%		MOROC	PORTU	----
		1975	D7	P62	93	%		MOROC	TRITO	----
		1980	D6	P57	91	%		IRAN	TRITO	----
V25	FOREIGN PROPERTY AS % OF GDP	1971	D7	P66	12.0	%		COLO	GHANA	----
		1975	D8	P78	12.6	%		MAURA	COSTA	----
		1978	D10	----	20.0	%		CONGO	SINGA	----
V26	GNP SHARE OF DEVELOPMENT AID	------	----	----	-----	-----		-------	-------	----
V27	SHARE IN NOBEL PRIZE WINNERS	1970-79	D5	P45	0.0	%		PARA	PHILI	----
V28	GDP SHARE OF MANUFACTURING	1970	D9	P82	23.8	%		MEXI	FINLA	----
		1975	D9	P86	24.9	%		FINLA	PHILI	----
		1978	D10	----	27.6	%		FRANC	AURIA	----

V29	EXPORT SHARE OF MANUFACTURES	1970	D2	P15	1.3	%	INDO	SRILA	----
		1975	D3	P24	2.8	%	PAPUA	SOMA	----
		1980	D6	P50	16.2	%	SENE	SRILA	----
V30	LACK OF CIVIL LIBERTIES	1975	D8	P74	6		PANA	POLA	----
		1980	D4	P38	4		NEPAL	ARGE	----
V31	LACK OF POLITICAL RIGHTS	1975	D7	P63	6		NIGRA	POLA	----
		1980	D5	P47	5		PARA	PHILI	----
V32	RIOTS	1970-74	D9	P84	14		LEBA	ETHIA	----
		1975-79	D9	P90	27		FRANC	TURKY	----
V33	PROTEST DEMONSTRATIONS	1970-74	D2	P15	0		PANA	RWAN	----
		1975-79	D6	P54	4		CHAD	UGADA	----
V34	POLITICAL STRIKES	1970-74	D9	P83	5		JAPAN	SOUAF	----
		1975-79	D10	P96	18		LEBA	FRANC	----
V35	MEMBER OF THE NONALIGNED MMT.	1970	----	----	0		PARA	PHILI	----
		1976	----	----	1		PANA	RWAN	----
		1981	----	----	1		PANA	RWAN	----
V36	MEMBER OF THE OPEC	1970	----	----	0		PARA	PHILI	----
		1975	----	----	0		PARA	PHILI	----
		1980	----	----	0		PARA	PHILI	----
V37	MEMBER OF THE OECD	1970	----	----	0		PARA	PHILI	----
		1975	----	----	0		PARA	PHILI	----
		1980	----	----	0		PARA	PHILI	----
V38	MEMBER OF THE CMEA	1970	----	----	0		PARA	PHILI	----
		1975	----	----	0		PARA	PHILI	----
		1980	----	----	0		PARA	PHILI	----
V39	MEMBER OF THE WTO	1970	----	----	0		PARA	PHILI	----
		1975	----	----	0		PARA	PHILI	----
		1980	----	----	0		PARA	PHILI	----
V40	MEMBER OF THE NATO	1970	----	----	0		PARA	PHILI	----
		1975	----	----	0		PARA	PHILI	----
		1980	----	----	0		PARA	PHILI	----
V41	GDP SHARE OF INVESTMENTS	1970	D2	P14	13.3	%	ELSA	UGADA	----
		1975	D4	P36	19.6	%	YENO	PAPUA	----
		1978	D2	----	13.6	%	KUWAI	AFGHA	----
V42	GDP SHARE OF AGRICULTURE	1970	D4	P37	16.4	%	PANA	ZAIRE	----
		1975	D4	P38	13.9	%	ZAMBI	CONGO	----
		1978	D4	----	10.9	%	PANA	NEWZ	----
V43	GDP SHARE OF INDUSTRY	1970	D7	P66	34.3	%	NORWY	USA	----
		1975	D7	P66	34.0	%	ECUA	SINGA	----
		1978	D9	----	41.6	%	NIGRA	ITALY	----
V44	GDP SHARE OF SERVICES	1970	D6	P55	49.3	%	NICA	GREC	----
		1975	D8	P73	52.1	%	ELSA	COSTA	----
		1978	D6	----	47.5	%	VENE	LESO	----
V45	HOMICIDES P. MIL. POPULATION	1970	D6	P54	17.0	1/MIL CAP	SINGA	HUNGA	F154

V46	SUICIDES P. MIL. POPULATION	1970	D1	P10	21.8 1/MIL CAP	PARA	ECUA	F2
V47	IMPORT PARTNERS	1970	R1	USA	31.9 %	PARA	SAUDI	----
		1970	R2	GFR	12.1 %	NORWY	ROMA	----
		1970	R3	JAPAN	7.9 %	IRAN	SRILA	----
		1980	R1	USA	36.7 %	PANA	PHILI	----
		1980	R2	JAPAN	10.4 %	PAPUA	PHILI	----
		1980	R3	GFR	8.4 %	NORWY	SAUDI	----
V48	EXPORT PARTNERS	1970	R1	USA	33.1 %	PANA	PHILI	----
		1970	R2	GFR	15.1 %	PANA	ROMA	----
		1970	R3	JAPAN	13.6 %	PAKI	SINGA	----
		1980	R1	USA	32.4 %	PANA	PHILI	----
		1980	R2	JAPAN	8.8 %	PAKI	PHILI	----
		1980	R3	GFR	5.5 %	PARA	URU	----
V49	PATENT SUPPLIERS	1972	R1	USA	219	NORWY	PHILI	----
		1972	R2	SWITZ	73	LEBA	POLA	----
		1972	R3	GFR	55	MOROC	UGADA	----
		1980	R1	USA	145	PAKI	PHILI	----
		1980	R2	FRANC	22	ZAIRE	SYRIA	----
		1980	R3	GFR	20	MOROC	SYRIA	----
V50	PROVENANCE OF FOREIGN FIRMS	1980	R1	USA	65.3 %	PARA	PHILI	----
		1980	R2	UNKI	7.9 %	PAPUA	PORTU	----
		1980	R3	JAPAN	4.8 %	MALAY	SINGA	----
V51	FILM SUPPLIERS	1980	R1	USA	298	NORWY	PORTU	F119
		1980	R2	ITALY	131	NICA	PORTU	F119
		1980	R3	FRANC	32	PAKI	PORTU	F119

PHILIPPINES (PHILI)

V1	INCOME PER CAPITA	1970	D3	P26	514 $/CAP	GHANA	HONDU	F147
		1975	D4	P33	608 $/CAP	LIBE	CAME	----
		1980	D4	P34	719 $/CAP	THAI	CAME	----
V2	TELEPHONES P. TSD. POPULATION	1970	D4	P34	7 1/TSD CAP	KENYA	YESO	----
		1975	D4	P37	11 1/TSD CAP	NICA	ZAMBI	----
		1980	D4	P33	15 1/TSD CAP	IVORY	PAPUA	----
V3	INFANT MORTALITY RATE	------	----	----	----- -----	-------	-------	----
V4	PHYSICIANS P. MIL. POPULATION	1971	D6	P52	369 1/MIL	LIBYA	JAMAI	F150
		1975	D5	P45	320 1/MIL	HONDU	SYRIA	----
V5	ADULT LITERACY	1970	D7	P65	82.6 %	PARA	YUGO	----
V6	DURATION OF SCHOOLING	1970	D7	P62	8.5 YR	COSTA	SRILA	----
		1975	D6	P59	8.7 YR	COSTA	DOMI	----
		1980	D6	P55	9.4 YR	MONGO	PORTU	----

V7	STUDENT ENROLLMENT RATIO	1970	D10	P93	19.8	%	NETH	ISRA	----
		1975	D8	P78	18.4	%	GREC	IRE	----
		1980	D9	P86	26.0	%	NORWY	NEWZ	----
V8	SHARE OF AGRICULTURAL LABOR	1970	D9	P81	54.9	%	MALAY	MOROC	F67
		1975	D8	P73	54.5	%	SYRIA	PAKI	----
		1981	D8	P82	49.9	%	PARA	PAKI	F46
V9	SHARE OF INDUSTRIAL LABOR	1975	D3	P25	19.4	%	THAI	GUATE	----
		1981	D2	P7	14.8	%	THAI	INDIA	F46
V10	SHARE OF SERVICE LABOR	1975	D4	P40	20.8	%	INDO	ECUA	----
		1981	D5	P39	28.8	%	GREC	KORSO	F46
V11	SHARE OF ACADEMIC LABOR	1975	D5	P43	5.2	%	TUNIS	ECUA	----
		1981	D4	P31	6.4	%	MOROC	SPAIN	F46
V12	SHARE OF SELF-EMPLOYED LABOR	1970	D8	P83	38.3	%	PANA	GREC	F67
		1975	D8	P71	41.5	%	HONDU	INDO	----
		1981	D8	P80	36.7	%	KORSO	GREC	F46
V13	MILITARY EXPENDITURES	1975	D6	P60	0.852	TSD MIL $	PERU	VENE	----
		1980	D6	P56	0.758	TSD MIL $	FINLA	PORTU	----
V14	MILITARY MANPOWER	1970	D6	P54	59	TSD CAP	MALAY	LAOS	----
V15	MEN AT AGE 20 - 30	1970	D9	P84	2716	TSD CAP	TURKY	MEXI	----
		1975	D9	P86	3477	TSD CAP	TURKY	THAI	F184
		1980	D9	P80	4004	TSD CAP	TURKY	UNKI	F22
V16	POPULATION	1970	D9	P87	36.85	MIL CAP	THAI	MEXI	F22
		1975	D9	P87	42.07	MIL CAP	THAI	FRANC	----
		1980	D9	P87	48.09	MIL CAP	THAI	FRANC	----
V17	GROSS DOMESTIC PRODUCT	1970	D7	P62	18.932	TSD MIL $	NEWZ	COLO	----
		1975	D7	P66	25.575	TSD MIL $	COLO	GREC	----
		1980	D7	P66	34.590	TSD MIL $	COLO	GREC	----
V18	SHARE IN WORLD IMPORTS	1970	D7	P62	3.874	1/TSD	ALGER	THAI	F30
		1975	D6	P59	4.154	1/TSD	MALAY	IRE	F30
		1980	D7	P62	4.044	1/TSD	ISRA	THAI	F30
V19	SHARE IN WORLD EXPORTS	1970	D7	P64	3.641	1/TSD	INDO	NEWZ	F30
		1975	D6	P60	2.618	1/TSD	GREC	THAI	F30
		1980	D7	P62	2.900	1/TSD	CUBA	THAI	F30
V20	GDP SHARE OF IMPORTS	1970	D5	P48	17.9	%	MOROC	SAUDI	F30
		1975	D6	P53	23.9	%	SUDAN	SWITZ	F30
		1980	D5	P49	23.4	%	SOUAF	MOROC	F30
V21	GDP SHARE OF EXPORTS	1970	D6	P52	15.9	%	UNKI	MADA	F30
		1975	D4	P38	14.5	%	AULIA	TANZA	F30
		1980	D5	P43	16.3	%	SENE	CHILE	F30
V22	EXPORT PARTNER CONCENTRATION	1970	D8	P76	41.7	%	BENIN	TRITO	----
		1975	D8	P73	37.4	%	GABON	JAMAI	----
		1980	D6	P55	27.5	%	VENE	MALAW	----
V23	TOTAL DEBT AS % OF GDP	1980	D7	P70	49.1	%	KENYA	VENE	----

V24	SHARE OF NEW FOREIGN PATENTS	1970	D7	P67	96 %	EGYPT	SYRIA	----
		1975	D5	P50	90 %	ISRA	BRAZI	----
		1980	D6	P53	90 %	ZIMBA	BRAZI	----
V25	FOREIGN PROPERTY AS % OF GDP	1971	D6	P60	10.7 %	NICA	HAITI	----
		1975	D7	P61	7.7 %	ELSA	ZAMBI	----
		1978	D7	----	7.5 %	IVORY	HAITI	----
V26	GNP SHARE OF DEVELOPMENT AID	------	----	----	----- -----	-------	-------	----
V27	SHARE IN NOBEL PRIZE WINNERS	1970-79	D5	P45	0.0 %	PERU	POLA	----
V28	GDP SHARE OF MANUFACTURING	1970	D8	P76	22.6 %	KORSO	NEWZ	----
		1975	D9	P86	24.9 %	PERU	SPAIN	----
		1980	D9	P85	24.8 %	MEXI	NICA	----
V29	EXPORT SHARE OF MANUFACTURES	------	----	----	----- -----	-------	-------	----
V30	LACK OF CIVIL LIBERTIES	1975	D6	P54	5	PARA	RWAN	----
		1980	D6	P52	5	PARA	POLA	----
V31	LACK OF POLITICAL RIGHTS	1975	D5	P43	5	PARA	PORTU	----
		1980	D5	P47	5	PERU	SIERA	----
V32	RIOTS	1970-74	D9	P88	20	JORDA	PORTU	----
		1975-79	D7	P69	5	LEBA	ARGE	----
V33	PROTEST DEMONSTRATIONS	1970-74	D9	P85	27	JAPAN	SOUAF	----
		1975-79	D9	P84	21	LAOS	SOUAF	----
V34	POLITICAL STRIKES	1970-74	D8	P74	2	GHANA	VISO	----
		1975-79	D3	P29	0	PARA	RWAN	----
V35	MEMBER OF THE NONALIGNED MMT.	1970	----	----	0	PERU	POLA	----
		1976	----	----	0	PARA	POLA	----
		1981	----	----	0	PARA	POLA	----
V36	MEMBER OF THE OPEC	1970	----	----	0	PERU	POLA	----
		1975	----	----	0	PERU	POLA	----
		1980	----	----	0	PERU	POLA	----
V37	MEMBER OF THE OECD	1970	----	----	0	PERU	POLA	----
		1975	----	----	0	PERU	POLA	----
		1980	----	----	0	PERU	POLA	----
V38	MEMBER OF THE CMEA	1970	----	----	0	PERU	PORTU	----
		1975	----	----	0	PERU	PORTU	----
		1980	----	----	0	PERU	PORTU	----
V39	MEMBER OF THE WTO	1970	----	----	0	PERU	PORTU	----
		1975	----	----	0	PERU	PORTU	----
		1980	----	----	0	PERU	PORTU	----
V40	MEMBER OF THE NATO	1970	----	----	0	PERU	POLA	----
		1975	----	----	0	PERU	POLA	----
		1980	----	----	0	PERU	POLA	----
V41	GDP SHARE OF INVESTMENTS	1970	D6	P57	21.2 %	ARGE	COLO	----
		1975	D9	P85	31.1 %	VENE	JORDA	----
		1980	D9	P84	30.5 %	GABON	CHINA	----

V42	GDP SHARE OF AGRICULTURE	1970	D6	P60	27.8	%	IVORY	SIERA	----
		1975	D6	P59	28.8	%	IVORY	EGYPT	----
		1980	D6	P56	23.2	%	TURKY	MALAY	----
V43	GDP SHARE OF INDUSTRY	1970	D6	P54	29.6	%	DENMA	URU	----
		1975	D7	P62	33.7	%	USA	INDO	----
		1980	D7	P69	36.9	%	MALAY	JAMAI	----
V44	GDP SHARE OF SERVICES	1970	D4	P31	42.6	%	EGYPT	NIGRA	----
		1975	D3	P25	37.5	%	NIGRA	UPVO	----
		1980	D3	P26	39.9	%	MALAY	MOZAM	----
V45	HOMICIDES P. MIL. POPULATION	------	----	----	-----	-----	-------	-------	----
V46	SUICIDES P. MIL. POPULATION	1970	D1	P3	6.7	1/MIL CAP	-------	NICA	F147
V47	IMPORT PARTNERS	1970	R1	JAPAN	30.5	%	MALAY	SINGA	----
		1970	R2	USA	29.3	%	NIGRA	SOUAF	----
		1970	R3	GFR	5.7	%	PARA	RWAN	----
		1980	R1	USA	23.6	%	PERU	SAUDI	----
		1980	R2	JAPAN	19.9	%	PERU	RWAN	----
		1980	R3	SAUDI	10.0	%	PAKI	SUDAN	----
V48	EXPORT PARTNERS	1970	R1	USA	41.7	%	PERU	SPAIN	----
		1970	R2	JAPAN	39.6	%	NICA	UPVO	----
		1970	R3	NETH	4.1	%	PARA	SENE	----
		1980	R1	USA	27.5	%	PERU	TRITO	----
		1980	R2	JAPAN	26.6	%	PERU	USA	----
		1980	R3	NETH	6.3	%	MOROC	UNKI	----
V49	PATENT SUPPLIERS	1970	R1	USA	364		PERU	PORTU	----
		1970	R2	JAPAN	68		MEXI	SYRIA	----
		1970	R3	SWITZ	50		PAKI	SINGA	----
		1980	R1	USA	379		PERU	PORTU	----
		1980	R2	SWITZ	76		COLO	TANZA	----
		1980	R3	JAPAN	70		NETH	TANZA	----
V50	PROVENANCE OF FOREIGN FIRMS	1980	R1	USA	62.2	%	PERU	PORTU	----
		1980	R2	JAPAN	13.3	%	INDO	COSTA	----
		1980	R3	UNKI	5.2	%	NORWY	SENE	----
V51	FILM SUPPLIERS	------	----	----	-----	-----	-------	-------	----

POLAND (POLA)

V1	INCOME PER CAPITA	------	----	----	-----	-----	-------	-------	----
V2	TELEPHONES P. TSD. POPULATION	1970	D7	P69	57	1/TSD CAP	BULGA	PANA	----
		1975	D7	P67	75	1/TSD CAP	USSR	ARGE	----
		1980	D7	P63	95	1/TSD CAP	PANA	YUGO	----

V3	INFANT MORTALITY RATE	1980	D3	P24	21.3	1/TSD	COSTA	HUNGA	----
V4	PHYSICIANS P. MIL. POPULATION	1970	D9	P85	1515	1/MIL	DENMA	BELGI	----
		1975	D9	P82	1712	1/MIL	USA	SWEDN	----
		1979	D8	P73	1743	1/MIL	KUWAI	AULIA	----
V5	ADULT LITERACY	1970	D10	P92	97.8	%	JAMAI	HUNGA	----
		1978	D10	----	98.8	%	SPAIN	HUNGA	----
V6	DURATION OF SCHOOLING	1970	D9	P85	10.4	YR	DENMA	ROMA	----
		1975	D9	P82	10.7	YR	IRE	SPAIN	----
		1980	D9	P84	11.0	YR	KORSO	ITALY	----
V7	STUDENT ENROLLMENT RATIO	1970	D9	P81	14.0	%	ARGE	UNKI	----
		1975	D8	P74	16.8	%	CHILE	PANA	----
		1980	D8	P71	17.3	%	CZECH	PERU	----
V8	SHARE OF AGRICULTURAL LABOR	1970	D6	P57	38.6	%	PORTU	PANA	----
		1978	D5	----	27.6	%	PORTU	PANA	----
V9	SHARE OF INDUSTRIAL LABOR	1970	D6	P58	34.7	%	SWEDN	LEBA	----
		1978	D9	----	38.8	%	PORTU	SPAIN	----
V10	SHARE OF SERVICE LABOR	1970	D2	P17	18.4	%	MOROC	SRILA	----
		1978	D3	----	22.2	%	TUNIS	JORDA	----
V11	SHARE OF ACADEMIC LABOR	1970	D7	P61	8.3	%	ARGE	CUBA	----
		1978	D7	----	11.4	%	PANA	AURIA	----
V12	SHARE OF SELF-EMPLOYED LABOR	1978	D3	----	13.3	%	SINGA	TRITO	----
V13	MILITARY EXPENDITURES	------	----	----	----- -----		-------	-------	----
V14	MILITARY MANPOWER	1970	D9	P85	314	TSD CAP	YUGO	INDO	----
		1975	D9	P87	435	TSD CAP	EGYPT	TURKY	----
		1980	D10	P91	421	TSD CAP	ITALY	EGYPT	----
V15	MEN AT AGE 20 - 30	1970	D9	P81	2448	TSD CAP	THAI	TURKY	----
		1975	D9	P83	3156	TSD CAP	KORSO	TURKY	----
		1980	D8	P76	3408	TSD CAP	IRAN	KORSO	----
V16	POPULATION	1970	D9	P82	32.53	MIL CAP	KORSO	EGYPT	----
		1975	D9	P82	34.02	MIL CAP	IRAN	KORSO	----
		1980	D9	P81	35.58	MIL CAP	BURMA	SPAIN	----
V17	GROSS DOMESTIC PRODUCT	------	----	----	----- -----		-------	-------	----
V18	SHARE IN WORLD IMPORTS	1970	D9	P83	10.869	1/TSD	AURIA	CZECH	F49
		1975	D9	P88	13.793	1/TSD	GDR	SWITZ	F49
		1980	D9	P81	9.307	1/TSD	GDR	MEXI	F49
V19	SHARE IN WORLD EXPORTS	1970	D9	P86	11.311	1/TSD	DENMA	CZECH	F30
		1975	D9	P87	11.734	1/TSD	GDR	AULIA	F30
		1980	D8	P75	8.516	1/TSD	ALGER	DENMA	F30
V20	GDP SHARE OF IMPORTS	------	----	----	----- -----		-------	-------	----
V21	GDP SHARE OF EXPORTS	------	----	----	----- -----		-------	-------	----

V22	EXPORT PARTNER CONCENTRATION	1970	D7	P66	35.3 %	HUNGA	VENE	----
		1975	D7	P66	31.5 %	BOLI	COLO	----
		1980	D7	P67	31.2 %	AURIA	PERU	----
V23	TOTAL DEBT AS % OF GDP	------	----	----	----- -----	-------	-------	----
V24	SHARE OF NEW FOREIGN PATENTS	1970	D1	P3	17 %	USSR	ROMA	----
		1975	D1	P5	34 %	GREC	CZECH	----
		1980	D1	P7	25 %	GDR	BULGA	----
V25	FOREIGN PROPERTY AS % OF GDP	------	----	----	----- -----	-------	-------	----
V26	GNP SHARE OF DEVELOPMENT AID	------	----	----	----- -----	-------	-------	----
V27	SHARE IN NOBEL PRIZE WINNERS	1970-79	D5	P45	0.0 %	PHILI	PORTU	----
V28	GDP SHARE OF MANUFACTURING	------	----	----	----- -----	-------	-------	----
V29	EXPORT SHARE OF MANUFACTURES	------	----	----	----- -----	-------	-------	----
V30	LACK OF CIVIL LIBERTIES	1975	D8	P74	6	PERU	ROMA	----
		1980	D6	P52	5	PHILI	SIERA	----
V31	LACK OF POLITICAL RIGHTS	1975	D7	P63	6	PERU	SAUDI	----
		1980	D7	P67	6	PAKI	RWAN	----
V32	RIOTS	1970-74	D7	P68	5	INDO	SYRIA	----
		1975-79	D5	P45	1	LESO	SIERA	----
V33	PROTEST DEMONSTRATIONS	1970-74	D7	P68	6	NICA	VENE	----
		1975-79	D9	P87	24	COLO	CHINA	----
V34	POLITICAL STRIKES	1970-74	D9	P85	8	ISRA	MOROC	----
		1975-79	D7	P63	1	NEPAL	ROMA	----
V35	MEMBER OF THE NONALIGNED MMT.	1970	----	----	0	PHILI	PORTU	----
		1976	----	----	0	PHILI	PORTU	----
		1981	----	----	0	PHILI	PORTU	----
V36	MEMBER OF THE OPEC	1970	----	----	0	PHILI	PORTU	----
		1975	----	----	0	PHILI	PORTU	----
		1980	----	----	0	PHILI	PORTU	----
V37	MEMBER OF THE OECD	1970	----	----	0	PHILI	ROMA	----
		1975	----	----	0	PHILI	ROMA	----
		1980	----	----	0	PHILI	ROMA	----
V38	MEMBER OF THE CMEA	1970	----	----	1	MONGO	ROMA	----
		1975	----	----	1	MONGO	ROMA	----
		1980	----	----	1	MONGO	ROMA	----
V39	MEMBER OF THE WTO	1970	----	----	1	HUNGA	ROMA	----
		1975	----	----	1	HUNGA	ROMA	----
		1980	----	----	1	HUNGA	ROMA	----
V40	MEMBER OF THE NATO	1970	----	----	0	PHILI	ROMA	----
		1975	----	----	0	PHILI	ROMA	----
		1980	----	----	0	PHILI	ROMA	----
V41	GDP SHARE OF INVESTMENTS	------	----	----	----- -----	-------	-------	----

V42	GDP SHARE OF AGRICULTURE	------	----	----	----- -----	-------	-------	----
V43	GDP SHARE OF INDUSTRY	------	----	----	----- -----	-------	-------	----
V44	GDP SHARE OF SERVICES	------	----	----	----- -----	-------	-------	----
V45	HOMICIDES P. MIL. POPULATION	1970	D3	P27	10.8 1/MIL CAP	SWEDN	BELGI	F154
		1975	D3	P27	10.4 1/MIL CAP	FRANC	ISRA	F154
V46	SUICIDES P. MIL. POPULATION	1970	D6	P57	112.5 1/MIL CAP	URU	CANA	F2
		1975	D6	P59	113.8 1/MIL CAP	SINGA	CANA	F2
V47	IMPORT PARTNERS	1970	R1	USSR	37.7 %	HUNGA	ROMA	----
		1970	R2	GDR	11.1 %	HUNGA	-------	----
		1970	R3	CZECH	8.6 %	HUNGA	ROMA	----
		1980	R1	USSR	33.1 %	HUNGA	ROMA	----
		1980	R2	GFR	6.8 %	NIGRA	SUDAN	----
		1980	R3	GDR	6.6 %	HUNGA	-------	----
V48	EXPORT PARTNERS	1970	R1	USSR	35.3 %	HUNGA	ROMA	----
		1970	R2	GDR	9.3 %	HUNGA	-------	----
		1970	R3	CZECH	7.5 %	KAMPU	ROMA	----
		1980	R1	USSR	31.2 %	NEPAL	ROMA	----
		1980	R2	GFR	8.6 %	PAPUA	PORTU	----
		1980	R3	GDR	6.9 %	HUNGA	ROMA	----
V49	PATENT SUPPLIERS	1971	R1	GFR	133	PAKI	ROMA	----
		1971	R2	SWITZ	69	PERU	SRILA	----
		1971	R3	FRANC	55	NETH	ROMA	----
		1980	R1	GFR	518	IRAN	ROMA	----
		1980	R2	USA	428	MOROC	ROMA	----
		1980	R3	FRANC	145	NIGRA	PORTU	----
V50	PROVENANCE OF FOREIGN FIRMS	------	----	----	----- -----	-------	-------	----
V51	FILM SUPPLIERS	1980	R1	USSR	36	MOZAM	VINO	F120
		1980	R2	USA	16	PAKI	RWAN	F120
		1980	R3	ITALY	9	NORWY	SINGA	F120

PORTUGAL (PORTU)

V1	INCOME PER CAPITA	1970	D7	P63	1618 $/CAP	MEXI	URU	----
		1975	D7	P66	1922 $/CAP	BRAZI	URU	----
		1980	D7	P63	2351 $/CAP	BRAZI	CHILE	----
V2	TELEPHONES P. TSD. POPULATION	1970	D8	P78	84 1/TSD CAP	HUNGA	IRE	----
		1975	D8	P74	113 1/TSD CAP	KAMPU	KUWAI	----
		1980	D7	P69	138 1/TSD CAP	HUNGA	BULGA	----
V3	INFANT MORTALITY RATE	1979	D3	P26	26.0 1/TSD	HUNGA	TRITO	----

V4	PHYSICIANS P. MIL. POPULATION	1975	D8	P71	1177	1/MIL	JAPAN	IRE	----
V5	ADULT LITERACY	1970	D5	P49	71.0	%	SINGA	PERU	F22
V6	DURATION OF SCHOOLING	1970	D7	P65	8.8	YR	PERU	KORSO	----
		1975	D7	P69	9.5	YR	TRITO	USSR	----
		1980	D6	P55	9.4	YR	PHILI	VINO	----
V7	STUDENT ENROLLMENT RATIO	1970	D7	P64	8.0	%	KORSO	EGYPT	----
		1975	D7	P62	10.5	%	DOMI	MEXI	----
		1980	D6	P59	11.3	%	ROMA	BRAZI	----
V8	SHARE OF AGRICULTURAL LABOR	1970	D6	P55	32.9	%	ZAMBI	POLA	F87
		1981	D5	P50	19.7	%	SPAIN	POLA	----
V9	SHARE OF INDUSTRIAL LABOR	1970	D8	P71	37.8	%	FRANC	NETH	F87
		1981	D9	P86	38.6	%	SYRIA	POLA	----
V10	SHARE OF SERVICE LABOR	1970	D5	P47	25.4	%	CZECH	BRAZI	F87
		1981	D6	P47	34.2	%	MEXI	SPAIN	----
V11	SHARE OF ACADEMIC LABOR	1970	D3	P26	4.0	%	GHANA	MOROC	F87
		1981	D5	P39	7.5	%	MALAY	MEXI	----
V12	SHARE OF SELF-EMPLOYED LABOR	1970	D5	P44	20.9	%	SINGA	ITALY	F87
		1981	D5	P49	20.4	%	ITALY	SPAIN	----
V13	MILITARY EXPENDITURES	1970	D7	P65	1.034	TSD MIL $	SOUAF	KORSO	----
		1975	D7	P63	0.959	TSD MIL $	VENE	MALAY	----
		1980	D6	P57	0.819	TSD MIL $	PHILI	ALGER	----
V14	MILITARY MANPOWER	1970	D8	P80	230	TSD CAP	CZECH	JAPAN	----
		1975	D8	P77	217	TSD CAP	CZECH	GDR	----
		1980	D7	P62	68	TSD CAP	SUDAN	SOUAF	----
V15	MEN AT AGE 20 - 30	1970	D5	P40	539	TSD CAP	SWITZ	GREC	----
		1975	D6	P55	644	TSD CAP	GREC	BULGA	F22
		1980	D5	P46	792	TSD CAP	BELGI	HUNGA	----
V16	POPULATION	1970	D6	P55	9.04	MIL CAP	GREC	CHILE	----
		1975	D6	P55	9.43	MIL CAP	CUBA	MOZAM	----
		1980	D6	P56	9.90	MIL CAP	BELGI	HUNGA	----
V17	GROSS DOMESTIC PRODUCT	1970	D6	P57	14.628	TSD MIL $	PERU	THAI	----
		1975	D6	P57	18.122	TSD MIL $	PAKI	CHILE	----
		1980	D6	P58	23.274	TSD MIL $	NEWZ	PAKI	----
V18	SHARE IN WORLD IMPORTS	1970	D7	P67	4.766	1/TSD	IRE	IRAN	----
		1975	D7	P61	4.229	1/TSD	IRE	CUBA	----
		1980	D7	P64	4.630	1/TSD	HUNGA	BULGA	----
V19	SHARE IN WORLD EXPORTS	1970	D6	P57	3.025	1/TSD	KORSO	ZAMBI	----
		1975	D6	P57	2.212	1/TSD	ISRA	NEWZ	----
		1980	D6	P56	2.318	1/TSD	TRITO	CHILE	----
V20	GDP SHARE OF IMPORTS	1970	D8	P76	25.7	%	NICA	IVORY	----
		1975	D6	P60	26.1	%	GREC	CHAD	----
		1980	D9	P83	38.5	%	SIERA	PAPUA	----

V21	GDP SHARE OF EXPORTS	1970	D5	P49	15.4 %	GUATE	NIGRA	----
		1975	D4	P35	13.2 %	CENTR	YUGO	----
		1980	D5	P47	18.8 %	SIERA	GUATE	----
V22	EXPORT PARTNER CONCENTRATION	1970	D3	P26	20.4 %	GREC	FRANC	----
		1975	D4	P36	21.2 %	MADA	MOROC	----
		1980	D2	P12	14.8 %	NEPAL	SINGA	----
V23	TOTAL DEBT AS % OF GDP	1980	D5	P50	37.4 %	SIERA	YENO	----
V24	SHARE OF NEW FOREIGN PATENTS	1970	D7	P61	95 %	PERU	ECUA	----
		1975	D8	P75	96 %	PAKI	IRAN	----
		1980	D8	P76	96 %	PAKI	COLO	----
V25	FOREIGN PROPERTY AS % OF GDP	1975	D3	P21	2.3 %	IRAN	THAI	----
		1978	D4	----	3.1 %	KORSO	MOZAM	----
V26	GNP SHARE OF DEVELOPMENT AID	------	----	----	----- -----	-------	-------	----
V27	SHARE IN NOBEL PRIZE WINNERS	1970-79	D5	P45	0.0 %	POLA	ROMA	----
V28	GDP SHARE OF MANUFACTURING	1970	D10	P97	33.3 %	BELGI	AURIA	F16
		1975	D10	P99	33.6 %	ARGE	-------	F16
		1980	D10	P98	36.3 %	JAPAN	CHINA	F16
V29	EXPORT SHARE OF MANUFACTURES	1970	D9	P88	61.3 %	BELGI	FRANC	----
		1975	D9	P90	68.1 %	FRANC	AURIA	----
		1980	D9	P85	68.6 %	FRANC	YUGO	----
V30	LACK OF CIVIL LIBERTIES	1975	D3	P27	3	MEXI	SRILA	----
		1980	D2	P18	2	PAPUA	SPAIN	----
V31	LACK OF POLITICAL RIGHTS	1975	D5	P43	5	PHILI	SINGA	----
		1980	D3	P21	2	PAPUA	SPAIN	----
V32	RIOTS	1970-74	D9	P88	20	PHILI	ARGE	----
		1975-79	D10	P99	129	IRAN	SPAIN	----
V33	PROTEST DEMONSTRATIONS	1970-74	D10	P95	67	KORSO	SPAIN	----
		1975-79	D10	P98	155	UNKI	SPAIN	----
V34	POLITICAL STRIKES	1970-74	D10	P92	15	ETHIA	PAKI	----
		1975-79	D9	P87	9	ITALY	NICA	----
V35	MEMBER OF THE NONALIGNED MMT.	1970	----	----	0	POLA	ROMA	----
		1976	----	----	0	POLA	ROMA	----
		1981	----	----	0	POLA	ROMA	----
V36	MEMBER OF THE OPEC	1970	----	----	0	POLA	ROMA	----
		1975	----	----	0	POLA	ROMA	----
		1980	----	----	0	POLA	ROMA	----
V37	MEMBER OF THE OECD	1970	----	----	1	NORWY	SPAIN	----
		1975	----	----	1	NORWY	SPAIN	----
		1980	----	----	1	NORWY	SPAIN	----
V38	MEMBER OF THE CMEA	1970	----	----	0	PHILI	RWAN	----
		1975	----	----	0	PHILI	RWAN	----
		1980	----	----	0	PHILI	RWAN	----

V39	MEMBER OF THE WTO	1970	----	----	0		PHILI	RWAN	----
		1975	----	----	0		PHILI	RWAN	----
		1980	----	----	0		PHILI	RWAN	----
V40	MEMBER OF THE NATO	1970	----	----	1		NORWY	TURKY	----
		1975	----	----	1		NORWY	TURKY	----
		1980	----	----	1		NORWY	TURKY	----
V41	GDP SHARE OF INVESTMENTS	1970	D7	P66	23.5	%	ITALY	BELGI	----
		1975	D3	P23	16.3	%	PAKI	USA	----
		1980	D6	P59	25.7	%	DOMI	PAPUA	----
V42	GDP SHARE OF AGRICULTURE	1970	D5	P43	18.0	%	CONGO	BOLI	F16
		1975	D4	P41	15.6	%	YUGO	IRE	F16
		1980	D4	P40	12.7	%	ECUA	IRE	F16
V43	GDP SHARE OF INDUSTRY	1970	D9	P87	41.6	%	LIBE	BELGI	F16
		1975	D9	P86	42.8	%	ARGE	SOUAF	F16
		1980	D9	P88	45.9	%	INDO	CONGO	F16
V44	GDP SHARE OF SERVICES	1970	D3	P24	40.4	%	UPVO	YUGO	F16
		1975	D4	P34	41.6	%	MADA	KORSO	F16
		1980	D4	P32	41.4	%	TRITO	CONGO	F16
V45	HOMICIDES P. MIL. POPULATION	1971	D4	P32	11.5	1/MIL CAP	BELGI	ISRA	F154
		1975	D6	P59	18.9	1/MIL CAP	SINGA	HUNGA	F148
V46	SUICIDES P. MIL. POPULATION	1971	D5	P44	81.0	1/MIL CAP	NETH	NORWY	F2
		1975	D4	P37	85.0	1/MIL CAP	UNKI	NETH	----
V47	IMPORT PARTNERS	1970	R1	GFR	15.5	%	NETH	SWEDN	----
		1970	R2	UNKI	14.0	%	MALAY	SWEDN	----
		1970	R3	ANGO	9.7	%	-------	-------	----
		1980	R1	GFR	11.6	%	NETH	SWEDN	----
		1980	R2	USA	10.9	%	MALAY	ROMA	----
		1980	R3	UNKI	8.8	%	OMAN	SENE	----
V48	EXPORT PARTNERS	1970	R1	UNKI	20.4	%	NIGRA	SRILA	----
		1970	R2	ANGO	12.5	%	-------	ZAIRE	----
		1970	R3	MOZAM	9.1	%	-------	-------	----
		1980	R1	UNKI	14.8	%	NORWY	DENMA	----
		1980	R2	GFR	13.5	%	POLA	ROMA	----
		1980	R3	FRANC	10.5	%	NETH	SAUDI	----
V49	PATENT SUPPLIERS	1970	R1	USA	430		PHILI	SIERA	----
		1970	R2	GFR	358		NORWY	SPAIN	----
		1970	R3	UNKI	223		KAMPU	SWEDN	----
		1980	R1	USA	501		PHILI	SINGA	----
		1980	R2	GFR	375		PAKI	SPAIN	----
		1980	R3	FRANC	313		POLA	SPAIN	----
V50	PROVENANCE OF FOREIGN FIRMS	1980	R1	USA	23.4	%	PHILI	SAUDI	----
		1980	R2	UNKI	23.2	%	PERU	SAUDI	----
		1980	R3	GFR	10.8	%	PAKI	SOUAF	----
V51	FILM SUPPLIERS	1980	R1	USA	131		PERU	ROMA	F118
		1980	R2	ITALY	66		PERU	SOMA	F118
		1980	R3	FRANC	59		PERU	ROMA	F118

ROMANIA (ROMA)

V1	INCOME PER CAPITA	------	----	----	----- -----		-------	-------	----
V2	TELEPHONES P. TSD. POPULATION	1970	D6	P60	32	1/TSD CAP	CUBA	COSTA	----
		1975	D7	P62	56	1/TSD CAP	VENE	YUGO	----
V3	INFANT MORTALITY RATE	1980	D3	P29	29.3	1/TSD	USSR	YUGO	----
V4	PHYSICIANS P. MIL. POPULATION	1971	D8	P78	1208	1/MIL	IRE	AULIA	----
		1975	D8	P74	1318	1/MIL	YUGO	NEWZ	----
		1980	D8	P69	1476	1/MIL	YUGO	NEWZ	----
V5	ADULT LITERACY	------	----	----	----- -----		-------	-------	----
V6	DURATION OF SCHOOLING	1970	D9	P85	10.4	YR	POLA	URU	----
		1975	D10	P91	11.2	YR	NETH	CANA	----
		1980	D9	P87	11.2	YR	ALBA	BELGI	----
V7	STUDENT ENROLLMENT RATIO	1970	D8	P72	10.1	%	HUNGA	CZECH	----
		1975	D6	P59	9.2	%	SINGA	TURKY	----
		1980	D6	P57	10.9	%	CHILE	PORTU	----
V8	SHARE OF AGRICULTURAL LABOR	------	----	----	----- -----		-------	-------	----
V9	SHARE OF INDUSTRIAL LABOR	------	----	----	----- -----		-------	-------	----
V10	SHARE OF SERVICE LABOR	------	----	----	----- -----		-------	-------	----
V11	SHARE OF ACADEMIC LABOR	------	----	----	----- -----		-------	-------	----
V12	SHARE OF SELF-EMPLOYED LABOR	------	----	----	----- -----		-------	-------	----
V13	MILITARY EXPENDITURES	------	----	----	----- -----		-------	-------	----
V14	MILITARY MANPOWER	1970	D8	P79	211	TSD CAP	GDR	CZECH	----
		1975	D8	P78	220	TSD CAP	GDR	THAI	----
		1980	D8	P80	215	TSD CAP	CZECH	CUBA	----
V15	MEN AT AGE 20 - 30	1970	D7	P69	1410	TSD CAP	CZECH	YUGO	----
		1975	D8	P72	1672	TSD CAP	PERU	COLO	----
		1980	D7	P63	1792	TSD CAP	ALGER	YUGO	----
V16	POPULATION	1970	D8	P73	20.25	MIL CAP	GDR	YUGO	----
		1975	D8	P74	21.25	MIL CAP	MOROC	YUGO	----
		1980	D8	P74	22.20	MIL CAP	MOROC	YUGO	----
V17	GROSS DOMESTIC PRODUCT	------	----	----	----- -----		-------	-------	----
V18	SHARE IN WORLD IMPORTS	1970	D8	P73	5.904	1/TSD	GREC	KORSO	F49
		1975	D8	P70	5.877	1/TSD	VENE	BULGA	F49
		1980	D8	P73	6.436	1/TSD	IRAN	INDIA	F49
V19	SHARE IN WORLD EXPORTS	1970	D8	P72	5.901	1/TSD	ARGE	BULGA	F30
		1975	D8	P70	6.095	1/TSD	KORSO	SINGA	F30
		1980	D7	P68	5.712	1/TSD	YUGO	SOUAF	F30
V20	GDP SHARE OF IMPORTS	------	----	----	----- -----		-------	-------	----

V21	GDP SHARE OF EXPORTS	------	----	----	----- -----	-------	-------	----
V22	EXPORT PARTNER CONCENTRATION	1970	D6	P52	28.6 %	IRAQ	CAME	----
		1975	D3	P24	18.0 %	IRAQ	SYRIA	----
		1980	D3	P28	18.4 %	ITALY	ZAMBI	----
V23	TOTAL DEBT AS % OF GDP	------	----	----	----- -----	-------	-------	----
V24	SHARE OF NEW FOREIGN PATENTS	1970	D1	P5	18 %	POLA	USA	----
		1975	D1	P10	37 %	CUBA	GDR	----
		1980	D2	P11	41 %	USA	CUBA	----
V25	FOREIGN PROPERTY AS % OF GDP	------	----	----	----- -----	-------	-------	----
V26	GNP SHARE OF DEVELOPMENT AID	------	----	----	----- -----	-------	-------	----
V27	SHARE IN NOBEL PRIZE WINNERS	1970-79	D5	P45	0.0 %	PORTU	RWAN	----
V28	GDP SHARE OF MANUFACTURING	------	----	----	----- -----	-------	-------	----
V29	EXPORT SHARE OF MANUFACTURES	------	----	----	----- -----	-------	-------	----
V30	LACK OF CIVIL LIBERTIES	1975	D8	P74	6	POLA	SAUDI	----
		1980	D8	P74	6	PAKI	RWAN	----
V31	LACK OF POLITICAL RIGHTS	1975	D9	P88	7	PANA	RWAN	----
		1980	D9	P90	7	NIGER	SOMA	----
V32	RIOTS	1970-74	D2	P19	0	PARA	RWAN	----
		1975-79	D2	P20	0	PARA	RWAN	----
V33	PROTEST DEMONSTRATIONS	1970-74	D4	P37	1	PARA	SAUDI	----
		1975-79	D6	P59	5	LIBYA	SWITZ	----
V34	POLITICAL STRIKES	1970-74	D3	P29	0	PARA	RWAN	----
		1975-79	D7	P63	1	POLA	SRILA	----
V35	MEMBER OF THE NONALIGNED MMT.	1970	----	----	0	PORTU	SOUAF	----
		1976	----	----	0	PORTU	SOUAF	----
		1981	----	----	0	PORTU	SOUAF	----
V36	MEMBER OF THE OPEC	1970	----	----	0	PORTU	RWAN	----
		1975	----	----	0	PORTU	RWAN	----
		1980	----	----	0	PORTU	RWAN	----
V37	MEMBER OF THE OECD	1970	----	----	0	POLA	RWAN	----
		1975	----	----	0	POLA	RWAN	----
		1980	----	----	0	POLA	RWAN	----
V38	MEMBER OF THE CMEA	1970	----	----	1	POLA	USSR	----
		1975	----	----	1	POLA	USSR	----
		1980	----	----	1	POLA	USSR	----
V39	MEMBER OF THE WTO	1970	----	----	1	POLA	USSR	F15
		1975	----	----	1	POLA	USSR	F15
		1980	----	----	1	POLA	USSR	F15
V40	MEMBER OF THE NATO	1970	----	----	0	POLA	RWAN	----
		1975	----	----	0	POLA	RWAN	----
		1980	----	----	0	POLA	RWAN	----

V41	GDP SHARE OF INVESTMENTS	------	----	----	----- -----		-------	-------	----
V42	GDP SHARE OF AGRICULTURE	------	----	----	----- -----		-------	-------	----
V43	GDP SHARE OF INDUSTRY	------	----	----	----- -----		-------	-------	----
V44	GDP SHARE OF SERVICES	------	----	----	----- -----		-------	-------	----
V45	HOMICIDES P. MIL. POPULATION	------	----	----	----- -----		-------	-------	----
V46	SUICIDES P. MIL. POPULATION	------	----	----	----- -----		-------	-------	----
V47	IMPORT PARTNERS	1970	R1	USSR	25.5	%	POLA	SYRIA	----
		1970	R2	GFR	8.2	%	PERU	SENE	----
		1970	R3	CZECH	8.1	%	POLA	USSR	----
		1980	R1	USSR	15.6	%	POLA	YUGO	----
		1980	R2	USA	7.4	%	PORTU	SINGA	----
		1980	R3	IRAQ	7.3	%	MADA	-------	----
V48	EXPORT PARTNERS	1970	R1	USSR	28.6	%	POLA	SUDAN	----
		1970	R2	GFR	9.0	%	PERU	SPAIN	----
		1970	R3	CZECH	7.1	%	POLA	USSR	----
		1980	R1	USSR	18.4	%	POLA	YUGO	----
		1980	R2	GFR	8.4	%	PORTU	SPAIN	----
		1980	R3	GDR	5.6	%	POLA	-------	----
V49	PATENT SUPPLIERS	1972	R1	GFR	151		POLA	SWITZ	----
		1972	R2	GDR	72		HUNGA	TANZA	----
		1972	R3	FRANC	71		POLA	SPAIN	----
		1979	R1	GFR	173		POLA	SWITZ	----
		1979	R2	USA	158		POLA	SWITZ	----
		1979	R3	GDR	67		HUNGA	-------	----
V50	PROVENANCE OF FOREIGN FIRMS	------	----	----	----- -----		-------	-------	----
V51	FILM SUPPLIERS	1980	R1	USA	30		PORTU	SINGA	F118
		1980	R2	USSR	22		INDIA	ANGO	F118
		1980	R3	FRANC	10		PORTU	RWAN	F118

RWANDA (RWAN)

V1	INCOME PER CAPITA	------	----	----	----- -----		-------	-------	----
V2	TELEPHONES P. TSD. POPULATION	1970	D1	P1	0	1/TSD CAP	-------	AFGHA	----
		1975	D1	P5	1	1/TSD CAP	NIGER	UPVO	----
		1980	D1	P3	1	1/TSD CAP	BURMA	ZAIRE	----
V3	INFANT MORTALITY RATE	1980	D7	P67	119.1	1/TSD	ZAIRE	MOZAM	F5

V4	PHYSICIANS P. MIL. POPULATION	1970	D1	P7	17	1/MIL	NIGER	MALI	----
		1975	D1	P10	25	1/MIL	CHAD	NEPAL	----
		1980	D1	P6	32	1/MIL	NIGER	NEPAL	----
V5	ADULT LITERACY	1980	D5	P49	49.7	%	KENYA	UGADA	F21
V6	DURATION OF SCHOOLING	1970	D3	P29	4.8	YR	IVORY	KENYA	----
		1975	D2	P16	3.8	YR	SIERA	SUDAN	----
		1980	D3	P21	5.7	YR	CENTR	LAOS	F35
V7	STUDENT ENROLLMENT RATIO	1970	D2	P13	0.2	%	MALI	TANZA	----
		1975	D1	P9	0.3	%	LAOS	CENTR	----
		1980	D1	P6	0.3	%	NIGER	UPVO	----
V8	SHARE OF AGRICULTURAL LABOR	1978	D10	----	93.1	%	BANGL	-------	F109
V9	SHARE OF INDUSTRIAL LABOR	1978	D1	----	3.2	%	-------	HAITI	F109
V10	SHARE OF SERVICE LABOR	1978	D1	----	2.8	%	-------	CAME	F109
V11	SHARE OF ACADEMIC LABOR	1978	D1	----	0.9	%	-------	COLO	F109
V12	SHARE OF SELF-EMPLOYED LABOR	1978	D8	----	38.9	%	GREC	DOMI	F109
V13	MILITARY EXPENDITURES	------	----	----	-----	-----	-------	-------	----
V14	MILITARY MANPOWER	1970	D1	P10	4	TSD CAP	NIGER	UPVO	----
		1975	D1	P9	4	TSD CAP	NIGER	MALAW	----
		1980	D2	P12	5	TSD CAP	GABON	UPVO	----
V15	MEN AT AGE 20 - 30	1970	D2	P16	205	TSD CAP	URU	NEWZ	F46
		1978	D3	----	402	TSD CAP	DENMA	FINLA	F22
V16	POPULATION	1970	D3	P28	3.68	MIL CAP	CHAD	NORWY	----
		1975	D3	P30	4.20	MIL CAP	CHAD	GUINE	----
		1980	D4	P32	5.05	MIL CAP	HAITI	DENMA	----
V17	GROSS DOMESTIC PRODUCT	------	----	----	-----	-----	-------	-------	----
V18	SHARE IN WORLD IMPORTS	1970	D1	P2	0.087	1/TSD	BURU	YENO	----
		1975	D1	P4	0.106	1/TSD	CENTR	NIGER	----
		1980	D1	P5	0.118	1/TSD	BURU	SOMA	----
V19	SHARE IN WORLD EXPORTS	1970	D1	P6	0.080	1/TSD	BURU	CHAD	----
		1975	D1	P5	0.048	1/TSD	BURU	UPVO	----
		1980	D1	P6	0.038	1/TSD	CHAD	NEPAL	----
V20	GDP SHARE OF IMPORTS	1970	D3	P25	13.2	%	UGADA	NIGRA	----
		1975	D3	P24	16.9	%	FRANC	GHANA	----
		1980	D4	P39	20.9	%	FRANC	NIGRA	----
V21	GDP SHARE OF EXPORTS	1970	D4	P33	11.4	%	SYRIA	SOUAF	----
		1975	D2	P14	7.4	%	SPAIN	ARGE	----
		1980	D1	P10	6.5	%	BRAZI	SUDAN	----
V22	EXPORT PARTNER CONCENTRATION	------	----	----	-----	-----	-------	-------	----
V23	TOTAL DEBT AS % OF GDP	1980	D2	P11	15.6	%	GUATE	URU	----

V24	SHARE OF NEW FOREIGN PATENTS	1971	D9	P90	100	%	NIGRA	SIERA	F19
		1975	D10	P92	100	%	NEPAL	SIERA	F19
		1980	D10	P94	100	%	KENYA	SIERA	F19
V25	FOREIGN PROPERTY AS % OF GDP	1971	D3	P26	4.5	%	IRAQ	TANZA	----
		1975	D4	P36	4.4	%	GREC	SOMA	----
		1978	D4	----	2.9	%	ETHIA	KORSO	----
V26	GNP SHARE OF DEVELOPMENT AID	------	----	----	----- -----		-------	-------	----
V27	SHARE IN NOBEL PRIZE WINNERS	1970-79	D5	P45	0.0	%	ROMA	SAUDI	----
V28	GDP SHARE OF MANUFACTURING	1970	D1	P3	2.8	%	LIBYA	LIBE	----
		1975	D5	P42	12.3	%	KENYA	PANA	----
		1980	D6	P56	15.6	%	JAMAI	HONDU	----
V29	EXPORT SHARE OF MANUFACTURES	1970	D1	P2	0.0	%	-------	SAUDI	----
		1975	D1	P7	0.2	%	NIGRA	YESO	----
V30	LACK OF CIVIL LIBERTIES	1975	D6	P54	5		PHILI	SENE	----
		1980	D8	P74	6		ROMA	SAUDI	----
V31	LACK OF POLITICAL RIGHTS	1975	D9	P88	7		ROMA	SOMA	----
		1980	D7	P67	6		POLA	SAUDI	----
V32	RIOTS	1970-74	D2	P19	0		ROMA	SAUDI	----
		1975-79	D2	P20	0		ROMA	SENE	----
V33	PROTEST DEMONSTRATIONS	1970-74	D2	P15	0		PERU	SENE	----
		1975-79	D4	P32	1		MAURA	SAUDI	----
V34	POLITICAL STRIKES	1970-74	D3	P29	0		ROMA	SAUDI	----
		1975-79	D3	P29	0		PHILI	SAUDI	----
V35	MEMBER OF THE NONALIGNED MMT.	1970	----	----	1		NIGRA	SENE	----
		1976	----	----	1		PERU	SAUDI	----
		1981	----	----	1		PERU	SAUDI	----
V36	MEMBER OF THE OPEC	1970	----	----	0		ROMA	SENE	----
		1975	----	----	0		ROMA	SENE	----
		1980	----	----	0		ROMA	SENE	----
V37	MEMBER OF THE OECD	1970	----	----	0		ROMA	SAUDI	----
		1975	----	----	0		ROMA	SAUDI	----
		1980	----	----	0		ROMA	SAUDI	----
V38	MEMBER OF THE CMEA	1970	----	----	0		PORTU	SAUDI	----
		1975	----	----	0		PORTU	SAUDI	----
		1980	----	----	0		PORTU	SAUDI	----
V39	MEMBER OF THE WTO	1970	----	----	0		PORTU	SAUDI	----
		1975	----	----	0		PORTU	SAUDI	----
		1980	----	----	0		PORTU	SAUDI	----
V40	MEMBER OF THE NATO	1970	----	----	0		ROMA	SAUDI	----
		1975	----	----	0		ROMA	SAUDI	----
		1980	----	----	0		ROMA	SAUDI	----
V41	GDP SHARE OF INVESTMENTS	1970	D1	P6	7.0	%	NEPAL	URU	----
		1975	D2	P16	14.4	%	URU	HAITI	----
		1980	D5	P47	23.4	%	FRANC	MADA	----

V42	GDP SHARE OF AGRICULTURE	1970	D10	P99	70.8	%	BURU	-------	----
		1975	D10	P94	49.3	%	CHAD	GUINE	----
		1980	D9	P89	45.2	%	MOZAM	BURMA	----
V43	GDP SHARE OF INDUSTRY	1970	D1	P2	7.1	%	BANGL	BURU	----
		1975	D2	P19	19.0	%	MADA	MALAW	----
		1980	D3	P24	22.0	%	KENYA	SIERA	----
V44	GDP SHARE OF SERVICES	1970	D1	P3	22.1	%	NEPAL	BURU	----
		1975	D2	P15	31.7	%	GHANA	GABON	----
		1980	D2	P14	32.8	%	NIGER	ETHIA	----
V45	HOMICIDES P. MIL. POPULATION	------	----	----	-----	-----	-------	-------	----
V46	SUICIDES P. MIL. POPULATION	------	----	----	-----	-----	-------	-------	----
V47	IMPORT PARTNERS	1970	R1	BELGI	19.7	%	BURU	ZAIRE	F142
		1970	R2	JAPAN	13.3	%	PAKI	SAUDI	----
		1970	R3	GFR	8.6	%	PHILI	SOUAF	----
		1980	R1	BELGI	15.8	%	BURU	ZAIRE	F142
		1980	R2	JAPAN	12.1	%	PHILI	SAUDI	----
		1980	R3	KENYA	10.7	%	-------	-------	----
V48	EXPORT PARTNERS	------	----	----	-----	-----	-------	-------	----
V49	PATENT SUPPLIERS	------	----	----	-----	-----	-------	-------	----
V50	PROVENANCE OF FOREIGN FIRMS	------	----	----	-----	-----	-------	-------	----
V51	FILM SUPPLIERS	1980	R1	INDIA	43		MOROC	SOMA	F119
		1980	R2	USA	33		POLA	SYRIA	F119
		1980	R3	FRANC	5		ROMA	SPAIN	F119

SAUDI ARABIA (SAUDI)

V1	INCOME PER CAPITA	1970	D8	P78	6013	$/CAP	ITALY	JAPAN	F4
		1975	D9	P86	9376	$/CAP	AULIA	NETH	----
		1980	D10	P92	11461	$/CAP	USA	GFR	----
V2	TELEPHONES P. TSD. POPULATION	1980	D6	P53	53	1/TSD CAP	CHILE	JAMAI	----
V3	INFANT MORTALITY RATE	1980	D7	P70	121.1	1/TSD	HAITI	GABON	F5
V4	PHYSICIANS P. MIL. POPULATION	1972	D5	----	304	1/MIL	IRAN	IRAQ	F2
		1975	D6	P53	498	1/MIL	SOUAF	ECUA	----
		1978	D6	----	597	1/MIL	OMAN	TURKY	----
V5	ADULT LITERACY	1980	D2	P15	24.6	%	AFGHA	LIBE	F21
V6	DURATION OF SCHOOLING	1970	D2	P20	3.7	YR	SENE	LAOS	----
		1975	D3	P27	5.0	YR	MALAW	BANGL	----
		1980	D3	P24	5.9	YR	BURMA	INDIA	----

V7	STUDENT ENROLLMENT RATIO	1970	D4	P37	1.7	%	CONGO	THAI	----
		1975	D5	P45	4.1	%	GUATE	TUNIS	----
		1980	D6	P49	7.3	%	PARA	GUATE	----
V8	SHARE OF AGRICULTURAL LABOR	------	----	----	-----	-----	-------	-------	----
V9	SHARE OF INDUSTRIAL LABOR	------	----	----	-----	-----	-------	-------	----
V10	SHARE OF SERVICE LABOR	------	----	----	-----	-----	-------	-------	----
V11	SHARE OF ACADEMIC LABOR	------	----	----	-----	-----	-------	-------	----
V12	SHARE OF SELF-EMPLOYED LABOR	------	----	----	-----	-----	-------	-------	----
V13	MILITARY EXPENDITURES	1975	D10	P92	7.239	TSD MIL $	NETH	ITALY	F62
		1980	D10	P95	17.571	TSD MIL $	JAPAN	FRANC	F62
V14	MILITARY MANPOWER	1970	D6	P56	65	TSD CAP	MOROC	CHILE	----
		1975	D7	P64	95	TSD CAP	PERU	BANGL	----
		1980	D6	P56	54	TSD CAP	TANZA	SOMA	----
V15	MEN AT AGE 20 - 30	------	----	----	-----	-----	-------	-------	----
V16	POPULATION	1970	D5	P45	6.20	MIL CAP	ECUA	SYRIA	F4
		1975	D5	P48	7.25	MIL CAP	KAMPU	SYRIA	----
		1980	D6	P52	9.23	MIL CAP	SYRIA	GREC	----
V17	GROSS DOMESTIC PRODUCT	1970	D8	P73	37.282	TSD MIL $	TURKY	VENE	----
		1975	D9	P81	67.973	TSD MIL $	ARGE	SWITZ	----
		1980	D9	P83	105.788	TSD MIL $	SWITZ	BELGI	----
V18	SHARE IN WORLD IMPORTS	1970	D6	P53	2.139	1/TSD	MOROC	EGYPT	----
		1975	D7	P65	4.636	1/TSD	ISRA	IRAQ	----
		1980	D9	P89	14.729	1/TSD	AURIA	SWEDN	----
V19	SHARE IN WORLD EXPORTS	1970	D8	P78	7.527	1/TSD	HUNGA	LIBYA	----
		1975	D10	P92	33.867	1/TSD	BELGI	CANA	----
		1980	D10	P95	54.666	1/TSD	ITALY	UNKI	----
V20	GDP SHARE OF IMPORTS	1970	D5	P49	18.4	%	PHILI	GHANA	----
		1975	D1	P8	10.7	%	ARGE	BRAZI	----
		1980	D6	P59	26.2	%	GREC	YUGO	----
V21	GDP SHARE OF EXPORTS	1970	D10	P98	61.1	%	LIBE	SINGA	----
		1975	D10	P98	75.1	%	TRITO	KUWAI	----
		1980	D10	P99	94.7	%	KUWAI	SINGA	----
V22	EXPORT PARTNER CONCENTRATION	1969	D4	P39	23.8	%	ZAMBI	TUNIS	----
		1975	D3	P30	19.6	%	ETHIA	JAPAN	----
		1980	D3	P20	17.4	%	BRAZI	FINLA	----
V23	TOTAL DEBT AS % OF GDP	------	----	----	-----	-----	-------	-------	----
V24	SHARE OF NEW FOREIGN PATENTS	------	----	----	-----	-----	-------	-------	----
V25	FOREIGN PROPERTY AS % OF GDP	1971	D8	P76	17.4	%	NIGRA	ZAMBI	----
		1975	D2	P16	1.6	%	MALI	LESO	----
		1978	D1	----	0.4	%	YUGO	AFGHA	----

V26	GNP SHARE OF DEVELOPMENT AID	1970	D10	P97	5.59	%	LIBYA	-------	----
		1975	D10	P97	7.50	%	KUWAI	-------	----
		1980	D10	P97	4.95	%	KUWAI	-------	----
V27	SHARE IN NOBEL PRIZE WINNERS	1970-79	D5	P45	0.0	%	RWAN	SENE	----
V28	GDP SHARE OF MANUFACTURING	1970	D3	P28	9.6	%	MALI	IRAQ	----
		1975	D1	P5	5.3	%	GUINE	LIBE	----
		1980	D2	P14	5.0	%	LESO	NIGRA	----
V29	EXPORT SHARE OF MANUFACTURES	1970	D1	P4	0.1	%	RWAN	ZAMBI	----
		1975	D2	P12	0.6	%	MAURA	ZAMBI	----
		1980	D2	P10	0.6	%	SOMA	ZAMBI	----
V30	LACK OF CIVIL LIBERTIES	1975	D8	P74	6		ROMA	SOMA	----
		1980	D8	P74	6		RWAN	SOUAF	----
V31	LACK OF POLITICAL RIGHTS	1975	D7	P63	6		POLA	SENE	----
		1980	D7	P67	6		RWAN	TANZA	----
V32	RIOTS	1970-74	D2	P19	0		RWAN	SOMA	----
		1975-79	D6	P53	2		LIBYA	SWITZ	----
V33	PROTEST DEMONSTRATIONS	1970-74	D4	P37	1		ROMA	YENO	----
		1975-79	D4	P32	1		RWAN	SUDAN	----
V34	POLITICAL STRIKES	1970-74	D3	P29	0		RWAN	SENE	----
		1975-79	D3	P29	0		RWAN	SENE	----
V35	MEMBER OF THE NONALIGNED MMT.	1976	----	----	1		RWAN	SENE	----
		1981	----	----	1		RWAN	SENE	----
V36	MEMBER OF THE OPEC	1970	----	----	1		LIBYA	VENE	----
		1975	----	----	1		NIGRA	VENE	----
		1980	----	----	1		NIGRA	UNARE	----
V37	MEMBER OF THE OECD	1970	----	----	0		RWAN	SENE	----
		1975	----	----	0		RWAN	SENE	----
		1980	----	----	0		RWAN	SENE	----
V38	MEMBER OF THE CMEA	1970	----	----	0		RWAN	SENE	----
		1975	----	----	0		RWAN	SENE	----
		1980	----	----	0		RWAN	SENE	----
V39	MEMBER OF THE WTO	1970	----	----	0		RWAN	SENE	----
		1975	----	----	0		RWAN	SENE	----
		1980	----	----	0		RWAN	SENE	----
V40	MEMBER OF THE NATO	1970	----	----	0		RWAN	SENE	----
		1975	----	----	0		RWAN	SENE	----
		1980	----	----	0		RWAN	SENE	----
V41	GDP SHARE OF INVESTMENTS	1970	D4	P31	16.1	%	LESO	CHILE	----
		1975	D2	P14	13.2	%	CHILE	URU	----
		1980	D5	P44	22.7	%	CANA	FRANC	----
V42	GDP SHARE OF AGRICULTURE	1970	D2	P14	5.7	%	DENMA	AULIA	----
		1975	D1	P3	1.0	%	KUWAI	SINGA	----
		1980	D1	P3	1.2	%	UNARE	SINGA	----

V43	GDP SHARE OF INDUSTRY	1970	D10	P98	63.4	%	ZAMBI	LIBYA	----
		1975	D10	P99	86.1	%	KUWAI	-------	----
		1980	D10	P99	78.1	%	KUWAI	-------	----
V44	GDP SHARE OF SERVICES	1970	D2	P11	30.9	%	INDIA	MAURA	----
		1975	D1	P2	12.9	%	-------	NEPAL	----
		1980	D1	P3	20.7	%	IRAQ	LIBYA	----
V45	HOMICIDES P. MIL. POPULATION	------	----	----	-----	-----	-------	-------	----
V46	SUICIDES P. MIL. POPULATION	------	----	----	-----	-----	-------	-------	----
V47	IMPORT PARTNERS	1969	R1	USA	18.8	%	PERU	SPAIN	----
		1969	R2	JAPAN	10.5	%	RWAN	UGADA	----
		1969	R3	LEBA	9.6	%	-------	-------	----
		1980	R1	USA	20.1	%	PHILI	SPAIN	----
		1980	R2	JAPAN	18.1	%	RWAN	USA	----
		1980	R3	GFR	9.1	%	PERU	SPAIN	----
V48	EXPORT PARTNERS	1969	R1	JAPAN	23.8	%	INDO	THAI	----
		1969	R2	ITALY	10.5	%	GREC	SOMA	----
		1969	R3	UNKI	8.7	%	LIBYA	TRITO	----
		1980	R1	JAPAN	17.4	%	PAPUA	THAI	----
		1980	R2	USA	15.5	%	NEPAL	SINGA	----
		1980	R3	FRANC	9.2	%	PORTU	TUNIS	----
V49	PATENT SUPPLIERS	------	----	----	-----	-----	-------	-------	----
V50	PROVENANCE OF FOREIGN FIRMS	1980	R1	USA	28.4	%	PORTU	SINGA	----
		1980	R2	UNKI	27.7	%	PORTU	SINGA	----
		1980	R3	NETH	10.2	%	GUATE	UNKI	----
V51	FILM SUPPLIERS	------	----	----	-----	-----	-------	-------	----

SENEGAL (SENE)

V1	INCOME PER CAPITA	1970	D3	P29	535	$/CAP	HONDU	CAME	----
		1975	D3	P30	512	$/CAP	HONDU	THAI	----
		1980	D3	P27	479	$/CAP	LIBE	BOLI	----
V2	TELEPHONES P. TSD. POPULATION	1970	D4	P37	8	1/TSD CAP	GUATE	ZAMBI	----
		1975	D4	P31	8	1/TSD CAP	CONGO	IVORY	----
		1979	D3	P24	8	1/TSD CAP	HONDU	CONGO	----
V3	INFANT MORTALITY RATE	1980	D9	P86	152.6	1/TSD	NIGER	YESO	F5
V4	PHYSICIANS P. MIL. POPULATION	1970	D3	P24	62	1/MIL	AFGHA	IVORY	----
		1975	D2	P21	62	1/MIL	MAURA	GUINE	----
		1978	D2	----	72	1/MIL	CAME	ZAIRE	----
V5	ADULT LITERACY	------	----	----	-----	-----	-------	-------	----

V6	DURATION OF SCHOOLING	1970	D2	P19	3.4	YR	MALAW	SAUDI	----
		1975	D2	P13	3.4	YR	SOMA	PAKI	----
		1980	D2	P11	3.8	YR	AFGHA	SUDAN	----
V7	STUDENT ENROLLMENT RATIO	1970	D4	P33	1.5	%	MOROC	MALAY	----
		1975	D4	P33	2.0	%	PAKI	ZAMBI	----
		1980	D4	P33	2.8	%	VINO	SRILA	----
V8	SHARE OF AGRICULTURAL LABOR	------	----	----	-----	-----	-------	-------	----
V9	SHARE OF INDUSTRIAL LABOR	------	----	----	-----	-----	-------	-------	----
V10	SHARE OF SERVICE LABOR	------	----	----	-----	-----	-------	-------	----
V11	SHARE OF ACADEMIC LABOR	------	----	----	-----	-----	-------	-------	----
V12	SHARE OF SELF-EMPLOYED LABOR	------	----	----	-----	-----	-------	-------	----
V13	MILITARY EXPENDITURES	1970	D3	P27	0.043	TSD MIL $	KENYA	ETHIA	F4
		1975	D3	P25	0.052	TSD MIL $	SRILA	GUATE	----
		1980	D3	P22	0.059	TSD MIL $	PARA	BOLI	----
V14	MILITARY MANPOWER	1970	D2	P19	7	TSD CAP	KENYA	CAME	----
		1975	D2	P17	7	TSD CAP	IVORY	ELSA	----
		1980	D2	P19	8	TSD CAP	PANA	CAME	----
V15	MEN AT AGE 20 - 30	1976	D4	P33	373	TSD CAP	ZAMBI	DENMA	F22
V16	POPULATION	1970	D4	P35	4.27	MIL CAP	ZAMBI	MALAW	----
		1975	D4	P36	4.98	MIL CAP	BOLI	ZAMBI	----
		1980	D4	P36	5.70	MIL CAP	BOLI	YENO	----
V17	GROSS DOMESTIC PRODUCT	1970	D3	P25	2.285	TSD MIL $	ELSA	SRILA	----
		1975	D3	P21	2.551	TSD MIL $	PANA	COSTA	----
		1980	D2	P19	2.731	TSD MIL $	YENO	BOLI	----
V18	SHARE IN WORLD IMPORTS	1970	D3	P27	0.581	1/TSD	JORDA	NICA	----
		1975	D3	P31	0.641	1/TSD	BOLI	ELSA	----
		1980	D3	P30	0.513	1/TSD	PAPUA	ZAMBI	----
V19	SHARE IN WORLD EXPORTS	1970	D3	P27	0.485	1/TSD	MADA	HONDU	----
		1975	D4	P36	0.525	1/TSD	CAME	COSTA	----
		1980	D3	P23	0.239	1/TSD	BURMA	TANZA	----
V20	GDP SHARE OF IMPORTS	1970	D7	P67	22.3	%	CAME	CHAD	----
		1975	D8	P73	30.7	%	KENYA	IRAQ	----
		1980	D8	P77	35.4	%	BENIN	KORSO	----
V21	GDP SHARE OF EXPORTS	1970	D6	P57	17.6	%	CENTR	BOLI	----
		1975	D8	P73	24.3	%	NIGRA	DOMI	----
		1980	D5	P43	16.1	%	SYRIA	PHILI	----
V22	EXPORT PARTNER CONCENTRATION	1970	D10	P92	57.0	%	BURU	HAITI	----
		1975	D9	P86	48.3	%	UPVO	SIERA	----
V23	TOTAL DEBT AS % OF GDP	1980	D6	P57	42.1	%	PAKI	TUNIS	----
V24	SHARE OF NEW FOREIGN PATENTS	------	----	----	-----	-----	-------	-------	----

V25	FOREIGN PROPERTY AS % OF GDP	1971	D9	P84	22.4 %	TOGO	GUINE	----
		1975	D9	P84	15.8 %	TOGO	CENTR	----
		1978	D9	----	15.5 %	HONDU	MALAY	----
V26	GNP SHARE OF DEVELOPMENT AID	------	----	----	----- -----	-------	-------	----
V27	SHARE IN NOBEL PRIZE WINNERS	1970-79	D5	P45	0.0 %	SAUDI	SIERA	----
V28	GDP SHARE OF MANUFACTURING	------	----	----	----- -----	-------	-------	----
V29	EXPORT SHARE OF MANUFACTURES	1970	D7	P62	18.7 %	COSTA	URU	----
		1975	D7	P62	14.5 %	KENYA	COLO	----
		1980	D5	P48	15.0 %	HONDU	PERU	----
V30	LACK OF CIVIL LIBERTIES	1975	D6	P54	5	RWAN	SIERA	----
		1980	D3	P29	3	NIGRA	SRILA	----
V31	LACK OF POLITICAL RIGHTS	1975	D7	P63	6	SAUDI	SIERA	----
		1980	D4	P36	4	LEBA	THAI	----
V32	RIOTS	1970-74	D8	P73	7	GUATE	VENE	----
		1975-79	D2	P20	0	RWAN	SINGA	----
V33	PROTEST DEMONSTRATIONS	1970-74	D2	P15	0	RWAN	SIERA	----
		1975-79	D2	P13	0	NIGER	SINGA	----
V34	POLITICAL STRIKES	1970-74	D3	P29	0	SAUDI	SIERA	----
		1975-79	D3	P29	0	SAUDI	SIERA	----
V35	MEMBER OF THE NONALIGNED MMT.	1970	----	----	1	RWAN	SIERA	----
		1976	----	----	1	SAUDI	SIERA	----
		1981	----	----	1	SAUDI	SIERA	----
V36	MEMBER OF THE OPEC	1970	----	----	0	RWAN	SIERA	----
		1975	----	----	0	RWAN	SIERA	----
		1980	----	----	0	RWAN	SIERA	----
V37	MEMBER OF THE OECD	1970	----	----	0	SAUDI	SIERA	----
		1975	----	----	0	SAUDI	SIERA	----
		1980	----	----	0	SAUDI	SIERA	----
V38	MEMBER OF THE CMEA	1970	----	----	0	SAUDI	SIERA	----
		1975	----	----	0	SAUDI	SIERA	----
		1980	----	----	0	SAUDI	SIERA	----
V39	MEMBER OF THE WTO	1970	----	----	0	SAUDI	SIERA	----
		1975	----	----	0	SAUDI	SIERA	----
		1980	----	----	0	SAUDI	SIERA	----
V40	MEMBER OF THE NATO	1970	----	----	0	SAUDI	SIERA	----
		1975	----	----	0	SAUDI	SIERA	----
		1980	----	----	0	SAUDI	SIERA	----
V41	GDP SHARE OF INVESTMENTS	1970	D3	P28	15.7 %	MADA	IRAQ	----
		1975	D3	P28	17.8 %	COLO	GUINE	----
		1980	D2	P12	14.1 %	AFGHA	BURU	----
V42	GDP SHARE OF AGRICULTURE	1970	D6	P54	24.1 %	LIBE	NICA	----
		1975	D7	P66	30.2 %	PAPUA	SRILA	----
		1980	D6	P55	22.7 %	NICA	TURKY	----

V43 GDP SHARE OF INDUSTRY	1970	D3	P28	20.2 %	KENYA	PARA	----
	1975	D3	P28	22.8 %	IVORY	INDIA	----
	1980	D3	P30	25.1 %	SYRIA	INDIA	----
V44 GDP SHARE OF SERVICES	1970	D9	P82	55.7 %	MEXI	NEWZ	----
	1975	D6	P56	47.0 %	TOGO	CENTR	----
	1980	D7	P70	52.2 %	DOMI	ELSA	----
V45 HOMICIDES P. MIL. POPULATION	------	----	----	----- -----	-------	-------	----
V46 SUICIDES P. MIL. POPULATION	------	----	----	----- -----	-------	-------	----
V47 IMPORT PARTNERS	1970	R1	FRANC	51.3 %	MOROC	TOGO	----
	1970	R2	GFR	6.5 %	ROMA	SOMA	----
	1970	R3	IVORY	5.0 %	MALI	-------	----
	1980	R1	FRANC	34.1 %	NIGER	TOGO	----
	1980	R2	NIGRA	7.4 %	NIGER	TOGO	----
	1980	R3	UNKI	6.5 %	PORTU	SOMA	----
V48 EXPORT PARTNERS	1970	R1	FRANC	57.0 %	NIGER	TOGO	----
	1970	R2	IVORY	6.6 %	UPVO	-------	----
	1970	R3	NETH	5.6 %	PHILI	THAI	----
V49 PATENT SUPPLIERS	------	----	----	----- -----	-------	-------	----
V50 PROVENANCE OF FOREIGN FIRMS	1980	R1	FRANC	67.9 %	MOROC	TOGO	----
	1980	R2	GFR	7.7 %	MEXI	SPAIN	----
	1980	R3	UNKI	5.8 %	PHILI	SPAIN	----
V51 FILM SUPPLIERS	------	----	----	----- -----	-------	-------	----

SIERRA LEONE (SIERA)

V1 INCOME PER CAPITA	1970	D2	P19	331 $/CAP	KENYA	TOGO	F4
	1975	D2	P18	325 $/CAP	ZAIRE	YENO	----
	1980	D2	P17	328 $/CAP	BENIN	MADA	----
V2 TELEPHONES P. TSD. POPULATION	1970	D3	P27	4 1/TSD CAP	MADA	THAI	----
	1975	D3	P23	4 1/TSD CAP	MALAW	TANZA	----
V3 INFANT MORTALITY RATE	1980	D10	P99	215.0 1/TSD	MALAW	KAMPU	F5
V4 PHYSICIANS P. MIL. POPULATION	1970	D3	P21	55 1/MIL	MAURA	KAMPU	----
	1980	D2	P14	58 1/MIL	MOROC	BENIN	----
V5 ADULT LITERACY	------	----	----	----- -----	-------	-------	----
V6 DURATION OF SCHOOLING	1970	D2	P18	3.1 YR	TANZA	MALAW	----
	1975	D2	P15	3.6 YR	PAKI	RWAN	----
	1980	D2	P13	4.3 YR	NEPAL	MOZAM	----

V7	STUDENT ENROLLMENT RATIO	1970	D3	P21	0.5	%	NIGRA	TOGO	----
		1975	D2	P14	0.6	%	MALI	HAITI	----
		1980	D2	P13	0.6	%	BURU	CENTR	----
V8	SHARE OF AGRICULTURAL LABOR	------	----	----	-----	-----	-------	-------	----
V9	SHARE OF INDUSTRIAL LABOR	------	----	----	-----	-----	-------	-------	----
V10	SHARE OF SERVICE LABOR	------	----	----	-----	-----	-------	-------	----
V11	SHARE OF ACADEMIC LABOR	------	----	----	-----	-----	-------	-------	----
V12	SHARE OF SELF-EMPLOYED LABOR	------	----	----	-----	-----	-------	-------	----
V13	MILITARY EXPENDITURES	1970	D1	P4	0.008	TSD MIL $	MALAW	COSTA	F4
		1975	D1	P3	0.010	TSD MIL $	LIBE	MALAW	----
		1980	D1	P2	0.012	TSD MIL $	-------	NIGER	F59
V14	MILITARY MANPOWER	1970	D1	P7	3	TSD CAP	MAURA	ELSA	----
		1975	D2	P12	5	TSD CAP	NICA	UPVO	----
		1980	D1	P3	2	TSD CAP	JAMAI	COSTA	----
V15	MEN AT AGE 20 - 30	1974	D2	P13	201	TSD CAP	BENIN	PARA	----
V16	POPULATION	1970	D2	P19	2.69	MIL CAP	HONDU	BENIN	----
		1975	D2	P20	3.05	MIL CAP	URU	NEWZ	----
		1980	D3	P21	3.30	MIL CAP	PARA	IRE	----
V17	GROSS DOMESTIC PRODUCT	1970	D1	P9	0.891	TSD MIL $	LIBE	HAITI	F4
		1975	D1	P7	0.990	TSD MIL $	BENIN	UPVO	----
		1980	D1	P8	1.081	TSD MIL $	BENIN	UPVO	----
V18	SHARE IN WORLD IMPORTS	1970	D2	P19	0.349	1/TSD	LAOS	MONGO	F30
		1975	D2	P14	0.204	1/TSD	PARA	BENIN	F30
		1980	D2	P12	0.202	1/TSD	BENIN	MALI	F30
V19	SHARE IN WORLD EXPORTS	1970	D3	P22	0.322	1/TSD	MAURA	PANA	F30
		1975	D2	P13	0.138	1/TSD	VISO	TOGO	F30
		1980	D2	P11	0.102	1/TSD	MAURA	MALI	F30
V20	GDP SHARE OF IMPORTS	1970	D9	P82	27.4	%	ALGER	KENYA	F30
		1975	D7	P69	29.2	%	TOGO	SYRIA	F30
		1980	D9	P82	37.6	%	MALAW	PORTU	F30
V21	GDP SHARE OF EXPORTS	1970	D8	P80	23.8	%	VENE	JAMAI	F30
		1975	D6	P54	19.1	%	SRILA	FINLA	F30
		1980	D5	P46	18.5	%	FRANC	PORTU	F30
V22	EXPORT PARTNER CONCENTRATION	1975	D9	P87	50.9	%	SENE	HONDU	----
V23	TOTAL DEBT AS % OF GDP	1980	D5	P48	37.3	%	GABON	PORTU	----
V24	SHARE OF NEW FOREIGN PATENTS	1970	D9	P90	100	%	RWAN	SINGA	----
		1974	D10	P92	100	%	RWAN	SOMA	----
		1980	D10	P94	100	%	RWAN	SINGA	----
V25	FOREIGN PROPERTY AS % OF GDP	1971	D8	P71	16.4	%	SINGA	DOMI	----
		1975	D8	P75	11.8	%	ECUA	MAURA	----
		1978	D8	----	10.1	%	KENYA	MALAW	----
V26	GNP SHARE OF DEVELOPMENT AID	------	----	----	-----	-----	-------	-------	----

V27	SHARE IN NOBEL PRIZE WINNERS	1970-79	D5	P45	0.0 %	SENE	SINGA	----
V28	GDP SHARE OF MANUFACTURING	1970	D2	P11	5.8 %	LESO	BURU	F16
		1975	D2	P14	5.8 %	LESO	IRAQ	F16
		1980	D2	P17	5.5 %	NIGRA	YENO	F16
V29	EXPORT SHARE OF MANUFACTURES	------	----	----	----- -----	-------	-------	----
V30	LACK OF CIVIL LIBERTIES	1975	D6	P54	5	SENE	SINGA	----
		1980	D6	P52	5	POLA	SINGA	----
V31	LACK OF POLITICAL RIGHTS	1975	D7	P63	6	SENE	SUDAN	----
		1980	D5	P47	5	PHILI	SINGA	----
V32	RIOTS	1970-74	D5	P43	1	NORWY	SINGA	----
		1975-79	D5	P45	1	POLA	SUDAN	----
V33	PROTEST DEMONSTRATIONS	1970-74	D2	P15	0	SENE	SOMA	----
		1975-79	D5	P49	3	NORWY	SWEDN	----
V34	POLITICAL STRIKES	1970-74	D3	P29	0	SENE	SINGA	----
		1975-79	D3	P29	0	SENE	SINGA	----
V35	MEMBER OF THE NONALIGNED MMT.	1970	----	----	1	SENE	SINGA	----
		1976	----	----	1	SENE	SINGA	----
		1981	----	----	1	SENE	SINGA	----
V36	MEMBER OF THE OPEC	1970	----	----	0	SENE	SINGA	----
		1975	----	----	0	SENE	SINGA	----
		1980	----	----	0	SENE	SINGA	----
V37	MEMBER OF THE OECD	1970	----	----	0	SENE	SINGA	----
		1975	----	----	0	SENE	SINGA	----
		1980	----	----	0	SENE	SINGA	----
V38	MEMBER OF THE CMEA	1970	----	----	0	SENE	SINGA	----
		1975	----	----	0	SENE	SINGA	----
		1980	----	----	0	SENE	SINGA	----
V39	MEMBER OF THE WTO	1970	----	----	0	SENE	SINGA	----
		1975	----	----	0	SENE	SINGA	----
		1980	----	----	0	SENE	SINGA	----
V40	MEMBER OF THE NATO	1970	----	----	0	SENE	SINGA	----
		1975	----	----	0	SENE	SINGA	----
		1980	----	----	0	SENE	SINGA	----
V41	GDP SHARE OF INVESTMENTS	1970	D4	P35	16.6 %	LIBYA	CAME	----
		1975	D2	P20	15.7 %	SRILA	GUATE	----
		1980	D3	P22	16.3 %	UNKI	BANGL	----
V42	GDP SHARE OF AGRICULTURE	1970	D7	P61	28.2 %	PHILI	SRILA	F16
		1975	D8	P76	35.5 %	CENTR	PARA	F16
		1980	D8	P73	31.4 %	PAKI	KENYA	F16
V43	GDP SHARE OF INDUSTRY	1970	D6	P59	30.3 %	SINGA	GREC	F16
		1975	D4	P32	23.6 %	PANA	JORDA	F16
		1980	D3	P25	22.1 %	RWAN	IVORY	F16

V44	GDP SHARE OF SERVICES	1970	D3	P26	41.5 %	YUGO	TANZA	F16
		1975	D4	P32	40.9 %	MOZAM	MADA	F16
		1980	D5	P50	46.5 %	ZAMBI	TURKY	F16
V45	HOMICIDES P. MIL. POPULATION	------	----	----	----- -----	-------	-------	----
V46	SUICIDES P. MIL. POPULATION	------	----	----	----- -----	-------	-------	----
V47	IMPORT PARTNERS	------	----	----	----- -----	-------	-------	----
V48	EXPORT PARTNERS	------	----	----	----- -----	-------	-------	----
V49	PATENT SUPPLIERS	1972	R1	USA	12	PORTU	SINGA	----
		1972	R2	UNKI	6	MALAY	SINGA	----
		1972	R3	ARGE	3	-------	-------	----
		1979	R1	SWITZ	9	-------	BANGL	----
		1979	R2	JAPAN	5	GFR	SINGA	----
		1979	R3	UNKI	4	PAKI	SINGA	----
V50	PROVENANCE OF FOREIGN FIRMS	1980	R1	UNKI	60.0 %	NIGRA	SOUAF	----
		1980	R2	-------	10.0 %	-------	-------	----
		1980	R3	-------	10.0 %	-------	-------	----
V51	FILM SUPPLIERS	------	----	----	----- -----	-------	-------	----

SINGAPORE (SINGA)

V1	INCOME PER CAPITA	1970	D7	P67	2238 $/CAP	CHILE	SOUAF	----
		1975	D7	P70	3246 $/CAP	SOUAF	GREC	----
		1980	D8	P72	4629 $/CAP	GREC	IRE	----
V2	TELEPHONES P. TSD. POPULATION	1970	D8	P73	68 1/TSD CAP	LEBA	SOUAF	----
		1975	D8	P77	141 1/TSD CAP	IRE	GDR	----
		1980	D8	P78	291 1/TSD CAP	GREC	ISRA	----
V3	INFANT MORTALITY RATE	1980	D2	P12	11.7 1/TSD	IRE	GDR	----
V4	PHYSICIANS P. MIL. POPULATION	1975	D7	P61	718 1/MIL	NICA	PANA	----
		1980	D7	P61	870 1/MIL	PANA	VENE	----
V5	ADULT LITERACY	1970	D5	P46	68.9 %	DOMI	PORTU	----
		1980	D8	P75	82.9 %	MEXI	VINO	----
V6	DURATION OF SCHOOLING	1970	D7	P68	9.2 YR	KORSO	YUGO	----
		1975	D7	P66	9.4 YR	PERU	TRITO	----
		1980	D7	P59	9.7 YR	DOMI	LEBA	----
V7	STUDENT ENROLLMENT RATIO	1970	D6	P60	6.7 %	DOMI	PANA	----
		1975	D6	P57	9.0 %	KUWAI	ROMA	----
		1980	D6	P51	7.8 %	GUATE	HONDU	----

V8	SHARE OF AGRICULTURAL LABOR	1970	D1	P6	4.3	%	USA	BELGI	----
		1975	D1	P6	2.9	%	KUWAI	USA	----
		1980	D1	P3	1.9	%	-------	KUWAI	----
V9	SHARE OF INDUSTRIAL LABOR	1970	D9	P83	40.6	%	AURIA	UNKI	----
		1975	D8	P76	37.5	%	LIBYA	AULIA	----
		1980	D10	P90	41.2	%	SPAIN	TUNIS	----
V10	SHARE OF SERVICE LABOR	1970	D10	P98	46.2	%	USA	-------	----
		1975	D10	P95	48.2	%	KUWAI	USA	----
		1980	D10	P92	47.7	%	JAPAN	CANA	----
V11	SHARE OF ACADEMIC LABOR	1970	D7	P67	8.9	%	AURIA	IRE	----
		1975	D8	P69	11.3	%	LIBYA	IRE	----
		1980	D6	P49	9.2	%	JAPAN	SYRIA	----
V12	SHARE OF SELF-EMPLOYED LABOR	1970	D4	P42	19.8	%	SPAIN	PORTU	----
		1975	D3	P24	15.0	%	FRANC	TRITO	----
		1980	D3	P26	12.5	%	KUWAI	POLA	----
V13	MILITARY EXPENDITURES	1970	D5	P46	0.250	TSD MIL $	MOROC	LIBYA	----
		1975	D5	P49	0.406	TSD MIL $	NEWZ	HUNGA	----
		1980	D6	P53	0.596	TSD MIL $	MEXI	FINLA	----
V14	MILITARY MANPOWER	1970	D4	P31	14	TSD CAP	NEWZ	ECUA	----
		1975	D5	P43	27	TSD CAP	URU	ANGO	----
		1980	D6	P53	50	TSD CAP	ANGO	ALBA	----
V15	MEN AT AGE 20 - 30	1970	D1	P9	170	TSD CAP	NICA	JORDA	----
		1976	D3	P19	241	TSD CAP	IRE	NEWZ	----
		1980	D2	P13	272	TSD CAP	IRE	PARA	----
V16	POPULATION	1970	D2	P13	2.08	MIL CAP	LIBYA	ALBA	----
		1975	D2	P14	2.26	MIL CAP	TOGO	ALBA	----
		1980	D2	P12	2.41	MIL CAP	CENTR	TOGO	----
V17	GROSS DOMESTIC PRODUCT	1970	D5	P45	4.656	TSD MIL $	GUATE	SYRIA	----
		1975	D5	P46	7.336	TSD MIL $	ECUA	BANGL	----
		1980	D5	P48	11.155	TSD MIL $	ECUA	BANGL	----
V18	SHARE IN WORLD IMPORTS	1970	D8	P77	7.414	1/TSD	CHINA	HUNGA	F43
		1975	D9	P81	8.949	1/TSD	YUGO	CZECH	F43
		1980	D9	P86	11.501	1/TSD	AULIA	BRAZI	F43
V19	SHARE IN WORLD EXPORTS	1970	D7	P68	4.954	1/TSD	MEXI	YUGO	F43
		1975	D8	P71	6.135	1/TSD	ROMA	SOUAF	F43
		1980	D9	P81	9.708	1/TSD	NORWY	VENE	F43
V20	GDP SHARE OF IMPORTS	1970	D10	P99	129.8	%	HUNGA	-------	F43
		1975	D10	P100	144.2	%	HUNGA	-------	F43
		1980	D10	P100	208.0	%	YENO	-------	F43
V21	GDP SHARE OF EXPORTS	1970	D10	P99	81.9	%	SAUDI	-------	F43
		1975	D10	P100	95.3	%	KUWAI	-------	F43
		1980	D10	P100	170.8	%	SAUDI	-------	F43
V22	EXPORT PARTNER CONCENTRATION	1970	D4	P34	21.9	%	MALAY	TANZA	F134
		1975	D3	P22	17.2	%	URU	IRAQ	F134
		1980	D2	P13	15.0	%	PORTU	THAI	F134
V23	TOTAL DEBT AS % OF GDP	------	----	----	----- -----		-------	-------	----

V24 SHARE OF NEW FOREIGN PATENTS	1970	D9	P90	100 %	SIERA	SOMA	----
	1977	D9	----	99 %	NIGRA	BURU	----
	1980	D10	P94	100 %	SIERA	TANZA	----
V25 FOREIGN PROPERTY AS % OF GDP	1971	D7	P70	16.1 %	COSTA	SIERA	----
	1975	D10	P93	30.1 %	GABON	JAMAI	----
	1978	D10	----	21.8 %	PERU	GABON	----
V26 GNP SHARE OF DEVELOPMENT AID	------	----	----	----- -----	-------	-------	----
V27 SHARE IN NOBEL PRIZE WINNERS	1970-79	D5	P45	0.0 %	SIERA	SOMA	----
V28 GDP SHARE OF MANUFACTURING	1970	D8	P71	20.4 %	NICA	TRITO	----
	1975	D9	P83	24.1 %	USA	FINLA	----
	1980	D10	P96	29.5 %	KORSO	JAPAN	----
V29 EXPORT SHARE OF MANUFACTURES	------	----	----	----- -----	-------	-------	----
V30 LACK OF CIVIL LIBERTIES	1975	D6	P54	5	SIERA	SOUAF	----
	1980	D6	P52	5	SIERA	SUDAN	----
V31 LACK OF POLITICAL RIGHTS	1975	D5	P43	5	PORTU	SPAIN	----
	1980	D5	P47	5	SIERA	SOUAF	----
V32 RIOTS	1970-74	D5	P43	1	SIERA	YENO	----
	1975-79	D2	P20	0	SENE	SOMA	----
V33 PROTEST DEMONSTRATIONS	1970-74	D6	P54	3	ECUA	TUNIS	----
	1975-79	D2	P13	0	SENE	SOMA	----
V34 POLITICAL STRIKES	1970-74	D3	P29	0	SIERA	SOMA	----
	1975-79	D3	P29	0	SIERA	SOMA	----
V35 MEMBER OF THE NONALIGNED MMT.	1970	----	----	1	SIERA	SOMA	----
	1976	----	----	1	SIERA	SOMA	----
	1981	----	----	1	SIERA	SOMA	----
V36 MEMBER OF THE OPEC	1970	----	----	0	SIERA	SOMA	----
	1975	----	----	0	SIERA	SOMA	----
	1980	----	----	0	SIERA	SOMA	----
V37 MEMBER OF THE OECD	1970	----	----	0	SIERA	SOMA	----
	1975	----	----	0	SIERA	SOMA	----
	1980	----	----	0	SIERA	SOMA	----
V38 MEMBER OF THE CMEA	1970	----	----	0	SIERA	SOMA	----
	1975	----	----	0	SIERA	SOMA	----
	1980	----	----	0	SIERA	SOMA	----
V39 MEMBER OF THE WTO	1970	----	----	0	SIERA	SOMA	----
	1975	----	----	0	SIERA	SOMA	----
	1980	----	----	0	SIERA	SOMA	----
V40 MEMBER OF THE NATO	1970	----	----	0	SIERA	SOMA	----
	1975	----	----	0	SIERA	SOMA	----
	1980	----	----	0	SIERA	SOMA	----
V41 GDP SHARE OF INVESTMENTS	1970	D10	P98	38.7 %	ALGER	JAPAN	----
	1975	D10	P96	37.6 %	NORWY	HUNGA	----
	1980	D10	P100	45.4 %	YENO	-------	----

V42	GDP SHARE OF AGRICULTURE	1970	D1	P2	2.3	%	-------	LIBYA	----
		1975	D1	P4	1.9	%	SAUDI	LIBYA	----
		1980	D1	P4	1.4	%	SAUDI	LIBYA	----
V43	GDP SHARE OF INDUSTRY	1970	D6	P57	30.2	%	BOLI	SIERA	----
		1975	D7	P67	34.5	%	PERU	NETH	----
		1980	D8	P77	39.0	%	ZIMBA	ZAMBI	----
V44	GDP SHARE OF SERVICES	1970	D10	P98	67.5	%	DENMA	JORDA	----
		1975	D10	P96	63.6	%	USA	PANA	----
		1980	D9	P89	59.6	%	SPAIN	FRANC	----
V45	HOMICIDES P. MIL. POPULATION	1970	D6	P52	16.8	1/MIL CAP	AULIA	PERU	F154
		1975	D6	P57	18.6	1/MIL CAP	AURIA	PORTU	F154
V46	SUICIDES P. MIL. POPULATION	1970	D5	P48	88.9	1/MIL CAP	NORWY	NEWZ	F2
		1975	D6	P57	111.5	1/MIL CAP	AULIA	POLA	F2
V47	IMPORT PARTNERS	1970	R1	JAPAN	19.4	%	PHILI	THAI	F134
		1970	R2	MALAY	18.6	%	-------	-------	F134
		1970	R3	USA	10.8	%	NEWZ	SOMA	F134
		1980	R1	JAPAN	17.8	%	OMAN	SRILA	F134
		1980	R2	USA	14.1	%	ROMA	SOMA	F134
		1980	R3	MALAY	13.9	%	-------	-------	F134
V48	EXPORT PARTNERS	1970	R1	MALAY	21.9	%	LAOS	MADA	F134
		1970	R2	USA	11.1	%	PARA	TANZA	F134
		1970	R3	JAPAN	7.6	%	PERU	UGADA	F134
		1980	R1	MALAY	15.0	%	-------	-------	F134
		1980	R2	USA	12.7	%	SAUDI	UNKI	F134
		1980	R3	JAPAN	8.1	%	MEXI	SUDAN	F134
V49	PATENT SUPPLIERS	1970	R1	USA	160		SIERA	SPAIN	----
		1970	R2	UNKI	46		SIERA	TRITO	----
		1970	R3	SWITZ	21		PHILI	TUNIS	----
		1980	R1	USA	152		PORTU	SPAIN	----
		1980	R2	JAPAN	140		SIERA	AULIA	----
		1980	R3	UNKI	80		SIERA	URU	----
V50	PROVENANCE OF FOREIGN FIRMS	1980	R1	USA	34.4	%	SAUDI	SPAIN	----
		1980	R2	UNKI	29.2	%	SAUDI	SWEDN	----
		1980	R3	JAPAN	7.7	%	PERU	-------	----
V51	FILM SUPPLIERS	1982	R1	USA	221		ROMA	SPAIN	F117
		1982	R2	INDIA	78		MAURA	TRITO	F117
		1982	R3	ITALY	25		POLA	SWITZ	F117

SOMALIA (SOMA)

V1	INCOME PER CAPITA	------	----	----	----- -----	-------	-------	----
V2	TELEPHONES P. TSD. POPULATION	1970	D2	P16	2 1/TSD CAP	INDO	VISO	----
V3	INFANT MORTALITY RATE	1980	D9	P90	154.9 1/TSD	ETHIA	BHUTA	F5
V4	PHYSICIANS P. MIL. POPULATION	1970	D2	P18	47 1/MIL	YENO	MAURA	----
		1973	D3	----	64 1/MIL	NIGRA	YENO	----
		1980	D2	P18	65 1/MIL	PAPUA	CAME	----
V5	ADULT LITERACY	1980	D1	P3	6.1 %	-------	YENO	F21
V6	DURATION OF SCHOOLING	1970	D1	P3	0.8 YR	BHUTA	YENO	----
		1975	D2	P12	3.1 YR	GUINE	SENE	----
		1980	D1	P6	2.9 YR	MAURA	GUINE	----
V7	STUDENT ENROLLMENT RATIO	1970	D2	P18	0.4 %	HAITI	ZAMBI	----
		1975	D2	P19	0.8 %	NIGRA	AFGHA	----
		1979	D2	P15	0.9 %	KENYA	HAITI	----
V8	SHARE OF AGRICULTURAL LABOR	------	----	----	----- -----	-------	-------	----
V9	SHARE OF INDUSTRIAL LABOR	------	----	----	----- -----	-------	-------	----
V10	SHARE OF SERVICE LABOR	------	----	----	----- -----	-------	-------	----
V11	SHARE OF ACADEMIC LABOR	------	----	----	----- -----	-------	-------	----
V12	SHARE OF SELF-EMPLOYED LABOR	------	----	----	----- -----	-------	-------	----
V13	MILITARY EXPENDITURES	------	----	----	----- -----	-------	-------	----
V14	MILITARY MANPOWER	1970	D4	P39	20 TSD CAP	LEBA	TANZA	----
		1975	D5	P44	30 TSD CAP	ANGO	NEPAL	----
		1980	D6	P56	54 TSD CAP	SAUDI	LAOS	----
V15	MEN AT AGE 20 - 30	------	----	----	----- -----	-------	-------	----
V16	POPULATION	1970	D2	P20	2.79 MIL CAP	BENIN	NEWZ	F4
		1975	D3	P24	3.13 MIL CAP	BENIN	IRE	----
		1980	D3	P28	4.61 MIL CAP	CHAD	ELSA	----
V17	GROSS DOMESTIC PRODUCT	------	----	----	----- -----	-------	-------	----
V18	SHARE IN WORLD IMPORTS	1970	D1	P5	0.136 1/TSD	CENTR	MALI	----
		1975	D1	P8	0.171 1/TSD	UPVO	CONGO	----
		1980	D1	P6	0.134 1/TSD	RWAN	MAURA	----
V19	SHARE IN WORLD EXPORTS	1970	D1	P9	0.099 1/TSD	CONGO	NIGER	----
		1975	D1	P10	0.102 1/TSD	HAITI	NIGER	----
		1980	D1	P9	0.071 1/TSD	CENTR	MAURA	----
V20	GDP SHARE OF IMPORTS	1970	D4	P31	14.2 %	IRAQ	SUDAN	----
		1975	D5	P42	21.3 %	HAITI	DOMI	----
		1980	D4	P31	18.2 %	IRAQ	MOZAM	----

V21	GDP SHARE OF EXPORTS	1970	D2	P20	9.8 %	URU	HAITI	----
		1975	D4	P32	12.3 %	EGYPT	NIGER	----
		1980	D2	P19	9.3 %	USA	MOZAM	----
V22	EXPORT PARTNER CONCENTRATION	1970	D9	P87	52.4 %	YENO	JAMAI	----
		1975	D10	P95	64.1 %	NIGER	CANA	----
		1980	D10	P99	69.9 %	MEXI	-------	----
V23	TOTAL DEBT AS % OF GDP	1980	D8	P73	50.1 %	VENE	TANZA	----
V24	SHARE OF NEW FOREIGN PATENTS	1971	D9	P90	100 %	SINGA	TANZA	F19
		1975	D10	P92	100 %	SIERA	TANZA	----
		1978	D4	----	78 %	ITALY	UNKI	F19
V25	FOREIGN PROPERTY AS % OF GDP	1971	D2	P19	3.3 %	URU	ETHIA	----
		1975	D4	P36	4.4 %	RWAN	KORSO	----
		1978	D7	----	8.4 %	DOMI	ECUA	----
V26	GNP SHARE OF DEVELOPMENT AID	------	----	----	----- -----	-------	-------	----
V27	SHARE IN NOBEL PRIZE WINNERS	1970-79	D5	P45	0.0 %	SINGA	SOUAF	----
V28	GDP SHARE OF MANUFACTURING	1970	D3	P25	9.3 %	INDO	MALI	F16
		1975	D1	P10	5.6 %	KUWAI	YENO	F16
		1979	D3	P25	7.0 %	TOGO	GHANA	F16
V29	EXPORT SHARE OF MANUFACTURES	1970	D4	P35	4.9 %	ALGER	TOGO	----
		1975	D3	P26	2.9 %	PERU	BURMA	----
		1980	D1	P8	0.5 %	IRAQ	SAUDI	----
V30	LACK OF CIVIL LIBERTIES	1975	D8	P74	6	SAUDI	SUDAN	----
		1980	D10	P92	7	MOZAM	VINO	----
V31	LACK OF POLITICAL RIGHTS	1975	D9	P88	7	RWAN	TOGO	----
		1980	D9	P90	7	ROMA	TOGO	----
V32	RIOTS	1970-74	D2	P19	0	SAUDI	SWEDN	----
		1975-79	D2	P20	0	SINGA	TOGO	----
V33	PROTEST DEMONSTRATIONS	1970-74	D2	P15	0	SIERA	TANZA	----
		1975-79	D2	P13	0	SINGA	TOGO	----
V34	POLITICAL STRIKES	1970-74	D3	P29	0	SINGA	SRILA	----
		1975-79	D3	P29	0	SINGA	SUDAN	----
V35	MEMBER OF THE NONALIGNED MMT.	1970	----	----	1	SINGA	SRILA	----
		1976	----	----	1	SINGA	SRILA	----
		1981	----	----	1	SINGA	SRILA	----
V36	MEMBER OF THE OPEC	1970	----	----	0	SINGA	SOUAF	----
		1975	----	----	0	SINGA	SOUAF	----
		1980	----	----	0	SINGA	SOUAF	----
V37	MEMBER OF THE OECD	1970	----	----	0	SINGA	SOUAF	----
		1975	----	----	0	SINGA	SOUAF	----
		1980	----	----	0	SINGA	SOUAF	----
V38	MEMBER OF THE CMEA	1970	----	----	0	SINGA	SOUAF	----
		1975	----	----	0	SINGA	SOUAF	----
		1980	----	----	0	SINGA	SOUAF	----

V39	MEMBER OF THE WTO	1970	----	----	0		SINGA	SOUAF	----
		1975	----	----	0		SINGA	SOUAF	----
		1980	----	----	0		SINGA	SOUAF	----
V40	MEMBER OF THE NATO	1970	----	----	0		SINGA	SOUAF	----
		1975	----	----	0		SINGA	SOUAF	----
		1980	----	----	0		SINGA	SOUAF	----
V41	GDP SHARE OF INVESTMENTS	1970	D2	P11	11.7	%	ETHIA	GUATE	----
		1975	D4	P34	18.2	%	UNKI	YENO	----
		1979	D3	P20	16.1	%	MALI	UNKI	----
V42	GDP SHARE OF AGRICULTURE	1970	D10	P96	59.4	%	NIGER	BANGL	F16
		1975	D10	P96	62.0	%	GUINE	BANGL	F16
		1979	D10	P98	60.0	%	NEPAL	GHANA	F16
V43	GDP SHARE OF INDUSTRY	1970	D2	P17	15.9	%	JORDA	CAME	F16
		1975	D1	P8	12.0	%	YENO	CHAD	F16
		1979	D1	P4	11.4	%	GHANA	BANGL	F16
V44	GDP SHARE OF SERVICES	1970	D1	P5	24.7	%	BURU	NIGER	F16
		1975	D1	P7	26.0	%	BURU	IRAQ	F16
		1979	D1	P8	28.6	%	GHANA	GABON	F16
V45	HOMICIDES P. MIL. POPULATION	------	----	----	----- -----		-------	-------	----
V46	SUICIDES P. MIL. POPULATION	------	----	----	----- -----		-------	-------	----
V47	IMPORT PARTNERS	1970	R1	ITALY	29.5	%	LIBYA	YUGO	----
		1970	R2	GFR	9.1	%	SENE	SPAIN	----
		1970	R3	USA	7.9	%	SINGA	SWEDN	----
		1980	R1	ITALY	34.5	%	LIBYA	AURIA	----
		1980	R2	USA	9.2	%	SINGA	THAI	----
		1980	R3	UNKI	7.9	%	SENE	SRILA	----
V48	EXPORT PARTNERS	1970	R1	SAUDI	52.4	%	LEBA	JORDA	----
		1970	R2	ITALY	26.1	%	SAUDI	SWITZ	----
		1970	R3	YESO	10.3	%	YENO	-------	----
		1980	R1	SAUDI	69.9	%	JORDA	SUDAN	----
		1980	R2	ITALY	12.9	%	LIBYA	SUDAN	----
		1980	R3	UNARE	5.4	%	-------	-------	----
V49	PATENT SUPPLIERS	------	----	----	----- -----		-------	-------	----
V50	PROVENANCE OF FOREIGN FIRMS	------	----	----	----- -----		-------	-------	----
V51	FILM SUPPLIERS	1982	R1	INDIA	162		RWAN	TANZA	F117
		1982	R2	ITALY	144		PORTU	SPAIN	F117
		1982	R3	-------	0		-------	-------	F117

SOUTH AFRICA (SOUAF)

V1	INCOME PER CAPITA	1970	D7	P68	2309	$/CAP	SINGA	GREC	----
		1975	D7	P69	2490	$/CAP	URU	SINGA	----
		1980	D7	P68	2597	$/CAP	URU	GABON	F35
V2	TELEPHONES P. TSD. POPULATION	1970	D8	P75	70	1/TSD CAP	SINGA	URU	----
		1975	D8	P69	78	1/TSD CAP	ARGE	BULGA	----
		1980	D7	P67	112	1/TSD CAP	COSTA	HUNGA	----
V3	INFANT MORTALITY RATE	1980	D6	P56	100.6	1/TSD	UGADA	PERU	F5
V4	PHYSICIANS P. MIL. POPULATION	1970	D7	P61	486	1/MIL	DOMI	BRAZI	----
		1973	D6	----	496	1/MIL	BOLI	SAUDI	----
V5	ADULT LITERACY	------	----	----	----- -----		-------	-------	----
V6	DURATION OF SCHOOLING	------	----	----	----- -----		-------	-------	----
V7	STUDENT ENROLLMENT RATIO	1970	D5	P50	4.5	%	PARA	COLO	----
		1973	D5	----	4.8	%	HONDU	TRITO	----
V8	SHARE OF AGRICULTURAL LABOR	1970	D5	P51	31.1	%	CUBA	ZAMBI	----
V9	SHARE OF INDUSTRIAL LABOR	1970	D6	P53	33.8	%	CANA	SWEDN	----
V10	SHARE OF SERVICE LABOR	1970	D6	P58	30.7	%	ITALY	CUBA	----
V11	SHARE OF ACADEMIC LABOR	1970	D4	P33	4.5	%	SYRIA	MALAY	----
V12	SHARE OF SELF-EMPLOYED LABOR	------	----	----	----- -----		-------	-------	----
V13	MILITARY EXPENDITURES	1970	D7	P64	1.033	TSD MIL $	VENE	PORTU	F4
		1975	D8	P78	2.150	TSD MIL $	GREC	INDO	----
		1980	D9	P83	2.905	TSD MIL $	LIBYA	BELGI	F62
V14	MILITARY MANPOWER	1970	D5	P46	40	TSD CAP	FINLA	COLO	----
		1980	D7	P63	70	TSD CAP	PORTU	SWEDN	----
V15	MEN AT AGE 20 - 30	1970	D8	P72	1686	TSD CAP	YUGO	CANA	----
V16	POPULATION	1970	D8	P77	22.47	MIL CAP	CANA	ARGE	----
		1975	D8	P78	25.47	MIL CAP	COLO	ARGE	----
		1980	D8	P79	28.61	MIL CAP	ARGE	ETHIA	F35
V17	GROSS DOMESTIC PRODUCT	1970	D8	P80	51.891	TSD MIL $	DENMA	MEXI	----
		1975	D8	P78	63.409	TSD MIL $	AURIA	NIGRA	----
		1980	D9	P81	74.296	TSD MIL $	NIGRA	SWITZ	----
V18	SHARE IN WORLD IMPORTS	1970	D9	P85	11.860	1/TSD	NORWY	DENMA	F52
		1975	D8	P78	8.322	1/TSD	CHINA	FINLA	F52
		1980	D8	P79	9.045	1/TSD	YUGO	GDR	F52
V19	SHARE IN WORLD EXPORTS	1970	D8	P75	6.857	1/TSD	INDIA	CHINA	F45
		1975	D8	P72	6.265	1/TSD	SINGA	FINLA	F45
		1980	D7	P69	6.287	1/TSD	ROMA	MALAY	F45

V20	GDP SHARE OF IMPORTS	1970	D7	P65	21.8 %	TUNIS	CAME	F208
		1975	D4	P39	20.4 %	ITALY	CANA	F208
		1980	D5	P47	23.3 %	GFR	PHILI	F208
V21	GDP SHARE OF EXPORTS	1970	D4	P34	11.9 %	RWAN	MALI	F209
		1975	D4	P40	14.8 %	TANZA	FRANC	F209
		1980	D5	P41	15.8 %	HAITI	SYRIA	F209
V22	EXPORT PARTNER CONCENTRATION	1975	D5	P46	23.3 %	GUATE	MOZAM	F133
V23	TOTAL DEBT AS % OF GDP	------	----	----	----- -----	-------	-------	----
V24	SHARE OF NEW FOREIGN PATENTS	1976	D2	P19	68 %	HUNGA	ARGE	----
V25	FOREIGN PROPERTY AS % OF GDP	------	----	----	----- -----	-------	-------	----
V26	GNP SHARE OF DEVELOPMENT AID	------	----	----	----- -----	-------	-------	----
V27	SHARE IN NOBEL PRIZE WINNERS	1970-79	D5	P45	0.0 %	SOMA	SPAIN	----
V28	GDP SHARE OF MANUFACTURING	1970	D8	P79	23.4 %	NEWZ	MEXI	F16
		1975	D8	P80	23.3 %	MEXI	USA	F16
		1980	D8	P80	22.6 %	MALAY	USA	F16
V29	EXPORT SHARE OF MANUFACTURES	------	----	----	----- -----	-------	-------	----
V30	LACK OF CIVIL LIBERTIES	1975	D6	P54	5	SINGA	SPAIN	----
		1980	D8	P74	6	SAUDI	SYRIA	----
V31	LACK OF POLITICAL RIGHTS	1975	D4	P31	4	MEXI	VISO	----
		1980	D5	P47	5	SINGA	SUDAN	----
V32	RIOTS	1970-74	D9	P90	37	ARGE	KORSO	----
		1975-79	D10	P97	87	ITALY	IRAN	----
V33	PROTEST DEMONSTRATIONS	1970-74	D9	P86	32	PHILI	GFR	----
		1975-79	D9	P84	21	PHILI	LEBA	----
V34	POLITICAL STRIKES	1970-74	D9	P84	6	PERU	ISRA	----
		1975-79	D10	P94	15	GHANA	LEBA	----
V35	MEMBER OF THE NONALIGNED MMT.	1970	----	----	0	ROMA	SPAIN	----
		1976	----	----	0	ROMA	SPAIN	----
		1981	----	----	0	ROMA	SPAIN	----
V36	MEMBER OF THE OPEC	1970	----	----	0	SOMA	SPAIN	----
		1975	----	----	0	SOMA	SPAIN	----
		1980	----	----	0	SOMA	SPAIN	----
V37	MEMBER OF THE OECD	1970	----	----	0	SOMA	SRILA	----
		1975	----	----	0	SOMA	SRILA	----
		1980	----	----	0	SOMA	SRILA	----
V38	MEMBER OF THE CMEA	1970	----	----	0	SOMA	SPAIN	----
		1975	----	----	0	SOMA	SPAIN	----
		1980	----	----	0	SOMA	SPAIN	----
V39	MEMBER OF THE WTO	1970	----	----	0	SOMA	SPAIN	----
		1975	----	----	0	SOMA	SPAIN	----
		1980	----	----	0	SOMA	SPAIN	----

V40	MEMBER OF THE NATO	1970	----	----	0		SOMA	SPAIN	----
		1975	----	----	0		SOMA	SPAIN	----
		1980	----	----	0		SOMA	SPAIN	----
V41	GDP SHARE OF INVESTMENTS	1970	D9	P87	28.7	%	ZAMBI	FINLA	----
		1975	D9	P88	32.5	%	ZAIRE	FINLA	----
		1980	D8	P78	28.8	%	PARA	TUNIS	----
V42	GDP SHARE OF AGRICULTURE	1970	D3	P24	8.1	%	ITALY	ALGER	F16
		1975	D3	P26	8.3	%	JAMAI	ALGER	F16
		1980	D3	P24	6.6	%	GABON	AULIA	F16
V43	GDP SHARE OF INDUSTRY	1970	D9	P82	40.3	%	ARGE	AULIA	F16
		1975	D9	P87	42.9	%	PORTU	LIBE	F16
		1980	D10	P92	53.1	%	GFR	TRITO	F16
V44	GDP SHARE OF SERVICES	1970	D7	P64	51.6	%	ECUA	BOLI	F16
		1975	D7	P63	48.8	%	TUNIS	GFR	F16
		1980	D3	P28	40.3	%	MOZAM	EGYPT	F16
V45	HOMICIDES P. MIL. POPULATION	------	----	----	----- -----		-------	-------	----
V46	SUICIDES P. MIL. POPULATION	------	----	----	----- -----		-------	-------	----
V47	IMPORT PARTNERS	1970	R1	UNKI	22.1	%	NIGRA	SRILA	F133
		1970	R2	USA	16.7	%	PHILI	THAI	F133
		1970	R3	GFR	13.9	%	RWAN	SYRIA	F133
V48	EXPORT PARTNERS	------	----	----	----- -----		-------	-------	----
V49	PATENT SUPPLIERS	------	----	----	----- -----		-------	-------	----
V50	PROVENANCE OF FOREIGN FIRMS	1980	R1	UNKI	71.0	%	SIERA	SRILA	----
		1980	R2	USA	14.1	%	NORWY	SRILA	----
		1980	R3	GFR	4.8	%	PORTU	SWEDN	----
V51	FILM SUPPLIERS	------	----	----	----- -----		-------	-------	----

SPAIN (SPAIN)

V1	INCOME PER CAPITA	1970	D8	P75	4078	$/CAP	TRITO	LIBYA	----
		1975	D8	P76	5062	$/CAP	TRITO	ITALY	----
		1980	D8	P75	5305	$/CAP	IRE	TRITO	----
V2	TELEPHONES P. TSD. POPULATION	1970	D9	P81	135	1/TSD CAP	GDR	CZECH	----
		1975	D9	P81	220	1/TSD CAP	ISRA	GREC	----
		1980	D8	P80	315	1/TSD CAP	ISRA	ITALY	----
V3	INFANT MORTALITY RATE	1980	D2	P11	11.1	1/TSD	BELGI	IRE	----
V4	PHYSICIANS P. MIL. POPULATION	1980	D10	P91	2305	1/MIL	GFR	GREC	----
V5	ADULT LITERACY	1970	D9	P82	90.2	%	CHILE	ARGE	----
		1981	D10	P92	92.6	%	THAI	POLA	----

V6	DURATION OF SCHOOLING	1970	D8	P71	9.7	YR	ARGE	CZECH	F4
		1975	D9	P82	10.7	YR	POLA	AULIA	----
		1980	D10	P93	11.5	YR	NETH	JAPAN	----
V7	STUDENT ENROLLMENT RATIO	1970	D7	P66	8.9	%	EGYPT	SYRIA	----
		1975	D9	P83	20.4	%	YUGO	NORWY	----
		1980	D9	P81	23.1	%	YUGO	AURIA	----
V8	SHARE OF AGRICULTURAL LABOR	1970	D5	P46	25.2	%	VENE	IRE	----
		1976	D4	P46	21.2	%	BULGA	IRE	----
		1979	D5	P48	19.6	%	IRE	PORTU	----
V9	SHARE OF INDUSTRIAL LABOR	1970	D9	P88	40.9	%	UNKI	CZECH	----
		1976	D10	P90	39.0	%	TUNIS	IRAN	----
		1979	D9	P88	39.4	%	POLA	SINGA	----
V10	SHARE OF SERVICE LABOR	1970	D6	P53	28.3	%	BRAZI	ITALY	----
		1976	D7	P58	31.9	%	COLO	MEXI	----
		1979	D6	P49	34.4	%	PORTU	FINLA	----
V11	SHARE OF ACADEMIC LABOR	1970	D5	P47	5.7	%	GREC	JAPAN	----
		1976	D6	P56	7.9	%	EGYPT	ALGER	----
		1979	D4	P33	6.6	%	PHILI	CHILE	----
V12	SHARE OF SELF-EMPLOYED LABOR	1970	D4	P39	19.4	%	FRANC	SINGA	----
		1979	D5	P52	21.7	%	PORTU	TURKY	----
V13	MILITARY EXPENDITURES	1970	D8	P76	2.245	TSD MIL $	SWITZ	BELGI	----
		1975	D9	P84	3.081	TSD MIL $	TURKY	NIGRA	----
		1980	D9	P87	3.753	TSD MIL $	SWEDN	AULIA	----
V14	MILITARY MANPOWER	1970	D9	P86	365	TSD CAP	INDO	BRAZI	----
		1975	D9	P85	375	TSD CAP	UNKI	IRAN	----
		1980	D9	P89	341	TSD CAP	UNKI	IRAQ	----
V15	MEN AT AGE 20 - 30	1970	D8	P79	2409	TSD CAP	KORSO	THAI	F22
		1974	D8	P79	2515	TSD CAP	IRAN	EGYPT	F186
		1981	D8	P73	2766	TSD CAP	BURMA	IRAN	F22
V16	POPULATION	1970	D9	P84	33.78	MIL CAP	EGYPT	TURKY	----
		1975	D9	P84	35.60	MIL CAP	KORSO	EGYPT	----
		1980	D9	P82	37.43	MIL CAP	POLA	KORSO	----
V17	GROSS DOMESTIC PRODUCT	1970	D10	P91	137.741	TSD MIL $	BRAZI	CANA	----
		1975	D9	P90	180.202	TSD MIL $	NETH	BRAZI	----
		1980	D10	P91	198.576	TSD MIL $	NETH	CANA	----
V18	SHARE IN WORLD IMPORTS	1970	D9	P87	14.206	1/TSD	DENMA	GDR	----
		1975	D9	P90	17.860	1/TSD	BRAZI	SWEDN	----
		1980	D9	P90	16.616	1/TSD	SWEDN	SWITZ	----
V19	SHARE IN WORLD EXPORTS	1970	D8	P80	7.613	1/TSD	LIBYA	NORWY	----
		1975	D8	P79	8.752	1/TSD	AURIA	NIGRA	----
		1980	D9	P84	10.382	1/TSD	KUWAI	INDO	----
V20	GDP SHARE OF IMPORTS	1970	D3	P23	12.8	%	HAITI	UGADA	----
		1975	D2	P20	15.5	%	BURU	INDO	----
		1980	D3	P23	16.1	%	AULIA	AFGHA	----

V21 GDP SHARE OF EXPORTS	1970	D2	P12	6.5 %	GREC	ETHIA	----
	1975	D2	P13	7.3 %	USA	RWAN	----
	1980	D3	P21	9.8 %	MOZAM	PANA	----
V22 EXPORT PARTNER CONCENTRATION	1970	D1	P8	14.1 %	INDIA	CONGO	----
	1975	D1	P10	13.7 %	JORDA	TANZA	----
	1980	D2	P17	16.5 %	FRANC	INDIA	----
V23 TOTAL DEBT AS % OF GDP	------	----	----	----- -----	-------	-------	----
V24 SHARE OF NEW FOREIGN PATENTS	1970	D3	P24	75 %	URU	SWITZ	----
	1975	D3	P28	79 %	YUGO	SWEDN	----
	1980	D4	P36	84 %	ISRA	TUNIS	----
V25 FOREIGN PROPERTY AS % OF GDP	1971	D3	P30	4.9 %	TANZA	UPVO	----
	1975	D4	P33	4.2 %	BOLI	GREC	----
	1978	D5	----	3.9 %	CHAD	TANZA	----
V26 GNP SHARE OF DEVELOPMENT AID	------	----	----	----- -----	-------	-------	----
V27 SHARE IN NOBEL PRIZE WINNERS	1970-79	D5	P45	0.0 %	SOUAF	SRILA	----
V28 GDP SHARE OF MANUFACTURING	1970	D9	P85	25.4 %	SWEDN	CHILE	----
	1975	D9	P88	25.2 %	PHILI	UNKI	----
V29 EXPORT SHARE OF MANUFACTURES	1970	D8	P80	51.3 %	JAMAI	NETH	----
	1975	D9	P86	63.7 %	BELGI	YUGO	----
	1980	D9	P82	62.4 %	BELGI	FRANC	----
V30 LACK OF CIVIL LIBERTIES	1975	D6	P54	5	SOUAF	TAIWA	----
	1980	D2	P18	2	PORTU	TRITO	----
V31 LACK OF POLITICAL RIGHTS	1975	D5	P43	5	SINGA	THAI	----
	1980	D3	P21	2	PORTU	SRILA	----
V32 RIOTS	1970-74	D10	P93	45	VISO	FRANC	----
	1975-79	D10	P100	177	PORTU	-------	----
V33 PROTEST DEMONSTRATIONS	1970-74	D10	P95	67	PORTU	GREC	----
	1975-79	D10	P99	366	PORTU	USA	----
V34 POLITICAL STRIKES	1970-74	D10	P93	16	PAKI	CANA	----
	1975-79	D10	P100	114	BOLI	-------	----
V35 MEMBER OF THE NONALIGNED MMT.	1970	----	----	0	SOUAF	SWEDN	----
	1976	----	----	0	SOUAF	SWEDN	----
	1981	----	----	0	SOUAF	SWEDN	----
V36 MEMBER OF THE OPEC	1970	----	----	0	SOUAF	SRILA	----
	1975	----	----	0	SOUAF	SRILA	----
	1980	----	----	0	SOUAF	SRILA	----
V37 MEMBER OF THE OECD	1970	----	----	1	PORTU	SWEDN	----
	1975	----	----	1	PORTU	SWEDN	----
	1980	----	----	1	PORTU	SWEDN	----
V38 MEMBER OF THE CMEA	1970	----	----	0	SOUAF	SRILA	----
	1975	----	----	0	SOUAF	SRILA	----
	1980	----	----	0	SOUAF	SRILA	----

V39	MEMBER OF THE WTO	1970	----	----	0		SOUAF	SRILA	----
		1975	----	----	0		SOUAF	SRILA	----
		1980	----	----	0		SOUAF	SRILA	----
V40	MEMBER OF THE NATO	1970	----	----	0		SOUAF	SRILA	----
		1975	----	----	0		SOUAF	SRILA	----
		1980	----	----	0		SOUAF	SRILA	----
V41	GDP SHARE OF INVESTMENTS	1970	D8	P70	24.4 %		KENYA	IRE	----
		1975	D7	P70	26.5 %		AURIA	ECUA	----
		1980	D4	P31	20.7 %		CHILE	INDO	----
V42	GDP SHARE OF AGRICULTURE	1970	D3	P27	10.5 %		ALGER	ZAMBI	----
		1975	D3	P28	9.3 %		ALGER	JORDA	----
		1980	D3	P26	7.1 %		AULIA	CHILE	----
V43	GDP SHARE OF INDUSTRY	1970	D8	P73	37.1 %		NETH	TRITO	----
		1975	D8	P76	37.4 %		FINLA	AULIA	----
		1980	D6	P59	34.2 %		NIGER	UNKI	----
V44	GDP SHARE OF SERVICES	1970	D7	P69	52.4 %		MADA	FINLA	----
		1975	D8	P78	53.3 %		FINLA	AURIA	----
		1980	D9	P88	58.7 %		NEWZ	SINGA	----
V45	HOMICIDES P. MIL. POPULATION	1970	D1	P10	6.3 1/MIL CAP		NORWY	DENMA	F148
		1975	D1	P8	6.3 1/MIL CAP		DENMA	NETH	F148
		1979	D3	P28	10.6 1/MIL CAP		FRANC	CZECH	F148
V46	SUICIDES P. MIL. POPULATION	1970	D3	P25	42.2 1/MIL CAP		THAI	TRITO	----
		1975	D2	P18	38.4 1/MIL CAP		COLO	COSTA	----
		1979	D2	P16	41.2 1/MIL CAP		GREC	VENE	----
V47	IMPORT PARTNERS	1970	R1	USA	19.0 %		SAUDI	TRITO	----
		1970	R2	GFR	12.7 %		SOMA	TURKY	----
		1970	R3	FRANC	9.4 %		MEXI	-------	----
		1980	R1	USA	13.0 %		SAUDI	UNKI	----
		1980	R2	SAUDI	9.5 %		PANA	SRILA	----
		1980	R3	GFR	8.2 %		SAUDI	TUNIS	----
V48	EXPORT PARTNERS	1970	R1	USA	14.1 %		PHILI	TRITO	----
		1970	R2	GFR	11.8 %		ROMA	SWEDN	----
		1970	R3	FRANC	10.3 %		NETH	UPVO	----
		1980	R1	FRANC	16.5 %		NIGER	ALGER	----
		1980	R2	GFR	10.2 %		ROMA	ALGER	----
		1980	R3	ITALY	7.8 %		IVORY	SWITZ	----
V49	PATENT SUPPLIERS	1970	R1	USA	1556		SINGA	SWEDN	----
		1970	R2	GFR	974		PORTU	SWEDN	----
		1970	R3	FRANC	811		ROMA	SWITZ	----
		1980	R1	USA	1909		SINGA	SRILA	----
		1980	R2	GFR	1593		PORTU	SWEDN	----
		1980	R3	FRANC	1159		PORTU	SWEDN	----
V50	PROVENANCE OF FOREIGN FIRMS	1980	R1	USA	27.9 %		SINGA	SWEDN	----
		1980	R2	GFR	16.7 %		SENE	SWITZ	----
		1980	R3	UNKI	16.1 %		SENE	SWITZ	----

V51	FILM SUPPLIERS	1980	R1	USA	147		SINGA	SRILA	F119
		1980	R2	ITALY	93		SOMA	SUDAN	F119
		1980	R3	FRANC	47		RWAN	SYRIA	F119

SRI LANKA (SRILA)

V1	INCOME PER CAPITA	1970	D1	P8	198	$/CAP	BURU	INDIA	----
		1975	D2	P11	223	$/CAP	INDIA	HAITI	----
		1980	D2	P12	267	$/CAP	INDIA	TANZA	----
V2	TELEPHONES P. TSD. POPULATION	1970	D3	P30	5	1/TSD CAP	LIBE	IVORY	----
		1973	D3	----	5	1/TSD CAP	MOZAM	GHANA	----
		1980	D2	P20	6	1/TSD CAP	TANZA	ANGO	----
V3	INFANT MORTALITY RATE	1979	D4	P38	37.7	1/TSD	URU	ELSA	----
V4	PHYSICIANS P. MIL. POPULATION	1972	D5	----	253	1/MIL	ELSA	SYRIA	----
V5	ADULT LITERACY	1971	D6	P57	77.6	%	VENE	PANA	----
		1981	D9	P83	86.1	%	COLO	PANA	----
V6	DURATION OF SCHOOLING	1970	D7	P62	8.5	YR	PHILI	PANA	----
		1975	D4	P40	7.3	YR	CAME	TURKY	----
		1980	D6	P58	9.5	YR	VINO	AURIA	F35
V7	STUDENT ENROLLMENT RATIO	1970	D4	P31	1.2	%	MADA	SUDAN	----
		1975	D3	P27	1.3	%	MADA	SUDAN	----
		1980	D4	P33	2.8	%	SENE	IVORY	----
V8	SHARE OF AGRICULTURAL LABOR	1971	D8	P71	50.1	%	IRAN	SYRIA	----
		1980	D8	P80	46.2	%	MOROC	PARA	----
V9	SHARE OF INDUSTRIAL LABOR	1971	D4	P38	26.0	%	PERU	SYRIA	----
		1980	D5	P42	28.8	%	AFGHA	CANA	----
V10	SHARE OF SERVICE LABOR	1971	D2	P21	18.8	%	POLA	INDO	----
		1980	D3	P17	19.5	%	PAKI	SYRIA	----
V11	SHARE OF ACADEMIC LABOR	1971	D4	P39	5.0	%	BRAZI	NICA	----
		1980	D4	P27	5.5	%	GUATE	DOMI	----
V12	SHARE OF SELF-EMPLOYED LABOR	1971	D6	P57	28.2	%	TURKY	ELSA	----
		1980	D6	P57	27.4	%	TURKY	VENE	----
V13	MILITARY EXPENDITURES	1975	D3	P23	0.046	TSD MIL $	ELSA	SENE	----
		1980	D2	P20	0.057	TSD MIL $	GABON	PARA	----
V14	MILITARY MANPOWER	1970	D3	P26	10	TSD CAP	YESO	HAITI	----
		1975	D4	P31	18	TSD CAP	DOMI	YESO	----
		1980	D4	P32	18	TSD CAP	GUINE	IRE	----
V15	MEN AT AGE 20 - 30	1971	D7	P66	1119	TSD CAP	NETH	CZECH	----
		1974	D7	P66	1171	TSD CAP	GDR	NETH	F2
		1981	D6	P59	1391	TSD CAP	GDR	PERU	----

V16 POPULATION	1970	D7	P64	12.52	MIL CAP	AULIA	NETH	----
	1975	D7	P65	13.50	MIL CAP	KENYA	NETH	----
	1980	D7	P64	14.74	MIL CAP	AULIA	VENE	----
V17 GROSS DOMESTIC PRODUCT	1970	D3	P26	2.482	TSD MIL $	SENE	JAMAI	----
	1975	D3	P28	3.014	TSD MIL $	JAMAI	ETHIA	----
	1980	D3	P29	3.936	TSD MIL $	ZAMBI	ETHIA	----
V18 SHARE IN WORLD IMPORTS	1970	D5	P43	1.172	1/TSD	IVORY	GHANA	F30
	1975	D4	P36	0.826	1/TSD	GUATE	DOMI	F30
	1980	D5	P44	0.992	1/TSD	BANGL	ECUA	F30
V19 SHARE IN WORLD EXPORTS	1970	D5	P45	1.090	1/TSD	JAMAI	GHANA	F30
	1975	D4	P38	0.638	1/TSD	ELSA	GUATE	F30
	1980	D4	P38	0.522	1/TSD	BOLI	URU	F30
V20 GDP SHARE OF IMPORTS	1970	D6	P55	19.5	%	NEWZ	GREC	F30
	1975	D6	P58	25.4	%	YUGO	GREC	F30
	1980	D10	P95	50.6	%	TRITO	BELGI	F30
V21 GDP SHARE OF EXPORTS	1970	D6	P55	17.1	%	PERU	CENTR	F30
	1975	D6	P53	18.9	%	UNKI	SIERA	F30
	1980	D7	P68	25.9	%	TUNIS	DENMA	F30
V22 EXPORT PARTNER CONCENTRATION	1970	D4	P36	22.8	%	LIBE	AURIA	----
	1975	D1	P6	11.7	%	INDIA	USSR	----
V23 TOTAL DEBT AS % OF GDP	1980	D7	P67	47.8	%	KORSO	ECUA	----
V24 SHARE OF NEW FOREIGN PATENTS	1970	D5	P43	89	%	NETH	BOLI	----
	1975	D5	P46	89	%	NETH	HAITI	----
	1980	D9	P84	98	%	IRE	ECUA	----
V25 FOREIGN PROPERTY AS % OF GDP	1971	D5	P41	6.5	%	PARA	CHAD	----
	1975	D2	P18	2.0	%	LESO	IRAN	----
	1978	D3	----	2.6	%	MOROC	ETHIA	----
V26 GNP SHARE OF DEVELOPMENT AID	------	----	----	-----	-----	-------	-------	----
V27 SHARE IN NOBEL PRIZE WINNERS	1970-79	D5	P45	0.0	%	SPAIN	SUDAN	----
V28 GDP SHARE OF MANUFACTURING	1970	D6	P58	16.7	%	PARA	TURKY	F16
	1975	D8	P71	20.1	%	GREC	CHILE	F16
	1980	D7	P67	17.7	%	INDIA	CANA	F16
V29 EXPORT SHARE OF MANUFACTURES	1970	D2	P16	1.4	%	PERU	BURMA	----
	1975	D4	P32	3.8	%	BOLI	LAOS	----
	1980	D6	P51	18.6	%	PERU	COLO	----
V30 LACK OF CIVIL LIBERTIES	1975	D3	P27	3		PORTU	THAI	----
	1980	D3	P29	3		SENE	THAI	----
V31 LACK OF POLITICAL RIGHTS	1975	D2	P20	2		LEBA	TRITO	----
	1980	D3	P21	2		SPAIN	TRITO	----
V32 RIOTS	1970-74	D6	P59	3		NEPAL	TUNIS	----
	1975-79	D8	P75	7		JAPAN	TUNIS	----
V33 PROTEST DEMONSTRATIONS	1970-74	D6	P59	4		NEWZ	SUDAN	----
	1975-79	D5	P42	2		PARA	TAIWA	----

V34	POLITICAL STRIKES	1970-74	D3	P29	0		SOMA	SUDAN	----
		1975-79	D7	P63	1		ROMA	TUNIS	----
V35	MEMBER OF THE NONALIGNED MMT.	1970	----	----	1		SOMA	SUDAN	----
		1976	----	----	1		SOMA	SUDAN	----
		1981	----	----	1		SOMA	SUDAN	----
V36	MEMBER OF THE OPEC	1970	----	----	0		SPAIN	SUDAN	----
		1975	----	----	0		SPAIN	SUDAN	----
		1980	----	----	0		SPAIN	SUDAN	----
V37	MEMBER OF THE OECD	1970	----	----	0		SOUAF	SUDAN	----
		1975	----	----	0		SOUAF	SUDAN	----
		1980	----	----	0		SOUAF	SUDAN	----
V38	MEMBER OF THE CMEA	1970	----	----	0		SPAIN	SUDAN	----
		1975	----	----	0		SPAIN	SUDAN	----
		1980	----	----	0		SPAIN	SUDAN	----
V39	MEMBER OF THE WTO	1970	----	----	0		SPAIN	SUDAN	----
		1975	----	----	0		SPAIN	SUDAN	----
		1980	----	----	0		SPAIN	SUDAN	----
V40	MEMBER OF THE NATO	1970	----	----	0		SPAIN	SUDAN	----
		1975	----	----	0		SPAIN	SUDAN	----
		1980	----	----	0		SPAIN	SUDAN	----
V41	GDP SHARE OF INVESTMENTS	1970	D5	P45	18.9 %		JORDA	DOMI	----
		1975	D2	P20	15.6 %		MALI	SIERA	----
		1980	D10	P94	33.8 %		TOGO	YUGO	----
V42	GDP SHARE OF AGRICULTURE	1970	D7	P63	28.3 %		SIERA	THAI	F16
		1975	D7	P67	30.4 %		SENE	THAI	F16
		1980	D7	P64	27.6 %		COLO	ELSA	F16
V43	GDP SHARE OF INDUSTRY	1970	D4	P38	23.8 %		TUNIS	CONGO	F16
		1975	D4	P39	26.4 %		HONDU	TOGO	F16
		1980	D5	P43	29.6 %		JORDA	PAPUA	F16
V44	GDP SHARE OF SERVICES	1970	D6	P51	47.9 %		BURMA	ELSA	F16
		1975	D5	P43	43.2 %		SUDAN	THAI	F16
		1980	D4	P39	42.8 %		UPVO	KORSO	F16
V45	HOMICIDES P. MIL. POPULATION	1980	D7	P67	22.9 1/MIL CAP		CANA	BULGA	F2
V46	SUICIDES P. MIL. POPULATION	1968	D8	----	171.9 1/MIL CAP		BELGI	SWITZ	----
		1977	D8	----	200.0 1/MIL CAP		SWEDN	GFR	----
		1980	D10	P91	289.8 1/MIL CAP		AURIA	DENMA	F2
V47	IMPORT PARTNERS	1970	R1	UNKI	14.1 %		SOUAF	SUDAN	----
		1970	R2	CHINA	13.2 %		-------	TANZA	----
		1970	R3	JAPAN	8.8 %		PERU	VENE	----
		1980	R1	JAPAN	12.8 %		SINGA	THAI	----
		1980	R2	SAUDI	10.5 %		SPAIN	ZAMBI	----
		1980	R3	UNKI	9.5 %		SOMA	TRITO	----
V48	EXPORT PARTNERS	1970	R1	UNKI	22.8 %		PORTU	SWEDN	----
		1970	R2	CHINA	12.7 %		-------	-------	----
		1970	R3	USA	7.3 %		NIGRA	SWITZ	----

V49	PATENT SUPPLIERS	1970	R1	UNKI	18		NIGRA	UGADA	----
		1970	R2	SWITZ	9		POLA	ARGE	----
		1970	R3	USA	5		UGADA	USSR	----
		1980	R1	USA	216		SPAIN	SWEDN	----
		1980	R2	UNKI	107		NIGRA	TRITO	----
		1980	R3	SWITZ	77		NEWZ	TUNIS	----
V50	PROVENANCE OF FOREIGN FIRMS	1980	R1	UNKI	75.5	%	SOUAF	TANZA	----
		1980	R2	USA	16.3	%	SOUAF	TANZA	----
V51	FILM SUPPLIERS	1980	R1	USA	39		SPAIN	SUDAN	F120
		1980	R2	UNKI	34		NORWY	ZAMBI	F120
		1980	R3	INDIA	13		LIBYA	SUDAN	F120

SUDAN (SUDAN)

V1	INCOME PER CAPITA	------	----	----	----- -----		-------	-------	----
V2	TELEPHONES P. TSD. POPULATION	1980	D1	P9	3	1/TSD CAP	INDO	CHINA	----
V3	INFANT MORTALITY RATE	1980	D8	P78	131.1	1/TSD	TURKY	PAKI	F5
V4	PHYSICIANS P. MIL. POPULATION	1970	D3	P27	70	1/MIL	IVORY	MOROC	----
		1975	D3	P28	89	1/MIL	BANGL	GHANA	F147
		1979	D4	P30	119	1/MIL	ZAMBI	YESO	F147
V5	ADULT LITERACY	------	----	----	----- -----		-------	-------	----
V6	DURATION OF SCHOOLING	1970	D2	P16	2.9	YR	GUINE	TANZA	----
		1975	D2	P16	3.8	YR	RWAN	BENIN	----
		1980	D2	P12	4.2	YR	SENE	NEPAL	----
V7	STUDENT ENROLLMENT RATIO	1970	D4	P31	1.2	%	SRILA	KAMPU	----
		1975	D3	P30	1.5	%	SRILA	LIBE	----
		1980	D3	P25	1.8	%	PAPUA	BENIN	----
V8	SHARE OF AGRICULTURAL LABOR	1973	D9	----	71.8	%	INDO	YENO	F46
V9	SHARE OF INDUSTRIAL LABOR	1973	D2	----	11.5	%	BANGL	CAME	F46
V10	SHARE OF SERVICE LABOR	1973	D2	----	13.9	%	YENO	THAI	F46
V11	SHARE OF ACADEMIC LABOR	1973	D2	----	2.8	%	THAI	PAKI	F46
V12	SHARE OF SELF-EMPLOYED LABOR	1973	D10	----	62.7	%	BOLI	CAME	F46
V13	MILITARY EXPENDITURES	------	----	----	----- -----		-------	-------	----
V14	MILITARY MANPOWER	1970	D5	P41	25	TSD CAP	TANZA	SWITZ	----
		1975	D6	P52	50	TSD CAP	ETHIA	ALBA	----
		1980	D7	P61	65	TSD CAP	JORDA	PORTU	----
V15	MEN AT AGE 20 - 30	1980	D7	P62	1506	TSD CAP	PERU	MOROC	F2

V16	POPULATION	1970	D7	P69	14.09	MIL CAP	KORNO	ALGER	F4
		1975	D7	P70	15.73	MIL CAP	TANZA	KORNO	F22
		1980	D8	P72	18.68	MIL CAP	ALGER	MOROC	F182
V17	GROSS DOMESTIC PRODUCT	------	----	----	-----	-----	-------	-------	----
V18	SHARE IN WORLD IMPORTS	1970	D4	P36	0.868	1/TSD	GUATE	TUNIS	F30
		1975	D5	P44	1.136	1/TSD	KENYA	JAMAI	F30
		1980	D4	P39	0.768	1/TSD	YESO	GUATE	F30
V19	SHARE IN WORLD EXPORTS	1970	D5	P42	0.950	1/TSD	GUATE	KENYA	F30
		1975	D4	P32	0.500	1/TSD	LIBE	PAPUA	F30
		1980	D3	P24	0.272	1/TSD	TANZA	NIGER	F30
V20	GDP SHARE OF IMPORTS	1970	D4	P34	14.3	%	SOMA	VENE	F30
		1975	D6	P52	23.8	%	UPVO	PHILI	F30
		1980	D4	P36	19.4	%	ECUA	GUATE	F30
V21	GDP SHARE OF EXPORTS	1970	D5	P46	14.8	%	DOMI	CHILE	F30
		1975	D3	P23	10.1	%	PERU	URU	F30
		1980	D2	P12	6.7	%	RWAN	UPVO	F30
V22	EXPORT PARTNER CONCENTRATION	1970	D2	P16	16.8	%	LEBA	FINLA	----
		1975	D2	P15	14.4	%	CHILE	SWITZ	----
		1980	D5	P40	22.0	%	IVORY	GABON	----
V23	TOTAL DEBT AS % OF GDP	1980	D9	P82	57.5	%	COSTA	PERU	----
V24	SHARE OF NEW FOREIGN PATENTS	------	----	----	-----	-----	-------	-------	----
V25	FOREIGN PROPERTY AS % OF GDP	1971	D1	P8	1.6	%	AFGHA	SYRIA	----
		1975	D2	P11	1.3	%	SYRIA	TURKY	----
		1978	D1	----	0.8	%	BANGL	SYRIA	----
V26	GNP SHARE OF DEVELOPMENT AID	------	----	----	-----	-----	-------	-------	----
V27	SHARE IN NOBEL PRIZE WINNERS	1970-79	D5	P45	0.0	%	SRILA	SYRIA	----
V28	GDP SHARE OF MANUFACTURING	1970	D2	P16	7.9	%	CENTR	ZAIRE	F16
		1975	D2	P19	7.1	%	TOGO	BURU	F16
		1980	D2	P21	5.9	%	MALI	CONGO	F16
V29	EXPORT SHARE OF MANUFACTURES	------	----	----	-----	-----	-------	-------	----
V30	LACK OF CIVIL LIBERTIES	1975	D8	P74	6		SOMA	TANZA	----
		1980	D6	P52	5		SINGA	TAIWA	----
V31	LACK OF POLITICAL RIGHTS	1975	D7	P63	6		SIERA	SYRIA	----
		1980	D5	P47	5		SOUAF	SYRIA	----
V32	RIOTS	1970-74	D7	P64	4		COLO	UGADA	----
		1975-79	D5	P45	1		SIERA	SWEDN	----
V33	PROTEST DEMONSTRATIONS	1970-74	D6	P59	4		SRILA	TAIWA	----
		1975-79	D4	P32	1		SAUDI	TUNIS	----
V34	POLITICAL STRIKES	1970-74	D3	P29	0		SRILA	SWITZ	----
		1975-79	D3	P29	0		SOMA	SWEDN	----

V35 MEMBER OF THE NONALIGNED MMT.	1970	----	----	1	SRILA	SYRIA	----
	1976	----	----	1	SRILA	SYRIA	----
	1981	----	----	1	SRILA	SYRIA	----
V36 MEMBER OF THE OPEC	1970	----	----	0	SRILA	SWEDN	----
	1975	----	----	0	SRILA	SWEDN	----
	1980	----	----	0	SRILA	SWEDN	----
V37 MEMBER OF THE OECD	1970	----	----	0	SRILA	SYRIA	----
	1975	----	----	0	SRILA	SYRIA	----
	1980	----	----	0	SRILA	SYRIA	----
V38 MEMBER OF THE CMEA	1970	----	----	0	SRILA	SWEDN	----
	1975	----	----	0	SRILA	SWEDN	----
	1980	----	----	0	SRILA	SWEDN	----
V39 MEMBER OF THE WTO	1970	----	----	0	SRILA	SWEDN	----
	1975	----	----	0	SRILA	SWEDN	----
	1980	----	----	0	SRILA	SWEDN	----
V40 MEMBER OF THE NATO	1970	----	----	0	SRILA	SWEDN	----
	1975	----	----	0	SRILA	SWEDN	----
	1980	----	----	0	SRILA	SWEDN	----
V41 GDP SHARE OF INVESTMENTS	1970	D2	P18	13.6 %	INDO	SYRIA	----
	1975	D3	P25	17.5 %	USA	BENIN	----
	1980	D3	P24	16.7 %	BANGL	UPVO	----
V42 GDP SHARE OF AGRICULTURE	1970	D9	P83	42.9 %	UPVO	MALI	F16
	1975	D9	P86	43.2 %	MOZAM	YENO	F16
	1980	D9	P81	36.3 %	MADA	GUINE	F16
V43 GDP SHARE OF INDUSTRY	1970	D2	P14	14.9 %	NIGER	CENTR	F16
	1975	D2	P11	13.8 %	LESO	BENIN	F16
	1980	D1	P8	13.9 %	BURMA	CENTR	F16
V44 GDP SHARE OF SERVICES	1970	D3	P29	42.2 %	CHAD	EGYPT	F16
	1975	D5	P42	43.0 %	TANZA	SRILA	F16
	1980	D7	P61	49.8 %	MOROC	GFR	F16
V45 HOMICIDES P. MIL. POPULATION	------	----	----	----- -----	-------	-------	----
V46 SUICIDES P. MIL. POPULATION	------	----	----	----- -----	-------	-------	----
V47 IMPORT PARTNERS	1970	R1	UNKI	16.5 %	SRILA	TANZA	----
	1970	R2	INDIA	13.1 %	EGYPT	AFGHA	----
	1970	R3	USSR	7.7 %	MALI	YENO	----
	1980	R1	UNKI	13.1 %	NIGRA	TANZA	----
	1980	R2	GFR	9.3 %	POLA	SYRIA	----
	1980	R3	SAUDI	7.7 %	PHILI	THAI	----
V48 EXPORT PARTNERS	1970	R1	USSR	16.8 %	ROMA	YENO	----
	1970	R2	INDIA	10.2 %	-------	AFGHA	----
	1970	R3	ITALY	9.9 %	NIGER	ZAIRE	----
	1980	R1	SAUDI	22.0 %	SOMA	KORSO	----
	1980	R2	ITALY	12.6 %	SOMA	TUNIS	----
	1980	R3	JAPAN	8.6 %	SINGA	UPVO	----
V49 PATENT SUPPLIERS	------	----	----	----- -----	-------	-------	----

V50	PROVENANCE OF FOREIGN FIRMS	------	----	----	----- -----		-------	-------	----

V51	FILM SUPPLIERS	1979	R1	USA	97	SRILA	SWEDN	F119
		1979	R2	ITALY	21	SPAIN	VENE	F119
		1979	R3	INDIA	17	SRILA	-------	F119

SWEDEN (SWEDN)

V1	INCOME PER CAPITA	1970	D10	P98	11851 $/CAP	DENMA	SWITZ	F147
		1975	D10	P97	13218 $/CAP	DENMA	SWITZ	F147
		1980	D10	P96	13916 $/CAP	NORWY	SWITZ	F147
V2	TELEPHONES P. TSD. POPULATION	1970	D10	P99	557 1/TSD CAP	SWITZ	USA	----
		1975	D10	P98	661 1/TSD CAP	SWITZ	USA	----
		1980	D10	P99	796 1/TSD CAP	USA	-------	----
V3	INFANT MORTALITY RATE	1980	D1	P1	6.9 1/TSD	-------	JAPAN	----
V4	PHYSICIANS P. MIL. POPULATION	1970	D9	P83	1362 1/MIL	FRANC	DENMA	F147
		1975	D9	P83	1716 1/MIL	POLA	NORWY	F147
		1980	D9	P87	2202 1/MIL	DENMA	MONGO	F147
V5	ADULT LITERACY	------	----	----	----- -----	-------	-------	---
V6	DURATION OF SCHOOLING	1970	D9	P90	10.8 YR	NETH	AULIA	----
		1975	D9	P84	10.8 YR	AULIA	ITALY	----
		1980	D9	P81	10.9 YR	JORDA	KORSO	----
V7	STUDENT ENROLLMENT RATIO	1970	D10	P95	21.4 %	ISRA	LEBA	----
		1975	D10	P96	28.8 %	ECUA	DENMA	----
		1980	D10	P98	36.9 %	CANA	ECUA	----
V8	SHARE OF AGRICULTURAL LABOR	1970	D2	P14	8.0 %	ISRA	SWITZ	----
		1975	D1	P11	6.0 %	USA	NETH	F102
		1981	D1	P10	5.5 %	GFR	CANA	F102
V9	SHARE OF INDUSTRIAL LABOR	1970	D6	P56	34.4 %	SOUAF	POLA	----
		1975	D8	P73	36.1 %	KUWAI	LIBYA	F102
		1981	D6	P50	31.3 %	USA	NETH	F102
V10	SHARE OF SERVICE LABOR	1970	D8	P78	38.2 %	AURIA	JAPAN	----
		1975	D8	P69	35.6 %	FRANC	NEWZ	F102
		1981	D7	P60	36.4 %	IRE	PANA	F102
V11	SHARE OF ACADEMIC LABOR	1970	D10	P96	19.3 %	USA	CZECH	----
		1975	D10	P98	22.2 %	ISRA	-------	F102
		1981	D10	P98	26.8 %	ISRA	-------	F102
V12	SHARE OF SELF-EMPLOYED LABOR	1970	D2	P18	8.9 %	UNKI	SWITZ	----
		1975	D1	P3	7.4 %	-------	USA	F102
		1981	D1	P11	7.5 %	USA	GFR	F102

V13 MILITARY EXPENDITURES	1970	D9	P83	3.402	TSD MIL $	INDIA	AULIA	----
	1975	D9	P88	3.507	TSD MIL $	AULIA	CANA	----
	1980	D9	P86	3.735	TSD MIL $	KORSO	SPAIN	----
V14 MILITARY MANPOWER	1970	D6	P60	75	TSD CAP	JORDA	SYRIA	----
	1975	D6	P59	75	TSD CAP	MOROC	MALAY	----
	1980	D7	P63	70	TSD CAP	SOUAF	BANGL	----
V15 MEN AT AGE 20 - 30	1970	D5	P47	664	TSD CAP	BELGI	CHILE	F22
	1975	D5	P52	621	TSD CAP	IVORY	GREC	F22
	1980	D4	P33	583	TSD CAP	ZIMBA	GUATE	F22
V16 POPULATION	1970	D5	P50	8.04	MIL CAP	AURIA	BULGA	F22
	1975	D6	P52	8.19	MIL CAP	MADA	BULGA	F22
	1980	D5	P48	8.31	MIL CAP	IVORY	ECUA	F22
V17 GROSS DOMESTIC PRODUCT	1970	D9	P84	95.283	TSD MIL $	SWITZ	AULIA	----
	1975	D9	P86	108.255	TSD MIL $	MEXI	AULIA	----
	1980	D9	P85	115.643	TSD MIL $	BELGI	AULIA	----
V18 SHARE IN WORLD IMPORTS	1970	D10	P91	21.108	1/TSD	SWITZ	BELGI	F30
	1975	D10	P91	19.650	1/TSD	SPAIN	BELGI	F30
	1980	D9	P89	16.345	1/TSD	SAUDI	SPAIN	F30
V19 SHARE IN WORLD EXPORTS	1970	D10	P91	21.659	1/TSD	SWITZ	BELGI	F30
	1975	D9	P89	19.837	1/TSD	SWITZ	IRAN	F30
	1980	D9	P90	15.516	1/TSD	SWITZ	BELGI	F30
V20 GDP SHARE OF IMPORTS	1970	D7	P63	21.0	%	YUGO	TUNIS	F30
	1975	D6	P55	24.7	%	SWITZ	AURIA	F30
	1980	D7	P62	27.0	%	UPVO	ELSA	F30
V21 GDP SHARE OF EXPORTS	1970	D7	P67	20.4	%	TANZA	GHANA	F30
	1975	D7	P70	24.0	%	KORSO	NICA	F30
	1980	D7	P65	24.9	%	CANA	TUNIS	F30
V22 EXPORT PARTNER CONCENTRATION	1970	D1	P4	12.5	%	GFR	URU	----
	1975	D1	P4	11.1	%	ARGE	GFR	----
	1980	D1	P7	12.2	%	BANGL	BURMA	----
V23 TOTAL DEBT AS % OF GDP	------	----	----	-----	-----	-------	-------	----
V24 SHARE OF NEW FOREIGN PATENTS	1970	D3	P29	79	%	FINLA	BRAZI	----
	1975	D3	P28	79	%	SPAIN	COLO	----
	1980	D3	P25	72	%	HAITI	SWITZ	----
V25 FOREIGN PROPERTY AS % OF GDP	------	----	----	-----	-----	-------	-------	----
V26 GNP SHARE OF DEVELOPMENT AID	1970	D6	P61	0.35	%	NORWY	DENMA	----
	1975	D8	P77	0.78	%	NETH	IRAN	----
	1980	D8	P71	0.78	%	DENMA	NORWY	----
V27 SHARE IN NOBEL PRIZE WINNERS	1970-79	D10	P98	5.0	%	BELGI	UNKI	----
V28 GDP SHARE OF MANUFACTURING	1970	D9	P84	25.0	%	FINLA	SPAIN	----
	1975	D10	P92	26.3	%	KORSO	BELGI	----
	1980	D8	P77	21.7	%	CHILE	COLO	----
V29 EXPORT SHARE OF MANUFACTURES	------	----	----	-----	-----	-------	-------	----

V30	LACK OF CIVIL LIBERTIES	1975	D1	P7	1		NORWY	SWITZ	----
		1980	D1	P7	1		NORWY	SWITZ	----
V31	LACK OF POLITICAL RIGHTS	1975	D1	P8	1		NORWY	SWITZ	----
		1980	D1	P8	1		NORWY	SWITZ	----
V32	RIOTS	1970-74	D2	P19	0		SOMA	TANZA	----
		1975-79	D5	P45	1		SUDAN	TANZA	----
V33	PROTEST DEMONSTRATIONS	1970-74	D8	P79	14		KAMPU	ETHIA	----
		1975-79	D5	P49	3		SIERA	SYRIA	----
V34	POLITICAL STRIKES	1970-74	D7	P64	1		NORWY	YUGO	----
		1975-79	D3	P29	0		SUDAN	SWITZ	----
V35	MEMBER OF THE NONALIGNED MMT.	1970	----	----	0		SPAIN	SWITZ	----
		1976	----	----	0		SPAIN	SWITZ	----
		1981	----	----	0		SPAIN	SWITZ	----
V36	MEMBER OF THE OPEC	1970	----	----	0		SUDAN	SWITZ	----
		1975	----	----	0		SUDAN	SWITZ	----
		1980	----	----	0		SUDAN	SWITZ	----
V37	MEMBER OF THE OECD	1970	----	----	1		SPAIN	SWITZ	----
		1975	----	----	1		SPAIN	SWITZ	----
		1980	----	----	1		SPAIN	SWITZ	----
V38	MEMBER OF THE CMEA	1970	----	----	0		SUDAN	SWITZ	----
		1975	----	----	0		SUDAN	SWITZ	----
		1980	----	----	0		SUDAN	SWITZ	----
V39	MEMBER OF THE WTO	1970	----	----	0		SUDAN	SWITZ	----
		1975	----	----	0		SUDAN	SWITZ	----
		1980	----	----	0		SUDAN	SWITZ	----
V40	MEMBER OF THE NATO	1970	----	----	0		SUDAN	SWITZ	----
		1975	----	----	0		SUDAN	SWITZ	----
		1980	----	----	0		SUDAN	SWITZ	----
V41	GDP SHARE OF INVESTMENTS	1970	D8	P73	25.6 %		IRE	DENMA	----
		1975	D7	P61	24.2 %		PARA	DOMI	----
		1980	D4	P35	21.4 %		NETH	BURMA	----
V42	GDP SHARE OF AGRICULTURE	1970	D1	P9	4.1 %		CANA	TRITO	----
		1975	D2	P11	4.4 %		NETH	CANA	----
		1980	D2	P12	3.2 %		USA	NETH	----
V43	GDP SHARE OF INDUSTRY	1970	D7	P70	35.9 %		FINLA	ZAIRE	----
		1975	D8	P73	36.2 %		NORWY	UNKI	----
		1980	D6	P52	31.5 %		NEWZ	MOROC	----
V44	GDP SHARE OF SERVICES	1970	D10	P92	60.0 %		NORWY	USA	----
		1975	D10	P91	59.4 %		NORWY	NETH	----
		1980	D10	P97	65.3 %		NETH	PANA	----
V45	HOMICIDES P. MIL. POPULATION	1970	D3	P24	8.3	1/MIL CAP	ITALY	POLA	F153
		1975	D4	P35	11.5	1/MIL CAP	NEWZ	GFR	F153
		1980	D4	P40	11.7	1/MIL CAP	GFR	AURIA	F153

V46	SUICIDES P. MIL. POPULATION	1970	D9	P89	222.6	1/MIL CAP	GFR	AURIA	F150
		1975	D8	P79	194.1	1/MIL CAP	JAPAN	SRILA	F150
		1980	D7	P69	193.7	1/MIL CAP	FRANC	CZECH	F150
V47	IMPORT PARTNERS	1970	R1	GFR	18.9	%	PORTU	SWITZ	----
		1970	R2	UNKI	13.8	%	PORTU	TOGO	----
		1970	R3	USA	8.7	%	SOMA	ZAMBI	----
		1980	R1	GFR	16.8	%	PORTU	SWITZ	----
		1980	R2	UNKI	11.9	%	NORWY	AULIA	----
		1980	R3	USA	7.3	%	PARA	UPVO	----
V48	EXPORT PARTNERS	1970	R1	UNKI	12.5	%	SRILA	TANZA	----
		1970	R2	GFR	11.7	%	SPAIN	UNKI	----
		1970	R3	NORWY	10.8	%	-------	-------	----
		1980	R1	GFR	12.2	%	NETH	SWITZ	----
		1980	R2	UNKI	10.0	%	JAMAI	TANZA	----
		1980	R3	NORWY	9.8	%	JAMAI	-------	----
V49	PATENT SUPPLIERS	1970	R1	USA	3846		SPAIN	TANZA	----
		1970	R2	GFR	2203		SPAIN	TURKY	----
		1970	R3	UNKI	1147		PORTU	TANZA	----
		1980	R1	USA	1037		SRILA	SYRIA	----
		1980	R2	GFR	792		SPAIN	UNKI	----
		1980	R3	FRANC	250		SPAIN	SWITZ	----
V50	PROVENANCE OF FOREIGN FIRMS	1980	R1	USA	28.8	%	SPAIN	SWITZ	----
		1980	R2	UNKI	23.2	%	SINGA	VENE	----
		1980	R3	GFR	11.2	%	SOUAF	TANZA	----
V51	FILM SUPPLIERS	1979	R1	USA	167		SUDAN	SWITZ	F120
		1979	R2	FRANC	45		NETH	SWITZ	F120
		1979	R3	UNKI	23		NICA	TANZA	F120

SWITZERLAND (SWITZ)

V1	INCOME PER CAPITA	1970	D10	P99	13759	$/CAP	SWEDN	-------	F147
		1975	D10	P98	14013	$/CAP	SWEDN	KUWAI	F147
		1980	D10	P97	15277	$/CAP	SWEDN	KUWAI	F147
V2	TELEPHONES P. TSD. POPULATION	1970	D10	P98	482	1/TSD CAP	CANA	SWEDN	----
		1975	D10	P97	613	1/TSD CAP	CANA	SWEDN	----
		1980	D10	P97	727	1/TSD CAP	CANA	USA	----
V3	INFANT MORTALITY RATE	1980	D1	P6	9.1	1/TSD	NETH	FRANC	----
V4	PHYSICIANS P. MIL. POPULATION	1975	D9	P87	1789	1/MIL	DENMA	GDR	F147
		1980	D10	P94	2439	1/MIL	GREC	BULGA	F147
V5	ADULT LITERACY	------	----	----	-----	-----	-------	-------	----
V6	DURATION OF SCHOOLING	------	----	----	-----	-----	-------	-------	----

V7	STUDENT ENROLLMENT RATIO	1970	D7	P70	10.0 %	CHILE	URU	----
		1975	D7	P69	13.6 %	SYRIA	EGYPT	----
		1980	D8	P76	20.5 %	VENE	IRE	----
V8	SHARE OF AGRICULTURAL LABOR	1970	D2	P16	8.1 %	SWEDN	AULIA	----
		1980	D2	P19	6.6 %	NETH	AULIA	----
V9	SHARE OF INDUSTRIAL LABOR	1970	D8	P78	40.0 %	NEWZ	AURIA	----
		1980	D7	P65	35.1 %	YUGO	FINLA	----
V10	SHARE OF SERVICE LABOR	1970	D9	P83	39.6 %	JAPAN	NETH	----
		1980	D9	P83	42.9 %	COSTA	GFR	----
V11	SHARE OF ACADEMIC LABOR	1970	D9	P83	12.3 %	UNKI	FRANC	----
		1980	D9	P84	15.4 %	CANA	USA	----
V12	SHARE OF SELF-EMPLOYED LABOR	1970	D2	P21	10.4 %	SWEDN	AULIA	----
		1980	D2	P16	9.7 %	GFR	FINLA	----
V13	MILITARY EXPENDITURES	1970	D8	P74	1.915 TSD MIL $	NORWY	SPAIN	----
		1975	D8	P75	1.805 TSD MIL $	SYRIA	KORSO	----
		1980	D8	P75	2.021 TSD MIL $	CHILE	INDO	----
V14	MILITARY MANPOWER	1970	D5	P41	25 TSD CAP	SUDAN	TUNIS	----
		1975	D4	P40	25 TSD CAP	LIBYA	TANZA	----
		1980	D4	P36	23 TSD CAP	LEBA	YESO	----
V15	MEN AT AGE 20 - 30	1970	D4	P38	528 TSD CAP	AURIA	PORTU	F22
		1975	D5	P42	500 TSD CAP	CAME	ECUA	F22
		1980	D3	P28	483 TSD CAP	BOLI	TUNIS	F22
V16	POPULATION	1970	D5	P46	6.27 MIL CAP	SYRIA	CAME	F22
		1975	D5	P43	6.41 MIL CAP	MALI	ANGO	F22
		1980	D5	P41	6.39 MIL CAP	UPVO	TUNIS	F22
V17	GROSS DOMESTIC PRODUCT	1970	D9	P83	86.270 TSD MIL $	BELGI	SWEDN	----
		1975	D9	P82	89.824 TSD MIL $	SAUDI	BELGI	----
		1980	D9	P82	97.619 TSD MIL $	SOUAF	SAUDI	----
V18	SHARE IN WORLD IMPORTS	1970	D9	P90	19.538 1/TSD	AULIA	SWEDN	----
		1975	D9	P88	14.635 1/TSD	POLA	BRAZI	----
		1980	D10	P91	17.725 1/TSD	SPAIN	CANA	----
V19	SHARE IN WORLD EXPORTS	1970	D9	P90	16.425 1/TSD	AULIA	SWEDN	----
		1975	D9	P88	14.787 1/TSD	AULIA	SWEDN	----
		1980	D9	P89	14.847 1/TSD	NIGRA	SWEDN	----
V20	GDP SHARE OF IMPORTS	1970	D9	P88	31.3 %	HONDU	COSTA	----
		1975	D6	P54	24.5 %	PHILI	SWEDN	----
		1980	D8	P78	35.8 %	KORSO	KENYA	----
V21	GDP SHARE OF EXPORTS	1970	D9	P83	24.8 %	HONDU	IRAN	----
		1975	D7	P68	23.9 %	INDO	KORSO	----
		1980	D8	P74	29.1 %	MAURA	TOGO	----
V22	EXPORT PARTNER CONCENTRATION	1970	D1	P10	14.6 %	CONGO	USSR	----
		1975	D2	P16	14.6 %	SUDAN	GHANA	----
		1980	D4	P32	19.7 %	DENMA	GHANA	----
V23	TOTAL DEBT AS % OF GDP	------	----	----	----- -----	-------	-------	----

V24	SHARE OF NEW FOREIGN PATENTS	1970	D3	P24	75	%	SPAIN	UNKI	----
		1975	D2	P21	72	%	ARGE	FINLA	----
		1980	D3	P27	75	%	SWEDN	FINLA	----
V25	FOREIGN PROPERTY AS % OF GDP	------	----	----	-----	-----	-------	-------	----
V26	GNP SHARE OF DEVELOPMENT AID	1970	D4	P33	0.14	%	IRAQ	ITALY	----
		1975	D2	P20	0.18	%	FINLA	ALGER	----
		1980	D3	P30	0.24	%	AURIA	USA	----
V27	SHARE IN NOBEL PRIZE WINNERS	1970-79	D10	P94	2.5	%	GFR	USSR	----
V28	GDP SHARE OF MANUFACTURING	------	----	----	-----	-----	-------	-------	----
V29	EXPORT SHARE OF MANUFACTURES	1970	D10	P99	88.3	%	GFR	-------	----
		1975	D10	P99	89.8	%	GFR	-------	----
		1980	D10	P99	88.9	%	ISRA	-------	----
V30	LACK OF CIVIL LIBERTIES	1975	D1	P7	1		SWEDN	UNKI	----
		1980	D1	P7	1		SWEDN	UNKI	----
V31	LACK OF POLITICAL RIGHTS	1975	D1	P8	1		SWEDN	UNKI	----
		1980	D1	P8	1		SWEDN	UNKI	----
V32	RIOTS	1970-74	D6	P53	2		NETH	TAIWA	----
		1975-79	D6	P53	2		SAUDI	BELGI	----
V33	PROTEST DEMONSTRATIONS	1970-74	D8	P74	9		MEXI	THAI	----
		1975-79	D6	P59	5		ROMA	AURIA	----
V34	POLITICAL STRIKES	1970-74	D3	P29	0		SUDAN	SYRIA	----
		1975-79	D3	P29	0		SWEDN	SYRIA	----
V35	MEMBER OF THE NONALIGNED MMT.	1970	----	----	0		SWEDN	TAIWA	----
		1976	----	----	0		SWEDN	TAIWA	----
		1981	----	----	0		SWEDN	TAIWA	----
V36	MEMBER OF THE OPEC	1970	----	----	0		SWEDN	SYRIA	----
		1975	----	----	0		SWEDN	SYRIA	----
		1980	----	----	0		SWEDN	SYRIA	----
V37	MEMBER OF THE OECD	1970	----	----	1		SWEDN	TURKY	----
		1975	----	----	1		SWEDN	TURKY	----
		1980	----	----	1		SWEDN	TURKY	----
V38	MEMBER OF THE CMEA	1970	----	----	0		SWEDN	SYRIA	----
		1975	----	----	0		SWEDN	SYRIA	----
		1980	----	----	0		SWEDN	SYRIA	----
V39	MEMBER OF THE WTO	1970	----	----	0		SWEDN	SYRIA	----
		1975	----	----	0		SWEDN	SYRIA	----
		1980	----	----	0		SWEDN	SYRIA	----
V40	MEMBER OF THE NATO	1970	----	----	0		SWEDN	SYRIA	----
		1975	----	----	0		SWEDN	SYRIA	----
		1980	----	----	0		SWEDN	SYRIA	----
V41	GDP SHARE OF INVESTMENTS	1970	D10	P94	32.3	%	JAMAI	YUGO	----
		1975	D6	P53	23.0	%	FRANC	MALAY	----
		1980	D7	P66	27.1	%	COSTA	THAI	----

SWITZ

V42	GDP SHARE OF AGRICULTURE	------	----	----	----- -----	-------	-------	----
V43	GDP SHARE OF INDUSTRY	------	----	----	----- -----	-------	-------	----
V44	GDP SHARE OF SERVICES	------	----	----	----- -----	-------	-------	----
V45	HOMICIDES P. MIL. POPULATION	1970	D2	P15	7.0 1/MIL CAP	DENMA	FRANC	F149
		1975	D3	P21	9.4 1/MIL CAP	IRE	FRANC	F149
		1980	D2	P16	9.4 1/MIL CAP	KUWAI	JAPAN	F148
V46	SUICIDES P. MIL. POPULATION	1970	D8	P80	183.4 1/MIL CAP	SRILA	FINLA	F147
		1975	D9	P86	222.9 1/MIL CAP	CZECH	DENMA	F147
		1980	D9	P82	253.7 1/MIL CAP	BELGI	FINLA	----
V47	IMPORT PARTNERS	1970	R1	GFR	29.9 %	SWEDN	YUGO	----
		1970	R2	FRANC	12.1 %	KAMPU	IRAQ	----
		1970	R3	ITALY	9.4 %	MADA	-------	----
		1980	R1	GFR	27.7 %	SWEDN	ALGER	----
		1980	R2	FRANC	12.3 %	MALI	ZAIRE	----
		1980	R3	ITALY	9.6 %	NIGER	SYRIA	----
V48	EXPORT PARTNERS	1970	R1	GFR	14.6 %	NORWY	TURKY	----
		1970	R2	ITALY	9.4 %	SOMA	TUNIS	----
		1970	R3	USA	9.0 %	SRILA	-------	----
		1980	R1	GFR	19.7 %	SWEDN	TANZA	----
		1980	R2	FRANC	9.2 %	ITALY	TOGO	----
		1980	R3	ITALY	7.9 %	SPAIN	VENE	----
V49	PATENT SUPPLIERS	1970	R1	GFR	4669	ROMA	USA	----
		1970	R2	USA	3090	PAKI	SYRIA	----
		1970	R3	FRANC	1147	SPAIN	-------	----
		1980	R1	GFR	1418	ROMA	TURKY	----
		1980	R2	USA	981	ROMA	TUNIS	----
		1980	R3	FRANC	537	SWEDN	USSR	----
V50	PROVENANCE OF FOREIGN FIRMS	1980	R1	USA	29.7 %	SWEDN	THAI	----
		1980	R2	GFR	21.1 %	SPAIN	TURKY	----
		1980	R3	UNKI	19.1 %	SPAIN	TOGO	----
V51	FILM SUPPLIERS	1980	R1	USA	258	SWEDN	TRITO	F118
		1980	R2	FRANC	90	SWEDN	TURKY	F118
		1980	R3	ITALY	55	SINGA	TRITO	F118

SYRIA (SYRIA)

V1	INCOME PER CAPITA	1970	D5	P41	821 $/CAP	PARA	NIGRA	F218
		1975	D6	P57	1334 $/CAP	COSTA	JAMAI	F217
		1980	D6	P53	1431 $/CAP	TURKY	COSTA	F217

V2	TELEPHONES P. TSD. POPULATION	1970	D6	P55	18	1/TSD CAP	PERU	BRAZI	----
		1975	D5	P47	22	1/TSD CAP	MONGO	TUNIS	----
		1980	D5	P45	32	1/TSD CAP	IRAN	ECUA	----
V3	INFANT MORTALITY RATE	------	----	----	----- -----		-------	-------	----
V4	PHYSICIANS P. MIL. POPULATION	1970	D5	P45	259	1/MIL	SRILA	HONDU	----
		1975	D5	P46	323	1/MIL	PHILI	IRAN	----
		1980	D5	P48	432	1/MIL	IRAN	CHINA	----
V5	ADULT LITERACY	1970	D3	P25	40.0	%	INDIA	ZAMBI	F28
V6	DURATION OF SCHOOLING	1970	D5	P48	7.3	YR	GHANA	COLO	----
		1975	D6	P55	8.5	YR	LESO	MALAY	----
		1980	D6	P52	9.2	YR	MALAY	MONGO	----
V7	STUDENT ENROLLMENT RATIO	1970	D7	P67	9.2	%	SPAIN	BOLI	----
		1975	D7	P68	12.1	%	CZECH	SWITZ	----
		1980	D8	P70	16.9	%	GREC	CZECH	----
V8	SHARE OF AGRICULTURAL LABOR	1970	D8	P73	50.9	%	SRILA	KORSO	F88
		1975	D7	P71	51.2	%	ECUA	PHILI	----
		1979	D6	P63	32.2	%	MEXI	DOMI	----
V9	SHARE OF INDUSTRIAL LABOR	1970	D5	P41	28.3	%	SRILA	IRAN	F88
		1975	D5	P46	28.0	%	COLO	CANA	----
		1979	D9	P84	38.4	%	KUWAI	PORTU	----
V10	SHARE OF SERVICE LABOR	1970	D1	P11	16.3	%	INDIA	HAITI	F88
		1975	D3	P23	16.2	%	THAI	HONDU	----
		1979	D3	P19	20.1	%	SRILA	MOROC	----
V11	SHARE OF ACADEMIC LABOR	1970	D4	P31	4.4	%	PARA	SOUAF	F88
		1975	D4	P35	4.6	%	YENO	TURKY	----
		1979	D6	P52	9.4	%	SINGA	GREC	----
V12	SHARE OF SELF-EMPLOYED LABOR	1970	D9	P93	40.6	%	INDO	PERU	F88
		1975	D7	P62	38.0	%	IRAN	ECUA	----
		1979	D7	P75	35.3	%	MEXI	KORSO	----
V13	MILITARY EXPENDITURES	1970	D6	P60	0.573	TSD MIL $	AURIA	VENE	F4
		1975	D8	P73	1.603	TSD MIL $	NORWY	SWITZ	----
		1980	D8	P77	2.088	TSD MIL $	INDO	NIGRA	F62
V14	MILITARY MANPOWER	1970	D6	P60	75	TSD CAP	SWEDN	ALGER	----
		1975	D8	P80	230	TSD CAP	THAI	JAPAN	----
		1980	D9	P84	250	TSD CAP	INDO	YUGO	----
V15	MEN AT AGE 20 - 30	1970	D4	P33	408	TSD CAP	FINLA	DENMA	F176
		1976	D5	P49	565	TSD CAP	MADA	IVORY	F191
		1981	D5	P42	762	TSD CAP	MOZAM	CUBA	F191
V16	POPULATION	1970	D5	P46	6.26	MIL CAP	SAUDI	SWITZ	F177
		1975	D5	P48	7.44	MIL CAP	SAUDI	AURIA	F176
		1980	D6	P52	8.98	MIL CAP	BULGA	SAUDI	F176
V17	GROSS DOMESTIC PRODUCT	1970	D5	P46	5.141	TSD MIL $	SINGA	URU	----
		1975	D5	P49	9.923	TSD MIL $	BANGL	MOROC	----
		1980	D5	P50	12.849	TSD MIL $	BANGL	MOROC	----

V18	SHARE IN WORLD IMPORTS	1970	D4	P40	1.075	1/TSD	PANA	VISO	----
		1975	D6	P51	1.854	1/TSD	COLO	PAKI	----
		1980	D6	P51	2.011	1/TSD	TUNIS	MOROC	----
V19	SHARE IN WORLD EXPORTS	1970	D4	P34	0.647	1/TSD	LEBA	LIBE	----
		1975	D5	P47	1.061	1/TSD	ECUA	GABON	----
		1980	D5	P45	1.056	1/TSD	ZAIRE	GABON	----
V20	GDP SHARE OF IMPORTS	1970	D6	P58	19.9	%	GREC	THAI	----
		1975	D8	P71	30.1	%	SIERA	TANZA	----
		1980	D8	P70	31.2	%	UNARE	COSTA	----
V21	GDP SHARE OF EXPORTS	1970	D4	P31	11.3	%	ECUA	RWAN	----
		1975	D5	P45	16.6	%	PANA	GUATE	----
		1980	D5	P42	16.0	%	SOUAF	SENE	----
V22	EXPORT PARTNER CONCENTRATION	1970	D3	P30	21.5	%	USA	ITALY	----
		1975	D3	P25	18.1	%	ROMA	ITALY	----
		1980	D10	P92	55.3	%	CENTR	HAITI	----
V23	TOTAL DEBT AS % OF GDP	1980	D2	P19	20.7	%	ETHIA	COLO	----
V24	SHARE OF NEW FOREIGN PATENTS	1970	D7	P67	96	%	PHILI	DOMI	----
		1975	D8	P79	97	%	IRE	MALAW	----
		1980	D7	P72	94	%	PANA	PAKI	----
V25	FOREIGN PROPERTY AS % OF GDP	1971	D1	P10	1.7	%	SUDAN	MALI	----
		1975	D1	P10	1.0	%	AFGHA	SUDAN	----
		1978	D1	----	0.8	%	SUDAN	TURKY	----
V26	GNP SHARE OF DEVELOPMENT AID	------	----	----	-----	-----	-------	-------	
V27	SHARE IN NOBEL PRIZE WINNERS	1970-79	D5	P45	0.0	%	SUDAN	TAIWA	----
V28	GDP SHARE OF MANUFACTURING	------	----	----	-----	-----	-------	-------	
V29	EXPORT SHARE OF MANUFACTURES	1970	D6	P53	10.9	%	BENIN	ARGE	----
		1975	D5	P45	7.8	%	KUWAI	CHILE	----
		1979	D4	P33	7.5	%	CONGO	BENIN	----
V30	LACK OF CIVIL LIBERTIES	1975	D10	P93	7		MONGO	UGADA	----
		1980	D8	P74	6		SOUAF	TANZA	----
V31	LACK OF POLITICAL RIGHTS	1975	D7	P63	6		SUDAN	TAIWA	----
		1980	D5	P47	5		SUDAN	TAIWA	----
V32	RIOTS	1970-74	D7	P68	5		POLA	MADA	----
		1975-79	D6	P60	3		NETH	TAIWA	----
V33	PROTEST DEMONSTRATIONS	1970-74	D5	P49	2		NIGER	VINO	----
		1975-79	D5	P49	3		SWEDN	URU	----
V34	POLITICAL STRIKES	1970-74	D3	P29	0		SWITZ	TANZA	----
		1975-79	D3	P29	0		SWITZ	TAIWA	----
V35	MEMBER OF THE NONALIGNED MMT.	1970	----	----	1		SUDAN	TANZA	----
		1976	----	----	1		SUDAN	TANZA	----
		1981	----	----	1		SUDAN	TANZA	----

V36 MEMBER OF THE OPEC	1970	----	----	0		SWITZ	TAIWA	----
	1975	----	----	0		SWITZ	TAIWA	----
	1980	----	----	0		SWITZ	TAIWA	----
V37 MEMBER OF THE OECD	1970	----	----	0		SUDAN	TAIWA	----
	1975	----	----	0		SUDAN	TAIWA	----
	1980	----	----	0		SUDAN	TAIWA	----
V38 MEMBER OF THE CMEA	1970	----	----	0		SWITZ	TAIWA	----
	1975	----	----	0		SWITZ	TAIWA	----
	1980	----	----	0		SWITZ	TAIWA	----
V39 MEMBER OF THE WTO	1970	----	----	0		SWITZ	TAIWA	----
	1975	----	----	0		SWITZ	TAIWA	----
	1980	----	----	0		SWITZ	TAIWA	----
V40 MEMBER OF THE NATO	1970	----	----	0		SWITZ	TAIWA	----
	1975	----	----	0		SWITZ	TAIWA	----
	1980	----	----	0		SWITZ	TAIWA	----
V41 GDP SHARE OF INVESTMENTS	1970	D2	P19	13.7 %		SUDAN	EGYPT	----
	1975	D8	P76	28.6 %		MALAW	KORSO	----
	1980	D6	P50	23.9 %		INDIA	OMAN	----
V42 GDP SHARE OF AGRICULTURE	1970	D5	P49	20.2 %		MOROC	COSTA	----
	1975	D5	P44	17.9 %		MOROC	BOLI	----
	1980	D5	P50	20.4 %		MOROC	DOMI	----
V43 GDP SHARE OF INDUSTRY	1970	D5	P44	25.7 %		MALAY	NICA	----
	1975	D4	P34	24.8 %		JORDA	THAI	----
	1980	D3	P29	24.6 %		MAURA	SENE	----
V44 GDP SHARE OF SERVICES	1970	D8	P77	54.1 %		BELGI	IRE	----
	1975	D9	P86	57.3 %		AULIA	FRANC	----
	1980	D8	P77	55.0 %		CHILE	NORWY	----
V45 HOMICIDES P. MIL. POPULATION	------	----	----	----- -----		-------	-------	----
V46 SUICIDES P. MIL. POPULATION	------	----	----	----- -----		-------	-------	----
V47 IMPORT PARTNERS	1970	R1	USSR	7.9 %		ROMA	INDIA	----
	1970	R2	CANA	7.3 %		USA	UNKI	----
	1970	R3	GFR	7.0 %		SOUAF	TANZA	----
	1980	R1	IRAQ	17.8 %		-------	TURKY	----
	1980	R2	GFR	10.8 %		SUDAN	TANZA	----
	1980	R3	ITALY	8.7 %		SWITZ	YUGO	----
V48 EXPORT PARTNERS	1970	R1	ITALY	21.5 %		LIBYA	YUGO	----
	1970	R2	LEBA	11.7 %		JORDA	-------	----
	1970	R3	USSR	8.7 %		INDIA	-------	----
	1980	R1	ITALY	55.3 %		EGYPT	AURIA	----
	1980	R2	ROMA	11.3 %		-------	-------	----
	1980	R3	USSR	5.6 %		GHANA	TURKY	----

V49 PATENT SUPPLIERS	1970	R1	SWITZ	29		CONGO	ZAIRE	----
	1970	R2	USA	23		SWITZ	TUNIS	----
	1970	R3	JAPAN	10		PHILI	USA	----
	1978	R1	USA	33		SWEDN	TRITO	----
	1978	R2	FRANC	25		PERU	ARGE	----
	1978	R3	GFR	18		PERU	-------	----
V50 PROVENANCE OF FOREIGN FIRMS	------	----	----	----- -----		-------	-------	----
V51 FILM SUPPLIERS	1980	R1	UNKI	47		PAKI	FINLA	F118
	1980	R2	USA	32		RWAN	TANZA	F118
	1980	R3	FRANC	26		SPAIN	VENE	F118

TAIWAN (TAIWA)

V1 INCOME PER CAPITA	------	----	----	----- -----	-------	-------	----
V2 TELEPHONES P. TSD. POPULATION	------	----	----	----- -----	-------	-------	----
V3 INFANT MORTALITY RATE	------	----	----	----- -----	-------	-------	----
V4 PHYSICIANS P. MIL. POPULATION	------	----	----	----- -----	-------	-------	----
V5 ADULT LITERACY	------	----	----	----- -----	-------	-------	----
V6 DURATION OF SCHOOLING	------	----	----	----- -----	-------	-------	----
V7 STUDENT ENROLLMENT RATIO	------	----	----	----- -----	-------	-------	----
V8 SHARE OF AGRICULTURAL LABOR	------	----	----	----- -----	-------	-------	----
V9 SHARE OF INDUSTRIAL LABOR	------	----	----	----- -----	-------	-------	----
V10 SHARE OF SERVICE LABOR	------	----	----	----- -----	-------	-------	----
V11 SHARE OF ACADEMIC LABOR	------	----	----	----- -----	-------	-------	----
V12 SHARE OF SELF-EMPLOYED LABOR	------	----	----	----- -----	-------	-------	----
V13 MILITARY EXPENDITURES	------	----	----	----- -----	-------	-------	----
V14 MILITARY MANPOWER	1970	D10	P93	522 TSD CAP	GFR	TURKY	F1
	1975	D10	P93	504 TSD CAP	PAKI	FRANC	F1
V15 MEN AT AGE 20 - 30	------	----	----	----- -----	-------	-------	----
V16 POPULATION	------	----	----	----- -----	-------	-------	----
V17 GROSS DOMESTIC PRODUCT	------	----	----	----- -----	-------	-------	----
V18 SHARE IN WORLD IMPORTS	------	----	----	----- -----	-------	-------	----
V19 SHARE IN WORLD EXPORTS	------	----	----	----- -----	-------	-------	----

V20 GDP SHARE OF IMPORTS	------	----	----	----- -----		-------	-------	----
V21 GDP SHARE OF EXPORTS	------	----	----	----- -----		-------	-------	----
V22 EXPORT PARTNER CONCENTRATION	------	----	----	----- -----		-------	-------	----
V23 TOTAL DEBT AS % OF GDP	------	----	----	----- -----		-------	-------	----
V24 SHARE OF NEW FOREIGN PATENTS	------	----	----	----- -----		-------	-------	----
V25 FOREIGN PROPERTY AS % OF GDP	------	----	----	----- -----		-------	-------	----
V26 GNP SHARE OF DEVELOPMENT AID	------	----	----	----- -----		-------	-------	----
V27 SHARE IN NOBEL PRIZE WINNERS	1970-79	D5	P45	0.0 %		SYRIA	TANZA	----
V28 GDP SHARE OF MANUFACTURING	------	----	----	----- -----		-------	-------	----
V29 EXPORT SHARE OF MANUFACTURES	------	----	----	----- -----		-------	-------	----
V30 LACK OF CIVIL LIBERTIES	1975	D6	P54	5		SPAIN	TUNIS	----
	1980	D6	P52	5		SUDAN	TUNIS	----
V31 LACK OF POLITICAL RIGHTS	1975	D7	P63	6		SYRIA	TANZA	----
	1980	D5	P47	5		SYRIA	UNARE	----
V32 RIOTS	1970-74	D6	P53	2		SWITZ	URU	----
	1975-79	D6	P60	3		SYRIA	CHINA	----
V33 PROTEST DEMONSTRATIONS	1970-74	D6	P59	4		SUDAN	BRAZI	----
	1975-79	D5	P42	2		SRILA	TANZA	----
V34 POLITICAL STRIKES	1970-74	D8	P78	3		NIGRA	BOLI	----
	1975-79	D3	P29	0		SYRIA	TOGO	----
V35 MEMBER OF THE NONALIGNED MMT.	1970	----	----	0		SWITZ	THAI	----
	1976	----	----	0		SWITZ	THAI	----
	1981	----	----	0		SWITZ	THAI	----
V36 MEMBER OF THE OPEC	1970	----	----	0		SYRIA	TANZA	----
	1975	----	----	0		SYRIA	TANZA	----
	1980	----	----	0		SYRIA	TANZA	----
V37 MEMBER OF THE OECD	1970	----	----	0		SYRIA	TANZA	----
	1975	----	----	0		SYRIA	TANZA	----
	1980	----	----	0		SYRIA	TANZA	----
V38 MEMBER OF THE CMEA	1970	----	----	0		SYRIA	TANZA	----
	1975	----	----	0		SYRIA	TANZA	----
	1980	----	----	0		SYRIA	TANZA	----
V39 MEMBER OF THE WTO	1970	----	----	0		SYRIA	TANZA	----
	1975	----	----	0		SYRIA	TANZA	----
	1980	----	----	0		SYRIA	TANZA	----
V40 MEMBER OF THE NATO	1970	----	----	0		SYRIA	TANZA	----
	1975	----	----	0		SYRIA	TANZA	----
	1980	----	----	0		SYRIA	TANZA	----
V41 GDP SHARE OF INVESTMENTS	------	----	----	----- -----		-------	-------	----

V42	GDP SHARE OF AGRICULTURE	------	---- ----	----- -----	------- -------	----
V43	GDP SHARE OF INDUSTRY	------	---- ----	----- -----	------- -------	----
V44	GDP SHARE OF SERVICES	------	---- ----	----- -----	------- -------	----
V45	HOMICIDES P. MIL. POPULATION	------	---- ----	----- -----	------- -------	----
V46	SUICIDES P. MIL. POPULATION	------	---- ----	----- -----	------- -------	----
V47	IMPORT PARTNERS	------	---- ----	----- -----	------- -------	----
V48	EXPORT PARTNERS	------	---- ----	----- -----	------- -------	----
V49	PATENT SUPPLIERS	------	---- ----	----- -----	------- -------	----
V50	PROVENANCE OF FOREIGN FIRMS	------	---- ----	----- -----	------- -------	----
V51	FILM SUPPLIERS	------	---- ----	----- -----	------- -------	----

TANZANIA (TANZA)

V1	INCOME PER CAPITA	1970	D2	P13	242	$/CAP	HAITI	BENIN	----
		1975	D2	P15	261	$/CAP	PAKI	BENIN	----
		1980	D2	P13	271	$/CAP	SRILA	HAITI	F35
V2	TELEPHONES P. TSD. POPULATION	1970	D3	P22	3	1/TSD CAP	PAKI	TOGO	----
		1975	D3	P23	4	1/TSD CAP	SIERA	TOGO	----
		1980	D2	P19	5	1/TSD CAP	MALAW	SRILA	----
V3	INFANT MORTALITY RATE	1980	D7	P62	107.4	1/TSD	GHANA	ZAMBI	F5
V4	PHYSICIANS P. MIL. POPULATION	------	----	----	-----	-----	-------	-------	----
V5	ADULT LITERACY	1978	D5	----	46.3	%	ALGER	TUNIS	----
V6	DURATION OF SCHOOLING	1970	D2	P16	2.9	YR	SUDAN	SIERA	----
		1975	D2	P20	4.3	YR	PAPUA	HAITI	----
		1980	D4	P31	7.4	YR	ZIMBA	ELSA	----
V7	STUDENT ENROLLMENT RATIO	1970	D2	P13	0.2	%	RWAN	MALAW	----
		1975	D1	P6	0.2	%	CHAD	UPVO	----
		1981	D1	P10	0.4	%	MALAW	ETHIA	----
V8	SHARE OF AGRICULTURAL LABOR	------	----	----	-----	-----	-------	-------	----
V9	SHARE OF INDUSTRIAL LABOR	------	----	----	-----	-----	-------	-------	----
V10	SHARE OF SERVICE LABOR	------	----	----	-----	-----	-------	-------	----
V11	SHARE OF ACADEMIC LABOR	------	----	----	-----	-----	-------	-------	----
V12	SHARE OF SELF-EMPLOYED LABOR	------	----	----	-----	-----	-------	-------	----

V13 MILITARY EXPENDITURES	1975	D4	P38	0.153	TSD MIL $	ZAMBI	BURMA	----
	1980	D5	P41	0.245	TSD MIL $	BURMA	KENYA	F62
V14 MILITARY MANPOWER	1970	D4	P39	20	TSD CAP	SOMA	SUDAN	----
	1975	D4	P40	25	TSD CAP	SWITZ	UGADA	----
	1980	D6	P55	53	TSD CAP	LIBYA	SAUDI	----
V15 MEN AT AGE 20 - 30	1978	D6	----	1197	TSD CAP	NETH	CZECH	----
V16 POPULATION	1970	D7	P66	13.27	MIL CAP	NETH	PERU	----
	1975	D7	P69	15.31	MIL CAP	PERU	SUDAN	----
	1980	D8	P71	18.58	MIL CAP	KORNO	ALGER	F35
V17 GROSS DOMESTIC PRODUCT	1970	D4	P33	3.214	TSD MIL $	ZAMBI	DOMI	----
	1975	D4	P32	3.989	TSD MIL $	ZAMBI	BURMA	----
	1980	D4	P33	5.027	TSD MIL $	GHANA	ZIMBA	----
V18 SHARE IN WORLD IMPORTS	1970	D4	P39	0.958	1/TSD	COSTA	PANA	F30
	1975	D4	P37	0.850	1/TSD	DOMI	GHANA	F30
	1980	D4	P34	0.598	1/TSD	JAMAI	ZIMBA	F30
V19 SHARE IN WORLD EXPORTS	1970	D4	P40	0.826	1/TSD	URU	UGADA	F30
	1975	D3	P29	0.425	1/TSD	LEBA	NICA	F30
	1980	D3	P23	0.255	1/TSD	SENE	SUDAN	F30
V20 GDP SHARE OF IMPORTS	1970	D8	P73	24.8	%	TOGO	BENIN	F30
	1975	D8	P71	30.1	%	SYRIA	KENYA	F30
	1980	D6	P54	24.7	%	CAME	ALGER	F30
V21 GDP SHARE OF EXPORTS	1970	D7	P66	20.2	%	AURIA	SWEDN	F30
	1975	D4	P38	14.5	%	PHILI	SOUAF	F30
	1980	D3	P23	10.2	%	PANA	ETHIA	F30
V22 EXPORT PARTNER CONCENTRATION	1970	D4	P34	21.9	%	SINGA	LIBE	F124
	1975	D1	P10	13.7	%	SPAIN	NEPAL	F124
	1980	D2	P10	13.8	%	GFR	NEPAL	F136
V23 TOTAL DEBT AS % OF GDP	1980	D8	P75	50.6	%	SOMA	BOLI	----
V24 SHARE OF NEW FOREIGN PATENTS	1972	D9	----	100	%	SOMA	UGADA	----
	1976	D10	P92	100	%	SOMA	UGADA	----
	1980	D10	P94	100	%	SINGA	UGADA	----
V25 FOREIGN PROPERTY AS % OF GDP	1971	D3	P28	4.7	%	RWAN	SPAIN	----
	1975	D5	P49	5.5	%	MEXI	BENIN	----
	1978	D5	----	3.9	%	SPAIN	BURU	----
V26 GNP SHARE OF DEVELOPMENT AID	------	----	----	-----	-----	-------	-------	----
V27 SHARE IN NOBEL PRIZE WINNERS	1970-79	D5	P45	0.0	%	TAIWA	THAI	----
V28 GDP SHARE OF MANUFACTURING	1970	D4	P32	10.1	%	TOGO	ZAMBI	F16
	1975	D4	P36	10.4	%	TUNIS	NIGER	F16
	1980	D4	P37	10.0	%	BURMA	NEPAL	F16
V29 EXPORT SHARE OF MANUFACTURES	1970	D6	P58	12.7	%	KENYA	TUNIS	----
	1975	D6	P57	12.0	%	MALI	MOROC	----
V30 LACK OF CIVIL LIBERTIES	1975	D8	P74	6		SUDAN	TOGO	----
	1980	D8	P74	6		SYRIA	TOGO	----

V31	LACK OF POLITICAL RIGHTS	1975	D7	P63	6		TAIWA	TUNIS	----
		1980	D7	P67	6		SAUDI	TUNIS	----
V32	RIOTS	1970-74	D2	P19	0		SWEDN	TOGO	----
		1975-79	D5	P45	1		SWEDN	ZAIRE	----
V33	PROTEST DEMONSTRATIONS	1970-74	D2	P15	0		SOMA	TOGO	----
		1975-79	D5	P42	2		TAIWA	AFGHA	----
V34	POLITICAL STRIKES	1970-74	D3	P29	0		SYRIA	THAI	----
		1975-79	D8	P73	2		PANA	CANA	----
V35	MEMBER OF THE NONALIGNED MMT.	1970	----	----	1		SYRIA	TOGO	----
		1976	----	----	1		SYRIA	TOGO	----
		1981	----	----	1		SYRIA	TOGO	----
V36	MEMBER OF THE OPEC	1970	----	----	0		TAIWA	THAI	----
		1975	----	----	0		TAIWA	THAI	----
		1980	----	----	0		TAIWA	THAI	----
V37	MEMBER OF THE OECD	1970	----	----	0		TAIWA	THAI	----
		1975	----	----	0		TAIWA	THAI	----
		1980	----	----	0		TAIWA	THAI	----
V38	MEMBER OF THE CMEA	1970	----	----	0		TAIWA	THAI	----
		1975	----	----	0		TAIWA	THAI	----
		1980	----	----	0		TAIWA	THAI	----
V39	MEMBER OF THE WTO	1970	----	----	0		TAIWA	THAI	----
		1975	----	----	0		TAIWA	THAI	----
		1980	----	----	0		TAIWA	THAI	----
V40	MEMBER OF THE NATO	1970	----	----	0		TAIWA	THAI	----
		1975	----	----	0		TAIWA	THAI	----
		1980	----	----	0		TAIWA	THAI	----
V41	GDP SHARE OF INVESTMENTS	1970	D7	P62	22.5 %		LIBE	BRAZI	----
		1975	D5	P44	21.1 %		DENMA	TRITO	----
		1980	D4	P39	22.0 %		ISRA	CAME	----
V42	GDP SHARE OF AGRICULTURE	1970	D8	P81	41.2 %		NIGRA	UPVO	F16
		1975	D9	P83	41.2 %		MADA	INDIA	F16
		1980	D10	P92	50.5 %		BENIN	ETHIA	F16
V43	GDP SHARE OF INDUSTRY	1970	D2	P19	17.3 %		CAME	INDO	F16
		1975	D2	P14	16.2 %		CAME	ETHIA	F16
		1980	D2	P12	15.7 %		ETHIA	YENO	F16
V44	GDP SHARE OF SERVICES	1970	D3	P26	41.5 %		SIERA	CHAD	F16
		1975	D4	P40	42.6 %		MALAY	SUDAN	F16
		1980	D2	P16	33.8 %		ETHIA	BANGL	F16
V45	HOMICIDES P. MIL. POPULATION	------	----	----	----- -----		-------	-------	----
V46	SUICIDES P. MIL. POPULATION	------	----	----	----- -----		-------	-------	----

V47 IMPORT PARTNERS	1970	R1	UNKI	21.3 %		SUDAN	UGADA	F124
	1970	R2	CHINA	13.6 %		SRILA	-------	F124
	1970	R3	GFR	9.4 %		SYRIA	THAI	F124
	1980	R1	UNKI	17.8 %		SUDAN	ZAMBI	F136
	1980	R2	GFR	10.1 %		SYRIA	TURKY	F136
	1980	R3	JAPAN	8.9 %		NIGRA	-------	F136
V48 EXPORT PARTNERS	1970	R1	UNKI	21.9 %		SWEDN	YESO	F124
	1970	R2	USA	9.6 %		SINGA	THAI	F124
	1970	R3	INDIA	7.3 %		EGYPT	-------	F124
	1980	R1	GFR	13.8 %		SWITZ	TURKY	F136
	1980	R2	UNKI	13.1 %		SWEDN	ZAIRE	F136
	1980	R3	INDO	7.0 %		-------	-------	F136
V49 PATENT SUPPLIERS	1972	R1	USA	15		SWEDN	TRITO	----
	1972	R2	GDR	7		ROMA	YUGO	----
	1972	R3	UNKI	6		SWEDN	URU	----
	1979	R1	UNKI	13		MALAW	AULIA	----
	1979	R2	SWITZ	8		PHILI	AURIA	----
	1979	R3	JAPAN	6		PHILI	UGADA	----
V50 PROVENANCE OF FOREIGN FIRMS	1980	R1	UNKI	73.6 %		SRILA	TRITO	----
	1980	R2	USA	8.0 %		SRILA	TRITO	----
	1980	R3	GFR	6.4 %		SWEDN	UGADA	----
V51 FILM SUPPLIERS	1980	R1	INDIA	52		SOMA	ISRA	F119
	1980	R2	USA	50		SYRIA	JORDA	F119
	1980	R3	UNKI	14		SWEDN	-------	F119

THAILAND (THAI)

V1 INCOME PER CAPITA	1970	D3	P24	453	$/CAP	MADA	GHANA	----
	1975	D4	P31	533	$/CAP	SENE	LIBE	----
	1980	D4	P33	692	$/CAP	ELSA	PHILI	F35
V2 TELEPHONES P. TSD. POPULATION	1970	D3	P27	4	1/TSD CAP	SIERA	GHANA	----
	1975	D4	P29	7	1/TSD CAP	HONDU	CONGO	----
	1980	D3	P27	11	1/TSD CAP	CONGO	ZAMBI	----
V3 INFANT MORTALITY RATE	1980	D5	P43	59.0	1/TSD	ALBA	MONGO	F5
V4 PHYSICIANS P. MIL. POPULATION	1970	D4	P36	119	1/MIL	BURMA	ZAMBI	----
	1975	D4	P34	120	1/MIL	HAITI	MALAY	----
	1980	D4	P34	148	1/MIL	GHANA	ZIMBA	----
V5 ADULT LITERACY	1970	D7	P63	78.6 %		PANA	PARA	F22
	1980	D9	P89	88.0 %		PANA	SPAIN	----
V6 DURATION OF SCHOOLING	1970	D5	P45	7.0	YR	MADA	BOLI	----
	1975	D5	P42	7.4	YR	TURKY	ELSA	----
	1980	D4	P35	7.9	YR	IRAN	ANGO	----

V7	STUDENT ENROLLMENT RATIO	1970	D4	P37	1.7 %	SAUDI	ALGER	----
		1975	D5	P43	3.4 %	GUINE	GUATE	----
		1980	D7	P62	13.5 %	HUNGA	MEXI	----
V8	SHARE OF AGRICULTURAL LABOR	1970	D10	P97	79.5 %	HAITI	NEPAL	F67
		1976	D8	P81	62.4 %	HONDU	TURKY	F103
		1980	D10	P96	70.9 %	HAITI	CAME	F103
V9	SHARE OF INDUSTRIAL LABOR	1976	D3	P22	18.9 %	HONDU	PHILI	F103
		1980	D1	P5	12.6 %	CAME	PHILI	F103
V10	SHARE OF SERVICE LABOR	1976	D3	P20	16.1 %	SUDAN	SYRIA	F103
		1980	D2	P11	14.0 %	TURKY	ZIMBA	F103
V11	SHARE OF ACADEMIC LABOR	1976	D2	P13	2.6 %	CAME	SUDAN	F103
		1980	D1	P9	2.5 %	CAME	AFGHA	F103
V12	SHARE OF SELF-EMPLOYED LABOR	1970	D6	P62	30.2 %	ELSA	MEXI	F67
		1976	D8	P77	45.6 %	INDO	BANGL	F103
		1980	D7	P70	31.4 %	MALAY	MEXI	F103
V13	MILITARY EXPENDITURES	1975	D6	P57	0.715 TSD MIL $	MOROC	AURIA	F62
		1980	D7	P67	1.417 TSD MIL $	PAKI	MALAY	----
V14	MILITARY MANPOWER	1970	D8	P75	175 TSD CAP	BULGA	GREC	----
		1975	D8	P79	227 TSD CAP	ROMA	SYRIA	----
		1980	D9	P83	234 TSD CAP	GDR	ETHIA	----
V15	MEN AT AGE 20 - 30	1970	D8	P80	2420 TSD CAP	SPAIN	POLA	F22
		1977	D9	----	3843 TSD CAP	PHILI	UNKI	F184
		1980	D9	P85	4188 TSD CAP	ITALY	FRANC	F184
V16	POPULATION	1970	D9	P86	36.37 MIL CAP	TURKY	PHILI	----
		1975	D9	P86	41.87 MIL CAP	TURKY	PHILI	----
		1980	D9	P86	46.46 MIL CAP	TURKY	PHILI	F35
V17	GROSS DOMESTIC PRODUCT	1970	D6	P59	16.471 TSD MIL $	PORTU	ALGER	----
		1975	D6	P60	22.334 TSD MIL $	LIBYA	KUWAI	----
		1980	D7	P64	32.138 TSD MIL $	LIBYA	COLO	----
V18	SHARE IN WORLD IMPORTS	1970	D7	P63	3.913 1/TSD	PHILI	CUBA	F30
		1975	D6	P57	3.608 1/TSD	NEWZ	LIBYA	F30
		1980	D7	P62	4.492 1/TSD	PHILI	HUNGA	F30
V19	SHARE IN WORLD EXPORTS	1970	D5	P50	2.263 1/TSD	GREC	PAKI	F30
		1975	D7	P61	2.713 1/TSD	PHILI	ARGE	F30
		1980	D7	P62	3.259 1/TSD	PHILI	ARGE	F30
V20	GDP SHARE OF IMPORTS	1970	D6	P58	19.9 %	SYRIA	CONGO	F30
		1975	D5	P47	22.4 %	NEWZ	BOLI	F30
		1980	D7	P64	27.5 %	ELSA	IVORY	F30
V21	GDP SHARE OF EXPORTS	1970	D3	P27	10.9 %	PARA	BURU	F30
		1975	D5	P44	16.2 %	MADA	PANA	F30
		1980	D5	P49	19.4 %	GUATE	ITALY	F30
V22	EXPORT PARTNER CONCENTRATION	1970	D5	P45	25.5 %	ELSA	LIBYA	----
		1975	D6	P59	27.8 %	BENIN	NICA	----
		1980	D2	P14	15.1 %	SINGA	USA	----
V23	TOTAL DEBT AS % OF GDP	1980	D3	P29	24.8 %	GREC	UPVO	----

V24	SHARE OF NEW FOREIGN PATENTS	------	----	----	----- -----	-------	-------	----
V25	FOREIGN PROPERTY AS % OF GDP	1971	D4	P35	5.9 %	NIGER	BOLI	----
		1975	D3	P21	2.3 %	PORTU	ALGER	----
		1978	D3	----	1.9 %	EGYPT	UPVO	----
V26	GNP SHARE OF DEVELOPMENT AID	------	----	----	----- -----	-------	-------	----
V27	SHARE IN NOBEL PRIZE WINNERS	1970-79	D5	P45	0.0 %	TANZA	TOGO	----
V28	GDP SHARE OF MANUFACTURING	1970	D6	P55	16.0 %	VENE	MOROC	----
		1975	D7	P64	18.0 %	MALAY	DENMA	----
		1980	D7	P70	19.6 %	GREC	AULIA	----
V29	EXPORT SHARE OF MANUFACTURES	------	----	----	----- -----	-------	-------	----
V30	LACK OF CIVIL LIBERTIES	1975	D3	P27	3	SRILA	TURKY	----
		1980	D3	P29	3	SRILA	TURKY	----
V31	LACK OF POLITICAL RIGHTS	1975	D5	P43	5	SPAIN	URU	----
		1980	D4	P36	4	SENE	ZIMBA	----
V32	RIOTS	1970-74	D7	P70	6	MADA	CHINA	----
		1975-79	D8	P79	8	PANA	UGADA	----
V33	PROTEST DEMONSTRATIONS	1970-74	D8	P76	10	SWITZ	CZECH	----
		1975-79	D8	P79	16	NICA	ARGE	----
V34	POLITICAL STRIKES	1970-74	D3	P29	0	TANZA	TOGO	----
		1975-79	D9	P89	10	NICA	IRAN	----
V35	MEMBER OF THE NONALIGNED MMT.	1970	----	----	0	TAIWA	TURKY	----
		1976	----	----	0	TAIWA	TURKY	----
		1981	----	----	0	TAIWA	TURKY	----
V36	MEMBER OF THE OPEC	1970	----	----	0	TANZA	TOGO	----
		1975	----	----	0	TANZA	TOGO	----
		1980	----	----	0	TANZA	TOGO	----
V37	MEMBER OF THE OECD	1970	----	----	0	TANZA	TOGO	----
		1975	----	----	0	TANZA	TOGO	----
		1980	----	----	0	TANZA	TOGO	----
V38	MEMBER OF THE CMEA	1970	----	----	0	TANZA	TOGO	----
		1975	----	----	0	TANZA	TOGO	----
		1980	----	----	0	TANZA	TOGO	----
V39	MEMBER OF THE WTO	1970	----	----	0	TANZA	TOGO	----
		1975	----	----	0	TANZA	TOGO	----
		1980	----	----	0	TANZA	TOGO	----
V40	MEMBER OF THE NATO	1970	----	----	0	TANZA	TOGO	----
		1975	----	----	0	TANZA	TOGO	----
		1980	----	----	0	TANZA	TOGO	----
V41	GDP SHARE OF INVESTMENTS	1970	D8	P78	26.2 %	ZAIRE	KORSO	----
		1975	D7	P65	25.4 %	MOROC	JAMAI	----
		1980	D7	P67	27.2 %	SWITZ	LIBE	----

V42	GDP SHARE OF AGRICULTURE	1970	D7	P63	28.3	%	SRILA	ELSA	----
		1975	D7	P68	31.5	%	SRILA	INDO	----
		1980	D7	P60	25.4	%	INDO	IVORY	----
V43	GDP SHARE OF INDUSTRY	1970	D5	P42	25.3	%	ECUA	MALAY	----
		1975	D4	P34	24.8	%	SYRIA	ELSA	----
		1980	D4	P39	28.5	%	LIBE	ZAIRE	----
V44	GDP SHARE OF SERVICES	1970	D5	P42	46.4	%	HONDU	ZAIRE	----
		1975	D5	P44	43.7	%	SRILA	EGYPT	----
		1980	D5	P47	46.1	%	MADA	NICA	----
V45	HOMICIDES P. MIL. POPULATION	1970	D10	P93	164.3	1/MIL CAP	COLO	GUATE	F148
		1975	D10	P96	287.7	1/MIL CAP	NICA	ELSA	F148
		1980	D10	P94	250.8	1/MIL CAP	VENE	GUATE	----
V46	SUICIDES P. MIL. POPULATION	1970	D3	P23	39.3	1/MIL CAP	GREC	SPAIN	----
		1975	D3	P22	44.9	1/MIL CAP	COSTA	IRE	----
		1980	D4	P31	74.3	1/MIL CAP	ITALY	ARGE	----
V47	IMPORT PARTNERS	1970	R1	JAPAN	37.6	%	SINGA	AFGHA	----
		1970	R2	USA	14.9	%	SOUAF	TUNIS	----
		1970	R3	GFR	8.5	%	TANZA	TOGO	----
		1980	R1	JAPAN	20.7	%	SRILA	UNARE	----
		1980	R2	USA	16.6	%	SOMA	TRITO	----
		1980	R3	SAUDI	9.9	%	SUDAN	USA	----
V48	EXPORT PARTNERS	1970	R1	JAPAN	25.5	%	SAUDI	ZAMBI	----
		1970	R2	USA	13.4	%	TANZA	TURKY	----
		1970	R3	NETH	8.6	%	SENE	UNKI	----
		1980	R1	JAPAN	15.1	%	SAUDI	UNARE	----
		1980	R2	NETH	13.2	%	OMAN	TRITO	----
		1980	R3	USA	12.7	%	NEWZ	UNARE	----
V49	PATENT SUPPLIERS	------	----	----	-----	-----	-------	-------	----
V50	PROVENANCE OF FOREIGN FIRMS	1980	R1	USA	36.0	%	SWITZ	TURKY	----
V51	FILM SUPPLIERS	------	----	----	-----	-----	-------	-------	----

TOGO (TOGO)

V1	INCOME PER CAPITA	1970	D2	P20	385	$/CAP	SIERA	NIGER	----
		1975	D3	P24	370	$/CAP	MADA	KENYA	----
		1980	D3	P22	406	$/CAP	KENYA	NIGER	----
V2	TELEPHONES P. TSD. POPULATION	1970	D3	P22	3	1/TSD CAP	TANZA	UGADA	----
		1976	D3	P23	4	1/TSD CAP	TANZA	UGADA	----
		1980	D2	P14	4	1/TSD CAP	PAKI	UGADA	----
V3	INFANT MORTALITY RATE	1980	D8	P73	123.7	1/TSD	LIBE	NIGRA	F5

V4	PHYSICIANS P. MIL. POPULATION	1970	D2	P14	36	1/MIL	BENIN	INDO	----
		1975	D2	P17	48	1/MIL	CAME	INDO	----
		1980	D2	P11	55	1/MIL	UGADA	MOROC	----
V5	ADULT LITERACY	1970	D1	P9	15.9	%	NEPAL	PAKI	F22
V6	DURATION OF SCHOOLING	1970	D4	P31	5.2	YR	KENYA	INDIA	----
		1975	D5	P48	7.8	YR	PARA	TUNIS	----
		1980	D8	P72	10.4	YR	MEXI	IRE	----
V7	STUDENT ENROLLMENT RATIO	1970	D3	P21	0.5	%	SIERA	GUINE	----
		1975	D3	P24	1.2	%	YESO	ZAIRE	----
		1980	D3	P28	2.2	%	NIGRA	YESO	----
V8	SHARE OF AGRICULTURAL LABOR	------	----	----	-----	-----	-------	-------	----
V9	SHARE OF INDUSTRIAL LABOR	------	----	----	-----	-----	-------	-------	----
V10	SHARE OF SERVICE LABOR	------	----	----	-----	-----	-------	-------	----
V11	SHARE OF ACADEMIC LABOR	------	----	----	-----	-----	-------	-------	----
V12	SHARE OF SELF-EMPLOYED LABOR	------	----	----	-----	-----	-------	-------	----
V13	MILITARY EXPENDITURES	1970	D1	P8	0.009	TSD MIL $	LIBE	NIGER	----
		1975	D1	P6	0.013	TSD MIL $	NEPAL	NIGER	----
		1980	D1	P9	0.022	TSD MIL $	JAMAI	MALAW	----
V14	MILITARY MANPOWER	1970	D1	P4	2	TSD CAP	COSTA	BURU	----
		1975	D1	P6	3	TSD CAP	PAPUA	NIGER	----
		1980	D1	P9	4	TSD CAP	MALAW	GABON	----
V15	MEN AT AGE 20 - 30	1970	D1	P2	107	TSD CAP	-------	JAMAI	F22
V16	POPULATION	1970	D2	P11	1.96	MIL CAP	JAMAI	LIBYA	----
		1975	D2	P13	2.23	MIL CAP	NICA	SINGA	----
		1980	D2	P13	2.53	MIL CAP	SINGA	ALBA	----
V17	GROSS DOMESTIC PRODUCT	1970	D1	P7	0.755	TSD MIL $	BENIN	LIBE	----
		1975	D1	P4	0.825	TSD MIL $	MALAW	LIBE	----
		1980	D1	P6	1.028	TSD MIL $	MALAW	BENIN	----
V18	SHARE IN WORLD IMPORTS	1970	D2	P15	0.196	1/TSD	PARA	NEPAL	----
		1975	D2	P11	0.191	1/TSD	NEPAL	MALI	----
		1980	D2	P17	0.268	1/TSD	LIBE	AFGHA	----
V19	SHARE IN WORLD EXPORTS	1970	D2	P17	0.175	1/TSD	NEPAL	MALAW	----
		1975	D2	P14	0.144	1/TSD	SIERA	MALAW	----
		1980	D2	P15	0.168	1/TSD	PARA	UGADA	----
V20	GDP SHARE OF IMPORTS	1970	D8	P72	24.5	%	AURIA	TANZA	----
		1975	D7	P68	29.1	%	IVORY	SIERA	----
		1980	D10	P93	48.6	%	MALAY	TRITO	----
V21	GDP SHARE OF EXPORTS	1970	D7	P68	20.7	%	GHANA	DENMA	----
		1975	D7	P61	21.0	%	ECUA	CHILE	----
		1980	D8	P75	29.6	%	SWITZ	IVORY	----
V22	EXPORT PARTNER CONCENTRATION	1970	D5	P49	28.2	%	PARA	GUATE	----
		1975	D8	P77	39.3	%	HUNGA	VENE	----
		1980	D4	P36	20.2	%	KUWAI	TURKY	----

V23	TOTAL DEBT AS % OF GDP	1980	D10	P96	92.2	%	ZAMBI	NICA	----
V24	SHARE OF NEW FOREIGN PATENTS	------	----	----	----- -----		-------	-------	----
V25	FOREIGN PROPERTY AS % OF GDP	1971	D9	P83	21.0	%	MALAY	SENE	----
		1975	D9	P82	15.0	%	VENE	SENE	----
		1978	D9	----	11.7	%	CENTR	ZAMBI	----
V26	GNP SHARE OF DEVELOPMENT AID	------	----	----	----- -----		-------	-------	----
V27	SHARE IN NOBEL PRIZE WINNERS	1970-79	D5	P45	0.0	%	THAI	TUNIS	----
V28	GDP SHARE OF MANUFACTURING	1970	D4	P31	10.0	%	IRAQ	TANZA	----
		1975	D2	P18	7.0	%	UGADA	SUDAN	----
		1980	D3	P24	6.7	%	CENTR	SOMA	----
V29	EXPORT SHARE OF MANUFACTURES	1970	D4	P37	5.6	%	SOMA	MADA	----
		1975	D4	P38	5.8	%	PANA	TRITO	----
		1980	D5	P40	10.1	%	UPVO	KUWAI	----
V30	LACK OF CIVIL LIBERTIES	1975	D8	P74	6		TANZA	USSR	----
		1980	D8	P74	6		TANZA	UGADA	----
V31	LACK OF POLITICAL RIGHTS	1975	D9	P88	7		SOMA	UGADA	----
		1980	D9	P90	7		SOMA	VINO	----
V32	RIOTS	1970-74	D2	P19	0		TANZA	UPVO	----
		1975-79	D2	P20	0		SOMA	TRITO	----
V33	PROTEST DEMONSTRATIONS	1970-74	D2	P15	0		TANZA	UGADA	----
		1975-79	D2	P13	0		SOMA	TRITO	----
V34	POLITICAL STRIKES	1970-74	D3	P29	0		THAI	TUNIS	----
		1975-79	D3	P29	0		TAIWA	TRITO	----
V35	MEMBER OF THE NONALIGNED MMT.	1970	----	----	1		TANZA	TUNIS	----
		1976	----	----	1		TANZA	TRITO	----
		1981	----	----	1		TANZA	TRITO	----
V36	MEMBER OF THE OPEC	1970	----	----	0		THAI	TUNIS	----
		1975	----	----	0		THAI	TRITO	----
		1980	----	----	0		THAI	TRITO	----
V37	MEMBER OF THE OECD	1970	----	----	0		THAI	TUNIS	----
		1975	----	----	0		THAI	TRITO	----
		1980	----	----	0		THAI	TRITO	----
V38	MEMBER OF THE CMEA	1970	----	----	0		THAI	TUNIS	----
		1975	----	----	0		THAI	TRITO	----
		1980	----	----	0		THAI	TRITO	----
V39	MEMBER OF THE WTO	1970	----	----	0		THAI	TUNIS	----
		1975	----	----	0		THAI	TRITO	----
		1980	----	----	0		THAI	TRITO	----
V40	MEMBER OF THE NATO	1970	----	----	0		THAI	TUNIS	----
		1975	----	----	0		THAI	TRITO	----
		1980	----	----	0		THAI	TRITO	----

V41	GDP SHARE OF INVESTMENTS	1970	D3	P24	15.1 %	PARA	BENIN	----
		1975	D8	P74	27.7 %	BRAZI	MALAW	----
		1980	D10	P93	33.4 %	ZAIRE	SRILA	----
V42	GDP SHARE OF AGRICULTURE	1970	D8	P78	33.8 %	CENTR	BURMA	----
		1975	D6	P55	26.6 %	LIBE	NIGRA	----
		1980	D6	P58	24.6 %	MALAY	INDO	----
V43	GDP SHARE OF INDUSTRY	1970	D4	P30	21.1 %	PARA	IVORY	----
		1975	D4	P40	26.5 %	SRILA	EGYPT	----
		1980	D4	P35	26.7 %	HONDU	COSTA	----
V44	GDP SHARE OF SERVICES	1970	D5	P40	45.1 %	COLO	HONDU	----
		1975	D6	P54	46.9 %	MOROC	SENE	----
		1980	D6	P57	48.7 %	MAURA	CENTR	----
V45	HOMICIDES P. MIL. POPULATION	------	----	----	----- -----	-------	-------	----
V46	SUICIDES P. MIL. POPULATION	------	----	----	----- -----	-------	-------	----
V47	IMPORT PARTNERS	1970	R1	FRANC	29.5 %	SENE	TUNIS	----
		1970	R2	UNKI	13.5 %	SWEDN	AURIA	----
		1970	R3	GFR	8.1 %	THAI	TUNIS	----
		1980	R1	FRANC	25.0 %	SENE	TUNIS	----
		1980	R2	NIGRA	15.9 %	SENE	-------	----
		1980	R3	NETH	9.0 %	CENTR	-------	----
V48	EXPORT PARTNERS	1970	R1	FRANC	28.2 %	SENE	TUNIS	----
		1970	R2	NETH	25.9 %	NIGRA	BELGI	----
		1970	R3	GFR	20.0 %	NICA	TUNIS	----
		1980	R1	NETH	20.2 %	BENIN	GFR	----
		1980	R2	FRANC	15.3 %	SWITZ	UNARE	----
		1980	R3	NIGRA	10.1 %	NIGER	-------	----
V49	PATENT SUPPLIERS	------	----	----	----- -----	-------	-------	----
V50	PROVENANCE OF FOREIGN FIRMS	1980	R1	FRANC	50.0 %	SENE	TUNIS	----
		1980	R2	NETH	14.7 %	MOZAM	GUATE	----
		1980	R3	UNKI	11.7 %	SWITZ	TURKY	----
V51	FILM SUPPLIERS	------	----	----	----- -----	-------	-------	----

TRINIDAD AND TOBAGO (TRITO)

V1	INCOME PER CAPITA	1971	D8	P73	3925 $/CAP	IRE	SPAIN	F4
		1975	D8	P75	4536 $/CAP	IRE	SPAIN	----
		1980	D8	P76	5589 $/CAP	SPAIN	ITALY	----
V2	TELEPHONES P. TSD. POPULATION	1971	D8	P71	61 1/TSD CAP	PANA	ARGE	----
		1975	D7	P65	63 1/TSD CAP	COSTA	USSR	----
V3	INFANT MORTALITY RATE	1979	D3	P27	26.4 1/TSD	PORTU	KUWAI	----

V4	PHYSICIANS P. MIL. POPULATION	1971	D6	P55	419	1/MIL	JAMAI	PARA	----
		1975	D6	P57	545	1/MIL	TURKY	CHILE	----
		1980	D7	P60	721	1/MIL	KORSO	PANA	----
V5	ADULT LITERACY	------	----	----	----- -----		-------	-------	----
V6	DURATION OF SCHOOLING	1975	D7	P66	9.4	YR	SINGA	PORTU	----
		1980	D8	P69	10.3	YR	ECUA	ARGE	----
V7	STUDENT ENROLLMENT RATIO	1971	D5	P45	3.1	%	IRAN	ELSA	F4
		1975	D5	P47	4.8	%	SOUAF	IRAN	----
		1980	D5	P43	5.2	%	BURMA	ALBA	----
V8	SHARE OF AGRICULTURAL LABOR	1975	D3	P31	12.7	%	AURIA	JAPAN	F67
		1980	D3	P25	8.0	%	NORWY	FRANC	F46
V9	SHARE OF INDUSTRIAL LABOR	1980	D10	P94	45.8	%	TUNIS	HUNGA	F46
V10	SHARE OF SERVICE LABOR	1980	D6	P56	35.8	%	DOMI	IRE	F46
V11	SHARE OF ACADEMIC LABOR	1980	D7	P60	10.5	%	EGYPT	YUGO	F46
V12	SHARE OF SELF-EMPLOYED LABOR	1975	D3	P27	15.3	%	SINGA	FINLA	F67
		1980	D3	P29	13.3	%	POLA	NEWZ	----
V13	MILITARY EXPENDITURES	1975	D2	P15	0.021	TSD MIL $	PANA	JAMAI	F62
		1980	D2	P16	0.031	TSD MIL $	GHANA	UPVO	----
V14	MILITARY MANPOWER	1975	D1	P2	1	TSD CAP	LESO	COSTA	----
		1980	D1	P2	1	TSD CAP	LESO	JAMAI	----
V15	MEN AT AGE 20 - 30	1975	D1	P3	97	TSD CAP	MAURA	KUWAI	----
		1982	D1	----	105	TSD CAP	-------	KUWAI	----
V16	POPULATION	1971	D1	P1	1.03	MIL CAP	-------	BHUTA	F4
		1975	D1	P3	1.01	MIL CAP	KUWAI	BHUTA	----
		1980	D1	P4	1.09	MIL CAP	GABON	BHUTA	----
V17	GROSS DOMESTIC PRODUCT	1971	D4	P39	4.043	TSD MIL $	CAME	TUNIS	----
		1975	D4	P35	4.581	TSD MIL $	GHANA	CAME	----
		1980	D4	P38	6.092	TSD MIL $	ZAIRE	CAME	----
V18	SHARE IN WORLD IMPORTS	1975	D5	P50	1.618	1/TSD	TUNIS	COLO	----
		1980	D5	P50	1.549	1/TSD	PERU	TUNIS	----
V19	SHARE IN WORLD EXPORTS	1975	D6	P56	2.002	1/TSD	MOROC	ISRA	----
		1980	D6	P56	2.043	1/TSD	COLO	PORTU	----
V20	GDP SHARE OF IMPORTS	1975	D10	P98	59.3	%	LIBE	HUNGA	----
		1980	D10	P94	49.9	%	TOGO	SRILA	----
V21	GDP SHARE OF EXPORTS	1975	D10	P97	70.7	%	LIBE	SAUDI	----
		1980	D10	P95	64.0	%	UNARE	LIBE	----
V22	EXPORT PARTNER CONCENTRATION	1971	D8	P77	42.2	%	PHILI	ZAIRE	----
		1975	D10	P97	68.3	%	CANA	DOMI	----
		1980	D10	P95	59.9	%	AFGHA	CANA	----
V23	TOTAL DEBT AS % OF GDP	1980	D1	P7	11.6	%	NIGRA	INDIA	----

V24	SHARE OF NEW FOREIGN PATENTS	1971	D8	P74	98	%	NICA	VENE	----
		1975	D7	P62	93	%	PERU	TUNIS	----
		1980	D6	P61	92	%	PERU	AULIA	----
V25	FOREIGN PROPERTY AS % OF GDP	1971	D10	P99	103.0	%	LIBE	-------	----
		1975	D10	P97	48.3	%	ZAIRE	PAPUA	----
		1978	D10	----	37.2	%	JAMAI	PAPUA	----
V26	GNP SHARE OF DEVELOPMENT AID	------	----	----	-----	-----	-------	-------	----
V27	SHARE IN NOBEL PRIZE WINNERS	------	----	----	-----	-----	-------	-------	----
V28	GDP SHARE OF MANUFACTURING	1971	D8	P74	20.6	%	SINGA	KORSO	F16
		1975	D5	P50	14.2	%	GHANA	HONDU	F16
		1980	D5	P48	13.4	%	KENYA	BOLI	F16
V29	EXPORT SHARE OF MANUFACTURES	1975	D4	P39	6.2	%	TOGO	UPVO	----
		1980	D3	P27	4.9	%	PARA	MADA	----
V30	LACK OF CIVIL LIBERTIES	1975	D2	P18	2		PAPUA	VENE	----
		1980	D2	P18	2		SPAIN	VENE	----
V31	LACK OF POLITICAL RIGHTS	1975	D2	P20	2		SRILA	TURKY	----
		1980	D3	P21	2		SRILA	TURKY	----
V32	RIOTS	1975-79	D2	P20	0		TOGO	UPVO	----
V33	PROTEST DEMONSTRATIONS	1975-79	D2	P13	0		TOGO	YESO	----
V34	POLITICAL STRIKES	1975-79	D3	P29	0		TOGO	URU	----
V35	MEMBER OF THE NONALIGNED MMT.	1976	----	----	1		TOGO	TUNIS	----
		1981	----	----	1		TOGO	TUNIS	----
V36	MEMBER OF THE OPEC	1975	----	----	0		TOGO	TUNIS	----
		1980	----	----	0		TOGO	TUNIS	----
V37	MEMBER OF THE OECD	1975	----	----	0		TOGO	TUNIS	----
		1980	----	----	0		TOGO	TUNIS	----
V38	MEMBER OF THE CMEA	1975	----	----	0		TOGO	TUNIS	----
		1980	----	----	0		TOGO	TUNIS	----
V39	MEMBER OF THE WTO	1975	----	----	0		TOGO	TUNIS	----
		1980	----	----	0		TOGO	TUNIS	----
V40	MEMBER OF THE NATO	1975	----	----	0		TOGO	TUNIS	----
		1980	----	----	0		TOGO	TUNIS	----
V41	GDP SHARE OF INVESTMENTS	1971	D10	P95	33.2	%	YUGO	HUNGA	----
		1975	D5	P44	21.1	%	TANZA	NICA	----
		1980	D9	P81	29.1	%	TUNIS	KENYA	----
V42	GDP SHARE OF AGRICULTURE	1971	D1	P10	4.8	%	SWEDN	NETH	F16
		1975	D1	P9	3.3	%	GFR	USA	F16
		1980	D1	P9	2.1	%	BELGI	GFR	F16
V43	GDP SHARE OF INDUSTRY	1971	D8	P74	37.6	%	SPAIN	UNKI	F16
		1975	D10	P93	56.7	%	ALGER	IRAN	F16
		1980	D10	P93	56.7	%	SOUAF	ALGER	F16

V44 GDP SHARE OF SERVICES	1971	D9	P86	57.6 %	NETH	URU	F16
	1975	D3	P29	40.0 %	NIGER	ALGER	F16
	1980	D4	P31	41.2 %	BURMA	PORTU	F16
V45 HOMICIDES P. MIL. POPULATION	1971	D8	P74	38.8 1/MIL CAP	COSTA	CUBA	F154
	1975	D8	P79	54.5 1/MIL CAP	COSTA	ECUA	F148
V46 SUICIDES P. MIL. POPULATION	1971	D3	P28	48.5 1/MIL CAP	SPAIN	ISRA	F2
	1975	D5	P42	90.1 1/MIL CAP	NETH	NEWZ	----
V47 IMPORT PARTNERS	1971	R1	USA	17.7 %	SPAIN	TURKY	----
	1971	R2	SAUDI	14.9 %	-------	-------	----
	1971	R3	LIBYA	13.3 %	-------	-------	----
	1980	R1	SAUDI	30.4 %	LIBE	YENO	----
	1980	R2	USA	26.8 %	THAI	UNARE	----
	1980	R3	UNKI	10.1 %	SRILA	UNARE	----
V48 EXPORT PARTNERS	1971	R1	USA	42.2 %	SPAIN	UGADA	----
	1971	R2	SWEDN	9.7 %	FINLA	NORWY	----
	1971	R3	UNKI	8.9 %	SAUDI	VENE	----
	1980	R1	USA	59.9 %	PHILI	VENE	----
	1980	R2	NETH	6.2 %	THAI	BELGI	----
V49 PATENT SUPPLIERS	1972	R1	USA	88	TANZA	TURKY	----
	1972	R2	UNKI	24	SINGA	USA	----
	1972	R3	ITALY	5	MEXI	-------	----
	1978	R1	USA	90	SYRIA	UGADA	----
	1978	R2	UNKI	7	SRILA	UGADA	----
	1978	R3	CANA	4	CUBA	-------	----
V50 PROVENANCE OF FOREIGN FIRMS	1980	R1	UNKI	43.1 %	TANZA	UGADA	----
	1980	R2	USA	37.7 %	TANZA	UGADA	----
	1980	R3	CANA	8.1 %	JAMAI	ZIMBA	----
V51 FILM SUPPLIERS	1978	R1	USA	202	SWITZ	TURKY	F120
	1978	R2	INDIA	66	SINGA	YENO	F120
	1978	R3	ITALY	24	SWITZ	TURKY	F120

TUNISIA (TUNIS)

V1 INCOME PER CAPITA	1970	D4	P38	789 $/CAP	ZAMBI	PARA	F4
	1975	D5	P48	1071 $/CAP	COLO	DOMI	----
	1980	D5	P50	1247 $/CAP	DOMI	PARA	----
V2 TELEPHONES P. TSD. POPULATION	1970	D6	P51	16 1/TSD CAP	MONGO	TURKY	----
	1975	D5	P48	23 1/TSD CAP	SYRIA	DOMI	----
	1980	D5	P44	30 1/TSD CAP	ZIMBA	IRAN	----
V3 INFANT MORTALITY RATE	1980	D6	P59	107.0 1/TSD	LIBYA	BURMA	F5

V4	PHYSICIANS P. MIL. POPULATION	1970	D4	P40	168	1/MIL	ALGER	MALAY	----
		1975	D4	P40	216	1/MIL	ALGER	INDIA	----
		1980	D4	P40	270	1/MIL	VINO	INDIA	----
V5	ADULT LITERACY	1980	D5	P43	46.5	%	TANZA	KENYA	----
V6	DURATION OF SCHOOLING	1970	D6	P60	8.2	YR	MONGO	COSTA	----
		1975	D5	P48	7.8	YR	TOGO	BRAZI	----
		1980	D5	P40	8.3	YR	CAME	ZAMBI	----
V7	STUDENT ENROLLMENT RATIO	1970	D5	P43	2.9	%	INDO	LIBYA	----
		1975	D5	P46	4.2	%	SAUDI	HONDU	----
		1980	D5	P45	5.5	%	ALBA	CONGO	----
V8	SHARE OF AGRICULTURAL LABOR	1975	D6	P53	37.5	%	IRAN	COSTA	----
		1980	D7	P67	33.9	%	DOMI	KORSO	----
V9	SHARE OF INDUSTRIAL LABOR	1975	D9	P87	38.9	%	ALGER	SPAIN	----
		1980	D10	P92	41.7	%	SINGA	TRITO	----
V10	SHARE OF SERVICE LABOR	1975	D4	P35	18.5	%	IRAN	GUATE	----
		1980	D3	P23	22.0	%	INDO	POLA	----
V11	SHARE OF ACADEMIC LABOR	1975	D4	P40	5.1	%	TURKY	PHILI	----
		1980	D1	P7	2.4	%	BANGL	CAME	----
V12	SHARE OF SELF-EMPLOYED LABOR	1975	D5	P45	29.3	%	VENE	KORSO	----
V13	MILITARY EXPENDITURES	1975	D4	P36	0.105	TSD MIL $	KENYA	ZAMBI	----
		1980	D4	P36	0.179	TSD MIL $	BANGL	ECUA	----
V14	MILITARY MANPOWER	1970	D5	P41	25	TSD CAP	SWITZ	NEPAL	----
		1975	D4	P35	20	TSD CAP	MOZAM	KUWAI	----
		1980	D5	P42	29	TSD CAP	URU	MOZAM	----
V15	MEN AT AGE 20 - 30	1970	D4	P31	321	TSD CAP	CHAD	FINLA	F2
		1976	D4	P38	426	TSD CAP	MALI	FINLA	F2
		1981	D4	P29	499	TSD CAP	SWITZ	AURIA	F2
V16	POPULATION	1970	D4	P40	5.13	MIL CAP	MALI	GUATE	F4
		1975	D4	P40	5.61	MIL CAP	YENO	UPVO	----
		1980	D5	P41	6.39	MIL CAP	SWITZ	KAMPU	----
V17	GROSS DOMESTIC PRODUCT	1970	D5	P40	4.048	TSD MIL $	TRITO	GHANA	----
		1975	D5	P41	6.010	TSD MIL $	GUATE	URU	----
		1980	D5	P44	7.970	TSD MIL $	GUATE	IVORY	----
V18	SHARE IN WORLD IMPORTS	1970	D4	P37	0.922	1/TSD	SUDAN	COSTA	----
		1975	D5	P49	1.567	1/TSD	VISO	TRITO	F57
		1980	D5	P50	1.720	1/TSD	TRITO	SYRIA	F30
V19	SHARE IN WORLD EXPORTS	1970	D3	P30	0.580	1/TSD	NICA	BOLI	----
		1975	D5	P44	0.977	1/TSD	ZAMBI	ZAIRE	F57
		1980	D5	P47	1.120	1/TSD	GABON	MOROC	F30
V20	GDP SHARE OF IMPORTS	1970	D7	P64	21.2	%	SWEDN	SOUAF	F4
		1975	D8	P75	32.8	%	IRAQ	NICA	F30
		1980	D9	P85	40.7	%	PANA	HONDU	F30

V21	GDP SHARE OF EXPORTS	1970	D4	P38	12.6 %	YUGO	FRANC	F4
		1975	D6	P56	19.7 %	FINLA	CANA	F30
		1980	D7	P67	25.8 %	SWEDN	SRILA	F30
V22	EXPORT PARTNER CONCENTRATION	1970	D4	P40	24.4 %	SAUDI	BELGI	F137
		1975	D3	P28	19.1 %	DENMA	ETHIA	----
		1980	D3	P25	18.1 %	ETHIA	ITALY	----
V23	TOTAL DEBT AS % OF GDP	1980	D6	P59	42.5 %	SENE	CHAD	----
V24	SHARE OF NEW FOREIGN PATENTS	1970	D8	P79	99 %	VENE	ZAMBI	----
		1975	D7	P62	93 %	TRITO	ZAIRE	----
		1980	D4	P38	85 %	SPAIN	URU	----
V25	FOREIGN PROPERTY AS % OF GDP	1971	D6	P56	10.2 %	INDO	BRAZI	----
		1975	D7	P63	8.4 %	ZAMBI	NIGRA	----
		1978	D6	----	4.7 %	MAURA	GUATE	----
V26	GNP SHARE OF DEVELOPMENT AID	------	----	----	----- -----	-------	-------	----
V27	SHARE IN NOBEL PRIZE WINNERS	1970-79	D5	P45	0.0 %	TOGO	TURKY	----
V28	GDP SHARE OF MANUFACTURING	1970	D3	P23	9.2 %	NEPAL	UGADA	F16
		1975	D4	P34	10.1 %	ALGER	TANZA	F16
		1980	D5	P50	13.7 %	BOLI	JORDA	F16
V29	EXPORT SHARE OF MANUFACTURES	1970	D6	P59	14.4 %	TANZA	COSTA	----
V30	LACK OF CIVIL LIBERTIES	1975	D6	P54	5	TAIWA	URU	----
		1980	D6	P52	5	TAIWA	UNARE	----
V31	LACK OF POLITICAL RIGHTS	1975	D7	P63	6	TANZA	UPVO	----
		1980	D7	P67	6	TANZA	UGADA	----
V32	RIOTS	1970-74	D6	P59	3	SRILA	YUGO	----
		1975-79	D8	P75	7	SRILA	USSR	----
V33	PROTEST DEMONSTRATIONS	1970-74	D6	P54	3	SINGA	AURIA	----
		1975-79	D4	P32	1	SUDAN	UPVO	----
V34	POLITICAL STRIKES	1970-74	D3	P29	0	TOGO	TURKY	----
		1975-79	D7	P63	1	SRILA	UGADA	----
V35	MEMBER OF THE NONALIGNED MMT.	1970	----	----	1	TOGO	UGADA	----
		1976	----	----	1	TRITO	UGADA	----
		1981	----	----	1	TRITO	UGADA	----
V36	MEMBER OF THE OPEC	1970	----	----	0	TOGO	TURKY	----
		1975	----	----	0	TRITO	TURKY	----
		1980	----	----	0	TRITO	TURKY	----
V37	MEMBER OF THE OECD	1970	----	----	0	TOGO	UGADA	----
		1975	----	----	0	TRITO	UGADA	----
		1980	----	----	0	TRITO	UGADA	----
V38	MEMBER OF THE CMEA	1970	----	----	0	TOGO	TURKY	----
		1975	----	----	0	TRITO	TURKY	----
		1980	----	----	0	TRITO	TURKY	----

V39 MEMBER OF THE WTO	1970	----	----	0		TOGO	TURKY	----
	1975	----	----	0		TRITO	TURKY	----
	1980	----	----	0		TRITO	TURKY	----
V40 MEMBER OF THE NATO	1970	----	----	0		TOGO	UGADA	----
	1975	----	----	0		TRITO	UGADA	----
	1980	----	----	0		TRITO	UGADA	----
V41 GDP SHARE OF INVESTMENTS	1970	D6	P50	19.7 %		UNKI	TURKY	----
	1975	D8	P78	29.3 %		KORSO	ISRA	----
	1980	D8	P80	29.0 %		SOUAF	TRITO	----
V42 GDP SHARE OF AGRICULTURE	1970	D5	P46	19.3 %		GREC	IRAN	F16
	1975	D5	P50	20.7 %		COSTA	DOMI	F16
	1980	D5	P45	16.1 %		KORSO	GREC	F16
V43 GDP SHARE OF INDUSTRY	1970	D4	P37	23.7 %		ELSA	SRILA	F16
	1975	D5	P50	30.8 %		GREC	NEWZ	F16
	1980	D7	P66	36.2 %		FRANC	AULIA	F16
V44 GDP SHARE OF SERVICES	1970	D9	P84	57.0 %		NEWZ	NETH	F16
	1975	D7	P62	48.5 %		NICA	SOUAF	F16
	1980	D6	P54	47.7 %		LESO	ZIMBA	F16
V45 HOMICIDES P. MIL. POPULATION	-------	----	----	----- -----		-------	-------	----
V46 SUICIDES P. MIL. POPULATION	-------	----	----	----- -----		-------	-------	----
V47 IMPORT PARTNERS	1970	R1	FRANC	34.7 %		TOGO	UPVO	F137
	1970	R2	USA	17.0 %		THAI	URU	F137
	1970	R3	GFR	8.5 %		TOGO	UGADA	F137
	1980	R1	FRANC	25.2 %		TOGO	UPVO	----
	1980	R2	ITALY	15.8 %		FRANC	ALGER	----
	1980	R3	GFR	9.5 %		SPAIN	VENE	----
V48 EXPORT PARTNERS	1970	R1	FRANC	24.4 %		TOGO	BELGI	F137
	1970	R2	ITALY	20.6 %		SWITZ	URU	F137
	1970	R3	GFR	9.7 %		TOGO	USA	F137
	1980	R1	GREC	18.1 %		-------	-------	----
	1980	R2	ITALY	15.8 %		SUDAN	TURKY	----
	1980	R3	FRANC	15.4 %		SAUDI	ZAMBI	----
V49 PATENT SUPPLIERS	1970	R1	FRANC	45		MOROC	CUBA	----
	1970	R2	USA	29		SYRIA	UGADA	----
	1970	R3	SWITZ	19		SINGA	VENE	----
	1980	R1	FRANC	73		MOROC	ZAIRE	----
	1980	R2	USA	42		SWITZ	TURKY	----
	1980	R3	SWITZ	21		SRILA	TURKY	----
V50 PROVENANCE OF FOREIGN FIRMS	1980	R1	FRANC	52.9 %		TOGO	UPVO	----
	1980	R2	-------	12.7 %		-------	-------	----
	1980	R3	-------	12.7 %		-------	-------	----
V51 FILM SUPPLIERS	-------	----	----	----- -----		-------	-------	----

TURKEY (TURKY)

V1	INCOME PER CAPITA	1970	D6	P52	1059	$/CAP	NICA	COSTA	----
		1975	D6	P55	1311	$/CAP	MALAY	COSTA	----
		1980	D6	P52	1353	$/CAP	PARA	SYRIA	----
V2	TELEPHONES P. TSD. POPULATION	1970	D6	P51	16	1/TSD CAP	TUNIS	ECUA	----
		1975	D6	P52	25	1/TSD CAP	PERU	ECUA	----
		1979	D5	P49	39	1/TSD CAP	CUBA	MALAY	----
V3	INFANT MORTALITY RATE	1980	D8	P77	131.0	1/TSD	INDIA	SUDAN	F5
V4	PHYSICIANS P. MIL. POPULATION	1970	D6	P56	455	1/MIL	PARA	NICA	----
		1975	D6	P56	542	1/MIL	DOMI	TRITO	----
		1980	D6	P55	613	1/MIL	SAUDI	PERU	----
V5	ADULT LITERACY	1970	D4	P30	51.3	%	ZAMBI	INDO	----
V6	DURATION OF SCHOOLING	1970	D6	P51	7.4	YR	COLO	ZAMBI	F4
		1975	D4	P40	7.3	YR	SRILA	THAI	----
		1981	D4	P29	7.3	YR	GHANA	ZIMBA	----
V7	STUDENT ENROLLMENT RATIO	1970	D6	P56	6.0	%	MEXI	INDIA	----
		1975	D6	P60	9.3	%	ROMA	KORSO	----
		1980	D5	P47	6.0	%	MOROC	JAMAI	----
V8	SHARE OF AGRICULTURAL LABOR	1970	D10	P91	72.0	%	INDO	INDIA	----
		1975	D9	P83	64.1	%	THAI	INDO	----
		1980	D9	P90	59.8	%	GUATE	AFGHA	F113
V9	SHARE OF INDUSTRIAL LABOR	1970	D2	P13	15.1	%	INDIA	ELSA	----
		1975	D3	P29	21.1	%	ELSA	MEXI	----
		1980	D3	P17	22.1	%	GUATE	ITALY	F113
V10	SHARE OF SERVICE LABOR	1970	D1	P6	9.6	%	NEPAL	INDIA	----
		1975	D2	P15	10.2	%	BANGL	YENO	----
		1980	D2	P9	13.6	%	INDIA	THAI	F113
V11	SHARE OF ACADEMIC LABOR	1970	D2	P17	3.3	%	DOMI	IRAN	----
		1975	D4	P38	4.7	%	SYRIA	TUNIS	----
		1980	D3	P21	4.5	%	ELSA	ZIMBA	F113
V12	SHARE OF SELF-EMPLOYED LABOR	1970	D6	P54	27.2	%	IRE	SRILA	----
		1975	D5	P39	26.6	%	COLO	VENE	----
		1980	D5	P54	24.1	%	SPAIN	SRILA	F113
V13	MILITARY EXPENDITURES	1975	D9	P83	3.058	TSD MIL $	BELGI	SPAIN	----
		1980	D8	P80	2.579	TSD MIL $	GREC	LIBYA	----
V14	MILITARY MANPOWER	1970	D10	P94	540	TSD CAP	TAIWA	FRANC	----
		1975	D9	P88	453	TSD CAP	POLA	BRAZI	----
		1980	D10	P96	517	TSD CAP	FRANC	VINO	----
V15	MEN AT AGE 20 - 30	1970	D9	P83	2647	TSD CAP	POLA	PHILI	F46
		1975	D9	P85	3276	TSD CAP	POLA	PHILI	F46
		1980	D8	P79	3945	TSD CAP	KORSO	PHILI	----

V16	POPULATION	1970	D9	P85	34.85	MIL CAP	SPAIN	THAI	----
		1975	D9	P86	40.08	MIL CAP	EGYPT	THAI	----
		1980	D9	P85	44.44	MIL CAP	EGYPT	THAI	----
V17	GROSS DOMESTIC PRODUCT	1970	D8	P72	36.907	TSD MIL $	NORWY	SAUDI	----
		1975	D8	P74	52.546	TSD MIL $	VENE	DENMA	----
		1980	D8	P73	60.121	TSD MIL $	VENE	KORSO	----
V18	SHARE IN WORLD IMPORTS	1970	D6	P56	2.693	1/TSD	COLO	CHILE	----
		1975	D7	P67	5.214	1/TSD	IRAQ	INDO	----
		1980	D6	P60	3.675	1/TSD	LIBYA	ISRA	----
V19	SHARE IN WORLD EXPORTS	1970	D5	P49	1.875	1/TSD	MOROC	GREC	----
		1975	D6	P51	1.599	1/TSD	PERU	EGYPT	----
		1980	D6	P51	1.458	1/TSD	PAKI	EGYPT	----
V20	GDP SHARE OF IMPORTS	1970	D1	P6	7.1	%	BRAZI	ARGE	----
		1975	D2	P17	13.2	%	MOZAM	NIGER	----
		1980	D2	P14	13.2	%	IRAN	JAPAN	----
V21	GDP SHARE OF EXPORTS	1970	D1	P6	4.6	%	USA	BURMA	----
		1975	D1	P4	3.9	%	MEXI	BURMA	----
		1980	D1	P5	5.1	%	BENIN	ARGE	----
V22	EXPORT PARTNER CONCENTRATION	1970	D3	P24	19.9	%	MAURA	GREC	----
		1975	D4	P39	21.8	%	MOROC	AURIA	----
		1980	D4	P37	20.8	%	TOGO	BELGI	----
V23	TOTAL DEBT AS % OF GDP	1980	D5	P45	33.9	%	BENIN	NIGER	----
V24	SHARE OF NEW FOREIGN PATENTS	1970	D5	P49	90	%	NORWY	BELGI	----
		1975	D7	P69	94	%	ELSA	EGYPT	----
		1980	D7	P65	93	%	MEXI	CANA	----
V25	FOREIGN PROPERTY AS % OF GDP	1971	D2	P12	2.4	%	MALI	LESO	----
		1975	D2	P13	1.4	%	SUDAN	BURMA	----
		1978	D2	----	0.9	%	SYRIA	MALI	----
V26	GNP SHARE OF DEVELOPMENT AID	------	----	----	-----	-----	-------	-------	----
V27	SHARE IN NOBEL PRIZE WINNERS	1970-79	D5	P45	0.0	%	TUNIS	UGADA	----
V28	GDP SHARE OF MANUFACTURING	1970	D6	P60	16.9	%	SRILA	COLO	F16
		1975	D6	P60	17.0	%	JAMAI	MOROC	F16
		1980	D8	P73	21.3	%	AULIA	UNKI	F16
V29	EXPORT SHARE OF MANUFACTURES	1970	D5	P44	8.4	%	CAME	MALI	----
		1975	D7	P65	22.4	%	COLO	COSTA	----
		1980	D7	P63	25.9	%	MOROC	CENTR	----
V30	LACK OF CIVIL LIBERTIES	1975	D3	P27	3		THAI	ANGO	----
		1980	D3	P29	3		THAI	UPVO	----
V31	LACK OF POLITICAL RIGHTS	1975	D2	P20	2		TRITO	VENE	----
		1980	D3	P21	2		TRITO	UPVO	----
V32	RIOTS	1970-74	D8	P78	9		NIGRA	BOLI	----
		1975-79	D10	P91	33		PERU	NICA	----
V33	PROTEST DEMONSTRATIONS	1970-74	D8	P72	8		GUATE	YUGO	----
		1975-79	D8	P73	11		JAMAI	AULIA	----

V34	POLITICAL STRIKES	1970-74	D3	P29	0		TUNIS	UGADA	----
		1975-79	D9	P83	6		INDIA	USA	----
V35	MEMBER OF THE NONALIGNED MMT.	1970	----	----	0		THAI	UNKI	----
		1976	----	----	0		THAI	UNKI	----
		1981	----	----	0		THAI	UNKI	----
V36	MEMBER OF THE OPEC	1970	----	----	0		TUNIS	UGADA	----
		1975	----	----	0		TUNIS	UGADA	----
		1980	----	----	0		TUNIS	UGADA	----
V37	MEMBER OF THE OECD	1970	----	----	1		SWITZ	UNKI	----
		1975	----	----	1		SWITZ	UNKI	----
		1980	----	----	1		SWITZ	UNKI	----
V38	MEMBER OF THE CMEA	1970	----	----	0		TUNIS	UGADA	----
		1975	----	----	0		TUNIS	UGADA	----
		1980	----	----	0		TUNIS	UGADA	----
V39	MEMBER OF THE WTO	1970	----	----	0		TUNIS	UGADA	----
		1975	----	----	0		TUNIS	UGADA	----
		1980	----	----	0		TUNIS	UGADA	----
V40	MEMBER OF THE NATO	1970	----	----	1		PORTU	UNKI	----
		1975	----	----	1		PORTU	UNKI	----
		1980	----	----	1		PORTU	UNKI	----
V41	GDP SHARE OF INVESTMENTS	1970	D6	P51	19.8 %		TUNIS	COSTA	----
		1975	D6	P57	23.7 %		MEXI	BOLI	----
		1980	D7	P64	26.4 %		HONDU	COSTA	----
V42	GDP SHARE OF AGRICULTURE	1970	D7	P70	29.7 %		MADA	CAME	F16
		1975	D7	P62	29.1 %		EGYPT	COLO	F16
		1980	D6	P55	22.7 %		SENE	PHILI	F16
V43	GDP SHARE OF INDUSTRY	1970	D5	P50	27.2 %		MOROC	EGYPT	F16
		1975	D4	P37	25.2 %		ELSA	HONDU	F16
		1980	D5	P47	30.4 %		ANGO	COLO	F16
V44	GDP SHARE OF SERVICES	1970	D4	P35	43.1 %		BENIN	GFR	F16
		1975	D6	P51	45.7 %		KENYA	VENE	F16
		1980	D6	P52	46.9 %		SIERA	VENE	F16
V45	HOMICIDES P. MIL. POPULATION	------	----	----	----- -----		-------	-------	----
V46	SUICIDES P. MIL. POPULATION	------	----	----	----- -----		-------	-------	----
V47	IMPORT PARTNERS	1970	R1	USA	19.4 %		TRITO	UNKI	----
		1970	R2	GFR	18.5 %		SPAIN	VENE	----
		1970	R3	UNKI	9.9 %		PAKI	-------	----
		1980	R1	IRAQ	15.2 %		SYRIA	BRAZI	----
		1980	R2	GFR	10.6 %		TANZA	UNKI	----
		1980	R3	IRAN	10.2 %		BURU	-------	----

V48 EXPORT PARTNERS	1970	R1	GFR	19.9 %		SWITZ	URU	----
	1970	R2	USA	9.6 %		THAI	ARGE	----
	1970	R3	SWITZ	7.5 %		AURIA	-------	----
	1980	R1	GFR	20.8 %		TANZA	UNKI	----
	1980	R2	ITALY	7.5 %		TUNIS	YUGO	----
	1980	R3	USSR	5.8 %		SYRIA	-------	----
V49 PATENT SUPPLIERS	1970	R1	USA	113		TRITO	UNKI	----
	1970	R2	GFR	97		SWEDN	URU	----
	1970	R3	FINLA	31		-------	-------	----
	1980	R1	GFR	112		SWITZ	YUGO	----
	1980	R2	USA	82		TUNIS	YUGO	----
	1980	R3	SWITZ	53		TUNIS	VENE	----
V50 PROVENANCE OF FOREIGN FIRMS	1980	R1	USA	28.8 %		THAI	UNKI	----
	1980	R2	GFR	14.4 %		SWITZ	ALGER	----
	1980	R3	UNKI	12.0 %		TOGO	URU	----
V51 FILM SUPPLIERS	1980	R1	USA	90		TRITO	VENE	F120
	1980	R2	FRANC	17		SWITZ	ARGE	F120
	1980	R3	ITALY	15		TRITO	ZAMBI	F120

UGANDA (UGADA)

V1 INCOME PER CAPITA	------	----	----	----- -----		-------	-------	----
V2 TELEPHONES P. TSD. POPULATION	1970	D3	P22	3	1/TSD CAP	TOGO	MADA	----
	1975	D3	P23	4	1/TSD CAP	TOGO	MOZAM	----
	1980	D2	P14	4	1/TSD CAP	TOGO	MALAW	----
V3 INFANT MORTALITY RATE	1980	D6	P55	100.5	1/TSD	INDO	SOUAF	F5
V4 PHYSICIANS P. MIL. POPULATION	1975	D2	P13	37	1/MIL	BENIN	CENTR	----
	1981	D2	P10	45	1/MIL	MALI	TOGO	----
V5 ADULT LITERACY	1980	D6	P52	52.3 %		RWAN	ZAIRE	F21
V6 DURATION OF SCHOOLING	------	----	----	----- -----		-------	-------	----
V7 STUDENT ENROLLMENT RATIO	------	----	----	----- -----		-------	-------	----
V8 SHARE OF AGRICULTURAL LABOR	------	----	----	----- -----		-------	-------	----
V9 SHARE OF INDUSTRIAL LABOR	------	----	----	----- -----		-------	-------	----
V10 SHARE OF SERVICE LABOR	------	----	----	----- -----		-------	-------	----
V11 SHARE OF ACADEMIC LABOR	------	----	----	----- -----		-------	-------	----
V12 SHARE OF SELF-EMPLOYED LABOR	------	----	----	----- -----		-------	-------	----
V13 MILITARY EXPENDITURES	------	----	----	----- -----		-------	-------	----

V14	MILITARY MANPOWER	1970	D4	P33	16	TSD CAP	ECUA	BOLI	----
		1975	D4	P40	25	TSD CAP	TANZA	URU	----
		1980	D2	P14	6	TSD CAP	IVORY	BURU	----
V15	MEN AT AGE 20 - 30	1969	D6	P50	691	TSD CAP	CHILE	CUBA	----
V16	POPULATION	1970	D6	P58	9.81	MIL CAP	BELGI	VENE	----
		1975	D7	P61	11.55	MIL CAP	IRAQ	MALAY	----
		1980	D6	P60	13.18	MIL CAP	MOZAM	IRAQ	F35
V17	GROSS DOMESTIC PRODUCT	------	----	----	-----	-----	-------	-------	----
V18	SHARE IN WORLD IMPORTS	1970	D3	P25	0.518	1/TSD	ETHIA	JORDA	F30
		1975	D2	P16	0.220	1/TSD	BENIN	BURMA	F30
		1980	D1	P7	0.143	1/TSD	MAURA	NEPAL	F30
V19	SHARE IN WORLD EXPORTS	1970	D5	P41	0.899	1/TSD	TANZA	GUATE	F30
		1975	D3	P25	0.305	1/TSD	ETHIA	MADA	F30
		1980	D2	P16	0.173	1/TSD	TOGO	PANA	F30
V20	GDP SHARE OF IMPORTS	1970	D3	P24	13.0	%	SPAIN	RWAN	F30
		1975	D1	P2	6.6	%	BANGL	USA	F30
		1980	D1	P1	0.9	%	-------	BURMA	F30
V21	GDP SHARE OF EXPORTS	1970	D8	P73	21.3	%	FINLA	ALGER	F30
		1975	D2	P18	8.8	%	MALI	ETHIA	F30
		1980	D1	P2	1.0	%	YENO	NEPAL	F30
V22	EXPORT PARTNER CONCENTRATION	1970	D3	P28	20.8	%	FRANC	USA	F124
		1975	D5	P50	24.4	%	PERU	YUGO	F124
V23	TOTAL DEBT AS % OF GDP	1980	D1	P2	2.1	%	-------	NEPAL	----
V24	SHARE OF NEW FOREIGN PATENTS	1971	D9	P90	100	%	TANZA	ZAIRE	----
		1975	D10	P92	100	%	TANZA	-------	----
		1980	D10	P94	100	%	TANZA	ZAMBI	----
V25	FOREIGN PROPERTY AS % OF GDP	1971	D3	P22	3.8	%	ETHIA	GREC	----
		1975	D1	P2	0.2	%	-------	YUGO	----
		1978	D1	----	0.1	%	-------	YUGO	----
V26	GNP SHARE OF DEVELOPMENT AID	------	----	----	-----	-----	-------	-------	----
V27	SHARE IN NOBEL PRIZE WINNERS	1970-79	D5	P45	0.0	%	TURKY	UPVO	----
V28	GDP SHARE OF MANUFACTURING	1970	D3	P23	9.2	%	TUNIS	INDO	F16
		1975	D2	P16	6.3	%	IRAQ	TOGO	F16
		1980	D1	P10	3.9	%	UNARE	CHAD	F16
V29	EXPORT SHARE OF MANUFACTURES	1975	D1	P3	0.0	%	CUBA	IRAQ	----
V30	LACK OF CIVIL LIBERTIES	1975	D10	P93	7		SYRIA	VINO	----
		1980	D8	P74	6		TOGO	URU	----
V31	LACK OF POLITICAL RIGHTS	1975	D9	P88	7		TOGO	VINO	----
		1980	D7	P67	6		TUNIS	URU	----
V32	RIOTS	1970-74	D7	P64	4		SUDAN	DOMI	----
		1975-79	D8	P79	8		THAI	GFR	----

V33 PROTEST DEMONSTRATIONS	1970-74	D2	P15	0		TOGO	UPVO	----
	1975-79	D6	P54	4		PERU	BURMA	----
V34 POLITICAL STRIKES	1970-74	D3	P29	0		TURKY	UPVO	----
	1975-79	D7	P63	1		TUNIS	UPVO	----
V35 MEMBER OF THE NONALIGNED MMT.	1970	----	----	1		TUNIS	YENO	----
	1976	----	----	1		TUNIS	UPVO	----
	1981	----	----	1		TUNIS	UNARE	----
V36 MEMBER OF THE OPEC	1970	----	----	0		TURKY	UNKI	----
	1975	----	----	0		TURKY	UNKI	----
	1980	----	----	0		TURKY	UNKI	----
V37 MEMBER OF THE OECD	1970	----	----	0		TUNIS	UPVO	----
	1975	----	----	0		TUNIS	UPVO	----
	1980	----	----	0		TUNIS	UPVO	----
V38 MEMBER OF THE CMEA	1970	----	----	0		TURKY	UNKI	----
	1975	----	----	0		TURKY	UNKI	----
	1980	----	----	0		TURKY	UNKI	----
V39 MEMBER OF THE WTO	1970	----	----	0		TURKY	UNKI	----
	1975	----	----	0		TURKY	UNKI	----
	1980	----	----	0		TURKY	UNKI	----
V40 MEMBER OF THE NATO	1970	----	----	0		TUNIS	UPVO	----
	1975	----	----	0		TUNIS	UPVO	----
	1980	----	----	0		TUNIS	UPVO	----
V41 GDP SHARE OF INVESTMENTS	1970	D2	P14	13.3 %		PERU	CHAD	----
	1975	D1	P2	7.6 %		ANGO	BURU	----
	1980	D1	P1	3.2 %		-------	GHANA	----
V42 GDP SHARE OF AGRICULTURE	1970	D10	P93	53.8 %		YENO	ETHIA	F16
	1975	D10	P100	72.2 %		NEPAL	-------	F16
	1980	D10	P100	73.1 %		GHANA	-------	F16
V43 GDP SHARE OF INDUSTRY	1970	D1	P9	13.7 %		BENIN	BURMA	F16
	1975	D1	P2	8.2 %		-------	BURMA	F16
V44 GDP SHARE OF SERVICES	1970	D2	P14	32.5 %		MAURA	BANGL	F16
	1975	D1	P4	19.6 %		NEPAL	KUWAI	F16
V45 HOMICIDES P. MIL. POPULATION	------	----	----	----- -----		-------	-------	----
V46 SUICIDES P. MIL. POPULATION	------	----	----	----- -----		-------	-------	----
V47 IMPORT PARTNERS	1970	R1	UNKI	32.2 %		TANZA	ZAMBI	F124
	1970	R2	JAPAN	11.5 %		SAUDI	USA	F124
	1970	R3	GFR	9.1 %		TUNIS	UNKI	F124
V48 EXPORT PARTNERS	1970	R1	USA	20.8 %		TRITO	UNKI	F124
	1970	R2	UNKI	20.6 %		PAKI	ZAMBI	F124
	1970	R3	JAPAN	10.8 %		SINGA	YENO	F124

V49	PATENT SUPPLIERS	1971	R1	UNKI	28		SRILA	AULIA	----
		1971	R2	USA	19		TUNIS	SRILA	----
		1971	R3	GFR	13		PERU	-------	----
		1980	R1	USA	11		TRITO	UNKI	----
		1980	R2	UNKI	8		TRITO	ZAMBI	----
		1980	R3	JAPAN	6		TANZA	UNKI	----
V50	PROVENANCE OF FOREIGN FIRMS	1980	R1	UNKI	71.0 %		TRITO	USA	----
		1980	R2	USA	11.0 %		TRITO	YUGO	----
		1980	R3	GFR	5.0 %		TANZA	USA	----
V51	FILM SUPPLIERS	------	----	----	----- -----		-------	-------	----

UNITED ARAB EMIRATES (UNARE)

V1	INCOME PER CAPITA	1981	D10	P99	28016 $/CAP	KUWAI	-------	F147
V2	TELEPHONES P. TSD. POPULATION	1981	D8	P76	231 1/TSD CAP	CZECH	GREC	F11
V3	INFANT MORTALITY RATE	------	----	----	----- -----	-------	-------	----
V4	PHYSICIANS P. MIL. POPULATION	------	----	----	----- -----	-------	-------	----
V5	ADULT LITERACY	------	----	----	----- -----	-------	-------	----
V6	DURATION OF SCHOOLING	1981	D6	P49	8.9 YR	BRAZI	VENE	----
V7	STUDENT ENROLLMENT RATIO	1981	D4	P34	2.9 %	IVORY	BANGL	----
V8	SHARE OF AGRICULTURAL LABOR	------	----	----	----- -----	-------	-------	----
V9	SHARE OF INDUSTRIAL LABOR	------	----	----	----- -----	-------	-------	----
V10	SHARE OF SERVICE LABOR	------	----	----	----- -----	-------	-------	----
V11	SHARE OF ACADEMIC LABOR	------	----	----	----- -----	-------	-------	----
V12	SHARE OF SELF-EMPLOYED LABOR	------	----	----	----- -----	-------	-------	----
V13	MILITARY EXPENDITURES	1981	D8	P72	1.915 TSD MIL $	ARGE	CHILE	F62
V14	MILITARY MANPOWER	------	----	----	----- -----	-------	-------	----
V15	MEN AT AGE 20 - 30	------	----	----	----- -----	-------	-------	----
V16	POPULATION	1981	D1	P2	1.06 MIL CAP	OMAN	GABON	F22
V17	GROSS DOMESTIC PRODUCT	1981	D7	P62	29.697 TSD MIL $	KUWAI	LIBYA	----
V18	SHARE IN WORLD IMPORTS	1981	D7	P66	4.767 1/TSD	BULGA	GREC	F30
V19	SHARE IN WORLD EXPORTS	------	----	----	----- -----	-------	-------	----

V20	GDP SHARE OF IMPORTS	1981	D7	P69	30.3 %	FINLA	SYRIA	F30
V21	GDP SHARE OF EXPORTS	1981	D10	P94	63.2 %	IRAQ	TRITO	F30
V22	EXPORT PARTNER CONCENTRATION	1981	D8	P73	35.9 %	CZECH	LIBYA	----
V23	TOTAL DEBT AS % OF GDP	------	----	----	----- -----	-------	-------	----
V24	SHARE OF NEW FOREIGN PATENTS	------	----	----	----- -----	-------	-------	----
V25	FOREIGN PROPERTY AS % OF GDP	------	----	----	----- -----	-------	-------	----
V26	GNP SHARE OF DEVELOPMENT AID	1981	D9	P89	2.60 %	IRAQ	KUWAI	----
V27	SHARE IN NOBEL PRIZE WINNERS	------	----	----	----- -----	-------	-------	----
V28	GDP SHARE OF MANUFACTURING	1981	D1	P8	3.8 %	GUINE	UGADA	F16
V29	EXPORT SHARE OF MANUFACTURES	------	----	----	----- -----	-------	-------	----
V30	LACK OF CIVIL LIBERTIES	1981	D6	P52	5	TUNIS	YENO	----
V31	LACK OF POLITICAL RIGHTS	1981	D5	P47	5	TAIWA	ZAMBI	----
V32	RIOTS	------	----	----	----- -----	-------	-------	----
V33	PROTEST DEMONSTRATIONS	------	----	----	----- -----	-------	-------	----
V34	POLITICAL STRIKES	------	----	----	----- -----	-------	-------	----
V35	MEMBER OF THE NONALIGNED MMT.	1981	----	----	1	UGADA	UPVO	----
V36	MEMBER OF THE OPEC	1981	----	----	1	SAUDI	VENE	----
V37	MEMBER OF THE OECD	------	----	----	----- -----	-------	-------	----
V38	MEMBER OF THE CMEA	------	----	----	----- -----	-------	-------	----
V39	MEMBER OF THE WTO	------	----	----	----- -----	-------	-------	----
V40	MEMBER OF THE NATO	------	----	----	----- -----	-------	-------	----
V41	GDP SHARE OF INVESTMENTS	1981	D8	P75	28.4 %	MALAY	PANA	----
V42	GDP SHARE OF AGRICULTURE	1981	D1	P2	0.7 %	KUWAI	SAUDI	F16
V43	GDP SHARE OF INDUSTRY	------	----	----	----- -----	-------	-------	----
V44	GDP SHARE OF SERVICES	------	----	----	----- -----	-------	-------	----
V45	HOMICIDES P. MIL. POPULATION	------	----	----	----- -----	-------	-------	----
V46	SUICIDES P. MIL. POPULATION	------	----	----	----- -----	-------	-------	----
V47	IMPORT PARTNERS	1981	R1	JAPAN	18.9 %	THAI	AFGHA	----
		1981	R2	USA	13.9 %	TRITO	GHANA	----
		1981	R3	UNKI	12.0 %	TRITO	-------	----
V48	EXPORT PARTNERS	1981	R1	JAPAN	35.9 %	THAI	ZAMBI	----
		1981	R2	FRANC	10.1 %	TOGO	UPVO	----
		1981	R3	USA	6.9 %	THAI	-------	----

V49	PATENT SUPPLIERS	------	----	----	-----	-----	-------	-------	----
V50	PROVENANCE OF FOREIGN FIRMS	------	----	----	-----	-----	-------	-------	----
V51	FILM SUPPLIERS	------	----	----	-----	-----	-------	-------	----

UNITED KINGDOM (UNKI)

V1	INCOME PER CAPITA	1970	D9	P84	7240	$/CAP	NEWZ	FINLA	----
		1975	D8	P80	7980	$/CAP	NEWZ	AURIA	----
		1980	D8	P79	8671	$/CAP	NEWZ	JAPAN	----
V2	TELEPHONES P. TSD. POPULATION	1970	D9	P90	251	1/TSD CAP	GFR	FINLA	----
		1975	D10	P90	364	1/TSD CAP	JAPAN	NETH	----
		1980	D9	P89	477	1/TSD CAP	GFR	AULIA	----
V3	INFANT MORTALITY RATE	1980	D2	P14	12.1	1/TSD	GDR	GFR	----
V4	PHYSICIANS P. MIL. POPULATION	------	----	----	-----	-----	-------	-------	
V5	ADULT LITERACY	------	----	----	-----	-----	-------	-------	
V6	DURATION OF SCHOOLING	1970	D10	P97	11.4	YR	NORWY	CANA	----
		1975	D10	P100	12.1	YR	NEWZ	-------	----
		1980	D10	P98	12.0	YR	FINLA	DENMA	----
V7	STUDENT ENROLLMENT RATIO	1970	D9	P82	14.1	%	POLA	BULGA	----
		1975	D8	P80	18.9	%	AURIA	BULGA	----
		1980	D8	P74	20.0	%	CUBA	VENE	----
V8	SHARE OF AGRICULTURAL LABOR	1971	D1	P2	3.1	%	-------	USA	F89
V9	SHARE OF INDUSTRIAL LABOR	1971	D9	P86	40.8	%	SINGA	SPAIN	F89
V10	SHARE OF SERVICE LABOR	1971	D10	P91	44.4	%	ARGE	CANA	F89
V11	SHARE OF ACADEMIC LABOR	1971	D8	P79	11.7	%	BELGI	SWITZ	F89
V12	SHARE OF SELF-EMPLOYED LABOR	1971	D2	P15	7.8	%	CANA	SWEDN	F89
V13	MILITARY EXPENDITURES	1970	D10	P95	19.058	TSD MIL $	FRANC	GFR	----
		1975	D10	P97	21.676	TSD MIL $	FRANC	GFR	----
		1980	D10	P97	24.252	TSD MIL $	FRANC	GFR	----
V14	MILITARY MANPOWER	1970	D9	P88	375	TSD CAP	BRAZI	PAKI	----
		1975	D9	P84	345	TSD CAP	YUGO	SPAIN	----
		1980	D9	P88	326	TSD CAP	IRAN	SPAIN	----
V15	MEN AT AGE 20 - 30	1971	D9	P90	3951	TSD CAP	ITALY	GFR	----
		1975	D9	P88	4072	TSD CAP	THAI	ITALY	----
		1980	D9	P82	4047	TSD CAP	PHILI	ITALY	----

V16	POPULATION	1970	D10	P91	55.42	MIL CAP	ITALY	NIGRA	----
		1975	D9	P90	55.89	MIL CAP	ITALY	MEXI	----
		1980	D9	P89	55.94	MIL CAP	VINO	ITALY	----
V17	GROSS DOMESTIC PRODUCT	1970	D10	P94	401.219	TSD MIL $	ITALY	FRANC	----
		1975	D10	P95	446.009	TSD MIL $	ITALY	FRANC	----
		1980	D10	P95	485.043	TSD MIL $	ITALY	FRANC	----
V18	SHARE IN WORLD IMPORTS	1970	D10	P98	65.881	1/TSD	FRANC	GFR	F30
		1975	D10	P96	58.646	1/TSD	ITALY	FRANC	F30
		1980	D10	P96	56.344	1/TSD	ITALY	FRANC	F34
V19	SHARE IN WORLD EXPORTS	1970	D10	P98	61.943	1/TSD	JAPAN	GFR	F30
		1975	D10	P96	49.549	1/TSD	NETH	FRANC	F30
		1980	D10	P96	55.178	1/TSD	SAUDI	FRANC	F34
V20	GDP SHARE OF IMPORTS	1970	D5	P46	17.7	%	MALI	MOROC	F30
		1975	D5	P49	22.7	%	BOLI	CAME	F30
		1980	D5	P41	21.6	%	NIGRA	PAKI	F34
V21	GDP SHARE OF EXPORTS	1970	D5	P50	15.7	%	NIGRA	PHILI	F30
		1975	D6	P52	18.5	%	ITALY	SRILA	F30
		1980	D6	P54	20.6	%	ELSA	COSTA	F34
V22	EXPORT PARTNER CONCENTRATION	1970	D1	P1	11.1	%	-------	PAKI	----
		1975	D1	P2	8.9	%	PAKI	ARGE	----
		1980	D1	P4	10.4	%	USSR	CHILE	----
V23	TOTAL DEBT AS % OF GDP	------	----	----	----- -----		-------	-------	----
V24	SHARE OF NEW FOREIGN PATENTS	1970	D3	P24	75	%	SWITZ	ARGE	----
		1975	D3	P24	78	%	FINLA	URU	----
		1980	D4	P32	78	%	SOMA	AURIA	----
V25	FOREIGN PROPERTY AS % OF GDP	------	----	----	----- -----		-------	-------	----
V26	GNP SHARE OF DEVELOPMENT AID	1970	D7	P69	0.39	%	DENMA	CANA	----
		1975	D4	P39	0.38	%	USA	GFR	----
		1980	D5	P45	0.35	%	NEWZ	CANA	----
V27	SHARE IN NOBEL PRIZE WINNERS	1970-79	D10	P99	17.5	%	SWEDN	USA	----
V28	GDP SHARE OF MANUFACTURING	1970	D10	P92	28.1	%	NETH	FRANC	----
		1975	D9	P90	25.8	%	SPAIN	KORSO	----
		1980	D8	P74	21.4	%	TURKY	CHILE	----
V29	EXPORT SHARE OF MANUFACTURES	------	----	----	----- -----		-------	-------	----
V30	LACK OF CIVIL LIBERTIES	1975	D1	P7	1		SWITZ	USA	----
		1980	D1	P7	1		SWITZ	USA	----
V31	LACK OF POLITICAL RIGHTS	1975	D1	P8	1		SWITZ	USA	----
		1980	D1	P8	1		SWITZ	USA	----
V32	RIOTS	1970-74	D10	P100	210		USA	-------	----
		1975-79	D10	P93	37		NICA	PAKI	----
V33	PROTEST DEMONSTRATIONS	1970-74	D10	P99	385		USSR	USA	----
		1975-79	D10	P97	143		ITALY	PORTU	----

V34	POLITICAL STRIKES	1970-74	D10	P100	113		USA	-------	----
		1975-79	D10	P93	13		ISRA	GHANA	----
V35	MEMBER OF THE NONALIGNED MMT.	1970	----	----	0		TURKY	UPVO	----
		1976	----	----	0		TURKY	URU	----
		1981	----	----	0		TURKY	URU	----
V36	MEMBER OF THE OPEC	1970	----	----	0		UGADA	UPVO	----
		1975	----	----	0		UGADA	UPVO	----
		1980	----	----	0		UGADA	UPVO	----
V37	MEMBER OF THE OECD	1970	----	----	1		TURKY	USA	----
		1975	----	----	1		TURKY	USA	----
		1980	----	----	1		TURKY	USA	----
V38	MEMBER OF THE CMEA	1970	----	----	0		UGADA	UPVO	----
		1975	----	----	0		UGADA	UPVO	----
		1980	----	----	0		UGADA	UPVO	----
V39	MEMBER OF THE WTO	1970	----	----	0		UGADA	UPVO	----
		1975	----	----	0		UGADA	UPVO	----
		1980	----	----	0		UGADA	UPVO	----
V40	MEMBER OF THE NATO	1970	----	----	1		TURKY	USA	----
		1975	----	----	1		TURKY	USA	----
		1980	----	----	1		TURKY	USA	----
V41	GDP SHARE OF INVESTMENTS	1970	D5	P49	19.4	%	DOMI	TUNIS	----
		1975	D4	P32	18.1	%	KENYA	SOMA	----
		1980	D3	P21	16.2	%	SOMA	SIERA	----
V42	GDP SHARE OF AGRICULTURE	1970	D1	P4	2.5	%	LIBYA	USA	----
		1975	D1	P6	2.4	%	LIBYA	BELGI	----
		1980	D1	P6	1.9	%	LIBYA	OMAN	----
V43	GDP SHARE OF INDUSTRY	1970	D8	P75	38.1	%	TRITO	ALGER	----
		1975	D8	P73	36.2	%	SWEDN	JAMAI	----
		1980	D6	P60	34.6	%	SPAIN	MEXI	----
V44	GDP SHARE OF SERVICES	1970	D9	P90	59.4	%	CONGO	NORWY	----
		1975	D10	P93	61.4	%	NETH	CANA	----
		1980	D10	P95	63.5	%	USA	NETH	----
V45	HOMICIDES P. MIL. POPULATION	1970	D2	P20	7.5	1/MIL CAP	FRANC	ITALY	F154
		1975	D5	P47	13.3	1/MIL CAP	CZECH	KUWAI	F154
		1980	D2	P22	9.7	1/MIL CAP	JAPAN	FRANC	F2
V46	SUICIDES P. MIL. POPULATION	1970	D4	P39	79.3	1/MIL CAP	ELSA	NETH	F2
		1975	D4	P35	74.7	1/MIL CAP	ISRA	PORTU	F2
		1980	D4	P37	87.9	1/MIL CAP	ARGE	NETH	F2
V47	IMPORT PARTNERS	1970	R1	USA	12.7	%	TURKY	VENE	----
		1970	R2	CANA	7.3	%	SYRIA	INDIA	----
		1970	R3	GFR	6.0	%	UGADA	UPVO	----
		1980	R1	USA	11.8	%	SPAIN	VENE	----
		1980	R2	GFR	11.1	%	TURKY	YUGO	----
		1980	R3	FRANC	7.7	%	BURU	YENO	----

V48	EXPORT PARTNERS	1970	R1	USA	11.1	%	UGADA	VENE	----
		1970	R2	GFR	6.0	%	SWEDN	CAME	----
		1970	R3	NETH	4.6	%	THAI	URU	----
		1980	R1	GFR	10.4	%	TURKY	BRAZI	----
		1980	R2	USA	9.5	%	SINGA	ARGE	----
		1980	R3	NETH	7.8	%	PHILI	-------	----
V49	PATENT SUPPLIERS	1970	R1	USA	12728		TURKY	URU	----
		1980	R1	USA	6726		UGADA	URU	----
		1980	R2	GFR	3929		SWEDN	URU	----
		1980	R3	JAPAN	2274		UGADA	-------	----
V50	PROVENANCE OF FOREIGN FIRMS	1980	R1	USA	52.6	%	TURKY	URU	----
		1980	R2	CANA	8.2	%	GUATE	USA	----
		1980	R3	NETH	6.1	%	SAUDI	-------	----
V51	FILM SUPPLIERS	------	----	----	-----	-----	-------	-------	----

UPPER VOLTA [5] (UPVO)

V1	INCOME PER CAPITA	1975	D1	P8	191	$/CAP	MALAW	BURU	----
		1980	D1	P7	200	$/CAP	BURMA	BURU	----
V2	TELEPHONES P. TSD. POPULATION	1970	D1	P7	1	1/TSD CAP	NIGER	YENO	----
		1975	D1	P5	1	1/TSD CAP	RWAN	AFGHA	----
V3	INFANT MORTALITY RATE	1980	D10	P94	160.4	1/TSD	MALI	YENO	F5
V4	PHYSICIANS P. MIL. POPULATION	1970	D1	P2	11	1/MIL	-------	ETHIA	----
		1976	D1	P4	19	1/MIL	NIGER	MALAW	----
		1980	D1	P3	21	1/MIL	ETHIA	MOZAM	----
V5	ADULT LITERACY	------	----	----	-----	-----	-------	-------	----
V6	DURATION OF SCHOOLING	1970	D1	P5	1.0	YR	NIGER	ETHIA	F4
		1975	D1	P2	1.2	YR	BHUTA	NIGER	----
		1980	D1	P1	1.6	YR	BHUTA	MALI	----
V7	STUDENT ENROLLMENT RATIO	1970	D1	P4	0.0	%	NIGER	YENO	----
		1975	D1	P6	0.2	%	TANZA	BURU	----
		1980	D1	P6	0.3	%	RWAN	LAOS	----
V8	SHARE OF AGRICULTURAL LABOR	------	----	----	-----	-----	-------	-------	----
V9	SHARE OF INDUSTRIAL LABOR	------	----	----	-----	-----	-------	-------	----
V10	SHARE OF SERVICE LABOR	------	----	----	-----	-----	-------	-------	----

---

[5] Also known as Burkina-Faso.

V11	SHARE OF ACADEMIC LABOR	------	----	----	----- -----		-------	-------	----
V12	SHARE OF SELF-EMPLOYED LABOR	------	----	----	----- -----		-------	-------	----
V13	MILITARY EXPENDITURES	1975	D2	P18	0.030	TSD MIL $	HONDU	NICA	----
		1980	D2	P17	0.032	TSD MIL $	TRITO	GABON	----
V14	MILITARY MANPOWER	1970	D1	P10	4	TSD CAP	RWAN	LIBE	----
		1975	D2	P12	5	TSD CAP	SIERA	HAITI	----
		1980	D2	P12	5	TSD CAP	RWAN	IVORY	----
V15	MEN AT AGE 20 - 30	1975	D4	P31	369	TSD CAP	NIGER	ZAMBI	----
V16	POPULATION	1970	D5	P43	5.38	MIL CAP	IVORY	ECUA	F4
		1975	D5	P41	5.64	MIL CAP	TUNIS	GUATE	----
		1980	D4	P40	6.15	MIL CAP	MALAW	SWITZ	----
V17	GROSS DOMESTIC PRODUCT	1972	D2	----	1.063	TSD MIL $	YENO	HONDU	----
		1975	D1	P9	1.077	TSD MIL $	SIERA	HAITI	----
		1980	D1	P9	1.227	TSD MIL $	SIERA	HAITI	----
V18	SHARE IN WORLD IMPORTS	1970	D1	P7	0.148	1/TSD	MALI	HAITI	----
		1975	D1	P7	0.166	1/TSD	HAITI	SOMA	----
		1980	D1	P10	0.175	1/TSD	BURMA	HAITI	----
V19	SHARE IN WORLD EXPORTS	1970	D1	P4	0.057	1/TSD	VISO	BURU	----
		1975	D1	P6	0.050	1/TSD	RWAN	CENTR	----
		1980	D1	P7	0.045	1/TSD	NEPAL	CENTR	----
V20	GDP SHARE OF IMPORTS	1970	D3	P28	13.8	%	FRANC	LIBYA	----
		1975	D6	P51	23.5	%	CAME	SUDAN	----
		1980	D7	P61	26.7	%	YUGO	SWEDN	----
V21	GDP SHARE OF EXPORTS	1970	D1	P8	5.1	%	BURMA	NEPAL	----
		1975	D1	P10	6.8	%	NEPAL	BRAZI	----
		1980	D2	P12	6.7	%	SUDAN	BURU	----
V22	EXPORT PARTNER CONCENTRATION	1970	D7	P62	33.7	%	INDO	CZECH	----
		1975	D9	P85	48.1	%	ECUA	SENE	----
		1980	D8	P70	32.9	%	ECUA	COSTA	----
V23	TOTAL DEBT AS % OF GDP	1980	D3	P30	25.1	%	THAI	ELSA	----
V24	SHARE OF NEW FOREIGN PATENTS	------	----	----	----- -----		-------	-------	----
V25	FOREIGN PROPERTY AS % OF GDP	1971	D3	P30	4.9	%	SPAIN	MOROC	----
		1975	D3	P26	3.1	%	MOZAM	MOROC	----
		1978	D3	----	2.0	%	THAI	INDIA	----
V26	GNP SHARE OF DEVELOPMENT AID	------	----	----	----- -----		-------	-------	----
V27	SHARE IN NOBEL PRIZE WINNERS	1970-79	D5	P45	0.0	%	UGADA	URU	----
V28	GDP SHARE OF MANUFACTURING	------	----	----	----- -----		-------	-------	----
V29	EXPORT SHARE OF MANUFACTURES	1970	D3	P29	3.1	%	BOLI	CHILE	----
		1975	D4	P41	6.3	%	TRITO	CHAD	----
		1980	D4	P38	9.9	%	PANA	TOGO	----
V30	LACK OF CIVIL LIBERTIES	1975	D4	P39	4		NIGRA	YENO	----
		1980	D3	P29	3		TURKY	GHANA	----

V31 LACK OF POLITICAL RIGHTS	1975	D7	P63	6	TUNIS	USSR	----
	1980	D3	P21	2	TURKY	BANGL	----
V32 RIOTS	1970-74	D2	P19	0	TOGO	VINO	----
	1975-79	D2	P20	0	TRITO	URU	----
V33 PROTEST DEMONSTRATIONS	1970-74	D2	P15	0	UGADA	YESO	----
	1975-79	D4	P32	1	TUNIS	VENE	----
V34 POLITICAL STRIKES	1970-74	D3	P29	0	UGADA	USSR	----
	1975-79	D7	P63	1	UGADA	USSR	----
V35 MEMBER OF THE NONALIGNED MMT.	1970	----	----	0	UNKI	URU	----
	1976	----	----	1	UGADA	VINO	----
	1981	----	----	1	UNARE	VINO	----
V36 MEMBER OF THE OPEC	1970	----	----	0	UNKI	URU	----
	1975	----	----	0	UNKI	URU	----
	1980	----	----	0	UNKI	URU	----
V37 MEMBER OF THE OECD	1970	----	----	0	UGADA	URU	----
	1975	----	----	0	UGADA	URU	----
	1980	----	----	0	UGADA	URU	----
V38 MEMBER OF THE CMEA	1970	----	----	0	UNKI	URU	----
	1975	----	----	0	UNKI	URU	----
	1980	----	----	0	UNKI	URU	----
V39 MEMBER OF THE WTO	1970	----	----	0	UNKI	URU	----
	1975	----	----	0	UNKI	URU	----
	1980	----	----	0	UNKI	URU	----
V40 MEMBER OF THE NATO	1970	----	----	0	UGADA	URU	----
	1975	----	----	0	UGADA	URU	----
	1980	----	----	0	UGADA	URU	----
V41 GDP SHARE OF INVESTMENTS	1970	D1	P8	11.4 %	HAITI	ETHIA	----
	1975	D7	P67	25.7 %	JAMAI	ARGE	----
	1980	D3	P25	17.3 %	SUDAN	PAKI	----
V42 GDP SHARE OF AGRICULTURE	1970	D9	P82	42.8 %	TANZA	SUDAN	F16
	1975	D8	P80	40.6 %	ANGO	MADA	F16
	1980	D9	P84	39.6 %	INDIA	MALI	F16
V43 GDP SHARE OF INDUSTRY	1970	D3	P24	18.6 %	MADA	MALAW	F16
	1975	D3	P23	20.7 %	KENYA	GHANA	F16
	1980	D2	P15	17.8 %	MOZAM	MADA	F16
V44 GDP SHARE OF SERVICES	1970	D3	P22	38.6 %	IRAN	PORTU	F16
	1975	D3	P26	38.7 %	PHILI	CHAD	F16
	1980	D4	P38	42.6 %	ZAIRE	SRILA	F16
V45 HOMICIDES P. MIL. POPULATION	------	----	----	----- -----	-------	-------	----
V46 SUICIDES P. MIL. POPULATION	------	----	----	----- -----	-------	-------	----

V47	IMPORT PARTNERS	1970	R1	FRANC	50.7 %	TUNIS	BELGI	----
		1970	R2	IVORY	10.8 %	-------	MALI	----
		1970	R3	GFR	6.1 %	UNKI	USA	----
		1980	R1	FRANC	39.3 %	TUNIS	EGYPT	----
		1980	R2	IVORY	11.5 %	MALI	-------	----
		1980	R3	USA	9.0 %	SWEDN	ZAIRE	----
V48	EXPORT PARTNERS	1970	R1	IVORY	33.7 %	MALI	SENE	----
		1970	R2	JAPAN	15.5 %	PHILI	USA	----
		1970	R3	FRANC	12.3 %	SPAIN	-------	----
		1980	R1	IVORY	32.9 %	-------	MALI	----
		1980	R2	FRANC	18.0 %	UNARE	YENO	----
		1980	R3	JAPAN	7.0 %	SUDAN	-------	----
V49	PATENT SUPPLIERS	------	----	----	----- -----	-------	-------	----
V50	PROVENANCE OF FOREIGN FIRMS	1980	R1	FRANC	60.0 %	TUNIS	GUINE	----
		1980	R2	-------	12.0 %	-------	-------	----
		1980	R3	-------	12.0 %	-------	-------	----
V51	FILM SUPPLIERS	------	----	----	----- -----	-------	-------	----

URUGUAY (URU)

V1	INCOME PER CAPITA	1970	D7	P64	1907 $/CAP	PORTU	CHILE	F4
		1975	D7	P68	2137 $/CAP	PORTU	SOUAF	----
		1980	D7	P67	2590 $/CAP	ARGE	SOUAF	----
V2	TELEPHONES P. TSD. POPULATION	1970	D8	P76	74 1/TSD CAP	SOUAF	HUNGA	----
		1975	D8	P71	90 1/TSD CAP	BULGA	HUNGA	----
		1980	D7	P65	99 1/TSD CAP	YUGO	COSTA	----
V3	INFANT MORTALITY RATE	1980	D4	P37	37.6 1/TSD	KORNO	SRILA	----
V4	PHYSICIANS P. MIL. POPULATION	1970	D8	P73	1062 1/MIL	YUGO	JAPAN	----
		1975	D8	P76	1407 1/MIL	NEWZ	AULIA	----
		1979	D9	P82	1869 1/MIL	LEBA	NORWY	----
V5	ADULT LITERACY	------	----	----	----- -----	-------	-------	----
V6	DURATION OF SCHOOLING	1970	D9	P85	10.4 YR	ROMA	ITALY	----
		1975	D8	P73	10.1 YR	JAMAI	YUGO	----
		1980	D7	P65	10.1 YR	JAMAI	PANA	----
V7	STUDENT ENROLLMENT RATIO	1970	D7	P70	10.0 %	SWITZ	HUNGA	F4
		1975	D8	P72	16.0 %	PERU	CHILE	----
		1980	D7	P67	16.1 %	BULGA	BOLI	----
V8	SHARE OF AGRICULTURAL LABOR	1975	D4	P38	17.9 %	FINLA	VENE	----
V9	SHARE OF INDUSTRIAL LABOR	1975	D6	P57	32.9 %	JAMAI	USA	----

V10	SHARE OF SERVICE LABOR	1975	D9	P80	40.9 %	ISRA	AULIA	----
V11	SHARE OF ACADEMIC LABOR	1975	D6	P60	8.3 %	ALGER	COSTA	----
V12	SHARE OF SELF-EMPLOYED LABOR	1975	D4	P36	25.5 %	LIBYA	COLO	----
V13	MILITARY EXPENDITURES	1970	D4	P39	0.109 TSD MIL $	ECUA	IRE	----
		1975	D4	P40	0.161 TSD MIL $	BURMA	ETHIA	----
		1980	D4	P39	0.193 TSD MIL $	ECUA	BURMA	----
V14	MILITARY MANPOWER	1970	D4	P36	18 TSD CAP	LIBYA	LEBA	----
		1975	D4	P40	25 TSD CAP	UGADA	SINGA	----
		1980	D5	P41	28 TSD CAP	ZAIRE	TUNIS	----
V15	MEN AT AGE 20 - 30	1968	D2	----	203 TSD CAP	IRE	RWAN	F2
		1975	D2	P10	192 TSD CAP	LIBYA	BENIN	F46
		1980	D1	P9	211 TSD CAP	BENIN	COSTA	F2
V16	POPULATION	1970	D3	P22	2.89 MIL CAP	NEWZ	IRE	F4
		1975	D2	P20	2.83 MIL CAP	LEBA	SIERA	----
		1980	D2	P16	2.91 MIL CAP	NICA	JORDA	----
V17	GROSS DOMESTIC PRODUCT	1970	D5	P47	5.512 TSD MIL $	SYRIA	ZAIRE	----
		1975	D5	P42	6.047 TSD MIL $	TUNIS	ZAIRE	----
		1980	D5	P42	7.536 TSD MIL $	DOMI	GUATE	----
V18	SHARE IN WORLD IMPORTS	1970	D4	P32	0.696 1/TSD	HONDU	CAME	----
		1975	D3	P29	0.612 1/TSD	NICA	BOLI	----
		1980	D5	P41	0.842 1/TSD	CAME	YENO	----
V19	SHARE IN WORLD EXPORTS	1970	D4	P39	0.743 1/TSD	CAME	TANZA	----
		1975	D4	P31	0.438 1/TSD	NICA	LIBE	----
		1980	D4	P39	0.531 1/TSD	SRILA	GHANA	----
V20	GDP SHARE OF IMPORTS	1970	D1	P10	9.6 %	ETHIA	NEPAL	----
		1975	D3	P22	15.7 %	INDO	FRANC	----
		1980	D3	P25	17.2 %	AFGHA	BURU	----
V21	GDP SHARE OF EXPORTS	1970	D2	P19	9.7 %	KORSO	SOMA	----
		1975	D3	P24	10.8 %	SUDAN	GREC	----
		1980	D3	P25	10.5 %	ETHIA	PAKI	----
V22	EXPORT PARTNER CONCENTRATION	1970	D1	P5	13.1 %	SWEDN	KAMPU	----
		1975	D3	P21	17.1 %	FRANC	SINGA	----
		1980	D3	P24	18.0 %	GREC	ETHIA	----
V23	TOTAL DEBT AS % OF GDP	1980	D2	P13	16.5 %	RWAN	LESO	----
V24	SHARE OF NEW FOREIGN PATENTS	1970	D2	P21	71 %	PAKI	SPAIN	----
		1975	D3	P24	78 %	UNKI	YUGO	----
		1980	D4	P38	85 %	TUNIS	BELGI	----
V25	FOREIGN PROPERTY AS % OF GDP	1971	D2	P18	2.9 %	INDIA	SOMA	----
		1975	D6	P56	7.0 %	PAKI	GUATE	----
		1978	D7	----	6.5 %	COLO	IVORY	----
V26	GNP SHARE OF DEVELOPMENT AID	------	----	----	----- -----	-------	-------	----
V27	SHARE IN NOBEL PRIZE WINNERS	1970-79	D5	P45	0.0 %	UPVO	VENE	----
V28	GDP SHARE OF MANUFACTURING	------	----	----	----- -----	-------	-------	----

V29	EXPORT SHARE OF MANUFACTURES	1970	D7	P64	19.9	%	SENE	GREC	----
		1975	D8	P75	29.5	%	ELSA	EGYPT	----
		1980	D8	P72	37.2	%	ELSA	GREC	----
V30	LACK OF CIVIL LIBERTIES	1975	D6	P54	5		TUNIS	VISO	----
		1980	D8	P74	6		UGADA	USSR	----
V31	LACK OF POLITICAL RIGHTS	1975	D5	P43	5		THAI	YENO	----
		1980	D7	P67	6		UGADA	USSR	----
V32	RIOTS	1970-74	D6	P53	2		TAIWA	LIBYA	----
		1975-79	D2	P20	0		UPVO	VENE	----
V33	PROTEST DEMONSTRATIONS	1970-74	D8	P78	12		CZECH	KAMPU	----
		1975-79	D5	P49	3		SYRIA	BANGL	----
V34	POLITICAL STRIKES	1970-74	D9	P87	9		MOROC	GREC	----
		1975-79	D3	P29	0		TRITO	VENE	----
V35	MEMBER OF THE NONALIGNED MMT.	1970	----	----	0		UPVO	USA	----
		1976	----	----	0		UNKI	USA	----
		1981	----	----	0		UNKI	USA	----
V36	MEMBER OF THE OPEC	1970	----	----	0		UPVO	USA	----
		1975	----	----	0		UPVO	USA	----
		1980	----	----	0		UPVO	USA	----
V37	MEMBER OF THE OECD	1970	----	----	0		UPVO	USSR	----
		1975	----	----	0		UPVO	USSR	----
		1980	----	----	0		UPVO	USSR	----
V38	MEMBER OF THE CMEA	1970	----	----	0		UPVO	USA	----
		1975	----	----	0		UPVO	USA	----
		1980	----	----	0		UPVO	USA	----
V39	MEMBER OF THE WTO	1970	----	----	0		UPVO	USA	----
		1975	----	----	0		UPVO	USA	----
		1980	----	----	0		UPVO	USA	----
V40	MEMBER OF THE NATO	1970	----	----	0		UPVO	USSR	----
		1975	----	----	0		UPVO	USSR	----
		1980	----	----	0		UPVO	USSR	----
V41	GDP SHARE OF INVESTMENTS	1970	D1	P7	11.3	%	RWAN	HAITI	----
		1975	D2	P15	13.5	%	SAUDI	RWAN	----
		1980	D3	P26	17.5	%	PAKI	USA	----
V42	GDP SHARE OF AGRICULTURE	1970	D4	P33	12.6	%	NEWZ	IRE	F16
		1975	D4	P36	12.0	%	PANA	ZAMBI	F16
		1980	D4	P34	9.7	%	MEXI	PANA	F16
V43	GDP SHARE OF INDUSTRY	1970	D6	P54	29.6	%	PHILI	BOLI	F16
		1975	D6	P56	32.1	%	CANA	CONGO	F16
		1980	D7	P63	35.0	%	MEXI	FINLA	F16
V44	GDP SHARE OF SERVICES	1970	D9	P87	57.8	%	TRITO	CONGO	F16
		1975	D9	P84	55.9	%	MEXI	AULIA	F16
		1980	D9	P81	55.3	%	COSTA	YENO	F16

V45	HOMICIDES P. MIL. POPULATION	1971	D7	P69	36.6	1/MIL CAP	YUGO	COSTA	F148
		1975	D7	P69	28.6	1/MIL CAP	CANA	FINLA	F148
		1978	D6	----	19.8	1/MIL CAP	AULIA	CANA	F148
V46	SUICIDES P. MIL. POPULATION	1971	D6	P55	104.1	1/MIL CAP	ARGE	POLA	----
		1975	D5	P49	101.4	1/MIL CAP	NORWY	ELSA	----
		1978	D5	----	104.2	1/MIL CAP	NETH	NEWZ	----
V47	IMPORT PARTNERS	1970	R1	BRAZI	15.0	%	-------	ARGE	----
		1970	R2	USA	12.9	%	TUNIS	ZAIRE	----
		1970	R3	ARGE	12.2	%	CHILE	-------	----
		1980	R1	BRAZI	17.3	%	PARA	ARGE	----
		1980	R2	IRAQ	12.8	%	MOROC	MADA	----
		1980	R3	ARGE	10.5	%	PARA	-------	----
V48	EXPORT PARTNERS	1970	R1	GFR	13.1	%	TURKY	ALGER	----
		1970	R2	ITALY	9.8	%	TUNIS	AURIA	----
		1970	R3	NETH	8.6	%	UNKI	-------	----
		1980	R1	BRAZI	18.0	%	-------	ARGE	----
		1980	R2	ARGE	13.4	%	BOLI	-------	----
		1980	R3	GFR	12.9	%	PERU	YUGO	----
V49	PATENT SUPPLIERS	1970	R1	USA	139		UNKI	VENE	----
		1970	R2	GFR	77		TURKY	AULIA	----
		1970	R3	UNKI	37		TANZA	VISO	----
		1980	R1	USA	57		UNKI	USSR	----
		1980	R2	GFR	30		UNKI	USA	----
		1980	R3	UNKI	27		SINGA	USA	----
V50	PROVENANCE OF FOREIGN FIRMS	1980	R1	USA	55.5	%	UNKI	VENE	----
		1980	R2	FRANC	9.0	%	GUINE	LEBA	----
		1980	R3	UNKI	6.9	%	TURKY	ZAIRE	----
V51	FILM SUPPLIERS	------	----	----	----- -----		-------	-------	----

USA (USA)

V1	INCOME PER CAPITA	1970	D10	P94	9392	$/CAP	NORWY	GFR	F210
		1975	D10	P92	10069	$/CAP	BELGI	GFR	F147
		1980	D9	P90	11368	$/CAP	BELGI	SAUDI	F147
V2	TELEPHONES P. TSD. POPULATION	1970	D10	P100	583	1/TSD CAP	SWEDN	-------	----
		1975	D10	P99	686	1/TSD CAP	SWEDN	-------	----
		1980	D10	P98	788	1/TSD CAP	SWITZ	SWEDN	----
V3	INFANT MORTALITY RATE	1980	D2	P15	12.6	1/TSD	GFR	NEWZ	----
V4	PHYSICIANS P. MIL. POPULATION	1970	D9	P88	1578	1/MIL	BELGI	GDR	F147
		1975	D9	P81	1630	1/MIL	NETH	POLA	F150
		1980	D8	P78	1822	1/MIL	CANA	NETH	F147

V5	ADULT LITERACY	1969	D10	P98	99.0	%	HUNGA	-------	F24
		1979	D10	P98	99.5	%	HUNGA	-------	F24
V6	DURATION OF SCHOOLING	1970	D10	P98	12.0	YR	CANA	NEWZ	----
		1975	D10	P98	11.9	YR	CHILE	NEWZ	----
		1980	D10	P90	11.4	YR	GDR	CHILE	----
V7	STUDENT ENROLLMENT RATIO	1970	D10	P100	49.4	%	CANA	-------	----
		1975	D10	P100	57.3	%	CANA	-------	----
		1980	D10	P100	56.0	%	ECUA	-------	----
V8	SHARE OF AGRICULTURAL LABOR	1970	D1	P4	3.2	%	UNKI	SINGA	F91
		1975	D1	P8	3.5	%	SINGA	SWEDN	F114
		1980	D1	P7	2.9	%	KUWAI	GFR	F90
V9	SHARE OF INDUSTRIAL LABOR	1970	D7	P66	36.5	%	JAPAN	ARGE	F91
		1975	D6	P60	33.0	%	URU	NETH	F114
		1980	D6	P48	31.2	%	MOROC	SWEDN	F90
V10	SHARE OF SERVICE LABOR	1970	D10	P96	45.3	%	CANA	SINGA	F91
		1975	D10	P98	48.5	%	SINGA	-------	F114
		1980	D10	P96	50.6	%	CANA	ITALY	F90
V11	SHARE OF ACADEMIC LABOR	1970	D10	P93	15.1	%	NETH	SWEDN	F91
		1975	D9	P80	15.0	%	NEWZ	CANA	F114
		1980	D9	P84	15.4	%	SWITZ	FRANC	F90
V12	SHARE OF SELF-EMPLOYED LABOR	1970	D1	P11	7.7	%	HUNGA	CANA	F92
		1975	D1	P6	8.7	%	SWEDN	NETH	F90
		1980	D1	P8	6.8	%	HUNGA	SWEDN	F90
V13	MILITARY EXPENDITURES	1970	D10	P99	152.009	TSD MIL $	GFR	-------	----
		1975	D10	P99	129.169	TSD MIL $	GFR	-------	----
		1980	D10	P99	144.175	TSD MIL $	GFR	-------	----
V14	MILITARY MANPOWER	1970	D10	P99	3070	TSD CAP	INDIA	USSR	F4
		1975	D10	P98	2128	TSD CAP	INDIA	USSR	----
		1980	D10	P99	2050	TSD CAP	INDIA	USSR	----
V15	MEN AT AGE 20 - 30	1970	D10	P96	14539	TSD CAP	JAPAN	USSR	F197
		1976	D10	P98	18481	TSD CAP	USSR	INDIA	F22
		1981	D10	P98	20909	TSD CAP	INDO	INDIA	F186
V16	POPULATION	1970	D10	P97	204.88	MIL CAP	INDO	USSR	F162
		1975	D10	P97	215.97	MIL CAP	INDO	USSR	F22
		1980	D10	P97	227.70	MIL CAP	INDO	USSR	F22
V17	GROSS DOMESTIC PRODUCT	1970	D10	P99	1924.159	TSD MIL $	JAPAN	-------	----
		1975	D10	P99	2174.559	TSD MIL $	JAPAN	-------	----
		1980	D10	P99	2588.420	TSD MIL $	JAPAN	-------	----
V18	SHARE IN WORLD IMPORTS	1970	D10	P100	129.030	1/TSD	GFR	-------	F55
		1975	D10	P100	116.484	1/TSD	GFR	-------	F30
		1980	D10	P100	125.291	1/TSD	GFR	-------	F30
V19	SHARE IN WORLD EXPORTS	1970	D10	P100	137.868	1/TSD	GFR	-------	F30
		1975	D10	P100	123.382	1/TSD	GFR	-------	F30
		1980	D10	P100	110.617	1/TSD	GFR	-------	F30

V20	GDP SHARE OF IMPORTS	1970	D1	P3	4.3 %	INDIA	MEXI	F55
		1975	D1	P3	6.9 %	UGADA	BURMA	F30
		1980	D1	P8	9.9 %	INDIA	CENTR	F30
V21	GDP SHARE OF EXPORTS	1970	D1	P5	4.4 %	INDIA	TURKY	F30
		1975	D2	P12	7.1 %	BRAZI	SPAIN	F30
		1980	D2	P18	8.5 %	MEXI	SOMA	F30
V22	EXPORT PARTNER CONCENTRATION	1970	D3	P29	21.0 %	UGADA	SYRIA	----
		1975	D4	P31	20.2 %	JAPAN	MALAY	----
		1980	D2	P15	15.6 %	THAI	FRANC	----
V23	TOTAL DEBT AS % OF GDP	------	----	----	----- -----	-------	-------	----
V24	SHARE OF NEW FOREIGN PATENTS	1970	D1	P6	27 %	ROMA	CZECH	----
		1975	D1	P7	35 %	CZECH	CUBA	----
		1980	D1	P10	40 %	BULGA	ROMA	----
V25	FOREIGN PROPERTY AS % OF GDP	------	----	----	----- -----	-------	-------	----
V26	GNP SHARE OF DEVELOPMENT AID	1970	D5	P51	0.32 %	GFR	NORWY	----
		1975	D4	P35	0.27 %	JAPAN	UNKI	----
		1980	D4	P34	0.27 %	SWITZ	JAPAN	----
V27	SHARE IN NOBEL PRIZE WINNERS	1970-79	D10	P100	53.8 %	UNKI	-------	----
V28	GDP SHARE OF MANUFACTURING	1970	D9	P88	25.7 %	CHILE	AULIA	----
		1975	D9	P82	23.5 %	SOUAF	SINGA	----
		1980	D8	P81	23.1 %	SOUAF	NEWZ	----
V29	EXPORT SHARE OF MANUFACTURES	------	----	----	----- -----	-------	-------	----
V30	LACK OF CIVIL LIBERTIES	1975	D1	P7	1	UNKI	COLO	----
		1980	D1	P7	1	UNKI	ECUA	----
V31	LACK OF POLITICAL RIGHTS	1975	D1	P8	1	UNKI	ARGE	----
		1980	D1	P8	1	UNKI	VENE	----
V32	RIOTS	1970-74	D10	P99	103	INDIA	UNKI	----
		1975-79	D10	P95	50	INDIA	ITALY	----
V33	PROTEST DEMONSTRATIONS	1970-74	D10	P100	624	UNKI	-------	----
		1975-79	D10	P100	581	SPAIN	-------	----
V34	POLITICAL STRIKES	1970-74	D10	P99	96	ITALY	UNKI	----
		1975-79	D9	P85	7	TURKY	ARGE	----
V35	MEMBER OF THE NONALIGNED MMT.	1970	----	----	0	URU	USSR	----
		1976	----	----	0	URU	USSR	----
		1981	----	----	0	URU	USSR	----
V36	MEMBER OF THE OPEC	1970	----	----	0	URU	USSR	----
		1975	----	----	0	URU	USSR	----
		1980	----	----	0	URU	USSR	----
V37	MEMBER OF THE OECD	1970	----	----	1	UNKI	-------	----
		1975	----	----	1	UNKI	-------	----
		1980	----	----	1	UNKI	-------	----

V38 MEMBER OF THE CMEA	1970	----	----	0		URU	VENE	----
	1975	----	----	0		URU	VENE	----
	1980	----	----	0		URU	VENE	----
V39 MEMBER OF THE WTO	1970	----	----	0		URU	VENE	----
	1975	----	----	0		URU	VENE	----
	1980	----	----	0		URU	VENE	----
V40 MEMBER OF THE NATO	1970	----	----	1		UNKI	-------	----
	1975	----	----	1		UNKI	-------	----
	1980	----	----	1		UNKI	-------	----
V41 GDP SHARE OF INVESTMENTS	1970	D4	P39	17.8	%	INDIA	NIGER	----
	1975	D3	P24	16.6	%	PORTU	SUDAN	----
	1980	D3	P28	18.0	%	URU	DENMA	----
V42 GDP SHARE OF AGRICULTURE	1970	D1	P5	2.7	%	UNKI	GFR	----
	1975	D1	P9	3.3	%	TRITO	NETH	----
	1980	D2	P11	2.8	%	GFR	SWEDN	----
V43 GDP SHARE OF INDUSTRY	1970	D7	P68	34.9	%	PERU	FINLA	----
	1975	D6	P60	33.2	%	IRE	PHILI	----
	1980	D6	P57	34.1	%	CANA	NIGER	----
V44 GDP SHARE OF SERVICES	1970	D10	P93	62.4	%	SWEDN	LESO	----
	1975	D10	P95	63.5	%	CANA	SINGA	----
	1980	D10	P94	63.1	%	JORDA	UNKI	----
V45 HOMICIDES P. MIL. POPULATION	1970	D9	P88	82.2	1/MIL CAP	VENE	COLO	F153
	1975	D9	P88	98.7	1/MIL CAP	PARA	COLO	F153
	1980	D9	P88	105.3	1/MIL CAP	ECUA	VENE	F147
V46 SUICIDES P. MIL. POPULATION	1970	D6	P62	114.6	1/MIL CAP	CANA	BULGA	F150
	1975	D7	P64	125.3	1/MIL CAP	CANA	BULGA	F150
	1980	D6	P49	118.0	1/MIL CAP	AULIA	NORWY	F147
V47 IMPORT PARTNERS	1970	R1	CANA	27.8	%	-------	SYRIA	----
	1970	R2	JAPAN	14.7	%	UGADA	AULIA	----
	1970	R3	GFR	7.8	%	UPVO	ZAIRE	----
	1980	R1	CANA	16.3	%	-------	HAITI	----
	1980	R2	JAPAN	13.1	%	SAUDI	VENE	----
	1980	R3	SAUDI	5.3	%	THAI	-------	----
V48 EXPORT PARTNERS	1970	R1	CANA	21.0	%	-------	VENE	----
	1970	R2	JAPAN	10.8	%	UPVO	YESO	----
	1970	R3	GFR	6.3	%	TUNIS	YUGO	----
	1980	R1	CANA	15.6	%	-------	VENE	----
	1980	R2	JAPAN	9.5	%	PHILI	BENIN	----
	1980	R3	MEXI	6.9	%	-------	-------	----
V49 PATENT SUPPLIERS	1970	R1	GFR	4434		SWITZ	USSR	----
	1970	R2	UNKI	2952		TRITO	VENE	----
	1970	R3	JAPAN	2625		SYRIA	-------	----
	1980	R1	JAPAN	7173		KORSO	CANA	----
	1980	R2	GFR	5767		URU	USSR	----
	1980	R3	UNKI	2440		URU	-------	----

V50 PROVENANCE OF FOREIGN FIRMS	1980	R1	UNKI	37.0	%	UGADA	ZAMBI	----
	1980	R2	CANA	19.4	%	UNKI	IRE	----
	1980	R3	GFR	9.1	%	UGADA	VENE	----
V51 FILM SUPPLIERS	------	----	----	-----	-----	-------	-------	----

USSR (USSR)

V1 INCOME PER CAPITA	------	----	----	-----	-----	-------	-------	----
V2 TELEPHONES P. TSD. POPULATION	1970	D7	P67	45	1/TSD CAP	CHILE	BULGA	F10
	1975	D7	P66	66	1/TSD CAP	TRITO	POLA	F10
	1980	D6	P59	89	1/TSD CAP	KORSO	ARGE	F10
V3 INFANT MORTALITY RATE	1980	D3	P28	28.8	1/TSD	KUWAI	ROMA	F5
V4 PHYSICIANS P. MIL. POPULATION	1970	D10	P99	2378	1/MIL	CZECH	-------	----
	1975	D10	P99	2883	1/MIL	CZECH	-------	----
V5 ADULT LITERACY	------	----	----	-----	-----	-------	-------	----
V6 DURATION OF SCHOOLING	1970	D7	P70	9.5	YR	LEBA	ARGE	----
	1975	D7	P69	9.5	YR	PORTU	KORSO	----
	1980	D7	P63	10.0	YR	PERU	CZECH	----
V7 STUDENT ENROLLMENT RATIO	1970	D10	P97	25.4	%	LEBA	GDR	----
	1975	D9	P85	22.2	%	NORWY	BELGI	----
	1980	D8	P77	21.2	%	IRE	PANA	----
V8 SHARE OF AGRICULTURAL LABOR	------	----	----	-----	-----	-------	-------	----
V9 SHARE OF INDUSTRIAL LABOR	------	----	----	-----	-----	-------	-------	----
V10 SHARE OF SERVICE LABOR	------	----	----	-----	-----	-------	-------	----
V11 SHARE OF ACADEMIC LABOR	------	----	----	-----	-----	-------	-------	----
V12 SHARE OF SELF-EMPLOYED LABOR	------	----	----	-----	-----	-------	-------	----
V13 MILITARY EXPENDITURES	------	----	----	-----	-----	-------	-------	----
V14 MILITARY MANPOWER	1971	D10	P100	3900	TSD CAP	USA	-------	----
	1975	D10	P99	4100	TSD CAP	USA	CHINA	----
	1980	D10	P100	4300	TSD CAP	USA	-------	----
V15 MEN AT AGE 20 - 30	1970	D10	P98	15440	TSD CAP	USA	INDIA	----
	1973	D10	----	17553	TSD CAP	JAPAN	USA	F46
V16 POPULATION	1970	D10	P98	242.76	MIL CAP	USA	INDIA	----
	1975	D10	P98	254.47	MIL CAP	USA	INDIA	----
	1980	D10	P98	265.54	MIL CAP	USA	INDIA	----
V17 GROSS DOMESTIC PRODUCT	------	----	----	-----	-----	-------	-------	----

V18	SHARE IN WORLD IMPORTS	1970	D10	P92	35.342	1/TSD	BELGI	CANA	F49
		1975	D10	P94	40.674	1/TSD	NETH	ITALY	F49
		1980	D10	P93	33.408	1/TSD	CANA	BELGI	F49
V19	SHARE IN WORLD EXPORTS	1970	D10	P93	40.806	1/TSD	NETH	ITALY	F30
		1975	D10	P94	38.021	1/TSD	CANA	ITALY	F30
		1980	D10	P94	38.302	1/TSD	NETH	ITALY	F30
V20	GDP SHARE OF IMPORTS	------	----	----	-----	-----	-------	-------	----
V21	GDP SHARE OF EXPORTS	------	----	----	-----	-----	-------	-------	----
V22	EXPORT PARTNER CONCENTRATION	1970	D2	P11	15.1	%	SWITZ	CHILE	----
		1975	D1	P8	12.4	%	SRILA	JORDA	----
		1980	D1	P3	9.8	%	PAKI	UNKI	----
V23	TOTAL DEBT AS % OF GDP	------	----	----	-----	-----	-------	-------	----
V24	SHARE OF NEW FOREIGN PATENTS	1970	D1	P2	6	%	-------	POLA	----
		1975	D1	P2	5	%	-------	JAPAN	----
		1980	D1	P2	2	%	-------	JAPAN	----
V25	FOREIGN PROPERTY AS % OF GDP	------	----	----	-----	-----	-------	-------	----
V26	GNP SHARE OF DEVELOPMENT AID	------	----	----	-----	-----	-------	-------	----
V27	SHARE IN NOBEL PRIZE WINNERS	1970-79	D10	P94	2.5	%	SWITZ	AURIA	----
V28	GDP SHARE OF MANUFACTURING	------	----	----	-----	-----	-------	-------	----
V29	EXPORT SHARE OF MANUFACTURES	------	----	----	-----	-----	-------	-------	----
V30	LACK OF CIVIL LIBERTIES	1975	D8	P74	6		TOGO	YUGO	----
		1980	D8	P74	6		URU	ZAIRE	----
V31	LACK OF POLITICAL RIGHTS	1975	D7	P63	6		UPVO	YUGO	----
		1980	D7	P67	6		URU	YENO	----
V32	RIOTS	1970-74	D9	P86	17		ETHIA	JORDA	----
		1975-79	D8	P75	7		TUNIS	ECUA	----
V33	PROTEST DEMONSTRATIONS	1970-74	D10	P98	289		FRANC	UNKI	----
		1975-79	D10	P95	74		INDIA	ISRA	----
V34	POLITICAL STRIKES	1970-74	D3	P29	0		UPVO	VENE	----
		1975-79	D7	P63	1		UPVO	AULIA	----
V35	MEMBER OF THE NONALIGNED MMT.	1970	----	----	0		USA	VENE	----
		1976	----	----	0		USA	VENE	----
		1981	----	----	0		USA	VENE	----
V36	MEMBER OF THE OPEC	1970	----	----	0		USA	VINO	----
		1975	----	----	0		USA	VINO	----
		1980	----	----	0		USA	VINO	----
V37	MEMBER OF THE OECD	1970	----	----	0		URU	VENE	----
		1975	----	----	0		URU	VENE	----
		1980	----	----	0		URU	VENE	----

V38 MEMBER OF THE CMEA	1970	----	----	1	ROMA	-------	----
	1975	----	----	1	ROMA	-------	----
	1980	----	----	1	ROMA	VINO	----
V39 MEMBER OF THE WTO	1970	----	----	1	ROMA	-------	----
	1975	----	----	1	ROMA	-------	----
	1980	----	----	1	ROMA	-------	----
V40 MEMBER OF THE NATO	1970	----	----	0	URU	VENE	----
	1975	----	----	0	URU	VENE	----
	1980	----	----	0	URU	VENE	----
V41 GDP SHARE OF INVESTMENTS	------	----	----	----- -----	-------	-------	----
V42 GDP SHARE OF AGRICULTURE	------	----	----	----- -----	-------	-------	----
V43 GDP SHARE OF INDUSTRY	------	----	----	----- -----	-------	-------	----
V44 GDP SHARE OF SERVICES	------	----	----	----- -----	-------	-------	----
V45 HOMICIDES P. MIL. POPULATION	------	----	----	----- -----	-------	-------	----
V46 SUICIDES P. MIL. POPULATION	------	----	----	----- -----	-------	-------	----
V47 IMPORT PARTNERS	1970	R1	GDR	14.7 %	-------	BULGA	----
	1970	R2	POLA	10.7 %	-------	CZECH	----
	1970	R3	CZECH	10.5 %	ROMA	-------	----
	1980	R1	GDR	9.7 %	-------	BULGA	----
	1980	R2	POLA	8.1 %	-------	CZECH	----
	1980	R3	CZECH	8.0 %	-------	-------	----
V48 EXPORT PARTNERS	1970	R1	GDR	15.1 %	-------	BULGA	----
	1970	R2	POLA	10.5 %	-------	CZECH	----
	1970	R3	CZECH	9.4 %	ROMA	-------	----
	1980	R1	GDR	9.8 %	-------	BULGA	----
	1980	R2	POLA	8.9 %	-------	BULGA	----
	1980	R3	BULGA	7.4 %	-------	-------	----
V49 PATENT SUPPLIERS	1970	R1	GFR	290	USA	YUGO	----
	1970	R2	FRANC	275	GFR	VISO	----
	1970	R3	USA	201	SRILA	-------	----
	1980	R1	USA	349	URU	VENE	----
	1980	R2	GFR	318	USA	VENE	----
	1980	R3	FRANC	194	SWITZ	-------	----
V50 PROVENANCE OF FOREIGN FIRMS	------	----	----	----- -----	-------	-------	----
V51 FILM SUPPLIERS	------	----	----	----- -----	-------	-------	----

VENEZUELA (VENE)

V1	INCOME PER CAPITA	1970	D8	P71	3767	$/CAP	GREC	IRE	F211
		1975	D8	P72	3867	$/CAP	GREC	IRE	F159
		1980	D7	P70	3841	$/CAP	GABON	GREC	F159
V2	TELEPHONES P. TSD. POPULATION	1970	D7	P65	39	1/TSD CAP	JAMAI	CHILE	----
		1975	D7	P61	53	1/TSD CAP	COLO	ROMA	----
		1979	D6	P55	58	1/TSD CAP	JAMAI	COLO	----
V3	INFANT MORTALITY RATE	1980	D4	P39	45.0	1/TSD	ELSA	LEBA	F5
V4	PHYSICIANS P. MIL. POPULATION	1970	D8	P70	921	1/MIL	ALBA	YUGO	F159
		1975	D8	P67	1074	1/MIL	LIBYA	KUWAI	F159
		1978	D7	----	1050	1/MIL	SINGA	EGYPT	F159
V5	ADULT LITERACY	1971	D6	P55	76.5	%	MEXI	SRILA	----
V6	DURATION OF SCHOOLING	1970	D6	P54	7.7	YR	ECUA	DOMI	----
		1975	D6	P52	8.1	YR	ZAMBI	KENYA	----
		1980	D6	P49	8.9	YR	UNARE	COLO	F35
V7	STUDENT ENROLLMENT RATIO	1970	D8	P75	10.9	%	COSTA	PERU	----
		1975	D8	P75	17.4	%	PANA	COSTA	----
		1980	D8	P75	20.2	%	UNKI	SWITZ	----
V8	SHARE OF AGRICULTURAL LABOR	1971	D5	P44	23.4	%	CHILE	SPAIN	F67
		1975	D4	P41	19.6	%	URU	BULGA	----
		1981	D4	P42	14.9	%	FINLA	CHILE	----
V9	SHARE OF INDUSTRIAL LABOR	1975	D6	P52	31.9	%	CANA	JAMAI	----
		1981	D6	P55	32.6	%	NETH	GREC	----
V10	SHARE OF SERVICE LABOR	1975	D8	P75	39.5	%	NEWZ	ISRA	----
		1981	D9	P78	42.5	%	AULIA	NETH	----
V11	SHARE OF ACADEMIC LABOR	1975	D7	P66	9.1	%	JAPAN	LIBYA	----
		1981	D6	P56	9.9	%	GREC	EGYPT	----
V12	SHARE OF SELF-EMPLOYED LABOR	1971	D7	P72	33.9	%	LEBA	KORSO	F67
		1975	D5	P42	27.9	%	TURKY	TUNIS	----
		1981	D6	P59	28.3	%	SRILA	ELSA	----
V13	MILITARY EXPENDITURES	1970	D7	P62	0.658	TSD MIL $	SYRIA	SOUAF	F4
		1975	D7	P62	0.951	TSD MIL $	PHILI	PORTU	----
		1980	D6	P59	0.883	TSD MIL $	ALGER	AURIA	----
V14	MILITARY MANPOWER	1970	D5	P49	45	TSD CAP	ETHIA	ZAIRE	----
		1975	D6	P55	55	TSD CAP	ALBA	JORDA	----
		1980	D6	P58	55	TSD CAP	LAOS	COLO	----
V15	MEN AT AGE 20 - 30	1970	D6	P54	758	TSD CAP	MALAY	HUNGA	F2
		1977	D7	----	1091	TSD CAP	IRAQ	AULIA	F2
		1980	D6	P55	1245	TSD CAP	NEPAL	AULIA	F2
V16	POPULATION	1970	D6	P59	10.28	MIL CAP	UGADA	HUNGA	F163
		1975	D7	P63	12.67	MIL CAP	NEPAL	KENYA	F23
		1980	D7	P65	15.02	MIL CAP	SRILA	CZECH	F23

V17 GROSS DOMESTIC PRODUCT	1970	D8	P75	38.727	TSD MIL $	SAUDI	NIGRA	----
	1975	D8	P73	48.995	TSD MIL $	INDO	TURKY	----
	1980	D8	P72	57.694	TSD MIL $	NORWY	TURKY	----
V18 SHARE IN WORLD IMPORTS	1970	D7	P69	5.016	1/TSD	IRAN	ARGE	F49
	1975	D7	P69	5.863	1/TSD	GREC	ROMA	F49
	1980	D7	P69	5.203	1/TSD	ALGER	MALAY	F49
V19 SHARE IN WORLD EXPORTS	1970	D9	P84	8.783	1/TSD	BRAZI	AURIA	F30
	1975	D9	P85	10.620	1/TSD	KUWAI	GDR	F30
	1980	D9	P82	9.980	1/TSD	SINGA	BRAZI	F30
V20 GDP SHARE OF IMPORTS	1970	D4	P34	14.3	%	SUDAN	YENO	F49
	1975	D4	P33	19.3	%	PAKI	MADA	F49
	1980	D3	P30	18.0	%	PERU	IRAQ	F49
V21 GDP SHARE OF EXPORTS	1970	D8	P79	23.7	%	COSTA	SIERA	F30
	1975	D9	P84	33.8	%	PAPUA	IRE	F30
	1980	D9	P81	33.6	%	ZAMBI	NIGRA	F30
V22 EXPORT PARTNER CONCENTRATION	1970	D7	P67	35.4	%	POLA	LAOS	----
	1975	D8	P78	39.4	%	TOGO	MALAW	----
	1980	D6	P54	27.3	%	COLO	PHILI	----
V23 TOTAL DEBT AS % OF GDP	1980	D8	P72	50.0	%	PHILI	SOMA	----
V24 SHARE OF NEW FOREIGN PATENTS	1970	D8	P74	98	%	TRITO	TUNIS	----
	1975	D4	P34	84	%	AURIA	LEBA	----
	1980	D5	P46	88	%	DOMI	YUGO	----
V25 FOREIGN PROPERTY AS % OF GDP	1971	D10	P91	29.0	%	ZAIRE	LIBYA	----
	1975	D9	P81	14.5	%	MALAW	TOGO	----
	1978	D8	----	9.2	%	CAME	CHILE	----
V26 GNP SHARE OF DEVELOPMENT AID	1970	D1	P11	0.00	%	NIGRA	FINLA	----
	1975	D2	P12	0.11	%	ITALY	FINLA	----
	1980	D2	P19	0.21	%	ALGER	FINLA	----
V27 SHARE IN NOBEL PRIZE WINNERS	1970-79	D5	P45	0.0	%	URU	VINO	----
V28 GDP SHARE OF MANUFACTURING	1970	D6	P54	15.9	%	JAMAI	THAI	----
	1975	D6	P57	15.9	%	ZAMBI	PAKI	----
	1980	D6	P59	16.2	%	HONDU	DENMA	----
V29 EXPORT SHARE OF MANUFACTURES	------	----	----	----- -----		-------	-------	----
V30 LACK OF CIVIL LIBERTIES	1975	D2	P18	2		TRITO	ELSA	----
	1980	D2	P18	2		TRITO	BANGL	----
V31 LACK OF POLITICAL RIGHTS	1975	D2	P20	2		TURKY	MALAY	----
	1980	D1	P8	1		USA	COLO	----
V32 RIOTS	1970-74	D8	P73	7		SENE	IRE	----
	1975-79	D2	P20	0		URU	YENO	----
V33 PROTEST DEMONSTRATIONS	1970-74	D7	P68	6		POLA	CHILE	----
	1975-79	D4	P32	1		UPVO	YENO	----
V34 POLITICAL STRIKES	1970-74	D3	P29	0		USSR	VINO	----
	1975-79	D3	P29	0		URU	YENO	----

V35	MEMBER OF THE NONALIGNED MMT.	1970	---- ----	0		USSR	VINO	----
		1976	---- ----	0		USSR	-------	----
		1981	---- ----	0		USSR	-------	----
V36	MEMBER OF THE OPEC	1970	---- ----	1		SAUDI	-------	----
		1975	---- ----	1		SAUDI	-------	----
		1980	---- ----	1		UNARE	-------	----
V37	MEMBER OF THE OECD	1970	---- ----	0		USSR	VINO	----
		1975	---- ----	0		USSR	VINO	----
		1980	---- ----	0		USSR	VINO	----
V38	MEMBER OF THE CMEA	1970	---- ----	0		USA	VINO	----
		1975	---- ----	0		USA	VINO	----
		1980	---- ----	0		USA	YENO	----
V39	MEMBER OF THE WTO	1970	---- ----	0		USA	VINO	----
		1975	---- ----	0		USA	VINO	----
		1980	---- ----	0		USA	VINO	----
V40	MEMBER OF THE NATO	1970	---- ----	0		USSR	VINO	----
		1975	---- ----	0		USSR	VINO	----
		1980	---- ----	0		USSR	VINO	----
V41	GDP SHARE OF INVESTMENTS	1970	D9 P89	29.5 %		FINLA	AURIA	----
		1975	D9 P84	30.8 %		PANA	PHILI	----
		1980	D6 P53	24.5 %		AULIA	BENIN	----
V42	GDP SHARE OF AGRICULTURE	1970	D3 P22	7.1 %		AURIA	ITALY	----
		1975	D2 P20	5.9 %		NORWY	GABON	----
		1980	D2 P20	5.8 %		NORWY	ALGER	----
V43	GDP SHARE OF INDUSTRY	1970	D8 P80	39.3 %		FRANC	ARGE	----
		1975	D9 P90	48.1 %		GFR	YUGO	----
		1980	D9 P89	47.1 %		CONGO	GFR	----
V44	GDP SHARE OF SERVICES	1970	D8 P75	53.6 %		CAME	BELGI	----
		1975	D6 P52	46.0 %		TURKY	DOMI	----
		1980	D6 P53	47.1 %		TURKY	PERU	----
V45	HOMICIDES P. MIL. POPULATION	1970	D9 P86	75.1 1/MIL CAP		ECUA	USA	F154
		1975	D9 P83	74.0 1/MIL CAP		ECUA	PARA	F154
		1980	D10 P91	117.4 1/MIL CAP		USA	THAI	----
V46	SUICIDES P. MIL. POPULATION	1970	D4 P35	65.1 1/MIL CAP		ITALY	ELSA	F2
		1975	D3 P27	47.1 1/MIL CAP		IRE	ITALY	F2
		1980	D2 P19	48.0 1/MIL CAP		SPAIN	COSTA	----
V47	IMPORT PARTNERS	1970	R1 USA	48.9 %		UNKI	GHANA	----
		1970	R2 GFR	9.0 %		TURKY	ARGE	----
		1970	R3 JAPAN	8.0 %		SRILA	YESO	----
		1980	R1 USA	48.1 %		UNKI	BURMA	----
		1980	R2 JAPAN	8.0 %		USA	YENO	----
		1980	R3 GFR	6.3 %		TUNIS	-------	----

V48	EXPORT PARTNERS	1970	R1	USA	35.4	%	UNKI	AULIA	----
		1970	R2	CANA	11.2	%	USA	JAMAI	----
		1970	R3	UNKI	4.8	%	TRITO	-------	----
		1980	R1	USA	27.3	%	TRITO	AULIA	----
		1980	R2	CANA	9.6	%	USA	-------	----
		1980	R3	ITALY	5.6	%	SWITZ	-------	----
V49	PATENT SUPPLIERS	1970	R1	USA	4363		URU	VISO	----
		1970	R2	UNKI	83		USA	ZAMBI	----
		1970	R3	SWITZ	77		TUNIS	YUGO	----
		1980	R1	USA	191		USSR	ZAMBI	----
		1980	R2	GFR	46		USSR	CANA	----
		1980	R3	SWITZ	30		TURKY	ZAIRE	----
V50	PROVENANCE OF FOREIGN FIRMS	1980	R1	USA	74.0	%	URU	ALGER	----
		1980	R2	UNKI	5.3	%	SWEDN	BELGI	----
		1980	R3	GFR	3.5	%	USA	ZAMBI	----
V51	FILM SUPPLIERS	1980	R1	USA	346		TURKY	YENO	F118
		1980	R2	ITALY	147		SUDAN	YUGO	F118
		1980	R3	FRANC	60		SYRIA	-------	F118

VIETNAM, NORTH (VINO)

V1	INCOME PER CAPITA	-------	----	----	-----	-----	-------	-------	----
V2	TELEPHONES P. TSD. POPULATION	-------	----	----	-----	-----	-------	-------	----
V3	INFANT MORTALITY RATE	1980	D6	P57	106.0	1/TSD	PERU	LIBYA	F5
V4	PHYSICIANS P. MIL. POPULATION	1980	D4	P38	241	1/MIL	BURMA	TUNIS	----
V5	ADULT LITERACY	1979	D8	P78	84.0	%	SINGA	COLO	----
V6	DURATION OF SCHOOLING	1980	D6	P55	9.4	YR	PORTU	SRILA	----
V7	STUDENT ENROLLMENT RATIO	1980	D4	P31	2.5	%	LIBE	SENE	----
V8	SHARE OF AGRICULTURAL LABOR	-------	----	----	-----	-----	-------	-------	----
V9	SHARE OF INDUSTRIAL LABOR	-------	----	----	-----	-----	-------	-------	----
V10	SHARE OF SERVICE LABOR	-------	----	----	-----	-----	-------	-------	----
V11	SHARE OF ACADEMIC LABOR	-------	----	----	-----	-----	-------	-------	----
V12	SHARE OF SELF-EMPLOYED LABOR	-------	----	----	-----	-----	-------	-------	----
V13	MILITARY EXPENDITURES	-------	----	----	-----	-----	-------	-------	----

		Year			Value	Unit			
V14	MILITARY MANPOWER	1970	D10	P92	452	TSD CAP	KORNO	GFR	----
		1975	D10	P96	643	TSD CAP	KORSO	VISO	F12
		1980	D10	P97	900	TSD CAP	TURKY	INDIA	----
V15	MEN AT AGE 20 - 30	------	----	----	-----	-----	-------	-------	----
V16	POPULATION	1980	D9	P88	53.74	MIL CAP	FRANC	UNKI	----
V17	GROSS DOMESTIC PRODUCT	------	----	----	-----	-----	-------	-------	----
V18	SHARE IN WORLD IMPORTS	------	----	----	-----	-----	-------	-------	----
V19	SHARE IN WORLD EXPORTS	------	----	----	-----	-----	-------	-------	----
V20	GDP SHARE OF IMPORTS	------	----	----	-----	-----	-------	-------	----
V21	GDP SHARE OF EXPORTS	------	----	----	-----	-----	-------	-------	----
V22	EXPORT PARTNER CONCENTRATION	------	----	----	-----	-----	-------	-------	----
V23	TOTAL DEBT AS % OF GDP	------	----	----	-----	-----	-------	-------	----
V24	SHARE OF NEW FOREIGN PATENTS	------	----	----	-----	-----	-------	-------	----
V25	FOREIGN PROPERTY AS % OF GDP	------	----	----	-----	-----	-------	-------	----
V26	GNP SHARE OF DEVELOPMENT AID	------	----	----	-----	-----	-------	-------	----
V27	SHARE IN NOBEL PRIZE WINNERS	1970-79	D5	P45	0.0	%	VENE	YENO	----
V28	GDP SHARE OF MANUFACTURING	------	----	----	-----	-----	-------	-------	----
V29	EXPORT SHARE OF MANUFACTURES	------	----	----	-----	-----	-------	-------	----
V30	LACK OF CIVIL LIBERTIES	1975	D10	P93	7		UGADA	YESO	----
		1980	D10	P92	7		SOMA	YESO	----
V31	LACK OF POLITICAL RIGHTS	1975	D9	P88	7		UGADA	YESO	----
		1980	D9	P90	7		TOGO	-------	----
V32	RIOTS	1970-74	D2	P19	0		UPVO	YESO	----
V33	PROTEST DEMONSTRATIONS	1970-74	D5	P49	2		SYRIA	BOLI	----
V34	POLITICAL STRIKES	1970-74	D3	P29	0		VENE	YENO	----
V35	MEMBER OF THE NONALIGNED MMT.	1970	----	----	0		VENE	-------	----
		1976	----	----	1		UPVO	YENO	----
		1981	----	----	1		UPVO	YENO	----
V36	MEMBER OF THE OPEC	1970	----	----	0		USSR	VISO	----
		1975	----	----	0		USSR	VISO	----
		1980	----	----	0		USSR	YENO	----
V37	MEMBER OF THE OECD	1970	----	----	0		VENE	VISO	----
		1975	----	----	0		VENE	VISO	----
		1980	----	----	0		VENE	YENO	----
V38	MEMBER OF THE CMEA	1970	----	----	0		VENE	VISO	----
		1975	----	----	0		VENE	VISO	----
		1980	----	----	1		USSR	-------	----

V39 MEMBER OF THE WTO	1970	----	----	0		VENE	VISO	----
	1975	----	----	0		VENE	VISO	----
	1980	----	----	0		VENE	YENO	----
V40 MEMBER OF THE NATO	1970	----	----	0		VENE	VISO	----
	1975	----	----	0		VENE	VISO	----
	1980	----	----	0		VENE	YENO	----
V41 GDP SHARE OF INVESTMENTS	------	----	----	----- -----		-------	-------	----
V42 GDP SHARE OF AGRICULTURE	------	----	----	----- -----		-------	-------	----
V43 GDP SHARE OF INDUSTRY	------	----	----	----- -----		-------	-------	----
V44 GDP SHARE OF SERVICES	------	----	----	----- -----		-------	-------	----
V45 HOMICIDES P. MIL. POPULATION	------	----	----	----- -----		-------	-------	----
V46 SUICIDES P. MIL. POPULATION	------	----	----	----- -----		-------	-------	----
V47 IMPORT PARTNERS	------	----	----	----- -----		-------	-------	----
V48 EXPORT PARTNERS	------	----	----	----- -----		-------	-------	----
V49 PATENT SUPPLIERS	------	----	----	----- -----		-------	-------	----
V50 PROVENANCE OF FOREIGN FIRMS	------	----	----	----- -----		-------	-------	----
V51 FILM SUPPLIERS	1979	R1	USSR	86		POLA	ETHIA	F118
	1979	R2	-------	0		-------	-------	F118
	1979	R3	-------	0		-------	-------	F118

VIETNAM, SOUTH (VISO)

V1 INCOME PER CAPITA	------	----	----	----- -----		-------	-------	----
V2 TELEPHONES P. TSD. POPULATION	1970	D2	P16	2	1/TSD CAP	SOMA	ZAIRE	----
	1973	D2	----	3	1/TSD CAP	PAKI	HAITI	----
V3 INFANT MORTALITY RATE	------	----	----	----- -----		-------	-------	----
V4 PHYSICIANS P. MIL. POPULATION	------	----	----	----- -----		-------	-------	----
V5 ADULT LITERACY	------	----	----	----- -----		-------	-------	----
V6 DURATION OF SCHOOLING	------	----	----	----- -----		-------	-------	----
V7 STUDENT ENROLLMENT RATIO	------	----	----	----- -----		-------	-------	----
V8 SHARE OF AGRICULTURAL LABOR	------	----	----	----- -----		-------	-------	----
V9 SHARE OF INDUSTRIAL LABOR	------	----	----	----- -----		-------	-------	----
V10 SHARE OF SERVICE LABOR	------	----	----	----- -----		-------	-------	----

V11	SHARE OF ACADEMIC LABOR	------	---- ----	----- -----	-------	-------	----
V12	SHARE OF SELF-EMPLOYED LABOR	------	---- ----	----- -----	-------	-------	----
V13	MILITARY EXPENDITURES	------	---- ----	----- -----	-------	-------	----
V14	MILITARY MANPOWER	1970	D10 P97	1000 TSD CAP	KORSO	INDIA	----
		1974	D10 P96	980 TSD CAP	VINO	INDIA	----
V15	MEN AT AGE 20 - 30	------	---- ----	----- -----	-------	-------	----
V16	POPULATION	------	---- ----	----- -----	-------	-------	----
V17	GROSS DOMESTIC PRODUCT	------	---- ----	----- -----	-------	-------	----
V18	SHARE IN WORLD IMPORTS	1970	D5 P42	1.124 1/TSD	SYRIA	IVORY	----
		1974	D5 P48	1.496 1/TSD	CHILE	TUNIS	----
V19	SHARE IN WORLD EXPORTS	1970	D1 P3	0.026 1/TSD	LAOS	UPVO	----
		1974	D2 P13	0.115 1/TSD	NEPAL	SIERA	----
V20	GDP SHARE OF IMPORTS	------	---- ----	----- -----	-------	-------	----
V21	GDP SHARE OF EXPORTS	------	---- ----	----- -----	-------	-------	----
V22	EXPORT PARTNER CONCENTRATION	------	---- ----	----- -----	-------	-------	----
V23	TOTAL DEBT AS % OF GDP	------	---- ----	----- -----	-------	-------	----
V24	SHARE OF NEW FOREIGN PATENTS	------	---- ----	----- -----	-------	-------	----
V25	FOREIGN PROPERTY AS % OF GDP	------	---- ----	----- -----	-------	-------	----
V26	GNP SHARE OF DEVELOPMENT AID	------	---- ----	----- -----	-------	-------	----
V27	SHARE IN NOBEL PRIZE WINNERS	------	---- ----	----- -----	-------	-------	----
V28	GDP SHARE OF MANUFACTURING	------	---- ----	----- -----	-------	-------	----
V29	EXPORT SHARE OF MANUFACTURES	------	---- ----	----- -----	-------	-------	----
V30	LACK OF CIVIL LIBERTIES	1975	D6 P54	5	URU	AFGHA	----
V31	LACK OF POLITICAL RIGHTS	1975	D4 P31	4	SOUAF	CONGO	----
V32	RIOTS	1970-74	D10 P92	40	KORSO	SPAIN	----
V33	PROTEST DEMONSTRATIONS	1970-74	D9 P90	44	ISRA	PAKI	----
V34	POLITICAL STRIKES	1970-74	D8 P74	2	PHILI	EGYPT	----
V35	MEMBER OF THE NONALIGNED MMT.	------	---- ----	----- -----	-------	-------	----
V36	MEMBER OF THE OPEC	1970	---- ----	0	VINO	YENO	----
		1975	---- ----	0	VINO	YENO	----
V37	MEMBER OF THE OECD	1970	---- ----	0	VINO	YENO	----
		1975	---- ----	0	VINO	YENO	----
V38	MEMBER OF THE CMEA	1970	---- ----	0	VINO	YENO	----
		1975	---- ----	0	VINO	YENO	----

V39	MEMBER OF THE WTO	1970	----	----	0		VINO	YENO	----
		1975	----	----	0		VINO	YENO	----
V40	MEMBER OF THE NATO	1970	----	----	0		VINO	YENO	----
		1975	----	----	0		VINO	YENO	----
V41	GDP SHARE OF INVESTMENTS	------	----	----	----- -----		-------	-------	----
V42	GDP SHARE OF AGRICULTURE	------	----	----	----- -----		-------	-------	----
V43	GDP SHARE OF INDUSTRY	------	----	----	----- -----		-------	-------	----
V44	GDP SHARE OF SERVICES	------	----	----	----- -----		-------	-------	----
V45	HOMICIDES P. MIL. POPULATION	------	----	----	----- -----		-------	-------	----
V46	SUICIDES P. MIL. POPULATION	------	----	----	----- -----		-------	-------	----
V47	IMPORT PARTNERS	------	----	----	----- -----		-------	-------	----
V48	EXPORT PARTNERS	------	----	----	----- -----		-------	-------	----
V49	PATENT SUPPLIERS	1972	R1	USA	32		VENE	ZAMBI	----
		1972	R2	FRANC	10		USSR	ZAIRE	----
		1972	R3	UNKI	7		URU	-------	----
V50	PROVENANCE OF FOREIGN FIRMS	------	----	----	----- -----		-------	-------	----
V51	FILM SUPPLIERS	------	----	----	----- -----		-------	-------	----

YEMEN, NORTH [6] (YENO)

V1	INCOME PER CAPITA	1970	D2	P11	209	$/CAP	INDIA	HAITI	----
		1975	D2	P19	336	$/CAP	SIERA	INDO	----
		1980	D3	P24	436	$/CAP	NIGER	INDO	F35
V2	TELEPHONES P. TSD. POPULATION	1970	D1	P7	1	1/TSD CAP	UPVO	ETHIA	----
V3	INFANT MORTALITY RATE	1980	D10	P96	169.6	1/TSD	UPVO	GUINE	F5
V4	PHYSICIANS P. MIL. POPULATION	1971	D2	P17	45	1/MIL	NIGRA	SOMA	----
		1976	D3	P25	68	1/MIL	SOMA	PAPUA	----
		1979	D3	P23	90	1/MIL	INDO	NIGRA	----
V5	ADULT LITERACY	1980	D1	P6	8.6	%	SOMA	NIGER	F21
V6	DURATION OF SCHOOLING	1970	D1	P3	0.8	YR	SOMA	NIGER	----
		1975	D1	P8	2.3	YR	MALI	AFGHA	----
		1980	D1	P9	3.4	YR	ETHIA	AFGHA	----

---

[6] Also known as Yemen Arab Republic.

V7	STUDENT ENROLLMENT RATIO	1970	D1	P4	0.0	%	UPVO	BENIN	----
		1975	D2	P16	0.7	%	HAITI	BENIN	----
		1980	D2	P18	1.2	%	CHINA	ZAIRE	----
V8	SHARE OF AGRICULTURAL LABOR	1975	D9	P88	76.4	%	SUDAN	CAME	----
V9	SHARE OF INDUSTRIAL LABOR	1975	D2	P17	13.4	%	INDO	HONDU	----
V10	SHARE OF SERVICE LABOR	1975	D2	P18	12.0	%	TURKY	SUDAN	----
V11	SHARE OF ACADEMIC LABOR	1975	D4	P30	4.3	%	ELSA	SYRIA	----
V12	SHARE OF SELF-EMPLOYED LABOR	1975	D9	P83	48.7	%	BANGL	MALI	----
V13	MILITARY EXPENDITURES	1980	D5	P43	0.329	TSD MIL $	KENYA	IRE	F35
V14	MILITARY MANPOWER	1970	D3	P29	13	TSD CAP	GUATE	NEWZ	----
		1975	D5	P49	42	TSD CAP	FINLA	LAOS	----
		1980	D5	P48	36	TSD CAP	MONGO	NORWY	----
V15	MEN AT AGE 20 - 30	------	----	----	----- -----		-------	-------	----
V16	POPULATION	1970	D4	P37	4.84	MIL CAP	FINLA	DENMA	----
		1975	D4	P39	5.32	MIL CAP	MALAW	TUNIS	----
		1980	D4	P37	5.82	MIL CAP	SENE	ZAMBI	----
V17	GROSS DOMESTIC PRODUCT	1970	D2	P12	1.012	TSD MIL $	HAITI	UPVO	----
		1975	D2	P14	1.787	TSD MIL $	JORDA	NEPAL	----
		1980	D2	P18	2.540	TSD MIL $	JAMAI	SENE	F35
V18	SHARE IN WORLD IMPORTS	1970	D1	P3	0.096	1/TSD	RWAN	CENTR	F30
		1975	D2	P19	0.323	1/TSD	MONGO	ETHIA	F30
		1980	D5	P42	0.903	1/TSD	URU	BANGL	F30
V19	SHARE IN WORLD EXPORTS	1970	D1	P1	0.010	1/TSD	-------	LAOS	F30
		1975	D1	P1	0.013	1/TSD	-------	LAOS	F30
		1980	D1	P1	0.012	1/TSD	-------	LAOS	F30
V20	GDP SHARE OF IMPORTS	1970	D4	P34	14.3	%	VENE	NIGER	F30
		1975	D9	P82	35.5	%	COSTA	HONDU	F30
		1979	D10	P99	67.0	%	IRE	SINGA	F30
V21	GDP SHARE OF EXPORTS	1970	D1	P2	1.3	%	-------	MEXI	F30
		1975	D1	P1	1.3	%	-------	BANGL	F30
		1979	D1	P1	0.6	%	-------	UGADA	F30
V22	EXPORT PARTNER CONCENTRATION	1970	D9	P86	51.9	%	ETHIA	SOMA	----
		1975	D9	P89	52.3	%	HONDU	IRE	----
		1980	D9	P82	42.4	%	NORWY	IRE	----
V23	TOTAL DEBT AS % OF GDP	1980	D6	P52	37.7	%	PORTU	CAME	----
V24	SHARE OF NEW FOREIGN PATENTS	------	----	----	----- -----		-------	-------	----
V25	FOREIGN PROPERTY AS % OF GDP	------	----	----	----- -----		-------	-------	----
V26	GNP SHARE OF DEVELOPMENT AID	------	----	----	----- -----		-------	-------	----
V27	SHARE IN NOBEL PRIZE WINNERS	1970-79	D5	P45	0.0	%	VINO	YESO	----

V28	GDP SHARE OF MANUFACTURING	1970	D1	P6	4.2 %	LIBE	NIGRA	----
		1975	D1	P10	5.6 %	SOMA	LESO	----
		1980	D2	P17	5.5 %	SIERA	IRAQ	----
V29	EXPORT SHARE OF MANUFACTURES	------	----	----	----- -----	-------	-------	----
V30	LACK OF CIVIL LIBERTIES	1975	D4	P39	4	UPVO	ZAMBI	----
		1980	D6	P52	5	UNARE	YUGO	----
V31	LACK OF POLITICAL RIGHTS	1975	D5	P43	5	URU	ZAMBI	----
		1980	D7	P67	6	USSR	YESO	----
V32	RIOTS	1970-74	D5	P43	1	SINGA	BENIN	----
		1975-79	D2	P20	0	VENE	YESO	----
V33	PROTEST DEMONSTRATIONS	1970-74	D4	P37	1	SAUDI	ZAIRE	----
		1975-79	D4	P32	1	VENE	ZAIRE	----
V34	POLITICAL STRIKES	1970-74	D3	P29	0	VINO	YESO	----
		1975-79	D3	P29	0	VENE	YESO	----
V35	MEMBER OF THE NONALIGNED MMT.	1970	----	----	1	UGADA	YESO	----
		1976	----	----	1	VINO	YESO	----
		1981	----	----	1	VINO	YESO	----
V36	MEMBER OF THE OPEC	1970	----	----	0	VISO	YESO	----
		1975	----	----	0	VISO	YESO	----
		1980	----	----	0	VINO	YESO	----
V37	MEMBER OF THE OECD	1970	----	----	0	VISO	YESO	----
		1975	----	----	0	VISO	YESO	----
		1980	----	----	0	VINO	YESO	----
V38	MEMBER OF THE CMEA	1970	----	----	0	VISO	YESO	----
		1975	----	----	0	VISO	YESO	----
		1980	----	----	0	VENE	YESO	----
V39	MEMBER OF THE WTO	1970	----	----	0	VISO	YESO	----
		1975	----	----	0	VISO	YESO	----
		1980	----	----	0	VINO	YESO	----
V40	MEMBER OF THE NATO	1970	----	----	0	VISO	YESO	----
		1975	----	----	0	VISO	YESO	----
		1980	----	----	0	VINO	YESO	----
V41	GDP SHARE OF INVESTMENTS	1970	D1	P2	0.4 %	-------	BURU	----
		1975	D4	P35	18.5 %	SOMA	PERU	----
		1980	D10	P99	43.9 %	JORDA	SINGA	----
V42	GDP SHARE OF AGRICULTURE	1970	D10	P92	52.2 %	MALAW	UGADA	----
		1975	D9	P87	43.6 %	SUDAN	MALI	----
		1980	D7	P69	29.0 %	CAME	PARA	----
V43	GDP SHARE OF INDUSTRY	1970	D1	P5	10.3 %	CHAD	LESO	----
		1975	D1	P6	11.3 %	BANGL	SOMA	----
		1980	D2	P12	15.7 %	TANZA	BURU	----
V44	GDP SHARE OF SERVICES	1970	D2	P19	37.5 %	GHANA	IRAQ	----
		1975	D5	P47	45.1 %	PAKI	HONDU	----
		1980	D9	P81	55.3 %	URU	AURIA	----

V45	HOMICIDES P. MIL. POPULATION	------	----	----	----- -----		-------	-------	----
V46	SUICIDES P. MIL. POPULATION	------	----	----	----- -----		-------	-------	----
V47	IMPORT PARTNERS	1970	R1	YESO	23.4 %		-------	-------	----
		1970	R2	AULIA	12.5 %		NEWZ	-------	----
		1970	R3	USSR	12.0 %		SUDAN	YUGO	----
		1980	R1	SAUDI	19.3 %		TRITO	JAPAN	----
		1980	R2	JAPAN	12.7 %		VENE	BOLI	----
		1980	R3	FRANC	7.9 %		UNKI	-------	----
V48	EXPORT PARTNERS	1970	R1	YESO	51.9 %		-------	SOMA	----
		1970	R2	USSR	31.7 %		SUDAN	YUGO	----
		1970	R3	JAPAN	11.8 %		UGADA	-------	----
		1980	R1	YESO	42.4 %		-------	-------	----
		1980	R2	FRANC	11.5 %		UPVO	GREC	----
		1980	R3	CHINA	9.3 %		PAKI	-------	----
V49	PATENT SUPPLIERS	------	----	----	----- -----		-------	-------	----
V50	PROVENANCE OF FOREIGN FIRMS	------	----	----	----- -----		-------	-------	----
V51	FILM SUPPLIERS	1980	R1	USA	50		VENE	YUGO	F117
		1980	R2	INDIA	40		TRITO	ALGER	F117
		1980	R3	-------	10		-------	-------	F117

YEMEN, SOUTH [7] (YESO)

V1	INCOME PER CAPITA	------	----	----	----- -----		-------	-------	----
V2	TELEPHONES P. TSD. POPULATION	1970	D4	P34	7	1/TSD CAP	PHILI	GUATE	----
		1973	D3	----	6	1/TSD CAP	GHANA	HONDU	----
V3	INFANT MORTALITY RATE	1980	D9	P87	153.3	1/TSD	SENE	CENTR	F5
V4	PHYSICIANS P. MIL. POPULATION	1968	D1	----	31	1/MIL	MALI	GUINE	----
		1976	D3	P32	109	1/MIL	MADA	LIBE	----
		1980	D4	P32	131	1/MIL	SUDAN	GHANA	----
V5	ADULT LITERACY	------	----	----	----- -----		-------	-------	----
V6	DURATION OF SCHOOLING	1970	D3	P26	4.3	YR	LIBE	CENTR	----
		1975	D4	P35	6.7	YR	NICA	ZAIRE	----
		1980	D3	P26	6.1	YR	INDIA	LIBE	----
V7	STUDENT ENROLLMENT RATIO	1970	D1	P8	0.1	%	CHINA	BURU	----
		1975	D3	P23	1.1	%	GHANA	TOGO	----
		1980	D3	P30	2.4	%	TOGO	LIBE	----

---

[7] Also known as People's Democratic Republic of Yemen.

V8	SHARE OF AGRICULTURAL LABOR	------	----	----	-----	-----	-------	-------	----
V9	SHARE OF INDUSTRIAL LABOR	------	----	----	-----	-----	-------	-------	----
V10	SHARE OF SERVICE LABOR	------	----	----	-----	-----	-------	-------	----
V11	SHARE OF ACADEMIC LABOR	------	----	----	-----	-----	-------	-------	----
V12	SHARE OF SELF-EMPLOYED LABOR	------	----	----	-----	-----	-------	-------	----
V13	MILITARY EXPENDITURES	------	----	----	-----	-----	-------	-------	----
V14	MILITARY MANPOWER	1970	D3	P24	9	TSD CAP	MADA	SRILA	----
		1975	D4	P32	19	TSD CAP	SRILA	BOLI	----
		1980	D4	P36	23	TSD CAP	SWITZ	BOLI	----
V15	MEN AT AGE 20 - 30	1970	D1	P6	118	TSD CAP	PANA	NICA	F2
		1977	D1	----	116	TSD CAP	CENTR	PANA	F2
V16	POPULATION	1970	D1	P8	1.44	MIL CAP	PANA	COSTA	F4
		1975	D1	P9	1.69	MIL CAP	PANA	COSTA	----
		1978	D1	----	1.85	MIL CAP	MONGO	LIBE	----
V17	GROSS DOMESTIC PRODUCT	------	----	----	-----	-----	-------	-------	----
V18	SHARE IN WORLD IMPORTS	1970	D3	P29	0.602	1/TSD	NICA	ELSA	F58
		1975	D3	P21	0.355	1/TSD	ETHIA	LIBE	----
		1980	D4	P38	0.744	1/TSD	COSTA	SUDAN	----
V19	SHARE IN WORLD EXPORTS	1970	D3	P25	0.430	1/TSD	ETHIA	MADA	F58
		1975	D2	P17	0.196	1/TSD	BURMA	MAURA	----
		1980	D3	P30	0.390	1/TSD	BANGL	ANGO	----
V20	GDP SHARE OF IMPORTS	------	----	----	-----	-----	-------	-------	----
V21	GDP SHARE OF EXPORTS	------	----	----	-----	-----	-------	-------	----
V22	EXPORT PARTNER CONCENTRATION	1970	D5	P42	24.6	%	BELGI	BRAZI	----
V23	TOTAL DEBT AS % OF GDP	------	----	----	-----	-----	-------	-------	----
V24	SHARE OF NEW FOREIGN PATENTS	------	----	----	-----	-----	-------	-------	----
V25	FOREIGN PROPERTY AS % OF GDP	------	----	----	-----	-----	-------	-------	----
V26	GNP SHARE OF DEVELOPMENT AID	------	----	----	-----	-----	-------	-------	----
V27	SHARE IN NOBEL PRIZE WINNERS	1970-79	D5	P45	0.0	%	YENO	YUGO	----
V28	GDP SHARE OF MANUFACTURING	------	----	----	-----	-----	-------	-------	----
V29	EXPORT SHARE OF MANUFACTURES	1976	D1	P7	0.2	%	RWAN	MAURA	----
V30	LACK OF CIVIL LIBERTIES	1975	D10	P93	7		VINO	-------	----
		1980	D10	P92	7		VINO	-------	----
V31	LACK OF POLITICAL RIGHTS	1975	D9	P88	7		VINO	ZAIRE	----
		1980	D7	P67	6		YENO	YUGO	----
V32	RIOTS	1970-74	D2	P19	0		VINO	ZAIRE	----
		1975-79	D2	P20	0		YENO	YUGO	----

V33	PROTEST DEMONSTRATIONS	1970-74	D2	P15	0		UPVO	AFGHA	----
		1975-79	D2	P13	0		TRITO	CENTR	----
V34	POLITICAL STRIKES	1970-74	D3	P29	0		YENO	ZAIRE	----
		1975-79	D3	P29	0		YENO	YUGO	----
V35	MEMBER OF THE NONALIGNED MMT.	1970	----	----	1		YENO	YUGO	----
		1976	----	----	1		YENO	YUGO	----
		1981	----	----	1		YENO	YUGO	----
V36	MEMBER OF THE OPEC	1970	----	----	0		YENO	YUGO	----
		1975	----	----	0		YENO	YUGO	----
		1980	----	----	0		YENO	YUGO	----
V37	MEMBER OF THE OECD	1970	----	----	0		YENO	YUGO	----
		1975	----	----	0		YENO	YUGO	----
		1980	----	----	0		YENO	YUGO	----
V38	MEMBER OF THE CMEA	1970	----	----	0		YENO	YUGO	----
		1975	----	----	0		YENO	YUGO	----
		1980	----	----	0		YENO	YUGO	----
V39	MEMBER OF THE WTO	1970	----	----	0		YENO	YUGO	----
		1975	----	----	0		YENO	YUGO	----
		1980	----	----	0		YENO	YUGO	----
V40	MEMBER OF THE NATO	1970	----	----	0		YENO	YUGO	----
		1975	----	----	0		YENO	YUGO	----
		1980	----	----	0		YENO	YUGO	----
V41	GDP SHARE OF INVESTMENTS	------	----	----	----- -----		-------	-------	----
V42	GDP SHARE OF AGRICULTURE	------	----	----	----- -----		-------	-------	----
V43	GDP SHARE OF INDUSTRY	------	----	----	----- -----		-------	-------	----
V44	GDP SHARE OF SERVICES	------	----	----	----- -----		-------	-------	----
V45	HOMICIDES P. MIL. POPULATION	------	----	----	----- -----		-------	-------	----
V46	SUICIDES P. MIL. POPULATION	------	----	----	----- -----		-------	-------	----
V47	IMPORT PARTNERS	1970	R1	IRAN	18.2	%	-------	JAPAN	----
		1970	R2	KUWAI	13.3	%	-------	-------	----
		1970	R3	JAPAN	10.5	%	VENE	-------	----
V48	EXPORT PARTNERS	1970	R1	UNKI	24.6	%	TANZA	AFGHA	----
		1970	R2	JAPAN	14.4	%	USA	BOLI	----
		1970	R3	THAI	8.6	%	LAOS	-------	----
V49	PATENT SUPPLIERS	------	----	----	----- -----		-------	-------	----
V50	PROVENANCE OF FOREIGN FIRMS	------	----	----	----- -----		-------	-------	----
V51	FILM SUPPLIERS	------	----	----	----- -----		-------	-------	----

YUGOSLAVIA (YUGO)

V1	INCOME PER CAPITA	------	----	----	----- -----		-------	-------	----
V2	TELEPHONES P. TSD. POPULATION	1970	D7	P62	36	1/TSD CAP	COSTA	COLO	----
		1975	D7	P63	60	1/TSD CAP	ROMA	COSTA	----
		1980	D7	P63	95	1/TSD CAP	POLA	URU	----
V3	INFANT MORTALITY RATE	1980	D3	P30	31.4	1/TSD	ROMA	JAMAI	----
V4	PHYSICIANS P. MIL. POPULATION	1970	D8	P71	1000	1/MIL	VENE	URU	F147
		1975	D8	P73	1238	1/MIL	IRE	ROMA	F147
		1980	D7	P68	1473	1/MIL	LIBYA	ROMA	F147
V5	ADULT LITERACY	1971	D8	P68	83.5	%	PHILI	GREC	F22
V6	DURATION OF SCHOOLING	1970	D7	P68	9.2	YR	SINGA	LEBA	----
		1975	D8	P73	10.1	YR	URU	ARGE	----
		1980	D8	P75	10.6	YR	KUWAI	HUNGA	----
V7	STUDENT ENROLLMENT RATIO	1970	D9	P85	15.9	%	NORWY	AULIA	----
		1975	D9	P82	20.0	%	BULGA	SPAIN	----
		1980	D9	P80	21.7	%	ARGE	SPAIN	----
V8	SHARE OF AGRICULTURAL LABOR	1971	D7	P67	46.9	%	BRAZI	NICA	F67
		1981	D6	P57	29.8	%	GREC	COLO	F75
V9	SHARE OF INDUSTRIAL LABOR	1981	D7	P63	34.9	%	FRANC	SWITZ	F75
V10	SHARE OF SERVICE LABOR	1981	D4	P27	24.3	%	PARA	HUNGA	F75
V11	SHARE OF ACADEMIC LABOR	1981	D7	P62	10.9	%	TRITO	PANA	F75
V12	SHARE OF SELF-EMPLOYED LABOR	1981	D4	P36	16.6	%	AULIA	JAPAN	F115
V13	MILITARY EXPENDITURES	------	----	----	----- -----		-------	-------	----
V14	MILITARY MANPOWER	1970	D9	P84	257	TSD CAP	EGYPT	POLA	----
		1975	D9	P83	270	TSD CAP	NIGRA	UNKI	----
		1980	D9	P86	258	TSD CAP	SYRIA	IRAN	----
V15	MEN AT AGE 20 - 30	1971	D8	P70	1550	TSD CAP	ROMA	SOUAF	F22
		1975	D8	P73	1841	TSD CAP	COLO	CANA	F22
		1980	D7	P65	1962	TSD CAP	ROMA	ZAIRE	F22
V16	POPULATION	1970	D8	P74	20.37	MIL CAP	ROMA	COLO	F22
		1975	D8	P75	21.37	MIL CAP	ROMA	ZAIRE	F22
		1980	D8	P75	22.30	MIL CAP	ROMA	CANA	F22
V17	GROSS DOMESTIC PRODUCT	------	----	----	----- -----		-------	-------	----
V18	SHARE IN WORLD IMPORTS	1970	D9	P81	8.658	1/TSD	BRAZI	AURIA	----
		1975	D8	P80	8.468	1/TSD	FINLA	SINGA	----
		1980	D8	P78	8.912	1/TSD	NORWY	SOUAF	----
V19	SHARE IN WORLD EXPORTS	1970	D7	P69	5.353	1/TSD	SINGA	MALAY	----
		1975	D7	P66	4.647	1/TSD	MALAY	INDIA	----
		1980	D7	P67	5.396	1/TSD	BULGA	ROMA	----

V20	GDP SHARE OF IMPORTS	1970	D7	P62	20.9 %	ELSA	SWEDN	----
		1975	D6	P57	24.9 %	AURIA	SRILA	----
		1980	D6	P60	26.4 %	SAUDI	UPVO	----
V21	GDP SHARE OF EXPORTS	1970	D4	P37	12.2 %	INDO	TUNIS	----
		1975	D4	P35	13.2 %	PORTU	AULIA	----
		1980	D4	P37	15.5 %	MALI	AULIA	----
V22	EXPORT PARTNER CONCENTRATION	1970	D2	P13	15.2 %	CHILE	ARGE	----
		1975	D5	P51	24.9 %	UGADA	KUWAI	----
		1980	D6	P57	27.7 %	MALAW	BENIN	----
V23	TOTAL DEBT AS % OF GDP	1980	D4	P34	26.7 %	BURMA	BRAZI	----
V24	SHARE OF NEW FOREIGN PATENTS	1970	D4	P33	82 %	ITALY	INDIA	----
		1975	D3	P24	78 %	URU	SPAIN	----
		1980	D5	P46	88 %	VENE	KORSO	----
V25	FOREIGN PROPERTY AS % OF GDP	1971	D1	P2	0.4 %	BURMA	NEPAL	----
		1975	D1	P3	0.3 %	UGADA	BANGL	----
		1978	D1	----	0.3 %	UGADA	SAUDI	----
V26	GNP SHARE OF DEVELOPMENT AID	------	----	----	----- -----	-------	-------	----
V27	SHARE IN NOBEL PRIZE WINNERS	1970-79	D5	P45	0.0 %	YESO	ZAIRE	----
V28	GDP SHARE OF MANUFACTURING	------	----	----	----- -----	-------	-------	----
V29	EXPORT SHARE OF MANUFACTURES	1970	D9	P83	55.3 %	NETH	LEBA	----
		1975	D9	P87	66.1 %	SPAIN	LEBA	----
		1980	D9	P87	70.2 %	PORTU	AURIA	----
V30	LACK OF CIVIL LIBERTIES	1975	D8	P74	6	USSR	ZAIRE	----
		1980	D6	P52	5	YENO	ZAMBI	----
V31	LACK OF POLITICAL RIGHTS	1975	D7	P63	6	USSR	AFGHA	----
		1980	D7	P67	6	YESO	ZAIRE	----
V32	RIOTS	1970-74	D6	P59	3	TUNIS	AULIA	----
		1975-79	D2	P20	0	YESO	CHAD	----
V33	PROTEST DEMONSTRATIONS	1970-74	D8	P72	8	TURKY	EGYPT	----
		1975-79	D7	P67	7	GUATE	ZAMBI	----
V34	POLITICAL STRIKES	1970-74	D7	P64	1	SWEDN	CONGO	----
		1975-79	D3	P29	0	YESO	ZAIRE	----
V35	MEMBER OF THE NONALIGNED MMT.	1970	----	----	1	YESO	ZAIRE	----
		1976	----	----	1	YESO	ZAIRE	----
		1981	----	----	1	YESO	ZAIRE	----
V36	MEMBER OF THE OPEC	1970	----	----	0	YESO	ZAIRE	----
		1975	----	----	0	YESO	ZAIRE	----
		1980	----	----	0	YESO	ZAIRE	----
V37	MEMBER OF THE OECD	1970	----	----	0	YESO	ZAIRE	----
		1975	----	----	0	YESO	ZAIRE	----
		1980	----	----	0	YESO	ZAIRE	----

V38 MEMBER OF THE CMEA	1970	----	----	0		YESO	ZAIRE	----
	1975	----	----	0		YESO	ZAIRE	----
	1980	----	----	0		YESO	ZAIRE	----
V39 MEMBER OF THE WTO	1970	----	----	0		YESO	ZAIRE	----
	1975	----	----	0		YESO	ZAIRE	----
	1980	----	----	0		YESO	ZAIRE	----
V40 MEMBER OF THE NATO	1970	----	----	0		YESO	ZAIRE	----
	1975	----	----	0		YESO	ZAIRE	----
	1980	----	----	0		YESO	ZAIRE	----
V41 GDP SHARE OF INVESTMENTS	1970	D10	P94	32.3	%	SWITZ	TRITO	----
	1975	D10	P92	33.5	%	EGYPT	LIBE	----
	1980	D10	P95	34.0	%	SRILA	MAURA	----
V42 GDP SHARE OF AGRICULTURE	1970	D4	P41	17.6	%	IRAQ	CONGO	F16
	1975	D4	P40	15.1	%	CONGO	PORTU	F16
	1980	D4	P38	12.2	%	CONGO	ECUA	F16
V43 GDP SHARE OF INDUSTRY	1970	D9	P84	41.0	%	AULIA	CHILE	F16
	1975	D10	P91	48.6	%	VENE	ALGER	F16
	1980	D9	P86	43.1	%	JAPAN	INDO	F16
V44 GDP SHARE OF SERVICES	1970	D3	P25	41.4	%	PORTU	SIERA	F16
	1975	D3	P22	36.3	%	MALAW	MAURA	F16
	1980	D5	P42	44.7	%	PAKI	PARA	F16
V45 HOMICIDES P. MIL. POPULATION	1969	D7	P66	33.9	1/MIL CAP	BULGA	URU	F149
	1980	D6	P55	17.3	1/MIL CAP	BELGI	ITALY	F147
V46 SUICIDES P. MIL. POPULATION	1969	D7	P71	138.6	1/MIL CAP	CUBA	JAPAN	F147
	1980	D7	P61	146.7	1/MIL CAP	CANA	JAPAN	F147
V47 IMPORT PARTNERS	1970	R1	GFR	19.7	%	SWITZ	ALGER	----
	1970	R2	ITALY	13.2	%	SOMA	HAITI	----
	1970	R3	USSR	6.7	%	YENO	-------	----
	1980	R1	USSR	17.9	%	ROMA	-------	----
	1980	R2	GFR	16.6	%	UNKI	ARGE	----
	1980	R3	ITALY	7.4	%	SYRIA	-------	----
V48 EXPORT PARTNERS	1970	R1	ITALY	15.2	%	SYRIA	FRANC	----
	1970	R2	USSR	14.4	%	YENO	ALGER	----
	1970	R3	GFR	11.8	%	USA	ZAMBI	----
	1980	R1	USSR	27.7	%	ROMA	ETHIA	----
	1980	R2	ITALY	9.3	%	TURKY	GFR	----
	1980	R3	GFR	8.7	%	URU	-------	----
V49 PATENT SUPPLIERS	1971	R1	GFR	140		USSR	ARGE	----
	1971	R2	GDR	82		TANZA	CHINA	----
	1971	R3	SWITZ	76		VENE	-------	----
	1980	R1	GFR	180		TURKY	ARGE	----
	1980	R2	USA	80		TURKY	ZAIRE	----
	1980	R3	ITALY	64		HONDU	-------	----
V50 PROVENANCE OF FOREIGN FIRMS	1980	R1	GFR	40.0	%	AURIA	BRAZI	----
	1980	R2	USA	14.2	%	UGADA	ZAIRE	----
	1980	R3	FRANC	11.4	%	LEBA	-------	----

V51 FILM SUPPLIERS	1981	R1	USA	77		YENO	ZAMBI	F117
	1981	R2	ITALY	30		VENE	BULGA	F117
	1981	R3	GFR	24		NETH	-------	F117

ZAIRE (ZAIRE)

V1 INCOME PER CAPITA	1975	D2	P17	288	$/CAP	BENIN	SIERA	----
	1980	D1	P9	228	$/CAP	BURU	INDIA	----
V2 TELEPHONES P. TSD. POPULATION	1970	D2	P16	2	1/TSD CAP	VISO	BENIN	----
	1975	D2	P12	2	1/TSD CAP	NIGRA	BENIN	----
	1980	D1	P3	1	1/TSD CAP	RWAN	AFGHA	----
V3 INFANT MORTALITY RATE	1980	D7	P66	116.6	1/TSD	IRAN	RWAN	F5
V4 PHYSICIANS P. MIL. POPULATION	1979	D3	P21	74	1/MIL	SENE	INDO	----
V5 ADULT LITERACY	1980	D6	P55	54.5	%	UGADA	JORDA	F21
V6 DURATION OF SCHOOLING	1970	D4	P38	6.2	YR	NICA	HONDU	----
	1975	D4	P35	6.7	YR	YESO	EGYPT	----
	1978	D3	----	7.2	YR	IVORY	GHANA	----
V7 STUDENT ENROLLMENT RATIO	1970	D3	P24	0.7	%	AFGHA	GHANA	----
	1975	D3	P24	1.2	%	TOGO	CAME	----
	1980	D2	P18	1.2	%	YENO	ZIMBA	----
V8 SHARE OF AGRICULTURAL LABOR	-------	----	----	-----	-----	-------	-------	----
V9 SHARE OF INDUSTRIAL LABOR	-------	----	----	-----	-----	-------	-------	----
V10 SHARE OF SERVICE LABOR	-------	----	----	-----	-----	-------	-------	----
V11 SHARE OF ACADEMIC LABOR	-------	----	----	-----	-----	-------	-------	----
V12 SHARE OF SELF-EMPLOYED LABOR	-------	----	----	-----	-----	-------	-------	----
V13 MILITARY EXPENDITURES	1975	D5	P44	0.238	TSD MIL $	ECUA	IRE	----
	1980	D4	P34	0.161	TSD MIL $	GUATE	BANGL	F59
V14 MILITARY MANPOWER	1970	D5	P49	45	TSD CAP	VENE	ALBA	----
	1980	D4	P40	26	TSD CAP	DOMI	URU	----
V15 MEN AT AGE 20 - 30	1980	D7	P66	2087	TSD CAP	YUGO	ARGE	F2
V16 POPULATION	1975	D8	P76	22.58	MIL CAP	YUGO	CANA	----
	1980	D8	P76	26.38	MIL CAP	CANA	COLO	----
V17 GROSS DOMESTIC PRODUCT	1970	D5	P49	5.777	TSD MIL $	URU	LIBYA	----
	1975	D5	P43	6.496	TSD MIL $	URU	IVORY	----
	1980	D4	P37	6.025	TSD MIL $	BURMA	TRITO	----

V18 SHARE IN WORLD IMPORTS	1970	D5	P49	1.606	1/TSD	JAMAI	LIBYA	----
	1975	D4	P40	0.996	1/TSD	BANGL	ZAMBI	----
	1980	D3	P26	0.411	1/TSD	ANGO	NICA	----
V19 SHARE IN WORLD EXPORTS	1970	D6	P55	2.490	1/TSD	EGYPT	KORSO	----
	1975	D5	P44	0.987	1/TSD	TUNIS	DOMI	----
	1980	D5	P45	0.821	1/TSD	GUATE	SYRIA	----
V20 GDP SHARE OF IMPORTS	1970	D9	P86	28.4	%	MAURA	HONDU	----
	1975	D9	P90	40.8	%	MAURA	MALAW	----
	1980	D2	P16	13.7	%	JAPAN	COLO	----
V21 GDP SHARE OF EXPORTS	1970	D9	P90	41.6	%	NETH	HUNGA	----
	1975	D9	P86	39.0	%	IRE	IRAN	----
	1980	D7	P70	26.7	%	DENMA	ZIMBA	----
V22 EXPORT PARTNER CONCENTRATION	1970	D8	P78	42.3	%	TRITO	COSTA	F206
	1978	D7	----	30.0	%	NETH	CAME	F206
V23 TOTAL DEBT AS % OF GDP	------	----	----	-----	-----	-------	-------	----
V24 SHARE OF NEW FOREIGN PATENTS	1970	D9	P90	100	%	UGADA	-------	----
	1975	D7	P62	93	%	TUNIS	CANA	----
	1980	D8	P80	97	%	HONDU	IRE	----
V25 FOREIGN PROPERTY AS % OF GDP	1971	D9	P90	26.7	%	HONDU	VENE	----
	1975	D10	P96	38.4	%	JAMAI	TRITO	----
	1978	D9	----	19.1	%	MALAY	CONGO	----
V26 GNP SHARE OF DEVELOPMENT AID	------	----	----	-----	-----	-------	-------	----
V27 SHARE IN NOBEL PRIZE WINNERS	1970-79	D5	P45	0.0	%	YUGO	ZAMBI	----
V28 GDP SHARE OF MANUFACTURING	1970	D2	P17	8.3	%	SUDAN	JORDA	----
	1975	D4	P32	10.0	%	CAME	ALGER	----
	1980	D1	P6	3.0	%	KUWAI	GUINE	----
V29 EXPORT SHARE OF MANUFACTURES	------	----	----	-----	-----	-------	-------	----
V30 LACK OF CIVIL LIBERTIES	1975	D8	P74	6		YUGO	ALBA	----
	1980	D8	P74	6		USSR	AFGHA	----
V31 LACK OF POLITICAL RIGHTS	1975	D9	P88	7		YESO	-------	----
	1980	D7	P67	6		YUGO	AFGHA	----
V32 RIOTS	1970-74	D2	P19	0		YESO	ZAMBI	----
	1975-79	D5	P45	1		TANZA	ZAMBI	----
V33 PROTEST DEMONSTRATIONS	1970-74	D4	P37	1		YENO	ZAMBI	----
	1975-79	D4	P32	1		YENO	FINLA	----
V34 POLITICAL STRIKES	1970-74	D3	P29	0		YESO	ZAMBI	----
	1975-79	D3	P29	0		YUGO	ZAMBI	----
V35 MEMBER OF THE NONALIGNED MMT.	1970	----	----	1		YUGO	ZAMBI	----
	1976	----	----	1		YUGO	ZAMBI	----
	1981	----	----	1		YUGO	ZAMBI	----
V36 MEMBER OF THE OPEC	1970	----	----	0		YUGO	ZAMBI	----
	1975	----	----	0		YUGO	ZAMBI	----
	1980	----	----	0		YUGO	ZAMBI	----

V37 MEMBER OF THE OECD	1970	----	----	0		YUGO	ZAMBI	----
	1975	----	----	0		YUGO	ZAMBI	----
	1980	----	----	0		YUGO	ZAMBI	----
V38 MEMBER OF THE CMEA	1970	----	----	0		YUGO	ZAMBI	----
	1975	----	----	0		YUGO	ZAMBI	----
	1980	----	----	0		YUGO	ZAMBI	----
V39 MEMBER OF THE WTO	1970	----	----	0		YUGO	ZAMBI	----
	1975	----	----	0		YUGO	ZAMBI	----
	1980	----	----	0		YUGO	ZAMBI	----
V40 MEMBER OF THE NATO	1970	----	----	0		YUGO	ZAMBI	----
	1975	----	----	0		YUGO	ZAMBI	----
	1980	----	----	0		YUGO	ZAMBI	----
V41 GDP SHARE OF INVESTMENTS	1970	D8	P76	26.1 %		MALAW	THAI	----
	1975	D9	P87	31.9 %		JORDA	SOUAF	----
	1980	D10	P92	32.8 %		EGYPT	TOGO	----
V42 GDP SHARE OF AGRICULTURE	1970	D4	P39	16.9 %		PERU	IRAQ	----
	1975	D5	P48	19.5 %		GREC	COSTA	----
	1980	D7	P67	28.8 %		HONDU	CAME	----
V43 GDP SHARE OF INDUSTRY	1970	D8	P71	36.5 %		SWEDN	NETH	----
	1975	D6	P53	31.6 %		DOMI	MAURA	----
	1980	D4	P40	28.8 %		THAI	BOLI	----
V44 GDP SHARE OF SERVICES	1970	D5	P43	46.6 %		THAI	KENYA	----
	1975	D7	P65	48.9 %		GFR	IVORY	----
	1980	D4	P37	42.4 %		BENIN	UPVO	----
V45 HOMICIDES P. MIL. POPULATION	------	----	----	----- -----		-------	-------	----
V46 SUICIDES P. MIL. POPULATION	------	----	----	----- -----		-------	-------	----
V47 IMPORT PARTNERS	1970	R1	BELGI	24.5 %		RWAN	FRANC	F142
	1970	R2	USA	10.7 %		URU	ALGER	----
	1970	R3	GFR	10.4 %		USA	-------	----
	1978	R1	BELGI	19.8 %		RWAN	NETH	F142
	1978	R2	FRANC	11.9 %		SWITZ	BELGI	----
	1978	R3	USA	11.6 %		UPVO	-------	----
V48 EXPORT PARTNERS	1970	R1	BELGI	42.3 %		-------	DOMI	F206
	1970	R2	ANGO	17.1 %		PORTU	-------	----
	1970	R3	ITALY	11.5 %		SUDAN	-------	----
	1978	R1	BELGI	30.0 %		-------	CENTR	F206
	1978	R2	UNKI	14.0 %		TANZA	ZAMBI	----
	1978	R3	SWITZ	10.1 %		AURIA	-------	----
V49 PATENT SUPPLIERS	1970	R1	SWITZ	25		SYRIA	GDR	----
	1970	R2	FRANC	19		VISO	BRAZI	----
	1970	R3	BELGI	17		-------	-------	----
	1979	R1	FRANC	20		TUNIS	PERU	----
	1979	R2	USA	19		YUGO	FINLA	----
	1979	R3	SWITZ	10		VENE	-------	----

V50	PROVENANCE OF FOREIGN FIRMS	1980	R1	BELGI	46.7 %	-------	CONGO	----
		1980	R2	USA	11.9 %	YUGO	ZAMBI	----
		1980	R3	UNKI	11.4 %	URU	-------	----
V51	FILM SUPPLIERS	------	----	----	----- -----	-------	-------	----

ZAMBIA (ZAMBI)

V1	INCOME PER CAPITA	1970	D4	P37	751 $/CAP	ECUA	TUNIS	----
		1975	D4	P36	726 $/CAP	CAME	ELSA	----
		1980	D4	P31	622 $/CAP	HONDU	ELSA	----
V2	TELEPHONES P. TSD. POPULATION	1970	D4	P39	9 1/TSD CAP	SENE	CONGO	----
		1975	D4	P37	11 1/TSD CAP	PHILI	EGYPT	----
		1980	D3	P27	11 1/TSD CAP	THAI	KENYA	----
V3	INFANT MORTALITY RATE	1980	D7	P62	110.5 1/TSD	TANZA	PAPUA	F5
V4	PHYSICIANS P. MIL. POPULATION	1971	D4	P37	120 1/MIL	THAI	ALGER	----
		1980	D3	P29	118 1/MIL	BANGL	SUDAN	----
V5	ADULT LITERACY	1969	D3	P28	47.3 %	SYRIA	TURKY	----
V6	DURATION OF SCHOOLING	1970	D6	P51	7.4 YR	TURKY	ECUA	----
		1975	D5	P50	8.0 YR	IRAQ	VENE	----
		1980	D5	P40	8.3 YR	TUNIS	BOLI	----
V7	STUDENT ENROLLMENT RATIO	1970	D2	P18	0.4 %	SOMA	CAME	----
		1975	D4	P34	2.1 %	SENE	BURMA	----
		1979	D3	P22	1.6 %	GHANA	AFGHA	----
V8	SHARE OF AGRICULTURAL LABOR	1969	D6	P53	31.3 %	SOUAF	PORTU	F93
V9	SHARE OF INDUSTRIAL LABOR	------	----	----	----- -----	-------	-------	----
V10	SHARE OF SERVICE LABOR	------	----	----	----- -----	-------	-------	----
V11	SHARE OF ACADEMIC LABOR	------	----	----	----- -----	-------	-------	----
V12	SHARE OF SELF-EMPLOYED LABOR	------	----	----	----- -----	-------	-------	----
V13	MILITARY EXPENDITURES	1975	D4	P36	0.105 TSD MIL $	TUNIS	TANZA	F59
		1980	D4	P32	0.125 TSD MIL $	NICA	GUATE	F59
V14	MILITARY MANPOWER	1970	D3	P27	12 TSD CAP	HAITI	GUATE	----
		1975	D3	P29	16 TSD CAP	PARA	DOMI	----
		1980	D3	P28	15 TSD CAP	PARA	CONGO	----
V15	MEN AT AGE 20 - 30	1969	D3	P23	258 TSD CAP	ELSA	DOMI	----
		1975	D4	P31	369 TSD CAP	UPVO	SENE	F2
V16	POPULATION	1970	D4	P34	4.25 MIL CAP	HAITI	SENE	----
		1975	D4	P36	4.98 MIL CAP	SENE	DENMA	----
		1980	D4	P38	5.83 MIL CAP	YENO	MALAW	----

V17	GROSS DOMESTIC PRODUCT	1970	D4	P31	3.190 TSD MIL $	ETHIA	TANZA	----
		1975	D3	P30	3.617 TSD MIL $	ETHIA	TANZA	----
		1980	D3	P28	3.627 TSD MIL $	PANA	SRILA	----
V18	SHARE IN WORLD IMPORTS	1970	D5	P46	1.437 1/TSD	KENYA	IRAQ	----
		1975	D5	P41	1.022 1/TSD	ZAIRE	ECUA	----
		1980	D4	P31	0.542 1/TSD	SENE	GHANA	----
V19	SHARE IN WORLD EXPORTS	1970	D6	P58	3.191 1/TSD	PORTU	ALGER	----
		1975	D5	P43	0.924 1/TSD	GHANA	TUNIS	----
		1980	D4	P40	0.651 1/TSD	GHANA	CAME	----
V20	GDP SHARE OF IMPORTS	1970	D8	P79	26.8 %	MALAW	ALGER	----
		1975	D9	P86	37.7 %	BENIN	MALAY	----
		1980	D7	P66	28.6 %	IVORY	NORWY	----
V21	GDP SHARE OF EXPORTS	1970	D10	P95	56.3 %	MAURA	LIBYA	----
		1975	D9	P81	32.9 %	IVORY	ALGER	----
		1980	D8	P80	33.5 %	HONDU	VENE	----
V22	EXPORT PARTNER CONCENTRATION	1970	D4	P38	23.4 %	AURIA	SAUDI	----
		1975	D5	P44	22.5 %	NEWZ	GUATE	----
		1979	D3	P29	18.5 %	ROMA	MADA	----
V23	TOTAL DEBT AS % OF GDP	1980	D10	P95	83.6 %	PANA	TOGO	----
V24	SHARE OF NEW FOREIGN PATENTS	1970	D8	P79	99 %	TUNIS	BURU	----
		1975	D9	P82	98 %	MALAW	NIGRA	----
		1980	D10	P94	100 %	UGADA	-------	----
V25	FOREIGN PROPERTY AS % OF GDP	1971	D8	P78	18.1 %	SAUDI	ECUA	----
		1975	D7	P62	8.1 %	PHILI	TUNIS	----
		1978	D9	----	11.9 %	TOGO	GUINE	----
V26	GNP SHARE OF DEVELOPMENT AID	------	----	----	----- -----	-------	-------	----
V27	SHARE IN NOBEL PRIZE WINNERS	1970-79	D5	P45	0.0 %	ZAIRE	ARGE	----
V28	GDP SHARE OF MANUFACTURING	1970	D4	P33	10.2 %	TANZA	BURMA	----
		1975	D6	P55	15.8 %	PARA	VENE	----
		1980	D7	P64	16.8 %	PARA	MOROC	----
V29	EXPORT SHARE OF MANUFACTURES	1970	D1	P5	0.2 %	SAUDI	CUBA	----
		1975	D2	P14	0.7 %	SAUDI	GABON	----
		1979	D2	P12	0.7 %	SAUDI	PAPUA	----
V30	LACK OF CIVIL LIBERTIES	1975	D4	P39	4	YENO	BOLI	----
		1980	D6	P52	5	YUGO	ZIMBA	----
V31	LACK OF POLITICAL RIGHTS	1975	D5	P43	5	YENO	ALGER	----
		1980	D5	P47	5	UNARE	ALGER	----
V32	RIOTS	1970-74	D2	P19	0	ZAIRE	ALGER	----
		1975-79	D5	P45	1	ZAIRE	BENIN	----
V33	PROTEST DEMONSTRATIONS	1970-74	D4	P37	1	ZAIRE	GDR	----
		1975-79	D7	P67	7	YUGO	CANA	----
V34	POLITICAL STRIKES	1970-74	D3	P29	0	ZAIRE	AULIA	----
		1975-79	D3	P29	0	ZAIRE	CZECH	----

V35	MEMBER OF THE NONALIGNED MMT.	1970	----	----	1	ZAIRE	-------	----
		1976	----	----	1	ZAIRE	-------	----
		1981	----	----	1	ZAIRE	ZIMBA	----
V36	MEMBER OF THE OPEC	1970	----	----	0	ZAIRE	-------	----
		1975	----	----	0	ZAIRE	-------	----
		1980	----	----	0	ZAIRE	ZIMBA	----
V37	MEMBER OF THE OECD	1970	----	----	0	ZAIRE	-------	----
		1975	----	----	0	ZAIRE	-------	----
		1980	----	----	0	ZAIRE	ZIMBA	----
V38	MEMBER OF THE CMEA	1970	----	----	0	ZAIRE	-------	----
		1975	----	----	0	ZAIRE	-------	----
		1980	----	----	0	ZAIRE	ZIMBA	----
V39	MEMBER OF THE WTO	1970	----	----	0	ZAIRE	-------	----
		1975	----	----	0	ZAIRE	-------	----
		1980	----	----	0	ZAIRE	ZIMBA	----
V40	MEMBER OF THE NATO	1970	----	----	0	ZAIRE	-------	----
		1975	----	----	0	ZAIRE	-------	----
		1980	----	----	0	ZAIRE	ZIMBA	----
V41	GDP SHARE OF INVESTMENTS	1970	D9	P86	28.4 %	GREC	SOUAF	----
		1975	D10	P98	40.5 %	HUNGA	ALGER	----
		1980	D5	P48	23.5 %	MADA	INDIA	----
V42	GDP SHARE OF AGRICULTURE	1970	D3	P28	10.7 %	SPAIN	FINLA	----
		1975	D4	P37	13.0 %	URU	PERU	----
		1980	D5	P43	14.6 %	ZIMBA	KORSO	----
V43	GDP SHARE OF INDUSTRY	1970	D10	P97	54.8 %	GFR	SAUDI	----
		1975	D9	P82	41.7 %	AURIA	JAPAN	----
		1980	D8	P78	39.1 %	SINGA	AURIA	----
V44	GDP SHARE OF SERVICES	1970	D2	P16	34.5 %	LIBE	INDO	----
		1975	D5	P49	45.3 %	HONDU	KENYA	----
		1980	D5	P49	46.3 %	NICA	SIERA	----
V45	HOMICIDES P. MIL. POPULATION	------	----	----	----- -----	-------	-------	----
V46	SUICIDES P. MIL. POPULATION	------	----	----	----- -----	-------	-------	----
V47	IMPORT PARTNERS	1970	R1	UNKI	23.6 %	UGADA	AULIA	----
		1970	R2	SOUAF	18.3 %	-------	MALAW	F144
		1970	R3	USA	9.7 %	SWEDN	-------	----
		1979	R1	UNKI	25.8 %	TANZA	BENIN	----
		1979	R2	SAUDI	15.2 %	SRILA	BRAZI	----
		1979	R3	SOUAF	11.3 %	MALAW	-------	F144
V48	EXPORT PARTNERS	1970	R1	JAPAN	23.4 %	THAI	BENIN	----
		1970	R2	UNKI	22.4 %	UGADA	AULIA	----
		1970	R3	GFR	11.8 %	YUGO	-------	----
		1979	R1	JAPAN	18.5 %	UNARE	CANA	----
		1979	R2	UNKI	13.3 %	ZAIRE	BOLI	----
		1979	R3	FRANC	11.5 %	TUNIS	-------	----

V49	PATENT SUPPLIERS	1970	R1	USA	46		VISO	AURIA	----
		1970	R2	UNKI	38		VENE	CANA	----
		1970	R3	SOUAF	14		MALAW	-------	----
		1979	R1	USA	17		VENE	AURIA	----
		1979	R2	UNKI	11		UGADA	ZIMBA	----
		1979	R3	SOUAF	8		ZIMBA	-------	----
V50	PROVENANCE OF FOREIGN FIRMS	1980	R1	UNKI	73.0 %		USA	ZIMBA	----
		1980	R2	USA	15.2 %		ZAIRE	ZIMBA	----
		1980	R3	GFR	3.4 %		VENE	-------	----
V51	FILM SUPPLIERS	1979	R1	USA	100		YUGO	ANGO	F119
		1979	R2	UNKI	37		SRILA	AULIA	F119
		1979	R3	ITALY	3		TURKY	-------	F119

ZIMBABWE (ZIMBA)

V1	INCOME PER CAPITA	1980	D4	P36	738 $/CAP	CAME	NICA	----
V2	TELEPHONES P. TSD. POPULATION	1980	D5	P42	29 1/TSD CAP	DOMI	TUNIS	----
V3	INFANT MORTALITY RATE	1980	D5	P49	79.0 1/TSD	BRAZI	IRAQ	F5
V4	PHYSICIANS P. MIL. POPULATION	1980	D4	P36	161 1/MIL	THAI	CONGO	----
V5	ADULT LITERACY	1980	D7	P69	68.8 %	KUWAI	BRAZI	F21
V6	DURATION OF SCHOOLING	1980	D4	P29	7.3 YR	TURKY	TANZA	----
V7	STUDENT ENROLLMENT RATIO	1980	D2	P20	1.3 %	ZAIRE	CAME	----
V8	SHARE OF AGRICULTURAL LABOR	1982	D9	----	63.7 %	AFGHA	INDIA	----
V9	SHARE OF INDUSTRIAL LABOR	1982	D2	----	16.2 %	INDIA	INDO	----
V10	SHARE OF SERVICE LABOR	1982	D2	----	15.7 %	THAI	HAITI	----
V11	SHARE OF ACADEMIC LABOR	1982	D3	----	4.5 %	TURKY	KORSO	----
V12	SHARE OF SELF-EMPLOYED LABOR	------	----	----	----- -----	-------	-------	----
V13	MILITARY EXPENDITURES	1980	D5	P49	0.454 TSD MIL $	JORDA	HUNGA	F62
V14	MILITARY MANPOWER	1980	D5	P45	35 TSD CAP	KAMPU	FINLA	----
V15	MEN AT AGE 20 - 30	1981	D4	P32	580 TSD CAP	AURIA	SWEDN	F2
V16	POPULATION	1980	D5	P44	7.14 MIL CAP	MALI	GUATE	----
V17	GROSS DOMESTIC PRODUCT	1980	D4	P35	5.266 TSD MIL $	TANZA	BURMA	----
V18	SHARE IN WORLD IMPORTS	1980	D4	P34	0.629 1/TSD	TANZA	PANA	F49

V19	SHARE IN WORLD EXPORTS	1980	D5	P43	0.713	1/TSD	KENYA	GUATE	F30
V20	GDP SHARE OF IMPORTS	1980	D6	P52	24.2	%	NIGER	CAME	F49
V21	GDP SHARE OF EXPORTS	1980	D7	P70	26.7	%	ZAIRE	FINLA	F30
V22	EXPORT PARTNER CONCENTRATION	------	----	----	----- -----		-------	-------	----
V23	TOTAL DEBT AS % OF GDP	1981	D3	P23	21.1	%	HAITI	PARA	----
V24	SHARE OF NEW FOREIGN PATENTS	1980	D5	P50	89	%	NEWZ	PHILI	----
V25	FOREIGN PROPERTY AS % OF GDP	------	----	----	----- -----		-------	-------	----
V26	GNP SHARE OF DEVELOPMENT AID	------	----	----	----- -----		-------	-------	----
V27	SHARE IN NOBEL PRIZE WINNERS	------	----	----	----- -----		-------	-------	----
V28	GDP SHARE OF MANUFACTURING	1980	D9	P90	25.5	%	BELGI	FINLA	F16
V29	EXPORT SHARE OF MANUFACTURES	------	----	----	----- -----		-------	-------	----
V30	LACK OF CIVIL LIBERTIES	1980	D6	P52	5		ZAMBI	ALGER	----
V31	LACK OF POLITICAL RIGHTS	1980	D4	P36	4		THAI	BHUTA	----
V32	RIOTS	------	----	----	----- -----		-------	-------	----
V33	PROTEST DEMONSTRATIONS	------	----	----	----- -----		-------	-------	----
V34	POLITICAL STRIKES	------	----	----	----- -----		-------	-------	----
V35	MEMBER OF THE NONALIGNED MMT.	1981	----	----	1		ZAMBI	-------	----
V36	MEMBER OF THE OPEC	1980	----	----	0		ZAMBI	-------	----
V37	MEMBER OF THE OECD	1980	----	----	0		ZAMBI	-------	----
V38	MEMBER OF THE CMEA	1980	----	----	0		ZAMBI	-------	----
V39	MEMBER OF THE WTO	1980	----	----	0		ZAMBI	-------	----
V40	MEMBER OF THE NATO	1980	----	----	0		ZAMBI	-------	----
V41	GDP SHARE OF INVESTMENTS	1980	D2	P14	15.1	%	HAITI	JAMAI	----
V42	GDP SHARE OF AGRICULTURE	1980	D5	P42	13.9	%	IRE	ZAMBI	F16
V43	GDP SHARE OF INDUSTRY	1980	D8	P76	38.3	%	EGYPT	SINGA	F16
V44	GDP SHARE OF SERVICES	1980	D6	P56	47.8	%	TUNIS	MAURA	F16
V45	HOMICIDES P. MIL. POPULATION	------	----	----	----- -----		-------	-------	----
V46	SUICIDES P. MIL. POPULATION	------	----	----	----- -----		-------	-------	----
V47	IMPORT PARTNERS	------	----	----	----- -----		-------	-------	----
V48	EXPORT PARTNERS	------	----	----	----- -----		-------	-------	----

V49	PATENT SUPPLIERS	1980	R1	SOUAF	41		-------	ZAMBI	----
		1980	R2	UNKI	34		ZAMBI	COSTA	----
		1980	R3	USA	33		FINLA	-------	----
V50	PROVENANCE OF FOREIGN FIRMS	1980	R1	UNKI	86.8	%	ZAMBI	ARGE	----
		1980	R2	USA	7.1	%	ZAMBI	CONGO	----
		1980	R3	CANA	2.5	%	TRITO	-------	----
V51	FILM SUPPLIERS	------	----	----	----- -----		-------	-------	----

APPENDIX

FOOTNOTES TO THE COUNTRY PROFILES

F1:   Excluding paramilitary forces.

F2:   Limited reliability.

F3:   See footnotes F1 and F2.

F4:   Not strictly comparable with figures for later years.

F5:   Estimate referring to 1975-1980.

F6:   Excluding Faeroe Islands and Greenland.

F7:   Including data for East Jerusalem and Israeli residents in certain other territories under occupation by Israeli military forces.

F8:   Member of CMEA but not participating in this organization since 1961.

F9:   Due to the secession of Bangladesh in 1971 this figure is not strictly comparable with the figures for later years.

F10: Excluding telephone systems of the military forces.

F11: Excluding Ras Al Khaimah.

F12: Due to the union of North and South Vietnam in 1976 this figure is not strictly comparable with the figures for later years.

F13: In spite of its withdrawal from the integrated military command of the NATO in the late 1960s, France has not left the NATO.

F14: In spite of its withdrawal from the integrated military command of the NATO between 1974 and 1980, Greece has never left the NATO.

F15: In spite of its low participation in the military activities of the WTO, Romania has not left the WTO.

F16: At current factor cost.

F17: Data refer to East Bank only.

F18: See footnotes F16 and F17.

F19: Since this figure is based on a total of less than 10 indigenous and foreign patents it must be considered as less reliable.

F20: Excludes investment in livestock.

F21: Estimated by UNESCO.

F22: Refers to the *de jure population,* i.e. the usual residents of the given country. For a discussion of the concept of *de jure population* see United Nations, *Demographic Yearbook, Historical Supplement,* New York, 1979, pp. 4, 5.

F23: Excluding Indian jungle population.

F24: Refers to the population aged 14 years and older.

F25: Persons with no schooling are defined as illiterates.

F26: Refers to Libyan population only.

F27: Estimate for the de jure population.

F28: Refers to national population only.

F29: Not strictly comparable with earlier or later years.

F30: Figure refers to *general trade: General imports* are the combined total of imports for direct domestic consumption and imports into bonded warehouses or free zones. *General exports* are the combined total of national exports and re-exports.

F31: Including exports of Luxembourg.

F32: Only exports of national produce.

F33: Including trade with monetary gold.

F34: See footnotes F30, F33, and F35.

F35: Not strictly comparable with figures for previous years.

F36: Excluding West Irian.

F37: See footnotes F4 and F36.

F38: Excluding trade for Okinawa prefecture.

F39: See footnotes F4, F30, and F38.

F40: Excluding the Canal Zone and the Free Zone.

F41: See footnotes F4 and F40.

F42: Including trans-shipments to and from West Malaysia.

F43: See footnotes F30 and F42.

F44: Figure adjusted to approximate trade of present customs area comprising Botswana, Lesotho, Namibia, South Africa, and Swaziland. Trade between these countries is excluded.

F45: See footnotes F30 and F44.

F46: Provisional figures.

F47: See footnotes F30 and F46.

F48: Fob value.

F49: See footnotes F30 and F48.

F50: Including imports of Luxembourg.

F51: Including imports of foreign aid.

F52: See footnotes F30, F44, and F48.

F53: Excluding certain petroleum imports.

F54: See footnotes F35 and F53.

F55: See footnotes F4, F30, and F48.

F56: See footnotes F9 and F30.

F57: See footnotes F30 and F35.

F58: See footnotes F4 and F30.

F59: Rough estimate.

F60: Uncertain data or SIPRI estimates of military expenditure.

F61: See footnotes F4 and F60.

F62: Uncertain data.

F63: See footnotes F4 and F62.

F64: Military expenditure as % of the gross national product.

F65: See footnotes F62 and F64.

F66: Based on figures for total and/or service labor both of which include members of the armed forces.

F67: Based on the 1958 International Standard Classification of Occupations (= ISCO-1958).

F68: Excluding Yukon, Northwest Territories, and Indians living on reserves.

F69: Based on figures for total and/or service labor which do not include domestic servants.

F70: See footnotes F46 and F69.

F71: Members of agricultural producers' co-operatives excluded from calculations.

F72: See footnotes F46, F69, and F71.

F73: Excluding unpaid family workers.

F74: Based on figures for total and self-employed labor both of which include members of the armed forces.

F75: Refers to persons 10 years of age and older.

F76: Based on labor force figures that exclude apprentices totaling 214900 persons.

F77: Excluding members of producers' co-operatives.

F78: See footnotes F76 and F77.

F79: Including data relating to certain territories under occupation by Israeli military forces.

F80: See footnotes F67 and F79.

F81: Based on labor force figures that exclude unreported female family helpers in agriculture.

F82: See footnotes F22, F46, and F81.

F83: Including unemployed persons.

F84: See footnotes F22 and F67.

F85: Excluding Canal Zone.

F86: Without adjustment for the undernumeration of the labor force.

F87: Figure refers to persons who have worked at least 15 hours during the week preceding the collection of the original census data.

F88: Refers to Syrian population only.

F89: Excluding Northern Ireland.

F90: Refers to persons 16 years of age and older.

F91: See footnotes F22, F83, and F90.

F92: See footnotes F22 and F90.

F93: See footnotes F46, F67, and F86.

F94: Refers to African population only.

F95: Refers to Egyptian population only.

F96: Refers to persons 15 years of age and older.

F97: See footnotes F95 and F96.

F98: Refers to persons 15 to 74 years of age.

F99: Official estimates.

F100: Refers to persons who have worked at least 20 hours per week.

F101: Excluding Jammu, Kashmir, Gilgit, Baltistan, Junagardh, and Manavadar.

F102: Refers to persons 16 to 74 years of age who have worked at least one hour per week.

F103: Based on labor force figures that exclude unpaid family workers who worked fewer than 20 hours during the week when the original data were collected.

F104: Refers to persons 12 to 64 years of age.

F105: Refers to persons 14 years of age and older.

F106: Refers to persons 10 to 79 years of age.

F107: Excluding Assam.

F108: See footnotes F46 and F107.

F109: Refers to persons 7 years of age and older.

F110: See footnotes F46 and F109.

F111: Refers to persons 10 to 69 years of age.

F112: See footnotes F46 and F111.

F113: Refers to persons 12 years of age and older.

F114: See footnotes F83 and F90.

F115: See footnotes F75 and F77.

F116: The information in this row does not exactly correspond to annex table II.19 of the source publication. A very obvious confusion of some of the data columns of this table has compelled us to make certain corrections that are based on annex table II.18 of the aforementioned source publication.

F117: Method of data collection is unknown. Three of the possible alternative methods are described in the footnotes F118, F119, and F120.

F118: Refers to films imported in the year stated.

F119: Refers to films approved by censor for public showing in the year stated.

F120: Refers to films commercially shown for the first time in the year stated.

F121: Based on data that exclude trade within the Customs and Economic Union of Central Africa comprising Cameroon, the Central African Republic, Congo, and Gabon.

F122: Exports of copper, iron ore, and nitrates are valued at cost of production and not at transaction values.

F123: Excluding trade of Faeroe Islands and Greenland.

F124: Based on data that exclude trade within the East African Community comprising Kenya, Tanzania, and Uganda.

F125: Based on data that exclude trade between Israel and the territories under occupation by Israeli military forces.

F126: Based on data that exclude trade between North and South Korea.

F127: Based on data that exclude trade with India.

F128: Excluding trade of the Canal Zone and of the Free Zone of Colon.

F129: Excluding trade of the Free Zone of Colon.

F130: Exports of bananas are underevaluated.

F131: See footnotes F128 and F130.

F132: See footnotes F129, F130, and F136.

F133: Refers to the Customs Union of Southern Africa, comprising South Africa, Botswana, Lesotho, Swaziland, and Namibia.

F134: Trade of Malaysia transported via Singapore is partly valued as import or export of Singapore. Hence the statistics of the trade partner distribution of Malaysia and Singapore are probably somewhat distorted.

F135: Refers to Belgium and Luxembourg.

F136: Not strictly comparable with information for previous years.

F137: Not strictly comparable with information for later years.

F138: Including exports to Luxembourg.

F139: See footnotes F137 and F138.

F140: See footnotes F121 and F138.

F141: Including exports to Botswana, Swaziland, Lesotho, and Namibia, all of which belong to the Customs Union of Southern Africa.

F142: Including imports from Luxembourg.

F143: See footnotes F121 and F142.

F144: Including imports from Botswana, Swaziland, Lesotho, and Namibia, all of which belong to the Customs Union of South Africa.

F145: Due to the secession of Bangladesh in 1971 there is only limited comparability with the information for later years.

F146: Including integrated special education.

F147: Based on population figures that refer to the *de jure population,* i.e. the usual residents of a given country. For a discussion of the concept of *de jure population* see United Nations, *Demographic Yearbook, Historical Supplement,* New York, 1979, pp. 4, 5.

F148: Including cases of death caused by legal interventions, such as executions or the suppression of riots.

F149: See footnotes F147 and F148.

F150: See footnotes F2 and F147.

F151: Based on counts of cases of death that refer to the Jewish population only.

F152: See footnotes F2, F147, F151, and F183.

F153: See footnotes F2, F147, and F148.

F154: See footnotes F2 and F148.

F155: See footnotes F2, F147, F148, F151, and F183.

F156: See footnotes F2 and F147.

F157: Based on population figures that exclude nomadic Indian tribes.

F158: See footnotes F148 and F157.

F159: Based on population figures that exclude the Indian jungle population.

F160: See footnotes F6 and F147.

F161: See footnotes F2, F6, and F147.

F162: See footnotes F4 and F22.

F163: See footnotes F4 and F23.

F164: See footnotes F23 and F35.

F165: See footnotes F6 and F22.

F166: Excluding nomadic Indian tribes.

F167: Excluding armed forces stationed outside the country, but including alien armed forces stationed in the area.

F168: Including the Indian-held part of Jammu and Kashmir.

F169: See footnotes F7 and F22.

F170: The population figures published in the *World Bank Atlas* (World Bank, Washington, D.C., several years) are much lower.

F171: Based on population figures that might be too high. See footnote F170.

F172: Including Palestinian refugees, but excluding Jordanian territory under occupation by Israeli military forces.

F173: Including Lebanese living outside the country but excluding non-resident foreigners and Palestinian refugees.

F174: See footnotes F4 and F173.

F175: See footnotes F4 and F85.

F176: Including Palestinian refugees.

F177: See footnotes F4 and F176.

F178: See footnotes F2 and F168.

F179: See footnotes F2, F148, and F157.

F180: See footnotes F2 and F157.

F181: See footnotes F35 and F172.

F182: See footnotes F22 and F35.

F183: Based on population figures that include East Jerusalem and Israeli residents in certain other territories under occupation by Israeli military forces.

F184: See footnotes F2 and F22.

F185: See footnotes F2, F22, and F23.

F186: See footnotes F22 and F46.

F187: See footnotes F2 and F166.

F188: See footnotes F2 and F168.

F189: Refers to Moslem population only.

F190: See footnotes F2 and F189.

F191: See footnotes F2, F22, and F176.

F192: See footnotes F2 and F172.

F193: See footnotes F2 and F85.

F194: See footnotes F22 and F23.

F195: Excluding Palestinian refugees in camps.

F196: Excluding armed forces overseas.

F197: See footnotes F22 and F196.

F198: Including the Indian-held part of Jammu and Kashmir, but excluding Sikkim.

F199: See footnotes F2 and F198.

F200: Including registered Palestinian refugees.

F201: See footnotes F2 and F200.

F202: Excluding Jammu, Kashmir, Gilgit, Baltistan, Junagardh, Manavadar, and federally administered tribal areas.

F203: See footnotes F46 and F202.

F204: Including certain territories under occupation by Israeli military forces.

F205: See footnotes F22 and F204.

F206: Figure refers to exports to Belgium and Luxembourg.

F207: Based on trade figures that refer to the Customs Union of Southern Africa, comprising South Africa, Botswana, Lesotho, Swaziland, and Namibia. Trade between these countries is excluded.

F208: See footnotes F30, F48, and F207.

F209: See footnotes F30 and F207.

F210: See footnotes F4 and F147.

F211: See footnotes F4 and F223.

F212: Based on population figures that exclude the Faeroe Islands and Greenland.

F213: See footnotes F147 and F212.

F214: Based on population figures that include the Indian-held part of Jammu and Kashmir.

F215: Based on population figures which exclude the Canal Zone.

F216: See footnotes F4 and F215.

F217: Based on population figures that include Palestinian refugees.

F218: See footnotes F4 and F217.

F219: Based on population figures that exclude Jammu, Kashmir, Gilgit, Baltistan, Junagardh, and Manavadar.

F220: See footnotes F35 and F159.

F221: Including events in territories under occupation by Israeli military forces.

F222: Excluding events in territories under occupation by Israeli military forces.

F223: Based on population figures that exclude the Indian jungle population.

F224: Based on population figures that exclude armed forces stationed outside the country but include alien armed forces stationed in the area.

LIST OF COUNTRIES

- Afghanistan
- Albania
- Algeria
- Angola
- Argentina
- Australia
- Austria
- Bangladesh
- Belgium
- Benin (formerly known as *Dahomey*)
- Bhutan
- Bolivia
- Brazil
- Bulgaria
- Burkina-Faso. See *Upper Volta.*
- Burma
- Burundi
- Cambodia. See *Kampuchea.*
- Cameroon
- Canada
- Central African Republic
- Chad
- Chile
- China, People's Republic of
- Colombia
- Congo, People's Republic of the
- Costa Rica
- Cuba
- Czechoslovakia
- Dahomey. See *Benin.*
- Denmark
- Dominican Republic
- East Germany. See *German Democratic Republic.*
- Ecuador
- Egypt
- El Salvador
- Ethiopia
- Finland
- France
- Gabon
- German Democratic Republic (also known as *East Germany*)

- Germany, Federal Republic of (also known as *West Germany*)
- Ghana
- Greece
- Guatemala
- Guinea
- Haiti
- Honduras
- Hungary
- India
- Indonesia
- Iran
- Iraq
- Ireland
- Israel
- Italy
- Ivory Coast
- Jamaica
- Japan
- Jordan
- Kampuchea (also known as *Cambodia*)
- Kenya
- Korea, North
- Korea, South
- Kuwait
- Laos
- Lebanon
- Lesotho
- Liberia
- Libya
- Madagascar
- Malawi
- Malaysia
- Mali
- Mauritania
- Mexico
- Mongolia
- Morocco
- Mozambique
- Nepal
- Netherlands
- New Zealand
- Nicaragua

- Niger
- Nigeria
- Norway
- Oman
- Pakistan
- Panama
- Papua New Guinea
- Paraguay
- Peru
- Philippines
- Poland
- Portugal
- Romania
- Rwanda
- Saudi Arabia
- Senegal
- Sierra Leone
- Singapore
- Somalia
- South Africa
- Spain
- Sri Lanka
- Sudan
- Sweden
- Switzerland
- Syria

- Taiwan
- Tanzania
- Thailand
- Togo
- Trinidad and Tobago
- Tunisia
- Turkey
- Uganda
- United Arab Emirates
- United Kingdom
- Upper Volta (also known as *Burkina-Faso*)
- Uruguay
- USA
- USSR
- Venezuela
- Vietnam, North
- Vietnam, South
- Yemen, North   (also known as *Yemen Arab Republic*)
- Yemen, South   (also known as *People's Democratic Republic of Yemen*)
- Yugoslavia
- Zaire
- Zambia
- Zimbabwe

ORGANIZATION AND USE OF THE COMPUTER DISKETTES

For statistical investigations beyond the level of exploratory data analysis the numerical information of this book is also offered on PC-diskettes of the *DOS-type*. This way, the information in this book can easily be processed by commonly used statistical software packages such as SAS, BMDP, SPSS/PC, or SPSS^x . To speed up the data processing by less powerful PC systems the data have been partitioned into 51 ASCII files named V1.DAT, V2.DAT, V3.DAT, ... , V51.DAT . Each of these ASCII files contains *all* the information referring to that variable Vx which is mentioned in the *filename* itself. The information contained in these files is stored in records of fixed length which are organized as follows:

Cols. 1-5: *Alphamerical field* that contains the *short name of the country* to which the record refers. The short names used in this field are identical to the ones used in the country profiles in chapter 4. *Missing values* are *nonexistent*. Names that have fewer than 5 characters are stored *left-aligned*. The remaining columns of the field are filled with blanks.

Col. 6: *Blank.*

Cols. 7-16: *Alphamerical field* that contains the *short name of the variable* to which the record refers. The short names used in this field are identical to the ones used in the variable descriptions in chapter 3. *Missing values* are *nonexistent*. Names that have fewer than 10 characters are stored *left-aligned*. The remaining columns of the field are filled with blanks.

Col. 17: *Blank.*

Cols. 18-21: *Numerical field without decimal point.* If the record refers to a *timeinterval* (e.g., record with information about V32 = Riots), the field contains the *first year* of this interval. If the record refers to a *timepoint* (e.g., record with information about V16 = Population), the field contains the *year* enclosing this time-point. Years are always coded in the usual 4-digit way. *Missing values* are *nonexistent*.

Col. 22: *Blank.*

Cols. 23-26: *Numerical field without decimal point.* If the record refers to a *timeinterval* (e.g., record with information about V32 = Riots), the field contains the *last year* of this interval. If the record refers to a *timepoint* (e.g., record with information about V16 = Population), the field contains the *year* enclosing this time-point, i.e., the information given in columns 18-21. Years are always coded in the usual 4-digit way. *Missing values* are *nonexistent*.

Col. 27: *Blank.*

Cols. 28-30: *Alphamerical field.* For the variables V47 to V51, which describe *exchange relations* and for which column 65 is coded as *I,* the field contains the *rank of the partner nation* to which the record refers. The ranks are coded as - - - , R1, R2, or R3, where - - - is the missing value code, R1 is the highest, and R3 the lowest rank. For the variables that describe *rank orders* or *reactions* and for which column 65 is coded as *A,* the columns 28-30 contain the missing value code - - - . All information is stored *left-aligned*. The remaining columns of the field are filled with blanks.

Col. 31:   *Blank.*

Cols. 32-36: *Alphamerical field.* For the variables V47 to V51, which describe *exchange relations* and for which column 65 is coded as *I*, the field contains the *short name of the partner nation* to which the record refers. The short names contained in this field are identical to the ones used in the country profiles in chapter 4. Occasional *missing values* are coded as - - - . For the variables that describe *rank orders* or *reactions* and for which column 65 is coded as *A*, the columns 32-36 contain the missing value code - - - . All information is stored *left-aligned.* The remaining columns of the field are filled with blanks.

Col. 37:   *Blank.*

Cols. 38-47: *Numerical field with a decimal point in column 44.* The field contains the *value* that is assigned to the timepoint/timeinterval, the variable, the country, and the rank of the partner nation mentioned between column 1 and column 37 of the record. Besides, there are *no missing values.*

Col. 48:   *Blank.*

Cols. 49-58: *Alphamerical field* containing the *unit* (e.g., $/CAP) assigned to the immediately preceding data field between the columns 38 and 47. *Missing values* are *nonexistent.* Information about units is always stored *left-aligned.* The remaining columns of the field are filled with blanks. Hence, columns 49-58 are *all blank* if they refer to a dimensionless variable.

Col. 59:   *Blank.*

Cols. 60-63: *Alphamerical field* containing references to *footnotes* which qualify the information of the corresponding record. The texts of these footnotes are listed in the appendix of this book. *Missing values* are coded as - - - . All information is stored *left-aligned.* The remaining columns of the field are filled with blanks.

Col. 64:   *Blank.*

Col. 65:   *Alphamerical field* describing the *type of the record* either by a code *I* or by a code *A*. *Code I* means that the record contains *interaction* data that describe *exchange relations.* Hence the columns 28-30 and 32-36 of the record contain meaningful information. *Code A* means that the record contains *attribute of nations* data referring to *reactions* or *rank orders. Missing value codes* are *nonexistent.*

The information on the diskettes can be used in *two* ways: Either it is processed directly by a *PC system* or it can be uploaded from the PC to a *mainframe computer* where it can be processed by a wide range of powerful statistical software. In both cases the user will have to transform the original information on the diskettes into a *standard data matrix.* Most statistical software packages will perform this task by a 4-step procedure of the following kind:

- *Step 1:* Read all information referring to those variables Va, Vb, ... , Vz that are needed for a given statistical analysis and pass this information to the following *step 2.*

- *Step 2:* Select those records that refer to a given *timepoint/timeinterval* and, if needed, a given *rank of a partner nation* and put these records for each variable Va, Vb, ... , Vz on a *separate* file Fa, Fb, ... , Fz. Each of these files should have the following structure:

Observation number	Short name of country	Value of Vx
1	.	.
2	.	.
.	.	.
.	.	.

To prevent difficulties with *step 4* the observations contained in these files should *not* differ by more than *2 years* from a file-specific timepoint/timeinterval 1970, 1975, 1980, 1970-1974, 1975-1979, or 1970-1979. This way it is ensured by the structure of the original data that each of the files Fa, Fb, ... , Fz contains *at most one* record referring to a given country.

- *Step 3:* Order the records of each file Fa, Fb, ... , Fz alphabetically by the *short names of the countries* to which these records refer. Since the original data on the diskettes are ordered this way *step 3* may be omitted if this order has not been destroyed by the previous two steps.

- *Step 4:* Join the records of the files Fa, Fb, ... , Fz by the *short names of the countries* to which the records refer. This way you will get a *single* file with the following structure:

Observation number	Short name of country	Value of Va	Value of Vb	. . .	Value of Vz
1	.	.	.		.
2	.	.	.		.
.	.	.	.		.
.	.	.	.		.

If each of the files Fa, Fb, ... , Fz contains *at most one* record referring to a given country the file resulting from the match-merging of *step 4* will have *not more than one* record per country. This means that *step 4* produces a standard data matrix if the data selection of *step 2* is done in an appropriate way.

TABLE A

CRITICAL VALUES $t_{N,p}$ FOR ONE - SIDED BINOMIALTESTS [1]

N =	p = .05	.10	.15	.20	.25	.30	.35	.40	.45	.50	.55	.60	.65	.70	.75	.80	.85	.90	.95
5	2	2	3	3	4	4	4	4	5	5	5	5	-	-	-	-	-	-	-
6	2	3	3	3	4	4	5	5	5	6	6	6	6	-	-	-	-	-	-
7	2	3	3	4	4	5	5	5	6	6	7	7	7	7	-	-	-	-	-
8	2	3	4	4	5	5	6	6	6	7	7	8	8	8	-	-	-	-	-
9	2	3	4	4	5	5	6	6	7	7	8	8	9	9	9	-	-	-	-
10	2	3	4	5	5	6	6	7	8	8	8	9	9	10	10	-	-	-	-
11	3	3	4	5	6	6	7	7	8	9	9	10	10	11	11	11	-	-	-
12	3	4	4	5	6	7	7	8	9	9	10	10	11	11	12	12	-	-	-
13	3	4	5	5	6	7	8	8	9	10	10	11	12	12	13	13	-	-	-
14	3	4	5	6	7	7	8	9	10	10	11	12	12	13	14	14	-	-	-
15	3	4	5	6	7	8	9	9	10	11	12	12	13	14	14	15	15	-	-
16	3	4	5	6	7	8	9	10	11	12	12	13	14	14	15	16	16	-	-
17	3	4	5	7	8	9	9	10	11	12	13	14	15	15	16	17	17	-	-
18	3	4	6	7	8	9	10	11	12	13	14	14	15	16	17	17	18	-	-
19	3	5	6	7	8	9	10	11	12	13	14	15	16	17	18	18	19	-	-
20	3	5	6	7	9	10	11	12	13	14	15	16	17	18	18	19	20	-	-
21	3	5	6	8	9	10	11	12	13	14	15	16	17	18	19	20	21	-	-
22	3	5	6	8	9	10	12	13	14	15	16	17	18	19	20	21	22	22	-
23	4	5	7	8	9	11	12	13	14	16	17	18	19	20	21	22	23	23	-
24	4	5	7	8	10	11	12	14	15	16	17	18	20	21	22	23	24	24	-
25	4	5	7	9	10	11	13	14	15	17	18	19	20	21	22	23	24	25	-
26	4	6	7	9	10	12	13	15	16	17	19	20	21	22	23	24	25	26	-
27	4	6	7	9	11	12	14	15	16	18	19	20	22	23	24	25	26	27	-
28	4	6	8	9	11	13	14	16	17	18	20	21	22	24	25	26	27	28	-
29	4	6	8	10	11	13	14	16	17	19	20	22	23	24	26	27	28	29	-
30	4	6	8	10	12	13	15	16	18	20	21	22	24	25	26	28	29	30	-
35	4	7	9	11	13	15	17	19	21	22	24	26	27	29	30	32	33	35	-
40	5	7	10	12	15	17	19	21	23	25	27	29	31	33	34	36	38	39	-
45	5	8	11	13	16	18	21	23	26	28	30	32	34	36	38	40	42	44	45
50	6	9	12	15	17	20	23	25	28	31	33	35	38	40	42	45	47	49	50

[1] If a series of N independent trials results in $t_{N,p}$ *or more* incidences of a given type of events it is assured at the *10% level of significance* that the probability of the occurrence of a *single event* is *higher than p*. $t_{N,p}$ = - means that N is too small for a test at the 10% level of significance. The values of $t_{N,p}$ in this table have been computed by means of the subroutine MDBIN of the IMSL program library, release 9.2.